Advance Praise

"Every country has its star institutional builders. Tan Sri Lin is a truly brilliant institutional builder and doer from his days as central banker, architect to the design and strengthening of Malaysia's financial system and advisor to all prime ministers. His masterly analysis of domestic and global events show through in his clear writings in this book, passionately written with verve, practical to a fault, and wonderfully told—from the biggest picture to the smallest institutional detail. Only one who has done it before firsthand knows how the system works, what to do, and how to fix it. No Asian writer has his command and authority on emerging market economic development from the ground up. This is truly the work of a master, teacher, and mentor—to be read and enjoyed by students and policy makers alike."

Andrew Sheng, Chief Adviser to the China Banking
Regulatory Commission and former Chairman,
Securities & Futures Commission, Hong Kong

"The style of the writing in this book will allow even a person who is not knowledgeable in finance or economics to comprehend the subject and enjoy reading the book. The topics covered are related to current issues and are loaded with lessons and advice. This book should be read by anyone wanting to make economic sense of the happenings in the financial markets and their effect on our lives."

Tun Ahmad Sarji, Chairman, PNB
(Permodalan Nasional Malaysia) and
former Chief Secretary to the Government of Malaysia

"When it comes to economics, I am very much a layman. That's why I have turned to my learned friend See-Yan's fortnightly column, and they have enabled me to make sense of what is going on around me. Now that they are compiled into a book, I would recommend it to all laymen like me who want to understand the forces at play that make us go up or down economically."

Tun Mohammed Hanif Omar, Deputy Chairman,
Genting Group and former Inspector-General of Police, Malaysia

"Essays on global economic and financial events are usually full of jargon that would put off most people after reading a few paragraphs. See-Yan cleans up the jargon and makes the concepts more comprehensible. Whether you are a student, academic, corporate executive, public official, or just a curious global citizen, See-Yan can help you relate to issues of global importance, and understand 'what are we to do' in our respective roles."

"Professor Lin's depth of knowledge and breadth of new strategic ideas are drawn from his extensive research and illustrative insights into management and leadership from a deep variety and culture of model practices. I would like to recommend to locals, world readers, and professionals, both in the public and private sectors, especially the banking sector, to read this book for its superior insights and superior execution."

"Tan Sri Lin's essay collection covers one of the most epochal periods for both the global economy and Malaysia's ongoing development journey. This backdrop gives See-Yan a rich and dramatic canvas to apply his sharp mind and deep experience. Dr. Lin indeed lived and lit up for us such interesting times with much gusto and in doing so brought the world to Malaysia and some of Malaysia to the world. This book is an indispensable record and compendium of a pivotal period, from one of the granddaddies of economic analysis in our region."

"See-Yan is a brilliant economist with a special knack for translating the complex into simple language. His objective economic analysis and his insights have helped us to better assess opportunities and anticipate challenges. This compendium of his essays, written for the noneconomist, will prove useful for any business leader or professional who desires to be more aware of the economic forces shaping the world today, especially fast-paced Asia."

"Professor Lin's insightful commentary will appeal to professors and students of economics. This highly readable book will serve as a useful reference for anyone seeking to understand economics from a global perspective. Tan Sri Lin, an accomplished economist, takes a bold stand on the many economic issues that he vividly portrays in the book. His balanced narrative offers ample room for the reader to arrive at his own solution to the ills afflicting the global economy."

"Having studied at Harvard University, and being part of the much decorated Bank Negara's top management during a period in which Malaysia had to confront several tumultuous financial turmoils, Lin See-Yan's knowledge and experience shines in this gem. The book is a synthesis of concepts and policies that blend with reality. While students and academics of monetary economics will benefit enormously from the breadth and depth of the analysis, it is a must-read for the nonspecialists as its presentation is simple, clear, and crisp."

Rajah Rasiah, Rajawali Fellow, Ash Center, Harvard Kennedy School,
Harvard University and Professor of Economics and
Technology Management, University of Malaya

"This book by one of Malaysia's most distinguished economists should be read by all in the Malaysian Economic Association and all academic staff for its deep analysis of how the country dealt with its macroeconomic policy at the most crucial moments."

Sheriff Kassim, President, Malaysian Economic Association and
former Secretary-General, Ministry of Finance, Malaysia

The Global Economy in Turbulent Times

LIN SEE-YAN

WILEY

Other Wiley Editorial Offices
John Wiley & Sons, 111 River Street, Hoboken, NJ 07030, USA
John Wiley & Sons, The Atrium, Southern Gate, Chichester, West Sussex, P019 8SQ,
United Kingdom
John Wiley & Sons (Canada) Ltd., 5353 Dundas Street West, Suite 400, Toronto, Ontario,
M9B 6HB, Canada
John Wiley & Sons Australia Ltd., 42 McDougall Street, Milton, Queensland 4064,
Australia
Wiley-VCH, Boschstrasse 12, D-69469 Weinheim, Germany

ISBN 978-1-119-05992-9 (Hardcover)
ISBN 978-1-119-05993-6 (ePDF)
ISBN 978-1-119-05994-3 (ePub)

Typeset in 10/12 pt, ITC Garamond Std Light by Aptara Inc., New Delhi, India

Printed in Singapore by C.O.S Printers Pte. Ltd.

10 9 8 7 6 5 4 3 2 1

To

Emily NH AMN

| Hsiu-Yi | Foong-Yi | Diaan-Yi | Jo-Yi |
| & Kevin | | & Tom | & KY |

And

Ashley Xuan   Zoe Qin

Joshua Di

The Loves of My Life

Contents

CURRENCY WARS

EDUCATION

REGIONAL PERSPECTIVES

MALAYSIAN MACROECONOMICS UNRAVELED

Royal Prelude

Tan Sri Dr. Lin See-Yan is one of Malaysia's most distinguished economists. I have long been an admirer of his career achievements and am an avid reader of his fortnightly column in *The Star* newspaper. Like me, his numerous readers will be delighted that these essays are now compiled into a book. These essays are characterized by a depth of analysis and breadth of coverage that can only come from someone with a sound understanding of the issues involved, and they are written in a style that is easy to read and can be understood by a nonspecialist.

Tan Sri Dr. Lin, I am proud to say, is a Perak-born, Harvard-educated economist. He served for many years as a central banker at Malaysia's Bank Negara, where he ended up as deputy governor for 14 years. Subsequently, he became a commercial banker, financier, and venture investor. Malaysia is fortunate to have had, and continues to have, his services. His perspectives on macroeconomics, finance, and economic matters in general are, therefore, no mere armchair cogitations but shaped in the crucible of real-world experience. In this, he differs from many others.

The chapters in this book address many of the important global issues of our time. Anybody with even the slightest interest in current economic matters and regional financial affairs should own and read this book. You will be richly rewarded. You will not find another book quite like it.

Sultan Nazrin Shah
Istana Iskandariah
Kuala Kangsar
Malaysia
January 9, 2015

Foreword

Tan Sri Dr. Lin See-Yan is certainly the most qualified to speak on the economy—both national and global.

We are living in turbulent times—both politically and economically. Political turbulence affects the economy and economic turbulence affects politics. The two cannot really be separated.

I remember Tan Sri Lin's contribution toward my thinking during the days when I was prime minister. His analytical mind managed to see things in depth and sharply. It is an uncommon gift.

I often read his essays in newspapers and magazines. Now he has put all of these essays in a book for everyone to read and learn.

I wish the leaders of Europe and America, as much as the leaders of Malaysia, would read what he has to say about the many wrong things that are happening to the world's economy.

I think many of us are in denial. We refuse to see the reality that is clearly evident before us. But reading the essays in this book might help us to acknowledge the truth.

I am no great believer of textbooks. I read them but I prefer to do my own thinking. This process is helped by reading some of the essays of See-Yan.

I recommend that this book be read by people entrusted with guiding and leading their societies and nations.

Tun Dr. Mahathir Mohamad
Prime Minister, Malaysia
1981–2003
1, Jalan P8H, Presint 8
62250, Putrajaya
October 13, 2014

Preface

In the twenty-first century, the economies of all of the world's nations are interconnected. What happens in one part of the globe has ripple effects that affect every other part. Even well-informed citizens often still see economic changes as being largely shaped by the actions of politicians and businesses close to home. Those who read through the 151 short chapters in this book will have their perspective on world economic events and the impact of those events on their own lives broadened greatly.

These chapters were originally written as freestanding short essays in Dr. Lin's column in *The Star* designed for an audience primarily in Southeast Asia, but the breadth of coverage makes them relevant to anyone in the world who is interested in global economic affairs. Many of the chapters deal explicitly with the global economy and the many high-level meetings, such as the G-20, that attempt to construct a global response to emerging economic challenges. A number of chapters are devoted to unraveling and explaining the United States' exposure to the recent Great Recession and the damage done by partisan politics. Others go in depth into the problems of Europe, ranging from the Greek bankruptcy to the dangers of deflation. Still other chapters deal with Japan's struggle through Abenomics to reverse the two decades of economic stagnation that resulted from the bursting Japanese stock market and real estate bubbles and the subsequent equivocating response of the Japanese government. Many chapters deal with issues such as the role of gold in the economic system and the effectiveness of the international monetary system. There is highly informed analysis of the various financial scandals that have erupted in recent years, such as the LIBOR scandal, and the fear felt by many of the expansion of shadow banking in many parts of the world.

Not surprisingly, given that the chapters were originally written for a Southeast Asian audience, there are many chapters that analyze the issues facing Malaysia, Indonesia, Thailand, Vietnam, the Philippines, Myanmar, and the ASEAN region as a whole. There are chapters on the economic challenges facing China and India and others on the BRICS (Brazil, Russia,

India, China, and South Africa) as a whole or individually. Not all of the chapters deal exclusively with economic issues. There are essays on some of the demographic and environmental challenges facing various parts of the globe, the problem of rising inequality and the emerging middle class, which is common to many countries, and issues concerning the quality of university education.

In all of these chapters, seemingly complex economic issues are explained without technical jargon in ways that any educated person can follow even if they have no background in economics. The analysis, however, does not sacrifice rigor in order to make the issues seem simpler or clearer. Most economists have trouble being both rigorous and clear, but Dr. Lin is a notable exception.

Dr. Lin See-Yan brings a unique background to these chapters. For much of his career, he was a central banker in Malaysia's Bank Negara. He was at the center of Malaysian inter-ministerial meetings on economic policy from very early in his career and for a very long period as deputy governor of the bank. During his time at Bank Negara, he took time out to come to Harvard University—originally to do a year of study for a master's in public administration from Harvard's Kennedy School, but he stayed on to do a PhD in economics in the Harvard Economic Department before returning to the bank. After retiring from the bank, he became chief executive officer of a publicly listed commercial bank. In addition, he served and continues to serve on numerous corporate boards in Malaysia as well as in the United States and elsewhere, and also on foundations and university boards. He has continued to be actively involved in economic policy, serving (among other positions) on the Prime Minister's Economic Council.

This book can be read from cover to cover, but for many readers it will serve two roles. It is an excellent reference book to be referred to when one wants to better understand the nature of the international monetary system, the reasons for deflation, or China's economic challenges. It is also a book for use as a very good university course on global economic issues.

Dwight H. Perkins
Harold Hitchings Burbank Professor of Political Economy, Emeritus
Harvard University
Chairman, International Academic Advisory Council, Jeffrey
Cheah Institute on Southeast Asia, Sunway University
September 15, 2014

Introduction

L in See-Yan has had a remarkable and inspiringly productive career and an exciting life as a prized government official, a leading business strategist, a top-notch research economist, a revered public intellectual, and a loving family man. He worked at Bank Negara from 1961 to 1994 (as the deputy governor in the last 14 years) and, after retirement, he has been active in business consultancy, support of the arts, and the upgrading of tertiary education in Malaysia. Most wonderfully for me, he has consistently been a dear friend, a guru, and a guide on matters of economic development in Malaysia, Asia, and the world.

Lin See-Yan has been particularly involved in strengthening academic ties between Harvard University (where he received his PhD) and Malaysian institutions. He is the first non-American to be a member of the Harvard Graduate School Alumni Council, and the first non-American chairman of that Council. He has worked closely with Professor Arthur Kleinman, Professor Dwight Perkins, and Professor Anthony Saich of Harvard Asia Center to help to establish the nonpartisan privately funded think tank, the Jeffrey Cheah Institute on Southeast Asia (JCI), in Kuala Lumpur to promote high-quality research on public policy choices in the region.

Lin See-Yan has worked as a highly valued adviser with every Malaysian prime minister, and continued to do so after he left Bank Negara. For over 50 years, through his wide global network of high-level policy analysts and his deep immersion in core domestic policy discussions, he has helped to brainstorm and address every major macroeconomic crisis that has confronted Malaysia and the world. In each case, he has lent his powerful analytical mind and sense of culture, history, and politics to help shape public policy responses to ameliorate the situation.

We are very fortunate that since 2008, Lin See-Yan has taken up the additional effort of public education through a biweekly column on economic affairs for *The Star* newspaper. This book is a selection of his essays on the main economic developments of the past six years, including the global financial crisis, the slow jobless economic recovery in the United States, and the stagnation of the eurozone countries. These excellent essays were written for the broad public in Malaysia, and thanks to the publication of this book, they are now also accessible to the public worldwide. The globalization of knowledge is a wonderful outcome indeed, and it is my great pleasure and honor to help disseminate Lin See-Yan's great wisdom for the wide world.

Jeffrey D. Sachs
Quetelet Professor of Sustainable Development
& Professor of Health Policy and Management
Director, Earth Institute
Special Adviser to UN Secretary-General Ban Ki-moon
Columbia University
New York, NY, USA
January 5, 2015

About the Book

The idea for the book came from friends and readers, from both professors and students as well. I am told that after reading the original essays (published in my fortnightly Saturday column, "What Are We to Do" in the *Star* newspaper in Malaysia), whenever they can, many have found them useful enough to save them every other Saturday for future reference. This gets messy to manage, as the file grows. What's really wanted is a well-organized single source of convenient reference, which they can readily resort to whenever they want or feel the need to. So many have encouraged me to compile the essays in some order: essentially to get them properly organized in a systematic and logical way for ease of reference and, just as important, convenient to locate.

Pressure to do so came by way of Tan Sri Rashid Hussain, who made me a friendly offer I couldn't possibly refuse: sponsorship by the Prime Minister's Exchange Fellowship Programme Malaysia to publish them in book form. John Wiley & Sons Singapore had since agreed to be the publisher. With that in place, I began to assemble the 151 essays that were written once a fortnight without fail since the last week of 2008. This date is significant in that since the onset of the 2008 Great Recession, I have been asked by many friends and corporates frequently enough to help explain simply what's going on, but also the meaning of economic and financial jargon used so very loosely in newspapers and magazines and on radio and TV—all these at a time when much of the news was deemed biased (in different ways depending on the source), and where the lines between gossip, fact, and opinion are unclear and not readily discernible.

There was, at that time, a growing demand for up-to-date, objective economic, business, and market news and independent analysis, written in a form most intelligent people can easily understand. As the recession deepened, the news coverage of interest expanded to include topics on political-economy, behavioral economics and social media, education, corporate governance, demography, and the environment. I gathered that what was really missing was reliable and intelligent news with objective, dependable analysis. Readers wanted to be well informed in order to better understand and become more aware of the world around them, especially on fast-emerging Asia. They needed insights about tomorrow's world and views by a wide range of experts and thinkers. My Saturday column took on these challenges to fill the need.

As I write, my primary aim is to help people better appreciate the world around them: not just about Malaysia, which is but a speck in our vast universe. We are just too small to be in a position to ignore what's really happening outside that can have such a profound impact—whether we like it or not—on what we do or plan to do: to help place breaking news, happenings, and opinions in context; to give insights into some moments of history; and indeed, for some, to even influence the course of the rest of this century. The goal is to get Malaysians, especially the young, to learn more about Asia and the rest of the world, and from the mistakes that others and we make; and to get them to be engaged and care enough to create a better world. More important, to watch the world change before our eyes as the rest of civilization looks to a source of trust, not just for information and analysis, but also for understanding and guidance: even some comfort.

My column's essays are rabidly nonpartisan. I hope they are versed in the highest standards, practices, and ethics of our craft. They are intended to always strike a balance with the idea that we often feel nothing really changes with the notion that yet, everything changes so fast; especially in the ever-evolving Internet on everything—the biggest change agent to hit the global economy in our lifetime. Finally, each essay hopes to initiate a conversation among readers and with leaders on serious problems surrounding us (especially in Asia), and how we should react and interact to make Malaysia a better place for all to work and live. These essays (now chapters) are committed to be a dependable guide: to inform, engage, and I hope, even delight readers along their journey through life.

And so my mission has been to write about what's current and topical in our complex world in simple language, so it's easy for most common folks to understand, and whenever called for, to clarify technical concepts and explain unfamiliar jargon to help nonbankers and noneconomists follow what they read in the popular press on world affairs. Essentially, the book is intended to be partly educational (to explain, clarify, and interpret); partly informative (to remind people it's important to be aware of happenings in the big world out there); and partly commentary (to express an objective opinion on happenings as I find them to need analysis). Over the years, I had gathered that the readers and regulars are rather wide ranging: from corporate executives to curious government officials; from teachers to university students; and from professionals to the usual "Saturday run-of-the-mill readers." I am surprised to learn even many stay-at-home mothers read them (however, they do complain that I sometimes get carried away and start using semi-technical language). So they keep me honest. I always end with the tagline, "What, then, are we to do?" That's pure commentary: how I see things as they evolve and what needs to be done. No holds barred. The idea is to provide enough information and a keen perspective to enable readers to judge for themselves the efficacy of public policies. I would have done this for six and a half years by the time this book goes to press.

See-Yan
Kuala Lumpur
March 31, 2015

Acknowledgments

I am grateful to many people and institutions whose support and encouragement made this book possible. Each made it better, but none bears any blame for its flaws. First among all has to be the late Tun Ismail Ali (Governor, Bank Negara Malaysia: Malaysia's Central Bank, 1962–1980), my mentor, a true gentleman and a dear friend, who impressed on me that there is beauty in saying something clearly and simply, and held me always to that high standard. I have gained enormously from his razor-sharp mind and particular attention to detail. His skepticism and constant questioning helped me build strong analytical skills and a certain meticulous care in precise drafting.

Indeed, no one really knows where our ideas come from. Supportive peer pressure and an academic environment are surely part of the answer. I remember with fondness my own teachers at Harvard, whose sensitivity to the tenderness of my skills nourished this growth over time. The very presence of Nobel laureates as early teachers, especially Professors Simon Kuznets, Wassily Leontief, and Kenneth Arrow, boosted my self-confidence, as did great textbook-name teachers, including Gottfried Harberler, John Kenneth Galbraith, Martin Feldstein, James Duesenberry, Richard Caves, Richard Cooper, Dale Jorgenson, Jerry Green, Hendrik Hauthakker, Stephen Marglin, Richard Musgrave, and of course, Alexander Gerschenkron, "the last man with all known knowledge." Above all, a colleague and good friend with whom I started to work in my early professional life and who later, at Harvard, became my teacher and mentor: Professor Dwight Perkins. He helped me better understand the importance of disciplined, synthesizing, and creative minds, and of delineating ethical minds. For me, Dwight sets the perfect example of always being able to strike an exquisite balance between critique and encouragement. I am honored and grateful that he wrote the Preface to this book. I thank him for his support, wisdom, kindness, and generosity over the years. Dwight remains a good friend.

I am especially indebted to HRH Sultan Dr. Nazrin Shah for his continuing support, encouragement, generosity, and guidance. It was Tuanku who constantly reminded me whenever we met to compile and organize the essays into a book. This way, the wealth of in-depth knowledge will be consolidated and made readily accessible, delivered at a one-stop single source. The intention is for the book to become an essential guide, engaging, informing, and hopefully delighting readers along the way. Without this pressure from Tuanku, I would not have done it. I am ever grateful to Tuanku for his confidence in me. Most of all, I deeply appreciate the Royal Prelude written by Tuanku to support and introduce the book. Most respectfully, I value his friendship, fellowship, and fraternity.

I started working for Tun Dr. Mahathir Mohamad when he was deputy prime minister in the mid-1970s and thereafter throughout his 22 years as prime minister. I've had the priceless good luck to learn from him what it means to be an effective and fearless leader. I've also had marvelous opportunities to absorb from Tun original insights about governance in practice and firm decision making, and about perceptions of the rapidly evolving political panorama of the Street and about tomorrow's world through the eyes of a seasoned street-smart politician. So it is with great pride that I express my appreciation to Dr. M (as he is known to many of us who work for him) for consenting to write the Foreword to this book.

I am particularly proud of my long association with Harvard University: first, as a graduate student (1969–1972 and 1976–1977) starting at the Kennedy School of Government as a Mason Fellow, then the Business School, and finally, the Economics Department of the Graduate School of Arts and Sciences, as well as with the Harvard Institute of International Development (and its predecessor, the Development Advisory Service). Thereafter, I was an active Harvard alumnus since 1993, as a member of Harvard's Graduate School Alumni Association Council (as its chairman, 2003–2005); 1998–2008, as member of the Harvard Alumni Association Council (serving, in addition, as its regional director for Asia, 2000–2010); 1998–2008, as founding deputy president, Association of Harvard University Alumni Clubs of Asia; and 2003–2006, as a member of Harvard's Visiting Committee on Asian Studies. And since 2002, I have served as the president of the Harvard Club of Malaysia. During this time, I came to be acquainted and later collaborated with Harvard Professor Jeffrey Sachs (now at Columbia University), whom I am honored and proud to call my friend—a man of remarkable dedication, optimism, and talent. I am inspired, as I seem to always be, by his vast area of interest and expertise. I thank Jeff most sincerely for writing the Introduction to this book, and extend to him my appreciation of his friendship.

Taken as a whole, this book benefited greatly from the support of my many friends in Malaysia and around the world. Each chapter relies in part on the mindfulness of colleagues, friends, and readers, as well as global academics and students with whom I had the pleasure of working for many years. Their contributions are mostly invisible, but their influence was enormously significant. Over the years, I have written and rewritten chapters in the book many times: each time, drawing on ideas and written texts of scholar-friends and influential writers I admire—in particular Nobel laureates Joseph Stiglitz, Paul Krugman, Robert Solow, Michael Spence, and Robert Mundell, and Professors Alan Blinder, Barry Eichengreen, and Martin Wolf as well as Harvard Professors Martin Feldstein, Larry Summers, Jorge Dominguez, Robert Barros, Henry Rosovky, Derek Bok, Howard Gardner, Ellen Langer, and Harry Lewis—each time, trying to make the ideas of interest reach an ever-expanding audience; each time, enlisting the patient advice of friends and scholars, as well as many writers and journalists in public affairs. All have enriched the book with their perceptive viewpoints, comments, and published texts. I am humbled by their help, guidance, and support. I should repeat that many of the ideas in this book are derived from the works of these scholars and many more, too numerous to mention by name. I am indebted to all of them: They have been invaluable in shaping this book. All errors and infelicities that are here are all my own. I take full responsibility for them.

A special thank-you goes to Tan Sri Rashid Hussain, chairman of the Program Pertukaran Fellowship Perdana Menteri Malaysia (the Prime Minister's Exchange Fellowship Programme Malaysia), for the Foundation's generous sponsorship to publish this book. Thanks are also due to Wah Seong Corporation for its continuing support.

Particular thanks are in order to my Eisenhower Fellow colleague, Datuk Mohd Nor Khalid (Lat), for taking time off to contribute the wonderful caricature featured in the cover design.

Last, but foremost, I am deeply indebted to my editor and friend, Ng Hon-Soon, whose skill, patience, and wisdom helped me finalize each chapter of this book. He read all the manuscripts with meticulous care and made invaluable suggestions. He has been an adviser and close friend for more than 25 years, and I owe him a great deal, personally and professionally. Hon-Soon has been singularly thoughtful in his suggestions about how to improve the book. He also did yeoman's work in research and fact checking, and assisted me to avoid technical errors, including helping to locate source materials that I had clearly forgotten.

I should also acknowledge the help of another old acquaintance, Soong Mun-Wai, a professional librarian and family friend, who has been of enormous help in this regard.

All errors remain mine. In no aspect of this book was I more fortunate than having Wong Lily to manage the draft manuscripts and getting them typed with meticulous care, often over and over again. She saw the manuscripts through from start to finish, shepherded the book's progress from submission to publication, and showed unerringly good judgment in ensuring each chapter was always completed on time, including attending to the subtlest details. I thank Lily for a job well done.

I owe special thanks to P. Gunasegaram, the former managing editor of *StarBizWeek* of Star Publications, for the opportunity to write my own column, "What Are We to Do," since December 2008. He and his executive team helped to instill in me the discipline of bringing this column out on time every fortnight. I appreciate their invaluable support and patience. I am also most grateful for the continuing enthusiastic assistance and direction received from his successors and their professional support teams, including Soo Ewe-Jin, Errol Oh, Shanmugam Murugasu, Anita Gabriel, Jagdev Singh Sidhu, and Thean Lee-Cheng, who had worked tirelessly to plan and coordinate in ensuring the timely publication of the column. I value their contributions and colleagueship.

I received extraordinary professional support in the production of the book. Jeremy Chia's and Kimberly Monroe-Hill's editorial skills have been invaluable in ensuring the book conforms with the best international practice. Also, they simply did a great job in putting together the notes, and index for the book. Along with their teammates Thomas Hyrkiel, Gladys Ganaden, and Nazneed Halim, they all exceeded reasonable expectations of effort and skill.

I do owe many thanks to many people, especially Harvard Professors Dwight Perkins, Jorge Dominguez, and Arthur Kleinman; and Tun Hanif Omar, Tun Ahmad Sarji, Tan Sri Thong Yaw Hong, Tan Sri Jeffrey Cheah, Tan Sri Rashid Hussain, Tan Sri Jawhar Hassan, Tan Sri Lim Kok Thay, Tan Sri Sidek Hassan, Tan Sri Andrew Sheng, Tan Sri Hamad Piah, Tan Sri Lim Wee Chai, Dato' Sri Robert Tan, Dato' Tan Chin Nam, Datuk Ali Kadir, Dato' Dr. Tan Tat Wai, Datuk Noor Azlan Ghazali, Dato' Ooi Sang Kuang, Dato' Siew Ka Wai, Professor Rajah Rasiah, Datuk Seri Dr Govindan Kunchamboo, Chew Gek Khim, Goh Peng Ooi, Raymond Kwong, Datuk Sulaiman Daud, Ong Kian Min, John Lim, Halim Din, Chan Cheu Leong, Mark Chang, Charles Lim, Ng Kay Yip, Gregory Poarch, my "Thursday lunch buddies," Jeffrey Toh, Lim Chee Sing, Cheah Kim Ling, Lee Guat Keow, Zoe Rai, and my exceptional colleague Datuk Professor Wing-Thye Woo for their unfailing support, assistance, encouragement, and generosity.

By no means least, I am grateful to my colleagues, students, and readers, from whom I learn how to be a better writer and become a more effective leader as well. The Roman proverb sums it up best: *Qui docet discet.* He who teaches, learns.

My greatest debt by far is to my wife, Emily. I am grateful for her unwavering care for our family over many, many years, as well as her sustained support and assistance of what I do. It is an infinite debt for which only Goethe could aptly find the right words: "A debt that can only be discharged through all eternity." This book is dedicated with love to her; also, to my kids and grandkids. They are the loves of my life.

Izmir, Turkey; Constanta, Romania
Nessebur, Bulgaria; Athens, Greece
October 4–10, 2014

That Was the World That Was (TW3)

CHAPTER 1

TW3 2008: The Year Free Markets Ran Amok[1]

I am writing from Boracay, with both my feet well-sunk into the powder-textured white sand on the best stretch of beach in the world, located south of the city of Manila. The weather was just nice enough for me to think about what to write for my second essay in *The Star* (the first was on December 20, 2008, now published as Chapter 101, "Getting 'Cangkul-Ready'") as another annus horribilis draws to a sad conclusion. Hence, TW3 2008, or that was the world that was in 2008.

Looking back, it's hard to summarize a year that blew hot and cold—both rather uncomfortable. The first half of the year reminds me of Malthus's challenge to the dwindling global supply of resources—oil, food, and other commodities. None foresaw (including me) that the crude oil price would rise so fast from its lows in early 2007 to US$87 a barrel on February 6, 2008, to US$100 on February 19, and then on to a high of US$145 on July 3, only to fall precipitously to US$31 by December 22 (US$44.60 on December 31, 2008). Similarly with crude palm oil: from a low of RM1,893 per tonne on January 30, 2007, to RM3,117 by end-2007 to a high of RM4,330 on March 3, 2008; the highest price reached in the second half of the year was RM3,600 on July 3, before falling to its lowest on October 24 at RM1,390 (RM1,629.50 on December 31).

Name the commodity, and we see similar sharp gyrating trends all within a calendar year. In the same vein, central banks saw the scepter of inflation and debated seriously on the trade-off between growth and inflation. The second half of the year turned it all around—by year-end, the talk had centered on how to avoid stag-deflation (Columbia University's Professor Nouriel Roubini's combination of *stagnation/recession* and *deflation*) or even depression (at worse, the Great Depression Mark II). Just as quickly, John Maynard Keynes has been disinterred and became the topic of conversation within the infamous Malaysian *tai-tai* network,[2] so I was told.

Politicians have since had a field day and decided that the state now has a proactive role beyond standing back, since the market no longer has all the answers. They do have good reasons.

Annus Horribilis

Indeed, 2008 was the year the system failed in the United States. Consider these contradictory phenomena: (1) **In this year,** US long-term interest rates were at their lowest in 500 years; but the year also saw the highest rates in 20 years; (2) **this year** was the worst for the US stock market in 70 years—yet, of the 10 best days experienced during this long period, 6 came in 2008; (3) **this year,** economists started off by worrying a lot about inflation but then switched to concerns about recession and deflation, all within a year; (4) **this year,** the US government started lending to businesses and banks in ways that they could never have borrowed before, as people feared widespread corporate and financial bankruptcies since the businesses and banks could not borrow to repay; and (5) **this year,** a few trusted Wall Street personalities defrauded their own kind (Madoff for a reported US$50 billion through a Ponzi-like fraud scheme, and lawyer Marc Stuart Dreier getting hedge funds to invest monies that eventually landed in his pockets). These glaring contradictions—all within a year—reflect the sentiments behind the title: "The Year Free Markets Ran Amok."

That's not all: (1) **This year,** in a dramatic turnaround to save the financial system, Washington practically nationalized federal government–guaranteed housing mortgage institutions, Fannie Mae and Freddie Mac, as well as the AIG group of insurance companies (including bailing out those who lent to Bear Stearns) and later, Citigroup; however, it allowed investment bank Lehman Brothers to fail with disastrous worldwide repercussions; (2) **this year,** the US securitization machine (which was heavily relied on previously to "prop up" the system) collapsed so badly that the financial system could not perform its traditional role of "bridging" lenders and borrowers—worse still, banks could no longer trust one another's balance sheet; as a consequence, government had to become lender of first and only resort; (3) **this year,** it took Washington most of the year to realize that the underlying problem of the banks and investment houses was one of solvency, not just illiquidity; (4) **this year,** most economists were caught flat-footed before they realized that the US recession had already started in December 2007, with optimists still thinking then that it wouldn't last longer than early 2009; (5) **this year,** with oil and commodity prices collapsing, inflation vanishing, and unemployment rising rapidly, the US Federal Reserve Bank (Fed) cut short-term interest rates rapidly to about zero by near year-end with 10-year Treasuries at close to 2 percent (not seen since Eisenhower years); but junk bond yields rose to

17 percent (i.e., about 1990 levels, the last time the banking system almost collapsed)—indeed, money has become so cheap that recently the US Treasury bills rate turned negative briefly (can you imagine, the government got paid for borrowing!); (6) **this year**, we began to see that the expected push of the Chinese and Indian locomotives could not be de-coupled from the ever-evolving global interdependence—that the BRIC nations' (Brazil, Russia, India, and China)[3] expansion was not sufficiently dynamic to offset the recession contagion originating in the United States and Europe, whose virulence has since surprised even those who supposedly had the prescience to foresee; and (7) **this year**, we saw a crisis of global proportions made in the West—from irresponsibility emanating not from "them" (for until now such crises only happen to "them" in Asia, Latin America, and Russia) but from indiscipline, profligacy, and regulatory failures of the United States and Europe, ironically with "them" as the creditors and the West, the debtors—and this list is not exhaustive.

What's in Store for 2009?

What, then, are the lessons? What are we to do? The thing that continues to puzzle and intrigue is how the two halves of 2008 could not have been more different and yet, they came together rather seamlessly within the same year. It does, however, point to the inadequacy of conventional wisdom to explain just how quickly the unthinkable can readily come to pass and just as quickly become the unremarkable. The big lesson: It is foolhardy to even offer to peer into 2009. We just don't know enough about the nature of the global transmission mechanism and the time taken for economic interdependence to work through on the financial front (failure of political governance to keep pace with tightening interconnections among markets, banks, and regulators), on the geopolitical side (the disappearing line between "them" and "us" regarding the origin of crisis) and in the wider context of a "cracked" established world economic order that is not working and not properly understood. Nevertheless, let's take stock and see where the unfolding financial crisis and current recession in the United States and Europe are leading us. My own take is as follows:

1. We are already witnessing (and most certainly feeling) a global recession, and it is likely to get worse.
2. US gross domestic product (GDP) will likely remain negative over most of the first half of 2009; the best-case scenario being negative until the end-2009. Recovery in late 2009 is still possible but will be weak (it's going to still feel like a recession) and is expected to be still rather weak in 2010. Unemployment could possibly peak at 9 percent

in 2010 (nowhere close to the 25 percent, and a 50 percent national income loss, as in 1929–1933).

3. Things have happened (and are still happening) that I have not seen in my 39 years as a working economist and banker: (a) the sharp amplitude of US stock market movements—value of the real (adjusted for inflation) S&P 500 Index tripled in 1995–2000, but by November 2008, it fell 60 percent from its 2000 peak (in 1924–1929, real stock prices tripled, and then fell 80 percent in 1929–1932); (b) the biggest housing bust since the Great Depression; (c) zero interest rates—and briefly, in December, negative rates—not seen since 1941; (d) global equity values estimated to be down by 50 to 60 percent in 2008—the year in which every asset class (stocks, real estate, commodities, even high-yield bonds) fell by significant double digits. Total paper wealth destruction could be in the region of US$30–35 trillion. The list goes on.

4. I don't see a Great Depression Mark II coming on.

Lessons

Here are 10 useful lessons from the Great Depression to think about:

1. Adjustment from the sharp downturn will be long and painful.
2. Credible solutions need to focus on demand and output, and in the process, avoid fixing prices and wages.
3. It is useful to have a willingness to explore new, lean-against-the-wind programs.
4. Time is of the essence in the politics of recovery—large direct spending fusions do serve to weaken downward spirals; recessions are prone to develop.
5. When spending during recessionary times, deflation is a worse enemy than inflation.
6. Do not engage in beggar-thy-neighbor policies.
7. When trust is shattered, economic stakeholders need firm leadership and confidence in an effective public authority to manage expectations and address the destructive deleveraging recession.
8. Economic mishaps can quickly eat up political capital since expectations are high to deliver quick results.
9. Need to address early the capitulation of underlying consumer spending since both income and wealth have been drastically reduced—the policy response needed is purposeful measures to fill the void left by retrenching consumers—that is, a massive fiscal stimulus.

10. **The key economic lesson**: The political will to do enough—that is, leadership to err on the side of doing too much to stimulate rather than doing too little and too late.

What, Then, Are We to Do?

The key to good leadership is to be ahead of the curve. For us in Malaysia, there is no doubt that the worst is yet to come—likely to come on after the Chinese New Year festivities in early 2009. Already, businesses and consumers are getting that "sinking feeling" regardless of what the economic numbers now show. One of the lessons from our short history of recessions and slowdowns is that things can smolder for a longer time than expected. As of now, confidence is still fragile, and whatever is being done, don't forget we are dealing with managing expectations, a psychological phenomenon.

People need to believe that public policies will do the whole job, not just plugging holes. As I see it, we are at most times more of an ostrich than a sage owl. Realistically, our macroeconomic adjustment is likely to be longer than shorter. Unfortunately, we are optimists by nature, already thinking too soon that we can discern a beginning of better days ahead. I assure you, there will be time for optimism, but not just yet. I fear we must expect macroeconomic weaknesses still to come and maybe even persist through most of 2009.

I realize, of course, it's hard to know what's going to happen next week, never mind the entire 2009. My gut feeling is that the overall economy is worse than what many people expect. The year 2008 saw the markets pushing the economy down; if so, 2009 will see the macroeconomy impacting the markets. Indeed, the process has already started—surely in the United States and Europe, and the impact is beginning to be felt in China, India, and Japan.

Through good and bad times, the Malaysian economy has always shown an innate resilience that eventually pulls the country through, mainly with firm leadership at the helm to restore confidence and, when needed, rejuvenate Keynes's "animal spirits" to help jump-start the economy.

But before this can happen, at a time like now, we need the type of leadership we deserve to stimulate activity through large-scale effective government spending to fill the gap created by softening consumer spending (because of declining wealth, stock prices and Bursa Malaysia market capitalization had fallen 45 percent between their high and low in 2008, with expectations of income loss), business downswing in profits and reduced earnings growth, if any, and the deleveraging of private balance sheets as the slowdown bites. The key push must be to generate employment since the economy will not stabilize until wealth and incomes are rebuilt in a sustained way. The full force of fiscal policy needs to be deployed to push for an early recovery through compensatory government spending to fill the void left by business and consumer withdrawal of spending and borrowing.

In earlier essays (published in *The Star* on December 20, 2008, and in *The Edge* on December 29, 2008), both now reproduced as Chapters 101 and 102, respectively, I proposed (and rationalized in some detail) the urgent need for a second stimulus program of RM30–40 billion over the next two to three years. This should give us the value-added jobs and evolving income we badly need, bearing in mind the lessons we can learn from the past. Indeed, we need to do more rather than less at a time of great uncertainty in the face of a rapidly expanding global recession, and at a time when the risks of pump-priming are minimal.

In times of complexity, I believe commonsense pragmatism has to prevail. I am optimistic about the macroeconomic choices now before us. The political and economic risks can be readily managed. The current and unfolding uncertain circumstances present the best time for Malaysia to spend smartly on projects with lasting benefits, and at the same time, add value and restructure the economy to build capacity in an environment of slowing and weakening economic conditions at home. We deserve more.

Boracay, Philippines
Kuala Lumpur
January 1, 2009

Notes

1. First published on January 3, 2009.
2. Refers to the proactive network of well-to-do and well-connected housewives (mainly *tai-tais*, usually rich or titled or both) with nothing better to do than organize regular get-togethers (usually lunches, sometimes dinners) at which they exchange the latest goings-on around town (and act as an online "breaking news") over a game of mah-jongg or afternoon tea.
3. This new grouping (first suggested by Jim O'Neill, then of Goldman Sachs, in 2001) comprises Brazil, Russia, India, and China—the rapidly rising major emerging "developing" nations. Together, they exceed 3 billion people (nearly 45 percent of world) and account for 25 percent of the global GDP on a purchasing power parity basis. South Africa was included as a member since December 2010, with the grouping consequently known as BRICS.

CHAPTER 2

2009: "Oxpicious" Year Ahead[1]

In January 2009, I have had many conference calls with friends overseas, stretching from Boston (Harvard and MIT) to New York (Columbia) to Washington, DC (Brookings) to get an updated feel of the prospective state of the United States, the eurozone, and Japanese economies. As expected, the economic situation had since changed for the worse with each passing day (especially the rapidly deteriorating unemployment situation) and that does not appear to have reached bottom. So I decided to round up the picture and revisited Association of Southeast Asian Nations (ASEAN)[2] (among the last to be really affected, except Singapore) to gauge the prevailing mood especially in this part of the world. I landed up in Chiang Rai, Thailand, over the February Chinese New Year festivities. Indeed, I am writing this from a tent (literally) along the Burma/Thailand/Laos Golden Triangle.

Ox Year

Here, this is also open season for astrologers/feng-shui masters/fortunetellers. For them, the year of the Rat (2008) was not good—we all know that. After all, the rat and water go together, and as everyone who follows this knows, water brings worries and provides fear. Worse, 2008 was also a year without fire—the element that drives the pursuit of money. This is not rocket science, of course. Nevertheless, their views have a general thrust that points in the same direction: There is no fire in the year of the Ox (2009), either. So don't expect all things related to money and banking to bounce back big-time this year! Now the plot thickens: Instead of water, the element influencing this year is yin-earth, and since the Ox is an earth animal, 2009 is really a double earth year, which is good (I think). This earthly combination promises harmony and stability, reconstruction and rebuilding, bringing opportunities for long-term gain. The last yin-earth-Ox year was 1949, with the world settling to a new order (People's

Republic of China came into being that year, so did the North Atlantic Treaty Organization (NATO); but it was also a time of the Cold War, with the USSR testing its first atom bomb that August).

I have it from a good source that President Obama is an Ox, born on a yin-earth day in 1961. So is Timothy Geithner, the new secretary of the US Treasury. Such double-earth people, according to my Túng Shu, the ancient Chinese almanac, are moderate, peaceful, charismatic, intellectual, and slim! For your information, President Bush is a yin-metal person who became president in 2001, a yin-metal year that saw great turbulence. There is more. A pure earth year points to the lack of conflict. But without fire (i.e., optimism), conservatism prevails. It also points to no early recovery—a year of cooling down, moving over time to stability. Without fire, the "earth" just cools. Finance and banking is considered a "metal" industry, and without fire, metal is quite useless. However, 2010 looks more promising—the Tiger is a wood sign that feeds fire! All this information is secondhand, of course. You get sucked into this sort of mood when you are situated in the Golden Triangle.

Reassessment

My reassessment is made after considering the following seven factors:

1. International Monetary Fund's (IMF) 2008 study of recessions over three decades had concluded that (a) recessions preceded by financial crises are deeper and longer; (b) recessions tend to be worse if the crisis is in banking; (c) nations hardest hit are those with "arm's-length" financial institutions (e.g., United States and Europe); and (d) recessions linked with banking crises last two times longer and the cumulative gross domestic product loss is four times larger. Overall, the evidence points to a severe global recession this time around.

2. The recession, which started in the United States in December 2007, has now bloated into a worldwide phenomenon. Job cuts have gained rapid speed as the global economy slides. In the United States, about 2.6 million jobs have already been lost in 2008. Job losses are widespread from Britain to the eurozone to China. The International Labour Organization had estimated that 51 million jobs will be lost by the end of this year, 2009. Recessionary influences are now globally driven. Revised IMF predictions for 2009 put the world on the precipice, and likely to slow to a standstill. Already, the United States, the eurozone, the United Kingdom, and Japan are in recession. Developing countries as a whole are not far behind.

3. Today's global business climate is at its worst since World War II (WWII) if recent survey results are to be believed. Sluggish demand is most pronounced in the goods-producing sectors. Both investor

and consumer sentiments have since turned pessimistic and are fast becoming a global phenomenon.

4. Throughout most of Asia, certainly in most ASEAN nations, governments have come out strongly to stimulate—in some cases, not just once, but already in the midst of a second recovery plan. As of now, the overall sentiment remains opportunistic.

5. Few would argue that the economic crisis (especially in the United States, the eurozone, and Japan) has grown worse. Earlier on, most thought the Keynesian way was simply the easiest way to go. With each passing month, it appears that the situation gets harder to resolve as the crisis gets more global and as decisions and their implementation take more and more time to effectively put on the ground—what economics Nobel laureate Paul Krugman calls "stuck in the muddle," echoing John Maynard Keynes, who wrote as the world plunged into the Great Depression: "But today we have involved ourselves in a colossal muddle, having blundered in the control of a delicate machine, the working of which we do not understand."[3]

6. Despite the severity of this crisis recession, there is scant evidence, so far, that it will soon develop into a depression (à la 1929–1933). Thus far, it is also unlikely that deflation (à la Japanese style in the 1990s) will set in (even in the United States). It is true that consumers and investors are spending less (if at all) and more wisely. Given the harsh economic climate, more firms are resorting to price cuts to lure buyers, and consumers are looking for real bargains and postponing spending. It is also true that lenders and consumers have become skittish about taking on new risks. This "wait and see" mentality continues to spark fears of deflation. The Obama stimulus package is intended to lead and reverse such sentiments.

7. Since September 2008, when events in the United States really turned sour, the government remains the only lender of first and last resort. Despite bold measures (especially by the Fed), markets are still nervous and stressed, and it remains true that no one really knows what's going to happen the next day. Similarly, the overall situation in the United Kingdom, the eurozone, and Japan has markedly deteriorated. Confidence remains fragile. Two key ingredients are needed now, more than ever, if any bold government stimulus is to work: return of confidence, especially for investors and consumers, and widespread ready access to bank credit. Both are still found wanting, despite governments and central banks doing their darndest to help. As the liquidity trap sets in (because of prevailing very low interest rates), monetary policy gets increasingly less potent while the fiscal policy options take time to pass and implement (if ever). In the meantime, Northeast Asia, ASEAN, and South Asia are getting very nervous, mainly because more nations fear getting into a worsening recession at home as the global side worsens.

On the surface, things might have appeared not to be as bad for some because of the lagged effects. The key risk involves the feedback loop between the financial and real sectors, which gets more adverse as the recession deepens. The case of Malaysia—which came through a sustained period of commodity price and electronics boom—had continued to record a credible macroeconomic performance right until the fourth quarter of 2008, especially the corporate results. This has tended to lull many, especially consumers, into a sense of complacency, which I am afraid could drag until early first quarter of 2009. There is no doubt that for countries like Malaysia, the worst is yet to come.

The Worst Is Yet to Come

Overall, those revisiting their outlook are revising it down. For some, it's now a matter of whether a country is technically in recession. But this is not really important from the point of view of public policy since most people— investors, businesspeople, exporters, and consumers—are already feeling the recessionary tendencies; indeed, people expect more gloomy news to emerge. As it plays out, most forecasters are now on their "worst-case" scenario for the world. Many, like me, don't really know what the new worst-case scenario is going to be like. But one thing is sure: at the "eye" (United States) of the recession, at best, there could be some sort of recovery by the fourth quarter of 2009, but I think this to be rather implausible. To be sure, I can't see real recovery before 2011; even so, unemployment will likely remain high (in double digits). For my friends in the United States, this outlook is a reasonable outcome given the historical perspective. Economics Nobel Laureate Paul Samuelson (basically, a cautious person) is reported to have said: "I suspect we won't see a recovery before 2012, and possibly even 2014. That more closely resembles the time frame it took Roosevelt from his inauguration in March 1933 to the eve of the WWII."[4] For us in emerging Asia, the deep, inner longing to grow and the deep hunger for new business opportunities remains intact, and politicians who lack the will to react swiftly and act boldly remain so at their own peril.

What, Then, Are We to Do?

"Don't curse the darkness; light a candle."
—Peter Benenson, founder of Amnesty International

We tend to associate Keynesian economics with just the concept of priming the pump (or jump-starting). In his landmark 1936 book, *General*

Theory of Employment, Interest and Money, Lord Keynes discusses the business cycle by introducing the emotive concept of "animal spirits," which lie at the very core of why the economy fluctuates up and down as it does in real life.[5] Many have offered interpretations of Keynes's intention (Professor Robert Shiller[6] of Yale being the latest) to embody the ideas of trust and confidence building, without which fiscal policy measures will not have their desired impact. It has a lot to do with consumer, investor, and businessman confidence inasmuch as it also deals with trust among all stakeholders in the economy. It would seem that Keynes wanted to convey the feeling that swings in confidence (trust) are not always logical. That's why business cycles are what they are—driven largely by animal spirits. When times are good, people feel optimistic and trusting, thereby helping to build a climate of confidence where they tend to act spontaneously and even let their guard down, since they feel instinctively that they will get to where they want to go. Over sustained periods of good times and growing confidence in the system (as the United States had for most of the 2000s), this almost blind trust was destroyed overnight by the mortgage bubble, and turned emotions into deep mistrust—their animal spirits are now at the lowest ebb. That is why any stimulative package has to be targeted to revive people's badly bruised animal spirits. The real danger here is that if recovery efforts are not bold enough or substantial enough to have a clear and present significant and visible impact on people's economic life, loss of confidence can deepen further and makes reviving it that much harder. That explains why the US efforts are now of such an enormous size!

For Malaysia, what is it that we now need to do to uplift our animal spirits in an "oxpicious" year? The Keynesian prescription would involve three key elements:

1. A second fiscal stimulus significantly larger than the first, based on the worst-case scenario in macroeconomic terms: It needs to be large enough, bold enough, and focused enough to boost public confidence. It could well involve a combination of spending and tax relief, targeted at job creation and credits directed to aid consumers.
2. Opportunity should be taken to embed into it a sufficiently large and targeted assistance package to help restructure the economy (through fiscal incentives, soft loans, and training grants) with a strong tinge of green.
3. Access to credit markets that had worked well in boom times when animal spirits were high. With financial institutions well capitalized and highly liquid, ready access to relatively inexpensive credit is vital to lift confidence not just for small and medium-sized enterprises but also for the larger businesses and exporters, especially in the form of working capital and trade finance.

This is the time to be bold and firm, at a time when all stakeholders expect the government to have the strong political will to act swiftly and with great focus on the depth and breadth of impact. The real danger is to come up short. This Keynesian approach through reviving the animal spirits points to the way forward on what really needs to be done. I have written extensively on (1) and (2) above in my earlier essays in *The Star* on the need for an overarching RM30–40 billion stimulative package. It must be stressed that a quick shot in the arm will not work. We need sustained productive spending on a large enough scale. If needed, we should bring the 10th Malaysia Plan projects forward, provided they are ready for implementation. Let's act unconventionally, as we have done in past crises.

Inflation and the budget deficit are the least of our worries today. Ready access to credit can be difficult at a time when lenders have turned significantly risk adverse, and since Bank Negara Malaysia (Central Bank) and the financial institutions have to act prudently to avoid situations of large nonperforming loans at a later date. This dilemma can be resolved with government lending through a special window at the Credit Guarantee Corporation (perhaps, an enhanced special access guarantee scheme) and through government-linked lending institutions to assist the larger businesses and exporters during this difficult time of great stress. Official interest rates are already low, and there is room for further cuts (if needed). What is important is for private lenders to keep the stream of credit flowing and to play their part in not unnecessarily raising the cost of credit, especially margins. For in the final analysis, without ready access to credit at relatively low cost at this time, the animal spirits will not turn positive to respond fast enough to meet public policy objectives. Speed and size are of the essence. Implementation is key, and it has to be swift. The idea is to strengthen and prepare the private sector for its confident return to resume driving the economy once the crisis is over.

Chiang Rai, Thailand
Kuala Lumpur
January 29, 2009

Notes

1. First published on January 31, 2009, as "An 'Oxpicious' Year Ahead?"
2. The Association of South-East Asian Nations, a grouping comprising Brunei, Indonesia, Malaysia, the Philippines, Thailand, and Singapore, as well as the Indo-Chinese States of Vietnam, Cambodia, and Laos, and since 1997, Myanmar (formerly Burma).

3. Paul Krugman, "Stuck in the Muddle," *International Herald Tribune* (January 24, 2009).
4. Interview with Nathan Gardels on January 20, 2009, and reproduced in the *Bangkok Post*'s "2009 Global Viewpoint," distributed by Tribune Media Services.
5. John Maynard Keynes, *General Theory of Employment, Interest and Money* (New York: Harcourt, Brace, 1936).
6. Robert Shiller, "Making Sense of the Madness," *Fortune* (December 22, 2008), pp. 67–68.

CHAPTER 3

Beware of PME in a Jobless 2009 Recovery[1]

This chapter is not on medicine. I have no interest in the medical dysfunction PME (premature ejaculation) that afflicts many males. I am concerned about the possibility of inflationary and rising debt pressures in the face of early "green shoots" from substantial global stimulus, which has led to talk of the early withdrawal of stimulus. Hence, PME, or premature exit. Don't be fooled. At this time, if there is irresponsible talk, this is it. Unfortunately, a lot of this is politics. Indeed, any early pullback of stimuli can—and very likely will—lead to a premature end to the buildup of growth in Asia. Sure, in the end, if we are not careful, the large stimuli arising from massive pump-priming and easy money can well lead to inflation and high debt. But the world, especially the United States, needs the fiscal red ink in order to get out of the bigger evil—recession that is threatening to turn into a depression. This piling on of money and massive debt saved the United States, but there is still growing unemployment. As I see it, both can be readily managed. If there is a potential problem, it's not because the United States, Europe, and Japan can't handle the debt or inflationary expectations. It's the politics that's messing things up—same in most of Asia, including here at home. Politicians like to play to the gallery. They only want to do what's popular. Tough times call for tough measures. It's also time for reform, and that's always difficult. The trouble is, what's always good in the long run isn't the best thing to do in the short run. That's why we need leaders who are not afraid to do the right thing, no matter how unpopular.

Fragile Global Recovery

By now—21 months after the recession began in the United States—the Federal Reserve Bank finally calls it "very likely over." But what is also clear is that even optimistic growth prospects in 2010 won't be enough to bring gross domestic product (GDP) back in the United States to its US$14 trillion precrisis peak. In contrast, with its last 10 recoveries, GDP bounced back to its previous levels within one year! It is equally clear that the United States is unlikely to recover its close-to 7 million lost jobs and US$14 trillion of wealth lost during the recession until, perhaps, 2015. Even now, continuing tight credit conditions, a less-than-stable real-estate sector, a still-fragile banking environment, and a jobless recovery pose real risks of a double-dip recession (warnings are coming from no less than Feldstein,[2] Roubini,[3] the International Monetary Fund (IMF),[4] Krugman,[5] and Stiglitz[6]).

The good news is inflation (certainly core inflation), as of now, is not a real threat; neither is the rising US debt or its depreciating dollar. Curiously enough, US consumers are saving—Harvard's Martin Feldstein[7] estimated that rising US savings is now equivalent to US$800 million in consumption forgone. To put it in perspective, US consumer spending is equal to the gross national products of China and India combined and then doubled! Globally, recovery appears on track. With inflation threat distant, monetary policy will remain easy. But sustained recovery requires renewed private spending in both personal consumption and business investment, especially the latter. Indeed, significant domestic demand gains, especially in emerging Asia and Latin America, are required in order to reestablish and sustain a stronger global expansion. Realistically, this remains very much an item on the wish list.

Latest information from the summer World Economic Forum in Dalian, China, indicated a mood of caution about global recovery, especially in China. While it is clear the global economic situation had stopped deteriorating, signs of significant sustainable growth are only here and there. Certainly, there will be no return to its former strength anytime soon. China and India remain a source of optimism, but elsewhere, including the United States, current recovery isn't likely—so far—to be sustainable. Many are worried about a W-type recovery. Even in China, Premier Wen Jiabao talks of pickup in activity as "remaining unstable, unconsolidated and imbalanced,"[8] in the face of uncertainty continuing to cloud global growth. Also, many still judge heavy reliance on sharp Asian consumption gains as premature, even unrealistic. Overall, the feeling is that Asia hasn't done enough heavy lifting and structural transformation to warrant any significant decoupling from the United States and Europe.

PME: A Bad Idea

The global economy is at last emerging from a severe downturn. Recovery is sluggish, and unwinding stimulus measures any time soon would derail the nascent upswing, and risk more unemployment worldwide. Exit policies only make sense once definite signs of recovery have taken hold and unemployment is set to fall in a sustainable manner. The call now must be to err on the side of continued expansionary policies. In the United States, fiscal stimulus spending is beginning to bite, giving significant boost to present-quarter growth, as the economy stabilizes. No one wants to repeat the mistake Japan made in the 1990s when premature tightening of policy short-circuited the recovery process. PME roils markets, adding unhelpful uncertainty to the direction of policy. The basic imperative is to solidify the foundations for self-sustaining recovery, led by private demand. This needs early return of confidence, continuing government support, and firm leadership to stay the course.

Not to Worry about Inflation and High Debt

Current preoccupation with inflation borders on hysteria. As I see it, this imminent danger is unlikely to be reduced by the PME of stimulus. Indeed, it could even exacerbate it since it could, in turn, provoke another round of fiscal and monetary intervention. Three good reasons not to worry right now include: (1) the world has massive excess capacity: the Organisation for Economic Co-operation and Development (OECD) estimated the potential GDP gap as exceeding 5 percent; (2) central banks have plenty of time to soak up excess stimulus and the record level of unused labor combined with rising productivity will prevent price pressures from building; and (3) at this time, even heavy public debt is sustainable. In the United States, real interest is at an all-time low. So, even a 100 percent debt/GDP ratio would only cost 2 percent of GDP. Surely, this can't be an unsupportable burden! The fundamental point is this: Underlying weakness in private demand is the root cause, not the massive fiscal and monetary expansion of liquidity; these policy measures are a consequence. This simply means PME can be unhelpful. What is needed is a coordinated exit strategy at the global level to unwind as the global expansion gathers strength and recovery is firmly established. The core ingredients have to be: credible monetary policy, committed fiscal responsibility, and coordinated rebalancing of global demand, away from the old ways of unfettered spending based on others' saving. This has to be an issue of concern for the forthcoming G-20 Summit to resolve.

Lesson from the 1930s

Recovery from the 1929–1932 Great Depression only returned the US economy to full employment after the outbreak of World War II. This is because the Great Depression was "W" shaped. Recovery in four years after Roosevelt took office (1933) was the fastest sustained growth period *ever* for the

United States—annual growth averaged over 9 percent; unemployment fell from 25 percent (1933) to 14 percent (1937). Growth faltered by a second sharp downturn in 1937–1938, and unemployment surged to 19 percent. Nobel laureate Milton Friedman had attributed this to premature monetary contraction. The Fed, which made the mistake of tightening monetary policy soon after the 1929 stock market crash, miscalculated again. It tightened prematurely in 1936 in the face of worries about its early "exit" strategy (familiar?). Tightening the monetary and fiscal levers sent the economy once again into freefall in the second trough of the W. This is what happens when policy makers withdraw support too early—return of economic decline or even panic could follow. This points to the need to carefully plan for its exit. Pressure from fiscal conservatives to cut deficits and slow monetary growth is often the main source of concern. Broadly, the real lesson is to find constructive ways to respond to the inevitable pressure to cut back on stimulus as the economy gathers greater strength. As I see it, realistically, the risk lies not so much in pulling back too soon (PME) but in dithering too long.

What, Then, Are We to Do?

Malaysia's nascent recovery remains fragile and has yet to see consistent and convincing evidence that the recovery is more than just "green shoots." The massive stimulus appears to be working but far too slowly in terms of the desired impact. Like the rest of the world, the root problem is lack of private demand, especially capital spending. Consumption is still hesitant. Export growth remains soft. But inflation is not a real problem. Both fiscal and monetary easing will have to continue. Fiscal deficit is rising, but I am not unduly worried as we still badly need the stimulus. Too many worry quite unnecessarily about the rising debt ratio. Frankly, I won't lose too much sleep over it. Both Krugman and Stigliz have a point: Accept the realities of today; we need to keep on stimulating to instill sufficient confidence in the enterprise sector to get private initiatives moving again—until the economy is on a solid path to recovery. We have to avoid a W-recovery; V-recovery is already off the radar screen. In the early 1990s, Belgium and Italy had debt ratios in triple digits—they are doing okay today.

Notwithstanding that, now is also the time to think about the long-term fiscal situation. To switch to austerity soon would surely short-circuit the nascent recovery and risk a 1937-like US recession-within-a-recession. I am of the view that we can constructively, dramatically improve the long-term fiscal situation without tightening prematurely. It is important in this stimulus phase not to crowd out the private sector. At this time, it is certainly not a bad thing to get rid of policies that aren't working to promote private initiative. It takes political courage to maximize the impact of stimulative spending. The focus must be to get the private sector moving again. Policy makers need to learn from past experiences, and respond constructively with much greater emotional attachment and commitment, without derailing recovery.

Kuala Lumpur
September 16, 2009

Notes

1. First published on September 19, 2009, as "Beware of PME."
2. Martin Feldstein, "The Fed Must Reassure Markets on Inflation," *Financial Times* (June 26, 2009).
3. Nouriel Roubini, "Increasing Risk of Double-Dip Recession," *Financial Times* (August 25, 2009).
4. Dominique Strauss-Khan, International Monetary Fund, "IMF Chief Warns Against Unwinding Stimulus Too Soon," *Bundesbank Conference*, Berlin, published in *Straits Times*, Singapore, September 5, 2009.
5. Paul Krugman, "Two More Years for Full Recovery," *Global Financial Crisis—The Way Forward Symposium*, organized by Securities Commission, Malaysia, published in *The Star*, Malaysia, August 11, 2009.
6. Joseph Stiglitz, "Warns of Economic Double-Dip," AEP interview published in *The Star*, Malaysia, September 9, 2009.
7. Feldstein.
8. Jiabao Wen, "China Will Stay the Course on Stimulus," addressing the *World Economic Forum* at Dalian, China, September 11, 2009.

CHAPTER 4

G-20 Summit, Pittsburgh 2009: Has "It Worked"?[1]

Amid cooled-down expectations that G-20 leaders face waning enthusiasm for bold measures, decisions at the conclusion of their summit in the last weekend of September were within expectations. The preamble to their communiqué declared "It worked." In their response to the global economic crisis: "Our forceful response helped stop the dangerous, sharp decline in global activity and stabilize financial markets."[2] That sounds rather presumptuous! Sure, there have been some successes. And this has been an unusual period of desperate cooperation. But, the process of repair and recovery remains incomplete even though the "Leaders' Statement" included this bold two-worded declarative sentence: "It worked."[3] There were many promises and more have since been made. For many nations, unemployment is still too high; clear signs of recovery in private demand are not here as yet; then, what real regulatory bank reforms since April 2009? Anyway, possible pitfalls that can trigger setbacks include growing losses on commercial real estate; need for the recapitalization of European banks; continuing reluctance of banks to lend; work on how to make global economy less susceptible to crisis (or a second dip); uncertainty about the needed political will back home to push the global agenda; restructuring global payments imbalances remains a serious problem.

G-20 Promises . . .

The G-20 leaders now promise to do much more, including (1) avoid premature withdrawal of stimulus; (2) plan for effective exit strategies; (3) launch new frameworks for strong, sustainable, and balanced growth; (4) shift from public to private sources of demand; (5) reform and strengthen financial regulation and act together to raise capital standards; (6) design, implement, and monitor plans for global rebalancing; (7) reform global institutional architecture, especially IMF and the World Bank; (8) phase out fossil-fuel subsidies; (9) fight protectionism and secure Doha Round deal in 2010; and (10) reach agreement on climate change at Copenhagen. The G-20 leaders scheduled to meet twice in 2010 (first in London and then South Korea) to indicate what they have done so far is only a start. It would appear that the G-20 leaders are sensitive to criticism that they lack political will to really act in earnest. They now have to live up to their commitments on the listed broad reform agenda. They also know that success requires coordinated global governance, which can only come through realistic global cooperation. So, much work still needs to be done. As of now, I would grade G-20's performance as "incomplete."

G-20: The New Champion

In this context, a key decision was to use G-20 as the new champion of the global economy and financial system: "We designated the G-20 to be the premier forum for our international economic cooperation. We established the Financial Stability Board [FSB] to include major emerging economies and welcome its efforts to coordinate and monitor progress in strengthening financial regulation."[4] It will replace the once elite G-7 of rich industrial nations. G-20 comprises the original G-7 (the United States, Canada, the United Kingdom, France, Germany, Italy, and Japan); six Asian nations (China, India, Indonesia, South Korea, Saudi Arabia, and Australia); six others (Russia, Brazil, Argentina, Mexico, South Africa, and Turkey); plus the European Union. Netherlands and Spain were observers for this occasion. Together, G-20 nations account for 85–90 percent of global income and 90–95 percent of world payments. The United Nations, the International Monetary Fund (IMF), and the World Bank also attend.

Some bemoan 85 percent of the world's nations are not represented, and Africa, the Middle East, and very poor nations are underrepresented. Symbolically, for the first time, this forum brings the system of cooperation up to date with structural changes in the global economy, to build a durable recovery. UK Prime Minister Gordon Brown went so far as to describe this move as offering "more chance of delivering results than anything since the Second World War."[5] Expectations are high. The focus is on how the leaders will enforce commitments countries make, which can involve peer reviews—although there will be no sanctions. Similar efforts were attempted in the past, but failed. Realistically, memories of having grappled with the deepest recession since 1929 can be short-lived.

New Global Growth Model

As I see it, five key challenges must be addressed to ensure that the world economy will be placed on a more stable and balanced growth path. This requires a new growth model that not only rebalances growth but also lifts the growth potential of all nations, especially the most vulnerable. First, commitment to support and implement stimulative programs until recovery is clearly secured. In the meantime, put in place a transparent and orderly process to withdraw the extraordinary fiscal, monetary, and financial sector support, for implementation when the time is right and coordinated globally. This should contain expectations and build confidence.

Second, a precondition for sustained growth requires reform in the distribution of global demand. This needs a practical global mechanism to avoid excessive payments, deficits, and surpluses, requiring (1) adjustments across the global economy, and (2) reform to raise growth potentials and avoid creation of asset bubbles. Increasing living standards in emerging markets remains a critical element.

Third, international financial institutions (especially the IMF and the World Bank) must be redesigned and strengthened to effectively deliver. This includes measures to rebalance power and reshape governance within them, to reflect today's realities in Asia in particular. This should boost their legitimacy in global development.

Fourth, programs to ensure benefits of recovery extend to the world's poorest. Their access to multilateral resources and involvement in broader development issues, including food security and aid effectiveness, remain critical in order not to leave them behind.

Fifth, support for global efforts at addressing issues on climate change, starting at the Copenhagen Climate Change Conference in December 2009. Urgency is needed to bridge the funding gap to support the adoption of technology, including its adaptation and mitigation action in developing nations. These can be facilitated by both private funding through international carbon markets and providing access to greater public resources.

Global Imbalances: What Next?

Somewhat lost in the heated outcry over the lack of definitive progress in financial regulation and supervision reform (especially curbs on banker's pay) is the critical issue of global imbalances—the root cause of the crisis. Jean-Claude Trichet, president of European Central Bank, stated, "If we don't correct them, we'll have the recipe for the next major crisis. And this of course would be totally unacceptable."[6] Indeed, these imbalances have deeper roots in global macroeconomic policy. Why is this so? Large and persistent deficits and surpluses (i.e., fundamental disequilibrium, in IMF-speak) are both bad. They generate even larger capital flows, which can become destabilizing. Simply put, current account surpluses mean excess of national savings over investment. These surpluses are invested abroad in private assets or piled up as foreign exchange reserves. They are rerouted through the global markets, raising liquidity worldwide and at home. Toxic assets would not pose such a threat had these surpluses been smaller and less persistent. Unfortunately, there is no international mechanism to allow these disequilibrating flows to adjust by themselves.

What, Then, Are We to Do?

Four key elements need to be addressed:

1. Are these imbalances self-correcting? To a degree, rebalancing is happening automatically because of the crisis. The Chinese surplus at 11 percent of gross domestic product at its peak will fall to 7 percent in 2009. In the United States, its deficit is likely to drop from its high of 6.5 percent to 3 percent this year. But, the underlying problem just won't go away. Both surplus and deficit countries have to separately adjust through their own mix of macroeconomic policies. There is no guarantee that these will act in concert to resolve the problem—only by accident. Hence, the need for global policy coordination, which is not easy, given these are very sensitive issues. Similarly, a US-only adjustment will not do.
2. The eurozone's problem is different since it, as a whole, runs a small deficit. But, there are large intra-cross-country imbalances within the zone. Besides, Germany runs a persistent surplus, like China. When it comes to surplus and deficit, the eurozone does not behave like one zone; each country's policy response is uncoordinated and nationalistic. This issue can only be resolved on a country basis and not as one currency area.
3. What then is the best policy approach? There is no one-size-fits-all solution. Each country will tailor-make its own adjustment policy—reflecting in reality what is happening now in the United States, Germany, the United Kingdom, France, China, and Japan. G-20 leaders were tongue-tied in finding the right words to reflect their collective stand: There exists a "compact that commits (the group) to work together to assess how policies fit together, to evaluate whether they are collectively consistent with more sustainable and balanced growth, and to act as necessary to meet our common objectives."[7] What gobbledegook!

4. Can this be policed? It can't. Caps on imbalances won't work in practice; neither would penalties should the cap be broken. In essence, the G-20 has no legitimacy here. The real issue is this: None of the surplus or deficit nations are ready to surrender sovereignty over macroeconomic policies in the future. Least of all, follow the advice of the IMF and under pressure from its peers. Not even for the common good and world economic stability!

All we know now is that G-20 leaders have started a conversation on this difficult but critical issue. It's just too early to know where this will lead by end 2010. Harvard's Martin Feldstein went so far as to call G-20's pledges "empty promises." He concluded: "In short, it would be wrong for investors or ordinary citizens around the world to have too much faith in G-20's promises to rein in monetary and fiscal policies, much less to do so in a co-ordinate way."[8]

Kuala Lumpur
September 30, 2009

Notes

1. First published on October 3, 2009, as "The Pittsburgh G-20 Summit: Has 'It Worked'?"
2. Group of 20 (G-20), "Leaders' Final Statement at Pittsburgh Summit: Framework for Strong, Sustainable, and Balanced Growth," G-20 Summit, Pittsburgh, September 24–25, 2009.
3. Ibid., para. 5.
4. Ibid., para. 19.
5. Gordon Brown, in his address to the G-20 Summit.
6. Jean-Claude Trichet, "Grouping Must Tackle Global Imbalance." He told Italy's Corriere della Sera, on September 27, 2009, that G-20's new role would allow a good combination of expert analysis and peer pressure.
7. Group of 20 (G-20), "Leaders' Statement."
8. Martin Feldstein, "The G-20's Empty Promises," *The Star*, Malaysia (September 19, 2009).

CHAPTER 5

TW3 2009: Growing Again, but Hold on Tight[1]

One thing is certain about 2009—it will change 2010.

I just returned from an extended trip to the United States, Japan, the Pearl delta, and Hong Kong. I sense increasingly encouraging signs that the world economy is in recovery. Rebound is, however, uneven. The latest Organisation for Economic Co-operation and Development (OECD) indicators point to stronger than previously expected growth of activity in France, Italy, Australia, and the United Kingdom. Tentative signals of expansion have emerged in Canada and Germany. Clearer signs of revival have become more visible in the United States and Japan, and in most other OECD nations. But the main driver is not the OECD. The combined output of its 30 developed members is expected to grow by about 2 percent in 2010 and in the region of 2.5–3 percent in 2011. That's poor recovery; it's not very encouraging. Outside, China is forecast to expand by 9–10 percent in 2010, and more of the same in 2011. Some say even higher. Activity in India and Indonesia is rather robust. Brazil and Russia have a way to go. Indeed, both the World Bank and the International Monetary Fund (IMF) have just raised their forecasts for East Asia: gross domestic product (GDP) growth of 6–7 percent in 2009 (up from 5½ percent) and accelerating to 7.5–8 percent in 2010. China's rapid growth is not just pulling the region along; it is acting like the world's locomotive. Nevertheless, governments remain cautious and conscious of the risks of any premature withdrawal of stimuli. There are still potential output-gaps out there. Also, there are concerns that the developed countries are converging to a slower growth equilibrium. It will take many years to bring unemployment and government debt back to their precrisis levels.

Dangers Lurk in 2010

As we enter the 2010s, doubts encircle the vigor and rhythm of the nascent 2009 recovery. So far, the fiscal stimuli and "abundant and cheap-liquidity" medicine seems to be taking hold. Fair enough; there can be still more widespread multiplier effects in the pipeline. While growing again, recoveries are not yet self-sustaining. The jobless recovery in the West continues to restrain consumer spending and hold down consumer confidence. Supply and demand remain fundamentally weak. Risks on the volatility of commodity markets (especially oil and food prices) remain high. Potential inflationary concerns down the line and continuing pressures on markets from soon-to-come interest rate hikes, and negative base-effects from premature stimulus withdrawal, bear heavily on investors' sentiment about the future. Worries about the knock-on impact of failures of States viz., United Arab Emirates (Dubai), Greece, Portugal, and Spain, add to uncertainties. All these have a strong bearing on growing fears of a possible "W"-type recovery—revival leading to a second dip, before a sustained rebound. Markets, investors, and consumers begin to worry even more with the call by Nobel laureates Paul Krugman[2] and Joseph Stiglitz[3] for another sizable "stimulus" for the United States because of a "significant" chance that activity will slacken in the second half of 2010, and growth will be unlikely to expand fast enough to create the jobs needed. Krugman stressed that new stimulus spending is needed or risk "many years of high unemployment."[4]

Optimism Is Not Good Enough

In a nutshell, having witnessed some of the worst in the past two years, the West is likely to remain in recession—already the output-gap is still rising. Even if, as some have estimated, this recession has permanently destroyed up to 10 percent of usable productive capacity, this gap won't shrink until 2011. No doubt, recent experience has taken a heavy toll on the Western psyche, leaving scars that will take years to mend. In contrast, the BRIIC countries (Brazil, Russia, India, Indonesia, and China) have since 2007 accounted for close to 50 percent of global growth, compared with 25 percent in 2000–2006 and 17 percent in the 1990s. Even so, they will take another 20 to 25 years to reach any semblance of parity with the West. Viewed differently, consumption in the United States and the eurozone totaled US$20 trillion, about 10 times that of China, and 18 times that of India.

As another exceptionally difficult year (2009) draws to a close, it is clear that glimmers of recovery seen at the macroeconomic level aren't adequately filtered down to everyday life. As a result, "Main Street" worldwide has been prone to what Keynes called herd-like waves of optimism and pessimism.

It is hard to say at this time whether the "green shoots" we now see will rekindle the spirit of optimism. For sure, optimism alone won't get us out of uncertainty. It needs to be founded in reality. Not unlike the West, Asian economic activity still depends on public policy support. The harsh reality is that the major developed nations remain Asia's largest market. Indeed, I am doubtful whether reality points to what someone labeled as "a calmer prosperity" still to come—or maybe more accurately, "a less prosperous calm" is in the making. Still, after two years, they are struggling to shed off much of the economic "baggage" they had created for themselves.

Picking through the Wreckage

The psychological baggage of the Great Depression was immense. Indeed, the damage was so traumatic, the scars so deep, that the Crash sapped the national psyche for risk and enterprise over two decades. Similarly, businesses and consumers today are suffering from post-traumatic stress. So fresh have been the memories of the past two years that indications of any new "failure" lead people to imagine the worst, relive old events, and take evasive action. That's why concerns about Dubai and Greece are so touchy. This is the psychological price people pay. Every loud "pop" now and then makes people run for cover. Since 2007, the vast majority of economists and analysts have a lot of egg on their faces. Be that as it may, they are still stuck with the problem that the unpredictable can happen. They say that "what you cannot forecast is a shock." If so, the recent crisis must be the most predicted shock in history! Economics continues to remain a dismal science. It is a fallacy that economic models (old or new), especially those with a base in history, are able to specify fundamental relationships in a complex globalized world. It will be foolish of me to even try to make predictions. Users of forecasts now know full well they cannot simply take them on trust.

Two Qualms to Unravel

But this I will do. Use experience and judgment to arrive at outcomes based on specific options and uncertainty. To me, until growth of nations is able to close the potential output gap, public policy in 2010 will remain loose. This is so because the following two areas of concern will shape prospective recovery worldwide.

First, what if the world really recovers but reverts to its old ways: The United States resumes consuming (by government and, maybe, even consumers) and Asia resumes supplying, with oil flowing to match demand. Just as unsustainable as before. Sure, global imbalances have since diminished, reflecting US economic weaknesses. China and India are importing relatively more. Is this the new trend? Unlikely. My sense is that with real recovery, China's export machine will be ramped up. Businesses revive and survive.

Second, US income and consumption rebuild slowly: Households save more (this is already happening) and government spending slackens, constrained by unsustainable deficits (a reality not easily avoided). The Chinese and Indian expansion is not powerful enough to decouple; there is no other growth machine. This appears to be the failed US–Euro strategy at G-20 in Pittsburgh.

G-20's "Framework for Strong Sustainable and Balanced Growth"—based on rest-of-world boosting domestic consumption to offset US savings—is now left hanging.[5] The Chinese and Indians definitely didn't buy it the way the United States had wanted through peer pressure. The global dilemma remains, with no real agreement on means to "force" nations' reform in ways they think don't serve their national interests. We saw this again at Copenhagen. So, I do agree it's premature to talk of stimulus withdrawal. Now is not the time to exit.

Indeed, what a difference 12 months of active public quantitative engagement makes. I see more of this to come. The battered world economy has since emerged in better shape than most had feared. Not even the politicians want to spoil this.

Growth Strategy—Competitiveness Matters

At home, what happens in the world economy looms large. The global crisis is Malaysia's wakeup call. The prime minister had articulated the need, objectives, and imperatives of the new economic model (NEM). I was privileged to have been asked to provide the "first cut" of the NEM during the 2010 budget dialogue in early June 2009. The next Malaysia has to be more balanced and more sustainable. One that favors private initiative, fastens private investment, fosters talent management in driving innovation, and foments competitiveness in all that it does.

What, Then, Are We to Do?

For 2010, six major areas need to be addressed in any strategic shift.

First, wide-ranging private business initiatives are needed to lead sustained recovery. Recognition of private investment's role (especially in the new growth areas of services and to rebuild and resecure supply chains) is vital. Not consumption directly. Unlike China, our consumers traditionally favor spending once permanent income is forthcoming. Don't put the cart before the horse. Sure enough, government stimulus is still needed until recovery is secured. Business confidence has to be nurtured. Lasting growth can only come with sustained flows of private capital. After that, government should be on tap, not on top.

Second, government's critical role remains at facilitating the continuing flow of private investment. Priority is to bring about ahead of demand, a visionary integrated transportation infrastructure, modern utilities, and related networks (including urban transit) to support the new growth areas. One "big bang" is needed. Like it or not, Asia and Southeast Asia are shrinking as a result of the rail and air revolution. To benefit, Malaysia can play a lead part in this vision.

Third, the new reality is dynamic innovation, competitive as hell worldwide. Catch-up is urgent and critical. As now structured (from research and development to venture capital; from life sciences to information technology and bio-tech), we are way, way behind. Innovation is strategic to our survival. It's no longer limited to new physical electronic products but includes all sorts of processes, systems, services, networks, interactions, entertainment forms, new means of communicating and collaborating, and design thinking. These are the new sorts of human talent–centered tasks that strategists and designers work on every day. We need to be part of the action.

Fourth, there is a talent war out there. We need to get real serious with talent management, from supplying to harnessing to importing. It's critical to implement clear policies to build a viable pool of global-savvy talent and niche skills. We do not appear to be a serious part of this movement. The global market for talent is highly choosy, mobile, and competitive.

Fifth, green growth addresses urgent and immediate economic and social needs within the new green global economy. Green is not just an option. It is a necessity. We have to reinvent and expand green stimulus elements, including energy efficiency, renewables, mass transit, new smart electricity grids, finance, and reforestation. New "green shoots" offer immense new opportunities for widespread small and medium-scaled enterprises' participation.

Sixth, the modern economy comprises privates for profit; the public (plus government-linked companies [(GLCs] for profit); and the nonprofits. Today, there is this burgeoning global movement of social enterprise that straddles all sectors. Reject Nobel laureate Milton Friedman's perspective that "the social responsibility of business is to increase profits." The timing is right for the NEM to cut four clear sectors. And, once and for all, banish the critique of GLCs misallocating resources and crowding out private initiatives, namely, private business, government per se, social enterprise (only the real strategic parts of GLCs), and nonprofits.

In the end, it all boils down to competitiveness being what really matters.

Obiter Dictum

One final observation: NEM in 2010 is all about change. In times of crisis, this change imperative is heightened. I can even understand the call for "all-at-once" overhaul. This is good politics. But frame-breaking change can't just be about getting things done now. Change is a process. Massive change has to be about getting the right outcomes, something rarely sorted out in a rush. They emerge from vigorous debate, from grappling with complex ideas and trade-offs, from changing mindsets, and from immersing in options and consequences. I will never argue against change. But achieving the right outcomes requires the right process. Ownership of it has to be bought in. Sound patience is advised.

On a lighter note, 2010 will be another stressful year. So, I am delighted turquoise is the chosen color for the year, in expectation of a stressful year ahead. This color is believed by the Chinese to be a "protective talisman, a color of deep compassion and healing, and a color of faith and truth, inspired by water and sky."[6] At least for now, we have a constant in 2010.

Hong Kong
Kuala Lumpur
December 24, 2009

Notes

1. First published on January 2, 2010, as "2010: Growing Again in 2010 But Hold on Tight."
2. Paul Krugman recommended more stimulus packages be put in place with higher inflation targets at the *World Capital Markets Symposium* in Kuala Lumpur on August 11, 2009.
3. Joseph Stiglitz suggested United States needs a second stimulus package in an interview in Singapore on December 21, 2009.
4. Krugman.
5. Group of 20 (G-20), "Leaders' Final Statement at Pittsburgh Summit: Framework for Strong, Sustainable, and Balanced Growth," G-20 Summit, Pittsburgh, September 24–25, 2009.
6. Pantone Color Institute. In a press release issued by the authority of color and color standards in the design industry, December 21, 2009.

CHAPTER 6

Summer 2010: In for a Bumpy Ride, Even a Double-Dip?[1]

The World Bank's "Global Economic Prospect Summer 2010 Report" carries both good and bad news.[2] The good news: Global economy will grow faster than previously forecast. It now expects global growth of between 2.9 percent and 3.3 percent this year, up from a January 2010 forecast of 2.7 percent. Developing economies will spearhead recovery, growing three times as quickly as their high-income counterparts from now until 2012. For developing countries in East Asia, the World Bank projects growth of 8.7 percent this year, then slowing down in 2011 and 2012. China is projected to be the fastest-growing economy—up by 9.5 percent this year and 8.5 percent in 2011. But for the rebound to endure, high-income nations need to seize opportunities offered by stronger growth elsewhere. The bad news: While markets have improved, reaction to a possible debt default and eventual contagion reflects fragility of the current situation. Indeed, market nervousness concerning the fiscal position of several European high-income countries poses a new challenge for the world economy. Upheaval in Europe simply means a double-dip recession can't be ruled out.

A Double-Dip?

Recent efforts from the International Monetary Fund (IMF) and other European institutions are expected to stave off a major European sovereign debt default. In this scenario, the World Bank expects high-income countries to grow just 2.1 to 2.3 percent this year—not enough to reverse last year's 3.3 percent GDP contraction. However, global economic growth could stall sharply if the European sovereign debt crisis produces a debt default or spurs loss of market confidence. If bond yields rose by 1 percentage point, projected world growth could slow to 2 percent this year and 0.7 percent in 2011. In the case of a full-fledged debt meltdown, high-income countries will expand by just 0.9 percent in 2010 and 0.6 percent in 2011. In this case, gross domestic product (GDP) of France, Germany, Italy, Spain, and the United Kingdom would fall sharply, causing a domino effect on exports to the rest of the European Union (EU) and the world. If Europe can avoid a debt crisis, signs of a steady recovery will continue. In the United States and Japan, the stimulus-led rebound is now being driven increasingly by more organic expansion, fueled by investment and consumer demand. That signals a more self-sustaining recovery and diminishes the risk of a double-dip recession. Historically, the only double-dip recession in modern times began during 1980 when the Fed slashed federal funds rate to 9 percent that April from 17.5 percent in July 1979. Inflation returned, so the Fed reversed course and pushed the rate above 19 percent by January 1981.

Europe is a different story. With growth last year now undermined by debt anxieties, the World Bank sees much weaker growth—even no growth for the EU as a whole if fiscal austerity, as now being promoted, comes to pass. Indeed, the fiscal situation in high-income countries in Europe and the United States is currently on an "unsustainable path, and there is a need for more rapid fiscal consolidation," says the World Bank.[3] This is not just to ensure sustainability of rich countries' public finances. But also, rapid cuts in public spending or tax hikes designed to return the rich countries' debt ratio to 60 percent of GDP by 2030 would benefit poorer economies. There will be a fall in export demand for sure, but this would be offset by improved financial positions, improved investment climate, and improved long-term interest rates. Over the longer term, these same factors can be expected to kick in a win-win situation. Nevertheless, Wall Street is convinced that fiscal tightening by European governments has dramatically shifted the macro-economic environment for the worse over the past five weeks. The world's leading hedge fund managers are already acting to reposition their funds for a double-dip recession. Many have begun to aggressively de-risk their portfolios. Others are closely monitoring their portfolios, preparing for growth to be far less than what people now expect.

The Deflation Dilemma

Since the Greece debacle, financial markets have been sending mixed signals. In essence, we see falling yields on US Treasury bills, suggesting that investors seem to worry more about economic stagnation and deflation. But we also see soaring gold prices, pointing to prospects of runaway inflation. This is confusing. A fair assessment suggests that as of today, deflation is the bigger danger in the big, rich nations, whereas inflation is of immediate worry in many emerging economies, and potentially a longer-term danger for the richer ones. Worries about consumer price deflation are resurfacing in the world's rich nations after weeks of market turmoil driven by Europe's fiscal crisis. The fears are most pronounced in Europe, where policy makers are under strong pressure to reduce unsustainable public debt, before any durable recovery can emerge. A combination of spending cuts and tax increases is likely to weigh down growth and feed deflation. In the United States, the eurozone, and Japan, deflation is uncomfortably close by, despite near-zero interest rates and other central bank actions. Year to April 2010, core consumer prices rose by 0.9 percent in the United States (lowest in four decades), by 0.7 percent in the eurozone, but fell by 1.5 percent in Japan, which has been battling falling prices for more than a decade. Money and credit growth are virtually stagnant or shrinking in all three places. Unemployment (especially among youths) is high, and large gaps remain between actual output and their potential. In the eurozone, new austerity programs will further sap domestic demand. The short-term consumer price outlook clearly points downward.

Deflation makes it harder for consumers, businesses, and government to pay off debts. Principal debt repayments are fixed, but deflation is marked by falling incomes. So, as deflation sets in, debt burden rises. Additionally, when prices fall, consumers put off purchasing in anticipation of still lower prices, driving the economy to a vicious cycle of weak spending and further sliding prices. Indeed, deflation is harder to fight because it is hard to stop. With interest rates near zero, policy makers can't use traditional rate cuts to spur growth and stop deflation. That's an acute worry.

Japan's ongoing fight against deflation suggests that preventing prices from falling is less well understood. Further budget belt-tightening suggests that interest rates will remain low for some time. This causes problems for emerging nations in terms of unwelcome capital inflows. Indeed, this makes it much more difficult for healthier economies to maintain financial stability. Many are already overheating, with rising consumer prices and asset bubbles.

The irony is that governments were the solution to the recent Great Recession. Now, they are the problem. The scale of sovereign debts has left rich-nation governments with less room to maneuver in any new downturn; most of them are being forced into austerity. The real danger lies in these fears reinforcing each other in a pernicious reversal of the dynamics of 2008 to 2009. Now, governments have become the problem that will drag the world economy down the path of deflation.

New Conventional Wisdom

After nearly two years of lockstep economic policy moves, the United States and Europe are going separate ways; with debt-wary Germany pressing for swift austerity on public spending and tax hikes while the United States preaches patience. The US administration is emblematic of this deepening rift over how best to secure a lasting economic recovery. This recent feud is best articulated by Nobel laureate Paul Krugman (supported by Nobel laureate Joseph Stiglitz), who calls it the "spread of a destructive idea."[4] After less than a year of weak recovery from the worst slump since World War II, it is not timely for governments to switch from supporting the economy and helping the jobless, to inflicting pain through fiscal austerity. Surely, not until the recovery is secure and self-sustainable. Lessons from the 1930s, when premature lifting of monetary and fiscal support led to a double-dip recession, must be applied. Germany's old scar is hyperinflation. What irked Krugman is the idea that what nascent economies really need now is even more suffering has become the new conventional wisdom. So much so that the European think tank, Organisation for Economic Co-operation and Development (OECD), has picked up this idea and suggested in its latest report that policy makers should stop promoting economic recovery and instead bring on raising interest rates, slashing spending, and hiking taxes.[5] Ironically, this flies in the face of what the global economy now really needs. OECD justifies its stand on two grounds: (1) need to head off inflation (certainly, inflationary expectations); yet, inflation is low and declining and OECD's own forecasts indicated no hint of an inflationary threat; and (2) need to cut spending to guard against the possibility that longer-term inflationary expectations could become unanchored. Fiscal austerity at a time of high unemployment must be a lousy idea; not only does it deepen the downturn but it does little to improve the budget outlook. On top of it all, OECD predicts that high unemployment will persist for years. It just doesn't make sense.

Indeed, the battle has taken a higher profile. Next week, the G-20 Summit of world leaders will be held in Toronto. In essence, the dispute boils down to one of sequencing. Gone was an earlier pledge—to maintain policy support until recovery is finally entrenched. In its place are statements stressing sustainable public finances and the need for some nations to accelerate the pace of consolidation. One thing is clear: Both the United States and Europe agree that current public debt levels are not sustainable. Their views differ on how and when to tackle them, quite obviously, colored by their memories of the 1930s—the United States fears premature lifting of fiscal and monetary support (and a double-dip), and Europe, fearful of runaway inflation, emphasizes fiscal restraint to restore confidence as a precondition for growth.

The rift goes beyond US–European politics—it's also in academia, as evidenced by the deep divide between prominent economists four months ago in the United Kingdom on this issue: those who assert that budget cuts should be postponed until the economy is out of the liquidity trap, and those who insist on immediate cuts (and hence, inflicting greater pain now) to achieve market credibility. Here Paul Krugman has a point: Currently, there is no evidence that the United States and the United Kingdom have any problems of access to markets. The world economy remains disturbingly fragile. Based on experience, premature fiscal tightening is as big a danger as delayed tightening can be. It is not clear that Europe is strong enough to absorb all that austerity. To be sure, a weaker Europe means a weaker global economy.

What, Then, Are We to Do?

Markets have been sending mixed signals. This is so because some markets move on shocks; some on macroeconomic trends; others on technical information; still others look for long-term value. But much of the recent fury and volatility of markets—rapid fall of the euro, tightening of bank rate spreads, tumbling stock indices, sharp swings in commodity markets—reflects new political risks. These include (1) market perception that governments are unwilling or unable to reform their economies—the Greek crisis saw governments paralyzed where inaction and delay made the problem worse; (2) market worries how soaring debts and budget deficits in the United States, Japan, and Europe are being handled—no evidence they are prepared for large tax increases or severe spending cuts, resulting in potential soaring inflation and debt defaults; (3) market concern on uncoordinated bank regulation reform—right now, the United States, EU, and Basle are all moving in different directions, at different speeds, and on different timelines.

There are other potential political risks—inability of governments to politically borrow more in the face of another shock crisis; apprehension that fiscal austerity could plunge economies into deflation, further raising unemployment and reviving recession; fear of competitive devaluations and global tariff war; and heightened sensitivity to connectivity among national and international economies so that local political sparks can light a global fire. So, the world is nervous for good reason. At this time, fundamentals are reasonably good. Unfortunately, political decisions are often unreasonably bad. Right now, that's what poses the highest risk to global sustainability.

Kuala Lumpur
June 18, 2010

Notes

1. First published on June 19, 2010, as "In for a Bumpy Ride: Perhaps Even a Double-Dip."
2. World Bank, *Global Economic Prospects Summer 2010* (Washington, DC: World Bank, 2010).

3. Ibid.

4. Paul Krugman, "The Pain Caucus," *International Herald Tribune* (June 1, 2010); "Does Fiscal Austerity Reassure Markets," *International New York Times* (June 14, 2010); and "That 30s Feeling," *International New York Times* (June 18, 2010).

5. Organisation for Economic Co-operation and Development (OECD), *Economic Outlook*, Issue 1 (2010), Paris.

CHAPTER 7

G-20 Summit, Toronto 2010: Reflects a Fragile Unity[1]

What a difference half a year makes. On the Pittsburgh G-20 Summit held in the fall of 2009, I concluded in Chapter 4: "Sure, there have been successes. And this has been an unusual period of desperate cooperation. But, the process of repair and recovery remains incomplete." What's worrisome is that the root cause of the recent global crisis was left unresolved, that is, the critical issue of global imbalances. "If we don't correct them, we'll have the recipe for the next major crisis. And this of course would be totally unacceptable." Indeed, these imbalances have deeper roots in global macroeconomic policy. I ended with four parting shots: (1) imbalances are not self-correcting; (2) the eurozone does not behave like one zone—each policy response is uncoordinated and nationalistic (no wonder the Greece crisis sparked off a new European crisis in March 2010); (3) no one-size-fits-all solution exists; each country will tailor-make its own solution, but this has to be well calibrated (why is no one surprised it wasn't?); and (4) there is no way to police this—none of surplus or deficit nations is ready to surrender sovereignty over its macroeconomic policies. G-20 had but started a conversation on these critical issues. The Toronto Summit ended at end-June 2010; its communiqué reflected, at best, a fragile unity. It's still too early to say where it will take us by year-end. I dare say, however, expectations of G-20 are way overrated.

The Toronto Accord

The boldness of the Pittsburgh Accord 2009 is, I guess, a product of the moment. When everyone wants the same thing—economic recovery—cooperation is easy: Indeed, it's free, no trade-offs here. In 2010, circumstances have drastically changed. Granted, many large, developed countries still have fiscal room to maneuver, while others have less, and some have none. Cooperation thus becomes more difficult as trade-offs have become increasingly more costly. The textbook case for fiscal coordination states simply: Surplus nations still with capacity to borrow should expand commensurate with available excess capacity; likewise, deficit nations with impending borrowing constraints should better manage whatever fiscal stimulus is left, consistent with fiscal constraints. In practice, however, the endgame is more complex because of politics. Continuing disagreement, which is what really happened in Toronto, raises the risk of a double-dip recession. Most glaring is the case of "bad boy" Germany in going for tightening fiscal policy despite its balance of payments surplus and oodles of unused borrowing capacity. However, the United Kingdom and Spain do look needlessly severe, even though they do have serious public debt problems. No doubt over the medium term, all should make a committed stand on fiscal austerity. But, at the same time, with nascent economic recovery—weak in the United States and feeble in Europe and Japan—this is no time to cut-your-nose-to-spite-your-face, with a head-on rush to fiscal retrenchment.

Nevertheless, despite initial difficulties in finding common ground, they did manage to agree on "differentiated and tailored" policies in two crucial areas. First, balance their contrasting priorities by pledging to halve budget deficits by 2013, without stunting growth. Second, clamp down on risky bank behavior without choking off lending. So, it was agreed:

> *Strengthening the recovery is key. . . . Recent events highlight the importance of sustainable public finances and the need for countries to put in place credible, properly phased and growth friendly plans to deliver fiscal sustainability, differentiated for and tailored to national circumstances.*
>
> *Advanced economies have committed to fiscal plans that will at least halve deficits by 2013 and stabilise or reduce debt-to-GDP ratios by 2016.*
>
> *Further progress is also required on financial repair and reform . . . [which] rests on four pillars. The first is a strong regulatory framework . . . ; second is effective supervision . . . ; third is resolution and addressing systemic institutions; and fourth is transparent internal assessment and peer review.*
>
> *We commit to strengthening the legitimacy, credibility and effectiveness of International Financial Institutions to make them even stronger partners . . . .*
>
> *. . . reiterate our support for bringing the World Trade Organization's Doha Development Round to a balanced and ambitious conclusion as soon as possible . . . and reiterate our commitment to a green recovery and to sustainable global growth.*[2]

Challenges and Risks

Overall, it was a polite agreement to disagree. For G-20, the agenda offered four challenges. First, the path to economic recovery. What's meant by "growth-friendly fiscal consolidation?" It seems to offer something to everyone—for the austerity hawks, fiscal retrenchment; and for the neo-Keynesians, one final fling at further stimulus. The real issue is, how fast to reduce government spending in the face of faltering recovery. Moving too fast runs the risk of a double-dip if private demand doesn't pick up the slack. Moving too slowly can lead to unsustainable debt load-ups, which can boost interest rates and threaten debt defaults à la Greece. What is really needed is to clearly demonstrate a will to reduce deficits without triggering a rapid slowdown in spending. Hence, priority must remain at safeguarding and strengthening the recovery. Indeed, G-20 acknowledged the dual risks facing global recovery: (1) risk that failure to "commit, communicate, and move forward," on clear, credible fiscal retrenchment plans could undermine the recovery; and (2) risk that a "rapid synchronized fiscal consolidation" could adversely impact prospects of a solid recovery. This "you have to be cruel-to-be-kind" strategy is disconcerting.

As I see it, it is important to realize that present conditions not only permit but also demand that the fiscal stimulus be extended. Interest rates remain at an all-time low; inflation is the least of the problems facing the United States, Europe, and Japan; and there are no signs of stress in the market for the US, Japanese, German, and French gilt-edged debt. But this "window" will not remain open for too long. In my view, the balance of risks favors keeping financial policy loose for the next 12 months. Recent data supports this. At the same time, a firm commitment to fiscal control is needed right now. This is urgently needed to restore confidence in the context of alarm over the outlook for debt being now so widespread.

Second, while G-20 agreed on the need for stronger financial regulation, actual details continue to be vague and lacking a solid deadline. In the end, it appears delay is better than diluting the new rules to meet the original deadline of end-2012: "There is a huge unfinished agenda"—(1) banks are given more time to adopt tougher global rules in a concession that the body tasked with coordinating reforms had said would safeguard the recovery and ultimately lead to stronger banks; (2) flexible timeline to build up higher levels of capital and liquidity, allowing breathing room for many banks still struggling from the recession; (3) time to ensure new regulations and pace of implementation do not cause undue market disruption; and (4) laid to rest plans to introduce a common tax on banks to shield taxpayers from paying for the next bailout.

Third, on free trade, G-20 backpedaled on pledges to press for a multilateral commitment to liberalization by end-2010 under the long-stalled Doha Round negotiations. This time they dropped the date and set no new one. In the end, politics (which favors protectionism) won the day.

Fourth, it's more of the same on G-20's commitment to a greener recovery and to sustainable global growth—just reaffirmation of support for the Copenhagen Accord and its implementation. For the most part, negotiations on all these matters were pushed off until the next meeting in Seoul at year-end. What a shame. Perhaps the time has come to make them responsible for what they say, as proposed by host Canadian Prime Minister at G-20. "Promises made by G-20 should be accompanied by a clear and transparent accounting of what each country will do and when," suggested Columbia's Professor Jeffrey Sachs.[3]

New Conventional Wisdom

Confronted with huge and growing fiscal deficits, a new conventional wisdom has emerged that priority should now be accorded to prompt fiscal tightening in the hope that this would prove expansionary. As I see it, this is indeed odd: Why might a sharp fiscal tightening promote recovery rather than undermine it?

Martin Wolf, in his July 1, 2010, column in the *Financial Times*, argued rather convincingly that the empirical basis for such an assumption is erroneous.[4] He cited a paper by Harvard's Professors Alberto Alesina and Silvia Ardagna, who concluded that smaller potential deficits improves confidence among businessmen and consumers, thus raising their spending and lowering the interest rate premium. At the same time, it increases the supply of labor, capital, and entrepreneurship. Its empirical underpinnings make the case that "fiscal adjustments based on spending cuts and no tax increases are more likely to reduce deficits and debt over gross domestic product (GDP) ratios than those based on tax increases." He also cited the study by Almunia et al., which concluded that fiscal stimulus was effective when tried.

Bear in mind that today we live in a Hobbesian world of survival of the fittest, with near-zero interest rates, where large nations are essentially mercantilist, businesses and households are credit constrained, unemployment is at an all-time high, and 60 percent of the world is affected by financial fragility. In this context, the view that early fiscal austerity will be strongly expansionary is at best, "heroic." Asia should brace itself to cope with downside risks, including being hit by spillover from the eurozone crisis and destabilizing capital flows bringing with it credit and asset bubbles.

Obiter Dictum

To be fair, the global economy and financial markets were recovering by end-2009. Into the second half of 2010, however, recovery is looking far less solid. If austerity in the eurozone succeeds, global turnaround will lose more steam. Even so, the International Monetary Fund (IMF) now forecasts (and assuming shocks from European debt problems continue) a no double-dip recession. World GDP growth would fall to 2.8 percent in 2011 as against 4.3 percent now forecast. This means very little growth (if at all) in Europe. China, India, and Brazil will still roar ahead. But there is a sense of reality that rebuilding global demand will take years. The IMF estimates the debt of advanced economies to be three times as large as the debt of emerging nations. No doubt, the United States remains focused on growth and job creation, and has made it clear that it will not be "the global consumer of last resort." Estimates are that the United States will reduce its fiscal deficit to 4.2 percent of GDP by 2013 (from 10.1 percent now). Bear in mind that public eurozone opinion has also shifted to erring on the side of prioritizing deficit reduction over short-term boosts to demand. Much could still change. But, for now, the rich G-20 nations are set to engage in the biggest synchronized fiscal adjustment (worth 1 percent of world GDP in 2011) in four decades.

What, Then, Are We to Do?

The "new normal" points to a diminishing capacity of the West to shape evolving events because of two missing links: lack of legitimacy of international institutions (viewed as a cover for Western hegemony) and, crucially, lack of trust among competing big nations, which makes their reform well-nigh impossible. This leaves the world in a "make-do and mend" mode— muddling through with ad-hoc deals and partnerships of convenience. A fast-moving geopolitical landscape leaves but one certainty—that is, uncertainty. We'll have to get used to having suboptimal options from now on.

Kuala Lumpur
July 15, 2010

Notes

1. First published on July 17, 2010, as "Toronto G-20 Summit Reflects a Fragile Unity."
2. Group of 20 (G-20). "The G-20 Toronto Summit Declaration," *G-20 Summit*, Toronto, Canada (June 26–27, 2010), paras. 4, 10, 17–22, 24, 38.
3. Jeffrey Sachs, "The Unaccountable G8," reproduced by *The Edge*, Malaysia (July 12, 2010).
4. Martin Wolf, "Why It Is Right for Central Banks to Keep Printing," *Financial Times* (June 23, 2010); and "The Global Game of 'Pass the Parcel' Cannot End Well," *Financial Times* (July 1, 2010). He concluded that the need to reduce fiscal deficit now will not work.

CHAPTER 8

IMF Meet, Fall 2010: A Cop-Out[1]

Maybe I am getting old. For 20 years since the early 1960s, I was a regular at the annual meetings of the International Monetary Fund (IMF). In those days, the annual meetings were eagerly awaited and exciting—serious systemic international monetary issues were usually taken up and resolved in corridors outside the main meeting. While concrete action was definitely lacking, the just-concluded mid-October meetings showcased the growing influence of emerging nations, who were on the verge of winning a greater share of IMF governance power. The flocking of a record number of private bankers and fund managers to gain insights from (and access to) policy makers from Asia, Africa, and Latin America offered the main excitement—a further testament to the growing importance of emerging markets where generous returns have drawn (and continue to draw) an uncomfortably heavy flow of investment monies from the United States and Europe. The mood was absorbing. But I sense the common thread was countries pursuing a national agenda in a fruitless effort to resolve major global problems. It is clear that no nation is really ready to act for the greater global good. So what else is new?

The main issue on the table was currencies—two to be precise: the US$ (US dollar) and the RMB (renminbi) or yuan. The US$ because it is deemed to be deliberately made too weak; and the RMB because it is deliberately managed too inflexibly (despite breaking away from its fixed parity with the US$ on June 19). Behind the squabbles much is at stake: viz. how to rebalance the global economy. The outcome was predictable—global economic cooperation was in tatters and the currency war (detailed in Chapter 73, "Currency Wars at a Time of Deficient Demand") is now destined to be picked up at the G-20 meetings in November in Seoul, after the weekend meetings broke up with no resolution.

Global Economic Adjustment

Let's step back. This year has gone messy. Policy makers had thought that having rescued the world from the brink of economic disaster they would by now be plotting an exit from stimulation rather than planning again to boost demand. IMF data pointed to an anemic global recovery after initially experiencing rather rapid growth, albeit uneven. As a result, gross domestic product (GDP) of the rich economies is still below pre-2008 levels. Stubbornly high unemployment is making lives uncomfortable and souring politics. The eurozone narrowly avoided igniting a second worldwide crisis in May following the "bailout" of Greece and possibly other highly indebted Euro-nations at risk of sovereign default. Continuing massive monetary easing by the United States and, until recently, the eurozone flooded global markets with US$ in particular, forcing emerging economies like Brazil, India, and Thailand to take steps to protect themselves from destabilizing capital inflows, including exchange market interventions. The IMF now touts capital controls. Japan intervened in the currency markets for the first time in six years to halt its yen from being further appreciated but with little success. Against this backdrop, the October 12 communiqué of the International Monetary and Financial Committee of the IMF stated firmly:

> *While the international monetary system has proved resilient, tensions and vulnerabilities remain as a result of widening global imbalances, continued volatile capital flows, exchange rate movements, and issues related to the supply and accumulation of official reserves. Given that these issues are critically important for the effective operation of the global economy and the stability of the international monetary system, we call on the Fund to deepen its work in these areas, including in-depth studies to help increase the effectiveness of policies to manage capital flows.*[2]

What a cop-out.

The Mechanics of Rebalancing

The IMF's economic counselor, Olivier Blanchard, is right in stating that "achieving a strong, balanced and sustainable world recovery was never going to be easy. . . . It requires two fundamental and difficult economic rebalancing acts."[3] The first is internal balancing. The recession arose because private demand collapsed; fiscal stimulus helped alleviate the fall in GDP—which has to eventually give way to fiscal consolidation; this means sustained growth needs private demand to resume and be strong enough to take over and lead. Second, external rebalancing. Most advanced nations (notably, the United States) that relied excessively on domestic demand must now restructure to depend more on net exports to grow; similarly, most emerging economies (mainly China), which depended largely on net exports, must now switch to rely increasing on domestic demand. Adjustment problems arose because both rebalancing acts moved too slowly.

On paper, what needs to be done is straightforward. The private sector of high-spending, high-deficit rich nations needs to deleverage quickly to reach the "new normal" referred to by this year's Per Jacobsson Foundation Lecture speaker, Mohamed El-Erian (chief executive officer of PIMCO, the world's largest bond fund manager). At the same time, economies with robust payment surpluses and strong investment opportunities need to let their exchange rates reflect the market and appreciate, while encouraging domestic demand to expand to offset the consequential drag from a fall in net exports.

In practice, what happened was overdone and undercooked. Aggressive monetary easing by reserve-issuing rich nations (again, notably the United States) flooded the world with cheap US$, pushing exchange rates of strong emerging nations to revalue (since the US$ as the world's anchor can't devalue on its own). Worse, capital recipients reacted stubbornly to accept the needed changes and acted to deflect the changes elsewhere. Hence, the currency "wars." Martin Wolf of the *Financial Times* sums it up best: "The United States wants to inflate the rest of the world, while the latter tries to deflate the United States."[4]

Frankly, the United States is getting desperate. The jobless recovery is not getting better fast. Debt deleveraging is moving too slowly. Monetary policy is up against Keynes's liquidity trap (further falls in interest rates can't stimulate demand). Inflation is low and falling. To avoid debt deflation, the Fed has reintroduced QE2 (quantitative easing, Mark 2). The objective is to avoid deflation. The Fed is determined to do what it takes to meet this goal. Whatever impact this has on the rest of the world is collateral damage. However, the World Bank has since warned that surging capital inflows threaten Asia's economic stability and fan fears of asset bubbles.

We can already see what's going to happen. On October 15, 2010, the chairman of the Fed sent a clear message, sledgehammered home by four phrases (in italics): The Fed takes its cues from two primary objectives: the *longer-run sustainable rate of unemployment* and the *mandate-consistent inflation rate,* adding what the Fed thinks of both right now: Inflation is *too low* and unemployment is *too high*. This means further QE2 is a given. The Fed will turn up its electronic printing pieces, create loads of US$, and buy trillions of US Treasury debt, as it is poised to do to resuscitate the US economy. The Fed is determined to do what it wants to and needs to—like it or not.

Problem Not One of Coordination

As I see it, what's unfolding are radically different views of the world. China does not accept that its undervalued exchange rate is a significant cause of global imbalances. Beijing goes on to suggest that the US external deficits and fiscal deficits are self-inflicted. The common view in the United States is Asia's excess savings created the US current account deficits. So the solution lies in Asia. It has come to a stage of not who blinks first, but who moves first if at all, and in what direction. So there is no deal. Other emerging nations are mostly caught in between: concerned about China's currency misalignment, which undercuts their exports, but worried at the same time that fund managers armed with lots of cheap US$ are driving their currencies higher in search of higher yields. No doubt, QE2 is potentially very stimulative, with expansive ramifications for the global economy. This is particularly so if it compels other central banks to follow suit in retaliation to protect their currencies' value and ward off inflation. But does QE2 really work? It comes out loud and clear at the IMF meetings that European central banks and politicians need lots of convincing.

Similar Problems, Different Paths

Despite almost identical problems—high unemployment and very low inflation—the Fed and the European Central Bank (ECB) walk vastly different paths in their policies. The chairman of the Fed attributed the unemployment to the sharp contraction in economic activity that occurred in the wake of the financial crisis and the continuing shortfall in aggregate demand since then, rather than structural factors. The Fed is wedded to using all tools at its disposal to lower long-term rates and goose growth to reduce the jobless. Hence, more QE2. The Europeans regard their unemployment as more structural, reflecting labor rules. Axel Weber, Germany's central bank chief, stresses often enough in the press that his reading of what happened in the (eurozone) labor markets during the crisis is largely structural and needs structural policies. Who's right? In the eurozone, there is a wide unemployment gap—from 4.3 percent in Austria to 20.5 percent in Spain. In the United States, there is growing concern that unemployment could become structural. The term *hysteresis* is now used to describe this dynamic in which the longer you remain jobless, the more your skills erode; as you get used to being out of work, you adjust your behavior, which makes reentry to work tougher. The real challenge is whether more QE spurs real investment, badly needed to bring down the jobless rate. In the United States, this gets more complicated because of viable attractive alternatives: including use as capital-protection against US$ debasement and inflation; and greater growth prospects in emerging countries. Nobel Laureate Joseph Stiglitz thinks QE is "ineffective in reviving the US economy . . . won't do much to stimulate business directly." For the ECB, "monetary policy cannot, by itself transform a jobless recovery into a job generating recovery."[5]

What, Then, Are We to Do?

The world appears on the brink of a nasty confrontation over exchange rates. China's central bank chief, Zhou Xiaochuan, realizes the yuan value will rise, but its strength must depend on gauging fundamentals like inflation, growth, and employment: "China would like to use more gradual ways to realise a balance between domestic and external demands. . . . We have a package to enhance internal demand including consumption, social security system reform, new investment in the rural areas."[6] But the United States is seeking to impose its will via the printing press. Frankly, there is no limit to the amount of US$ the Fed can create. At its heart, the currency war appears more like a skirmish. The real problem lies in there being no political will to really reform the international monetary system. The core of the system is unstable and unsustainable. Reckless risk taking can once again lead to widespread collateral damage. The communiqué after the IMF meeting spoke of countries working "cooperatively," but says nothing on how to find lasting agreement on the issues that divide them.

Kuala Lumpur
October 20, 2010

Notes

1. First published on October 23, 2010, as "IMF Meet '10—A Cop-Out."
2. International Monetary Fund (IMF), "Communiquè of the 22nd Meeting of the IMF and the International Monetary and Financial Committee of the IMF's Board of Governors" (October 9, 2010), p. 3.
3. Olivier Blanchard, Foreword to the *World Economic Outlook, October 2010: Recovery, Risk and Rebalancing* (Washington, DC: IMF, 2010), p. xiii.
4. Martin Wolf, "Why America Is Going to Win the Global Currency Battle," *Financial Times* (October 14, 2010).
5. Joseph Stiglitz, "The Federal Reserve's Relevance Test," reproduced in *The Edge*, Malaysia (October 18, 2010).
6. Kristina Cooke and Paul Eckert, "Fast Yuan Revaluation No Panacea, Zhou Says," Reuters (October 12, 2010), reporting remarks by Zhou Xiaochuan, Governor, People's Bank of China at the IMF meetings in Washington, DC.

CHAPTER 9

G-20 Summit, Seoul 2010: Much Ado about Nothing[1]

The recent G-20 Seoul Summit was a disappointment. Because expectations were carefully managed down, most were really not surprised to be disappointed. When all is said and done, nothing really happened. G-20 succeeded in assisting the traditional and emerging powers to agree to disagree. Pretty much more of the same—each country will continue doing whatever it was already doing. Much ado about nothing, really, except the willingness to keep talking and worrying. President Obama puts it best at the Summit: "The work that we do here is not always going to seem dramatic. It's not always going to be immediately world changing. But step by step what we are doing is building stronger international mechanisms and institutions that will help stabilize the economy, ensure economic growth, and reduce some tensions."

On global trade imbalance, the British prime minister added: "The key thing is being discussed in a proper multilateral way without resort to tit-for-tat measures and selfish policies." Let's hope it was not a multilateral monologue! The communiqué reflected "rewarmed" pronouncements of good intentions. While understandably short of actionable solutions, it did at least seem to acknowledge the difficulties of the situation. Not surprisingly, G-20 reiterated its commitment to work together toward strong, sustainable, and balanced (SSB) growth, and to take additional measures to achieve shared objectives.

After dramatically forging a sense of unity during the crisis, the G-20 has now splintered, with competitive policies and rancor taking place instead of taking on coordinated policy actions. While the leaders were sidetracked from making the strong decisions, a new report from the International Monetary Fund (IMF) suggested that much more forceful action on imbalances is going to be needed, and soon, with prospects of deficits in the advanced nations likely to double by 2014 if nothing is done now. All the G-20 Summit managed to produce was a final document in which leaders agreed on various measures to achieve economic stability, none of them specific enough to act on or be enforced.

The Seoul Action Plan

The G-20 launched the Seoul Action Plan (SAP), shaped "with unity of purpose," to ensure "unwavering commitment to cooperation," with each member making "concrete policy commitments" to deliver all three objectives of SSB growth.[2] Specifically, commitments were made to act in five policy areas.

Monetary and exchange rate policies: The G-20 Group will move toward "more market-determined exchange rate systems and enhance exchange rate flexibility to reflect underlying economic fundamentals"—which China claims it's already doing.[3] The group will also "refrain from competitive devaluation of currencies"—which the United States denies its QE2 (second round of quantitative easing) is engaged in, and helps mitigate "the risk of excessive volatility in capital flows facing some emerging market economies" by allowing the use of "carefully designed macro-prudential measures"—sanctioning for the first time capital controls that are increasingly being imposed by the likes of Korea, China, Brazil, the Philippines, and Thailand, flooded with foreign capital (arriving mostly from cheap excess dollars from QE2 in search of higher yields), thus avoiding being considered global scofflaws.

Structural reforms: The G-20 Group will "implement a range of structural reforms to boost and sustain global demand, . . . contribute to global re-balancing . . .; and strengthen multilateral co-operation to promote external sustainability and pursue the full range of policies conducive to reducing excessive imbalances and maintaining current account imbalances at sustainable levels."[4] Since the last summit in 2009, commitments like these ran into insurmountable problems of not being able simultaneously to agree on specific policies to achieve their ambitions, nor a timetable, nor an enforceable mechanism to ensure that everyone plays ball. Leaders in Seoul expressed the conviction that this time would be different: They promised to assess imbalances by nebulous-sounding "indicative guidelines," to be developed by the Framework Working Group (assisted by the IMF) and discussed by finance ministers in the first half of 2011. This time, G-20 talks of "a shared responsibility . . . [where] members with sustained, significant external deficits pledge to undertake policies to support private savings and where appropriate undertake fiscal consolidation, while maintaining open markets and strengthening export sectors. Members with sustained significant external surpluses pledge to strengthen domestic sources of growth."

But without effective coordinated cooperative action, unsustainable imbalances will eventually be adjusted by market forces with the inevitable result of making things harder all round. The risk now is for adjustment to be messier than it needs to be. Where market forces are not allowed to prevail (as in China), the temptation for politicians (in the United States and Europe) to try to force adjustment through tariffs and import barriers can only grow. I now sense a pervasiveness that the G-20 has reached the limit of cooperative efforts toward global rebalancing. With advanced economies barely plodding along while emerging nations are enjoying robust growth, reconnecting the different approaches to policies required will become increasingly more difficult. Bear in mind that the Germans are still growing after rejecting US advances in 2009 to join the US spending stimulus.

China is growing smartly, having rejected counsel from three US administrations to abandon its currency discipline. Even the United Kingdom and France are pursuing more fiscal restraint. Only the United States is determined to keep both the fiscal (hopefully) and monetary spigots open, while blaming everyone else for its jobless recovery. Meanwhile, China, India, and other Asian economies fear that rather than spurring more growth in the United States, QE2 is flooding the developing world with more dollars than they are able to efficiently absorb, producing uncertain exchange rate volatility to the detriment of their external trade and sending the world's dollar-denominated commodity prices climbing with serious impact on domestic inflation.

Agreeing to measurable targets for external imbalances is bound to prove difficult. Already, before the Summit, China and Germany had rejected specific targets for current accounts (amounting to new controls on trade and capital flows, which go against three decades of US policy against barriers to the free flow of money and goods)—just as other groups of countries had refused in 2009 to sign up to specific stimulus targets. As a compromise, the vague notion of "indicative guidelines" was set to usher in the year ahead of squabbling about the right indicators to use. The underlying problem, as I see it, lies in forcing nations to agree when they have irreconcilable differences over their global economic approaches and domestic policy prescriptions. In practice, no country is willing to cede sovereignty of its basic economic policies to a multilateral agency. The follow-through is bound to raise serious problems.

Fiscal policies: Advanced economies will formulate and implement "clear, credible, ambitious and growth friendly medium-term fiscal consolidation plans."[5] Like it or not, the conflict between the new-world approach (essentially Keynesian, involving continuing stimulus with fiscal adjustments over the medium term when economic recovery is entrenched) and the old-world approach (largely Hayekian—i.e., fiscal consolidation to address the deficit and debt problems now because "it is good for confidence, consumption, and investment today," according to the president of the

European Central Bank) is real and here to stay. Its resolution, in my view, heightens the urgent need for serious global coordination of polices, especially monetary policy.

Financial reforms: The G-20 Group is committed to take action "to raise standards and ensure national authorities implement global standards developed to deter, consistently, in a way that ensures a level playing field . . . and avoids fragmentation of markets, protectionism and regulatory arbitrage; . . . [and] will implement fully the new bank capital and liquidity standards and address too-big-to-fail problems."[6] As I understand it, officials will finalize a package of capital surcharges and other safety measures next year (i.e., 2011).

IMF reform: The G-20 made a historic breakthrough in granting a greater voice to developing nations on the governance of the IMF at the expense of Europe. This ensures that quotas and management composition at the IMF are "more reflective of new global economic realities." China will become the third-largest member of the 187-strong institution. Horse-trading is still ongoing on the final recomposition of the boards and to pursue "all outstanding governance reform issues at the World Bank and IMF."

Trade and development policies: The G-20 Group reaffirms its commitment to "free trade and investment; . . . [and] will refrain from introducing, and oppose protectionist actions in all forms and recognize the importance of a prompt conclusion of the Doha negotiations."[7] However, it offered no advice on how to resolve serious tensions between the rich and poor nations that tanked the talks in the first place.

The Seoul Development Consensus (SDC) for Shared Growth

The SDC is intended to steer international development away from financial handouts to broaden the factors that promote economic growth, especially in infrastructure. It stands in contrast to the 1989 Washington consensus, which focused on fiscal discipline, privatization, and trade liberalization. The SDC envisages (1) rich countries to engage poor nations as equal partners and allows them to set their own strategic course; (2) no one-size-fits-all formula for development success—that is, leaves nations to design and implement development strategies tailored to individual needs and circumstances; and (3) a multiyear action plan focusing on infrastructure, private investment, and jobs, and food security for poor countries. In an unprecedented step, a panel of 12 nations was created to work in 2011 on measures to mobilize infrastructure financing. On these, G-20 promised to deliver! As I see it, the SDC's pragmatic and pluralistic view of development is appealing enough. But it avoided setting numerical targets that can hold richer nations to account in areas such as opening up markets to exports from the developing world.

What, Then, Are We to Do?

It's a pity the G-20 lacks leadership this time around. Without doubt, faltering US influence will produce a vacuum. But the fact remains that the United States is still the world's largest economy, the issuer of its sole reserve currency, and its lone military superpower. Future leadership is now tied to US policies and priorities to lead the global economy. To begin with, US primacy and credibility can be regained only with robust all-round economic performance. As someone just remarked: The United States needs to start punching above its weight rather than below it. It is also a fact that on current trends, emerging markets and developing nations will account for 60 percent of global gross domestic product within six years. It's a different world ahead. This heightens the need to find a "new normal," whereby the US relationship with China and the new world remains central in the challenges going forward. As Professor Lawrence Summers puts it this week: "Our wisdom, their wisdom, the way in which we interact is going to be of the utmost importance."[8]

Leaderless, the G-20 now shapes up as the least ineffective global forum—not enough to keep another crisis away, or deal with one when it arrives. Live with it. We just have to wait and see.

Kuala Lumpur
November 18, 2010

Notes

1. First published on November 20, 2010, as "The G-20 Seoul Summit: Much Ado About Nothing."
2. Group of 20 (G-20), "The Seoul Action Plan (SAP)," G-20 Summit, Seoul, South Korea, November 12, 2010, paras. 4, 5.
3. Ibid., para. 6.
4. Ibid., para. 10.
5. Ibid., para. 8.
6. Ibid., para. 9.
7. Ibid., para. 7.
8. Lawrence Summers (White House National Economic Council Director), addressing the *Wall Street Journal* CEO Council, Washington, DC, on November 17, 2010.

CHAPTER 10

TW3 2010: The World Trichotomized[1]

I am often asked: What's happening to the world? Indeed, the world seems so messed up we can't take anything for granted. It does look like the world is not simply just dichotomized, anymore. We are used to talking of north versus south, haves versus have-nots, developed versus developing. All this has changed since Thomas Friedman's (*International New York Times*) discourse that the world is flat; but Harvard's Pankaj Ghemawat has since demonstrated that the world is not really flat.[2] What's going on? But if this is true, why is there no convergence? What's in store for the future? Before we begin the new year, I intend to devote my last essay for 2010 to throw some light on these important questions, and what we can look forward to in 2011.

State of the World Economy

As I see it, the situation in the United States blows hot and cold. By December 2010, the US economy reached a crossroad as a flurry of data showed consumption may be recovering fast enough to sustain growth in 2011, despite weaker investment, continuing high unemployment, and a gloomy housing outlook. What's promising is inflation continues to fall (core personal consumption prices rose only 0.9 percent in October). This prompted former Fed Chairman Paul Volcker to conclude the economic outlook is for continuing but limited increases in economic activity for the next year or more. He added that inflation is not a problem next year. It won't be a problem for several years—indeed, he doesn't see a possibility that a deflation will take place. Over a period of time, price stability will be conducive to a strong economy. Make no mistake, President Barack Obama is worried, too. What is a danger is that we are stuck in a "new normal" where unemployment rates stay high in the face of continuing high corporate profits where businesses learned to do more with less.

However, the tax package awaiting approval in Congress could give a noticeable boost to economic activity next year—providing a second stealth stimulus package without antagonizing lawmakers reluctant to spend more to spur growth. The total package could amount to US$900 billion (larger than the first stimulus package in 2009) of spending and tax cuts over the next two years. In the third quarter of 2010, the economy was stalling at 2.5 percent (2.5 percent in the second quarter of 2010). "This gives us a chance to do what most people thought wasn't going to be possible in this environment, which is to provide a real forward lift to the economy relatively quickly," according to Lawrence Summers (director of the US National Economic Council).

Economists have since grown more optimistic, seeing a stronger expansion in the first half of 2011, with growth picking up speed as the year progresses (as much as 3.5 percent) in 2011. Odds of a double-dip recession are now cut to 15 percent. Data released in recent days point to a recovery that is gathering steam in the fourth quarter of 2010 (shoppers' purchases were up 0.8 percent in November and core wholesale prices rose at a milder 0.3 percent), pointing to growth of 3.5 percent in the final quarter. Nevertheless, while the fourth quarter of 2010 is shaping up rather decently, the Fed continues to view the pace of recovery as still too slow to bring down the 9.8 percent unemployment rate. Its US$600 billion bond-buying program (QE2) is expected to continue.

The euro-area remains under siege. Greece and Ireland are in the International Monetary Fund's (IMF) intensive care. The fiscal crisis threatens to engulf the peripheral PIIGS (Portugal, Ireland, Italy, Greece, and Spain). Yet, for all its sovereign bond risk turmoil, overall, its real economy is stabilizing. The Organisation for Economic Co-operation and Development (OECD) think tank raised its forecast growth in the 16-member nations sharing the euro to 1.8 percent for 2010 (2 percent in the fourth quarter of 2010), slow by US standards but acceptable for the aging continent. Growth across the euro-bloc will soften before picking up again: It is expected to average 1.6 percent in 2011 and 1.8 percent in 2012.

Eurozone growth slowed markedly in the third quarter of 2010 as Germany's rapid growth spurt lost momentum, intensifying pressure on Europe's weakest economies. This deceleration reduced opportunities for the PIIGS to grow out of the current crisis by exporting to its neighbors. It also showed the eurozone lagging behind the United States, which is doing much better. So, recovery will be modest in the next two years, as deficit-reduction plans weigh on growth and large imbalances in the peripheral European nations with high debt are wound down. This fans concerns of a widening chasm between Germany's buoyant prospects and continuing struggles of the PIIGS economies. It highlights a dualism in Europe—between core countries mainly in northern Europe and the eurozone laggards, which have since become a source of serious concern.

Although Germany is doing well, it may not be enough to save others in the eurozone. This perception of the eurozone drifting apart has been and remains a driver of the sovereign debt crisis. Continuing market jitters about the situation is one of the main risks to play out in 2011.

The outlook for stronger growth in Europe faces two big threats. First, fiscal tightening is expected to begin with vigor next year. But there are already enough signs of intensifying social unrest. Second, there is growing tension in Europe's peripherals (viz. PIIGS). Ireland and Greece are in recession, with debt-overhang ratios exceeding 100 percent. The austerity required of them is unlikely to be readily met. Spain and Italy are barely growing, and they, too, need to tackle their budget deficits, with ratios too high to be sustainable. Portugal has only started to act on its deficit. Delays have kept its economy afloat but made bond investors rather nervous. The PIIGS account for 35 percent of the euro-area economy (18 percent without Italy). Their fragility has not so far outweighed the strength of the entire region. However, they have outsized effects on monetary policy simply because of their impact on confidence, especially in the bond markets. It is interesting that Germany and the European Central Bank (ECB) have taken a tag-team approach to keeping the eurozone afloat: The former supports the zone's economy and the ECB, its financial markets. One key success of the euro has been its financial integration, so much so that its banks are now heavily exposed to each other's debts. So, more trouble in the peripheral European nations could easily spread, with dire consequences for the eurozone as a whole.

Since the Great Recession, the emerging economies have been by far the biggest contributor to global expansion. From Guangzhou to Sao Paulo, from Bangalore to Incheon, the big emerging economies have been roaring ahead, even as the United States and Europe are mired in deep recession. Spare capacity was rapidly used up, and fear of bubbles (from capital inflows following continuing monetary easing in the United States and Europe) was replaced by broader overheating and fear of inflation.

China and India led the way with sustainable high growth rates and with even higher imports, as did Brazil, where rising consumer demand packed shopping centers, and imports in November surged 44 percent. But inflation lurks. Nowhere has the economic mood been so ably lifted as in emerging East Asia (Northeast Asia plus ASEAN-6[3]), led by China. Emerging East Asia's gross domestic product (GDP) grew by 8 percent annually since 2004 (9 percent in 2010) and is expected to continue to rise by 7.5 percent in 2011. China will expand by 10 percent this year (+9.1 percent in 2009) and 9 percent next year. Similarly, ASEAN-6—according to the Asian Development Bank—will grow by 5 percent in 2011 after expanding 7.5 percent in 2010 (1.3 percent in 2009). In contrast, growth in the United States in 2010 is expected at 2.8 percent (–2.6 percent in 2009) and 3.5 percent in 2011. Eurozone GDP contracted by 5.2 percent in 2009, and is set to recover by 3.2 percent this year, with growth of 1.4 percent in 2011.

But inflation worries are causing a policy dilemma. High food and energy prices plus capacity constraints in the face of the Fed's quantitative easing (QE2) will force central banks to raise interest rates more aggressively. But higher interest rates to fight inflation will attract even more funds. Inflation is highest in India (9 percent) and Brazil (6 percent): in China, 4.5 percent; South Korea, 4 percent; Indonesia, 5.7 percent; Malaysia, 2.5 percent; To ensure interest is kept at rates appropriate to their particular circumstances, some emerging Asian economies have resorted to selective controls to offset the impact of continuing inflows of cheap monies.

Manufacturing activity strengthened significantly in China and India in November, underlying a widening gap between two of Asia's largest economies and the rest of the region. Not unlike Europe, Asia is being dichotomized into two economic camps as growth steams ahead in China and India, but grows at a slower pace in much of emerging Asia or stays relatively flat, as in Japan. But unlike Europe, where its life-wire (Germany) is moderating, emerging Asia's big brothers are pushing ahead: China recorded in November its seventh successive month of manufacturing expansion. Similarly, India registered a blistering 8.9 percent growth in the third quarter of 2010, its third in a row exceeding 8 percent. India's continuing expansion is fueled by rapidly rising demand within the Asian community, thus sharing prosperity through reversing the tide in the directional flow of goods and services.

Focus has sharply swiveled to Asia: Before, we mainly worried about the Christmas and New Year seasons in the United States and Europe. Now we also look at Ramadan, Diwali, and Chinese New Year. There is a clear surge in intraregional trade in Asia, which grew at an average annual rate of 13.4 percent from 2000 to 2009, valued at US$1 trillion. Nearly 50 percent of Asian exports (ex-Japan) now go to other Asian nations, more than the current demand for Asian exports from the United States, Europe, and Japan combined. Another 17 percent goes to rest of the world, meeting largely Russian and Brazilian demand. The main driver of this drama: China and India. In 1916, Nobel laureate Rabindranath Tagore (Indian poet) roamed from Calcutta to Tokyo in search of "one Asia." The poet's vision was misty. Yet, by end of the century, Asia is knit together in a value-adding manufacturing supply chain stretching 5,000 kilometers from Seoul to Penang to Mumbai.

Importing Pessimism

As I see it, the world has changed, and dramatically so, since the great recession. The outlook for 2011 and beyond rests on what happens in three great areas: the United States, Europe, and emerging economies. Fair enough—Japan is still an economic heavyweight, but it has ceased to be dynamic and is unlikely to surprise. Unfortunately, all three are heading in different directions with different growth prospects and having noncompatible policy choices. The outcome depends on how increasing chances for friction play out.

The United States and Europe avoided depression by working together with a shared economic philosophy. Now, both are preoccupied with clear domestic demands. They have since adopted wholly opposite strategies to deal with them: The United States is continuing to stimulate until recovery is secured (i.e., falling unemployment) before tackling its fiscal and debt issues; the eurozone is dead-on fiscal austerity and consolidation, subjecting profligate members to tough fiscal adjustments now in exchange for assistance. The United States is continuing loose monetary policies, and the eurozone concerns with sovereign debt defaults encourage a continuing flow of virtually costless funds to emerging economies in search of higher returns. Such massive capital inflows infuriate large, emerging economies' central banks, which are reluctant to raise interest rates (and attract even more such funds) so needed to dampen rising inflation. Therein lies the policy dilemma for each of the three.

What, Then, Are We to Do?

Bear in mind that over the next five years, emerging economies are expected to account for one-half of global growth, but only 13 percent of the increase in net global public debt. This simply means that given divergent goals of policy, the world economy is unlikely to give any priority to global rebalancing (which is so badly needed) in favor of more of the same. The consequence: the widening gap between debt-ridden United States and Europe and thrifty big, emerging nations. It need not be this way, of course. The United States and Europe can work out a deal to better regulate the financial system, with the United States starting early enough to put its fiscal house in order and Europe institutionalizing the euro and putting its banking system on a more sustainable footing.

On their part, major emerging economies can start rebalancing their macroeconomic policies, including adjusting the exchange rate to better reflect underlying market conditions. This, of course, is the best-case scenario. But I won't bet on it. I see continuing friction ahead, leading to more uncertainties in terms of policy actions, but unfortunately, with little effective international collaboration and coordination. That's life, I guess. In times of stress, subjecting national interest to the noble greater global interest is asking too much. So Asia stands ready for another year of importing pessimism.

Kuala Lumpur
December 17, 2010

Notes

1. First published on December 18, 2010, as "The World Trichotomized."
2. Thomas Friedman, *The World Is Flat—A Brief History of the Globalized World in the 21st Century* (New York: Allen Lane, 2005); Pankaj Ghemawat, "Why the World Isn't Flat," *Foreign Policy* (February 14, 2007), pp. 54–60.
3. Comprising Indonesia, Malaysia, the Philippines, Singapore, Thailand, and Vietnam.

CHAPTER 11

Prospects 2011: As the World Turns[1]

I am back. Missed my last column in *The Star* as I had to put in a "bionic" spine on March 6. Technically, I underwent a major surgery to resolve degenerative lumbar kypho-scoliosis, causing severe multilevel spinal stenosis. Simply put, I had to fuse lumbar vertebrae #L2, L3, L4, L5, and S1 (the secrum). The outcome: I now have 10 screws in my lower back, and these are held together by two 8-inch titanium rods. It took eight hours of surgery, so I now have sort of a "bionic" lower spine. That does sound awesome, but I am fine—walking and sleeping without pain; a trade-off I assumed in exchange for a rather stiff and inflexible lower back. No more golf for me, I am afraid. But no problems in continuing with my qigong.

The past week was not all bad. On March 19, I was conferred the Honorary Doctorate in Economics by Universiti Sains Malaysia, at which I have served as its Pro-Chancellor for the past 10 years (2000–2010). It was an honor I deeply appreciated. Then, on March 23, I was awarded the Brand Laureate Brand Personality Award, 2010–2011, for achievements in economics and finance. That's rather sobering since I have also been associated with (sitting on the boards of directors, mainly) some of the best Malaysian and foreign brands over the past 17 years: Jobstreet, Mid-Valley MegaMall, Genting and Resorts World, Silverlake, Top Glove, Fraser and Neave, Coca-Cola, Great Eastern Life, Straits Trading, and Cabot of Boston.

State of the World

Just as economic expansion is stabilizing in the long-troubled United States and the eurozone, concerns are now emerging on the economic health of Asia and the Middle East. The unfolding disaster in Japan following the March 11 earthquake and tsunami, along with the continuing turmoil in the Middle East, have raised new concerns and uncertainties over economic prospects in these regions, including their impact on food and commodities' prices, especially oil. As events turned, the US economy now appears healthier, with growth slowly gathering strength and consumers cautiously borrowing again. But, it's still a sluggish recovery, with high unemployment at 8.9 percent, albeit its lowest in nearly two years, and a struggling housing market. Let's face it: US households are still carrying far too much debt. Relative to income, families' debt today is nearly twice as high as in the 1980s. Borrowing relative to disposable income after tax today stands at 120 percent. To return to normal (70 percent), debt would need to be cut by some US$6 trillion (or 45 percent of gross domestic product [GDP]). The deleveraging process still has a ways to go. Much is said about the bounce that could come from improving profitability of corporate America, if the cash finds its way into increased capital spending and employment. But with companies still uncertain about the future, that's not happening. So, like it or not, the anemic recovery may yet require another jolt of new stimulus. That won't come easy, if at all.

The eurozone, on the whole, will see very moderate growth—certainly lower than the United States according to the World Bank, which talks of 2011 as a year of deceleration.[2] In Europe, you get a mixture of some growth in Germany and France, and very soft recoveries (if at all) in debt-ridden Portugal, Greece, Ireland, and Spain. The risks lie in the impact of continuing emphasis to contain inflation, while helping to keep the region's most indebted nations afloat. The United Kingdom, in the midst of austerity, is now struggling. With markets unnerved by further rating downgrades on Greek and Spanish debt, the effective capacity of the European rescue funds has since been bumped up to €500 billion (US$700 billion), with many strings attached to whip eurozone laggards into shape through vigorous economic and fiscal workouts (including putting into law a pledge to get a grip on public debt). The intention is to prevent its sovereign risk woes from spreading beyond Portugal. Despite these steps, markets are not convinced. Europe is seen to continue to muddle and fuddle.

Where does this leave the rest of the world? The World Bank's January 2011 outlook talks of emerging and developing countries (EDCs) expanding at nearly twice (6 percent) the rate of global growth in 2011, and more than double the 2.4 percent expected for high-income nations.[3] Still, the overall pace of growth is not strong enough to give global recovery a solid traction. Even so, the World Bank says that "serious tensions and pitfalls persist in the global economy, which in the short-run could derail the recovery to different degrees." These threats include the eurozone financial market crisis, volatile capital flows, and rising prices of commodities, especially food and fuel. Alongside are affordability issues, where poverty impacts could intensify with dire consequences for social and political stability.

Impact of Oil

But the world has since changed with new concerns coming from Asia and the Middle East. The Arab world has seen unprecedented political unrest as its people sought to bring down long-standing regimes, resulting of late in a new "war" in Libya. As the region is a crucial supplier of oil, its price assumes a new risk. The world faces the prospect of another bumpy ride if oil prices persist on current levels. This time is more alarming because oil prices are rising out of fear that global supply lines are being disrupted. Not because demand for oil is racing ahead along with the price. The World Bank says this surge in prices would dent growth in EDCs by 0.2–0.4 percentage point. Overall, this is unlikely to be large enough to derail the strong recovery we now see in EDCs. But a spike to US$150 or even US$200 a barrel would present a serious risk. For March, the price stood at US$90–120. Yet a lot more can still go wrong. As I see it now, consumers can withstand a moderate rise in oil prices. But at anything above US$150, we are in unchartered waters and can cause panic, which, in turn, could lead to a double-dip recession in the West and high inflation in the East. It's a risk that has to be taken seriously. However, oil prices have a firm floor (underpinned by demand) but a soft ceiling because of spreading unrest. If the recent rise proves temporary, the world economy can shrug off its effects with relative ease. If the price rise persists, outlook could darken quickly.

MENA

The Middle East and North Africa (MENA) produce more than one-third of the world's oil. The spread of unrest across the region threatens widespread supply disruption. Sure, the oil market has many buffers today: government stockpiles, high commercial stocks, and Saudi Arabia's ample spare capacity to pump more. Yet, more disruption can't be ruled out. The joker in the pack could be Saudi Arabia, which bears many characteristics that had fueled unrest elsewhere, including a large pool of disillusioned youth. Despite spending US$36 billion to "buy-off" dissent, the kingdom continues to face demand for reform. Furthermore, a second threat could come from gradual dwindling of spare capacity.

All point to a continuing high premium for oil. Today, the world is less vulnerable to damage from higher oil, but not immune. The conventional rule of thumb is a 10 percent rise in oil price will cut world growth by one-quarter of one percentage point. The World Bank puts global growth in 2011 at 3.3 percent (3.9 percent in 2010), but its impact on inflation, especially in EDCs, is much more serious.[4] The United States, facing low inflation now, sits rather comfortably. Even so, US consumer confidence fell sharply once gasoline went past US$3 a gallon. It's now at US$3.38. But Europe, already getting more unsettled with inflationary expectations, could overreact and tighten too far, which could push its still-fragile economies back into recession. The worst hit will be EDCs; many of them (India, Brazil, and China) are facing problems of high inflation and rising inflationary expectations. Most serious is impact on the poor, which has led many governments to subsidize both food and fuel. This has already put enormous pressure on the budgets of India and Brazil. But the biggest damage lies in MENA itself, where subsidies on food and fuel are increasingly used to quell unrest. Fuel importers, such as Egypt, face enormous challenges in bankruptcy from spiraling oil prices and ever-growing subsidies. At worst, the risks are secular with dearer oil and political uncertainty feeding on each other. So the world remains shakier than we all realize.

And Then, There's Japan

As of now, the serious Japanese situation appears to be under control. There have been disruptions, of course, but not so disastrous as to cause real difficulties for the world economy as a result of earthquake and tsunami. Nevertheless, two areas of some concern remain. The first has to do with effects of nuclear plants, which contribute up to 30 percent of total electricity generated in Japan. In the event of catastrophe, the shortage of electricity and rolling power outages would adversely affect economic activities, which, in turn, could lead to cutbacks in imports and exports. These have attendant effects on other economies, especially in Asia. The second deals with fears over Japanese supply chain disruptions. Some multinationals have begun to halt output due to shortage of parts from Japan. Especially hit are high-tech, automotive, and steel industries, including electronic and raw materials for making semiconductors.

For example, Japan accounts for 90 percent of the world's supply of bismaleimide triazine, a key material used in the production of printed circuit boards used in chips for tele-handsets. Japan is also a large suppler of silicon wafers used for semiconductors. It is home to many manufacturers of glass substrates, a key material in making liquid-crystal-display panels used in smartphones, tablet computers, and TVs.

These disruptions are already affecting businesses that run "just-in-time" inventory processes with very little slack. Undoubtedly, the short-term is likely to see disruptions. Japan is in urgent need to import coal, LNG, and oil products to restore energy consumption, but damaged storage tanks, ports, and refineries make it difficult to absorb fuel and raw materials that foreign suppliers are prepared to rush in. All these would slow auto, technology, and ship-building industries worldwide.

Cost of rebuilding has been variously estimated at US$150–250 billion (Kobe 1995 earthquake damage cost US$100 billion). The upper end is about 4 percent of GDP. The government now talks of at least US$200 billion, in line with World Bank's estimate of US$122–235 billion. Reconstruction will take years, with safer new structures of higher quality. This should begin to boost GDP later this year—pushing up further demand for oil even as unrest in MENA raises supply fears. Higher oil prices are always bad news for Asia and the world.

A Word on China

China's new economic roadmap sets a low 7 percent annual growth for 2011–2015; it's expected to grow 8 percent this year (10.3 percent in 2010). For the past five years, growth target was 7.5 percent, but actual annual growth was 11.2 percent. This is intended to signal the government's desire to adjust the economic structure to bridge the wealth gap and to engineer a shift from an investment/export–led growth model to one led by its own domestic engine, mainly private consumption. The emphasis is on quality of growth, not its speed. Part of restructuring includes building 10 million affordable homes in 2011 and 36 million units in 2011–2015. That's enough to house the combined population of France, Australia, and Canada. My own view is that Chinese officials are convinced a slowdown is already in the works. To rebalance its economy, less weight is being placed on manufacturing and exports, and more on building services and getting domestic spending as the new growth engine. So it's not a matter of whether growth will indeed slacken, but when.

What, Then, Are We to Do?

Recent empirical work by Prof. Barry Eichengreen (Berkeley) and Shin Kwanho (Korea University) concluded that fast-growing economies slow down when per-capita income reaches US$16,500.[5] China will be there in 2014 if it continues growing 10 percent a year. Generally, slow growth comes sooner when (1) a higher ratio of elderly people is active in the labor force; (2) manufacturing's share of labor exceeds 20 percent; (3) its currency is undervalued; and (4) imbalances and excesses in manufacturing exports eventually force a deceleration (Korea in the 1990s). China displays all these symptoms. So if there is a lesson from history, is China's slackening growth really imminent? Certainly that's what China's new vision is. I am reminded of what Thomas Edison once said (to words of this effect): Vision without execution is a hallucination.

Kuala Lumpur
March 24, 2011

Notes

1. First published on March 26, 2011, as "As the World Turns."
2. World Bank, *Global Economic Prospect: Navigating Strong Currents*, Vol. 1 (Washington, DC: World Bank, January 2011), and *East Asia and Pacific Economic Update: Navigating Turbulence, Sustaining Growth*, Vol. 2 (Washington, DC: World Bank, 2011).
3. Ibid.
4. Ibid.
5. Barry Eichengreen (University of California, Berkeley) and Shin Kwanho (Korea University) studied in 2010, 39 episodes in which fast-growing economies with per-capita income of US$10,000 or more experienced sharp and persistent economic slowdowns.

CHAPTER 12

A Check-up at Mid-Year, 2011[1]

My early 2011 essays in *The Star* were set in a rather optimistic mood, hoping it would be a stress-free year for the world economy. Early in January, the financial crisis seemed to be well contained and the euro sovereign-debt crisis had become less acute. The US economy was poised to be better able to tackle unemployment. Investors began building up their equities and sold some bonds they had bought as cover for troubled times. The main worry, then, was to await progress by the major emerging countries in slowing down growth, which otherwise was pushing commodity prices further up. But that was not to be.

MENA Jasmine Revolution

First, came the Arab Spring. Few would have imagined that among the many Middle East and North Africa (MENA) unpopular governments, Tunisia would be the first to face a serious attempt to foment an Eastern European–style velvet revolution. Since December 17 last year, when a jobless youth set himself on fire in protest, spontaneous reactions spread nationwide. On January 11, protests in Tunis galvanized near-moribund opposition into action, bringing about the president of 23 years' dramatic scuttle into exile on January 14. Some Egyptians jokingly called it a Tunami.

Unexpectedly, a Tunisia-tinted jasmine revolution tidal wave soon hit Egypt. The nationwide protest on January 25 turned out to be the largest act of civil disobedience in 30 years of President Mubarak's rule. Mubarak was eventually toppled on February 11. The scent of jasmine spreads next to Libya. After 41 years of violent capricious rule, Mr. Gaddafi faced a popular uprising on February 22, after a blood-soaked week of unrest. By March 22, the no-fly-zone set up under a UN mandate covered most of the rebel-held eastern coastal region. Today, the war rages on.

What started in Tunisia has certainly caught fire—satellite TV, mobile phones, the Internet, and Twitter continue to relay giddy news across the Maghreb along the Mediterranean's southern coast, on even through Saudi Arabia to the Gulf and Yemen. Plainly, many are nervous. Jordan is sullen, Syria defiant, Algeria unstable, and Yemen seething—on the verge of civil war. Undoubtedly, the Arab Spring puts oil markets on edge. Pinpointing its impact is complicated since oil prices were already rising because of the rosier economic outlook at the close of 2010. Nevertheless, a good part of this year's 25 percent rise (reaching US$115/barrel for Brent) reflected worries over supply. The rule of thumb holds that a 10 percent rise in oil prices reduces 0.25 percentage point off global growth. At the start of 2011, global growth was set at 3.5 to 4 percent. This implies world growth would fall overall by at least 0.5 percentage point. But that's not all. Crises generate much uncertainty: Businesses postpone investments and hiring, and investors seek the refuge of bonds at the expense of equities. Oil prices remain hard to predict. Lord Keynes once argued that faced with uncertainties, businessmen rely on conventional wisdom that the existing state of affairs will continue indefinitely. I am afraid events of the past two months have poured cold water on this assumption.

Japan's Earthquake and Tsunami

Second, the earthquake and tsunami on March 2011 and the consequent nuclear accident badly hit the world's third-largest economy, which was already hardly growing. Its share of world output has been shrinking; but at 9 percent it remains big enough for the impact on Japan's growth to noticeably affect global gross domestic product (GDP). Moreover, ripple effects on the rest of the world can also be significant since Japan is a critical supplier of components to the global electronic and automotive supply chain—from hardened glass on the iPad to vital parts for gearboxes to Volkswagen. As a result, many makers of such parts have had to slow or miss shipments. The collateral damage has been wide and far beyond, causing shutdowns from South Korea to Southern California to the South of France. This does not include a range of wider, fuzzier costs. The disaster forced the utility company to schedule power cuts; if the cuts last, it could depress industrial output by as much as 14 percent. Most important is the loss of consumer confidence. Most troublesome are harmful rumors and its psychological impact as a result of radiation concerns. Already many hotels and restaurants have stopped importing fresh fish and related food from Japan. Furthermore, the price of memory chips has jumped, with chain effects on the cost of end products around the world.

Eurozone Concerns Grow

Third, across the Mediterranean, the eurozone's debt crisis came back in full swing. Markets fretted about the long-expected bailout for Portugal, after Lisbon rejected the March 23 austerity measures. Possible write-downs of Irish bank debt by the new government in Dublin were another concern. By the second quarter of 2011, fears mounted about the eurozone's debt situation following crushing electoral defeat for Spain's ruling party, compounded by in-fighting in Europe over whether Greek government bonds should be restructured and new warnings on credit downgrades. On May 20, Fitch lopped three notches off Greece's rating to B+ and warned any measure of default would have far reaching implications on financial stability worldwide. Moreover, Standard & Poor's (S&P) had on June 14 downgraded Greece once again to CCC, the world's lowest sovereign credit rating ever. Immediately, Greek 10-year yields jumped to 17 percent, higher than the Portuguese (10.7 percent) and the Irish (11.3 percent). Furthermore, S&P also lowered its outlook on Italy's US$1.9 trillion government debt to negative. Still, the yield difference or spread between 10-year German bunds and similar Greek bonds was 1,402 basis points, close to a record. Even Germany, Europe's economic powerhouse, is now showing some signs of fatigue.

US Economy: Worse than It Looks

Fourth, my teacher and mentor at Harvard, Professor Martin Feldstein, recently concluded that the US economy is in a worse shape than suggested by the first quarter 2011 growth of just 1.8 percent (3.1 percent in the fourth quarter of 2010).[2] He made four points: (1) two-thirds of it reflected inventories build-up and not final sales; (2) consumer spending really hardly rose; (3) the economy slid in April, and May retail sales suffered its first drop in 11 months; (4) each US$ of stimulus spent in 2008 and 2009 added much less than a US$ to GDP. Two other problems worried him: (1) lack of an explicit plan to deal with the budget deficit and rising national debt (60 percent of GDP), and (2) incoherent policy on the US$ value. All these add to the lack of business confidence to make entrepreneurial investments and new expansions to generate employment. As always, Marty makes a compelling case.

Global Growth Revisited

It is already well known that the disaster in Japan, the violence in MENA, the eurozone's fiscal strains, and the "soft patch" in the US second quarter 2011 growth are bad for the global economy. But it's hard to tell how bad.

This lack of clarity can be as harmful as the disruptions and war. One gauge of uncertainty is the increase in stock market gyrations. Japan's so-called fear gauge (the VXJ-index of stock market volatility) rose 22.4 percent on the day following the earthquake and tsunami. On the other hand, the recent US stock volatility was—in hindsight, relatively mild. The Dow Jones Industrial Average had fallen for six consecutive weeks—the largest losing streak since 2002—leaving the index below 12,000 for the first time since March. But the Dow was down only 6.7 percent from its April high, just over 1 percentage point a week. The Dow still remains up 3.2 percent for 2011. Just a year ago, investors reacted more negatively amid a similar mix of worries; they knocked the Dow down 14 percent from late April through early July. On the knowledge that last year's troubles didn't last, investors reacted this time with less anxiety. The US equivalent of the "fear index" (the VIX) remained quiet at below 20, well far from panic (30–40). Be that as it may, businesses don't like uncertainty—managers defer decisions to invest and hire, missing opportunities to create employment.

The World Bank's revised June forecasts place world growth as moderating to 3.2 percent in 2011 and recovering to 3.6 percent in 2012.[3] Latest OECD lead indicators also show more or less the same trends—a mild loss of momentum in most economies, notably France and Italy as well as Brazil and India.[4] High-income nations are seen to grow at 2.2 percent this year and 2.7 percent in 2012, compared with nearly three times the pace (6.3 percent and 6.2 percent respectively in 2011 and 2012) in the emerging countries. Embedded in the World Bank forecasts, US growth was cut to 2.6 percent this year, pointing to a growth pause in the second quarter of 2011, but there is little prospect (so far) of a double-dip. The eurozone will grow more slowly at 1.2 percent. But emerging nations, although also slackening, continue to maintain a strong pace, accounting for about one-half of global demand for oil, while China alone absorbed 40 percent of world's metal supplies. Oil prices were up 37 percent in 2010; copper up to record high, with mining companies struggling to meet demand. Nevertheless, China's growth will slow down to 9.3 percent this year (10.3 percent in 2010) and to 8.7 percent in 2012. Latest indications are that a soft landing remains in sight for China. India will grow at 8 percent in 2011 and 8.4 percent next year.

The Threat of Inflation

While developed economies have to contend with high unemployment and Europe's debt crisis and fiscal austerity, many emerging nations with strong expansions, notably China, India, and Brazil, have to deal with rising inflation, brought about in part by rising food and commodity prices and strong capital inflows, and partly by the inability to remove fiscal stimulus enacted earlier. Real interest rates remain low (or negative) in many countries. For the developing countries, inflation was 7 percent in May from a year earlier. In India, official inflation in May is now 9.1 percent, Indonesia 6 percent, South Korea 4.2 percent, and China 5.5 percent (above official target of 4 percent). Vietnam, Asia's worst inflation performer, suffered a surge to 20 percent in April. For many of them, consumer prices have eased somewhat in May due to better harvests (India), increased wheat exports (Ukraine), appreciating currencies, softening oil prices, and the impact of tightening monetary policies (India). Credit Suisse's "surprise index," which measures the difference between inflation announcements and consensus forecasts, turned downward in May, indicating consumer price rises may be moving downward. This reflected, in the end, decelerating growth in Asia from last year's breakneck expansion. Western markets for Asian exports are also weakening.

Make no mistake, Asian inflation is not going away. The slowdown may have taken the sting off the problem for the time being. Look at "core" inflation indices, which strip out volatile elements of food and energy prices; they have continued to move up in many countries, even as headline (overall) inflation softened. Structurally, underlying price pressures remain a worry in Asia—if nothing else, they are grossly underestimated by price control measures in particular. In both China and India, loan growth may have slowed but they remain above nominal GDP growth. This oversupply of credit continues to fan inflation. Then, there are the ever-present cost-push factors: Input prices are getting more expensive and wages are rising across the region. So, inflation is a very much underrated longer-term threat that continues to require close monitoring and decisive action by central banks and finance ministries. It will most certainly flare up when you least expect, in particular once growth deaccelerates (or fails to definitely decelerate) or surprise "shocks" reappear.

What, Then, Are We to Do?

Expectation is for growth to return to the precrisis trend. In the first quarter of 2011, GDP growth was 4.6 percent (4.8 percent in the fourth quarter of 2010), supported mainly by expansion in manufacturing and services. There are increasing signs that the second quarter of 2011 is already hitting a soft patch: April's industrial production contracted 2.2 percent from a year ago (on a month-to-month basis, it fell 7.6 percent); orders in the electrical and electronics sector have since slowed down and so has capital spending. Also, activity in services appears to have slackened. This is not unique to Malaysia. Business sentiment at Asia's top businesses fell to 71 in the second quarter of 2011 from 80 in the first quarter of 2011, hitting its lowest since the third quarter of 2010, according to Reuters' Asia Corporate Sentiment Index. An index above 50 indicates a positive outlook. The consensus is for a weak second quarter of 2011 stretching to the third quarter of 2011, but with rapid recovery in the fourth quarter of 2011. Sentiment in Southeast Asia has turned cautious, with China and India remaining the more optimistic. The World Bank's April forecast for Malaysia of 5.1 percent (range being 3.8–5.7 percent) for 2011 appears now on the high side—hitting the middle of the range is more likely, in the region of 4.5–5 percent for the year as a whole. The situation needs close monitoring.

Kuala Lumpur
June 16, 2011

Notes

1. First published on June 18, 2011, as "A Check-up at Mid-Year."
2. Martin Feldstein, "The US Economy Is Worse Than You Think," *Asian Wall Street Journal* (June 13, 2011). Professor Feldstein was chairman for the Council of Economic Advisors under US President Ronald Reagan.
3. World Bank, *Global Economic Prospects* (Washington, DC: World Bank, June 2011).
4. Organisation for Economic Co-operation and Development (OECD), *Future Global Shocks—Improving Risk Governance* (Paris: OECD, June 2011).

CHAPTER 13

Gloomy Outlook Takes Its Toll, 2011–2012[1]

With every passing day, the shelf-life of the eurozone's rescue package is getting shorter. On July 21, eurozone leaders agreed to a second Greek bailout (details in Chapter 49, "Greek Bailout Mark II: It's a Default"). European parliaments have yet to complete ratification to expand the €440 billion bailout fund (European Financial Stability Facility—EFSF). Already, talk has shifted to expanding the EFSF in the light of escalation of the crisis. Frankly, the fund is just not large enough to halt the contagion. It's a matter of market confidence really—the larger, the better. About one-half of the fund is already committed or utilized—with more demands coming on. Greece will miss the deficit targets for this year and next despite austerity, showing the drastic steps taken to avert bankruptcy are not enough. The crisis is boiling over. Eurozone ministers have since delayed the release of €8 billion cash scheduled for October 13, threatening to revisit the deal where private bondholders may be asked to take a higher "haircut." This has rattled markets and raised fears of an imminent messy default. Estimates are that with a 60 percent haircut (21 percent now) for private bondholders, Greek banks would suffer another €27 billion write-down, wiping out their capital. Inevitably, the fallout will have much wider repercussions and fuel turmoil for Spanish and Italian debt, not to mention Irish and Portuguese.

The Contagion

The world economy once again stands on a knife's edge. As finance leaders gathered at end-September, they all want to look forward. But markets and investors are forcing them to peer down the precipice into the abyss as growth in advanced economies slackened sharply and emerging nations

77

grappled with inflation in the face of a fast deteriorating eurozone debt crisis, wondering how to make the needed adjustments to restore confidence. Continuing uncertainty and worries about the global economic outlook fueled a rush into safe assets. The eurozone is seen to be on the brink of recession. Its prospects have been hit by sharp falls in consumer and business confidence amid the escalating eurozone debt crisis, as well as fiscal austerity measures across the continent and pessimism about US growth. Germany's slowdown is worrisome because of its role as Europe's powerhouse. Gathering pessimism came to a head as global equities tumbled on September 22 (Thursday) as the Federal Reserve's (Fed) gloomy outlook ("There were significant downside risks to the economic outlook")[2] caused investors to sell stocks in a widespread flight to safety. The United Kingdom's FTSE (All World) Index fell by as much as 23 percent from its May high, signifying a bear market as it fell through the 20 percent threshold. US and UK stocks were not yet in bear territory but German and French equities have since been there. The sell-off was mooted by a big move into government bonds. Benchmark German 10-year bond yields hit an all-time low of 1.65 percent while US Treasuries fell to 1.77 percent, the lowest level since 1946. On a day reminiscent of 2008, Asian stocks and currencies tumbled, reflecting foreign capital repatriation, with the Indonesian stock market plunging 9 percent, the Australian dollar falling below US dollar parity, and the Hong Kong Hang Seng index settling at its lowest point since July 2009.

Amid market tumult, investors were left wondering what to do in October. The third quarter had been painful and volatile. The Dow finished the quarter down 12.1 percent; the S&P 500 fell 14 percent. Many had hoped for a second-half rebound after spring's soft patch, only to be confronted with worries the developed economies could be heading for a possible double-dip recession. There is also a new fear: weakness in emerging market economies, especially China. During the third quarter, markets were tossed to and fro on a daily (even hourly) basis, reflecting developments in Europe and the United States. In August and September, the Dow industrials rose or fell by more than 1 percent on each of 29 days; on another 15 days, the daily moves were more than 2 percent. The last time the market saw this was in March/April 2009. The "fear index" (VIX volatility index) reflecting market instability was up 160 percent over the third quarter, finishing at above 40 (normal 15–20) at end-September.

The Problem Is Europe

The damage was worse in Europe. The main German and French stock indices both lost more than 25 percent of their value in the third quarter, the largest quarterly loss since 2002. Asian stocks also took a pounding, experiencing double-digit losses. The Hong Kong Hang Seng index lost 21 percent. Even gold—usually the refuge—suffered a collapse in September from its record high of US$1,920 per troy ounce in August. The safety was in US Treasuries, German bunds, and UK gilts. Yields didn't matter—for now it's just preservation of capital. As I see it, the sovereign risk crisis is compounded by much weaker growth among the "core" nations, and increasing market stress. In the United States, it has just managed to avoid recession, with little buffer to insulate itself from any fallout from a European event. Complications can also come from a bursting bubble in the Chinese property market, rattling Chinese banks with ripple effects on world markets.

US and European stocks tumbled when markets opened in the new fourth quarter, with S&P 500 entering the bear market as Europe postponed a vital tranche drawing to debt-stricken Greece. Wall Street fell about 2 percent on October 3 (Monday), extending Friday's decline to a 13-month low as investors feared the crisis would lead the United States into a new recession. With this drop, the benchmark S&P 500 had fallen past 20 percent, putting it in bear territory. In Europe, banking stocks dived as investors slashed their exposure on worries the authorities are unable to contain the debt crisis. The Stoxx Europe 600 index tumbled 2.8 percent, hitting its lowest since October 2008; Stoxx Europe 600 banks finished 4.3 percent lower. The eurozone's problem is one of market confidence rather than solvency.

In Asia, most regional markets in the third quarter suffered their biggest falls since the Lehman's collapse in 2008, with Tokyo losing 11 percent and Hong Kong 21 percent. Since then, South Korea dropped 3.6 percent, Hong Kong another 3.4 percent, India's Sensex 1.8 percent, the Nikkei, 1.1 percent, and Australia, 0.6 percent.

Italy's latest downgrade—a three-notch cut by Moody's to A2 with continued negative outlook—reflected as much the eurozone's inability to spur market confidence, as it does Italy's failure to promote growth. Without a comprehensive response to the crisis, the risk of a downward spiral remains. In the past days, European stocks posted hefty gains as policymakers were reported to be prepared to help recapitalize European banks, in an effort to reduce uncertainty. The International Monetary Fund (IMF) had estimated Europe needed €100–200 billion. Priority remains with Spain and Italy, which are basically solvent but lack credibility. The prospect of the IMF coming in alongside the EFSF to buy Spanish and Italian bonds boosted sentiment.

Default by Greece?

Greece will miss the targets set just two months ago. The 2012 approved budget predicts a deficit of 8.5 percent of gross domestic product (GDP) for 2011, well short of the 7.6 percent target. For 2012, the deficit is set at 6.8 percent, short of the target of 6.5 percent, reflecting the sluggish economy. Its 8.5 percent target remains a challenge in the current environment. GDP is expected to fall by 5.5 percent in 2011, pushing unemployment to 16 percent, and a further GDP shrinkage of 2.0 to 2.5 percent is in prospect. The 2011 shortfall meant Greece would need another €2 billion just to bridge the gap. Greece is now off-track, reflecting disappointing revenues and missed targets. On September 21, it acted to raise taxes, speed up public layoffs, and cut some pensions. Ongoing austerity measures are already deeply unpopular, with dire consequences on the social fabric of the economy.

My mentor and teacher at Harvard, Martin Feldstein, believes the only way out is for Greece to default and write down its debt by at least 50 percent.[3] This strategy of default and devalue is standard fare for nations in Greece's shoes. But this hasn't happened because "Greece is trapped in the single currency." So why are the political leaders trying to postpone the inevitable? He offered two sensible reasons: (1) banks and other financial institutions in Germany and France have large exposures to Greek debt, and time is needed to build capital; and (2) default would induce sovereign defaults in other countries and runs on their banks. The EFSF is just not large enough to bail out Italy and Spain. Europe's politicians hope to buy enough time (2 years) for Spain and Italy to prove they are financially viable. As I see it, both these nations don't have another two years to prove their worth. The markets will decide the fate of Greece (and possibly Spain and Italy), not the other way around.

The Shadow of Recession

IMF's September forecast pointed to growth in emerging economies exceeding 6 percent in 2011 and 2012, but with the advanced nations sliding to below 2 percent.[4] On current trends, the latter prediction is perhaps closer to 1 percent. I think the outlook for the eurozone is deteriorating fast: At best, it is already in the throes of a severe slowdown, at worst, a relapse into recession. The European Commission recently stated growth is at a virtual standstill, with eurozone GDP rising by 0.2 percent in the third quarter of 2011 and 0.1 percent in the fourth quarter of 2011. Pain will be most intense in the south (no growth in Italy in 2011 and 2012), where the pressure of austerity is greatest.

But the "core" economies are also hurting. The IMF estimated German growth would slow down from 2.7 percent in 2011 to 1.3 percent in 2012. The short-term outlook is even worse. According to Markit Economics, the eurozone's factory activity fell to a 25-month low of 48.5 (a reading below 50 indicates contraction). Indications are economic conditions will deteriorate.

Germany's index fell in September with overall activity just above 50—the worst performance in two years. France's index stood at 48.2; Italy, 48.3—both in contraction territory. Other eurozone states reported steeper contractions. All reflected lackluster domestic demand and falling export sales. The vicious feedback loop between growth, debt concerns, and banking woes is now in train. One thing is certain. More sluggish growth will make it harder to achieve fiscal targets. Rising risk of recession will damage efforts to deal with the debt crisis.

The Fed's latest assessment for the US economy to falter needs to be taken seriously. Citing anemic employment, depressed confidence, and financial risks from Europe, its chief (Ben Bernanke) urged Congress not to cut spending too quickly in the short term even as the Fed grapples with fiscal consolidation over the medium term. The IMF expects the United States to grow by 1.5 percent in 2011 (less than 1 percent in the first half of 2011) and 1.8 percent in 2012.[5] The short-term outlook isn't looking better.

Uncertainty about the outcome of the eurozone's sovereign debt crisis has undermined US business and consumer confidence and helped to slow economic growth. Indeed, the business cycle monitoring group ECRI concluded last week that the US economy is tipping into a new recession. Latest data are mixed after a dismal August. US manufacturing managed to keep expanding and employment strengthened in September, but the tone has not been sufficiently robust to dispel fears of another downturn. Sure, the United States was not in recession in the third quarter of 2011, but the lack of new orders remains of concern. While even sluggish job growth is welcome, the government's belt-tightening is likely to prove a significant drag on the economy. The Fed's commitment to ensure recovery continues will reassure. But if Europe falters badly, there is little the Fed can do.

Housing Ignored

Over the past 35 years, housing has added value to US GDP. Empirically, in the two years following most recessions, housing adds about 0.5 percentage point to US GDP growth. So far, the contribution has been negative. This is so because: (1) home prices dropped 2.5 percent this year; since its 2005 peak, home prices have fallen 31.6 percent; (2) the United States lost US$7 trillion (close to one-half of GDP) in the value of homes Americans own; homeowners' equity has since fallen to 38.6 percent of home values; and (3) home starts are at an all-time low—and still falling. The housing bust weighs heavily on consumers, making them more reluctant to spend. Innovative ways to unleash housing are needed.

What, Then, Are We to Do?

Looks like the world remains in bad shape. It is also a dangerous place with growing uncertainty, high volatility, and increasing social unrest. Europe, in particular, is in a high-risk gamble. I worry that European politicians may learn the hard way in trying to outsmart the markets.

Kuala Lumpur
October 7, 2011

Notes

1. First published on October 8, 2011, as "The Gloomy Outlook Takes Its Toll."
2. US Federal Reserve Bank Statement on September 22, 2011, following its Federal Open Market Committee meeting. It also announced that through June 2012, the Fed would buy US$400 billion in Treasury bonds at the long end of the market (6- to 30-year maturities) and sell an equal amount of 3-years' duration or less. The aim is to put further "downward pressure on longer-term interest rates and help make broader financial conditions more accommodative."
3. Martin Feldstein, "Europe's High-Risk Gamble," reproduced in *The Star*, Malaysia (September 29, 2011). Harvard Professor Feldstein was chairman of the Council of Economic Advisors under US President Ronald Reagan.
4. International Monetary Fund (IMF), *World Economic Outlook: Slowing Growth, Rising Risks* (Washington, DC: IMF, September 2011).
5. Ibid.

CHAPTER 14

G-20 Summit, Cannes 2011; APEC, Honolulu 2011: Without Gusto![1]

When President Nicolas Sarkozy of France assumed the presidency of G-20 for 2011, I was delighted for, alas, international monetary reform would take center stage. That's what he promised. I felt it's high time leadership was put to bear on an issue of critical international concern, where the Americans had for years "feared to tread"—for obvious reasons: to protect US national interest to preserve (as long as feasible) an archaic international monetary system with the US$ as its centerpiece and which has outlasted its usefulness.

But this was not to be. Political turmoil in Greece had added fuel to the European financial chaos, with the G-20 meeting scrambling to arrange (and rearrange) emergency measures aimed at preventing the eurozone sovereign debt crisis from contaminating the rest of Europe and the global economy. As they gathered in Cannes on November 3–4, leaders from G-20 faced high expectations to confront the festering European turmoil. Instead, the two-day summit in this Mediterranean resort largely resulted in more pressure on Europe to respond more forcefully before the crisis deepened. The United States, China, and others were worried that Europeans might fail to avert a collapse of the Greek economy, bringing with it sovereign default and corporate bankruptcies that would inevitably send shock-waves through the global financial system. Priority was placed to quickly resolve the evolving European crisis. It was clear that the weight of the crisis had overshadowed other policy goals of the G-20 Summit.

G-20 and France

France's president had hoped to use the G-20 to burnish his reputation as a global statesman. I gathered Mr. Sarkozy had intended to focus the G-20 agenda on French ideas for reducing global imbalances. Instead, he found himself in the midst of a gathering euro-storm, now focused on Greece's sudden decision to call a referendum on its bailout. Behind the scenes, France was itself subject to growing economic stress. The market's verdict on France's finances had since grown increasingly harsh. The spread between the yields on German and French 10-year triple-A government bonds had widened to a euro-era record of 1.95 percentage points.

France is a triple-A-rated nation in name only because its debt is in danger of spiraling out of control. Forecast by Fitch Ratings at 86.8 percent of gross domestic product (GDP) in 2013, it is the highest among triple-A-rated nations. Its recent sharp economic downturn has exposed a €8 billion gap in France's efforts to reduce its budget deficit to 4.5 percent of GDP in 2012 from 7.1 percent in 2010—more than twice the permissible limit of 3 percent. At 45 percent of GDP, France is already among the most highly taxed in OECD. The recent report by the Lisbon Council ranked France 13th out of 17 for its overall health, including growth potential, unemployment, and consumption; and 15th for progress on economic adjustments, including reducing the budget deficit and unit labor cost.

G-20 and Italy

It's quite clear that G-20's prime concern is Italy. The country is increasingly unable to raise debt at affordable cost, and its prime minister was struggling to push through austerity measures in the face of mounting labor unrest amidst an unfriendly parliament. It was also clear the eurozone isn't equipped to deal with the collapse of Italy. At G-20, although they had indicated a willingness to co-operate, non-European leaders had made it clear they want the eurozone to first rely on its own resources to resolve the crisis. Nevertheless, Europeans did consider seeking outside help, in particular to boost their bailout fund, including asking the International Monetary Fund (IMF) for cooperative support. But not one bit. The very hint of boosting the IMF's role underscored deepening worries about the adequacy of Europe's own response. In the end, G-20 leaders agreed only to explore options, including voluntary contributions and using its Special Drawing Rights (SDRs) in some fashion. Just kick the can down the road!

G-20 Has Little to Show

As in the previous year, an all-too-familiar G-20 meeting ended with a long list of promises made, many of which reflected a rehash of old ones; with most promises made and then broken in the past, and still others not known to be kept. However, one key step did emerge: Italy, the focus of most worries in the European (and indeed the world) markets agreed to permit the IMF to monitor its progress with fiscal reforms. This is as drastic a step as can be expected, given the biggest fear among Europeans is that markets will cease financing Italy, causing a meltdown the eurozone would be quite powerless to stop. European leaders had hoped G-20 would conclude with an endorsement of their plan, announced a week before, that would boost confidence in the markets. It included new efforts to recapitalize European banks, an upgraded bailout scheme for Greece, and an increase in funding available to the eurozone's bailout fund, the European Financial Stability Facility (EFSF). There was also the hope to enhance EFSF's capacity through parallel "investments" from non-European G-20 members. G-20 had noted the European Central Bank's (ECB) refusal to act as lender of last resort— and to provide financing to help leverage the EFSF's €440 billion into something much larger, which had led the Europeans to pursue the non-Europeans with large surpluses, such as China. As the eurozone crisis deepened, much of the wider G-20 agenda to encourage "strong, stable and balanced" global growth fell by the wayside at this time. As I understand it, it would appear the stronger economies, including China, Germany, Canada, and Brazil, did agree to limit efforts at fiscal tightening and possibly do more to boost demand at home. This marked a reversal from last year's summit, which centered on fiscal deficit reduction.

The G-20 Pact

The more important conclusions reached at the summit included the following:[2]

- Commitment to working together and taking decisions to reinvigorate economic growth, create jobs, ensure financial stability, and promote social inclusion, and to coordinate their actions and policies.
- An Action Plan for Growth and Jobs to address short-term vulnerabilities and strengthen foundations for growth. Advanced economies committed to adopt policies to build confidence and support growth, and implement clear and credible measures at fiscal consolidation.
- Commitment by (1) countries whose public finances remain strong to take discretionary measures to support domestic demand; (2) countries with large current surpluses commit to reforms to raise domestic demand coupled with greater exchange rate flexibility; and (3) all commit to further structural reforms to raise output in their countries.
- Commitment to strengthen the social dimension of globalization.
- A taskforce will be set up to work with priority on youth unemployment.

- Commitment to promote a more stable and resilient international monetary system.
- Agreement to (1) ensure the SDRs basket composition continues to reflect the global role of currencies, (2) review the composition of the SDRs basket in 2015, or earlier, and (3) make progress toward a more integrated, even-handed, and effective IMF surveillance.
- Commitment to move rapidly toward more market-determined exchange rate systems, avoid persistent exchange rate misalignments, and refrain from competitive devaluation.

Despite the cheering about Europe's debt deal and G-20s role in pressuring Europe to act swiftly, worries continue to mount that the world can't succeed without stronger growth. Europe and the United States are virtually at a standstill. At the present pace of muted expansion, unemployment will stay high and incomes stall. Debt-saddled nations will have an even tougher time generating enough revenue to pay bills and service debt. This would spark more default fears or even higher borrowing rates in Italy, Greece, and others under pressure. Latest projections point to the eurozone flirting with recession in 2012. Even in Asia, a critical engine of recovery, prospects are dimming.

Yet, nations remain divided on enacting new measures to boost growth or continue focus on deficit reduction. Weak nations like Italy and Greece are under intense pressure to adopt severe austerity schemes in the face of enormous suffering by its people who fall victim to weakened social safety nets and reduced cash flows. Toward this end, the G-20 commitments fall far short. Markets worldwide have since responded; their verdict: continuing sell-off of bonds and shares, and continuing high cost of borrowing by Italy and Spain.

APEC's Honolulu Declaration

Following the goings-on at G-20, the 21-member Asia-Pacific Economic Co-operation (APEC) Economic Leaders met in Honolulu on November 12–13, 2011, to bolster their economies and lower trade barriers as they seek to prop up global growth and shield themselves against fallout from Europe's debt crisis. They adopted the Honolulu Declaration in which leaders agreed to take concrete steps toward building a "seamless regional economy" to generate growth and create jobs in three priority areas: (1) strengthening regional economic integration and expanding trade, (2) promoting green growth, and (3) advancing regulatory convergence and cooperation.[3] APEC leaders gathered at a time when "growth and job creation have weakened and significant downside risks remain, including those arising from the financial challenges in Europe and a succession of natural disasters in the region." Against this uncertain backdrop, the forum had something more concrete to focus on than the usual bromides about extending free trade. This reflected in part frustration with the long-running (entering its eleventh year with no end in sight) world trade talks, and in part, a desire to snap out of the poor global economic outlook. There is also a broader influence from concern about how best to grow and create jobs.

The Trans-Pacific Partnership (TPP), a proposed free trade pact covering nine APEC members (the United States, Australia, New Zealand, Vietnam, Singapore, Malaysia, Brunei, Chile, and Peru) account for 35 percent of the world economy, is unique—making it the blueprint for future global trade agreements since it had taken on new issues including green technologies and the digital economy. Agreement was reached on the broad outline of a deal, with a final agreement in sight for 2012. Since then, three more APEC members (Japan, Canada, and Mexico) have expressed interest to join. Together, this would create a market of 800 million, the largest trade deal for the United States. The aim is to eventually cover all 21 members of APEC, which accounts for more than one-half of the world's economic output. According to APEC: "We recognize that further trade liberalization is essential to achieving a sustainable global recovery in the aftermath of the global recession of 2008–09." An expanded TPP would provide the much-needed boost. But no trade agreement in the Pacific is complete without China. Looks like a power-play between the United States and China is in the works. As such, optimism about its potential benefits needs to be tempered.

At the conclusion of APEC, leaders agreed to: (1) address two key next generation trade and investment issues, viz. commitment to help the small and medium-sized enterprises grow and plug into global production chains, and to promote effective market-driven innovative policies; (2) develop by 2012 a list of environmental goods (including solar panels, wind turbines, and energy-efficient light bulbs) that contribute to green growth on which members resolved to reduce tariffs to 5 percent or less by end 2015, and to also eliminate nontariff barriers; and (3) take steps by 2013 to implement good regulatory practices. They also pledged to phase out "inefficient fossil-fuel subsidies and to aspire to reduce aggregate energy use by 45 percent by 2035."

What, Then, Are We to Do?

In the end, the question remains how far leaders will be able to turn promises into action. The biggest problem on the Asia-Pacific horizon remains Europe, where fiscal turmoil centered on Italy and Greece will continue to surprise and send shockwaves worldwide. As feared, both summits ended with a whimper, eclipsed by the Italian and Greek sovereign debt drama. All the leaders wanted to do was to kick the can down the road!

Kuala Lumpur
November 18, 2011

Notes

1. First published on November 19, 2011, as "G-20, Cannes' 11 and APEC, Honolulu: Without Gusto."
2. Group of 20 (G-20), "G-20 Cannes Summit Communiqué." *G-20 Summit*, Cannes, France, November 4, 2011.
3. Asia Pacific Economic Co-operation (APEC), "19th APEC Economic Leaders Meeting Honolulu Declaration." *APEC Meeting*, Hawaii, November 13, 2011.

CHAPTER 15

TW3 2011: Annus Horribilis[1]

As the world recovered in 2010 from the throes of the 2008/2009 recession, it turned lackluster in 2011—dragged down by the downturn as the debt crisis in peripheral Europe engulfed its neighbors, in the face of flattish growth in the United States and a mild contraction in Japan. All this pulled down demand for exports and, with it, slower growth in the emerging and developing (E&D) world. A horrible and a hugely disappointing year. For the second time in three years, global recovery stands at risk. That was the world that was (TW3) in 2011.

Storm Clouds Gather

The world has become an increasingly dangerous place. Thousands of people have taken to the streets to protest, including on Wall Street, London, and Warsaw. Global activity weakened in the course of 2011 and became even more uneven. Since midyear, confidence has fallen sharply, and downside risks have grown and are still evolving.

Against the backdrop of a world immersed in imbalances, a barrage of shocks hit the global economy this year: the devastating Japanese earthquake and tsunami, and the Arab Spring unrest in many parts of oil-producing Middle East and North Africa. The US economy slackened, reflecting political impotence; the eurozone debt crisis blew out of hand, encountering major turbulence; and markets were subject to major sell-off of risky sovereigns. These imposed unprecedented risks with adverse spill-over to the real economy, already fragile with the jobless recovery.

As the crisis persisted, the impact on rich economies proved to be even more intractable than expected, and the process of reform even more complicated and difficult. Prospects for E&D economies have become more uncertain, although growth this year should remain reasonably robust. Growth in emerging Asia remained strong but had since moderated, reflecting a weak United States and Europe. Growth was also affected by supply shocks, and slower-than-expected recovery in private demand in rich nations. More recently, fiscal austerity in the United States and Europe and the deepening sovereign debt crisis fanned financial volatility and adversely affected consumer and investor sentiments. Also, domestic demand in Asia has begun to soften, driven by tightening policies to fight inflation, although it had remained sufficiently robust to continue to contribute to global growth. Looking forward, downside risks remain considerable.

Poor Rich World

The global economy had been deteriorating by the month. Succeeding reviews had downgraded global performance, so that by September, the International Monetary Fund's (IMF) *World Economic Outlook* moderated world growth to 4 percent through 2012, from 5 percent in 2010. Rich nations would grow at an anemic pace (1.6 percent in 2011 and 1.9 percent in 2012), while E&D economies would slacken but still register a solid pace of 6 percent through 2012.[2] Since then, reviews in November by the Asian Development Bank and then the World Bank had further revised forecasts downward, culminating in the most bearish outlook to date by the Organisation for Economic Co-operation and Development (OECD) in late November: putting rich nations' growth in 2012 at 1.6 percent (1.9 percent in 2011), reflecting growth of 1.5–2 percent in the United States through 2012, no growth in the eurozone, and a flattish outcome in Japan.[3]

But growth in China, India, and Indonesia will remain robust in 2012: China would still expand at 8.5 percent (9.3 percent in 2011); India at 7.2 percent (2011: 7.7 percent); and Indonesia at 6.1 percent (2011: 6.3 percent).

Even so, latest indicators show continued weakening in manufacturing and services activity in both the rich and poor nations, reflecting (1) growing lack of confidence in Europe, (2) poor sentiment on US leadership to unlock the congressional gridlock, and (3) as of now, E&D markets feeling the intense pressure of weakening overseas demand for their exports.

As I write, the outlook is much darker today than it was in early December. Underlying it all is the deepening eurozone crisis, with contagion again threatening to engulf Italy and Spain, and lapping at the door of France; although of late, US retail and car sales seemed a bit more upbeat, maybe because it has been down for so long. But, as forecasters fret, not all in the rich world is suffering. German employment hit another post-unification high in October, highlighting a disconnect between its prosperity and the pain in most of the eurozone's periphery. True, forecasts are constantly being revised down, but by now most economists expect the rich OECD economies to grow by as low as 1 percent in 2012, with Europe going into recession in the fourth quarter of 2011 or first quarter of 2012. The great concern is for the downturn in Europe to exacerbate stresses in the debt and bank funding markets, creating a vicious downward spiral akin to 2008 with rising probability of a collapse of the euro. Most observers, including myself, expect the euro to just about survive, but not because the leadership is capable of solving the underlying problems.

United States, Eurozone, and Japan

Most economists expect a modest US recovery in an election year. With unemployment still high and growth above Europe on the back of better consumer spending, latest survey data pointed to continuing low growth (2 percent against 1.7 percent in 2011, but no recession) with nothing to be excited about. Given another disappointing year, the engine of global growth has moved decisively to the large E&D economies, notably China. It's a pretty dicey situation—a few mis-turns here or there, especially in the eurozone, could raise domestic risks considerably, with the potential to derail US recovery and renew fears among financially fragile households and investors. The Fed singled out turmoil in Europe's volatile financial markets as the biggest risk to the outlook. With the eurozone already in recession, the United States is expected to struggle to maintain even its current modest growth pace.

In the eurozone, the OECD expects growth to collapse: –1 percent in the fourth quarter of 2011 and –0.4 percent in the first quarter of 2012 (+0.2 percent in the third quarter of 2011), and then slowly recover to 1.8 percent by the fourth quarter of 2013.[4] But nothing is cast in stone. There is still time for decisive action to shore up stricken credibility and avert a far worse outlook. So far, its own crisis had scared off investment and eaten into business and consumer confidence. Europe's factories are feeling the brunt of the stress, while government austerity and job losses are depriving corporates of demand and crunching exports. Markit's Eurozone Composite Purchasing Managers' Index (which measures changes in business activity) showed private business contracting for the third month in November. Italy is facing the worst (fourth quarter of 2011 to contract by 1 percent), while growth in both France and Spain is likely to slacken by 0.5 percent. Germany contracted as well in November, sinking for the first time in 2½ years. All point to the eurozone facing recession. Forging a fiscal compact to save the euro risks making the whittling down of debt tougher than it needs to be. Pro-growth reforms are sidelined as deficit cutting takes hold; worse, the eurozone periphery is made to bear the heaviest burden in correcting imbalances that lie at the heart of euro's existential crisis. As I see it, Germany needs to stop tightening and adopt mildly expansionary policies to get growth going again to save the euro. There is already excessive austerity at a time when economies are contracting; it dampens the outlook. Austerity merely compounds economic weaknesses and does nothing to improve competitiveness and trade imbalances; moreover, it wrecks havoc with public finances.

The gloom over Japan had been bad, reflecting "structural pessimism." Its economy rebounded from the recession triggered by the devastating tsunami and nuclear disaster in March, and the subsequent supply chain disruption (+6 percent in the third quarter of 2011). Since then, the effects of the high yen and slowdown in overseas demand are weighing on business sentiment. The December Tankan survey dipped negative, indicating Japanese exports are getting hammered.[5] But the index also suggested some good news: The key auto sector showed a strong rise, and there's improvement in sentiment among nonmanufacturers, supported by private consumption. Things are beginning to look better—OECD expected Japan's gross domestic product (GDP) growth to pick up in 2012 to up to 2 percent growth, against –0.3 percent in 2011.

Rich Poor World

All across China, India, and the rest of Asia, the eurozone crisis is being felt, especially in export-oriented manufacturing, prompting fears that falling overseas demand and financial disruptions could once again cause a steep drop in growth and loss of wealth as it did during the 2008/2009 recession. Still, emerging East Asia's economic momentum remains robust. But the region now faces greater risks as the eurozone's debt problems worsen, and a fragile US economy could turn wary, unleashing devastating consequences. Already, business sentiment among Asian's top corporates fell in the fourth quarter of 2011 to its lowest in two years, with fears over global slack and rising costs being the risks to the outlook. More recently, financial volatility dampened investor confidence and consumer sentiment. Domestic demand has since softened, although it continued to remain a reliable contributor to growth. GDP in developing East Asia would expand 8.2 percent in 2011, and 7.8 percent in 2012 (9.7 percent in 2010). Slackening growth reflected lower demand for exports, tightening monetary conditions, and lower manufacturing, especially in electronics. Recent events intensified investors' concerns over growth and stability, and triggered capital outflows toward safer havens; stock markets lost value. Within Asia, China and India expanded the fastest, although evolving developments have not been encouraging. In Southeast Asia, Indonesia's GDP expanded 6.4 percent in 2011 (against 6.1 percent in 2010) and is expected to grow steadily in 2012 (6.3 percent). World Bank estimated activity in Malaysia had also slackened: 4.3 percent in 2011 (7.2 percent in 2010), and 4.5 to 5 percent in 2012.

High reserves and current surpluses would protect most of East Asia from possible renewed financial stress. Looking forward, East Asia needs to balance between growth and fighting off the impact of uncertainty. The region is likely to hold off further policy tightening, ready to ward off negative effects. Their strong fiscal positions also leave space for stimulus when needed.

China

In China, overall growth remains still heavily dependent on exports. Growth will slacken to 9.2 percent this year. But manufacturing activity contracted in December, while foreign direct investment fell for the first time in 28 months. China faces severe foreign trade restrictions in the first quarter of 2012 due to the "grim and complicated" global outlook. For 2012, "growth momentum remains weak, with additional downside risks from exports and property market not yet fully filtering through." With Europe already in recession, the United States struggling with a fragile recovery, and Japan battered, China's exports have flagged, with expectations of worse to come. Domestically, there is no growth in property starts, electricity output is slackening, and exports in November and December are likely to be awful.

These have since triggered a shift in policy focus to expand domestic demand, including a stronger yuan—fiscal policy in 2012 will be more proactive and monetary policy more accommodative. Social spending will rise, reflecting the "inclusiveness" of development. Low-income housing construction will pick up. "Targeted easing" will also help prop up small manufacturers. They signal preparedness to move aggressively to stoke consumption. Both OECD and the World Bank are optimistic that China will grow at 8.5 percent in 2012, its slowest pace in a decade, and 9.5 percent in 2013. The World Bank and the IMF considered China's banking system able to withstand exchange rate and interest rate shocks, including significant spillover from eurozone debt restructuring. I would err with caution because China still needs to rebalance—from exports bias to consumption driven—as the transition can be disruptive.

What, Then, Are We to Do?

The year 2012 is fraught with uncertainty. Things will become more unsettling before they get better. Unfortunately, uncertainty extends beyond nations and regions to worries about political stability and global economic order, eroding the quality of public goods. It's no coincidence all these are happening simultaneously, adding to anxiety that comes with the loss of once-dependable anchors. We just don't know how things will pan out—what is evolutionary and what will be sudden, even disruptive. Experts have varying views on what to look for, what to expect, and where and how best to change and adapt. The economic and financial or social and political dynamics are complex. What's going to happen in 2012? Even by the first quarter of 2012? Psychologist and Nobel Laureate economist Daniel Kahneman believes, "There are domains in which expertise is not possible—and in long-term political forecasting, it's been shown that experts are just not better than a dice-throwing monkey."[6] So take your pick!

Kuala Lumpur
December 19, 2011

Notes

1. First published on December 31, 2011.
2. International Monetary Fund (IMF), *World Economic Outlook: Slowing Growth, Rising Risks* (Washington, DC: IMF, September 2011).
3. Asian Development Bank (ADB), *Asian Economic Monitor* (Manila: ADB, December 2011); World Bank, *East Asia and Pacific Economic Update: Navigating Turbulence, Sustaining Growth*, vol. 2 (Washington, DC: World Bank, November 2011); Organisation for Economic Co-operation and Development (OECD), *Economic Outlook, No. 90* (Paris: OECD, November 28, 2011).
4. OECD, *What Is the Economic Outlook for OECD Countries?* (Paris: OECD, November 28, 2011).
5. Bank of Japan, *Tankan Survey* of business sentiment among large manufacturers deteriorated to –4 in December 2011 from +2 in September. The index is calculated by subtracting the percentage of companies reporting business conditions are bad from those saying they are good. The December index shows Japanese companies getting hammered by the strong yen and weakening overseas demand.
6. Daniel Kahneman, "10 Questions," psychologist and Nobel Laureate economist on why people don't make rational choices, *Time* (December 5, 2011).

CHAPTER 16

G-20 Summit, Los Cabos 2012 GJAP: More of the Same[1]

I have just returned from the Shadow G-20 meeting of the International Policy Advisory Group convened by the Asian Development Bank (led by President Haruhiko Kuroda) and the Earth Institute of Columbia University (under the direction of its president, Professor Jeffrey Sachs). Its theme: the global economy in uncertain waters—question marks over fiscal sustainability, financial stability, structural adjustment, and global environmental adjustment. The gathering of about 30 global scholars (including Mr. Daniel Cohen, adviser to the president of France) deliberated for two days with the view of being better placed to influence the outcome on key global issues confronting G-20 leaders at its June 18–19, 2012, meeting in Mexico.

As they met, they were no better off than where they left off last November in Cannes, France, facing heightened risks from Europe that threatens to cripple the global economy. As it turned out, this time the stakes were even higher, as growth in both the rich and emerging nations was now slackening in sync. Not surprisingly, the G-20 meeting turned out to be a nonevent—with a declaration that is full of "sound and fury, signifying nothing." The G-20, accounting for two-thirds of the world's population and 85 percent of global output, was expected to press for swift and decisive action by Europe to resolve the turmoil. This time, some leaders did push to steer the agenda's focus away from fiscal austerity toward more definite steps to spur growth, so critical to global recovery. Said an Organisation for Economic Co-operation and Development senior official: "The fire is in Europe right now and it is affecting the system as a whole. It is no longer just a European issue."[2] Realistically, G-20 leaders can only hope that their discussions will be taken further at key gatherings of European leaders as they work toward the European Union (EU) Summit. But time is not on their side. Contagion lurks.

Los Cabos GJAP

As in Cannes, G-20 was not expected to do more than urge the eurozone urgently to resolve the crisis. The communique[3] made no real new commitments, only a renewed (and reworded) commitment to ensure that the crisis does not spiral out of control: "We are committed to adopting all necessary policy measures to strengthen demand, support global growth and restore confidence, . . . enhance jobs creation as reflected in the Los Cabos Growth and Jobs Action Plan (GJAP). We will implement all our commitments in a timely manner and rigorously monitor their implementation."[4] Unfortunately, they are short on real actions to be taken. This plan, however, did envisage policy actions to be focused on the following:

- Addressing the sovereign debt and banking crisis in the euro area
- Ensuring financial stability
- Boosting demand and growth, and reducing high unemployment
- Ensuring the pace of fiscal consolidation supports economic recovery
- Dealing with geopolitical risks that can lead to a spike in oil prices
- Ensuring emerging markets maintain sustainable economic growth
- Resisting protectionism and keeping markets open

To promote confidence, G-20 agreed on the following:

1. Euro-area members of G-20 (EAM-G20) will take all necessary measures to safeguard the integrity and stability of the area, and support growth, ensure financial stability, and promote fiscal responsibility.
   - EAM-G20 will move to get a more integrated financial architecture, covering banking supervision and recapitalization, and deposit insurance.
   - Foster adjustment through reforms to strengthen competitiveness in deficit countries, and to promote demand in surplus nations.
   - EAM-G20 will support growth, including making better use of European financial means, such as the European Investment Bank (EIB), project bonds, and structural funds, for more targeted investment.
2. Fiscal policies in G-20 will be consistent with real economic recovery.
3. Monetary policies will focus on economic growth with price stability.
4. Should conditions significantly deteriorate, G-20 nations stand ready to coordinate and implement new measures to support demand.
5. Emerging markets' policies will support demand with price stability.
6. G-20 will further rebalance global demand by pushing demand in surplus nations, rotating demand to the private sector in countries with fiscal deficits, and raising savings in deficit countries.

7. G-20 reaffirms its shared interest in a strong and stable international monetary system and support for market-determined exchange rates.

But what real mechanisms are being devised and used to really boost confidence?

IMF War Chest

The International Monetary Fund's (IMF) resources were raised at G-20 by new BRICS (comprising Brazil, Russia, India, China, and South Africa) pledges—US$43 billion from China; US$10 billion each from India, Russia, and Brazil; US$10 billion from Mexico; US$5 billion from Turkey; and US$1 billion from a number of smaller nations, raising total new commitments to US$456 billion. The new cash boost would nearly double the IMF's real lending ability to around US$700 billion. These resources are being made available for crisis prevention and resolution by meeting potential financing needs of all IMF members, and not earmarked for European use. There was expressed concern about signing off on new loans to the IMF for use to backstop the eurozone. Emphasized the Canadian finance minister: "The situation is not that we're dealing with impoverished countries here. The reality is that we have non-European G-20 nations that have a lot of hesitation in dedicating resources to the wealthy European countries."[5] The new pledges were made on the understanding that the IMF would move promptly forward on governance reform to enhance the say of developing and emerging nations.

BRICS Initiative

BRICS advanced the idea of pooling foreign exchange reserves through multilateral currency swap arrangements in the face of new threats that the evolving European crisis would spill over into the global economy. Swaps—allowing central banks to lend each other currencies on demand to help boost liquidity and keep markets well funded—represent emergency measures at a time of crisis. They are also viewed as part of a broader move away from overreliance on the US dollar and the euro, toward the IMF. Similar arrangements are already in place under the Chiang Mai Initiative among ASEAN+3 (China, Japan, and South Korea), which last month agreed to double its size to US$240 billion. Also, Russia is setting aside US$40 billion to stimulate in the event the eurozone crisis escalates and spreads, to support "socially needy people" and "systemically vital enterprises."

Growth Compact

G-20 leaders have fundamental disagreements on most key economic issues: high taxes or low; larger central bank bond portfolios or smaller;
more government or less; more growth or less austerity. The Los Cabos
GJAP was high at expressing fine sentiments, but it lacked details on
actual mechanisms for real action. Like it or not, Europeans face a huge
dilemma over Greece. Its new coalition wants to extend by "at least two
years" to 2016 the budget deficit targets Athens must achieve; it's also
proposing tax cuts and other measures over the next four years to support the unemployed and low-income groups hit hard by five years of
recession, including: freeze on the 150,000 public-sector job cuts; pay two
years of unemployment benefits instead of one; revise the 22 percent cut
in minimum wage; give income tax relief to the low-income brackets; and
reduce sales tax on restaurants and agriculture. Realistically, the troika
(EU, European Central Bank [ECB], and IMF) can be expected to offer
some adjustments, but no radical rewrite of bailout terms; Germany will
continue to resist. Greece's gross domestic product (GDP) will contract
by more than 6 percent this year with no turnaround signs. The jobless
rate is at a record high, especially among youth. Greece is now on a collision course with international creditors. It can't force internal devaluation
through falling wages, nor create enough growth to allow existing debt
to be serviced. Prospects remain dismal. Ironically, Greece is no longer at
the center of the crisis. The fate of the euro will be decided in Spain and,
certainly, in Italy.

On paper, G-20 is now committed to push for more growth. The ongoing crisis serves as a new test of G-20's power to coordinate global action.
In the 2008–2009 crisis, its quick and coordinated global moves at stimulation helped reverse the global disaster. Now, there is little ammunition left
to fight a potential new slump. Europe and the United States are struggling
with crushing debts and political stalemate. Emerging nations' growth is
slackening, in part because of growing uncertainty risks, and in part because of troubles in Europe and the United States.

Be that as it may, France is committed to push for euro-wide growth,
and wants the EU to agree before end-2012 on growth-boosting measures worth €120 billion, and appears prepared to trade off with Germany
in soft-pedaling its call to issue mutualized debt in the euro-bloc. This
growth compact will comprise a combination of €55 billion in unused EU
structural funds, €4.5 billion in project bonds to be deployed in areas such
as new technologies, renewal energy, transport, and other infrastructure,
and €60 billion in new resources to be raised by leveraging a €10 billion
increase in EIB's capital. The idea is then to enlarge this by end-2012 to
raise more new funds to create jobs for youth. This compact is pathetically

inadequate. It looks like a face-saving device for Mr. Hollande, admits Mr. Cohen, his adviser. Nobel Laureate Paul Krugman refers to this as part of the "great abdication."[6]

What, Then, Are We to Do?

The impact of good news gets briefer each time. Of late, good news gets a half-life in 24-hour live markets. Spain's bank bailout rallied markets and investors' sentiment for only half a day on June 11. The following week-end of the Greek election—with an outcome as good as could have been hoped—did not buoy the markets for half a morning. It fizzled because the election changed nothing. Such has been the influence of European decisions—doing the minimum to address each crisis as it comes along, so that expectations are now so low that they hardly disappoint markets. As it happens, the downturn in the eurozone's private sector is becoming more entrenched, with falling new orders and rising jobless levels denting confidence. June is the fifth consecutive month activity across the entire euro-zone declined, dragging down heavyweights Germany and France, and increasing calls for ECB action support. The eurozone's north–south divide is likely to worsen. Consumer spending will support growth in Germany and France, while austerity programs will contribute to contractions in Spain, Italy, and Greece. This doesn't look good.

Growing discontent reflects the need to do more, and more radically: We know fiscal austerity needs to be relaxed; a credible growth compact is needed to complement the fiscal compact; and the EU badly needs a fiscal union with debt mutualization (euro-bonds, i.e., collective eurozone borrowing). In addition, the time has now come to implement a banking union (integrated eurozone bank governance system), starting with euro-wide deposit insurance and bank recapitalization schemes. And, the EU needs to move toward greater political integration, with or without Greece. There is nothing new here that's not in GJAP.

But Germany is known to actively resist its key elements. How did Greece, the birthplace of democracy, come to have a parliament full of hammers, sickles, and swastikas? Yet, more than 50 percent of Greeks voted for stronger European unification. In his latest column, Krugman reminds us once again of the lessons from 1931 (when bank panic in Austria was allowed to spread globally) and from 1937 (when the United States shifted far too soon from fiscal stimulus to austerity, plunging the recovering economy into a double-dip recession), which, if not well learned, will land the world once again in catastrophe, simply because it is politically expedient to adopt the line that "avoiding economic disaster is somebody else's responsibility." What a shame. True, it's more about politics than economics. Electoral politics can readily spoil the best efforts to salvage the euro. Just too many things can go wrong.

New York
Kuala Lumpur
June 28, 2012

Notes

1. First published on June 30, 2012, as "Los Cabos 'Growth & Jobs Action Plan': More of the Same."
2. Angel Gurria, Secretary General of Organisation for Economic Co-operation and Development at G-20 Summit on June 18, 2012.
3. Group of 20 (G-20), "Leaders Declaration," G-20 Summit, Los Cabos, Mexico, June 19, 2012.
4. Group of 20 (G-20), "The Los Cabos Growth and Jobs Action Plan," G-20 Summit, Los Cabos, Mexico, June 19, 2012.
5. Jim Flaherty, Canadian Finance Minister, told Canadian television on June 18, 2012.
6. Paul Krugman, "Another Bank Bailout," *International Herald Tribune* (June 12, 2012).

CHAPTER 17

APEC, Vladivostok 2012:
A New Perspective[1]

The 20th Asia Pacific Economic Cooperation (APEC) meeting among 21 nations in the Pacific Rim has come and gone—not with a bang, but a whimper. It was held on an island off the Russian seaport of Vladivostok, September 8–9, 2012. The timing wasn't good. The summit was overshadowed by (1) continuing diplomatic strains across the region (tensions over territorial claims and disputes over the future direction of trade initiatives) and beyond (security issues and continuing social unrest in the Middle East); and (2) economic uncertainties in Europe as its leaders grapple and struggle to resolve the 3½-year-old "debt" crisis amid a double-dip recession in the eurozone, sparking concerns about the global economic downturn.

APEC accounts for 40 percent of the world's population, 54 percent of economic output, and 44 percent of total trade. It has the world's three largest economies—the United States, China, and Japan. Yet, there wasn't much APEC could do about the strong headwinds to economic recovery globally, other than declaring: "In such circumstances, we are resolved to work collectively to support growth and foster financial stability, and restore confidence."[2] How lame has global leadership become! But life goes on.

APEC Declaration

Over the past 10 years, APEC trade has risen four times and foreign direct investments in the region are up more than 20 percent a year. But the global economy has recently faced serious downside risks. Financial markets had remained "fragile, while public deficits and debts in some advanced economies are creating strong headwinds to economic recovery globally. The events in Europe are adversely affecting growth in the region."[3] Nevertheless, the

Vladivostok Leaders' Declaration strongly affirmed 12 commitments to do the following:[4]

1. Promote trade and investment liberalization and facilitation.
2. Strengthen domestic demand, facilitate job creation, reduce high public deficits and debts, and implement structural reforms.
3. Support European efforts to safeguard integrity of the eurozone.
4. Reduce imbalances by strengthening deficit (in external payments) economies' public finances, and surplus nations' domestic demand and greater exchange rate flexibility.
5. Move more rapidly toward market-determined exchange-rate regimes.
6. Avoid persistent exchange rate misalignments, and refrain from competitive currency devaluation.
7. Ensure long-term fiscal sustainability while recognizing the need to support recovery within the available fiscal space.
8. Strengthen the multilateral trading system as embodied in World Trade Organization (WTO) and work toward the successful conclusion of the Doha Development Round.
9. Address the next generation of trade and investment issues to further integrate APEC economies and trade expansion.
10. Continue efforts to improve investment climate in the region.
11. Promote green growth and seek practical trade-enhancing solutions to address global environment challenges, including ensuring that actions to protect the environment are not used as an excuse to introduce protectionist measures.
12. Fight against corruption to enhance openness and transparency, and combat fraud, bribery, and misuse of public resources.

These commitments offer nothing new—a mere restatement of past commitments and intentions. So, what else is new?

Free and Open Markets

Russia, as its host, was especially keen for the dialogue to focus on freeing up trade and investment flows to help stimulate economic growth, taking into account the new realities of Russia's accession to the WTO. In particular, concern was expressed, and rightly so, on growing signs of protectionism, global food security, "duties" in green technology, "chokepoints" hampering the expansion of reliable supply chains, and development of market-driven innovation policies. APEC addressed these concerns with eight new resolutions:

1. Refrain through end-2015 from raising new barriers to investment and to trade in goods and services (including rollback of protectionist measures), as well as from imposing new export restrictions or implementing WTO-inconsistent measures.
2. Rule out limiting food exports, and underline the importance of maintaining open markets to ensure reliable food supplies, despite severe drought that had damaged crops in the United States, Russia, and Australia (major global wheat and other food suppliers).
3. Raise sustainable food production and productivity (including through adopting innovative technologies and biotechnology), further facilitating trade and developing food markets, enhancing food safety, improving access to food, and improving farmers' welfare.
4. Endorse the "List of 54 Environmental Goods" that directly contribute to green growth, on which import duties will be reduced to no more than 5 percent by 2015, including equipment for renewable energy, waste treatment, and environment monitoring. (To promote further green growth in ASEAN, I understand Indonesia pushed hard but failed to include crude palm oil in the final list [which was expanded to 54 from 25 in one day!].)
5. Promote further energy efficiency and cleaner energy supplies as a priority to boost both sustainable development and energy security and reduce carbon emissions. Toward this end, develop a workable action plan to reduce by 45 percent APEC's energy intensity by 2035.
6. Reaffirm its commitment to an APEC-wide target of 10 percent improvement in supply-chain performance by 2015 in terms of reducing time, cost, and uncertainty of moving goods and services throughout the region. Progress has since been made at addressing chokepoints in supply chains through targeted capacity building and concrete steps taken in making supply chains more reliable, resilient, safe, efficient, transparent, diversified, and intelligent; and greater progress is expected through 2014.
7. Remain committed to encourage innovation and the building of capacity to innovate. Toward this end, it will promote effective, non-discriminatory, and market-driven domestic innovation policies by implementing innovative practices in 2013 that will assist economies to integrate these commitments into their domestic policy framework.
8. Take steps in 2012 to enhance practical and sustainable educational collaboration, especially in cross-border cooperation and facilitation of exchanges in education and through bilateral agreements within the region to enhance the mobility of students, researchers, and education providers. APEC recognizes education to be the essential driver of innovative growth.

APEC Integration

The Free Trade Area of the Asia-Pacific (FTAAP) is a major instrument to further APEC's agenda for regional integration. Various sectional-regional undertakings are in the pipeline. China, Japan, and South Korea have begun intense work to form a free-trade group with ASEAN (the Association of Southeast Asian Nations)[5] known as ASEAN+3[6] free-trade area while the United States is leading an initiative with Canada, Australia, Vietnam, and eight other countries toward a Trans-Pacific Partnership (TPP). Unlike traditional free trade, as I understand it, this pact is reported to focus on stronger protection for intellectual property and stronger and longer patent protection that ironically would possibly "restrict" competition to the detriment of consumers. The TPP talks have since, however, experienced a major setback with the recent withdrawal of Japan. Recognizing this, APEC directed its ministers to continue to facilitate APEC's role as an incubator of FTAAP in providing leadership to bring the parties together. As host, Russia—whose trade with the European Union (EU) accounts for about half of its total trade—is already shifting its strategy in practice toward Asia-Pacific. Then, there is its creation of a common market with Belarus and Kazakhstan. This and the Customs Union and Common Economic Space agreements (which are already implemented), as well as the prospective Eurasian Economic Union, are all designed as an integral part in shaping its regional and international agenda, especially as a seamless bridge between the EU and APEC across a vast area, including development of Siberia and its Far East.

Russia: According to new Russian president, Vladimir Putin, this approach now provides a "transport profile" for integration, aimed at building an efficient system for managing logistical risks and diversifying trade routes.[7] Already, modern ports are being built in the Russian Far East, including investments to modernize transportation and shipping infrastructure, and improving customs and other cross-border facilities.

Assessment by APEC's Business Advisory Council concluded that the new Russian initiatives will raise traffic flow between Europe and APEC across Russian territory by no less than fivefold by 2020. These new routes can prove to be more cost competitive compared with traditional routes through the Suez Canal and Straits of Malacca, and can offer advantages of speed and safety. This is the new challenge. In addition, there is the opportunity to promote real sustainable growth.

For the future, the quality of growth matters. This simply means placing more emphasis on innovation and the development of human capital, taking advantage of new partnerships, removing barriers to the movement of ideas, expertise, and technology, coordinating scientific policy, and jointly shaping innovative markets. Education holds the key. Russia can provide a network of universities to promote student and teacher exchanges and create an environment for greater academic mobility. Russia has since proposed forming a common educational space for the Asia-Pacific region, offering broad opportunities to join forces in advancing APEC's common creative goals.

What, Then, Are We to Do?

With each passing G-20 meeting, questions are raised about APEC's long-term mission to create a region-wide free-trade area, as competing trade and educational groupings emerge. The new Russian initiatives offer a fresh perspective. No doubt, Russia, the United States, and the European Union are all looking toward Asia and China in particular, where continuing robust economic development is providing the engine of activity and future drive. At the summit, Russia advertised its vast country and resources, and advanced its unique location as the new gateway and technology hub for Asia to European-wide markets. The time has come to reassess APEC in this new perspective. We know China (with its new infrastructure investments in Russia's agriculture, energy, railways, and roads) and Japan (investments in gas supply and LNG plant on Russia's Pacific coast) already have a head start. Can the United States and Europe afford to be left behind?

Kuala Lumpur
September 20, 2012

Notes

1. First published on September 22, 2012, as "APEC '12 Vladivostok: A New Perspective."
2. Asia Pacific Economic Cooperation (APEC), "2012 Leaders' Declaration," APEC Meeting, Vladivostok, Russia, September 9, 2012.
3. Ibid.
4. Asia Pacific Economic Cooperation (APEC), "Vladivostok Declaration—Integrate to Grow, Innovate to Prosper," APEC Meeting, Vladivostok, Russia, September 9, 2012.
5. Comprises Brunei, Indonesia, Malaysia, the Philippines, Singapore, Thailand, the Indo-Chinese States of Vietnam, Cambodia, Laos, and Myanmar.
6. ASEAN plus China, Japan, and South Korea.
7. Vladimir Putin, at the 2012 APEC Meeting in Vladivostok, Russia, on September 9, 2012.

CHAPTER 18

TW3 2012: A Tough Year with a Bleak Outlook[1]

The year 2012 is coming to a close, leaving behind many problems. Most are man-made, originating in politics. Yet, sadly, there are no major political leaders who have the credibility, charisma, and strength of character to garner the needed political resolve to set their own nations or the world on the righteous path of sustainable development.

The reelection of US resident Barack Obama helped a little. As I write, even if he is able to persuade opposition Republicans in Congress to a deal to avoid the looming "fiscal cliff" (self-inflicted arrangement involving US$600 billion of indiscriminate tax hikes and "sequester" cuts in military and welfare spending, bringing on a 3 percent reduction in 2013 fiscal deficit), the resulting cuts and taxes will invariably become a drag on growth—estimated by most to be at least 1 percent of gross domestic product (GDP) in 2013. The downside risk to global growth is likely to be exacerbated by the spread of ongoing austerity to most advanced nations. Thus far, the recessionary fiscal drag has been centered on the eurozone periphery and the United Kingdom. Latest indicators point to it spreading to the eurozone's core (including Germany and France) and Japan. This only confirms the International Monetary Fund's (IMF) contention that continuing excessive front-loading of fiscal austerity will work to dim global growth prospects in 2013. The recent near-simultaneous leadership changes in China, Japan, and South Korea offer East Asia a fresh opportunity for reconciliation after a period of tension. The region's three biggest economies now appear to be confidently over the hump—following the Japanese and South Korean elections last week and Beijing's leadership "jockeying" resolved by last month. But, realistically, they continue to face headwinds from a stumbling world economy. North Korea's rocket launch last week adds to regional uncertainty. So does continuing unrest in Syria and Middle East, in general. Critical to the well-being of nations is how they will use this opportunity to get their ties back on track.

Enter 2013

The year 2013 is a big step following a tough year. To me, six events had dominated 2012: (1) Europe held the world's fate in its unsteady hands for most of the year. It took the European Central Bank (ECB) President Mario Draghi's promise "to do whatever it takes to save the euro" to rid the sting out of the crisis, with a later pledge of "unlimited" bond buying;[2] (2) impact of the war in Syria and Morsi's uneasy presidency in Egypt; (3) leadership transition in four of the world's five largest economies, with "elections" in the United States, France, Japan, and China ushering in promises of new approaches to politics and policy making; (4) serious political disputes in the East Asia seas; (5) recent massive anti-Putin unrest in Russia; and (6) serious transformation moves in Myanmar. They still continue to dominate in the new year. For the moment, it is too soon to tell what their politics will bring in 2013. But one thing is for sure. Global business gloom has deepened since the third quarter of 2012 and is likely to persist.

I think there are some important lessons. First, investment risks have turned more political. US businesses today have more than US$1 trillion in cash reserves and committed facilities awaiting investment. For them, the nightmare is Washington staying gridlocked, four days before falling off the cliff. Hopefully, like before, the game of chicken ends at the last minute. Second, even a small economy like Greece (barely 2 percent of the eurozone economy) can have a material impact on global business sentiment as the "Grexit" drama showed. Third, the European episode pointed out clearly that governments can't simply cut and grow. One of the important takeaways from 2012 is that it is critical to always focus on the big picture and not be grappled by event risks as these come and go. As a US civil rights activist once said: "For all its uncertainty, we cannot flee the future."[3] So as we step into 2013, nations just have to embrace risks and learn to manage and live with them. Scurrying away will not help.

OECD Slashes Forecast

Paris-based rich-nations' think tank, Organisation for Economic Co-operation and Development (OECD), said in mid-December that its Composite Leading Indicators (CLIs) point to widely differing growth outlooks among its 34 member states.[4] Signs are of a modest pickup in the United States and the United Kingdom, slowdown in Canada and Russia, and deepening recession in the eurozone (including significant slackening in Germany and France) and in Japan, and possibly Brazil. OECD's CLIs are designed to provide early signals of turning points between economic expansion and slowdown, based on extensive data that have a reliable history of signaling changes in activity. Overall, barring the worst fears won't come to pass, combined OECD GDP will only rise 1 to 1.5 percent in 2013, not much change from 2012, with a modest pickup of 2 to 2.5 percent in prospect for 2014. Not unlike IMF forecast, OECD growth will only expand if the eurozone deals seriously with its political and debt crisis, and the United States finds a timely credible path to avoid the cliff. Absent such actions, world growth would slide into another downturn, with deepening recession in the eurozone periphery, and contraction or stagnation at the core and related advanced nations. What's needed is "very careful policy steering."[5] Eurozone manufacturing kept contracting in November for a sixteenth month. Data show signs of recession extending into 2013 as policy makers struggle to come to grips with the long-standing crisis. For businesses and investors, the October Markit survey concluded that in 2013, companies can expect challenging sales and profits, causing many to focus on cost cutting.

Eurozone

On December 6, the European Central Bank (ECB) slashed its forecast on the eurozone for 2013, signaling another difficult year ahead. Echoing the IMF,[6] it now expects growth ranging from a decline of 0.9 percent to a growth of 0.3 percent next year (–0.5 percent in 2012). Level of uncertainty was reflected in its first attempt to forecast 2014—at 1.2 percent: "Gradual recovery should start later in 2013" (GDP shrank 0.1 percent in the third quarter of 2012 and –0.2 percent in the second quarter of 2012). As the eurozone slipped into recession for the second time in four years, Germany's growth slowed down to 0.2 percent in the third quarter of 2012 (0.3 percent in the second quarter of 2012); expectation is for it to expand 0.4 percent in 2013 (from 1.6 percent in 2012). However, Germany faces a "favorable environment on the back of expansionary monetary policy." Expect some revival later on in the second half of 2013, following a better-than-expected jump in investor sentiment in December 2012. Industrial output in Germany fell 2.4 percent in October (–1.6 percent in September); France reported a 0.6 percent drop while Spain and Portugal had increases of 1.2 percent and 4.8 percent respectively. France is facing conditions much worse than Germany—it is fast becoming aligned with its southern neighbors of Spain and Italy. Germany, given its openness, cannot "prosper alone; it has a particular interest in the welfare of its partners." Nevertheless, the eurozone's peripheral shows little sign of recovery: GDP continues to shrink because of fiscal austerity, euro's excessive strength, and severe credit crunch. Already, social and political backlash against more austerity is becoming overwhelming with strikes, riots, violence, and rise of extremist politics. They just need to grow. Another year of muddling through only revives old risks in a more virulent form in 2013 and beyond.

The United States

Growth in the United States remained anemic at 1.5 to 2 percent for most of 2012. Political and policy uncertainties abound. Fiscal worries are centered on four key areas: taxes, spending, stimulus, and borrowing:

1. The United States needs a package exceeding US$1 trillion in revenues over 10 years and to set in motion a tax-reform process in 2013 to limit tax deductions and lower rates for businesses and individuals.
2. The United States needs to pass a package of spending cuts with less generous social benefits, reductions in health spending, and cuts in selected mandatory programs, including the military.
3. Some short-term stimulus measures must be taken, especially on infra-structure projects, education, and research and development.
4. The debt ceiling must be raised now. Already, with continuing impasse even at this late hour, forecasters are downgrading growth expectations for 2013.

"It's a dangerous situation," says Nobel Laureate Paul Krugman: "The opposition is lost and rudderless, bitter and angry . . . as it lashes out in the death throes of the conservative dream."[7]

All this is happening at a time of significant game changes boosting the outlook: (1) housing is recovering haltingly; (2) manufacturing reengineering is under way; (3) third quarter of 2012 growth is up 3.1 percent (1.3 percent in the second quarter of 2012), with consumer spending rising 1.6 percent and unemployment down to 7.7 percent, its lowest since 2008; (4) pent-up demand is awaiting clarity on the future fiscal pathway to be unleashed; and (5) future is in energy transformation, especially from low-cost shale oil and gas. But first, the daunting task to regain business and consumer confidence needs to begin now. Because of continuing uncertainty, consensus forecast chances of 24 percent for greater than 3 percent growth in 2013, same as chances of a recession. On the whole, they expect growth of 2.3 percent in 2013, better than three months ago. But, this won't materially help the 12 million jobless. Even by 2014, unemployment is unlikely to be lower than 6.5 to 7 percent.

East Asia and Pacific (EAP)

The World Bank's December update places growth in China and developing East Asia at 7.5 percent in 2012 (against 8.3 percent in 2011) in the face of weak external demand.[8] Growth in EAP is still the highest among the developing world and constituted 40 percent of global growth; but is set to recover to 7.9 percent in 2013. EAP (excluding China) will grow 5.6 percent in 2012, 1 percent higher than in 2011 due mainly to a rebound of activity in Thailand, strong growth in the Philippines, and relatively modest slowdown in Indonesia and Vietnam. Malaysia held a steady course. For the entire region, easy fiscal and monetary policies supported growth. Next year, the region will benefit from continued strong domestic demand and the mild expected global recovery, especially in the second half of 2013.

I agree with the World Bank that most EAP nations have retained strong underlying macroeconomic fundamentals and should be better able to withstand external shocks. But many risks remain, including open vulnerabilities in the eurozone that could readily lead to renewed financial market volatility, and global slowdown; United States falling off the fiscal cliff, resulting in a loss of growth push for EAP; potential hostility arising from political territorial tensions in the Asian seas; and fallout from unexpected developments in Syria and the Middle East.

However, the robust growth in services this year reflects strong domestic support derived from continuing rising incomes. As these trends gather strength, services can be expected to emerge as a new growth driver in EAP. For the region, the latest business sentiment surveys have turned positive for the fourth quarter of 2012, reversing two consecutive quarters of declines, while global uncertainties remained the biggest concern for the region's firms.

China is expected to grow by 7.9 percent in 2012 (9.3 percent in 2011), the lowest since 1999, due mainly to lower domestic demand growth reflecting the 2011 stabilization measures. The World Bank expects China to expand 8.4 percent in 2013 fueled by fiscal stimulus and faster effective implementation of large investment projects. Indications are that the recent slowdown has now bottomed out: Third quarter of 2012 GDP rose 7.4 percent, below the historical trend and lowest in 14 quarters, but its quarter-over-quarter growth reached a 9.1 percent annual rate in the third quarter of 2012. Growth is, however, expected to slacken to 8 percent in 2014 as productivity and labor force growth tail off. Consumer prices will likely continue to fall, averaging 2.8 percent in 2012, but will rise moderately to 3.3 percent in 2013 as growth picks up and the lagged effects of easy monetary policies in the second half of 2011 take hold. China's policy challenge is to balance the trade-off between supporting growth and reforming. But, priority remains at implementing targeted tax cuts, health and social welfare spending, and large-scale social housing to support consumption.

What, Then, Are We to Do?

After a tough 2012, geopolitical uncertainties will engulf 2013. Consumers, corporations, and investors are bound to remain cautious and risk adverse—even scared at times. But prospects in EAP look bright, and the region continues to have ample fiscal space to counter the impact of unforeseen external shocks. Much of the global economic uncertainty is still being generated in Europe. It's messy there right now, but the recovery of Europe will come—someday, hopefully soon. Today, the ratio of stock market value to GDP averaged worldwide at 80 percent. In peripheral Europe, this ratio ranged from 23 percent in Greece to 38 percent in Portugal—akin to where Asian counterparts were in 1998. Italy's total stock market value is today about the same as Apple's. Ruchir Sharma of Morgan Stanley made these and other insightful comments in the *Financial Times*, with this refrain: Is Italy worth no more than Apple?[9] Food for thought. Look at it this way. We all have to keep the perspective in approaching 2013 in order to avoid our own self-made "cliff."

Kuala Lumpur
December 27, 2012

Notes

1. First published on December 29, 2012, as "Bleak 2013 Outlook as Asia Remains Resilient."
2. Mario Draghi, in the event the euro spirals out of control again, Draghi promises in July 2012 to do "whatever it takes" to save it, including potentially unlimited bond purchases.
3. Barbara Jordan, American civil rights activist.
4. Organisation for Economic Co-operation and Development (OECD), *Economic Outlook* (Paris: OECD, December 2012).
5. David Lipton, speaking at the Royal Institute of International Affairs at Chatham House in London on December 12, 2012.
6. International Monetary Fund (IMF), *World Economic Outlook: Coping with High Debt and Sluggish Growth* (Washington, DC: IMF, October 2012).
7. Paul Krugman, "Political Party in Ruins," *International Herald Tribune* (December 15, 2012).
8. World Bank, *East Asia and Pacific Economic Update: Remaining Resilient*. vol. 2 (Washington, DC: World Bank, 2012).
9. Ruchir Sharma, "Why 2013 Will Be the Year Europe Bounces Back," *Financial Times* (December 19, 2012).

CHAPTER 19

2013: Breadth of Global Slowdown Disconcerting[1]

It's disconcerting. We now have a Goldilocks situation—not too hot, not too cold. The speed limit on global growth has slackened, with no further boost from the emerging markets to offset the continuing slack in advanced economies. The world economy is just moving along with nothing much to shout about.

The year started badly, with fiscal cliffs lurking in the United States and a toxic situation in Europe. But the worst didn't happen. Yes, US politicians bungled about, but disaster was avoided. The Cyprus bailout turned into a bail-in; nevertheless, government bond yields surprisingly fell across the troubled eurozone periphery as recession persisted. Yet, it could not prevent a slowdown worldwide. Global growth sank below 2.5 percent in the first half of 2012. Any expected rebound has since faded.

First quarter of 2013 gross domestic product (GDP) growth in the United States and China turned disappointing. However, Japan's economy is rebounding, reflecting fiscal and monetary stimuli with the yen tumbling against US$ and euro. Unemployment in Europe remained unrelentlessly brutal, reflecting the deepening recession. In April, an important index of global economic activity fell to its lowest level since October 2012, suggesting that the world economy is barely managing to accelerate.

Europe remains in bad shape. The European Central Bank (ECB) is reported to continue to see downside risks surrounding the economic outlook, including the possibility of "weaker-than-expected domestic and global demand and slow or insufficient implementation of structural reforms." Emerging market growth is now at its weakest since the third quarter of 2011, as global demand for manufactures and services further declined. Growth in emerging Asia (most robust source of push) appears to be trending lower or stabilizing. Indeed, most are still struggling to get out of the "middle-income trap" where economies risk stagnation at middle-income levels and struggle to scale higher to become rich. Growth in Latin America is also showing signs of fatigue, with the passing of commodities boom as slackening Asian demand hits economies from Bogota to Brasilia. When so many parts of the world are performing below expectations, it is difficult to locate an engine of global demand where so many things can still go wrong.

OECD and IMF Downgrade

The Organisation of Economic Co-operation and Development (OECD) had expressed disappointment that the global economy is moving too slowly, although at multiple speeds, in its recent semiannual Economic Outlook.[2] As a group, OECD revised its first quarter of 2013 GDP 0.4 percent higher than in the fourth quarter of 2012, when output was flat. Its activities would advance 1.2 percent in 2013, lower than 1.4 percent forecast six months ago and 1.4 percent in 2012. OECD, however, cuts its global forecast to 3.1 percent this year, against 3.2 percent in 2012, taking a more pessimistic view on China, repeating concerns by International Monetary Fund (IMF) following disappointing Chinese first quarter of 2013 GDP performance and a number of continued sluggish indications in April and May. The IMF had, in April 2013, expected the world to grow by 3.3 percent this year, little changed from the 3.2 percent expansion experienced in 2012 and 3.6 percent forecast for 2013 in October 2012. It observed that the global economy is experiencing a "three-speed recovery," with Europe lagging behind the United States and large emerging economies and acting as a continuing drag on growth. According to the IMF, "Europe has to do better." The IMF has since revised down projections of global growth for 2013 and a better outcome in 2014.[3] So what else is new? Both the IMF and OECD had repeatedly missed their forecasts: They overestimated the will of the United States and Europe to reform, and even ignored their own warnings on the dire need for emerging Asia to adopt a new model for more sustainable growth. This time, the IMF trimmed its own growth forecast for China, flagging concerns about the rapid rise in total social financing (TSF), the widest measure of credit, including bonds and informal lending, and about a decisive reform impetus to contain vulnerabilities and move to a more sustainable growth path that is "more balanced, inclusive, and green."

China

The IMF's lowered forecast shaved a quarter of 1 percentage point off its April 2013 projection of 8 percent for China to 7.75 percent, still higher than the government's target of 7.5 percent. In the first quarter of 2013, GDP slowed to 7.7 percent, below what most analysts had expected. Indicators for April and May had been lackluster: They showed exports, investments, and industrial output all decelerating. In the short-run, recent TSF expansion (up 51 percent so far this year) together with mild activity pickup in Japan, are expected to lift China's growth in the second half of 2013. But in the longer-term, the new leadership appears determined to rebalance the economy to bring about higher quality growth that will improve living standards and incomes, and seriously address fundamental problems like widening income inequality and environmental degradation. No doubt, rapid growth of TSF is a major source of concern, with accumulation of debt bringing on substantial risks, including asset price bubbles and potentially destabilizing defaults. Much of this is happening in shadow banking (i.e., lending outside the regulated system), which had expanded rapidly in recent years.

To me, this sharp rise and spread of TSF raise concerns about the quality of investment and its impact on repayment capacity, especially in the unregulated system. Its growth had become "too dependent on continued expansion of investment, much of it by the property sector and local government" (IMF). I agree with the IMF assessment: Reining in TSF growth is a "priority and will require further tightening of prudential oversight."[4]

This, if implemented well, will pose the dilemma of a further slowdown in activity as a result of slowing the pace of lending to avoid deepening financial problems. There will be ripple effects, harming commodity producers in Latin America and Africa, farmers in the United States, and machinery makers in Europe who count on China for exports. But China has little choice but to support the transition to a more sustainable growth path. Indeed, the IMF is right to warn that while China still has significant policy space and financial capacity to rebalance for stability even in the face of adverse shocks, the "margins of safety are narrowing and a decisive impetus to reforms is needed." The IMF was "assured by the leadership that policy focus will be on the financial sector and fiscal overhauls."

China grew at its slowest pace for 13 years in 2012. Latest May data points to growth remaining unconvincing, with momentum losing pace toward a slower second quarter of 2013. It would seem the new leadership could even tolerate growth slipping to 7 percent, provided the economy and employment remain stable.

The United States

GDP annual growth averaged less than 2 percent since the Great Recession, which is 4 percentage points (or US$600 billion) below the pace of recovery from prior deep recessions, as in 1981–1982. Today's unemployment at

7.6 percent is twice as high. The 2009–2012 stimulus averaged +6 percent of GDP (US$1.2–1.5 trillion) annually. Yet, it was not really effective.

Even so, the US economy has proved surprisingly resilient in the face of budget cuts and tax hikes. GDP rose by 2.4 percent in the first quarter of 2013, less than previously estimated, as slower inventory buildup and cutbacks in public spending overshadowed the biggest gain in consumer purchases since end-2010. The boost to household wealth from rising home values and stock prices is making Americans feel more comfortable. So the outlook is more favorable as the economy moves beyond the current soft patch. Consumer spending (70 percent of GDP) rose 3.4 percent in the first quarter of 2013 despite previous fiscal tightening and lagged effects of earlier tax increases. But it is not yet ready to assume its previous role of global consumer of last resort.

However, concern has arisen that any premature tightening by the Fed would not only raise interest rates but also carry the substantial risk of slowing, even ending, the delicate recovery that still carries unemployment of 7.6 percent, and cause inflation to fall. Economic conditions are still not good—certainly not good enough for unemployment to hit 5.5 percent, which the Fed considers optimal, until 2017. Forecasts expect growth in the next two quarters to be slower than 2 percent, since the economy has yet to feel the full squeeze of sequester cuts and the fiscal drag. So it is refreshing that Standard & Poor's (S&P) did give the United States a vote of confidence, citing economic resilience and monetary creditability as factors that drove the better outlook to "stable" from "negative," while maintaining its AA+ credit rating.

Europe

The eurozone has been in double-dip recession since late 2011. The downturn intensified into the fourth quarter of 2012. Recession had since deepened in the first quarter of 2013, as investment and exports plunged. GDP fell 1.1 percent from a year earlier; it is now revised downward by the IMF to shrink by 0.6 percent this year and rise by 1.1 percent in 2014. Recent business surveys suggest GDP would contract for a seventh straight quarter in the second quarter of 2013, extending the region's longest postwar recession.

Much of its fragility owes something to austerity. Inflation is expected to average 1.3 percent in 2014 (1.4 percent in May), well below ECB's target of 2 percent. The economy is grappling with a record slump, as unemployment, at 12.2 percent (18 percent in Portugal and 25 percent in Spain and Greece) in April, reached a record high of 19.4 million as austerity measures continued to damp domestic demand. The index of manufacturing remains in contraction but is deteriorating more gradually. Youth unemployment was 60 percent in Spain and Greece and +40 percent in Italy.

The situation in the eurozone remains challenging, with few signs of a possible stabilization. There is growing realization that stagnation and political turmoil in Italy and beyond are eroding Europe's way of life and its global relevance. Observers also worry that the eurozone could sink into prolonged stagnation of the kind that gripped Japan for two decades. So, the European Union (EU) badly needs to finish the reforms it had started.

However, bank credit remains tight. The IMF had urged the ECB to act more aggressively to stimulate lending to struggling enterprises in Spain, Italy, Portugal, and Greece. OECD alluded that "since the eurozone is doing worse, the ECB should do more." For the moment, there remains deep concern about prospects for the eurozone. Germany will grow only 0.3 percent this year, at half the IMF's previous forecast, and 1.5 percent in 2014. Although France is expected to escape recession in the second half of 2013 (GDP fell in the fourth quarter of 2012 and first quarter of 2013), activity will decline 0.2 percent in 2013, with growth accelerating to 0.8 percent in 2014. It has a jobless rate of 11 percent, double Germany's, the largest EU member.

Japan

GDP rose faster than expected at 4.1 percent in the first quarter of 2013. Stronger growth was helped by higher private capital spending. Consumers are becoming more upbeat. Equities have since surged, helping to maintain the needed momentum as the government moves to implement the "third arrow" of structural reform to support growth, to complement monetary and fiscal stimulus already in place. This aggressive program has sent the yen plunging around 20 percent since November. The Japanese economy appears to be in a firm recovery track. The IMF expects GDP to grow 1.6 percent in 2013 and 1.4 percent in 2014. Consumer confidence in May is at its highest level since 2007. Monetary policy is being kept steady to calm market volatility so that it won't pose a significant risk to recovery prospects. The economy appears to be in a sweet spot, for now.

What, Then, Are We to Do?

World growth fell from 5.1 percent in 2010 to 3.7 percent in 2011 and then to 3.2 percent last year. The structural crisis (2008–2009) is not over; recession is but one of its many effects. A lot more is still happening, following disruption of key markets, including in finance and labor. Adjustments can take 5 to 10 years. Five years after the onset of recession, we still have an output "gap" in the United States and Europe, reflecting too much wastage of human capital (high unemployment), underutilization of industrial capacity, and under-access to technologies. That's why mature economies grow so slowly. What's worrisome is their impact on the big emerging economies—Brazil, Russia, India, China, and South Africa (BRICS) and South Korea—which are also slowing down.

The challenge here is to make growth sustainable. You can't do so solely by driving consumption. You need to create employment that's productive and innovative: a challenge requiring painful reform and discipline to effectively implement. Already, big economies are stumbling trying to adjust. Europe doesn't do this well.

China has taken the first big step—accepting lower but quality growth. Let's set the perspective on the scale of China. Its US$8.5 trillion economy is half the size of the United States. China growing at 7 percent is like the United States growing at 3½ percent. China can create a Greece in 12½ weeks! Since 2010, China has created an India!

ASEAN economies are also struggling—much of its growth is fueled by consumption, not by trade and foreign direct investment. So, if I put all of these together, the world still has a way to go, struggling below trend at 3 percent growth a year. This scenario won't change much any time soon. Three catch-phrase challenges will dominate: human capital issues, operational excellence, and innovation. So, there is potential, but government constraints will act to hold growth back as mature economies recover at their own pace while emerging nations settle into a more sustainable pace.

Kuala Lumpur
June 14, 2013

Notes

1. First published on June 15, 2013, as "Breadth of Global Slowdown Disconcerting."
2. Organisation for Economic Co-operation and Development (OECD), *Economic Outlook* (Paris: OECD, June 2013).
3. International Monetary Fund (IMF), *World Economic Outlook: Hopes, Realities and Risks* (Washington, DC: IMF, April 2013).
4. David Lipton, the International Monetary Fund's first deputy managing director, speaking in Beijing on May 29, 2013, at the conclusion of the IMF's annual review of the Chinese economy.

CHAPTER 20

TW3 2013: Tension and Risks; a Peek at 2014[1]

It's that time of the year again—to look back over the past 12 months, take stock and review, and assess the outlook for next year, especially for emerging Asia (EA) and ASEAN. The year 2013 was not a good one—most quarterly reviews ended with a downgrade. In April last year, the IMF's forecast was for global GDP to grow by 4.1 percent in 2013; while GDP of advanced economies (AEs) was expected to expand at 2.0 percent and EA, 7.9 percent. ASEAN-5 (Indonesia, Malaysia, the Philippines, Thailand, and Vietnam) would raise gross domestic product (GDP) by 6.2 percent. By June 2013, the outlook further dimmed. In its October review, growth prospects were again downgraded (indeed, in 9 out of the last 10 updates) so that by this December, the consensus estimate by the major reviewers was for the world economy to grow by only 2.9 percent in 2013; AEs by less than 1 percent, and EA, 6.0 percent (with ASEAN-5 rising by only 5.1 percent).[2]

Much of the downward revision reflected continuing basic fiscal challenges and uncertainties in the United States and Europe, and the marked slackening of growth in the major emerging market economies (EMEs) and its spillover effects. Still, EA as a group managed to grow at six times the pace of AEs and against ASEAN-5, five times. This significant growth-rate gap reflects poorly on the recovery process in AEs.

Similarly, it was a bruising year for Asian bonds, stocks, and currencies, whose markets were long one of the world's hottest investment destinations. Foreign investors have since started to retreat. Bond prices are on course to fall, as interest rate expectations rise, while stocks have underperformed its peers in the rest of the world. Most Asian currencies (except China's renminbi or yuan) have tumbled—Indonesia's rupiah was down about 20 percent, and the Indian rupee, 11 percent so far this year. This big shift reflected the gradually slackening growth throughout most of Asia and worries that the United States may soon trim its quantitative easing (QE3)

119

efforts that have supported inflows of cheap funds into riskier markets. Cumulatively, outflows from bond funds focused on emerging Asia markets have totaled US$22 billion since May when talk of US tapering (slowing down of US Fed purchases of bonds) first began. Interest in Asian currency-denominated bonds has since declined—most bond indices have dropped significantly for the first time since 2000. For stocks, 2013 has also been lackluster. Benchmark for the region (MSCI Asia ex-Japan index) was up only 2.2 percent to date, against a rise of 27 percent for US S&P 500—even Stoxx Europe 600 index was up 11 percent to date. Gold price fell to a three-year low at US$1,187 on December 20.

Emerging Asia 2013

Like everyone else, Paris-based OECD (Organisation for Economic Co-operation and Development—the "rich boys" club) cut its December global growth forecast for 2013 as EMEs, including EA and Latin America, cooled off.[3] The world economy will most likely rise by 2.7 percent this year (against 2.9 percent by the International Monetary Fund (IMF) and Asian Development Bank [ADB]).[4] That's down from 5.4 percent in 2007, before the global recession hit. Sure, EMEs (including China) have cooled off; Europe still remains fundamentally in the doldrums; and the United States continues to face fiscal uncertainties.

In the midst of it all, the world's most powerful central bank (the US Fed) has been contemplating easing up on its extraordinary stimulative efforts, with potentially serious global ramifications. It finally decided to take its foot off the gas come January 2014. So, the IMF says global growth is in "low gear," with continuing high rates of unemployment especially among its youth. All these translate to lower living standards in the face of little inflation.

Collectively, growth among EMEs has fallen 3 percentage points since 2010 to only 4.5 percent this year, with Brazil, China, and India accounting for two-thirds of the fall. Growth in EA was downgraded 2 percentage points this year alone, to 6 percent in 2013. As I see it, global growth is still basically weak, but its underlying dynamics are changing, with much downside risk.

For EA, the risks that are now most worrisome include: (1) US Fed's plans to taper and eventually exit its QE3 stimulus program; (2) China's attempt to meet irreconcilable targets of stable growth and structural reform; and (3) the China–Japan political stand-off. The mere talk of QE3 tapering had already sparked off increases in, and fueled expectations of, further higher interest rates, as well as slowing down of capital inflows to EMEs, especially EA.

As for China, there is growing expectation that its economy will expand more slowly over the medium term, with widespread implications for commodity exporters and income growth among the EMEs. Finally, the territorial dispute between Japan and China is very real, with deep-rooted social, cultural, and psychological underpinnings.

Outlook for 2014

Most expect a better 2014. From the United States to Europe to Japan, monetary authorities have been pumping cheap funds into their economies and keeping loan rates at near zero. Once-red-hot China has since revived, with the help of public funds invested in projects through easily available funds from state-owned banks. The world economy now appears to be improving, with growth forecast at 3.5 percent in 2014. Prospects in the United States and Japan look more upbeat, with Europe appearing to be recovering but at a tepid pace from depressed levels—my impression is for the euro-area to face the prospect of a lost decade. In Japan, Abenomics remains very much a work in progress.

While the United States is bouncing back, it is still blighted by polarized politics that could yet extract a heavy economic toll. Tiger (Tracking Indexes for the Global Economic Recovery) has shown improvement from its recent lows in mid-2012, pointing out that the global economy is "being borne along by surging business and consumer confidence in advanced economies, and stabilization in the growth of emerging markets."[5]

Consequently, I see 2014 as a year of broader economic recovery, but with more market volatility as global monetary conditions are tightened. AEs are forecast to grow somewhat stronger at just below 2 percent despite softening in the euro-area. Still, its pace is less than a third that of EA. China and others in EA are coming off cyclical peaks and are now projected to grow at 6.2 percent as a whole, below the elevated levels seen in recent years. Despite uncertainties in the global environment, indicators in more dynamic East Asia are positive, boosting its growth rate in 2014 to 6.7 percent (same as in 2013), driven mainly by continuing strong performance in China and South Korea. ASEAN-5's growth performance is likely to be maintained.

While EMEs have regained some of the momentum they lost earlier this year, particularly China, many of them remain vulnerable to a loss of private sector confidence or capital flight. To be fair, the volatility of capital flows engendered by the Fed's vacillations on its tapering measures has added to the difficult external environment these nations continue to face. In addition, US political dysfunction leading to "mistakes" in fiscal policy can derail the fragile global upswing, as the recovery is still tenuous.

The United States

A gradual acceleration of economic activity is in prospect for 2014, with GDP growth expected at 2.6 percent (after a strong 4.1 percent in the third quarter of 2013, which brought unemployment down to 7 percent in November), with little inflation to speak of. Thank goodness the Fed's tapering and support in Congress for a budget deal are on the way. Uncertainty over public policy that has overshadowed business and consumer sentiment since 2008 is now much reduced. But, Washington politics will still remain uncertain. The Fed just announced plans to cut its monthly purchases of securities from US$85 billion in December to zero by late 2014 in a series of small steps, starting with a US$10 billion cut in January 2014. The tapering pace is notably slow. December marks the fifth anniversary of the Fed's QE experiment in near-zero interest rates and other extraordinary monetary adventures. There are risks, of course. Cheap cash that continues to be pumped into the global financial system will flow into stocks, bonds, and commodities. Already, Wall Street has become the world's most expensive stock market. Their prices can escalate and become unsustainable, raising risks of a crash. Moreover, prolonged easy money can cause inflation over the long run. Overall, even at reduced levels, QE3 bond purchases will contribute to stimulate growth and help offset spending cuts.

The Fed's message is clear: (1) tapering does not change the outlook for interest rates—short rates will remain firmly anchored at near zero, and (2) interest rates will start to rise only after the economy approaches full employment, which will be beyond 2015. These simply mean monetary conditions will remain stimulative for a while longer. Medium-term prospects thus look positive even though fiscal policy remains at risk. Based on latest indications, I expect a less destructive Washington political environment in 2014, with fiscal headwinds subsiding. After all, the United States can't rely forever on monetary policy to save the day.

Europe

Frankly, economic conditions in the 17-nation eurozone are not good. After enduring two recessions since 2009, GDP rose 0.1 percent in the third quarter of 2013 after rising 0.3 percent in the second quarter of 2013. From a year earlier, the economy contracted 0.4 percent. GDP in the fourth quarter of 2013 is expected at 0.2 percent so that the euro-area will contract 0.4 percent in 2013. Indications are that it will grow tentatively at 0.3 percent in the first quarter of 2014 and by 1 percent for 2014 as a whole. This is optimistic, since Europe still lacks a reliable engine of growth. Indeed, there is even concern about the core—France, Netherlands, and Germany. French GDP fell 0.1 percent in the third quarter of 2013; in Germany, GDP rose only

0.3 percent in the third quarter of 2013 (against 0.7 percent in the second quarter of 2013), while the Dutch economy rose a mere 0.1 percent. The eurozone's GDP, reflecting its southern peripheral, is still 3 percent below prefinancial crisis level now in its fifth year. Unemployment remained near record high of 12.1 percent in October, with a scant 0.7 percent inflation.

The outlook for euro-area remains fragile; it is still being dragged down by fiscal fatigue because of aggressive fiscal tightening, especially in the South that is front-loaded, and tight credit conditions reflect heightened credit risks and poor bank balance sheets. Of immediate concern is the risk of deflation—a prolonged fall in wages, prices, and value of assets (such as stocks and homes). The recent cut by the European Central Bank of its benchmark refinancing rate to a record low of 0.25 percent was meant to reduce any risk of the economy falling into deflation. Unfortunately, without cataclysmic policy change, the eurozone will muddle through in the foreseeable future. However, of late, I sense there has been a change in mood with the hope that Europe has turned the corner. Unfortunately, this still has not been translated into a self-fulfilling increase in spending.

Japan

Recovery in Japan has been spurred by Abenomics (Chapter 60: "Abenomics: Japan Comes Alive Again," provides interesting details). GDP rose 1.1 percent in the third quarter of 2013 after a robust, broad-based growth of 3.3 percent in the first half of 2013. The economy is expected to expand by 3.4 percent in the fourth quarter of 2013 and then by 4.4 percent in the first quarter of 2014 before contracting by 4 percent in the second quarter of 2014 with the onset of higher value-added tax (VAT) in April 2014 and again in 2015. But sustainability of the current cyclical upswing will depend on: (1) success at fiscal consolidation to reform Japan's poor fiscal condition with the VAT hike, and (2) implementing a credible package of structural reform measures to transform the economy with the aim of making it more competitive. A US$67 billion stimulus program was recently approved to help boost GDP by 1 percent and create 250,000 jobs. For 2014 as a whole, GDP is forecast to rise by 1.6 percent (1.7 percent in 2013), with 2 percent inflation (1.1 percent in November 2013).

China

EA has grown significantly, becoming a force to be reckoned with globally. The improving global environment is good for Asia (which accounts for some 40 percent of global GDP) in the face of an expanding and stable China. I believe Beijing's main policy objectives for 2014 are to promote stable output growth while pushing key structural reforms—two apparently mutually exclusive objectives. In practice, Beijing can have its cake and eat it, too, over the next 10 years, only if it is prepared to sacrifice faster growth for broad-based reforms—that is, lower its sights on high growth while being relentless in its pursuit of reforms. The IMF forecasts China to grow by 7.3 percent in 2014 (7.7 percent in 2013), below those by OECD (8.2 percent), World Bank (7.7 percent), and the ADB (7.5 percent). Realistically, I expect China to be prepared to go as low as 7 percent while shooting for 7.5 percent, because it has to come to terms with its problems of high debt and excess capacity as it switches to the new economic model driven by consumer demand.

The recent Third Plenum reforms set China's economic direction for the next 10 years (Chapter 139: "China: The Third Plenum Reforms Are Well Received but the New Deal Flashes Danger Signals" contains details). I believe prospects for serious reform (briefly, letting the market play a decisive role in allocating resources, granting farmers' property rights, introducing greater competition, forging urban-rural integration, elevating private sector's role and expanding opportunities for small and medium-sized enterprises, and setting up a sustainable social welfare system) are now better than at any time since 1990s, for four reasons: (1) the leadership is committed to the new economic model based on consumption, (2) its leadership is already well-positioned to forge change, (3) China can't afford to delay reforms, and (4) there is a need to meet high expectations for a sustainable increase in income and a better way of life. With reform, China will emerge the better for it.

India

India's outlook is more uncertain; its prospects are dependent on the outcome of the May 2014 elections. Much better global economic conditions and improved sentiment for exports are expected to support a gradual recovery in the face of a steadfast fight against inflation (11.24 percent in November 2013). GDP growth in 2014 is expected at between 5.1 percent (IMF) and 5.7 percent (ADB), against 4.7 percent in 2013 and a potential growth rate of 6 percent. The economy appears to have bottomed out, with many signs of "green shoots" springing up in industry.

ASEAN-5

Growth in Southeast Asia moderated in 2013, reflecting political tensions in Thailand, the devastation wrought by Typhoon Haiyan on the Philippines, and the impact of widening current account deficit in Indonesia. Despite these setbacks, the outlook is for ASEAN-5 to pick up and steadily expand at 5.5 percent in 2014, against 5.1 percent in 2013.[6] Inflation would likely hold steady at 4.4 percent next year (4.8 percent in 2013).

What, Then, Are We to Do?

Looks like the world's three largest economies—the United States, China, and Japan—are all in decent shape to grow in 2014. How fast they will expand and how long it can last, nobody really knows. The past offers a clue. In the 1980s, world growth averaged 3.4 percent; in the 1990s, 3.2 percent—so it's not unreasonable to use 3.3 percent as the plausible trend. Growth in 2001–2010 was well above this at 3.7 percent, reflecting mainly the surge in commodity prices and abundant cheap money inflows or, in short, a favorable external environment. In their book, *Who Needs to Open the Capital Account*, authors Olivier Jeanne, Arvind Subramanian, and John Williamson concluded that over the medium-term (averaging over booms and slumps) "growth has little association with capital flows," except for foreign direct investment.[7] Favorable external environment does fuel growth in the short run, but its long-term effects are questionable. I believe the day of reckoning always comes. According to Jeanne et al.: "Those that borrow most suffer the biggest growth collapses from 'sudden stops' of capital." This is true in recent history, and it's true in the turmoil affecting EMEs today—those benefiting from the largest hot-money inflows (Brazil, India, Indonesia, Turkey, and South Africa) experienced the greatest currency declines and market volatility. The impact of US tapering withdrawal, while significant in the short run, should not "keep policy makers awake at night." Lament over fleeing hot money and falling commodity prices is just over inconsequential "noise." There is life after QE3!

Kuala Lumpur
December 24, 2013

Notes

1. First published on December 28, 2013, as "A Peek at 2014—There Is Life after QE3."
2. International Monetary Fund (IMF), *World Economic Outlook: Transitions and Tensions* (Washington, DC: IMF, October, 2013).
3. Organisation for Economic Co-operation and Development (OECD), *Economic Outlook* (Paris: OECD, December, 2013).

4. Asian Development Bank (ADB), *Asian Development Outlook Update* (Manila: ADB, December 2013).
5. Chris Giles, "Global Economy 'Back on Track,'" *Financial Times* (October 7, 2013). Quoting Professor Eswar Prasad of the Brookings Institute, Giles writes: "The Tiger index combines measures of real economic activity, financial variables and indicators of confidence, according to the degree to which they are all moving up or down at the same time."
6. ASEAN-5 refers to ASEAN's five largest nations: Indonesia, Malaysia, the Philippines, Thailand, and Vietnam.
7. Olivier Jeanne, Arvind Subramanian, and John Williamson, Capsule Review: *Who Needs to Open the Capital Account? Foreign Affairs* (September/October 2012).

Spring 2014 Stock Take: Complex Risks Ahead[1]

World economic activity picked up in the second half of 2013 and continued to expand into the first quarter of 2014; it can be expected to improve further in 2014–2015. This assessment is contained in the International Monetary Fund's (IMF) April 2014 *World Economic Outlook* update, which rolled back marginally from its January 2014 forecast when it was a bit more optimistic before the Ukraine crisis.[2] This has exacerbated Russia's sharp economic downturn (following sanctions by the United States and Europe), while the IMF worries about contagion beyond Europe. Even so, the IMF still thinks the global recovery has become not only stronger but also broader. Indeed, the "various brakes that hampered growth are being slowly loosened. Fiscal consolidation is slowing and investors are less worried about debt sustainability." But the IMF also points to the sharp downturn in some leading emerging market economies (EMEs), including Argentina, Brazil, South Africa, and Turkey, which acted as a drag on global output growth. Their predicament was rooted in domestic policy shortcomings, tighter financial conditions, and a pullback in investment.

The Assessment

The IMF had projected global growth to strengthen to 3.6 percent in 2014 and then to nearly 4 percent in 2015 (from 3.1 percent in 2012–2013), with much of the impetus coming from advanced economies (led by the United States), where growth is expected to improve by nearly 1 percentage point to 2.25 percent in 2014–2015. But this growth will be uneven. Even so, global trade will rebound so much that its growth, expected at 4.3 percent in 2014 and 5.3 percent in 2015 (against only 2.8 percent in 2012 and 3 percent in 2013), will exceed world growth of real activity for the first time since 2012—which is as it should be. Key drivers included some relaxation of fiscal tightening in the face of still highly easy monetary conditions. Economic growth is expected to be strongest in the United States at 2.2 percent this year (1.3 percent in 2013). In the stressed euro-area, growth is projected to remain weak but certainly fragile with low inflation as domestic demand is held back, reflecting high debt and tepid credit demand. Japan is in a similar situation with Abenomic stimulus facing challenges, including deflation, which is worrisome. Some growth moderation is in prospect.

Growth in EMEs will continue to pick up, but only modestly—the result of the confluence of two opposing forces: rising export growth (lifted by stronger activity in advanced economies [AEs] and by currency deprecia-tion) in the face of continuing weakness in investment and tightening finan-cial conditions compared with the outlook in October 2013. This weakening cyclical momentum will continue. Nevertheless, EMEs are expected to con-tribute more than two-thirds of global expansion—with projected growth rising from 4.7 percent in 2013 to nearly 5 percent in 2014 and 5.3 percent in 2015. The April 2014 World Bank's East Asia and Pacific (EAP) Economic Update expects the recovery of AEs' demand to help bolster growth in export-dependent Asia—developing EAP economies are now expected to grow by 7.1 percent in 2014, about the same as in 2013 but much slower than the average 8 percent from 2009–2013.[3] ASEAN-4 (Indonesia, Malaysia, Philippines, and Thailand) will slide back to expand at 5.3 percent in 2014 (5.8 percent in 2013), while the Mekong-4 (Cambodia, Laos, Myanmar, and Vietnam) will maintain steady growth at 7.2 percent this year (7.4 percent in 2013). Overall, ASEAN-10 as a whole will still expand at a pace 2 percentage points higher than world growth.

I expect EAP economies to continue to serve as the world's main growth engine, even as they adjust to tightening global financial conditions. These economies demonstrated how "flexible currencies will help East Asia deal with external shocks, including potential capital flow reversals. In addition, most countries have adequate reserves to cover temporary trade and exter-nal shocks" (World Bank). Despite the major sell-off in emerging markets earlier this year, EAP economies withstood the resulting capital outflows following US Fed's scaling back of quantitative easing. It would appear "the tailwinds from improving trade will offset the headwinds from the tighten-ing of global financial markets" (World Bank). Nevertheless, EAP economies continue to remain vulnerable, including commodity price volatility, geopo-litical tensions in Eastern Europe, and ongoing country elections in the face of slowdown in foreign investment inflows. China, too, can be expected to pull its weight despite slowdown in the first quarter of 2014 (gross domestic product [GDP], rising only 7.4 percent).

Both the IMF and World Bank expect growth will moderate to "soft-land" at 7.3 to 7.6 percent in 2014–2015. This assumes the Chinese authorities will gradually (1) rein in rapid credit growth, (2) embark on ongoing structural reforms to deliver more inclusive growth, (3) implement the longer-term reform blueprint, and (4) promote more sustainable economic expansion. Prospect of growth falling below 7.5 percent target is real and likely to be met with temporary easy policies, for which it has much room to maneuver, while ensuring gradual transition to a more balanced growth path. For India, the IMF expects GDP to strengthen to 5.4 percent in 2014 and 6.4 percent in 2015, based on concerted efforts to revive investment and push exports given the recent rupee depreciation. Uncertainty remains as general elections continue.

The Risks

Since its October 2013 review, the IMF reports that previous overall downside risks have diminished a bit, except for the following: (1) emerging market risks have taken a turn for the worse—pivoted around concerns about fundamentals among its weaker members; poorer investor sentiment relative to improved returns in advanced markets; higher risks of capital flow reversals and disorderly currency depreciation; and tightening financial conditions; (2) higher risks to activity from below-target inflation reflecting tepid demand; and (3) resurfacing of geopolitical risks, including growing uncertainty from deteriorating Ukraine and territorial disputes between China and Japan, and China and ASEAN. Overall, the IMF concludes: "The balance of risks, while improved, remains on the downside." This is expected to dampen prospects for investment and weigh in on growth over the next 18 months in the face of a global recovery that is still fragile. Old risks will persist. For the EMEs, changing external environment will undoubtedly give rise to more financial volatility and pose continuing challenges as US monetary policy returns to normalcy (raising the cost of capital) and as renewed bouts of higher risk aversion befall investors.

The situation in Russia and Ukraine is particularly serious. Persisting political impasse could spark new flights to safety in global markets. Intensifying sanctions and countersanctions are bound to disrupt trade and finance, including markets for oil and gas, food, and basic metals. Already, the IMF has slashed Russia growth for 2014 to 1.3 percent (down from 2 percent in January 2014 and 3 percent in October 2013). Outlook doesn't look good for the entire Europe, which is already preoccupied with repairing bank balance sheets. EMEs also face formidable risks. Although they are diverse as a group, they nevertheless share some common priorities, each with its own peculiar attendant risks: (1) exchange rates have to continue to remain flexible to facilitate adjustment and avoid financial disruption—the trade-off being more inflation and a loss in reserves; (2) monetary policy may prematurely tighten at the expense of growth; (3) likewise, fiscal policy also has to rein in budget deficits, raising concerns over the size of public debt and its servicing; and (4) pressure on structural reforms, which can't be put off to rebalance in order to remain competitive. Still, further slowdown remains a risk, because continuing uncertainties will cause capital flows to slow or reverse. So, EMEs stand ready to face sporadic market turmoil and reduce externally induced vulnerabilities.

What, Then, Are We to Do?

The US National Bureau of Economic Research—the arbiter of business cycles, recently concluded that the US economy started to expand again in June 2009, just over 58 months ago. Although this current stretch of growth is the longest post–World War II, its 6.7 percent jobless rate is the highest on record at this stage in the modern era. GDP annual growth averaged 1.8 percent, one-half the pace of the previous three expansions. This relative stagnation explains why the recovery could chug along without overheating. The US Fed now believes that this growth run will last through 2016. Indeed, several mysteries have arisen about the recovery, which generated not just slow growth and low productivity but low inflation and a faster fall in unemployment than expected. It's not surprising that the IMF has since endorsed this secular stagnation hypothesis as possibly the new normal, noting that the real interest rate necessary to revive demand has declined significantly and is likely to remain depressed. Indeed, inflation has been below target not just in the United States but in the major AEs as well, and is likely to fall further this year. Uncertainty about direction of the benchmark short-term rate (already near zero since 2008) is not helpful. Investors wonder if the world still needs more stimuli to counter the many varied risks ranging from deflation to geopolitical tension. Indeed, there is no strong basis to assume that further reduction in interest rates will resolve the situation. Yet without robust growth expansion, growth in EMEs is likely to slacken in the face of inadequate demand despite continuing easy money. What's really needed is a creative new strategy, framed to resist secular stagnation rather than just rely on more of the same—easy money.

Kuala Lumpur
April 25, 2014

Notes

1. First published on May 3, 2014, as "Spring '14 Stock Take: Risks Ahead for World Economy."
2. International Monetary Fund (IMF), *World Economic Outlook: Recovery Strengthens, Remains Uneven* (Washington, DC: IMF, April 2014).
3. World Bank, *East Asia and Pacific Economic Update: Preserving Stability and Promoting Growth* (Washington, DC: World Bank, April 2014).

Trouble with the Global Economy

PART II

Trouble with the
Global Economy

CHAPTER 22

The Paradox of Thrift[1]

The year 2008 was a disaster for savers. We are taught from a young age that we should always save; that saving is a discipline in prudence. Indeed, it's a virtue. Stock markets the world over have since plummeted, with the value of investments having fallen by about 50 percent, estimated to be now US$30 trillion below its peak. The prices of bonds and commercial property have also plunged. Those who diversified to commodities, hedge funds, and private equity fared no better. Even those who only saved with banks had to worry about the safety of these institutions, including the "branded" banks (so much so that governments in many countries have had to step in to guarantee bank deposits). Worse, the value of most people's main item of wealth—their home—has fallen sharply. This is my eighth recession—I have not seen anything quite like this.

Savings

The savers' pain can be ascertained from pooled portfolio investments: American mutual funds were reported to have lost US$2.4 trillion in the first 10 months of 2008. The value of US pension funds dropped by US$2 trillion during the 18 months prior to October 2008. This was before Black October 2008, when the New York Dow Jones Industrial Index virtually collapsed. From its high in October 2007, the Dow took only 503 days to fall 50 percent, a full 320 days faster than the Nikkei took to fall 50 percent after the Japanese bubble burst. The Bank of England estimated that close to US$3 trillion was lost in credit-related instruments that dragged down the financial system in the first place. All these losses are just a portion of what was lost worldwide. Of course, a good deal of these losses fell on many who were able to cope, especially the wealthy. But many others were not so lucky—those elderly and retired, those on pension plans, those fixed-income savers, those who are about to retire, and those who have mortgages that are now higher than the diminished value of their homes. Latest reports indicated that house prices in the United States fell 18.5 percent in 2008, the biggest fall in 21 years. Americans were told that saving pays in the long run; most also borrowed on the premise that their house value can only go up. They now wonder why they even bothered. Although not as bad, the overall situation in Asia (including Malaysia) runs along similar lines. Furthermore, interest rates have fallen so very sharply that interest income (which for many is also taxed) can no longer support savers in deposits and bonds.

Aggregate Demand

According to Lord Keynes, the root cause of downturns, especially recessions, is insufficient aggregate demand.[2] The rationale is clear. When total demand for goods and services falls, business sales decline. In turn, lower sales lead to cutbacks in production and, eventually, workers are laid off. Falling profits and rising unemployment further depress demand, causing a feedback loop very much like what we are seeing now, certainly in the United States and Europe.

The situation will only reverse when definite action is taken to raise total demand. Very much like Newton's law at work: Objects in a state of motion will remain in motion unless an external force is applied to stop it. According to Nobel Laureate Friedrich Hayek, a contemporary of Lord Keynes, Keynes was guided by one central idea—that is, that general employment is always positively correlated with the aggregate demand for consumer goods. He argued that government should intervene to maintain aggregate demand and full employment, the objective being to smooth out the business cycle. In recessions, he asserted that governments should borrow and spend. Output of goods and services in any economy comes from four sources: consumption, investment, government purchases, and exports/imports. Any rise in demand can only come from any of these sources (or some combination thereof). In a downturn, strong forces are at work to keep such spending down.

Since the US recession started in December 2007, these forces have moved (and spread) so very rapidly that the world as a whole is now in recession; indeed, it is the force of global recession that now drives down economic activity around the world. We know that consumers' confidence in the United States, Europe, and Japan, as well as in Russia and Brazil, is now at its record lows. For the consumer (the driving force, together with business, behind the Bush "bubble" expansion of 2001–2008), uncertainty looms large in the face of significant loss of wealth, and soon, even the flow of income as unemployment rises. When it comes to discretionary spending, whether buying a new house, car, or high-definition TV, a wait-and-see attitude has set in. Consumers like to spend smarter. From the perspective of the economy as a whole, a recession or downturn is not the best time to save more.

Thrift

Keynes spoke of a paradox of thrift. When households and businesses save more, they are consuming less, so that aggregate demand falls, which eventually leads to lower national income. This, in turn, works to deepen the downturn in the short-term. So, saving more now—contrary to a recent Citibank survey's report that Malaysians are not saving enough—is not a good idea. Malaysians are already among the world's high savers.[3] In 2007, gross national savings accounted for 39 percent of gross national product (GNP) and expected at 38 percent or thereabouts in 2008. Even in a recession year (1998) when gross domestic product (GDP) contracted (–7.5 percent), Malaysians saved even more at 42 percent of GNP. In contrast, American savings turned negative for one quarter in 2005 and have since been estimated at about 1 percent of disposal income in 2008. The British and Japanese saved about 2.5 percent, and squirrel-like Germany, 11 percent. Most economists (including myself) would regard saving more now as undesirable. In the context of a global recession, governments would rather people consume more and not save more. This is easier said than done. That is unlikely to happen without a hard jolt when most households are uncertain about the future outlook (regarding jobs). The tendency (especially in Asia, and now, even in the United States) is to save, and save more if they can, even though their recent experience at holding onto their wealth is far from encouraging. Keynes is frequently reported to have remarked: Whenever you save five shillings, you put a man out of work for the day (1936). Hence, governments are keen to stimulate and do their darnedest to get consumers and businesses to sustain their spending power.

Japan and Germany

It is said that recession could well be the "penance for past profligacy." Yet high saving and low private debt have not protected Germany and Japan from recession. Indeed, prudence has not spared them. Why? Both had avoided credit excesses, consumer overspending, house-price bubbles, and balance of payments deficits. The trouble is that they had thrived (and accumulated surpluses) on the backs of the persistent spending of others, especially the United States and the rest of Europe. When these nations started to cut back because of recession, Japan and Germany suffered badly as a consequence. Japan's exports fell by 45.7 percent this January, the sharpest fall in more than 40 years. It highlighted the severe impact of the global recession on demand for Japanese products. Germany, Europe's largest economy, posted a sharp GDP contraction in late 2008 as crucial exports collapsed. The lesson: Both of these persistent surplus nations had become too reliant on exports and investments to drive their prosperity. When foreign orders contracted sharply, they went into a tailspin.

Technically, both Japan and Germany should still have immense capacity to drive domestic demand. Unfortunately, their instinct for saving hardens in a recession. Japan's "lost decade" of the 1990s offers valuable lessons in managing the risk of deflation. Indeed, Japan's experience provides an insight into how thrift can take hold of consumption with disastrous impact. As its economy has weakened, consumers are not ready to spend more as they see their wealth shrink and begin to worry more and more about jobs. Firms can also become big savers in uncertain times. For Japan, inflows of capital strengthened the yen, squeezed profits on exports, and made businesses more and more reluctant to invest. Between 2001 and 2007, per-capita consumer spending was reported to have risen by a mere 0.2 percent. With recession spreading globally, Japan's economy is now on a free fall as domestic consumption can no longer be relied on to pick up the slack. Part of this reflects widespread distrust of the Japanese pension and banking systems. Its aging population is not helping consumption, either. Fears of a second lost decade now permeate Japanese society.

What, Then, Are We to Do?

Global recovery requires a fundamental shift in attitudes worldwide in order to facilitate multilateral adjustment: "Shopaholic" deficit nations (notably the United States) will need to save a bit more, while surplus nations (especially Japan, although Germany and China appear to be starting to spend more) need definitive and massive efforts at stimulating aggregate demand in a very effective way. Most important, Japan, Germany, and China need to change their mind-sets that demand has to come from somewhere else (traditionally, the United States), when their own domestic economies should be the locomotive. This would require changing the basic parameters of each country's comfort zone.

Manila
Kuala Lumpur
February 26, 2009

Notes

1. First published on February 28, 2009.
2. John Maynard Keynes, *General Theory of Employment, Interest and Money* (New York: Harcourt Brace and Company, 1936).
3. Citibank's Financial Quotient (Fin-Q) 2008 survey reported that only 2 in 5 (39%) Malaysians actually save, and less than 1 in 3 (28%) make and stick to a monthly budget.

CHAPTER 23

Deflation Is Not an Option[1]

Hello, from Xiamen University. Like most large Chinese cities, Xiamen is crowded, and summer is not its best month. This week, the city hosts the Asia Financial Management Association international conference. Away from the maddening crowd, the university campus offers respite to reflect on the frightening prospect of deflation, which can readily evolve from the impact of deep global recession and lower commodity prices. I am often asked: What's so wrong about deflation? Falling prices (as opposed to inflation) should be positive, since it raises the purchasing power of the ringgit. That's clearly a simplistic and very naive micro-view.

World Economy

Some perspective is useful. The current US recession is past 17 months old (already the longest since World War II). It is expected to be still there in the next six months, the Fed chairman's "green shoots" notwithstanding.[2] After all, gross domestic product (GDP) in the United States had contracted in excess of 6 percent per annum in each of the past two quarters, the worst six-month performance in 50 years. To be sure, as of now, although the outlook in the United States and China seems to be better, prospects in most of the eurozone (including the United Kingdom and Germany) and in Japan have not brightened much.

The International Monetary Fund's (IMF) update this week predicted a "long and severe recession" for Asia's wealthier but export-oriented economies.[3] Prospects for an imminent rebound are weak. Realistically, latest data show a mixed picture: In the United States, conditions begin to look up on the back of tentative signs of firmer household spending, the beginning of some signs of stabilization in the housing market, and in what appears to be a sharp inventory correction. Optimists point to the recent surge in stock markets around the world as a clear signal, since this is regarded by many as a leading indicator of things to come. This is a myth. After all, these markets did not see the meltdown coming last year.

Nobel Laureate Paul Samuelson is reported to have said it best: The stock markets predicted at least 12 of the last 2 recoveries, and 9 of the last 5 recessions. Even the US Fed admitted this week that activity is likely to remain weak for a time. But there are "headwinds"—US private investment remains weak and conditions in commercial real estate are poor; unemployment could reach 9 percent very soon and will rise further before it gets better; the banking system still needs fixing and bank loans remain tight (the IMF's recent estimates put losses in the financial sector at US$4.1 trillion); US private sector debt remains high (112 percent of GDP in 1976, 295 percent in 2008), while the financial debt picture is no better (rose from 16 percent to 121 percent over the same period); and private savings (up to 4.2 percent currently) can rise further as households begin to restore lost wealth (to match net worth at mid-2007, they have to save or make capital gains of US$13 trillion; matching the mid-2005 net worth will still require US$6.6 trillion).

"Green Shoots": Just out of Freefall

The brutal truth is: "Less-worse" is not recovery. The world is not out of the woods yet; there are no clear signs of stabilization. Sure, as Fed Chairman Ben Bernanke testified this week, the economic outlook has "improved moderately as the US recession appears to be losing steam," in the face of some positive "tentative signs."[4] But he also warned that even when the United States recovers, growth will remain below its long-run potential for some time.

In my view, the optimistic consensus forecast of positive growth by the third quarter of 2009, +2 percent in the fourth quarter of 2009, and about 2 percent in year 2010 is not realistic. The financial system is far from healthy; private deleveraging has about just begun; and the rebalancing of global demand has barely started. Even the Fed chairman conceded that "financial markets are still fragile and there will not be sustainable recovery without stabilization of the financial system and credit markets; and much more needs to be done to make further progress on this front."[5] Frankly, the reality is this: No one really knows what the year-end is going to bring. There is just too much uncertainty.

I think Columbia's Professor Nouriel Roubini's outlook makes good practical sense: –2 percent by the fourth quarter of 2009 and +0.5 percent in 2010; that is, "Even if we are technically out of a recession, we are going to feel like we are in a recession."[6] The IMF's recent update reflects similar views. What, then, has changed in the last few months? Two things: The risk of an L-shaped near-depression is reduced; and for the first time, we now begin to see positive risks in the global economic outlook as well as many negative risks (including something new: a possible H1N1 flu pandemic). Indeed, the whole situation remains rather confusing.

Worst-Case Scenario: Deflation?

But make no mistake. The risk of deflation is still there, with the odds falling, I think, to 15 to 20 percent after the aggressive US and Chinese stimuli programs and the coordinated actions with many others. After all, even the US Fed chairman admitted this week that "we expect the recovery will only gradually gain momentum and that economic slack will diminish slowly."[7] The Fed is also focused "like a laser beam on an exit strategy, to keep inflation low."[8] For 2009 as a whole, the consensus is for consumer prices to fall in the United States and Japan (close to zero now in both), while inflation in the eurozone will be flat. For the Organisation for Economic Co-operation and Development (OECD), consumer prices rose 0.9 percent for year ended March 2009—the lowest in 38 years. Reflecting the global recession, most countries in East Asia expect inflation to fall to historic low levels (including in China, South Korea, Taiwan, Thailand, Singapore, and Malaysia); even high-inflation nations like Indonesia and the Philippines will experience significant price declines. This is not surprising, given the collapse of industrial production, sharp fall in commodity prices, rising unemployment, and low utilization of existing capacity.

In the United States, the eurozone, and Japan, there are real concerns of deflation with potentially serious consequences for especially economies with over-indebted borrowers. The risks include (1) raising already large excess capacity (stimuli on infrastructure in particular will add further to this excess); (2) rising unemployment and huge wealth losses that can ironically work to raise savings; (3) falling demand and profits, rising risk aversion, and tight credit in the face of mounting fiscal deficits and soaring debt, with dire impact on incomes and consumption; and (4) flight from riskier borrowers, which can result in a vicious downward spiral of weakening foreign direct investment flows, falling output, and deteriorating asset quality.

This global recession is unlike any the world has ever seen. It creates uncertainty at every turn. Indeed, its exceptional and unpredictable dynamics raise doubts about the outcome of recovery when it does come. What is disturbing is the dynamics of the price discovery process, given uncertainties surrounding the timing of return to normalcy (i.e., sustainable fiscal clarity, viable market interest rates, and solvent financial system and credit market). For Japan, its recent experience in achieving such normalcy is scary. Indeed, the prospect of another "lost decade" is frightening. Whatever eventually happens in the United States, on whose final demand the world has come to depend, is critical. In the worst-case scenario, the real risks hinge on a shallow and hesitant economic turnaround in the face of insufficient progress at (1) deleveraging, (2) rebalancing global demand, and (3) inducing private-led revival, at a time when the financial system and credit market remain far from healthy. Deflation can take off in such an environment to the detriment of a solid recovery. In such an environment, the recent stock market "surge" can well become a "dead-cat bounce," heading south once again before too long.

Deflation Woes

Most of us, especially those who were old enough in the mid-1970s, know what inflation is and how destructive it can be. Some may even have painful memories. Deflation is something new in Asia; it only happened in Japan. For a decade after the stock market and real estate bust in 1990, Japan bumped along at just 0.5 percent growth a year, in the face of a deflation (including in wages) that so very slowly brought down unemployment that the period was dubbed "the lost decade." For the younger generation, both phenomena are abstracts.

Persistent falling prices and the expectation that they will continue to fall reflect a broken economy. In today's context, it can be serious enough to destabilize the recession and derail any prospect of early recovery in a number of critical ways.

First, deflation raises the real rate of interest, that is, the nominal rate adjusted for inflation. In practice, with inflation, the real rate is less than the nominal rate; with deflation, the real rate is higher than the nominal rate. In the United States, since short-term rates are already close to zero, there is no room to bring nominal rates down further to offset the higher real rate. So deflation simply raises the real yield on cash, thus encouraging more saving (a virtue, surely), which is precisely what you don't need in recessionary times. Hence, the **paradox of thrift** (Keynes).[9] Moreover, higher real rates discourage credit-based purchases by consumers and businesses. This weakens demand, leading to further falls in prices, which exacerbate the recession.

Second, deflation increases the real value of debt. In the same way, inflation helps debtors by driving down their real value. If the price level falls significantly, borrowers will really feel a double whammy: Real debt servicing will rise relative to income (as wages fall with deflation); and deflation also brings with it a higher loan-to-value for homeowners as house values fall. This can lead to loan defaults. Similarly, rising real debt weakens business balance sheets and affects their access to more credit. It encourages businesses to deleverage to clean up their balance sheets. This, of course, makes business sense. But, if all businesses did the same, we would have a financial crisis on our hands—hence, the **paradox of deleveraging** (Krugman).[10]

Third, deflation will bring with it the **paradox of falling wages** (Krugman). To save jobs in a recession (a good thing), workers are prepared to accept lower wages. If all businesses did this, no one gains any competitive advantage. But falling wages worsen the recession, since falling incomes adversely affect household and business debt, raise mortgage payments in real terms, and dampen their propensity to spend, with disastrous impact on recession in the face of rising real interest rates. As indicated earlier, falling wages in Japan brought about the "lost decade"—wages fell by more than 1 percent a year from 1997 to 2003.

Fourth, deflation also brings damaging effects on the expectations of consumers and businesses. Essentially, with deflation comes the psychological impact of expecting prices to fall some more. This can well bring on a potential downward spiral of declining prices to further weaken confidence, making real recovery that much more difficult. Crucial to breaking the downward cycle is changing expectation among shoppers and businesses alike that prices will keep tumbling.

What, Then, Are We to Do?

Perhaps the Japanese experience can offer an invaluable lesson. As of now, the prospective behavior of consumers and businesses remains deeply uncertain. The dynamics of the range of risks to be managed are as complex as they are global. As indicated earlier, it is possible that the United States, the eurozone, and even today's Japan could find themselves in the situation of Japan in the mid-1990s—that is, unable to power a sustainable strong recovery and requiring further stimuli. What is clear is that stabilizing the recession is not good enough. A really strong recovery is needed. This could mean much stronger stimulus, much stronger action to restore confidence in the financial system and credit market, and much stronger job-creation measures. By learning from Japan's mistakes, the United States and the eurozone can avoid a dismal decade.

Xiamen, China
Kuala Lumpur
May 8, 2009

Notes

1. First published on May 8, 2009.
2. In mid-March 2009, Fed Chairman Ben Bernanke told CBS's *60 Minutes* that he detected "green shoots" of economic recovery. Since then, this phrase has sprouted and blossomed. Indeed, on one day in the week ended May 3, it was reported that Bloomberg carried 118 articles and research reports from many sources in which this metaphor was deployed.
3. International Monetary Fund (IMF), *World Economic Outlook Update* (Washington, DC: IMF, April 2009).
4. Fed Chairman Ben Bernanke, in prepared testimony to the Congressional Joint Economic Committee on May 5, 2009.
5. Ibid.
6. Professor Nouriel Roubini, in an interview with *Newsweek*'s Lally Weymouth in New York on April 29, 2009.
7. Bernanke's comments, May 5, 2009.
8. Ibid.
9. For more details, see Chapter 22.
10. Paul Krugman, "Falling Wage Syndrome," *International Herald Tribune* (May 3, 2009).

CHAPTER 24

Reality Check on Economic Models[1]

Since the 1970s, mainstream research on major macroeconomic issues (growth and inflation, boom and bust, etc.) has been grounded in individual behavior. Their best and brightest became Nobel Laureates (e.g., Robert Lucas of University of Chicago in 1995 and George Akerlof of University of California at Berkeley in 2001). The results were rigorous; indeed, the macroeconomic models are certainly that. Their roots date back to Professor Irving Fisher (Keynes's contemporary), who determined behavior of the market in rational, mathematical terms. But policy makers and the public want them to be illuminating and useful, that is, being realistic. What we got was anything but that. To begin with, the idea of finding a single theory encompassing all of human behavior was not realistic. What emerged was based on the "efficient market" hypothesis—that everyone acts rationally and has perfect information so that the market accurately prices the real value of "goods" transacted.[2] Concepts like equity, ethics, and values are regarded as sloppy sociological constructs. In the real world, however, much of what brings about business opportunities and causes instability in the global economy results from the failure of assumptions such as these. Indeed, herd behavior, panic, asset mispricing, imperfect information, and irrational exuberance have resulted in the mess we now witness.

Failure of Models

The arrogance of it all is that these models claim to have solved the problem of instability. Admittedly, there could be periodic recessions but no gigantic collapse—whatever happens is predictable and can be handled; indeed, precautionary steps can be taken to prevent them. How wrong they were! Sure enough, the intellectual edifice fell into disrepute in the summer of 2008. What's unsettling is that the current crisis has not fitted into any of the standard models about business cycles. Nor has it submitted to textbook solutions. Mostly, they failed to point out fundamental weaknesses of financial markets. They could not foresee such a major crisis. Now, they quarrel on appropriate policies and on the likely course of future events. What's stark is the contrast between the real economy that produces goods and services and the financial intermediation markets in securities, banking, mutual funds, and other services. The causal relationship between them still remains a mystery, as is the solution. The puzzle remains because this crisis originated in very frightened financial markets with their toxic products.

Minsky's Challenge

Looking back, it was Hyman Minsky (a mid-twentieth-century economist) who confronted conventional theory and argued that the financial system played a big role in exaggerating the business cycle. This is so because (1) investors, banks, and consumers extrapolate the future as though it is like the recent past; and (2) after a period of stable growth, they develop a misguided confidence that such benign conditions will continue. This led them to borrow more (and banks to lend more in the face of accommodating easy money), thus raising the riskiness of the system's collapse. At this stage, it doesn't take much change in the fundamentals on investor attitudes to cause the system to unravel. Once prices start to drop, the downward cycle rapidly collapses. Minsky's challenge to blind faith in free markets offers an important lesson: If markets are not always right, then Wall Street's vested interest needs to be vigorously challenged—however loudly it may complain. One thing is clear: I do not believe in the market's self-healing ability.

Markets Don't Have All the Answers

Even before the crises, there were already strong hints that a hands-off approach by government was not the only way to manage an economy. Sure, Russia's past was not a good example. But China's government-managed capitalism appears to be doing fine. The modern financial system as we know it from history originated from a series of innovations in seventeenth-century Netherlands. Dutch finance and ideas eventually crossed the English Channel and built the stock market, financed global trade, and established the Bank of England, the nucleus of "Anglo-Saxon" capitalism. When the British system failed, the center crossed the seas once again. New York and Washington replaced London and Amsterdam. Its modern version runs the world today. The Dutch introduced version 1.0 around 1620; the British, 2.0 in about 1700; the United States set up version 3.0 in 1945. As an operating system, it did work pretty well most of the time. Not everyone shared the benefits, and there are environmental and social costs to rapid progress. But the system has a built-in tendency to crash. Since the Dutch tulip bubbles in 1637, the system was prey to excesses.

Now, we have the great unraveling—easily one of the worst. Liberal capitalism has proven to be risky, unequal, and destabilizing. When things go wrong, the less powerful often pay a high price—ask the Russians or the Argentinians. No question, the system as we know it now needs to be debugged. We are in the midst of its current evolution. We are, in a sense, still in unknown territory—facing new situations and taking measures not tried before. As I see it, now more than ever, version 4.0 in 2009 has to be one in which the needs of the many come before the greed of the few. Even in crisis, some form of capitalism remains favored—private enterprise, competition, and consumer choice will need to continue as the key drivers. That's still the best way to allocate and price goods and services. But there should also be a better way to regulate, monitor, and police the orderly conduct of financial services. We know only too well that the market no longer has all the answers.

Risk and Morals

In economics, technology has become king with an impact not unlike the benevolent Prometheus. Morality adapted to its demands. Faith in the market—the midwife of technological innovation—was a result of this. Debt became a factor to be leveraged (a metaphor from engineering), thus turning "getting into debt" (by being highly leveraged) as desirable. In contrast, the virtuous Chinese savers are being castigated for failing in their "duty" to spend more, and not less. According to Lord Skidelsky (Keynes's noted biographer), the key in the transition to a debt-fueled economy was the redefinition of uncertainty as risk. Whereas managing uncertainty was traditionally a moral matter, hedging against risk became regarded as just a legitimate technical issue. This, in practice, abolished the need for moral concerns. Hence, the active deployment of quants (mathematical whiz-kids) to develop new risk-free instruments (getting the sting out of debt) that confronted the barriers of prudence and self-restraint. These "merchants of debt" (as Minsky called them) offered a full range of risk preferences. Because growing competition steadily drove down the cost of risk, the future became (theoretically at least) virtually risk free! As we know it now, this brought the world onto the edge of complete disaster. It is now up to the evolving reformed regulatory framework to reestablish moral responsibility back to where it belongs, without the comfort of moral-hazard-rescue by governments.

What, Then, Are We to Do?

About 150 years ago, Darwin's *The Origin of Species* detailed how evolution- ary selection operated through the survival of the fittest. The lesson for us lies in Darwin's recognition that extinction is an integral part of evolution. Similarly, adverse macroeconomic conditions reduce the survival chances of enterprises in the same way that bad weather limits biodiversity. Viewed positively, the demise of weak ventures can—and do—lead to creative de- struction (Schumpeter), with capital being reallocated to more productive areas. For Darwin, the species that are most responsive to change will sur- vive. This precludes us from selecting the more macho eagles and bears as worthy exemplars—though noble and smart, they are collectively endan- gered. In reality, there is only one evolutionary superstar left on offer: the ever-adaptable humble crawler, the beetle!

Kuala Lumpur
June 25, 2009

Notes

1. First published on June 27, 2009.
2. According to University of Chicago Professor Eugene Fama (1969): "A market in which prices always fully reflect available information is called efficient." This basic assumption, which underlies the efficient market hypothesis, notes that prices are reliable reflections of eco- nomic reality, which has since become problematic. A new generation of economic scholars, many with roots at Professor Paul Samuelson's Massachusetts Institute of Technology, started pointing out the prob- lems, including Nobel Laureates Joseph Stiglitz and Robert Shiller. The 1987 stock market crash gave them all the ammunition they needed.

CHAPTER 25

Commodity and Asset Prices Are Up; Can Inflation Be Far Behind?[1]

In a previous essay in *The Star*, I wrote on how ironically the sovereign-risk "shoe" is now on the other foot (reproduced in Chapter 76, "The Kiss of Debt"). Historically, sovereign-risk concerns reflected profligacy in emerging market economies: Russia, Argentina, and Pakistan were notable examples. Today, the money-printing machines in the United States, the eurozone, the United Kingdom, and Japan are running overtime to assume the "crown."

We all know there is no such thing as a free lunch. This time, severe crises took their toll on those with a history of high living and fiscal indiscretion, ignoring reforms in good times. What a difference a generation makes. The contrast is provided by BRIICs (Brazil, Russia, India, Indonesia, and China). A year ago, with their fiscal and financial houses in good order, BRIICs were busy stimulating their economies. Their main worry then was to push for a fairer global economic order. But, one year on, their situation is ironic: They share three things in common—they are big and growing fast; they have inflation; and they have strengthening currencies thrust upon them. These days, their concerns are on rising commodity prices, overheating, asset bubbles, and inflation.

Paradox of a Symmetrical Recovery

Now more than ever, the 2009 Greek debt tragedy points to gathering risks in the global economic outlook. As of now, global recovery remains anemic, uneven, and in need of policy support. It is as though the world is still dichotomized, but with a big twist. In developed economies, recovery is there but growth remains modest with high unemployment and large fiscal deficits. Having been at the epicenter, sluggish growth in the United States can gather strength, but Europe will now come out of recession more slowly. Of concern is excess global liquidity, which will now grow even more, lifting commodity prices, bloating risky assets, and adding to inflationary pressure. Worse, scars of battered consumers remain in the face of strained and stressed fiscal dilemmas.

In emerging economies, especially BRIICs, the picture is amazingly different. Most are in a V-shaped recovery and many approaching normalcy. Asia ex-Japan is slated to grow 8 percent this year and prospects are for good times to continue. Despite it all, they have recovered with impressive speed. China persisted and grew by 8.7 percent in 2009 (13 percent in 2007); and by the first quarter of 2010, growth was already back up to 11.9 percent, prompting concerns of overheating. India—the more self-contained of the lot—managed 7.2 percent in 2009 and should comfortably clear 8 percent this year.

As a result, inflation is gathering strength in many parts of Asia ex-Japan and in other BRIICs. Inflation in India is already up 10 percent; China, 3 percent; Brazil, 10 percent; Russia, 8 percent; Indonesia, 4 percent. Asset prices have also surged, earning the attention of policy makers especially in China and India. China would do well to keep inflation no higher than 5 percent in 2010, and India, less than 8 percent. Yet, in the lead-up to recession, emerging economies were already becoming increasingly hitched up to the United States and European "shopping cart." Asia's exports share of output rose to 47 percent (from 37 percent) over 10 years pre-crisis. This shows their growing dependence on external demand, not less. When much of this demand disappeared overnight at end-2008, it didn't take Asia too long to be back exporting again. So much for decoupling. But this time, Asia found options. Commodity exporters, like Brazil, Indonesia, Russia, and Australia, and commodity importers, China, Japan, Europe and South Korea, found opportunities to reinforce each other. Such feedback loops built greater interdependence. It seems Asia was only unruffled—not shaken, just stirred.

Commodities

Commodities posted in 2009 the biggest annual gains in four decades, led by doubling in copper, sugar, and lead prices. Oil prices gained 78 percent. The S&P Index of 24 raw materials rose 50 percent in 2009, the highest since at least 1971. Many attribute this rapid price rise to the "super-cycle," fanned by abundant global liquidity and strong demand from China and India in the face of 20 years of underinvestment in raw materials production. The weak US dollar also played a part.

Good times ended abruptly with the financial crisis. But the conundrum became more complicated when prices rebounded strongly, lifted by higher production costs and strong economic growth in BRIICs. Prices of food commodities were also higher. According to experts, the food crisis has moved from lunch and dinner to breakfast. Among the "breakfast commodities," only milk prices remained low. Last year saw tea prices at all-time high; cocoa at 30-year high; sugar, 29-year high; coffee, near 11-year high; and orange juice, highest in 18 months. Sharp increases in these "soft commodity" prices contrast with relatively depressed prices for most agricultural commodities, including wheat, rice, soybean, and corn. Price divergences reflected fundamentals at play. Supply disruptions, not demand, were driving the rally.

But longer term, food prices are on a rising trend, driven by compelling fundamentals: years of underinvestment because of low prices prior to early 2000s; structural rise in demand because increased population demanded a diet richer in meat; and onslaught of biofuels. With economic recovery, high food prices are here to stay. Unlike oil and base metals, supply response of agricultural commodities to high prices is speedy: Farmers react each planting season. Farmers say there is no better fertilizer than high prices. In 2008, farmers' prompt response was aided by good weather; consequently wheat, corn, and soybean output expanded and prices halved! Until May 2010, *The Economist*'s overall commodity price index was up 22 percent, with food prices staying quite flat. Industrial commodities had risen 61 percent, nonfood agriculture, 74 percent, and metals, 56 percent. The Greece crisis temporarily halted the rising trend. Experts say that over the next 18 months, commodity prices will resume rising with economic recovery, lots of cheap money, and rapid BRIIC growth. Like it or not, high commodity prices will persist.

Asset Bubbles

In emerging countries, there is growing concern about too much liquidity (domestic and global) driving asset prices, which can lead to bubbles and inflation. So much so that Brazil and Taiwan introduced capital controls to better manage capital inflows. The International Monetary Fund (IMF) had since concluded that advanced countries may be responsible for creating bubbles in stock markets in emerging nations: Its studies found (1) a positive link between domestic liquidity (money) and stock values; and (2) an even stronger relationship between stock values and global liquidity (hot money).[2] There is also a strong link between liquidity (money) and house prices in all countries. However, the role of foreign money inflows doesn't appear significant. Hot money has little to do with China's frothy property market; it's homemade, it seems.

As someone who knows the goings-on in China, another friend, Professor Fan Gang (National Economic Research Institute, Beijing), has since expressed concern about rising commodity prices and food supply disruptions, even though he views the inflation outlook with limited immediate risk. Consumer prices rose 2.2 percent in first quarter of 2010 and 2.8 percent in April. But real estate prices are more worrisome—land prices more than doubled in 2009 and property prices were up 12.8 percent in April 2010. China's massive stimulus plus explosive credit expansion resulted in a 31 percent rise in money supply in April.

Even so, liquidity conditions are expected to remain easy, simply because balance sheets of consumers and enterprises remain healthy, with prudent leverage, even though more savings have moved into real estate. Most observers regard properties as not yet bubbly. Even so, Chinese authorities raised banks' reserve requirements (ratio of deposits kept at central bank) three times to moderate bank lending. Also, directives were issued to calm markets, including prohibiting developers from accepting deposits on uncompleted properties. China is not alone in this. Countries like Canada, Australia, India, and Singapore have similar concerns. In emerging economies, central banks readily use nontraditional "macro-prudential tools" to do the job, including credit allocation, arm-twisting (moral suasion), and favoring some with credit and discriminating against others. There is no shortage of ideas to fix property bubbles.

Inflation and the Quantity Theory of Money

Over the past 30 months, the global economy has been subject to two major shocks: (1) the buildup of enormous unutilized capacity. Global output had fallen by 5 to 6 percent since 2008. As expected, inflation in developed nations fell from about 4 percent in 2008 to less than 1 percent in 2009. It has since started to act up with rises in commodity prices. The IMF still thinks global inflation will remain low in 2010. (2) But, the crisis also injected enormous amounts of low-cost liquidity (money) into the global system. Fiscal stimuli and quantitative easing (printing money) in the United States, Europe, Japan, China, and India together pumped in liquidity estimated at 4 to 5 percent of global gross domestic product (GDP). Isn't all this money inflationary?

Many are familiar with the quantity theory of money (QTM)—this principle simply states that the general price level will rise in proportion to the increase in supply of money (i.e., cash and bank deposits in private hands). So if money supply rose by (say) 5 percent last year, inflation is likely to increase by about 5 percent this year (i.e., with a lag). But Lord Skidelsky (a noted Keynes biographer) nevertheless reminds us that QTM only works at full employment. If there is unutilized productive capacity, part of the rise in money supply is absorbed to produce new goods and services, instead of spending on existing output. That is noninflationary. Furthermore, flooding the economy with lots of central bank money does not necessarily mean private deposits (generated from spending or bank lending) will rise by the same proportion. Japan in the 1990s had lots of money pumped into the economy; yet, money supply rose by only 7 to 8 percent. Hence, the lost decade of no growth and no inflation (even deflation). We see similar trends in recent experience with quantitative easing in the United States and Europe.

What, Then, Are We to Do?

The lesson is clear: What matters is not the printing of money but spending it. Once spent, the bundle of paper money is activated to produce goods and services. Any central bank can create money but it can't ensure money will be spent or loaned out. Private money locked up in banks doesn't increase the needed money supply; new money simply replaces the old sterilized by recession. So, pump priming should be allowed sufficient time to work through the real economy: First, to use up existing capacity (hence, little or no inflation) and then, build new capacity to propel new growth. That is why any premature exit of fiscal stimuli just damages the recovery process.

We already see results of successful money creation in BRIICs and many others. Asymmetrical recovery demonstrated that, away from the epicenter, emerging economies were able to translate money they print into money spent. At this stage of the growth cycle, presence of significant output gaps means there is little pressure on resources, since firms can readily raise output and look to higher volumes instead of prices. Rising Asia is experiencing the "sweet spot" of the cycle as output and profits rise, while inflation remains under wraps.

As recovery proceeds, monetary policy needs to tighten, removing loose policy settings put into place during recession. Rising interest rates should not constrain the performance of risk assets driven in an improving economy. As I see it, risk of policy error tends to be "too little too late," erring on the side of policy that is too loose for fear of choking off recovery prematurely, or unsettling markets (and vested interests) ill-equipped to handle change.

Kuala Lumpur
May 20, 2010

Notes

1. First published on May 22, 2010.
2. International Monetary Fund (IMF), *Global Financial Stability Report* (Washington, DC: IMF, April 2010).

CHAPTER 26

A New Hazard: Double-Dip Deflation[1]

More than a year ago (May 9, 2009), I wrote "Deflation Is Not an Option," worried as the world was then of the possible coming to pass of the worst-case scenario—"The brutal truth is: Less-worse is not recovery. The world is not out of the woods yet."[2] But by late September 2009, things had begun to brighten up. The Pittsburgh G-20 Summit pronounced triumphantly that the vast global stimuli "had worked"—indeed, it rescued the world from knife's edge in the most severe recession since the Great Depression. What a difference a year makes. In May of this year, I wrote "PIIGS Can't Fly: The Trouble with Greece," brought about by Greece's insolvency spreading ripple effects all over the eurozone.[3] Overall, the Greece debacle casts a long shadow over market sentiment, which has since become dormant, as of now. Many risks still remain.

Double-Dip Talk amid Unusual Uncertainty

It is amazing how fast things do change. In mid-June 2010, I wrote "Summer 2010: In for a Bumpy Ride, Even a Double-Dip?" reflecting the fragility of the evolving situation. In the face of a weakening economy, premature tightening raises the risk of a relapse into recession.[4] Markets have since moved with greater volatility, essentially nervous about fiscal deterioration in the United States and many eurozone nations, and a darkening growth outlook outside Germany. Any upheaval there raises further the risk of a double-dip.

Indeed, Wall Street has since become increasingly convinced fiscal tightening by the United Kingdom and eurozone nations and recent lack of confidence in the United States have dramatically shifted global macroeconomics for the worse. I hear many leading fund managers are already acting to reposition their funds for a double-dip recession—just in case. Some have even started to aggressively de-risk their portfolios.

How real is the risk of a double-dip? For sure, recovery has lost momentum. US second quarter of 2010 gross domestic product (GDP) growth is lackluster at 2.4 percent annual pace, down from 3.7 percent in the first quarter of 2010, and below expectations. Key components exports and consumption contributed less to growth than in the first quarter of 2010. In the 12 months since the onset of recession, the economy grew just 2.3 percent. In contrast, during the equivalent period after the 1981–1982 recession, output rose 5.6 percent.

It is clear the initial boost to demand from inventory buildup has faded. The housing bust still casts a long shadow. US home sales fell 27.2 percent in July to a 15-year low. Households are saving more to work off debts. Worse, firms, fearful of the future, are preferring to squeeze yet more output from existing employees. So, unemployment is stuck at 9.5 percent, even though US corporations are flush with cash. Yet, bank credit is scarce. Bankers have turned risk-adverse. All these stand in the way of a wholesome recovery. Little wonder businesses are reluctant to hire with such "unusual uncertainty," as Fed Chairman Ben Bernanke puts it. No doubt, risk of double-dip has since increased. So much so the Fed recently made a U-turn to counter a weakening US recovery by resuming quantitative easing (dubbed QE2) through reinvesting cash from nearly US$1.3 trillion of maturing mortgage-linked debt. By buying new debt, the Fed pushes bond prices up and long-term interest rates down (since bond yields move inversely to prices). This way, it increases money supply and stimulates growth as credit eases. The message to the market is clear: The Fed will do everything and anything to put a backstop on risk of double-dip! But, as Columbia's Professor Nouriel Roubini aptly describes it, "Whatever letter of the alphabet US economic performance ultimately resembles, what is coming will feel like a recession."[5]

A History Lesson

According to Professor Michael Boskin of Stanford, double-dip downturns are technically more the rule than exception.[6] The US 2001 recession was one brief, mild double-dip. Within the current recession, there is already a double-dip: a dip at the start of 2008, some growth, another long deep dip, then renewed growth. Another dip is still possible—it will represent a triple-dip, but not yet an outright second recession, which is what most are concerned about. In Europe, in the early 1980s, the United Kingdom, Japan, Germany, and Italy all had double-dips. History suggests economies seldom grow out of recessions continuously, without occasional subsequent falls. Dips—double, triple, and even quadruple—have been part of US recessionary experience since World War II. So, it should not be surprising to see another decline in growth before sustained stronger growth emerges.

Deflation Is Poorly Understood

I note the Fed has become concerned over the long time it will take the United States to achieve full recovery (and restore the 8 million odd jobs lost since the onset of recession) as economic growth turned more sluggish. In addition, the downside risk of a double-dip recession and a deflationary spiral has since increased. Fears of deflation on the back of a still-faltering inflation and worries about the recession's return is now the flavor of the month.

What is deflation? Why worry about it? Deflation refers to persistent and sustained falls in prices. It is usually associated with the Great Depression and its cause—a sharp drop in demand. With it, incomes, consumer prices, and asset prices fall. Interest rates move toward zero. But the cost to borrowers in servicing doesn't fall, sucking life out of the economy and pushing prices further down. This bad situation gets worse. In 1932, US consumer prices fell 10 percent; between 1929 and 1933, they fell 27 percent.

The most recent experience is in Japan, but it pales in comparison. Rather than being deep, destructive, and concentrated in a few years, Japanese deflation is a mild drawn-out affair. Consumer prices faltered for 15 years, but never by more than 2 percent a year. It has been a morass but not a destructive downward spiral. Why? Economics don't have a way to rationalize steady multiyear flat deflation. Japan remains a puzzle because its problems have persisted for so long. Some turn to the psychology of households and businesses for the answer—if people believe prices will fall, they act to create the environment that becomes self-fulfilling. Government plays a role through intervention to keep the economy from going through the floor. Other explanations include consumers who are aging and thus more inclined to save for old age instead of spending.

But deflation is not all bad. For some, falling prices are good because incomes and assets can buy more. Such "good deflation" occurred in the United States from 1870 to 1890 in the face of strong economic growth, during a period of rising productivity and technological innovation. Falling electronic goods prices are a modern-day example of good deflation. However, deflation has its bad side—falling prices are associated with falling wages, rising unemployment, and falling asset prices. In the United States in the 1930s and more recently in Japan, deflation reflected that economic collapse and rising unemployment were made worse by high debt and falling asset prices. This delays spending and weakens economic activity. In today's environment of high household and public debt, deflation raises the real value of debt in the face of falling asset prices and declining incomes and public revenues. To the extent that households and governments attempt to reduce their debt burden by cutting spending and selling assets, a "debt deflation" spiral can set in; so will a double-dip recession. With "core" inflation (i.e., excluding fuel and food) now below 1 percent in the United States, the eurozone, and Japan, and headline inflation falling again, it is little wonder deflation worries resurfaced. The key to inflation outlook lies in capacity utilization. Historically, inflation falls or remains weak when business capacity utilization is well below normal (as in the 2008–2009 recession).

The bottom line is simple: As long as recovery in the United States, the eurozone, and Japan remains anemic and excess capacity in industry and labor markets remains high, inflation will likely fall further. If major developed nations return to recession, risk of deflation will rise. As a general rule, deflation favors cash and government bonds over equities, property, and corporate bonds, as well as defensive shares like utility stocks. It's now clear that more aggressive QE2 and sticky service prices are being relied on to break the back of possible sustained deflation. But with oodles of global spare capacity, I see risks favoring deflation rather than a return bout of inflation.

Concern but Not Panic

Make no mistake; threat of deflation is taken seriously on Wall Street. Bond fund heavyweights like Mohamed El-Erian of PIMCO (who manages US$1 trillion-plus in assets) bet the United States has a 25 percent chance of falling into deflation. Put it this way: If I told you that my kid has chicken pox and there is a one-in-four chance of passing it on, would you allow your kid to come over and play? To many, the United States faces a serious risk of falling into deflation. As slowdown takes hold, consumer prices fell 0.1 percent in June after falling 0.2 percent the month before. Growing increasingly wary of deflation (which eats into corporate profits and raises real borrowing costs), many fund managers are prompted to hedge against stock falls, while buying interest-bearing assets. Indeed, it has altered behavior by encouraging firms to accumulate cash, unthinkable a year ago.

Investors pile onto public bonds where fixed interest payments provide good returns when prices and stocks are falling. Investors are positioned well ahead of the Fed. This surge in bonds has pushed yields to multiyear lows; 10-year US Treasuries yield dropped to a 20-month low of 2.418 percent in late August, while its 2-year yield marked an all-time low of 0.498 percent.

I think there is still room down; yields are still too high. After all, yield on 10-year Treasuries is still 1.7 percentage points higher than the Japanese. In the eurozone (considered more prone to deflation than the United States) the gap is still 1.5 percentage points. As I see it, bond investors are slow to catch on, as Japanese were when deflation began. Since late 1992, average Japanese inflation was negative 0.1 percent, but it took 6 years for yield on 10-year bonds to move from 5 percent to less than 2 percent. Today, it's 0.9 percent. The question remains: Are US bonds selling at too high a price? Only time will tell.

Biflation

The risk of deflation varies between regions. Japan is already in deflation. The risk is highest in the eurozone because recent fiscal tightening and hard-line approach to monetary easing imply rising risk of a faltering economy. In contrast, big nations in Asia (notably China and India) have had strong growth with less spare capacity, and hence higher inflation; the risk of deflation is much less. That's the real world where biflation exists—that is, where deflation and inflation coexist in different parts of the world. They even exist in different parts of the same economy—rising prices for globally traded commodities and falling prices for homes and autos bought with credit domestically.

What, Then, Are We to Do?

As I see it, anxiety about double-dip deflation is well founded. The Fed has sent the right signal—one of concern but not panic. It is unclear that more stimulus will create more jobs, suggesting unemployment may have deeper roots. What's happening in the United States, the eurozone, and Japan points to a hard slog ahead. Asia seems able to hold itself. But clearly, its ability to decouple from the developed world has still to be fully tested. Much interdependency remains. Yet, not so long ago, the United States was confidently moving forward and the eurozone was the laggard. The US dollar was riding high as investors fled from the euro's debt crisis. Within months, the roles were reversed, with Asia still squeezed in the middle—but confident and kicking. This underlines the critical point for public policy: Economic fortunes of the United States, Europe, and Asia are as tightly bound as ever.

Kuala Lumpur
August 26, 2010

Notes

1. First published on August 28, 2010, as "Threat of a Double-Dip Deflation."
2. For details, see Chapter 23.
3. For details, see Chapter 47 (first published on May 8, 2010, as "PIIGs Can't Fly: The Greek Tragedy.")
4. For details, see Chapter 6.
5. Nouriel Roubini, "Double-Dip Days," *The Edge Malaysia* (July 26, 2010).
6. Michael Boskin, "Double-Dip Recession a Part of Recovery Process," *The Straits Times Singapore* (July 30, 2010).

CHAPTER 27

The "New Normal"[1]

I particularly like the annual Per Jacobsson Lecture. Per was the managing director of the International Monetary Fund (IMF); he died in May 1963. In September 1963, I joined the IMF, where I remained for about a year. Per's long shadow dominated its work, starting with the creation of the Finance Committee of League of Nations working alongside Sir Arthur Salter, Maurice Frere, and Jean Monnet. At the annual meetings of the IMF/World Bank, the Per Jacobsson Lecture is delivered by the very best from anywhere in the world to share their experiences and beliefs. Last October, Mr. Mohamed El-Erian spoke on "Navigating the New Normal in Industrial Countries."[2] He is the chief executive officer and co-chief investment officer of PIMCO, the world's largest bond fund manager.

New Normal for the United States

Mr. El-Erian coined the term "new normal" in 2009, which has since become widely used. It now means many different things to many different people. Indeed, it has spawned applications in almost every field: in technology (referring to its transformative power), lifestyle (US women getting fatter); medicine (early puberty in girls); management (constant change); higher education (less state financial support); the new rich (show-off its purchasing power); the Internet (new mind-sets for innovation); and so on.

For El-Erian, the economic crisis of 2008 changed everything. He used the new normal to codify for the United States a new era of slower growth with much higher than normal unemployment; increased government regulation in the face of wide-ranging banking reform and fiscal austerity; and decreased US role in the global economy. There is no returning to "business as usual." The United States, Europe, and the world now need a reconfiguration of mind-sets, institutions, and approaches. Those who recognize this early and act on it will fare better this year: "a year that promises both the best and worst of times for businesses."

How the new normal will shape up will depend on its reaction to and interaction with a number of challenges. In my view, the US economy is today still facing the aftershock and lagged effects of major policy and institutional changes since the crisis; a new political configuration; and continuing disarray in the financial services industry. In the process, we can begin to see the convoluted impact from the interplay of factors like the healing of financial markets and the second-round effects of the European debt crisis; continuing high unemployment; and reconfiguration of the medium-term landscape, bearing in mind that sooner rather than later, the United States will need to credibly tackle its deficits and debt.

All these get very complicated in terms of where the eventual outcome will be. Suffice to say that the United States is already in for a very bumpy ride to the new normal. Much of the growth we have seen is artificial—the result of the biggest fiscal and monetary stimuli in US history. The stimulus was not designed well enough to get back to a strong self-sustaining growth path. And now that most of the 2008–2009 packages have ended, the new expansionary programs have begun to hold back any backslides. At some point, private-sector initiative and entrepreneurship will need to take over as the engine of growth.

Even so, growth today remains anemic—a recovery muddling along at too slow a pace to create enough new jobs or become a durable expansion. Overall, the size of the economy still hasn't surpassed its last peak in the fourth quarter of 2007, three years on. Unlike the recovery in the 1980s, this time the rebound reached 5 percent for one quarter before decelerating to today's unrecovery-like speed. Gross domestic product (GDP) in the fourth quarter of 2010 is expected to rise at a 3.5 percent annual clip. For 2011, forecasters have now shifted their predictions to 3 percent-plus growth. Statistically, growth is here and there. But for most Americans, it still feels like recession. The US economy needs to grow at 2.5 to 3 percent a year to keep unemployment from rising. The rule of thumb is: The economy needs to grow two extra points over a year to bring unemployment down one point. Nobel Laureate Paul Krugman suggested that even with 4 percent growth a year from now on, US unemployment would be "close to 9 percent at end-2011 and still above 8 percent at end-2012. . . . Whatever the recent economic news, we're still near the bottom of a very deep hole."[3]

Unemployment, including underemployment, stands at a high 17.5 percent. Unemployment among 20-somethings is at least 15 percent. In the new normal, consumers' purses still hold the key; they continue to face strong headwinds. High unemployment has changed their behavior.

The financial crisis also left behind loads of debt. Some 5.5 million US households are tied to mortgages that are 20 percent higher than their home values. Consumers have since been spending relatively less, leading to feeble consumption growth. Deleveraging (reducing gearing up on debt) explains why growth since 2009 has been so slow. Consumption accounts for 70 percent of US GDP, and it grew less than 2 percent so far. Overall, household debt is too high—90 percent of GDP (last seen in 2005); it will take years to return to 80 percent, last seen in 2002–2003.

Underlying it all is its low savings rate. Deleveraging is slowly working. Personal savings peaked at 6.3 percent in July, but have since fallen to 5.3 percent reflecting much pent-up demand. Rising savings is good in time. The trouble is the transition. History suggests that savings need to be 8 to 10 percent to make a credible comeback. It's not yet there. How the United States adjusts to the new normal hinges on how it addresses four new challenges:

1. How far will the balance shift from markets to government? More government is a reality, even though their involvement in markets is still noncommercial. Nevertheless, businesses will now need to factor in more influential public policy risk.
2. How is this growing involvement to be financed? Markets get edgy with worries of crowding out and rising debt servicing. In the end, the United States needs fiscal austerity and budget surpluses. History teaches this is easier said than done.
3. How will the US role in the global economy change? The United States provides two global public goods: US dollars as reserve currency and deep and transparent financial markets. Both are today questionable; the more the world does, the less their exposure to US assets. The United States needs to get off denial and lead international monetary reform efforts.
4. How far will de-risking the financial system go? This is politically driven. At risk is the flow of credit that lubricates activity. The old normal was a world where credit flowed freely. Now, with ever-present systemic risk, credit will no longer be easy, and its cost will rise. There is still the inflation risk.

New Normal for the Eurozone

Global crises have dramatically changed the eurozone's economic orientation. Growth reflected disappointing performance in the United States, the eurozone, and Japan. They all share a common trait: All are mired in debt, sucking their capabilities and constraining their efforts at remedial measures. Credible growth remains elusive. The eurozone is also confronted with a policy dilemma—a choice between fiscal restraint now and continuing stimulus to secure sustainable growth. Unlike the United States (which chose growth now and tackling the budget deficit later), most eurozone nations opted for (or were forced into) fiscal austerity now, hoping budget discipline would help growth more than renewed stimulus.

The eurozone's choice is based on fear, according to European Central Bank's (ECB) Jean-Claude Trichet, of the "solid anchoring of inflationary expectations." Even now, policy makers are grappling with the surge in global food and commodity prices before inflation hits, as in mid-2008. European obsession with inflation is far, far more intense than in the United States, where job creation is the number one issue. For Europe, fiscal austerity and debt reduction is the new normal—to fend off inflation in the face of rising risks from sovereign debt contagion and euro's survival. The spread to Portugal, Spain, even Italy, is of serious concern. So much so that Mr. Otmar Issing (much-respected former ECB chief economist) warned that Europe's reaction, coupled with unsound fiscal policies in some nations, threatens the survival of the monetary union. He concluded: Financial rescue of Greece and Ireland risks setting in motion an unstoppable momentum toward a "transfer union," and gives rise to potential for blackmail on more solid member states. The resulting tensions may prove fatal for the euro. There are no easy answers. An unbalanced recovery (Germany now expands rather solidly) with peripheral nations lagging far behind could upset the balance, enhancing the risks.

New Normal for Emerging Nations

The disparity in growth between the United States, Europe, Japan, and emerging nations is well known. Less well known are Asia's three biggest developing nations (China, India, and Indonesia) witnessing the emergence of a viable middle class. The chase to join this evolving consuming class has become the new normal in Asia. As I see it, this year could mark the tipping point when Asia's export-led growth turns inward toward more self-generated growth. Not only in China (1.4 billion people), but nations including India (1.2 billion), Indonesia (240 million), Thailand (66 million), Vietnam (89 million), and, less obvious, Philippines (98 million) have gathered enough growth momentum to spin a growing consuming class. Its emergence beyond the prosperity that exists in Japan, South Korea, Taiwan, Singapore, Hong Kong, and Malaysia will have far-reaching consequences.

"Consuming China" now has about 300 million people with significant discretionary spending; their "GDP" is equivalent to two-thirds the size of Germany's. China is not alone. India, with a middle class of about 75 million (200 million by 2015), is like China in 2001. Indonesia now has a middle class not far behind India's. Together, they are witnessing something new—a growing consuming class outside the big urbans. And as reported in the *Financial Times,* Nomura estimated that by 2014, retail sales in China might surpass the United States.[4] The new normal in Asia is for growth to be increasingly driven by the newly empowered and aspirational middle class. Today, China purchases more cars and mobile phones than the United States, and soon will buy more computers. Realistically, Asia's middle class is not yet ready to spur global expansion. But it will soon enough drive a larger share of Asia's growth.

What, Then, Are We to Do?

Even in economics, the new normal is viewed differently, depending on whether you are American, European, or Asian. But one thing is for sure: It means fundamental change to face new realities following the 2008–2009 Great Recession. For Malaysia, the new normal is reflected in national transformation programs to elude the middle-income trap (for details, see Chapter 109, "The Mystique of National Transformation"), and (1) transform Malaysia into a high income, inclusive, and sustainable economy through invigorating the private sector; and (2) enter a new era of higher growth, driven by rising productivity from innovation and smart human resource deployment. To succeed, the underlying drivers must be very robust in practice. This is not going to be easy. I think the government has a good grasp of the issues it needs to tackle to set the new normal. Success will depend on dynamic leadership intent on bringing about change. We'll have to wait and see.

Kuala Lumpur
January 27, 2011

Notes

1. First published on January 29, 2011.
2. Mohamed El-Erian, "Navigating the New Normal in Industrial Countries," *Per Jacobsson Foundation Lecture* (October 20, 2010).
3. Paul Krugman, "Deep Hole Economics," *International Herald Tribune* (January 3, 2011).
4. David Pilling, Kathrin Hille, and Amy Kazmin, "Asia: The Rise of the Middle Class," *Financial Times* (January 4, 2011).

CHAPTER 28

Muddling Through the Inflation[1]

In Chapter 11, I wrote: "Just as economic expansion is stabilizing in the long-troubled United States and the eurozone, concerns are now emerging on the economic health of Asia and the Middle East. The unfolding disaster in Japan . . . , along with the continuing turmoil in the Middle East, have raised new concerns and uncertainties over economic prospects in these regions, including their impact on food and commodity prices, especially oil."[2] As the world turns, what has not changed is the underlying inflation, which continues to threaten global stability, albeit with different tempos between the West and the East.

Indeed, recent developments have only exacerbated the price trends. US jobs recovery gained speed in March 2011. Many herald this as recovery taking root. Half a million Americans have found jobs since early 2011. Unemployment fell to a two-year low of 8.8 percent, from 10.1 percent two years ago. That's an improvement. Lest it's forgotten, 6.1 million people are still out of work and the percentage of Americans without work for at least six months rose to 45.3 percent from 43.9 percent. Jobs recovery remains weakest on record. One commentator labeled it as nothing more than an *economic sugar rush*—built on expansionary monetary and fiscal policies that are unsustainable.

To me, the situation is uncomfortably reminiscent of last spring. Back then, corporates were starting to hire again, before events like euro-debt crisis and fading US stimulus program injected uncertainty, and business confidence fell to cut short the recovery. It is not difficult to imagine rising food and energy costs, supply chain disruptions, and government cuts could do the same this year. The long history of financial crises shows they inflict long-lasting damage. It does look like the US recovery is on second gear, even though workers' paychecks have been flat. All the stimulus did was to paper-over price pressures that have been building up, slowly but surely. The Fed has to deal with it, sooner rather than later.

United States and Eurozone Inflation

In the United States, inflation rises steadily: Cost of living rose more than forecast in February 2011, led by the highest food prices since 2008 and rising fuel costs. The consumer price index (CPI) gained 0.5 percent (highest since June 2009). Year-on-year, CPI rose 2.1 percent (1.6 percent a year ago). Energy costs were up 3.4 percent over January, the most since December 2010. Food costs rose 0.6 percent. What's of concern is that across the food chain, rising prices are being passed on. Prices paid at the farm and factory gate surged 1.6 percent in February. The food in the producer price index rose 3.9 percent, biggest gain since 1974 (with fresh vegetables up 49 percent).

Since then, the world is confronted with new uncertainties, spreading unrest in the Middle East and worse-than-expected effects of Japanese earthquake/tsunami in the face of robust global growth in manufacturing. US price pressures are ticking up, with inflationary expectations rising from 2.8 percent in December 2010 to 3.2 percent in March 2011 (University of Michigan's consumer survey).[3] While demand overall remains soft, supply matters. Anxiety over the flow of oil and food and interruptions in the supply chain are bound to exert more upward pressure on prices.

The eurozone is similarly impacted. Factory gate prices in February 2011 posted their sharpest annual gain (12.8 percent) in nearly 2½ years, putting pressure on the European Central Bank (ECB) to raise interest rates soon. Inflationary pressures are also broadening: Year-on-year, producer prices of intermediate goods were up 8.1 percent in February; factory gate prices, excluding construction and energy, rose 4.5 percent; for nondurable consumer goods, they were up 2.6 percent, the biggest rise since October 2008. Latest surveys indicate factory gate prices rose at record levels in March 2011. The eurozone headline inflation (including food and oil prices) has been above the ECB's "below but close to 2 percent" limit since December 2010. The ECB has had its benchmark interest rate at 1 percent since May 2009. Unlike the United States, the ECB focuses on "headline" inflation against the Fed's "core inflation," which excludes food and energy prices. For Europeans, you can't put "core" prices on the dinner table.

That's why the Fed is more relaxed about inflation. So far, the Fed didn't have to choose between fighting inflation and fighting unemployment, its twin mandates, and has kept the credit spigot open (through QE2). But recent cross-currents are putting more pressure on inflation in the face of still stubbornly high unemployment. Because monetary policy works with a lag, the Fed needs to tighten well before it hits the 2 percent target. The Fed's ability to maintain public confidence in keeping inflationary expectations appropriately "anchored" is critical. However, the latest University of Michigan's respected consumer survey points to rising inflationary expectations in the United States.[4]

Emerging Developing Countries (EDCs)

Inflation is much more serious in the EDCs. In particular, the BRIICs—Brazil, Russia, India, Indonesia, and China—may be growing too fast. Inflationary pressures could be getting out of hand. With gross domestic product (GDP) growing at 6.5 to 7 percent, unutilized excess capacity is growing thin. Furthermore, massive capital inflows (reflecting cross-border flows of QE2's easy money and a weak US$) have piled on the pressure. Investors flocked to EDCs markets, bringing with them much-needed capital but also the risk of fanning inflation.

Rising food and oil prices and the impact of Japanese earthquake/tsunami have compounded the problem. The Libyan war and supply disruptions created a "fear" factor that has since driven oil prices beyond US$120 this week. Rising food prices are just as worrisome, since they hit mainly the poor. The cost of food was one key reason for the recent upheaval in the Middle East (especially in Tunisia, Egypt, and Libya)—and even in countries without political disruptions. Rising food prices pose social strains and stresses on the poor, who badly need budgetary support at a time that is trying for most EDCs.

The fight against inflation is already weighing in on EDCs, from China to India, South Korea, to Indonesia. The World Bank recently estimated EDCs in East Asia will grow at 8.2 percent in 2011, slower than 9.6 percent in 2010.[5] The post-Japanese earthquake/tsunami global PMI (purchasing managers' index) surveys surprisingly now point to robust growth in manufacturing worldwide. The main concern is the inflationary threat coming from rapid rise in imports prices, as these are being increasingly passed on. This optimism is pervasive: The US index stood at a 27-year high, pointing to a strong manufacturing performance in the first quarter of 2011. Similar growth for the eurozone averaged 8 percent in the quarter. Data for East Asia show the authorities' efforts to cool down appear to be paying off somewhat. PMI for China was 53.4 in March (index exceeding 50 denotes expansion), and for India, 57.9.

China, India, Other Asia

In Asia, inflation is expected to exceed 5 percent this year (4.4 percent in 2010). Chinese inflation remained stubbornly high at 4.9 percent in February 2011, surpassing the government's target of 4 percent. Food prices (up 11 percent) have been the main driver of inflation. Pressure will mount, as March data are expected to be harsher. So, more anti-inflationary measures can be expected, following four interest rates hikes since October 2010, and increases in banks' reserves to squeeze lending. Costs at the factory gates rose 7.2 percent in February (6.6 percent in January 2011) as global commodity prices soared. The main threat to social stability rests with containing inflationary expectations. In India, food prices are rising at double digits (wholesale prices were up 10.05 percent for week ended March 12; 9.4 percent in previous week), exerting pressure on the authorities to rein in broader inflation. Headline inflation was up 8.23 percent in February, reflecting also higher fuel prices (+12.8 percent). Interest rates were raised a fortnight ago for the eighth time.

The policy stance remains strongly anti-inflationary. Food and fuel subsidies to maintain social stability will impinge on an already stressed Indian Budget. For most of other Asia, containing inflation remains top priority. In South Korea, consumer prices rose 4.7 percent in March, the fastest since October 2008 (and above the central banks' target band of 2–4 percent) and are expected to rise above 5 percent in the second quarter of 2011. Interest rates were last raised in January 2011, the fourth time since July 2010. Similarly, March inflation was high in Indonesia (6.65 percent), Vietnam (13.9 percent), and Singapore (4 percent), but subdued in Thailand (3.1 percent) and Malaysia (2.9 percent). Nevertheless, policy makers are busy taking proactive measures to contain inflation in addition to monetary policies, including increasingly unaffordable subsidies, price control, and other social payments to assist the poor. Many countries are also resorting to sorts of capital controls to ensure portfolio inflows do not destabilize domestic conditions. Central banks in India, South Korea, Thailand, Indonesia, Singapore, and Malaysia were known to have intervened to avoid rapid exchange rate appreciation inconsistent with underlying fundamentals, as one-off demand for the region's assets intensifies.

Latin America

Across Latin America, inflation is accelerating on the back of strong consumer demand and because soaring commodity prices have pushed food prices higher. Indeed, International Monetary Fund (IMF) estimates much of Latin America, including Brazil, Argentina, and Chile, which rebounded with help from strong demand for their commodities' exports, may now be growing too fast.[6] There are already signs of overheating. Latin America's economy will grow by 4.5 percent in 2011, after expanding 6.1 percent in 2010. It's worrisome that policy makers have assumed the food commodity price boom will soon pass. I think it's a mistake to chalk this all up to cyclical factors—prices for copper and grains have risen simply because of a business cycle upswing. Indeed, current high prices could persist for much longer because of rapid urbanization and a mushrooming middle-class in China, India, and Brazil. Already, inflation in Brazil topped 6 percent in February 2011 for first time since November 2008. Housing prices in major cities have doubled in just two years, and its currency strengthened 10 percent over the past year.

The Subsidy Spree

As prices for food and fuel climbed across Asia and Latin America, governments are adding or extending subsidy programs, price controls, and other ad hoc fixes that I fear will only make inflationary pressures worse. India extended longstanding subsidies on diesel and cooking fuels and additional subsidies for food. Even rich Hong Kong and Singapore are offering cash handouts and tax rebates, and so on as inflation exceeds target rates. These moves follow earlier steps in China to provide subsidies and use price controls to combat rising prices. For most EDCs, leaving the market mechanism to adjust is not an option. The poor just need help. Unfortunately, these programs can only add pressures to drive prices higher. They encourage consumers to spend more, which, in turn, fuels inflation. Similarly, price controls create market distortions and discourage producers from producing more. In the end, governments end up just kicking the can down the road. Another downside is that these policies are expensive. In Malaysia, subsidies and price controls cost RM14.2 billion (US$4.7 billion) in 2010, nearly 9 percent of government revenues. As consumers get used to subsidies and price caps, they want more. In the end, these policies are just not sustainable.

What, Then, Are We to Do?

The global economic outlook begins to look grim as inflationary pressures accelerate and growth headwinds mount. Trade-offs between pushing growth and fighting inflation get real. It's a mistake to assume rising commodity prices are just temporary. Like all risks, they need to be well managed. A US$10 oil price rise trims global growth by 0.5 percentage point over 12 months. It's already up at least US$30 since November. This could trim off up to 1.5 to 2 percentage points in 2011 growth, if the present price persists. That's scary. The biggest risk is a rerun of 1970s stagflation, if monetary conditions continue to stroke demand, while supply remains tight reflecting decades of underinvestment, monopolies in extractive industries, mounting unrest in key commodity producers, and rising inflationary expectations. There are many reasons to be skeptical—even pessimistic. The Asian Development Bank warns: High inflation is a direct threat to stable and inclusive growth.[7] I can't agree more.

Kuala Lumpur
April 7, 2011

Notes

1. First published on April 9, 2011, as "Muddling Through the Inflation Calculus."
2. For details, see Chapter 11: "Prospects 2011: As the World Turns."
3. University of Michigan's consumer survey in the first quarter of 2011 pointed to long-term inflationary expectations rising from 2.8 percent in December 2010 to 3.2 percent in March 2011.
4. Ibid.
5. World Bank, *Global Economic Prospects* (Washington, DC: World Bank, April 2011).
6. International Monetary Fund (IMF), *World Economic Outlook* (Washington, DC: IMF, April 2011).
7. Asian Development Bank (ADB), *Asian Development Outlook* (Manila: ADB, April 2011).

CHAPTER 29

It's a Dangerous World out There[1]

I delivered the 19th Tun Dr. Ismail Oration at the 46th Malaysia-Singapore Congress of Medicine in Kuala Lumpur on Thursday, July 12, 2012.[2] Here are some excerpts.

In Search of Safe Haven

The surest sign that all is not well about the global economy is when investors rush to buy gilt-edged or sovereign bonds of the United States, Germany, the United Kingdom, and Japan. Indeed, they are even prepared to "pay" (after adjusting for inflation) the German and Japanese governments for the privilege of holding their two-year bonds, which earn them practically nothing. They will even lend to the United States, Germany, and the United Kingdom for 10 years in exchange for bonds yielding a nominal 1.5 percent a year. What they receive is a return below the target inflation rate set by central banks! In the eurozone, only Germany enjoys this privilege. People are just scared of the dangers out there. They expect either years of stagnation or imminent disaster. Either way, they feel uncomfortable with the global outlook, so they opt to pay for safety. For them, what matters today is return *of* capital, *not* return *on* capital. I have been in this business for 50 years. I have seen crises come and go. Not even the Great Depression pushed bond yields down this far. History suggests that investing in low-yielding Treasuries is not a good deal. In 1945, I recall investors took in 2 percent a year on 10-year Treasuries. Over the next 35 years, they earned effectively a negative return of 2.3 percent a year after inflation. That's a bad deal. Still, investors continue to do it. To set the current perspective: Since 2009, US$1 trillion have moved into bond funds. Foreigners today hold 43 percent of US Treasuries. Official institutions (mainly in Asia and Middle East) own US$3.5 trillion worth of them. That's a big deal. What's frightening is that these low rates will persist. Last week, central banks in Europe, the United Kingdom, Denmark, and China moved in sync to ease monetary conditions, keeping interest rates still lower, reflecting grave disquiet about the future.

What Went Wrong?

Why is this so? What's going on? As I see it, what's happening is a combination of: (1) slackening economic growth, (2) rising risk of financial disaster, (3) collapse of trust in politics, and (4) an unwillingness of governments to reform to really raise competitiveness. All these in combination work to add on uncertainty. They raise risks associated with a loss of confidence in politicians, many of whom are still in denial, and in their lack of will to take tough decisions.

Slackening Global Growth

The first challenge involves the slackening of global growth. This time, the situation has become more serious—growth in rich and emerging nations is slackening in sync—that is, in tandem. The world's factories are running out of steam. In June 2012, services and industrial production fell across most of Asia and in the United States and Europe. Job data worsened—pointing to a continuing weak global outlook, which the International Monetary Fund (IMF) now considers to have become "more worrisome."[3] Recovery in the United States remains "tepid," vulnerable to contagion from the evolving euro crisis. In June, US manufacturing and services activity contracted for the first time in three years, further denting confidence in a global economy that is already feeling the recessionary effects of European and Chinese slowdown. Also, new orders posted their biggest monthly drop in more than a decade, indicating faltering demand. Some of the fragility is coming from outside the United States, signaling that it is catching the slowdown that is well under way in Europe, China, India, Russia, and Brazil.

The latest IMF assessment of the United States remains "regrettably" tentative.[4] It cites strong headwinds persisting in private consumption as households continue to deleverage—that is, unwind their debt. Job creation has slowed, while business investment seems to have lost some momentum.

Further compounding concerns is the present danger of going over, by year-end, the "fiscal cliff"—so called because of two cliff-like budgetary cuts involving the equivalent of 4 percent of US gross domestic product (GDP), viz. expiring temporary tax cuts and automatic spending cuts. There is also the need to raise the US$16.4 trillion debt ceiling. If no political accommodation is reached, the bipartisan US Congressional Budget Office predicted it would provoke a US recession in 2013. As I see it, such political brinksmanship could prove disastrous.

Europe is showing no signs of an early recovery. Already, at least seven eurozone economies are in recession. Germany and France are slipping, with the slowdown getting more entrenched and businesses getting less optimistic. Eurozone GDP fell in the past quarter, with output held flat in the first quarter of 2012 after shrinking in the fourth quarter of 2011. Of concern are signs that Germany is succumbing to spreading recessionary forces, as activity in manufacturing and services turned for the worse in June 2012. More worrisome is unemployment in the eurozone, which hit a record 11.1 percent in May, with close to 18 million out of work, and is likely to rise further to 12 percent. Youth employment matters most. The young are being left behind as never before. Once this gap emerges, history suggests it tends to persist and is difficult to close. The situation is getting more dangerous with jobless rates for those under 25 at record highs: One in two young Greeks and Spaniards are out of work; youth unemployment in Italy, at 35 percent, is four times the older jobless rate. It is 22 percent in both the United Kingdom and France. The outlook for jobs in Europe looks lousy. Across the world, Europe remains the epicenter of global concern. Much of its problems reflect the counterproductive nature of the cult of austerity, involving draconian cuts in public services and living standards. This compact has since proved economically ineffective, socially disruptive, and I think, politically naive. Simply put, you just can't cut and grow. Austerity depresses growth, reduces jobs, and makes it more difficult to reduce deficits, thereby risking pushing the economy into a self-defeating vicious cycle.

Furthermore, activity in the biggest emerging market—**China**—appears to have cooled. In June 2012, China's factory activity shrank at the fastest pace in seven months. New export orders fell to depths last seen three years ago. Growth in the services sector also slackened in June, expanding the slowest in 10 months. This sector, which is fast approaching one-half of China's GDP, has so far weathered global contraction well. It is likely to benefit from the rebalancing of activity in favor of services and consumption. As of now, Asian policy makers are under pressure to shield their economies from the protracted global slowdown. In China, the policy to revive growth will likely front-load public spending on social welfare, social housing, and social infrastructure. All told, we are in for a rough ride.

Rising Risk of Financial Disaster

The second challenge involves the rising risk of financial disaster. The longer the eurozone crisis drags on, the higher the risk of financial catastrophe. After two years (and 19 summits), the leaders of the eurozone finally agreed on some important steps to save the euro. But they are not enough, as reflected in its impact, which has gotten more brief with each round of talks. The recent June 28, 2012, summit rally lasted about a day: The euro gained nearly 2 percent against the US dollar; major European stock markets rose more than 4 percent; and Spanish and Italian bond yields fell sharply. But this reflected more about how low market expectations were than about the measures announced. It took only the weekend for investors to reverse sentiment, realizing the measures lack commitment.

Indeed, Finland and the Netherlands are already withholding support. German opposition is challenging the measures' constitutionality. It marked yet another in a string of rallies that quickly faded. Be that as it may, the Summit seems to be—in my view—on the right track. It severed the disastrous link (or the economists' "deadly embrace") between banks and governments, by allowing the bailout funds to be used (1) to buy up sovereign bonds **directly,** (2) to recapitalize banks **directly,** and (3) to appoint a euro-wide banking regulator **by year-end.**

No doubt, lack of details adds uncertainty on their implementation. Already two major problems had since surfaced that can complicate matters: First, the bailout "firewall" fund, European Stability Mechanism, will require to triple its present size to be effective. Second, ceding sovereignty by national bank regulators to the euro-wide regulator will be tough to sell. Sure, the Summit has taken a big step, but markets need to be convinced that the European Central Bank will come on board. Continuing political dysfunction will fuel turmoil, amplifying the eurozone's design flaws. Europe remains vulnerable to rising risks from the next fallout on the euro.

Increasing Political Challenges

The third challenge dwells into the space of politics. More than at any time in recent history, the global economy's fate is tied to the capriciousness of politicians. As I see it, the final outcome rests more on politics, not economics. Compounding concerns over the health of the US economy, the IMF had cautioned—correctly, I think—on the danger of going over the "fiscal cliff," calling on politicians to act early. My understanding is that this is not going to happen anytime soon. In Europe, time and again, eurozone leaders only make critical decisions on situations of dire stress—they just don't take difficult steps in normal times. Bear in mind also that Europe can't act without Germany. But few realize how vulnerable Germany is. True, Germany is large and its economy is doing better than most. However, the economies of France, Italy, and Spain combined are twice its size. Its debt-to-GDP ratio is already 81 percent. Germany has committed 6.5 percent of GDP to the various rescue measures. In addition, if all pledges to the bailout funds were added up, and potential central bank "losses" in the event of a euro breakup counted in, Germany's total "casualty" bill could reach 30 to 40 percent of GDP. So, Germany does have high risks at stake in the euro. Sure, its resources are not limitless. To be fair, it is the biggest beneficiary of the euro, running consistently huge payments surpluses within the region. But Germany does have domestic problems. Politically, despite the continuing crisis and bailout fatigue, a recent Forsa poll[5] showed 54 percent of Germans support the euro. However, 75 percent is against a "United States of Europe"—which requires ceding more sovereignty to the European Union; 59 percent is opposed to budgetary control by Brussels; and 66 percent is against any joint eurozone debt liability, or euro bonds. In the end, the reality remains that the European Union is a collective of nation states with notable economic, financial, social, and cultural divergences. Left to their own devices, they are vulnerable to recurrent bickering, disruptive posturing, and differing visions of the future. Even in the best of times, progress toward economic integration is slow and hesitant, and steps to political integration, painful. As always, this can quickly change in a crisis. Hence, the inherent dangerous risks of European politics.

Reforming Governance

The fourth challenge involves serious reforms to raise competitiveness after falling behind in productivity gains. As I see it, there is a bigger picture to preserve the euro. It involves shifting from austerity to a far greater focus on economic growth and instituting supply-side reforms to raise competitiveness. This needs to be complemented by a banking union (i.e., a single banking regulator with joint means to recapitalize and resolve weak banks, including deposit insurance); and then, some form of limited debt union. Realistically, this is still far off. Europeans, I think, are not yet ready for full political union. So, reform to overhaul their governance, economies, and finances is not going to happen anytime soon. So, expect more crises to erupt.

What, Then, Are We to Do?

By creating policy paralysis, political brinksmanship is stalling global growth. The cost of failed, deeply divisive policies extends well beyond economics to engulf social justice. **Naive politics** of confrontation can bring about a double-dip recession in the United States in 2013. Naive politics in pushing for more austerity, and in doing more kicking-the-can-down-the-road, will cause the recession to persist in Europe. Naive politics definitely ferment uncertainty and undermine public confidence. Together, they will sap business and consumer resolve to spend, spread unemployment, stall economic expansion in the advanced rich, and bring about subpar growth among the vast BRICS economies of Brazil, Russia, India, China, and South Africa. So, I am afraid naive politics will make the world a far, far more dangerous place than it already is.

Kuala Lumpur
July 12, 2012

Notes

1. First published on July 14, 2012.
2. See Yan Lin, "It's a Dangerous World Out There," *19th Tun Dr Ismail Oration at the 46th Malaysia-Singapore Congress of Medicine*, Kuala Lumpur, Malaysia, July 12, 2012.
3. International Monetary Fund (IMF), *World Economic Outlook* (Washington, DC: IMF, April 2012).
4. International Monetary Fund (IMF), Statement at end of annual economic consultation with authorities in the United States in July 2012 (part of regular assessment), Washington, DC.
5. Germans Shun Giving More EU Powers," *The Edge Financial Daily* (July 5, 2012).

CHAPTER 30

"Risk-Off" Episodes[1]

Events do develop rapidly in the midst of uncertainty. So I thought it best today to update readers on what's going on in the world. My recent essays in *The Star* covered a wide variety of subjects, ranging from what G-20 leaders did in Vladivostok to the serious malpractice of manipulating the London Interbank Offered Rate (LIBOR); from the snoozing global economy to efforts by the European Central Bank (ECB) and Fed to stimulate economic activity with more quantitative easing; from recession in the eurozone to Europeans struggling to save the euro and bring down unemployment. For sure, the course of global growth has gone worse. So what else is new?

Global Economy Snores

The world economy is now at its most fragile since the 2008 financial crisis, according to the Organisation for Economic Co-operation and Development (OECD),[2] the Paris-based 34-member rich world's think tank. Last week, the World Trade Organization (WTO)[3] forecast that world trade will grow by a mere 2.5 percent this year, based on data showing global trade volume rose by just 0.3 percent in the second quarter of 2012 (2.1 percent in the first quarter of 2012). Growth is dragged down mainly by Europe to less than half of the previous 20-year average. Its forecasts are based on a consensus 2.1 percent world growth in 2012 and 2.3 percent in 2013.

Still, many risks remain on the downside. OECD puts the blame squarely on the eurozone. So, too, is the row between China and Japan over disputed islands in nearby seas. China and Japan are Asia's largest economies: Two-way trade between them rose 14.3 percent to a record US$345 billion in 2011. Merchandise trade slowed in most major global economies in the second quarter of 2012, with outright contractions in all major European nations and in India, Russia, and South Africa (key emerging BRICS economies, the others being China and Brazil).

OECD's 40-year-long correlation established between trade and growth points to a slackening of world trade being accompanied by a fresh lurch lower for world growth. Its Composite Leading Indicators (CLIs)[4] show that most major economies will continue to slow down in the coming months. The CLIs (which have a good track record) suggest that it will take many months before global growth recovers. Indeed, they show that the loss of momentum will persist in the coming quarters in most major OECD nations and rest of the world.

Among the developed nations, economic contraction in the eurozone is set to continue. CLIs for the United States and Japan also fell; they were unchanged for China and India, but that for Russia declined. OECD's CLIs are designed to provide an early warning signal of turning points between expansion and contraction in economic activity. They are based on a wide range of data that have a history of signaling changes in activity. Overall, OECD concluded that the combined GDP of G-20 leading economies rose by only 0.6 percent in the second quarter of 2012, against 0.7 percent in the first quarter of 2012. And so the world begins to shrink.

Central Bank Fix

The outlook is grim. The policy game of kicking the can down the road hasn't worked, as the can gets heavier. Central bank stimulus is not enough to fix the ailing global economy amid a deepening sense of doom. Fiscal measures are needed to boost growth. Since midyear, financial markets have rallied on the hope that central banks will be there to backstop adverse developments with new buckets of cash. In the eurozone, euphoria followed the ECB's September 6 readiness to buy unlimited quantities of short-dated government bonds of nations signed up for rescue. This was followed on September 13 with the US Fed (Federal Reserve, its central bank) agreeing to buy additional US$40 billion of mortgage debt securities monthly in a third round of quantitative easing (QE3) while the Bank of Japan unexpectedly increased its asset-purchase fund to US$1 trillion on September 19. These moves helped to calm markets, but they are not a game-changer. I don't see how the extra stimulus can cancel out downside risks emanating from the persisting euro-crisis, impending fiscal cliffhanger tightening in the United States, and slackening growth in emerging markets. Easy money merely buys time. That's not enough to resolve deep-rooted problems. Serious downside risks remain.

Both the OECD and the International Monetary Fund (IMF) have since scaled back expectations for global growth—their outlooks have gotten worse since the Vladivostok G-20 Summit in September 2012. The United States is notably weaker, emerging economies are visibly weaker, and the eurozone is still the weakest of them all. With global trade stalling, prospects have dimmed that exports will help buoy the US economy. Indeed, the trade shift has taken a big toll on the US outlook. What's needed is for G-20 governments to speed up on steps already committed to boost domestic demand, support growth, and cut unemployment. Since then, Italy was forced to raise its budget deficit after revisions to growth forecasts indicated the economy will shrink by 2.4 percent in 2012, with no recovery in sight in 2013. Spain, despite raising value-added tax (VAT) and freezing pensions, is likely to deepen its recession that began at the end of last year. Finally, there is the ever-present danger of "currency wars," attendant on rounds of central bank easing. Already Brazil, Turkey, and Peru have taken steps to keep easy money from flooding in and driving up their currencies. I understand central banks in Malaysia, South Korea, Thailand, Singapore, and the Philippines are closely monitoring developments, ever ready to "smooth-out" market movements if capital inflows become disruptive.

Rich Nations' Woes

The Eurozone

The eurozone remains at the heart of the persisting slump. The ECB's decision to support distressed economies by purchasing bonds only buys time to implement tough measures needed to resolve the crisis. Policy challenges are daunting amid a deepening recession as front-loaded fiscal austerity takes hold. They just have too much to do: establishing a banking union, fiscal union, and economic union while needing to pursue macroeconomic policies to restore growth and foster external rebalancing and reform to enhance competitiveness. And they need to do all these in the midst of monetary "hawks," worried about open-ended bailout funding; austerity fatigue in the eurozone periphery; political-social unrest, including resurgence of Spanish Catalan secessionism; and possibly even a Greek exit before Spain and Italy can be appropriately ring-fenced.

Recent indicators continue to paint a bleak picture for Europe. Manufacturing activity shrank for the fourteenth straight month in September, suggesting prospects are slim for a quick return to growth. It's entering a period of recession, after three quarters of negative or flat growth. Joblessness in the 17-nation eurozone was 11.4 percent in August (18.2 million unemployed, highest since euro's inception in 1999), while 25.5 million were out of work in the wider 27-nation European Union. Joblessness will exceed 19 million by early 2014, or about 12 percent. Eurozone GDP fell 0.2 percent in the second quarter of 2012, and recession is expected to persist in the second half of 2012. According to the European Commission, confidence among eurozone consumers and businesses fell for a sixth straight month in September to its lowest level in three years, while bank credit flows stayed weak. Worse, the data painted an overwhelmingly negative picture even in the "core" countries (Germany, France, Netherlands, and Austria) that had largely withstood the effects of the crisis until recently. For Germany, there was a sixth successive rise in unemployment (2.91 million) in September (6.8 percent). Decline in manufacturing activity, however, eased in Germany in September, but steepened markedly in France. Slackening manufacturing, reflecting postponing investments and fiscal austerity, is expected to act as a severe drag on growth in the second half of 2012.

United States

US economic growth was much weaker than previously estimated in the second quarter of 2012, as drought cut into inventories against a backdrop of slowing manufacturing activity. GDP rose by a mere 1.3 percent in the second quarter of 2012, the slowest pace since the third quarter of 2011, down from previous estimates of 1.7 to 2 percent. It also reflected weaker consumer and business spending. Outlays in residential housing and export growth were also less robust. Indicators are that the third quarter of 2012 will show modest improvement despite housing coming out of a six-year slump and manufacturing expanding surprisingly in September amid slower global demand.

However, US CEOs are now as bleak about the outlook as they were in the aftermath of the last recession.[5] Business confidence fell to its lowest point since the third quarter of 2009. They now view the jobs outlook as dismal. Latest job report wasn't good, either.

In response, the Fed intends to vigorously pursue QE3: "Without further policy accommodation, economic growth might not be strong enough to generate sustained improvement in labor market conditions."[6] Since interest rates are already so low and for so long, the new move is unlikely to achieve much, given the prolonged and disturbing weakness in domestic demand. IMF warned that the United States will move into recession and contract 2 percent in 2013 if Congress doesn't avert the fiscal cliff of automatic spending cuts and tax increases.[7] Still, the Fed had chosen to err on the side of expansion to support the flagging recovery. Like its counterpart in Europe, the Fed has bought time for politicians to get their act together. Both Bernanke and Draghi know the risks involved; they obviously think they are worth taking. Only time will tell.

Japan

Japan's prospects for continuing economic recovery were set back with a 1.3 percent fall in industrial output in August to a 15-month low, reflecting slowing sales to its leading export market (China) and also to crisis-hit

Europe. I am now at Keio University, and Japanese friends tell me the economic outlook is somber, despite recent positive retail sales and a slight fall in unemployed. GDP rose 0.2 percent in the second quarter of 2012 (1.3 percent in the first quarter of 2012) and is likely to stall for the rest of the year as the boost from reconstruction-related demand fizzles, and because of poor European demand, subdued Chinese growth, and the strong yen.

For 2012, GDP will rise about 2 percent, but growth will peter out in 2013 (1.6 percent) and 2014 (below 1 percent) in the face of softening manufacturing activity and headwinds from slackening global demand. Manufacturing output hovered at its lowest level in 16 months. Its political dispute with China can only make things worse. For the Japanese (and the Chinese), it's an emotional issue—with deep historical, cultural, and people roots. I sense (being physically in Tokyo) that the issue just won't simply go away—things can get worse before they get better.

China

China's economy continues to soften and domestic investment is unlikely to expand significantly in the fourth quarter of 2012. Its GDP rose 7.6 percent in the second quarter of 2012 (8.1 percent in the first quarter of 2012), marking the slowest pace in more than three years. The economy continues to "cool," estimated to rise by 7.4 percent in the third quarter of 2012, reflecting contracting demand in key overseas markets (notably Europe) and sluggish home credit expansion. Manufacturing activity rose slightly in September but remained in "contractionary territory" for the eleventh consecutive month, suggesting persistent slowing of the economy. New export orders fell at the fastest rate since March 2009. As a result, the workforce in manufacturing shrank but mildly.

Beijing faces mounting pressure to stimulate to rekindle growth. It's acting cool as it wants to promote "stable growth." As I understand it, new infrastructure projects approved in early September add up to 1 trillion yuan (US$160 billion), or 2.1 percent of 2011 GDP. Government stimulus to cushion the downshift appears to be in train with stepped-up approvals of many "infrastructure projects," but the pace of implementation is not expected to be as rapid given tight monetary conditions, cautious bank lending, and restrained fiscal spending. Besides, rather than exacerbate previous imbalances, China is pushing for a "new normal" to stabilize annual growth at 7 to 7.5 percent, and avoid yet another round of investment-fueled growth. This time, stress would be placed on social housing, social safety nets, and social infrastructure and education. Expectation is for GDP to rise 7.5 percent in 2012, China's weakest full-year growth since 1999.

What, Then, Are We to Do?

Recent data highlighted continuing vulnerabilities in East and Southeast Asia. Sure, their economies are growing well. So far, at least. They have learned that the impact of the West's slump can get to be far reaching and their policy responses (more QEs and protectionist moves) potentially damaging. Withdrawal of demand from Asian exports has had profound consequences on growth and employment in China, Indonesia, Taiwan, South Korea, Vietnam, Malaysia, and India. So have their easy money flows and protectionist measures.

Asia must learn lessons from past indiscriminate, large-scale stimulus efforts. Governments need to preserve enough firepower just in case the slowdown deepens and persists. The time has come to take out some insurance—and err on the side of easier policies. When trying to lift growth, focus on efforts at building social infrastructure and institutions (affordable housing, welfare safety nets, education, and helping people left behind). Finally, worry also about the revival of "currency wars" following in the guise of rounds of central bank stimulus—cheap and abundant money tends to drive up artificially the value of Asian currencies. The world has become a more dangerous place. We can't take our eyes off the ball. Protecting the national interest requires policy makers to be always vigilant.

Tokyo, Japan
October 4, 2012

Notes

1. First published on October 6, 2012.
2. Angel Gurrie, Secretary General, Organisation for Economic Co-operation and Development (OECD). Told Reuters on September 18, 2012, in Beijing, China, when releasing its Composite Leading Indicators report.
3. World Trade Organisation (WTO) Secretariat, in a statement on September 19, 2012, releasing its "2012 global trade outlook" in Singapore.
4. Gurrie.
5. Business Rountable, "CEO Economic Outlook Index," a Survey of 138 CEOs (August 30 to September 14, 2012), New York City, September 26, 2012.
6. Ben Bernanke, in a speech delivered at the *Federal Reserve Bank of Kansas City Economic Symposium* in Jackson Hole, Wyoming, August 3, 2012.
7. Christine Lagarde, managing director, International Monetary Fund, *CBS Evening News* interview with Scott Pelley, October 1, 2012, Washington, DC.

CHAPTER 31

Now's Not the Time for Austerity[1]

Since 2008, policy debate continues to be centered on the correct mix between austerity and growth, and the need for fiscal sustainability, or what economists call budgetary consolidation—that is, measures to ensure that government budgets are balanced over time so that the servicing of rising debts is sustainable, without passing on too great a burden to future generations. The focus of public policy is now directed at the pace of fiscal retrenchment—that is, how best to bring down deficits and debt to provide for "more growth and less austerity," according to French President Francois Hollande, in order to provide sufficient leg room to create more jobs and ease human misery.[2]

In today's circumstance, it is proven that nations "can't cut and grow." Already the International Monetary Fund (IMF) concluded this spring that the "US is tightening fiscal policy too much, too fast and it's in the wrong place . . . and these spending cuts are both unwise and unnecessary."[3] It added that Spain had no need for "upfront heavy-duty fiscal consolidation"; it just needs more time to better manage its fiscal squeeze. Indeed, the time has come for Europe to decide how to better support demand; how to better balance the pace of fiscal consolidation with the need for growth; and how best to ensure surplus nations can contribute more to demand as deficit economies undergo adjustment. I think the time is now right for Europe to relax its self-defeating policy of universal austerity and push harder on structural reforms to raise competitiveness and create jobs. As the eurozone contracted for the twentieth time this May, the European Union (EU) Commission president is reported to have declared that austerity has reached its natural limits of popular support and should ease back. Makes sense.

Austerity

In economic terms, I don't see austerity as being a policy designed to punish moral failings, nor is it an expression of outrage over high taxes and high public spending. In the spirit of Hayek, the purpose behind austerity is to (1) be prudent in order to prepare for the rainy day (to fight crises or wars); and (2) ensure hard-earned taxpayers' money is spent to benefit society (that every dollar spent will add more than a dollar to domestic output). A lesson from recent crises points to the realization that nations are in reality poorer than they had hoped to be, leading to the need to cut their coat according to the size of the cloth. But these are not normal times.

At this point, the economic case for austerity—to slash public spending in the face of weak economic conditions, has collapsed. As Nobel Laureate Professor Paul Krugman (Princeton) had pointed out: (1) claims that spending cuts would boost employment by promoting business confidence have broken down; and (2) claims that there is a redline of debt beyond which nations cross at their own peril are erroneous.[4] The clearest case is the United Kingdom, whose economy has since contracted in 5 out of the past 10 quarters. Unemployment stands at a stubborn 8 percent. In today's circumstance in the United States and Europe, where interest rates are trapped at near zero, Professors Brad DeLong (Berkeley) and Lawrence Summers (Harvard) have observed in the *Financial Times* that government deficits can quite easily pay for themselves through higher economic growth.[5] These are not normal times. Like it or not, unemployment today is high almost everywhere in the United States and Europe; indeed, about 25 percent of world's 15- to 24-year-olds is neither studying nor working. In the United States, nearly 12 million are without jobs and still looking for work, 3 million of them for a full year or more. So much so that Sony Kapoor, a fellow at the London School of Economics, termed *austerity* as "mindless, arithmetically nonsensical, politically tone-deaf, socially risky, intellectually indefensible, and financially unsustainable."[6] Concludes Krugman: "It's tragic as austerity has destroyed millions of jobs and ruined many lives. And it's time for a U-turn."[7]

Growth and Austerity

When should a nation need to worry about the size of its public debt? In a 2010 study, Harvard professors Carmen Reinhart and Kenneth Rogoff (R&R) argued that growth slows dramatically once the ratio of government debt to gross domestic product (GDP) exceeds 90 percent.[8] They found that public debt had little effect on growth until debt reaches 90 percent; growth then drops sharply, which never made much sense to me. Unfortunately, this finding served as an important intellectual touchstone in support of austerity policies in the United States and Europe.

It has been cited by politicians ranging from archconservative US Congressman Paul Ryan to UK Chancellor of the Exchequer George Osborne.

But their results have since been challenged in a 2013 study by researchers Thomas Herndon, Michael Ash, and Robert Pollin (H,A&P) of University of Massachusetts at Amherst, who pointed to data errors, miscalculations, and unsupportable statistical techniques (since acknowledged by R&R).[9] Taken together, H,A&P concluded that R&R were wrong about austerity: Once past 90 percent, growth may be moderately slower but this was not true under all circumstances; and deficit-funded spending was most effective in injecting demand back to the economy. While not suggesting governments should borrow and spend profligately, "judicious deficit spending remains the single most effective tool we have to fight against mass unemployment caused by severe recessions."

Recent research by R&R, along with findings by austerity proponents, "does nothing to contradict this fundamental point." As I see it, the fundamental problem lies with causality: Certainly the state of the economy affects the fiscal position, just as taxes, spending deficits, and debt can affect growth. But, it is a statistical fact that correlation does not establish causation. Simply because high debt and low growth go together could well reflect debt accumulation that follows from slow growth. Indeed, slow GDP growth could readily cause a rising debt load. H,A&P showed that causality runs more dependably from growth to debt than vice versa. Recent increases in deficits and debt in the United States and Europe were a consequence of financial crisis; debt was not the cause of the growth collapse.

Research errors in economics are not uncommon. I well recall my economics professor at Harvard, Nobel Laureate Kenneth Arrow, had to correct a mistake in the proof of his famous impossibility theorem. That's why it's vital no policy measure should ever be based solely on a single empirical result. It needs robust evidence. In a recent opinion piece reported by Reuters and published in the *Financial Times*, R&R charged that politicians and pundits have "falsely equated our finding of a negative association between debt and growth with an unambiguous call for austerity," and emphasized (1) their message was merely that "debt matters for countries' long-term growth prospects"; and "our advice has been to avoid withdrawing fiscal stimulus too quickly"; (2) "our call to politicians to rethink current efforts to shrink debts"; and (3) "a sober reassessment of austerity is the responsible course for policy makers."[10] Sounds reasonable enough. All in all, empirical evidence merely suggests that high debt/GDP ratio eventually can impede long-term growth. So, fiscal consolidation needs to be phased in gradually as the economy recovers. No need for unusually harsh measures at this time of stress. Albert Einstein's dictum is right: Compound interest is the most powerful force in the universe—not through the happy accumulation of wealth but through the agonizing enslavement of debt!

The IMF About-Face

In an about-face, the IMF had recently warned that some leading economies—the United States, United Kingdom, and Germany, had adopted fiscal policies that were too tight for their own good and for the wider world. The United Kingdom should consider "greater flexibility" in pursuing deficit reduction.[11] This is a reversal for the IMF, which, as a member of the troika (together with the European Union and the ECB, the European Central Bank), had insisted that austerity forms an integral part of any bailout package. I see it as a victory for common sense that the IMF reverses its past mistakes and has sought less severe deficit reduction measures largely in these three economies, which it had deemed to have "fiscal space." It now recognizes the harsh impact on growth of deficit cutting and that debt reduction is a task best left until countries are out of recession; the IMF: To decisively avoid that dangerous downside, policy makers must act now to strengthen the prospects for growth. But these countries don't appear to be listening and are unlikely to change course, simply because they owe no debt to the IMF. The United Kingdom was even harshly warned to be "playing with fire" if it allowed stagnation to continue.[12] However, the IMF had insisted it is not looking for stimulus elsewhere. It does not want to slow austerity plans in bailout nations. It's a pity. Obviously, the IMF is placed in a difficult spot, making no country happy. In the end, as a practical matter, the IMF is simply worried about collecting its debt.

A Cri de Coeur

Winston Churchill is reported to have once said: It is not enough that we do our best; sometimes we have to do what is required. And, what is required is growth and job creation. Perhaps, because of the mistakes of what had happened in the United Kingdom and the eurozone, and hardships have since become more widespread, policies need to revert to those more obvious and practical options, recognizing the misery deficit cutting is causing—that is, go for the moderate, middle ground, sensible fiscal approaches. Sure, too much public debt will have its costs on growth, but let's not stop there—costs depends on the reasons that debt was accumulated in the first place and the present trajectory of the economy. As I see it, it's just not worth provoking a crisis to forestall another that is unlikely to come. The lesson of R&R's hasty conclusions is not to look for black holes when these are not there. I do understand you can't cut and grow. I do understand what it means to print money. I have been there. I also understand the overuse of euphemisms like *fiscal consolidation* and *fiscal retrenchment*. Now's not the time for more austerity. The reality is simply that we urgently need to grow and create jobs.

What, Then, Are We to Do?

As the Bank for International Settlements (BIS), which counts the world's leading central banks as members and is dubbed "the central banks' central bank," emphasized in its annual report in the last week of June: "Ours is a call for acting responsibly now to strengthen growth and avoid even costlier adjustment down the road. . . . Monetary policy has done its part!"[13] More it can't do and shouldn't do lest it compounds the risks already created. To be fair, central banks on their own can't do what ECB's Mario Draghi promised: "Do whatever it takes" to return struggling economies to health again. It's wishful thinking. Returning to stability and prosperity is a shared responsibility. It's now up to politicians to do their share of hard but essential work of adjustment—to reform still-sluggish economies to strong and sustainable growth (BIS). Although I do understand Draghi's aim was for the ECB to stop market speculation from tearing down the euro. Indeed, Europe needs to create more dynamic growth to create jobs and cut record unemployment, currently at 12.2 percent in the eurozone. By setting policy rates at close to zero and expanding their balance sheets through large bond purchases (thus pushing lots of money into the financial system), central banks have made it easy for the private sector to expand and governments to fund deficits, thereby—unfortunately—making it convenient to put off badly needed reforms to shore up creditworthiness. This can't go on. Central banks need to refocus. Governments must now hasten to oil the economy's wheels through labor market reforms to raise productivity. Private debt overhang must be restructured and cleared (i.e., deleveraged), and calcified economic structures and institutions must be repaired and reformed. This has to be done now. Not to reform is not an option.

Kuala Lumpur
June 27, 2013

Notes

1. First published on June 29, 2013, as "Now Is Not the Time for Austerity."
2. Francois Hollande, addressing journalists in Paris at the start of his second year as president of France on May 16, 2013.
3. International Monetary Fund (IMF), *World Economic Outlook: Hopes, Realities and Risks* (Washington, DC: IMF, April 2013).
4. Paul Krugman, "Time to Reverse the Destructive Turn Towards Austerity," *New York Times*, as reported in *Business Times*, Singapore (May 10, 2013).

5. Chris Giles and Robin Harding, "Austerity Is hurting but Is It Working?" *Financial Times,* as reported in *The Edge Financial Daily*, Kuala Lumpur (April 29, 2013).

6. Sony Kapoor, in Twitter on April 23, 2013, and reported in *The Edge Financial Daily*, Kuala Lumpur (April 24, 2013).

7. Krugman.

8. Carmen M. Reinhart and Kenneth Rogoff, "Growth in a Time of Debt," *American Economic Review*, Papers and Proceedings (2010), p. 100.

9. Thomas Herndon, Michael Ash, and Robert Pollin, "Does High Public Debt Consistently Stifle Economic Growth? A Critique of Reinhart and Rogoff" (April 15, 2013).

10. Carmen M. Reinhart and Kenneth Rogoff, "We Never Advocated Austerity: Harvard Dons," *Reuters*, as reported in *Business Times*, Singapore (April 29, 2013); Carmen M. Reinhart and Kenneth Rogoff, "Austerity Is Not the Only Answer to a Debt Problem," *Financial Times* (May 2, 2013).

11. International Monetary Fund, at the annual health check on the British economy in early May 2013, London.

12. Oliver Blanchard, "The Chief Economist of IMF: IMF Likely to Renew Call for Relaxation of Austerity," *Financial Times* (May 11, 2013).

13. Bank for International Settlements (BIS), *Annual Report, 2013*, Basel, Switzerland (June 2013).

CHAPTER 32

The World Economy: Growing Pains and Bubbly Worries[1]

Two recent reports offered somber, certainly sober reading: World Bank's June 2014 update—"Global Economic Prospects: Shifting Priorities, Building for the Future," and the Bank for International Settlements' (BIS) 84th Annual Report, 2013–2014, released at end-June (BIS in Basel acts as the central banks' banker).[2] They convey two important messages. First, as the global economy got off to a bumpy start this year, World Bank now has to trim its global growth forecast amid a weaker outlook all round. Second, BIS is concerned that today's buoyant financial markets are out of sync with the wobbly economic and worsening geopolitical outlook. This disconnect is worrisome. Let me sound a warning and draw some lessons for public policy.

The Worldwide Wobble

After nearly five years into their recovery from a deep recession, advanced nations still look disappointingly feeble, even fragile. The harsh winter in the United States, along with the ever-deteriorating Ukraine conflict, and worsening confrontation in the larger Middle East landscape, has chilled the world economy's outlook for this year. The World Bank now cuts global gross domestic product (GDP) growth to 2.8 percent in 2014, from 3.2 percent forecasted in January 2014. "We are coming to a period where growth is going to be more difficult to achieve than in the past everywhere, including in emerging markets," according to its lead author, Andrew Burns, on June 11, 2014. Growth in emerging markets is expected to slacken from the earlier estimate of 5.3 percent to 4.8 percent in 2014, with East Asia and Pacific (EAP) expanding at 7.1 percent (7.2 percent, previously).[3] Their prospects are marred with uncertainty and will likely face headwinds arising from the inability of many nations to enact badly needed reform measures, the rise in military conflict, and the specter of higher interest rates to come.

The World Bank had also projected growth in China, India, Russia, and Brazil to further slow down this year. High-income economies (HEs), similarly, have had a disappointing first half of 2014. Still, growth among the three majors (the United States, Europe, and Japan) is expected to pick up as the impact of government spending cuts recedes, labor markets improve, and pent-up demand starts to flow through these HEs. They can be expected to provide the much-needed global push with some momentum, just as their developing counterparts have failed to accelerate. As of now, recent setbacks are expected to be temporary; the 2015 estimate for world growth remains unchanged at 3.4 percent.

US GDP, after shrinking 2.9 percent in the first quarter of 2014 (worst since the first quarter of 2009 when economy shrank 5.4 percent) following abnormally cold weather, which hampered investment and exports, now appears to be rebounding—June added 288,000 new jobs, bringing the total so far to 1.4 million, the best six-month stretch since 2006. Unemployment has fallen to 6.1 percent, the lowest in six years. Gauges of industrial production, retail sales, and durable goods orders all posted credible gains in the second quarter of 2014, though it's still unclear how strong the rebound in the works is.

Job growth since has been lackluster, with unemployment slowly declining. This, coupled with rising wealth (S&P 500 index was up 30 percent in 2013), is boosting demand and more hiring—all expected to lead to stronger growth. Surveys point to a strong pickup in business investment in the second half of 2014, which has thus far lagged recovery. Inflation has stayed low. In all, the World Bank places US growth in 2014 at 2.1 percent (lower than 2.8 percent in January), with a 3 percent growth in 2015.

The Eurozone

The euro-area is still in the early phases of recovery, after its GDP contracted by 0.4 percent in 2013 and 0.6 percent in 2012. Surveys signaled some cooling-down in business sentiment, reflecting tepid growth since its exit from recession in the first quarter of 2013. To date, GDP growth averaged only 0.2 percent a quarter; the second quarter of 2014 growth remained feeble. Recovery has been uneven. Growth is driven by German output, which expanded by 3.3 percent in the first quarter of 2014, while the French economy (second largest) stagnated and Italy (third largest) contracted. Unemployment remained high: 11.6 percent in May 2014, with 5.1 percent in Germany against 12.6 percent in Italy and 25.1 percent in Spain.

Overall, GDP growth in euro-area is now projected at 1.1 percent for 2014—I think it's still too high. Persistent low euro-wide inflation ("lowflation") remains of concern, presenting a particular threat to high indebtedness (both public and private) in most periphery economies, including Portugal.

Japan

Japan is out-of-sync among the "big three"—its strong first quarter of 2014 GDP acceleration (5.9 percent) reflected one-off front loading of consumer demand before April's sales tax hike. But activities have since stabilized. Growth is forecast at 1.3 percent for 2014 (against 1.2 percent by Bank of Japan [BoJ]), with inflation (1.4 percent in May) broadly in line with 2 percent target. BoJ's second quarter of the 2014 Tankan business confidence survey sagged for the first time in six quarters because of the tax hike.

Developing Countries

Developing countries (DCs) have, for many years, led world growth, expanding at about four times the rate for the Organisation for Economic Co-operation and Development (OECD) rich nations. This growth model is not sustainable—growth has since slackened in the first quarter of 2014, reflecting fundamental weaknesses. But there are signs of a modest strengthening. For 2014, DCs' GDP will rise 4.8 percent (a step down from 5.3 percent in January), with EAP growing at 7.1 percent and EAP ex-China/India, at 2.9 percent. Most of the slowdown reflected China's weakness.

China

China's GDP rose 7.4 percent in the first quarter of 2014, 7.5 percent in the second quarter of 2014, or 7.4 percent in the first half of 2014, reflecting the impact of "mini-stimulus breaks" to aid small enterprises and to push targeted infrastructure. For 2014, the World Bank projected growth of 7.6 percent, higher than the median forecast of 7.3 percent in the AFP May survey (against 7.7 percent in 2013, same as in 2012). Nonetheless, the World Bank warns of a possible Chinese "hard landing" (10 percent fall in investment cuts 3 percentage points off growth), which could weigh down EAP's outlook and hurt commodity exporters. There is also "growing concern" over China's fragile real estate market.

Out of Step

For the past 18 months, financial markets in stocks and bonds, commodities, and derivatives have enjoyed a broad-based rally reflecting investor optimism, in the face of abundant cheap money emanating from easy expansionary monetary policies over extended periods. At the same time, even as global growth firmed, economic recovery is still way below its precrisis level. World growth rose 3 percent in the first quarter of 2014, weaker than the 4 percent average growth between 1996 and 2006. In most HEs, GDP, productivity and employment remained below their precrisis peaks, indeed below their potential. Policies aimed at boosting domestic demand were stunted by the huge overhang of debt.

In 2013, debt exceeded 100 percent of GDP in most OECD rich nations, including the United States. Yet, in 2013, the US S&P 500 index rose 30 percent, and Japan's Nikkei, by 57 percent; Malaysia's Bursa was up 11 percent. The US Dow Jones Industrial Average has since exceeded 17,000 (up 3 percent until July 3, 2014, and 14 percent higher than a year ago), and S&P 500 index to 1,985 (its 25th record high this year). Indeed, S&P 500 finished 2013 with a price-earnings multiple of 25 times 10 years' earnings, well above the historical average of 16 times.

Investor optimism stems from (1) commitment by the Fed, European Central Bank, and BoJ to keep interest rates low—near zero to assist nations to recover from recession; and (2) easy access to loads of easy money in the face of low and uneven growth, and geopolitical unrest and uncertainty. Overall, there is the sense of a puzzling disconnect between the markets' buoyancy and tepid economic development globally, warns the BIS. According to its general manager: "Financial markets are euphoric in the grip of an aggressive search for yield . . . and yet investment in the real economy remains weak while the macroeconomic and geopolitical outlook is still highly maintained. . . . Thus, higher debt translates into greater financial fragility and financial cycles that may become increasingly disruptive."[4] In other words, dangerous new bubbles are in the works even before the global economy fully recovers. Investors desperate to earn returns aggressively drive up prices of stocks and other assets with little regard for risk. That's how bubbles are created. Doesn't take much to burst them.

What, Then, Are We to Do?

The world remains a dangerous place. Predicting future growth is notoriously hard. But this is the seventh consecutive year that the World Bank (the Fed and the International Monetary Fund as well) has been too optimistic. Their models overstate the impact of monetary easing—especially the bond purchasing—and understate the negative impact of capital misallocation with its near-zero interest cost. By distorting stock and bond prices, central banks have been financing government deficits without really doing much for growth to create jobs or stimulating animal spirits.

It's hard to know the payoff or damage down the road of such massive flows of cheap and easy money. We now know the payoff is not faster growth, with all of the attendant harm of disruptions when interest rates eventually rise or when bubbles start to burst—as they will one day, as BIS has since warned. Then there is the damage from inequitable income distribution. So, too, governments should do more to improve the performance of their economies, including raising productivity and getting banks to raise more capital to cushion against new risks, especially arising from financial imbalances.

BIS is right that high debt levels indicate potential trouble. We readily forget lessons from recent history. Temptation to postpone adjustments can be still irresistible. "Financial booms sprinkle the fairy dust of illusory riches," warns BIS. The world is already comfortable with a growth model that relies too much on debt, which, over time, according to BIS, "sows the seeds of its own demise." We need to seriously heed these warnings.

Kuala Lumpur
July 24, 2014

Notes

1. First published on July 26, 2014.
2. World Bank, *Global Economic Prospects: Shifting Priorities, Building for the Future* (Washington, DC: World Bank, June 2014); Bank for International Settlements, *84th Annual Report, April 1, 2013, to March 31, 2014,* Basel (June 9, 2014).
3. Andrew Burns, at the release of the World Bank June report on June 11, 2014, in Washington, DC.
4. Jamie Caruana, General Manager of Bank for International Settlements, interview ahead of the release of its annual report in Basel on June 30, 2014.

CHAPTER 33

What's Up Is Down[1]

Yes, the United States Democrats are down. Back at Harvard recently, I witnessed the humiliating defeat of the Democrats at this November's midterm elections. Most experts at Harvard and Wall Street were unconvincing in telling me why the Democrats lost so badly at a time when the economy is doing well, while Republicans had been so completely wrong about almost everything. Even my friend, Nobel Laureate Paul Krugman, was down; he could only say: "The Republican triumph surely lies in the discovery that obstructionism bordering on sabotage is a winning political strategy. This was, it turned out, bad for America but good for Republicans." What most voters felt was that "the man in the White House wasn't delivering prosperity—and they punished his party."[2]

Studies show that mature stock markets don't really care much about elections.[3] So the stock market is up, just as down jackets are up from Boston's Newbury Street to New York's Fifth Avenue. Indeed, the puffer coat (not unlike the stock market) has now become a phenomenon—it's flying off shelves the fastest ever, reflecting both function and high style—guys just want to look cool and stay warm, as do stock traders. Even traditional makers of the puffer jacket (a British term that has caught on in the United States to describe horizontally baffled down coats) have combined their technical knowledge with heightened design to produce jackets warm enough to brace the February Boston cold, but light and lean enough to keep the ego warm, too. Since sinking into negative territory for the year in mid-October, the US stocks have staged a strong rebound, lifted by growth in the third quarter of 2014 earnings and upbeat economic indicators. Looking ahead, corporate revenues, just like the puffer, will remain light and lean because of the strong dollar (as many S&P 500 companies derive significant revenues from overseas) in the face of an unsettling and increasingly uncomfortable global backdrop.

Why the "Fall Fall"?

This fall's (mid-October) stock market "flash crash" ructions really hurt. What actually caused the plunge in equities, bond yields, and the US dollar remains largely unexplained. Finding out why may seem academic now, with the US stocks scaling new heights and the dollar strengthening close to its 2010 peak. Yet, for investors coming to terms with the market outlook (and the prospect of more volatility), much depends on a better understanding of what led to the scale of this fall's fall unrest. What really happened? Since mid-September 2014, equities had been falling. By early October, bond yields and the US dollar joined in, with all falling precipitously over the next fortnight. Then, on October 15, the US market went crazy. Reflecting strong demand, US Treasury bond prices had already been rising (hence, yields falling) following poor economic reports. By late morning, 10-year bond yields went into freefall and plummeted from above 2 percent to below it (1.86 percent)—that's after a 20-basis-point fall earlier in the morning. The same happened in Europe. At one point, yield on German 10-year bonds fell to as low as 0.72 percent (reminiscent of yen bonds). Within minutes, the markets rebounded. I am told that a trader who just took a toilet break then would have missed the entire episode. US 10-year Treasury futures leaped 2.5 percent (the biggest rise within a day since 2009); the US dollar followed, with the second biggest drop in five years. Equities came close to completing a 10 percent correction from their peak! The VIX (fear index) leaped above 30 on October 15. Why?

There are many theories, of course.[4] But the most credible, I think, involves the behavior of speculators (especially hedge funds) who had bet on yields and the US dollar to rise. As bond prices quickly rose, it became just too painful to hold onto their short positions. The rush to close out became sell-fulfilling; once the shorts were covered, the market rebounded. This explanation seems sensible. Others rest on the complex interaction among technical and exogenous factors (including wrong-guessing the Fed; hedge funds being placed at the wrong end of the stick with court decisions; caught having to sell Treasuries against their better judgment); or the impact of so-called calendar effects (buybacks, having strongly supported the markets, were held back—because of poorly timed regulatory compliance—at the same time as the pullback in equities). Each of these explanations offers different lessons, including: avoid excessively crowded trades; avoid buying or selling in a hurry by investing for the longer term; and avoid reading too much into official announcements—whether data or policy. Officials are not omniscient.

GDP and the Market

Studies by investment management firms (Vanguard and Morningstar) based on data over the past 90 years have established little correlation between GDP growth (whether past or prospective) and what stocks will do next, or for that matter, with returns on stocks or profit margins or tactical stock allocations.[5] Market moves are rarely intuitive. Indeed, they are counterintuitive in reality—studies I have seen show that most of the time, the economy and the stock market move out of sync with each other. Traders will advise that the biggest drivers of future stock direction are changes in investor sentiment, which cannot be readily measured. What really matters isn't what the economy is or is not doing, but how the economy is doing relative to how investors feel (whether optimistic or pessimistic). However, valuation (stock prices relative to earnings) can offer an indication of what stocks will do tomorrow—up to a point. The higher today's valuations, the lower future returns are likely to be—that's intuitive. Today's valuations are already on the high side. S&P 500 traded in October 2014 at close to 25.7× average earnings (inflation adjusted) against an average 16.5× since 1880 (14.1× over the last 10 years; 13.5× over the past 5; and 15.8× expected earnings over next 12 months), according to Yale's Nobel Laureate Robert Shiller.[6] On this metric, investors will do well to temper their expectations of future returns. My take is that today's markets are too complex to distill into one convenient, clear, predictive metric. Nobel Laureate behavioral economist Daniel Kahneman has rightly observed that there are domains in which expertise is not possible.[7] Stock picking is one.

Time for a "Melt-Up"?

The mid-October meltdown has come and gone. The US stocks have since inched up steadily to record levels as equity bulls continued to be encouraged by buoyant corporate earnings and broadly positive economic news, including the third quarter of 2014 GDP growth of 3.9 percent (4.6 percent in the second quarter of 2014) with unemployment down to 5.8 percent. Chinese equities outperformed following the start of the linkage between Hong Kong and Shanghai stock markets while the ruble rallied strongly as Russia pressed ahead with plans to fully float its currency. However, investors in Europe are holding their breath. With growth in the eurozone flattening, traders are keeping faith that the European Central Bank (ECB) will succeed in propping up markets, and eventually reviving the still troubled currency bloc. There's a long way to go. And yet, Europe's stock markets, while broadly lagging behind major competitors in the United States and

Japan, are far from experiencing the turmoil seen in late-2011. European stocks have since bounced back from the mid-October sell-offs, leaving the EuroStoxx index down less than 8 percent from its post-crisis peak and marginally lower for the year. S&P 500 is up 10 percent this year, and the Nikkei, up more than 7 percent. Investors were assured by ECB's commitment that rate-setters are united by plans to massively expand its balance sheet (up by €1 trillion). Many believe this will eventually lead to massive purchases of government debt in a US Fed–style program of quantitative easing (QE).

In the meantime, a number of columnists (including Anatole Kaletsky of Reuters) have suggested that a stock market boom is just starting because (1) the financial crisis is finally over; (2) economic policies worldwide are now more predictable (thus unlikely to cause disruptions); (3) technology is rapidly value-adding, stimulating investment and reviving consumer demand; and (4) inflation will stay low. Furthermore, falling oil prices are on balance good for stocks, and slumping economies in Europe and Japan are finally getting their act together.[8] Europe in particular is shifting toward more active policy stimulus: (1) French and Italian governments are determined to run deficits (regardless of EU rules); and (2) ECB has committed to do whatever is needed to effectively implement the new QE. These moves will make structural reforms easier and more effective for the first time in Europe. Even so, equity prices are bound to fluctuate. Boom and bust are inevitable since improving economic conditions encourage speculative excesses, which eventually adjust as greed gives way to fear.

Others, including Jeff Sommer of the *New York Times* and Michael Mackenzie of the *Financial Times*, are more cautious in their assessment. To them, too much has been made by Wall Street about how the United States can prosper and stand alone as eurozone and Japan face intractable problems.[9] And, as China wrestles with slower growth and the outlook dims for the likes of Brazil and Russia. Despite this unsettling backdrop, it has been suggested that the US equities still look good and stand to attract overseas buyers, partly because a rising US dollar helps boost the value of the United States holdings for foreign investors. However, looking deeper into S&P 500's recent performance brings out a less-than-soothing picture: The market rebound has been led largely by defensive stocks. Equity bulls extol the boost to demand from cheaper oil prices. But the internal dynamics of the broader market suggests investors are still waiting for stronger sales growth that can only come from sustained recovery of demand. Hence, investors should not expect a smooth ride. Bear in mind, the stock market is subject to *mean reversion*—the notion that what goes up must come down (and vice versa), with returns and valuations tending toward a mathematical middle ground. Valuations of S&P 500 stocks are already too high. History suggests that once valuations are stretched, the market adjusts to poorer returns. The US stocks returned 9.6 percent in annualized dividends over the past 20 years; the expectation is only 6.6 percent annualized over the next 5 years as the market has become more expensive.

What, Then, Are We To Do?

Stocks will outperform bonds, which are worth holding only because they reduce the risk of big falls in investment portfolios. In the end, expect lower stock returns in dividends. And, be prepared for unexpected problems, even if they are caused by good news. It's time to temper expectations.

A word of caution. Among global markets, Europe looks cheap. The Stoxx Europe 600 trades at 13.9× analysts' expected earnings for next year. This is a discount to S&P 500's ratio of 16×, pointing to better returns on euro-stocks. But faith in the ECB could be tested in the coming months: with (1) potential deflation heaping pressure on ECB to act boldly; and (2) political uncertainty surrounding ECB's ability to actively pursue QE. All these simply point to things getting worse before they get better. Bear in mind that when an investment relies on what a central bank might do, that's risky. Also amplifying this concern is the softening global economic outlook.

Kuala Lumpur
November 27, 2014

Notes

1. First published on November 29, 2014.
2. Paul Krugman, "Triumph of the Wrong," *New York Times* (November 11, 2014).
3. "The Stock Market Doesn't Care about Elections," *New York Times* (November 4, 2014).
4. James Mackintosh, "Mystery Lingers about the Causes of the 'Fall Fall,'" *Financial Times* (November 17, 2014).
5. Joe Davis, Chief economist of asset manager Vanguard, "A Growing Economy Doesn't Guarantee That Shares Will Rise," *Asian Wall Street Journal* (November 10, 2014), p. 35.
6. Ibid., p. 35.
7. Daniel Kahneman, "10 Questions," interview with *Time* (December 5, 2011).
8. Anatole Kaletsky, "Time for a 'Melt-up'—The Coming Global Boom," *Edge Financial Daily* (November 17, 2014).
9. Jeff Sommer, "What Goes Up Must at Least Slow Down," *New York Times* (November 2, 2014); Michael Mackenzie, "Short View," *Financial Times* (November 7, 2014).

The United States: Jobless Recovery

PART III

The United States: Jobless Recovery

CHAPTER 34

Jackson Hole "Gunfight" Shoots Blanks[1]

Twenty-five years ago, as a central banker, I used to attend the Jackson Hole, Wyoming, annual monetary symposium organized by the Kansas City Federal Reserve Bank. Those days, the tone used to be unusually policy heavy. The meetings tended to focus on loftier academic research, including new ideas in practical monetary matters and empirical work in rendering monetary policy more "scientific." As years passed, the research became increasingly mathematical. More recently, this symposium assumed a high profile—featuring prominent names in monetary policy formulation, application, and forecasting. Always, the center of attraction is the Fed chairman's keynote address.

The 2010 meeting in late August didn't disappoint. Not unlike the previous two years, Fed Chairman Ben Bernanke's statement was anxiously awaited. This time for indications on the economic outlook in the face of anemic US activity, and the direction monetary policy would take to get the US economy off what Harvard Professor Lawrence Summers labeled "a statistical recovery and a human recession." Keenly awaited are views of critics on both sides of the economic divide. As he spoke, more lukewarm news was released: US hiring and manufacturing output cooled in August 2010, indicating companies were scaling back as US recovery showed signs of stumbling. Indications are private payrolls rose by 47,000 (71,000 in July) while unemployment rose to 9.6 percent. Others showed that household purchases stagnated and services (largest part of the economy) decelerated.

The Official Line

Chairman Bernanke confirmed what many (myself included) had predicted: "The country's recovery has softened more than expected," and the Fed stood ready to take further steps (if needed) to spur the slowing economy, including resuming buying larger amounts of long-term debt. Nothing we don't already know. The latest sign of more trouble came when the Department of Commerce revised its second quarter 2010 gross domestic product (GDP) growth downward to 1.6 percent (from a 2.4 percent pace). The United States needs growth of 2.5 percent just to keep unemployment stable.

Bernanke painted a sober picture that growth had been "too slow" and unemployment "too high." But he tried to reassure: (1) "preconditions for growth in 2011 are in place," with handoff from fiscal stimulus and inventory restocking (for consumer spending and business investment) appearing "to be underway"; and (2) risk of "undesirable rise in inflation and of significant growth in inflation seems low." This is not unexpected. The Fed badly needs to show its relentlessness in preventing a double-dip deflation. He pledged to boost monetary stimulus should the economy continue to deteriorate. However, he avoided comment on the appropriate stance of fiscal policy in the circumstance.

Incoming data confirmed the United States was moving at a pace lower than most members of the US Federal Open Market Committee (FOMC) projected earlier. Back-to-back quarters of growth below 2 percent are likely to put more downward pressure on inflation, which is already lower than its desired targets. It is obvious Bernanke will be vigilant against driving the economy to Japan-like deflation. The Fed definitely likes to see faster growth than what most private economists perceived for the rest of this year. I wrote in Chapter 26, "A New Hazard: Double-Dip Deflation," that Wall Street is taking the possibility of a double-dip deflation seriously enough to act on it. Goldman Sachs is reported to have put the likelihood at 25 to 30 percent, a substantial risk, but adds, possibly unlikely.

As Bernanke spoke, his counterparts in the United Kingdom and the European Central Bank (ECB) echo the same optimism, although somewhat more guarded. Bank of England admitted more monetary stimulus may be required to sustain the fragile recovery as the United States activity cools and the debt crisis threatens the eurozone, while at home deleveraging remains incomplete and considerable spare capacity has yet to be worked off. It admitted that monetary policy appears "too weak and unreliable to moderate credit and asset price boom without inflicting unacceptable collateral damage on activity." The Bank is examining new methods to do the job better, including closer coordination between monetary policy and macro-prudential actions to avoid "pull-me-push-you" results.

The ECB sees Europe being on the brink of a self-sustaining recovery at a time when fiscal consolidation is placed top of the political agenda: There is not much concern for renewed recession but performance will be somewhat weaker going forward. President Jean-Claude Trichet (of the ECB) urged governments to think long term to reassure markets that an orderly transition from high debt and the recent economic fallout will take place without compromising growth. The challenge years ahead are to "ensure that they do not turn into another lost decade." This long-term approach makes a lot of sense. In the meantime, it would be "wise" to keep its policy of making available unlimited liquidity until year-end.

Uncomfortable Monetary Math

Worries about double-dip deflation abound. Outside the Fed, there is growing fear on risks of continuing Fed quantitative easing (QE) outweighing its benefits. Professor Alan Blinder of Princeton (a former Fed vice chairman) thinks it has a low return period, and maybe diminishing returns to scale. This is because what's accomplished came from the "announcement effect" on market expectations. Little to do with the purchases of securities themselves. It has been estimated that US$100 billion of Treasury purchases may lead to only 0.1 percentage point fall in long-term rates.

What would it take to get consumers spending again? At the beginning of the crisis, Goldman Sachs had estimated that QE would need to inject US$4–5 trillion worth of credit to do the job. But this policy, plus Congress's US$800 billion stimulus, have not gone the way it was intended. Even if it succeeded in preventing a worst-off outcome, it didn't last. The economy is slipping again. Meanwhile, the Fed's balance sheet had bloated to US$2.3 trillion from only US$850 billion pre-crisis.

What's the future impact when the Fed finally unwinds to exit? Given the present mood of US Congress, another major fiscal stimulus package looks unlikely. That leaves QE2 (Mark 2 version) to do the job. Central banks in the United States, Europe, and Japan have already slashed interest rates to near zero. Dare they move to negative interest rates? At this time, this is too much to expect.

Which raises the question: Is fiscal policy now really impotent? Empirical evidence confirms fiscal policy (especially when enacted in concert with monetary policy) can have as strong an impact on economic activity and inflation as do monetary actions. I sense a breath of fresh air in Professor Eric Leeper's (Indiana University) suggestion that fiscal "alchemy" must mimic monetary science to provide a new way out of the conundrum. It is true that modern monetary research and practical policy making are sufficiently blended to make monetary policy "scientific."[2] Similarly, tax and budget policies need the same independence of action as monetary policy to expand the nation's repertoire of policy tools to tackle the complex, dynamic problems facing the world today.

To cope with looming stresses, which demographic shifts are exerting on ever-rising government spending on pension and health care programs, fiscal policy needs to be freed from politics. US politicians have debated to death whether to raise taxes or cut benefits to Social Security and Medicare retiree pension and healthcare programs. The problems raise new challenges as the Baby Boom generation retires. Be that as it may, central bankers need to pay heed to taxation and budgeting in the future as the stresses from such financial obligations intensify. Just as there is an understanding central bank decisions should be made independently without political interference, financial markets need to be able to look forward confidently to expect fiscal policy to be formulated in response to any slowdown in economic growth or fall in inflation.

New Insights

Two other studies were debated. Carmen Reinhart (University of Maryland) and Vincent Reinhart (American Enterprise Institute) examined severe dislocations over the past 75 years, including 15 crises since World War II as well as the Great Depression and 1973 oil shock.[3]

Their results warned that the future is likely to bring only hard choices, and included: (1) GDP growth tends to be much lower during the decade following the crises, and unemployment much higher—indeed, in 10 of 15 episodes, unemployment never fell back to pre-crises level; (2) house prices took years to recover and deleveraging debt is often delayed and protracted; (3) big changes in long-term macroeconomic indicators take place well after the crisis is over; (4) history shows a failure to provide sufficient stimulus (slow growth becomes self-fulfilling); and (5) economic contraction (and slow recovery) can dent aggregate supply—indeed, political quick fix often impairs, rather than improves. Lessons point toward more prudent post-crisis policy to (1) be alert of threats to supply and demand, not just demand; (2) beware of impatience for the worst to have past as the dust settles—but the shock is more likely to be "deep and persistent, not temporary." Bernanke's optimism at attempting to restore employment to pre-crisis levels may prove premature, if history lessons are to be learned.

The other study by James H. Stock (Harvard) and Mark W. Watson (Princeton) discusses inflation, which has fallen so sharply, feeding new fears the economy is at risk of deflation.[4] This cycle still has room to fall in 2011. So much so, Bernanke reiterated the Fed would "strongly resist deviations from price stability in the downward direction." Stock and Watson found US recessions to be associated with falling inflation, except during the jobless recovery from the 2001 recession in 2004 when inflation rose. This exception remains a mystery. Could it happen again?

What, Then, Are We to Do?

In the good old days, Jackson Hole was a cowboy town with saloons and gunfights. Today, it's a holiday resort; mock shootouts are staged for summer tourists. The Fed's tepid pledge to do all it can to shoot down double-dip deflation sounded rather desperate. After all, its remaining arsenal might not do the job: more aggressive buying of Treasuries; lower rates banks earn on excessive reserves; and raising inflation targets. Their collateral damage is of increasing concern. That's why Bernanke ruled out the third, more radical step. But what's worrying the markets is that when push comes to shove, Bernanke could be shooting blanks in the absence of supportive fiscal policy moves. Lost confidence can be self-fulfilling. History does not appear to be on his side.

Kuala Lumpur
September 1, 2010

Notes

1. First published on September 4, 2010.
2. Eric M. Leeper, "Monetary Science, Fiscal Alchemy," *Federal Reserve Bank of Kansas City Jackson Hole Symposium*, August 26–28, 2010, which challenged the Fed to focus more attention on the large fiscal deficits. Fiscal stress had to be dealt with.
3. Carmen Reinhart and Vincent Reinhart, based on a paper, "After the Fall," presented at the *Federal Reserve Bank of Kansas City Jackson Hole Symposium*, August 26–28, 2010.
4. James H. Stock and Mark W. Watson, "Modeling Inflation after the Crisis," *Federal Reserve Bank of Kansas City Jackson Hole Symposium*, August 26–28, 2010.

CHAPTER 35

The United States Is No Longer AAA[1]

Standard & Poor's (S&P) had on August 5, 2011, cut the US long-term credit rating by a notch to AA-plus (from AAA). This unprecedented move reflected concerns about the US budget deficits and rising debt burden. It called the outlook negative, indicating that another downgrade is possible in the next 12 to 18 months. According to S&P, the August 2 debt deal approved by US Congress, which raised the debt ceiling beyond US$14.3 trillion and cut spending by US$2.1 trillion, didn't go far enough: "It's going to take a deal about twice the size to stabilize the debt-to-GDP ratio." It also stressed what it saw as the inability of the US political establishment to commit to an adequate and credible debt reduction plan: "The effectiveness, stability, and predictability of American policymaking and political institutions have weakened at a time of ongoing fiscal and economic challenges."

Moody's Investors Service and Fitch Ratings haven't followed S&P's move, causing a split rating. They had earlier (August 2) affirmed their AAA credit ratings for the United States while warning that downgrades were possible, grading the outlook as negative. At the same time, China's only rating agency (Dagong Global Credit Rating) downgraded the United States from A-plus to A, saying the deal won't solve underlying US debt problems or improve its debt servicing ability over the long run.

US Downgrade

What does a rating downgrade mean? For the United States, it will affect its borrowing costs eventually, and immediately, investor opinion of US assets. According to Sifma (a US securities industry trade group), the downgrade could add up to 0.7 of 1 percentage point to US Treasury yields, thereby increasing funding costs for US public debt by some US$100 billion. But the US dollar has a special position as the numeraire of global transactions; it is also a reserve currency and often regarded as a safe haven in times of uncertainty.

Ironically, in the recent sell-off in equities worldwide following the S&P downgrade, the US government bond was a big beneficiary. Its benchmark 10-year bond yields fell 21 basis points on Monday, August 8, to 2.35 percent, the biggest one-day drop since January 2009; by Wednesday, it was 2.14 percent, the lowest yield on record. Two-year US Treasuries yield touched a record low of 0.23 percent, and then fell further to 0.184 percent on Wednesday. In the panic, Treasuries appear to be still the way to go.

With the downgrade, the United States no longer warrants the top-tier rating it has enjoyed since 1941 (Moody's has had a AAA on the United States since 1917). At AA+, the United States is still considered to have a "strong" ability to service its debt. Only Canada, Germany, France, and the United Kingdom still carry triple-A at S&P. The downgrade didn't affect US short-term rating, which remains at A-1+, the highest at S&P. In a follow-through, S&P downgraded numerous government-related enterprises (notably Fannie Mae and Freddie Mac, which together hold more than one-half of US mortgages), 73 investment funds (fixed income funds, hedge funds, etc.), and 10 insurance companies for their large holdings of Treasuries. But banks were spared on the implicit "too big to fail" policy of the government.

Nevertheless, the US bond market retains widespread appeal. At more than US$35 trillion at end-March 2011, this market is broad, liquid, and deep. The Treasuries market alone has US$9.3 trillion debt outstanding. But in the end, the market decides. Consider Japan—S&P downgraded it in 2002. Today, Japan is still able to borrow freely and cheaply. As of August 9, interest rate on Japan's 10-year bonds stood at just 1.045 percent, and 30-year, at below 2 percent. In practice, for the United States, a double-A-plus still works like a de facto triple-A.

Immediate Global Sell-off

When markets opened following the weekend downgrade, a global panic sell-off in equities took over. There was a lot of fear and uncertainty in the markets, reflecting a confluence of three main factors: (1) uncertainty about the US economy faltering, raising the risk of a double-dip recession; (2) worries that the downgrade could further undermine US consumer confidence and business spending, adding another layer of anxiety on the global economic outlook; and (3) fear that the eurozone debt crisis will spin out of control, spooking investors.

All this took its toll. Stock markets plunged around the world with funds flowing into havens, such as gold (up 60 percent since 2010, surpassing US$1,800 a troy ounce), Swiss francs (up 24 percent against euro and 32 percent on US$ over the past year), and ironically, US Treasuries. In Asia, markets closed at their lowest levels in about a year. Key benchmarks in

Hong Kong, Seoul, Mumbai, and Sydney skidded for the fifth consecutive day. Shares in China, Taiwan, and South Korea plunged sharply before recovering some ground. All closed nearly 4 percent lower on Monday. In Hong Kong, the Hang Seng Index had its worst day since the 2008 financial crisis, falling another 5.6 percent on Tuesday; it had fallen by 16.7 percent in the past six sessions, or more than 20 percent from its recent peak. South Korea's Kospi was down 3.6 percent and Indonesia's main stock exchange fell 3 percent. At its close, Bursa Malaysia's Kuala Lumpur Composite Index lost another 1.7 percent on August 9 (–1.8 percent on previous day). Japan's Nikkei fell 2.2 percent to its weakest level since the March earthquake. India's Bombay stock index declined 1.6 percent, its fifth drop in a row.

The Dow Jones Industrial Average (DJIA) recovered 1.5 percent on Tuesday after a record 635 points fall (–5.5 percent) in sell-offs on Monday. The German DAX closed further down 5 percent and the Paris CAC 4.7 percent lower while the FTSE 100 in London fell another 3.4 percent. The Stoxx Europe 600 index ended 1.4 percent higher, following a 4.1 percent slide on Monday, although underlying sentiment remained extremely fragile. The VIX ("fear" index), which tracks stock market volatility, reached its highest since the initial Greek debt crisis in May 2010. It rose 20 percent to 38.5 on Monday afternoon and then to 40.5 on Tuesday, reflecting extreme fear and emotional trading. It measures the price investors pay for protective options on the S&P 500 index. After Monday's sharp share-price drop and the previous week's poor performance, China and Hong Kong aren't the only markets at or near bear territory. Stocks in Germany and France are now down more than 20 percent (definition of a bear market), from highs reached in the previous year. India's benchmark Bombay Sensex is down 20 percent, and Japan's Nikkei is off 16.5 percent.

A day after US stocks received a boost from the Fed to keep interest rates low until 2013, markets in the United States and Europe resumed their plunge on Wednesday. The fear: Politicians across the Atlantic won't be able to manage the significant headwinds buffeting the US and European economies. Woes were focused on France, where its bank stocks plunged amid worries it may lose its triple-A status. The Paris CAC-40 index fell 5.4 percent. In the United States, the DJIA was down 4.62 percent (–520 points), wiping out Tuesday's surge. The Fed had run out of bullets. Asian stocks advanced Wednesday with sentiment helped by a strong Wall Street rebound. However, gains in most markets lacked the passion observed on the way down. Hong Kong was up 2.3 percent, South Korea, 0.3 percent, and Taiwan, 3.3 percent. All three were still down more than 10 percent so far in August. Japan was up 1.1 percent, Australia, 2.6 percent, and China, 0.9 percent. But Stoxx Europe 600 was down 3.7 percent. Expectations are for the markets to remain choppy. On Thursday, most Asian markets were back in negative territory. But Europe closed stronger (up about 3 percent), and the DJIA surged by 4 percent (+423 points).

European Contagion

Italy and Spain, the eurozone's third and fourth largest economies, have a combined gross domestic product (GDP) of nearly €2.7 trillion, about 30 percent of the eurozone's total. For nearly two years, the European Union has been trying to stem the unfolding debt crisis. The July 21 Greek bailout bought some time—not much—to ward off further contagion. The European Central Bank's (ECB) decision Sunday (August 7) to buy Italian and Spanish debt represents a watershed in EU's continuing battle against turning ECB into the lender of last resort. The ECB has insisted the main responsibility to act lies with national governments. Given worries of a new bout of contagion sweeping European and global markets, the ECB defended the new intervention as restoring the "normal functioning of markets through a better transmission of monetary policy." The ECB's continued bond-buying brought benchmark Spanish borrowing costs for 10-year bonds down to 5.019 percent on Tuesday, close to their lows for the year. Italian 10-year bond yields also fell to a one-month low of 5.143 percent. Both countries' yields had approached 6.5 percent last week—a level that eventually escalated to push Greece, Ireland, and Portugal into bailouts. Analysts estimate that the ECB could have bought up to €10 billion, a small fraction relative to the size of Spain and Italy's debt markets. Italy's debt alone is €1.8 trillion.

Market sentiment aside, the purchases did little to change the fundamental backdrop in Europe, where economic growth has slowed even in the "core" nations of Germany and France. Signs of stress remain despite the positive market reactions to the ECB's decision. Deposits at the ECB, for example, hit a 2011 high of €145 billion on Monday, reflecting banks' reluctance to lend interbank, preferring the safety of the ECB. There is a limit to how deeply the ECB can be drawn into the fiscal misadventures of its members. Concerns are mounting on the French economy because of its high debt levels (85 percent of GDP, already above the United States and rising) and weak growth prospects. Germany, in much better shape, isn't immune, either. Already, the cost of insuring German bonds against default using credit-default swaps (CDSs) rose above 85 basis points, higher than insuring UK bonds for the first time on Tuesday, despite the London riots. There is growing concern that the new austerity measures in Italy and Spain will slacken their struggling economies, plagued also by social unrest.

What's Wrong with the US Economy?

The recession ended two years ago. The stumbling recovery may turn out to be the worst ever. Most indicators are not reassuring—unemployment at 9.1 percent is still too high and jobs creation too slow; GDP growth is faltering, income growth continues lagging behind; household wealth is falling; banks are not lending enough; and consumer expectations have not been positive. In the last eight recoveries, lost jobs were regained within two years of recession's end. This recovery is still seven million jobs below peak employment in 2008 and about two million fewer than if unemployment was held below 8 percent.

The US economy will remain lackluster for some years because of: heavy household debt, a financial system deeply scarred by mortgages, and a dysfunctional political establishment. Heavy household debt and a dismal job market have hurt consumers' confidence, further dampening their willingness to spend. The only bright spot is exports, reflecting the weak US dollar and still-booming emerging economies. Unexpectedly, the pace of growth in US services fell in July to its lowest level since February 2010. Taken alongside disappointing manufacturing data, the services sector showed up an economy with weak hopes of a rebound in the second half of 2011, after an anemic first half. According to Harvard's Professor Martin Feldstein, the US economy is really balanced on the edge. There is now a 50 percent chance that it could slide into a new recession. Even Harvard's Lawrence Summers now concedes: The odds of the economy going back into recession are at least one in three.

The US problem is more a job and growth deficit than an excessive budget deficit. The diagnosis of the run-up in debt—out-of-control spending by the federal government—is exaggerated. Indeed, the "cure" of severe spending cuts is likely to make recovery more difficult. The real problem lies in the fall-off in tax revenue. From 20 percent of GDP in 1998–2001, tax revenue has fallen steadily: averaging just 17 percent of GDP from 2002 to 2008, and then, to below 15 percent in 2009 to 2010. About 50 percent of the rise in deficit was due to the downturn because of "automatic stabilizers," reflecting cyclical revenue falls and higher spending to assist the unemployed and other transfers to help the poor. They contribute to demand and assist to "stabilize" the economy.

What, Then, Are We to Do?

The US rating downgrade is a warning bell. On present trend, its debt burden is unsustainable and the US political system seems unable to reverse it. To do so, it needs faster growth; it can't cut its way to growth. What's required is tax reform and a will to restore revenues back to the 20 percent of GDP trend—a prospect most Republicans have castigated. At issue is not the US government's capacity to service its debt, John Kay of the *Financial Times* pointed out. It is the "willingness of the government to repay."[2] If sovereign borrowers meet their obligations, it is only because "they want to."

Kuala Lumpur
August 12, 2011

Notes

1. First published on August 13, 2011.
2. John Kay, "Remember that a Loan to the King Does Not Always Pay," *Financial Times* (August 10, 2011).

CHAPTER 36

"Occupy Wall Street" Goes Global[1]

Since its obscure beginnings, the "Occupy Wall Street" (OWS) movement has spread its wings, joining the "Indignant" of Spain (a movement born on May 15 when a Madrid rally sparked a worldwide campaign focused on outrage over high unemployment and opposition to the financial elite). The OWS group, which has camped out in lower Manhattan's Zuccotti Park (near Wall Street), now in its fifth week, has a valid complaint: Its young social-media-connected generation is losing faith in traditional structures of government and business, arguing it has been betrayed and denied opportunity. "We got sold out; banks got bailed out" was their chant as thousands marched from Wall Street to Times Square.

Inspired by these movements, rallies rippled across the globe in the weekend of October 15, targeting 951 cities in Europe, Africa, Asia, Australia, and North and South America to take part in the demonstration. It's unclear how long protestors plan to stay. Some fear this could only be the beginning, as the world faces a systemic rise in anger, protest, and political volatility that could last for years. With Middle East unrest stirring again, a winter of discontent looks likely. It's not easy to pinpoint the underlying cause of their woes. Check out their websites: They seem to demonstrate against corporate greed (bank bailouts and bonuses) and income inequality (government cutbacks). Worldwide they demand a more fair and equal society.

Since the 2008 financial crisis, US bank profits were up 136 percent, but bank lending, down 9 percent. Indeed, bank lending has fallen in 10 of the past 12 quarters. To the OWS demonstrators, banks haven't fulfilled their part of the social bargain: bailouts for Wall Street in exchange for lending on Main Street. While banks now have more capital, they still aren't lending. Lending will continue to shrink. Banks say the demand isn't there. But 73 percent of small businesses say they are still being affected by the credit crunch. As I see it, banks remain very much risk adverse. Unlike in medicine, banks don't have the ability to quarantine financial contagion. There is a dangerous world out there. What also irks protestors are Wall Street bonuses, which have returned, while ordinary workers suffered retrenchment and job insecurity with little help from Washington. A recent New York State report had predicted that the financial industry will likely lose another 10,000 jobs by end-2012, a decline of 17 percent since August 2011.[2] That's on top of the 4,100 jobs lost since April and 22,000 since early 2008. Overall, New York–area employment in finance and insurance had declined by 8.9 percent since late 2006.

The OWS movement has gained widespread support and encouragement, including from economics Nobel Laureates such as Joseph Stiglitz: "We have too many regulations stopping democracy and not enough regulations stopping Wall Street from misbehaving. We are bearing the cost of their misdeeds. There's a system where we have socialized losses and privatized gains"; and Paul Krugman: "Wall Street pay has rebounded even as ordinary workers continue to suffer from high unemployment and falling real wages. Yet, it's harder than ever to see what, if anything, financiers are doing to earn that money—and their outrage has found resonance with millions of Americans. No wonder Wall Street is whining."[3] Harvard's historian, Niall Ferguson, regarded the movement "still worth taking seriously" even though he had concluded: "So occupying Wall Street is not the answer to this generation's problems. The answer is to occupy the Tea Party. . . . Call it the Iced Tea Party. Way cool."[4] Even the incoming president of the European Central Bank (Mario Draghi) has expressed support. However, the *Times* of London has since labeled the protests "Passionate but Pointless."

US Inequality

By far, the cause of OWS's frustration and outrage is best articulated in my friend Jeffrey Sachs's (Columbia University) latest book: *The Price of Civilization*.[5] In the United States, the top 1 percent of households accounted for almost 25 percent of all household income. The last time this happened was in 1929. In the first three decades of the twentieth century, rapid industrial development raised income and wealth at the top, while mass immigration set the low bar. Then came the 1929 Great Depression and the New Deal four years later, which railed against "a small group (who) had concentrated into their own hands an almost complete control over other people's property, other people's money, other people's labor—and other people's lives." But prosperity wasn't always accompanied by large-scale inequality. The 1950s and 1960s brought about rapid economic growth and a narrowing of inequality as a result of a more robust social safety net, fresh New Deal measures, World War II (WWII), and the vigorous postwar recovery, which reversed the 1920s inequalities.

Since the 1970s, the United States has tasted the fury of globalized competition but failed to grapple effectively with it. The deterioration in Main Street's earning prospects was papered over for the next 20 years by debt—mortgage debt and consumer credit. Bear in mind median earnings of male workers peaked way back in 1973. The US collects less tax as a percentage of national income (25 percent in 2009) than most advanced European nations (40 to 50 percent). This reflected partly the Republican's one-idea approach: Cut taxes permanently and impose fiscal austerity, often at the expense of lost competitiveness (reflecting insufficient public investment in education, infrastructure, and human capital). OWS young demonstrators have a valid argument to make: They are frustrated trying to find a place in an economy where there is one job for every five job seekers, and where youth unemployment is 18 percent. So much for the cliché of Wall Street vs. Main Street: The greedy 1 percent uses the hard-done-by 99 percent. The wider middle class fears its prosperity has evaporated, demanding for a way to deliver growth once more. It's about time Americans get wise to the source of their economic woes—it's a few hundred miles south of Wall Street.

US Poverty

According to the US Census Bureau, there are now more poor persons in America than at any other time in the 52 years such records were kept. More than 15 percent of US families live below the poverty line in 2010. The line is set at US$22,000 a year for a family of four. This reflected the high unemployment rate of 9.1 percent—6.5 million jobs were lost in the recent recession. An additional three million Americans would fall below the poverty line if not for doubling up; that is, adult children who can't afford life on their own return to live with their parents. Today marks the first time in 20 years when US employment (as a percentage of population) has fallen below the rate in advanced European nations like the United Kingdom, Germany, and the Netherlands. The average weekly earnings (adjusted for inflation) of a typical US blue-collar worker are lower today than in 1964. Indeed, median inflation-adjusted family income rose only about a fifth as much between 1980 and 2007 as it did in the generation following WWII.

The US poverty profile is unlikely to change soon. That is why people are protesting. Many believe the current anger against autocrat politicians, bankers, and elites is symptomatic of fundamental shifts in the structure of US (and indeed, global) population. Already, there are strains caused by aging populations driving up budget costs, reducing growth, and blocking jobs from younger people. Coincidentally, both the boomerang generation and the Baby Boomers are demonstrating together in OWS, as they could very well end up in a political battle for dwindling government benefits. That is, the elderly fight to keep their entitlements (Social Security and Medicare) to ward off poverty, and the younger population pushes for spending on education and training to avoid falling into it. Demographic issues are driving much of what we see today. A win-win is to continue pressuring the richest Americans to carry a larger share of the load. Despite congressional resistance, many wealthy in the United States do see it's in their interest to foster a less-divisive society.

Smart Government

While the benefits of globalization are clear and, I think, well appreciated (especially the rapid spread of technology embodied in the Internet and mobile telephony, and reduced poverty in emerging nations), the real problems associated with it are less well understood but nevertheless need to be urgently addressed. Globalization has (1) raised the scope for tax evasion; (2) led to a loss of competitiveness among the less educated in advanced nations, particularly in the United States; and (3) fueled contagion, especially in finance.

In his latest book, Jeffrey Sachs pushed hard for a highly effective government to deal with these problems. Smart public policies are needed to (1) promote high-quality education; (2) raise productivity by building modern infrastructure and inculcating science and technology; and (3) cooperate globally to regulate cross-border issues (e.g., finance and environment). His proposal is controversial at this time since it calls for more government, not less, especially in the United States, where economic inequality has reached a high not seen since the Great Depression. Sachs also points to growing signs worldwide that people are fed up with governments that cater for the rich and the powerful, and ignore everyone else. They call for greater social justice (not confined to the Arab Spring; also serious protests from Tel Aviv to London to Santiago to Sydney, and all over Europe, and now, in New York), and also more inclusive politics, rather than corrupt politics. There are even calls for higher taxes on the very rich across nations (the United States has proposed the rich to pay more taxes; several European governments have talked of a new wealth tax; the European Commission has suggested a new financial transactions tax to raise US$75 billion a year).

Sachs refers to the most successful well-balanced economies today being in Scandinavia—using high taxes to support smart public services, balancing economic prosperity with social justice and environmental sustainability. Sachs bemoaned that for 30 years, the United States has been going "in the wrong direction, cutting the role of government in the domestic economy rather than promoting the investments needed to modernize the economy and workforce." It all started when President Reagan declared in 1980: Government is not the solution to our problems—it is the problem. Today, the solution lies in how the United States is going to fund its future competitiveness through building skills and raising productivity to fight for markets in the twenty-first century. This is also the way to go for the eurozone.

What, Then, Are We to Do?

Historically, Americans haven't been inclined to be aggressive enough to riot, as the Europeans, over inequality (contrast the protests in Rome, Athens, Madrid, and London with those in New York). But the United States is in a new situation now, where protestors are getting desperate in the face of intransigency, especially the uncompromising Tea Party. It is hard to rule that out when the American Dream is very much at stake. At worst, I think the present situation can result in an economic malaise that lasts for decades. It makes politics most unpredictable.

There is already political paralysis. But dramatic shifts in policy are possible. My Harvard teacher, Nobel Laureate Professor Michael Spence—who shares a concern about rising inequality—once told me that we have seen an evolution from one propertied man, one vote; to one man, one vote; to one person, one vote; trending to one US$, one vote. The rise of ideologues in a modern guise is also probable, as we saw in the 1930s. I am afraid this is the new reality. We have to deal with it.

Kuala Lumpur
October 20, 2011

Notes

1. First published on October 22, 2011.
2. Thomas DiNapoli, New York State Comptroller, *New York State Comptroller Report*, released on October 11, 2011, New York City.
3. Joseph Stiglitz, in a statement in New York City to support OWS mass protests on October 2, 2011; Paul Krugman, "Losing Their Immunity," *International Herald Tribune* (October 18, 2011).
4. Niall Ferguson, "Blame the Baby Boomers," *Daily Beast* (October 11, 2011).
5. Jeffrey Sachs, *The Price of Civilization—Reawakening American Virtue and Prosperity* (New York: Random House, 2011).

CHAPTER 37

Lessons from Marx to Market[1]

Today, we still face not just about the worst recession since the 1930s, but a challenge to the rich West's economic order. The poverty of orthodox economics is now exposed. It showed up capitalism as fundamentally flawed. Karl Marx had contentiously labeled capitalism as inherently unstable. Sure, some of Marx's predictions had failed: no dictatorship of the proletariat; nor has the state withered away. Even among Americans, it's reported just 50 percent surveyed were positive on capitalism; 40 percent were not. Young people are markedly more disillusioned. So, the recent vogue for Marx should not surprise now that the euro stands on the precipice of collapse; and Jeffrey Sachs's *The Price of Civilization* points to US poverty levels not seen since 1929.[2] Indeed, the Vatican's *L'Osservatore Romano* recently praised Marx's diagnosis of income inequality. Brazil elected a former Marxist guerrilla, Dilma Rousseff, as president in 2010. Marx may still be misguided, but his written pieces can be shockingly perceptive.

Marx and Global Disorder

Examine the daily European headlines: There is the specter of a possible Greek default, an impending explosive bank-made disaster, the imminent collapse of the euro—all reflecting a bewildering mixture of denial, misdiagnosis, and bickering undermining European policy response. As Mohamed El-Erian (chief executive officer of PIMCO, the world's largest bond fund manager) observed: "Rather than proceeding in an orderly manner, today's global changes are being driven by disorderly forces of deleveraging emanating from a Europe in deep financial crisis and an America seemingly unable to restore sustained high rates of gross domestic product (GDP) growth and job creation."[3]

We see a crisis that has shaken the foundations of the prevailing international economic order. It is remarkable that in "Das Kapital," Marx diagnosed capitalism's instability at a time when his contemporaries and predecessors

(Adam Smith and John Stuart Mill) were mostly enthralled by its ability to serve human wants. George Magnus (UBS Investment Bank) wrote: "Today's global economy bears some uncanny resemblances" to what Marx foresaw.[4] According to Magnus, Marx had predicted that enterprises would need fewer workers as productivity rose, creating an "industrial reserve army" of unemployed whose very presence exerts downward pressure on wages.

Reality comes home readily with US unemployment still at 8.5 percent (13.3 million jobless). Nearly 5.6 million Americans have been out of work for at least six months, 3.9 million of them for a year or more. Last September, US Census Bureau data showed that median income (adjusted for inflation) in the United States fell from 1973 to 2010 for full-time male workers aged 15 and above. True, the condition of blue-collar US workers is still a far cry from the subsistence wage and "accumulation of misery" that Marx figured. Don't forget, Marx delighted in bashing French economist Jean-Baptiste Say, who postulated that markets will always match supply and demand—hence, gluts don't arise. Against this conventional wisdom, Marx argued that overproduction is endemic to capitalism simply because the proletariat isn't paid enough to buy up the supply that capitalists produce. Recent experience showed that the only way middle America managed to maintain consumption in the last 10 years was to overborrow. When the housing market collapsed, consumers were left with crippling debt they can't service. The resulting default is still being played out.

Marx also predicted capitalism sows the seeds of its own destruction. Unbridled capitalism tends toward wild excesses. The 2007–2008 Wall Street crisis had demonstrated how reckless deregulation (for example, in allowing banking leverage to rise unabatedly) proved disastrous for the financial system, attracting extensive moral hazard in massive bailouts. "The Republican Party is en route to destroy capitalism," radical geographer Professor David Harvey had contended, "and they may do a better job of it than the working class could." Now once again, we see unbridled capitalism threatening to undermine itself. European banks—financially weak but politically powerful—are putting on the pressure to rescue their balance sheets. We see the same in the United States as homeowners struggle to stay afloat while renegotiating their mortgages. Similarly, creditor nations (e.g., Germany and China) are trying to shift the pain of rebalancing onto debtor nations, even though squeezing them threatens to be counterproductive and, eventually, cause economic disaster. Even so, prolonged economic weakness is contributing to rethinking on the value of capitalism. Countries scraping for scarce demand are now resorting to currency wars. America's Senate has even turned protectionist. Within Europe, the crisis turmoil is encouraging ugly nationalists, some racist. Their extremism is mild against the wrecking horrors of Nazism. Even so, it's unacceptable.

Unbalanced Times Ahead

The outlook for 2012 is dismal (for details, see Chapter 15, "TW3 2011: Annus Horribilis"): recession in Europe, anemic growth at best in the United States, and a significant slowdown in emerging nations. We also know the world is far from decoupled. Export economies in Asia (South Korea, Taiwan, and China) and commodity exporters (Indonesia, Malaysia, and Brazil) are already feeling the pain.

What's going to happen in Europe is critical. The eurozone is already in recession. Germany's economy contracted in the fourth quarter of 2011 at a time the region is looking to its biggest economy to give the zone a lift. Add to this, continuing credit crunch, sovereign debt problems, lack of competitiveness, and intensifying fiscal austerity—we have a serious downturn ahead.

Downside risks in the United States can be as serious—fiscal drag, ongoing financial unwinding among households in the face of stagnant incomes, weak job creation, losses on wealth, rising inequality, and political gridlock. In Japan, weak governance will show up soon enough. Rising inequality is impacting domestic demand big time! This is also fueling popular protests around the world, bringing with it social and political instability—adding further risks to economic performance. Turmoil in the Middle East gathers geopolitical risks of its own making—persistent high oil prices will constrain growth.

On present course, conditions will get worse before they get any better. Policy makers are running out of options. Monetary policy is already less effective—and ineffective where problems stem from insolvency (as in Europe) rather than liquidity. Fiscal policy is now well constrained. Whatever central bankers do, they cannot resolve problems best fixed by politicians—such as incoherent US deficit politics or Europe's fractured institutions, and crucially, its lack of political will to act firmly. Eventually, papering over solvency problems and reform issues will give way to more painful and disorderly restructurings, including exit from the euro. History teaches that financial crises are followed by years of weakness and stress. But some of the pain is self-inflicted. Clarity on the eurozone's future needs strong political leadership. There is really no excuse for US fiscal paralysis as politicians bicker and dawdle. Indeed, even deeper austerity is quite unnecessary; it brings a vicious circle of decline, squeezing demand and raising unemployment, thereby hurting revenues, sustaining large deficits, and draining away confidence.

Lessons from Japan

Japan has been experiencing the West's current woes for 20 years ever since its asset bubble burst in early 1990s. Will Europe and the United States suffer a similar "Japanese" future? There are important lessons. First, get out of denial: Admit past mistakes and take on new challenges for the future. Japan had refused to admit its economic model has since failed. Similarly, Europeans are not ready to give up their welfare safety net even though already buried in huge debt. The United States, in preserving "free markets," wouldn't build badly needed infrastructure because of aversion to state intervention. Let's face it: New realities need new ideas. Second, recognize that the problems are really structural. Japanese politicians continue to rely on orthodox pump priming in the face of excessive regulations (which stymied competition) and believe its high savings will finance it. All it did was to pile up more debt—up to 200 percent of GDP. The United States and Europe are now in a similar boat. Continuing Fed stimuli missed tackling underlying problems—the United States needs smarter approaches to resolve the mortgage quagmire, and to extensively retrain misfit unemployed. The eurozone needs reforms for a more integrated Europe to spur growth. Instead, governments bury their heads in the sand of Tobin taxes (a small financial transactions tax to discourage speculation) and other such diversions. Third, embrace globalization—which Japan has yet to seriously acknowledge, while the rest of Asia had become more integrated. The United States is still "fighting" globalization—in my view, it harbors an anti-trade mentality in the face of deficit politics. Similarly, Europe indulges too intensely in intraregional trade; it needs to build a competitive multilateral non-European network. Finally, firm political leadership is critical. Psychologist and Nobel Laureate Daniel Kahneman[5] pointed to behavioral economics showing people are "influenced by all sorts of superficial things in decision making," and so they procrastinate. Japan personifies procrastination. Likewise, political gridlock gripping the United States and Europe led to more "kicking the can down the road," instead of seriously changing national policy. Japan's history teaches political will as vital in instigating change—without it, the West will likely turn "Japanese." Ignore it and history may well repeat itself.

Middle Classes Also Rise

The growing irrelevance and mistrust of politicians and governments are the result of massive economic slowdown and wasteful public spending. Emerging markets, in contrast, have kept growth consistently going while keeping fiscal affairs well under control. The political woes in China and India and even Malaysia (and possibly in Brazil and Indonesia) reflect, in my view, the early stirrings of political demands by the growing emerging middle class. The World Bank had estimated that the middle class (people earning between US$60 and US$400 a month) trebled to 1.5 billion between 1990 and 2005 in developing Asia, and by one-third to 362 million in Latin America. Estimates by Asian and African Development Banks showed similar trends in Africa, Latin America, and China in 2008.

As Marx had said: "Historically, the bourgeoisie played a most revolutionary part" in Europe. I see it in the emerging markets—that same but softer revolution is now at hand. Middle-class values are distinctive. Surveys showed the middle classes consistently are concerned with free speech and fair elections, with opportunities and corruption. Success of Mr. Aana Hazare's campaign against graft in India, and of street protests in Dalian and Xiamen in China over environmental abuses and the crash by high-speed trains, are some cases in point. Unlike unrest in the Middle East, middle-class activism in India, China, Brazil, and Chile is not aimed at bringing governments down. Rather, there is an attempt to reform government, not to replace it—so far, at least—aimed against unaccountable, nontransparent, and undemocratic politics.

What, Then, Are We to Do?

Recession made plain the need for smarter government and highlighted weaknesses in designing policy to address issues on fairness and burden sharing. There is lots to learn and much to put right. I see an extraordinarily uncomfortable year ahead, with a wide range of possible outcomes, many unpleasant. The eurozone casts the darkest shadow hanging over the world economy. The US outlook is darkened by political uncertainty. The West is now being challenged to deliver not just growth (while necessary, it is insufficient given high unemployment and income and wealth inequalities) but "inclusive growth" for greater social justice.

There is a deep sense that capitalism has become unfair. Calls for a fairer system will not go away. As Marx would insist, they will spread and grow louder. Ironically, unlike emerging economies, the West is not equipped to deal with structural and secular changes—after all, their recent history has been predominantly cyclical. Grasping the ways in which Marx was right marks the first step toward making things acceptable. The longer they fail to adjust, the higher the risks. So expect more volatility, unusual strains, and even odd outcomes. But looking at the cup as half-full, the global paradigm shifts, when they do come, will also present opportunities, not just risks. That can help ease the agony. But it won't make up for politicians' mistakes. Welcome to 2012!

Kuala Lumpur
January 12, 2012

Notes

1. First published on January 14, 2012.
2. Jeffrey Sachs, *The Price of Civilization—Reawakening American Virtue and Prosperity* (New York: Random House, 2011).

3. Mohamed El-Erian, "The New International Economic Disorder," *The Edge Financial Daily*, Kuala Lumpur (December 27, 2011).
4. George Magnus, "Give Karl Marx a Chance to Save the World," *Bloomberg View* (August 29, 2011).
5. Daniel Kahneman, "10 Questions," *Time* (December 5, 2011).

CHAPTER 38

Sachs and Krugman on the Global Crisis[1]

I met up with two old friends during the past month.

Professor Jeffrey Sachs at Columbia University was back in Kuala Lumpur after a long absence as orator of the Tan Sri Lim Goh Tong Memorial Public Lecture at University of Malaya on October 23. Besides being an old friend—he was my freshie during our PhD studies at Harvard in the late 1970s—Jeff is a fantastic and outstanding economist. Prior to moving to New York, Jeff spent over 20 years at Harvard University (where he was appointed full professor of economics at 25, the youngest ever), most recently as director of the Centre for International Development and Galen Stone Professor of International Trade. At Columbia, Jeff serves as director of the Earth Institute, Quetelet Professor of Sustainable Development, and professor of Health Policy and Management.

He is special adviser to United Nations Secretary General on the Millennium Development Goals, having first held that position under his predecessor. He is cofounder of Millennium Promise Alliance, and a director of the Millennium Villages Project. He authored three *New York Times* bestsellers. Jeff is widely considered as the world's leading expert on economic development and its fight against poverty. He was twice named among *Time*'s 100 most influential world leaders and was called by the *New York Times* probably the most important economist in the world, and by *Time* the world's best-known economist. A recent survey by the *Economist* ranked Sachs among the world's three most influential economists of the past decade. His syndicated monthly newspaper column appears in more than 80 countries. For the past 25 years, Jeff has advised dozens of heads of state and governments on economic strategy in the Americas, Europe, Asia, Russia, Africa, and Middle East.

Professor Paul Krugman of Princeton University was back in Singapore to deliver the Sim Kee Boon Institute of Financial Economics Public

Lecture at Singapore Management University on November 7. I last met Paul formally about 10 years ago when I moderated a dialogue between Dr. Mahathir Mohamad, Malaysia's former prime minister, and him in Kuala Lumpur. When I reminded him of it, his immediate response was, "My God!" That was it. I have since met up with him on a few occasions in New York.

Paul is one of the preeminent economists of our time, having won the 2008 Nobel Prize in Economic Science for his groundbreaking work on international trade and economic geography. For his early work, the American Economic Association awarded him its 1991 John Bates Clark medal, given to the "economist under 40 who is adjudged to have made significant contribution to economic knowledge." Today, he is best known worldwide as a regular op-ed columnist for the *New York Times*, where he speaks the truth as he sees it. He calls a spade a spade, often in the most blunt terms. I enjoy his works a lot. The author (and editor) of more than 20 books, Paul's most recent—*End This Depression Now!*—is a call for action.[2] In it, Paul sends a convincing message to all who are affected by the recent Great Recession— a quick, strong recovery is just a step away, he says, "if only our leaders can find the intellectual clarity and political will" to end the depression now. He is widely recognized as a pioneer in basic economic studies and founder of a groundbreaking new theory in international trade.

Sachs: Confucian Man

Jeff's public lecture was titled: "Macroeconomic Challenges in the US, Europe, and China."[3] I had the distinct pleasure to introduce Jeff—the man. Here's what I said: "In a nutshell, he is an outstanding economist; as a friend, he is a fantastic human being." What is not reflected in the write-up, however, is Jeff's character and his colorful career—I have always known Sachs to be never afraid of controversy. Indeed, I think he welcomes it—I recall him confronting European unions during the first oil shock in the 1970s; facing angry New York bankers over his proposed "hair-cuts" amid the Latin American debt crisis in the 1980s; and confronting fighting-fit Russian leftists when the USSR turned to become more capitalist. That's the character of the man—he loves sinking his teeth into the heart of crises and sticking to his guns.

When Jeff first published his book, *The End of Poverty*, in 2005, my friend Jared Diamond (Pulitzer Prize–winning author of *Guns, Germs and Steel*) called Jeff "that rare phenomenon: an academic economist famous for . . . his practical work in helping poor countries become richer." Jeff wrote yet another bestseller three years later. Last year, he wrote his most recent bestseller, *The Price of Civilization*.[4] By now, Jeff has become a seasoned author and a much-sought-after speaker, having matured in my view from an "accomplished academic economist" to a "wise problem-solver."

Confucius describes wisdom as when you are aware of what you know and maintain that you know it, and when you do not, to acknowledge your ignorance. First, according to Confucius, a wise man reads and learns everything he can, and suspends judgment when in doubt; he is cautious in what he says. In that way, his mistakes will be few. Second, a wise man widens his experience, but is bewarned of hazardous places and always gives heed to where he wanders. In that way, he will seldom have occasion for regret. Third, a wise man lets experience guide his words and actions. In that way, he let actions reinforce his words. That's the Jeff I know.

That's why you will find his latest book to be wise in the ways of the world; it's down to earth and realistic about life. In it, Jeff warns that the United States is experiencing the greatest degree of inequality among high-income democracies, where the top 1 percent of households takes almost one-quarter of all household income—a share not seen since the 1920s. The media has since picked this up under the caption: "the greedy 1 percent versus the hard-done-by 99 percent."

This widening gap between the rich and the poor places Jeff once again at the very center of controversy in the recent US election campaign. His conclusion: that the United States needs highly effective government in the era of globalization. Put simply, the United States now needs more government, not less. But, he argues, government governance needs to be modernized and smart in order to be able to meet new challenges in an interconnected world economy. This remains hotly debated. But Jeff is a Confucian man of principle, who—as one—will always have something to say that is worth listening to; but men of words are not necessarily men of principle. He who cares for his fellowmen needs to be bold, but the bold may not necessarily care for their fellowmen. So, you have a bold and principled man, one who is not afraid to innovate and expose fresh ideas to back up what he says. For his many contributions as a Harvard alumnus, the Harvard Graduate School of Arts and Sciences Alumni Council, of which I was its Chairman, awarded the Harvard Centennial Gold Medal to Jeff in 2007 for his many contributions for the betterment of mankind.

In Sachs's latest book, he talks about what *Time* now labels the "Screwed Generation," the young generation aged 35 and below who are screwed, not once, but thrice-over, whether they like it or not: (1) their household income is down 68 percent from a quarter century ago; (2) their unemployment rate is 12 to 14 percent in the United States (almost double the national average) compared with 50 percent in Spain and Greece, 35 percent in Italy, and 22 percent in France and United Kingdom, but well above 8 percent in Germany; and (3) this "screwed generation" is now loaded with huge debts, handed down by "senior Boomers" to their offspring, who will have to pay it off through higher taxes, less infrastructure and social spending, and the prospect of painfully slow growth.[5]

Sachs's Focus

At the said Lim Goh Tong Memorial Public Lecture and the private lunch thereafter, Jeff made seven points that are of public interest:

1. On Keynesian theory resorting to fiscal deficits to stimulate growth, he said: "I don't think it would work and I don't think it has worked. . . . We should make our economic policies with a 10-year horizon, not a three-month horizon. . . . We should ask ourselves what kind of investment, education and environmental management we want. Then, we will end up closer to where we want to be."
2. On quantitative easing, Jeff said: "Short-term financial stimulus is dangerous because "the overhang of bad debts is unpayable."
3. Jeff attributes the current crisis to high fiscal debts in the high-income nations. "We don't have a global crisis; we have a world that is operating at these two speeds: slow in the high-income world and rather fast in the developing countries." So the gap is narrowing, but the ride toward convergence is bumpy because adjustments in the United States and Europe to this reality have not been smooth: "This is the legacy of tax cuts, social spending cuts, lack of investment in infrastructure, training, and regulation."
4. The United States created a housing bubble that went bust in 2007, making unemployment miserable: "The federal government has put interest rates to near zero; but none of it works. The only thing we haven't tried is a structural look at our situation. It would require raising taxes, and ready access to quality education is the ticket for the lower and middle-income classes to move upwards."
5. "The situation in Europe is much more complicated because it has a shared currency . . . but Northern Europe is doing well."
6. "China will grow financially in the next 20 years . . . its biggest crisis is environmental. The slowdown in China is due to the massive catch-up."
7. Jeff expressed reservations on Malaysia's Lynas rare-earth processing project (to both prime minister and members of Parliament in Parliament), stating its national value-added appears marginal amid safety and environmental concerns.

Krugman: The Liberal

At the Sim Kee Boon Institute of Financial Economics Public Lecture titled "Global Economic Outlook: Preventing the Next Economic Crisis," Paul Krugman spent much time tracing the key causes of the crisis, concluding that although the United States has some of the tools needed to avert another crisis, they are still not ready enough to prevent the next crisis; but it would make sense to be better prepared to deal with it when it does come. "A lot more needs to be done."[6] Some of his thoughts bear repeating:

1. The crisis had its roots both in banking and the massive household debt. The advent of "shadow" banking, involving entities such as hedge funds, private equity, insurance companies, etc., not classified as banks but functioning like banks, had rendered regulation ineffective.
2. The 2010 Dodd–Frank regulations lack the needed punch to do the job. "The rules lack clarity . . . (and required) more mechanical definitions of what constitutes a regulated financial institution."
3. New regulations lacked effective resolution authority; "systematically important institutions" are poorly identified (you only know it when you see it); derivatives need to be better and smarter regulated; and consumer protection has yet to be fully worked out.
4. Much of real estate household debt would need to be "forgiven." At the private lunch, Paul (clearly an Obama supporter, couldn't hold back his great delight on an "amazing victory") counseled the president to use his new mandate to "hang tough" on the looming fiscal cliff (a self-imposed deadline involving US$600 billion of spending cuts and higher taxes early in 2013 if there is no deal to fix the budget deficit), which could push the United States back into recession: "No deal is better than a bad deal."

What, Then, Are We to Do?

We have heard the views of two big guns—they don't come any bigger. Their concern is centered on a possible global double-dip recession. For all practical purposes, the eurozone is already in recession (gross domestic product of –0.1 percent in the fourth quarter of 2012, following –0.2 percent in the second quarter of 2012). Industrial production dropped the most in more than three years in September (–2.5 percent for 17-nation eurozone), led by a 12.6 percent fall in Ireland, 12 percent in Portugal, 2.1 percent in Germany, and 2.7 percent in France.

If there is no deal to resolve the fiscal cliff, the nonpartisan Congressional Budget Office estimates the US economy will contract by 0.5 percent in 2013. As Honeywell chief executive officer David Cote stated in an interview at the recent US Business Roundtable—they're playing with nitroglycerin. If they go off the cliff, it would spark a recession that's a lot bigger than economists think—it could turn into a conflagration. All this uncertainty continues to hold back the economy. As I see it, it's not a fiscal crisis, it's a political crisis brought on by US and European politicians' intransigence, taking the world economy hostage. The consequence: back into recession. When will they ever learn?

Kuala Lumpur
November 16, 2012

Notes

1. First published on November 17, 2012.
2. Paul Krugman, *End This Depression Now !* (New York: W.W. Norton & Company, 2012).
3. Jeffrey Sachs, "Macroeconomic Challenges in the US, Europe and China," The Tan Sri Lim Goh Tong Memorial Public Lecture, Faculty of Business and Accountancy, University of Malaya, Kuala Lumpur, October 23, 2013.
4. Jeffrey Sachs, *The Price of Civilization—Reawakening Virtue and Prosperity after the Economic Fall* (London: Vintage Books, 2012).
5. "Generation Screwed—'Boomer America' Never Had It So Good. As a Result, Today's Young Americans Have Never Had It So Bad," *Time*, New York (July 22 and 30, 2012).
6. Paul Krugman, "Global Economic Outlook: Preventing the Next Economic Crisis." The Sim Kee Boon Institute for Financial Economics Public Lecture, Singapore Management University, Singapore, November 7, 2012.

CHAPTER 39

Life after Keynes with the Double-Dip[1]

Barack Obama was reelected US president this November. He had inherited (and managed) the Great Recession that devastated the rich economies for the greater part of 2008–2009. He still struggles over a jobless recovery (which, for most, feels like recession for all practical purposes) in the face of a double-dip recession in Europe in four years and slackening growth in the emerging world. Great crises are a reminder that we just don't know what the future brings.

John Maynard Keynes (1883–1946) never tried to conceal that he knew more than most people, according to John Kay of the *Financial Times*.[2] Yet he knew the limits of his knowledge: About these matters—the prospect of a European war, the price of copper 20 years hence—there is no scientific basis on which to form any calculable probability whatever. We simply do not know. True enough. He made these observations in 1921 and 20 years later, the United Kingdom was engaged in a desperate and bloody war with Germany and Japan. This may sound obvious but bear in mind the financial disaster in recent times was born in the hubris that financial markets are almost flawless machines that can readily manage risk and adjust, and government regulation only works to make them inefficient.

J. M. Keynes

In his book, *Keynes: The Return of the Master*, Professor Robert Skidelsky, a noted economic historian whose three-volume biography of Keynes was published in 1983, 1992, and 2000, pointed to the relevance of Keynesian economics in today's world.[3] He argues that one just can't miss the connections: (1) recent collapse of banking and credit stemmed from similar mistakes Keynes witnessed in the 1920s, and (2) government recovery stimuli worldwide reflected his precept that when confidence is shattered in private markets, the only remedy was "state intervention to promote and subsidize new investment"—necessarily by deficit spending.

According to Skidelsky, the positive factor today is that "we have Keynes's writing, so that governments needn't repeat the mistakes of early 1930s—of cutting public spending when private spending was falling." Readers tell me that they watch Stephanie Flanders's BBC TV series *Masters of Money* and come away confused; why none of the master political economists she has profiled (Keynes, Hayek, and Marx) has the answer to resolve problems plaguing the world today. All of them—in different ways—offer their own explanations of how the mess came about, but little in the way of realistic solutions. But all were in awe of Keynes—as a moral philosopher, a side of him of which most were unaware.

He had an intellectual affinity with artists—being part of the Bloomsbury Group of famous artists and writers, including Virginia Woolf, E. M. Forster, and George Bernard Shaw. He was the antithesis of the ivory-tower intellectual. His economic thinking reflected directly his own experience running a sort of proto–hedge fund speculating in currencies and commodities. His track record was mixed—he had his ups and downs like most of us. He made money in the 1920s by shorting currencies but lost heavily betting against sterling when the Bank of England raised interest rates. His Bloomsbury friends shared his varied record in managing money. He lost big in the Great Depression but made it all back in the 1930s. According to Skidelsky, his net worth was about US$20 million (in today's terms) when he died.

Free-Market Fundamentalism

Arthur Koestler once labeled communism as "the God that failed." At the other end is *free-market fundamentalism*: belief that only free financial markets—in old-fashioned banking, new-fangled investments, and free international flow of trade—could deliver steady, sustainable growth. Government's relationship with markets is supposed to be distant and supportive, not controlling. This hands-off approach spawned recent disastrous innovations, including securitized mortgages and collateralized debt obligations (CDOs), and encouraged regulators to ignore excess leveraging while central bankers watched from the sidelines as asset price bubbles grew and eventually burst. Confidence in cross-border financial freedom proved just as misguided. Conventional wisdom was that free global financial markets can efficiently absorb whatever cash trade surpluses or central banks created. That proved as valid as trust in Madoff or the unsinkable *Titanic*. Europe is now in double-dip recession, and in the United States, a jobless anemic growth. Banks and nations had to be rescued and money-men are in the doghouse. It's as though fundamentalists have been mugged by reality.

Friedrich Hayek

Nobel Laureate Friedrich Hayek, a Keynes contemporary, stated that Keynes was misguided by one central faulty idea: that general employment was always positively correlated with the aggregate demand for consumer goods. Keynes had argued that government should intervene to push aggregate demand and maintain full employment through smoothening out business cycles. During recessions, it should borrow and spend. Keynes's thinking was, of course, a decisive departure from classical economics, simply because arbitrary "macro-constructs" like aggregate demand have no basis in microeconomics of human behavior.

According to Hayek, Keynes consistently threw overboard all the traditional theory of price determination and of distribution, the backbone of economic theory, and in consequence, in my opinion, seems to have ceased to understand any economics. Bear in mind that classical economics up until then emphasized a balanced budget and restraint in fiscal spending. It is clear why Keynes's popularity endures in the US Congress. He provided "intellectual cover" for their spending spree. Indeed, Hayek viewed boom and bust as primarily a monetary phenomenon, promoted by governments' artificial creation of money and credit. According to Hayek, no one spends your money better than you spend your own.

Irving Fisher

Irving Fisher was Keynes's British contemporary; Keynes called Fisher the "great grandparent" of his own theories on how money influenced the real economy (and laid the foundation, in my view, for much of modern monetary economics). As parallels to the Great Depression multiply, Fisher is today relevant again. As it was then, the United States is now awash with debt. No matter that it is mostly "inside" debt owed by Americans to other Americans. As the underlying collateral falls in value and incomes shrink, the real burden of debt rises. Debts can go bad, weakening banks, forcing asset sales, and driving prices down further.

Fisher showed how such a spiral could turn mere busts into depressions. In 1933, he wrote: "Overinvestment and overspeculation . . . have far less serious results were they not conducted with borrowed money." As I see it, Fisher's debt deflation theory appeared to have shaped the Fed's response to the recent crisis, especially the decision to bail out Bear Stearns in March 2008 in order not to trigger a cycle of falling asset prices and default.

Unfortunately, Fisher is now almost forgotten by the public—only remembered, perhaps, for the worst stock market call in history. In October 1929, he was certain there would be no bear market, and declared that stocks had reached a "permanently high plateau." Fisher was by then a rich man but lost everything in the Depression. Yet, Fisher's 1933 essay, "The Debt Deflation Theory of Great Depressions," was avidly rediscovered, post-2008.[4] Fisher died soon after Keynes, and still remains in his shadow. Keynes's advocacy of aggressive fiscal policy overcame the limitations of Fisher's purely monetary remedies for the Depression.

Karl Marx and Milton Friedman

As for Karl Marx—well, the world did try his theory, too, and I dare say, few want to repeat the experience. Be that as it may, capitalism basically works, warts and all. Communism does not. Nobel Laureate Milton Friedman represented the odd contradiction as a free-market interventionist. A passionate advocate of small state economics, he believed governments have only a minor role in preventing (and solving) crises through manipulating money supply by following the simple monetary rule: Hold growth in money supply constant at 4 percent (or thereabouts) annually. When asked before his death in 2006 how to make the United States more prosperous, he said: "Three things—promote free trade, school choice for all children, and cut government spending."

Keynesianism

Keynes is now the name to invoke. For 25 years after his death in 1946, Keynes achieved a sort of posthumous veneration as the founder of a credible economic cult. This happened on both sides of the Atlantic and across party lines. It was Republican President Nixon who declared: "We are all Keynesians now."

But times have changed. His economics was vulnerable to debunking and, with time, to rebunking. For 30 years since the 1970s, Keynes's reputation languished. Keynesianism and its implicit warning that free markets have inherent limitations, and therefore demand regulation, remained in vogue from World War II until the mid-1970s. This was followed by its near-complete abandonment by Prime Minister Margaret Thatcher and US President Ronald Reagan in the 1980s.

Many of the problems that developed since then derived from the assumption that risk can be predicted, measured, priced, and then managed. The hallmark of Keynesianism was recognition that this efficient markets theory—the notion that markets synthesize all that is known and that needs to be known about current conditions and hence can be left to regulate themselves—is seriously flawed. Reality inevitably sets in. First comes a long period of excess in risk taking, where credit spirals out of control. This ultimately proves unsustainable, and with the resulting bust the process of credit expansion goes violently into reverse, causing catastrophic damage typically taking many years to recover.

What's unique in the current maelstrom is exploding debt. Never before has the crisis brought on such all-encompassing and rapid rise in public indebtedness to unthinkable levels. Already, three members of G-7 (world's richest nations) have debt in excess of 100 percent of gross domestic product (GDP), with Japan at more than 200 percent. Three of the remaining four are inching close by. Almost everywhere, target dates for fiscal consolidation are being pushed further into the future. Far from climbing out of the hole, Western economies are sinking ever deeper into it. Already, there is political stalemate over whether to tax more or spend less. Austerity in Europe has plunged it into a double-dip recession. It's clear governments cannot cut and grow. The United States is stuck with a fiscal cliff dilemma (a self-imposed deadline involving US$600 billion of automatic spending cuts and higher taxes early in 2013), to be followed later by another battle to raise the debt ceiling. The other Keynesian notion suppressed by free-marketers is the danger of rising income inequality. According to Skidelsky, for Keynes this phenomenon tends to promote speculation by the rich to get richer and the poor to reduce consumption—a stance for stagnation or worse. The only way for the majority to maintain their place is to borrow, with dire undesirable consequences.

The world has moved on since the 1930s when Keynes evolved his theories. As I see it, there was never a timeless Keynes. There is, instead, an adapting and evolving Keynes, who had ideas to suit all occasions. He supported President Roosevelt's New Deal measures in Depression-stricken United States in the 1930s (although he fretted that stingy Secretary Harold Ickes didn't spend enough on public works and, hence, saddled the United States with a less-than-robust recovery). His emphasis was on investment as the motor to boost effective demand to sustain employment (including stimulating consumption, when needed).

He was a pragmatist: "Practical men were often the slaves of some defunct economist," he wrote. Keynes invented a sort of macroeconomic way of thinking about the economy that we use today. True to this tradition, Nobel Laureate Joseph Stiglitz argued that Keynes believed markets are finitely not self-correcting, but also in a severe downturn, monetary policy was unlikely to be effective (Keynes worried about the liquidity trap—an inability to induce credit creation despite very low interest rates).[5] For now, Stiglitz maintains that more aggressive fiscal policy is required because of the huge overhang of household debt and high uncertainty, viz. largest possible stimulation for each dollar spent, especially to make good on past underinvestment in technology and infrastructure while assuring a constant flow of credit.

What would Keynes say today? According to Skidelsky, he would have advised the United States not to move too fast on financial reform, since recovery hinged on building trust and building business confidence. Too much reform too soon "will upset the confidence of the business world and weaken their existing motives to action," he wrote. Wait until recovery is secured. Keynes would have valued balance, which makes good sense.

What, Then, Are We to Do?

Often quoted is Keynes's "In the long run, we are all dead"—an admonition against irresponsibility of doing nothing by relying obstinately on the self-correcting power of markets. His benchmark? If the economy can expand by any such measures, do it! This justifies government action not only for short-term expediency but also in the long run. Keynes encouraged fresh approaches rather than take refuge in inert doctrinaire purity. That's the way to go.

Kuala Lumpur
December 13, 2012

Notes

1. First published on December 15, 2012.
2. John Kay, "A Wise Man Knows One Thing—the Limits of His Knowledge," *Financial Times*, London (November 30, 2011).
3. Robert Skidelsky, *Keynes: The Return of the Master* (New York: Public Affairs, 2009).
4. Irving Fisher, *The Debt Deflation Theory of Great Depressions* (East Ford, CT: Martino Publishing [Reprint], 2001).
5. Joseph Stiglitz, "Keynes Is Back but Read History Carefully," *Straits Times*, Singapore (November 22, 2012).

CHAPTER 40

Growth Dims after the "Cliff"[1]

It was a close shave. It even passed the January 31 midnight deadline. But in the end (as always with politicians), the United States avoided falling off the fiscal cliff in the new year with, again, Band-Aid half-measures. The International Monetary Fund (IMF) is right: US actions to avoid the cliff did not go far enough to address the nation's long-term fiscal deficit and debt problems. More remains to be done to put US public finances back on a sustainable path without harming the still-fragile recovery.

For Moody's, the United States needs to do much more to lift its Aaa debt rating from the current negative outlook. Of course, it did bring in the first major tax increase on high earners in 20 years. But this is not enough to provide a basis for meaningful improvement in its debt ratios over the medium term. Most economists concede that the deal will negatively impact growth and blunt efforts to create more jobs, but will likely avoid the most feared, a double-dip recession. Still, much uncertainty remains.

"Cliff" Deal

Major elements of the compromise deal included:

- Raise tax rates to 39.6 percent on income over US$400,000. For earners below this threshold, the lower 2012 tax rates will now become permanent.
- Limit the value of personal exemptions/deductions.
- Raise capital gains/dividends tax to 20 percent (from 15 percent).
- Raise the estate tax to 40 percent (from 35 percent) for assets of more than US$5 million.
- Delay US$110 billion in spending cuts for two months, including on defense.
- Lapse in payroll tax cuts (6.2 percent).

- Extending unemployment benefits for another year.
- Extending tax breaks for research and development (R&D), and for interest on student loans.

Also included in the deal were no hike in milk prices and extension of certain farm subsidies. Left out, however, were disaster-relief funds.

Overall, the upshot is a minus. US growth was already expected to be rather flat before the cliff—it will rise at about the 2012 rate in 2013—that is, 1.5 to 2 percent. This deal could shave off 1.4 percentage points in potential gross domestic product (GDP), and hold back job creation by up to 700,000. Much of the restraint reflected the rise in payroll taxes (pulling out US$113 billion in otherwise spending on consumption), in delayed spending cuts, and in higher income taxes. There is more to come.

US Debt Ceiling

Potentially, the most ominous hurdle to come is the need to raise the debt ceiling of US$16.394 trillion. As I see it, by the end of February 2013, US Treasury is likely to be unable to pay all its bills unless Congress authorizes to boost the borrowing limit. I also understand that on March 1, 2013, the across-the-board spending cuts of the fiscal cliff (now deferred) are scheduled (i.e., sequestered) to begin slicing into military and social programs. By March 27, a government shutdown looms (as it did in August 2011, to the point where the United States was on the brink of default before hammering out a last-minute deal), unless Congress approves funding government operations for the rest of the fiscal year ending September 2013.

In the wake of the recriminations and unpleasantness of the recent fiscal cliff fiasco, another nail-biting last-minute showdown looks inevitable. At risk is whether the United States has the ability to pay its bills. Already, the US president has shown a new assertiveness that he will not negotiate over the debt ceiling this time around, arguing Congress has the obligation to pay the bills for previously approved spending. A lot is at stake. Bear in mind, Standard and Poor's has placed a negative outlook on US AA+ rating, while Fitch Ratings, like Moody's, maintains an Aaa rating for the United States, with a negative outlook.

Budget Deficit

It is important to note that the deal does little to the US fiscal deficit. The nonpartisan CBO (Congressional Budget Office) had estimated in early 2011 that in order to hold its share of debt to GDP, the United States needs US$4 trillion in spending cuts and new tax revenues over the next 10 years. In August 2011, ceilings on spending were set on about one-third of federal spending in order to save US$1 trillion. That's US$3 trillion more to go. This latest deal is estimated to bring in new revenues of US$600 to US$650 billion. There are no spending cuts as yet—that's in the works. So, a big hole still remains. The federal debt stands today at 73 percent of GDP. If nothing happens, this ratio will rise by year-end to 79 percent—that's double what it was in 2000. The United States has to face the reality of higher taxes and lower social benefits down the road.

Ideological Divide

As I understand it, for Republicans the compromise cliff deal reflected a violation of the antitax orthodoxy that has defined the party. Its Senate leader has since laid out the position: The tax issue is finished, over, completed. Now the task is to tackle our spending addiction. Republicans appear to want big spending cuts, including on Medicare and Social Security pensions as a condition for raising the debt ceiling. For most Democrats, the focus must include some increases in tax revenue from tax reform (i.e., eliminating deductions and exemptions). They want a balanced approach to non-tax revenue and spending reductions. The trouble is, there is a left and a right, but without a magnet to pull them together. At this time, lurking in the background, I am afraid, is the deeper reality—there doesn't seem to be anything even approaching a consensus. In the absence of an evolving new center, there is a need for a fresh mind-set to (1) fix (reform) the tax system and (2) change entitlement programs. Trust across the aisle is really crucial for this to happen.

US Economy

Sure, the deal has avoided its worst-case scenario—it could have precipitated a recession. But consumers now have less to spend (because of higher income and payroll taxes) in the face of the welcome extension of unemployment benefits, while businesses are accorded a raft of tax breaks to encourage them to invest. The deal's net effects result in a tap on the brakes, with the economy still growing too slowly to bring down unemployment quickly. Mohamed El-Erian of PIMCO (world's largest bond fund manager) sums it up best: The deal avoids the more extreme risks of the fiscal cliff, but it doesn't enhance in any durable manner the medium-term economic outlook, nor provide a foundation for better economic governance by Congress. The US economy has been growing since mid-2009, in contrast to the dismal ways of Europe, United Kingdom, or Japan. GDP per head has not returned to the pre-recession level (and won't do so until 2014). Unemployment, at 7.8 percent, won't fall below 6 percent before 2016. The prognosis is stable but quite uncertain.

The benchmark used to discern the pace at which the economy will grow without inflation is the potential GDP. As a guide, unemployment falls 0.5 percentage point for every 1 percentage point rise in GDP above the long-term trend (2 to 2.5 percent per annum). Today, actual GDP growth lags behind potential. Fed Chief Ben Bernanke predicted that "effects of the crisis . . . should fade as the economy heals." But it also faces headwinds such as rising income inequality and eroding education competencies. Plenty of uncertainty still remains. Make no mistake. Washington is dysfunctional. Recent experience offers little prospect that US politics can accomplish anything significant in the first quarter of 2013. The upshot is painfully slow growth this year as the economy struggles to gain momentum. Corporations are holding back, fearing political fights will slacken recovery. Following an earlier slide in business confidence, consumer sentiment plummeted in December. We can expect investors, businesses, and consumers to remain on edge as the debt ceiling battle begins. Uncertainties abound, affecting markets and the economy—they make everyone edgy and cautious about spending.

Growth Update

Chapter 18, "TW3 2012: A Tough Year with a Bleak Outlook," was written before the cliff deal was struck. Since then, economies of US, China, and emerging markets have decoupled deeper from Europe where it wallows at various stages of recession and fiscal disarray. Survey data published in early 2013 point starkly to this divide. Markit has its US and China Manufacturing Purchasing Managers' Index coming in above the 50 index level (>50 indicating expansion), with US manufacturing activity in December 2012 growing at its fastest rate in seven months; growth also picked up in China as well as in Brazil.

But factory activity slowed down in the eurozone in December as new orders tumbled. It remained entrenched in a steep downturn. German activity shrank for the tenth straight month while French data fell in all but one of the past 17 months; the slump in Spain deepened. The eurozone is in a double-dip recession since 2009 and its GDP contracted again in the fourth quarter of 2012. Manufacturers look to be in for a tough 2013. The eurozone unemployment hit 11.8 percent in November 2012, with the number nudging close to 19 million—the nineteenth rise in a row; the rate for young unemployed (age 24 and below) hit 24.4 percent, the highest since records began in 1995. Spain recorded the highest unemployment (26.6 percent), worse than Greece. But for those under 25, both nations hit about 57 percent.

In the United States, the budget and debt ceiling wrangling still casts a long shadow, but so far has not dispelled the modest recovery; the US dollar has even begun to strengthen vis-à-vis the euro and yen. Asia and the BRICS (Brazil, Russia, India, China, and South Africa), especially Northeast Asia, offer their own challenges that could affect global stability. Only China has the clout to make a difference globally on its own. It is now beginning to emerge stronger. The others face a variety of challenges, ranging from inflation to inadequate FDI (foreign direct investment) inflows to labor unrest. Given strong regional rivalries and a lack of trust, problems are bound to fester, leading to complications down the road. Overall, ongoing politics, eurozone instability, fragile economies, and climate change (and rising greenhouse emissions) present a curious mix of risks and concerns. This week, extreme weather showed its ugly head as Australia grappled with destructive wildfires, and temperatures in China plunged to a 28-year low. The rising risk has to be mitigated. But, underlying it all is a growing fear that politicians will continue to fail to address fundamental problems. As a result, businesses and consumers have since become more pessimistic about the political-economic outlook. It just reflects the loss of confidence in leadership, especially over public governance. It is not surprising that for businesses and investors, severe wealth gaps, unsustainable public finances, and dangers posed by severe weather present the biggest threats confronting the world today.

What, Then, Are We to Do?

The advanced West, including the United States, has been on an unsustainable fiscal path for years. Economists at the Bank for International Settlements (the world's central banks' bank) in public discussions had predicted that unless radical reforms are adopted, the public debt of the United States, France, and Greece will reach over 400 percent of GDP by 2040, with Germany's rising above 300 percent.[2] Similarly, the ratio for Japan will be in the 600 percent range. Of course, this is merely extrapolatory.

Creditors would have stopped lending long before these levels are reached. The message is clear: The West is effectively bankrupt. The depth of the problem goes beyond Bush tax cuts, or Obama's stimulus, or European wasteful excesses, or Greek tax avoidance. Indeed, it can be traced back to the Great Depression and the rise of Keynesian macroeconomics, which, over the years, encouraged governments to spend and borrow beyond smoothing business cycles, and offered politicians a convenient way to meet electoral promises without raising taxes. The reality is that they did not get to where they are now by accident. It's deep-rooted and goes beyond technicalities. In the final analysis, policy makers and politicians need to address the "social contract" in the context of the welfare state, and the philosophy underpinning the politics and political institutional infrastructure. Basically, they have to ascertain what government should provide and how it can be restrained from overreaching. I envy the Scandinavians, as they appear to have come to terms with this fundamental issue and are happy to pay for it.

Kuala Lumpur
January 10, 2013

Notes

1. First published on January 12, 2013.
2. Bank for International Settlements (BIS), Annual Report 2012, Basel, Switzerland.

CHAPTER 41

An Inconvenient Truth: QE Withdrawal Syndrome[1]

It's done. The markets swallowed it hook, line, and sinker—it's just a matter of time to let the "food" fight it out inside. I refer to the morsel fed by Fed Chairman Ben Bernanke on May 22, 2013, when he told the US Congress: "If we see continued improvement and we have confidence that that is going to be sustained, then we could at the next few meetings take a step down in our pace of purchases." As to be expected, markets ignored the "if" and the "could" and freaked out with the usual knee-jerk reaction, as though the Fed would start winding down later in the year the QE3 easy-money policies (currently at a US$85 billion monthly clip in asset purchases) and bring them to a halt by mid-2014.

Investors fled stocks and bonds, fretting that the era of ultra-low interest rates and abundant easy central bank cash may soon end, resulting in interest rate hikes and falling bond prices. The stock markets gyrated. Markets the world over recoiled. All of this suggests that the sell-off reflected investor addiction to cheap money. As such, withdrawal is bound to be fertile and volatile. Financial markets have since calmed, their anxiety eased based on analyses from seasoned Fed watchers and assurances from the most senior Fed officials on what the Fed actually meant.

It turns out, not surprisingly, that markets simply overreacted. Indeed, Bernanke has demonstrated once again his determination to ensure that history will not accuse him of tightening policy too soon. It's quite clear now the doves are firmly in charge at the Fed. What a self-inflicted mess! Imagine the uproar when the Fed does act, as it eventually must. Now that it has happened, higher interest rates that followed are here to stay. This will make it even more difficult for the Fed to get to where it wants the labor situation to settle before it begins to taper (scale back) bond purchases. Nevertheless, rates are still abnormally low, certainly off historic lows. And, will remain low. The global economy is unlikely to grow much faster than today's sluggish pace of around 3 percent.

Current State of Play

The United States

The US economy is experiencing life of sorts. It has been growing painfully at a slow pace of 2 percent that had persisted since recession ended in 2009. The current picture is now one of "modest" (not "moderate") growth. Gross domestic product (GDP) rose at a revised subpar 1.1 percent in the first quarter of 2013 and an estimated 1.7 percent in the second quarter of 2013, suggesting that the horizon is looking brighter: Capital goods orders were up; June auto sales were the best since November 2007; housing surged; new private-sector jobs jumped; jobless rate fell to 7.4 percent, lowest since December 2008; real wages rose after a decade of falling income; and for the first time, bank credit rose to record highs (after shrinking in 2009 and 2010).

But dark clouds remain: The sequester (automatic cuts in government spending) and freeze on discretionary public spending continued to take its toll to shrink (GDP)—still, there are no signs of political course correction; then, there is also the spike in oil prices. We now begin to see the damage politicians have wreaked on pensioners and cities (e.g., Detroit)—indeed nationwide. As a result, consumption spending isn't doing too well—its 1.8 percent pace was down from 2.3 percent in the first quarter of 2013. It's not enough; the US economy will need help—just as well the Fed's QE3 program will continue to ease monetary conditions until "substantial improvement in the labor markets" brings unemployment to 6.5 percent, which is still a long way off.

Europe

Europe remains in recession. The endless fiscal austerity hasn't worked, and unemployment—especially among youth—remains a serious problem in the eurozone where the jobless rate hit 12.2 percent in May, leaving more than 19.3 million out of work. Youth unemployment is at record highs: Greece, 62 percent; Spain 56 percent; Portugal, 38 percent; Italy, 38 percent; France, 28 percent; even Germany, 7 percent.

Of late, the long-suffering eurozone may be tentatively emerging from recession: Manufacturers in Germany and France appear to be ramping-up production to meet rising demand, while the credit crunch seems to be easing, with credit to consumers becoming more available. But the upturn is slow and uneven, even fragile.

Growth in Germany is picking up, while French GDP is still contracting, but at a slower pace in the face of rising manufacturing activity. These are still early signs. The region remains vulnerable as high unemployment persists. After two years of recession, economic confidence improved for a third month in July, reflecting some optimism, especially in Germany, France, and Italy, which together account for two-thirds of the eurozone's industrial output.

Japan

Japan's Abenomics appears to be bearing fruit but still has a way to go to bring about a durable recovery. So far the pro-growth and anti-deflation policies have raised business confidence to slowly reverse 15 years of paltry growth and falling prices, using a combination of spending, easy money, and a planned overhaul of Japan's decaying economy.

It has since fired the first of Abenomics' "three arrows": installed a new central bank chief who began to flood the economy with easy money à la Fed's QE (quantitative easing) style. The second arrow using expansionary fiscal policy has only been partially fired: There is already some fiscal stimulus but still awaiting the medium-term plan to cut taxes and spending (fiscal consolidation). To keep the recovery on track, the third arrow of wide-ranging reforms has to be fired soon to include measures to raise competitiveness, bring on more women into the workforce, and deregulate the economy. So far, only modest and timid measures have been introduced. Structural reforms are critical to avert a debt crisis.

Emerging Markets

Emerging markets are taking a breather following China's slowing economic momentum. Indeed, both the International Monetary Fund (IMF) and Asian Development Bank have since marked down their growth forecasts for most developing Asian nations. In 2011, emerging Asia's GDP rose more than four times as fast as US; last year, it was almost three times as fast. This year, however, some of the shine has come off the Asia story since economic activity in China and ASEAN-5 (Indonesia, Malaysia, Philippines, Thailand, and Vietnam) has slackened significantly. The mood has yet to lift. Collectively, emerging Asia may just match last year's pace of 6.5 percent. That's the best they can do for now, considering the cost of borrowing will rise and investment capital is already migrating westward. Don't forget East Asia's 10 largest exporters' growth slowed to a halt in the second quarter of 2013, led by a 9 percent fall in exports to Europe. Exports make up 35 percent of the region's GDP. An early rebound is not in the cards for Asia.

China

China's growth, in particular, was markedly down: It was 7.7 percent in the first quarter of 2013 (against 7.9 percent in the fourth quarter of 2012), and then eased to 7.5 percent in the second quarter of 2013 (the ninth slow quarter in the past 10); for 2013 as a whole, it could be 7 percent, below the planned target of 7.5 percent.

Consider China's own analysis: "The global economy is in the middle of a major adjustment, and the domestic and international environment is highly complicated . . . we need to prepare for all kinds of complicated and difficult situations . . . (including be) on the lookout for financial risks and address the overcapacity that plagues some industries."[2] The Chinese economy rose steadily in the first half of 2013; prices were stable, and employment largely satisfactory.

According to Premier Li Keqiang, China has three bottom-line considerations: GDP, inflation, and jobs. In addition, China is concerned about the recent piling of local government debt (an estimated US$1.75 trillion at end 2010), a key source of financial worry. Its policy tactic: Macro policy should be stable, micro policy should be flexible, and social policy should support the bottom line. All of them should be coordinated. Also, China will need to coordinate the tasks on stabilizing growth, restructuring the economy, and promoting reforms.

In all, I sense it's steady as it goes into the second half of 2013. It will continue to hold back from large-scale stimulus in favor of smaller efforts, including tax exemption for small businesses; speedup of investment in railways; and maintaining a stable yuan to help exporters. I also sense its underlying to-do list will include huge social housing expansion, relaxation of the rigid (and troublesome) "hukou" household registration system, and strengthening land rights to assist farmers. So, there's still much to worry about and very much more to do.

BRICS

Brazil, Russia, India, China, and South Africa have lots of hype heaped on them, but they are not doing too well. Not unlike China, the GDP of Brazil, Russia, and South Africa will slacken to grow by barely 2.5 percent each this year. India's economy will stabilize and expand at about 4 to 5 percent (3.2 percent in 2012).

As a group, BRICS badly needs to seriously implement basic reforms to rebalance their economies and really adjust to face the new realities reflecting the passing of the commodity super-cycle—and like it or not, to also deal with the impact of tapering (scaling back) of US Fed QE3 in 2014, in addition to managing their own macroeconomic problems of inflation and overheating (and in the case of others, overcapacity and lack of demand), and external imbalances.

Tapering Is Not Tightening

There has since been a dawning realization among investors that tapering is not the same as tightening. Just because the Fed could reduce the quantum of bonds it buys, it's not the same as lifting interest rates. As I see it, bond buying is not a preset course; expectations that the Fed will opt to "taper-lite" are still very much intact. Rates will stay low, at least until the jobless rate falls to 6.5 percent or lower, as long as inflation stays tame and as head-winds continue to inconvenience the economy. According to the Fed chief: "You can only conclude that highly accommodative monetary policy for the foreseeable future is what's needed in the US economy."[3]

Nevertheless, uncertainty remains and volatility rules. Dow Jones Industrial Index fell 101 points by midday on August 6. For the market, money managers are now back on the hunt for yields. Key to this renewed appetite is the Fed's continuing accommodation to keep interest rates close to zero. There is thus a growing demand for high-income-generating stocks such as utilities, real-estate investment trusts (REITs), and energy-focused companies known as master limited partnerships (MLPs), which pay out high dividends or generate other income. Investors are focused on total return-yield plus growth. MLPs are mainly US-based companies that own and operate pipelines (mainly in oil and gas). While MLPs do trade like regular stocks, their corporate structure attracts favorable tax treatment and typically requires them to distribute most of their cash flow.

What, Then, Are We to Do?

What happened on May 22, 2013, serves an important lesson: Cheap and abundant QE monies, which can be addictive, must eventually end. It's just a question of when. All this is happening at a time of "The Great Deceleration" (*Economist*) in emerging markets. The IMF's recent studies concluded that QE3 had "more muted effects" than QE1 and QE2 on emerging markets in terms of exchange rates and systemic financial stability.[4] Indeed, capital inflows have been ample but not alarming.

Nevertheless, the still-massive flows remain of legitimate concern especially for currencies judged out-of-sync; economies at near full capacity; and nations with small, fragile capital markets. Asia's emerging economies have a proven track record of being strong enough to deal with any fallout from QE3—in or out. Today, they have the tools and ample reserves to adequately manage these capital flows, including the impact of QE3 exit. It's just a matter of whether developed nations are determined enough politically to do what it takes, especially when QEs are being used instead of more "fundamental reforms."

Summers vs. Yellen: It's a two-horse race for the next chairman of the Fed who will assume office in the throes of a likely QE3 exit: either Professor Lawrence Summers of Harvard University or Dr. Janet Yellen, the Fed's vice chair. Both are eminently qualified: Gender should not be an issue. I am acquainted with both of them.

I first met Larry in early 1990s when he was an integral part of the 1990s "Washington Consensus" (the Wall Street–Washington nexus devoted to promoting global free-capital flows). We became friends when he was appointed Harvard president in 2001, while I served as Harvard Alumni Association's Regional Director for Asia. A distinguished theoretical economist and original thinker, he can be depended on for independence of thought and ingenuity. He is not easy to pigeonhole.

I first met Janet when she was on the Harvard Economics faculty and was one of five examiners at the final round of my economics doctoral thesis defense in the fall of 1977. As a former central banker, I sense Janet will be a safe pair of hands, having been active on the Fed Board for nine years, where she is known to have displayed consistent good judgment and was always cool under fire. I am told she has this unique ability to disagree without being disagreeable.

Larry is more colorful and controversial. Close to Wall Street, he has wide experience in broad macroeconomic policy making, which is a huge plus for a Fed chairman, who is expected to get the private sector on board to help push growth and jobs. Larry's special talent is an ability to provoke, put forth fresh viewpoints on tough economic issues, and take unpopular decisions. So it's between Janet as the dependable choice and Larry as the gamble. I think Larry's "closeness" to the president can tip the scale. But Janet has the ability to really rally the team as a team at the Fed. She represents continuity of policy. I wish them well.

Kuala Lumpur
August 7, 2013

Notes

1. First published on August 10, 2013.
2. Politburo of the Chinese Community Party, in a statement on July 30, 2013, to address rising concerns about the uncertain economic outlook, Beijing, China.
3. Ben Bernanke, speaking at a conference held by the National Bureau of Economic Research on July 12, 2013, at Harvard University, Boston.
4. International Monetary Fund (IMF), a series of staff papers presented for discussion at the IMF.

CHAPTER 42

An Unnecessary Disaster Spawns Market Fears[1]

As I travel across Spain and Portugal, the focus of my concerns was on how to identify and best manage risk emanating from the great growth deceleration in emerging Asia in the face of "Abenomic" expansionary thrusts and threat of QE (quantitative easing) tapering by US Fed, which resulted in a massive withdrawal of funds from Asian markets. As I write, the threat of US fiscal impasse is once again upon us in early October 2013.

Already, US government has been shut down for 16 days, and in just another working day, US Treasury's October 17 deadline to raise the debt ceiling (US$16.7 trillion) will pass. At this late hour, US politicians are still grappling with how to reopen the shuttered government and avoid a potentially calamitous failure for the first time to service on time the nation's debt obligations. The standing of the United States (trust in the US signature) is at risk. Five years after the 2008 crisis, the debt standoff has plunged markets into uncertainty, a showdown not dissimilar to the 2011 brush with calamity.

Many readers have asked why this was allowed to happen, and asked to be better informed of the implications of such madness, which for even the most knowledgeable are just too vast and dynamic to fully fathom. Some scary views from experts: "would wreak havoc in the world economy and financial markets" (JP Morgan Chase); "would trigger failures in collateral markets" (PIMCO, world's largest bond fund manager); "would be negative, very negative for US economy and world economy" (European Central Bank); "utterly catastrophic" (Deutsche Bank); "would be at risk of tipping, yet again, into recession" (International Monetary Fund); "would be a disastrous event for the developing world, and that in turn will greatly hurt the developed economies as well" (World Bank); and "consequences for the market are dangerously unpredictable" (Sifma, a US lobby group for financial firms trading in Treasuries). How did this come about? I should explain.

Why So?

The answer can be traced to the radicalization of the US Republican Party. Senator Harry Reid (US Senate majority leader) attributes it to the emergence of a Banana Republican mind-set. I am told the core group orchestrating the impasse and fiscal standoff comprises 20 to 30 most conservative Republicans in the House of Representatives (mostly from the South, Midwest, and Plains states) who have gained strength and prominence with its ultraconservative Tea Party wing.

New York Times columnist Nicholas D. Kristof likened this group to the infamous "Gang of Four" who ruled China during the hard-time communist isolation years of the 1970s.[2] He labeled this hard-core group (and its sympathizers) "Gang of 40," who has since forced government to shut down and is now flirting with a debt default without any appreciation of its catastrophic consequences. Economics Nobel Laureate Paul Krugman outlines the group's psychological profile best by quoting from Thomas Mann and Norman Ornstein's 2012 book, *It's Even Worse Than It Looks*: "an insurgent outlier—ideologically extreme; contemptuous of the inherited social and economic policy regime; scornful of compromise; unpersuaded by conventional understanding of facts, evidence and science; and dismissive of the legitimacy of its political opposition."[3] Krugman concluded: "They are also deeply incompetent." I should add that such politicians are not unique to the United States. We do also find them all over Asia, including ASEAN and Malaysia.

Debt Armageddon

Most of US government is closed for business, first in nearly two decades. Europe has yet to fix its broken currency regime, while Japan is evolving at walking pace. China is decelerating. The other BRICS (Brazil, Russia, India, and South Africa) keep on faltering. They all don't seem to change. Yet, none of these has dimmed the resurgence of political brinksmanship in the United States. The situation could yet worsen if Congress fails to raise its borrowing limit by October 17, raising the chilling prospect of a default, starting with Treasury bills.

Alternatively, the Treasury could be forced to balance the budget abruptly (as it can no longer borrow), requiring savage spending cuts (equivalent to about 4 percent of gross domestic product [GDP]), which could send the United States (and with it, the world) into recession once more. The current situation is strange and tense. Unfortunately, it's not about the inability of the United States to pay its bills. It is self-inflicted political dysfunction that makes them unwilling to do so.

Fears for the solvency of the United States have begun to hit the market; investors again fear collateral damage. With Congress stuck in a highly partisan deadlock (with the president insisting no negotiations on the debt ceiling and Republicans insisting on defunding or delaying Obamacare—the Affordable Care Act—as a condition to break the impasse), financial markets are not pleased. The dollar has weakened and US stocks have now fallen. The Dow Jones Industrial Index rose nearly 3 percent toward the end of last week and was only marginally lower on Monday (October 14). The mood is queasy. Stock markets in Asia have been mostly resilient, with mixed performance last week. But there are already signs of investors and banks moving out of the US dollar, even as yields on short Treasuries rise. Amid anxiety over near-term finances, US debt that is due within a month has risen well above those for similar bonds that don't mature for another six months.

Given what's at stake, expectation was for a much stronger reaction. After all, Wall Street's "fear gauge" (the VIX index) has yet to react in a significant way. It's not that markets have become desensitized to political turmoil. I think investors are just lulled by previous experience of similar wrangling in 2011 and 2012, which ended in agreement. The bet is that, this time, too, sanity will eventually prevail. "A debt default cannot happen," concluded Jamie Dimon, chief executive officer and chairman of JP Morgan Chase. But there will be significant damage if it really happens.

Still, political brinksmanship is intense. It would appear neither side is prepared to default. After all, the House did vote 407–0 on October 5 to provide back pay to all furloughed federal workers once the shutdown ends. But neither side is ready to settle as yet, either. What's worrisome now is not just whether the United States would default, but also, can the United States be relied on in the future not to jeopardize the "extraordinary privilege," as a French minister once put it, of borrowing cheap in the world's most trusted currency.

The Impact

It is important to understand that the entire global financial architecture rests, to a large extent, on the US$ (as reserve currency and anchor intervention currency in global money and forex markets) and US Treasury bonds (TBs). Treasuries are important because (1) all other assets are valued relative to TBs; (2) TBs are regarded as havens—they are supposed to be riskless; (3) TBs are the most liquid (markets for them are deep and broad)—as good as cash; (4) TBs act as sterling collateral for borrowers to put up to secure short-term financing; and (5) TBs carry no "cross-default" provisions—unlike bank loans, missing a payment on TBs does not automatically place other TBs in default.

The US TBs market, with a value of US$11.6 trillion, is bigger than the government bond markets of Germany and the United Kingdom combined. The US government will reach its borrowing limit on October 17, when Congress will need to approve new borrowing to avoid running out of cash. Its budget is in deficit, equivalent to about 4 percent of GDP. Cash flow requires this financing gap to be bridged. Government has hovered just below the US$16.7 trillion limit since end-May, using various extraordinary measures to free up cash to meet payment obligations. Treasury has about US$30 billion in working cash, which would be used up in a few days.

Republicans are demanding a one-year delay (or scale-back or funding cut) of Obamacare before they agree to lift the ceiling. The president has refused to negotiate, stating that since Congress had already approved all spending, it has to honor its obligations. Setting such a precedent would be dangerous. The worst-case scenario? Default is unprecedented. It will cause investor alarm and possibly send TBs yields sharply higher, raising the cost of public debt, imperiling the tepid economic recovery, and triggering a global financial meltdown. In practice, about 30 percent of US government payments will be missed. This is most serious indeed.

There is precedent for a government shutdown. The 1995–1996 experience provides a guide for how lost government output will affect the economy. If the period is brief, it will likely shave 1.4 percentage points off the fourth quarter of 2013 GDP for a four-week shutdown. It's tiresome but manageable. If it really persists, Washington will be paralyzed, condemned to chronic uncertainty. But the fight over the legal borrowing limit is much more troublesome, since repercussions of a default are both global and unpredictable.

It is a major blow to confidence and threatens the stability of financial markets because of the role played by TBs as conduits of liquidity for the entire system. Simply put, a default would undermine investors' belief that the United States always makes good its debt. The direct impact would be a sell-off of short-term TBs (which has already started) with knock-on effects on equities and US dollar. About US$1.5 trillion of TBs are outstanding at the end of the second quarter of 2013.

The secondary impact is just as serious. TBs are the collateral of choice in both the US$2.6 trillion "bilateral-repo" market and the US$1.8 trillion "tri-party repo" market, both important sources of overnight funding. Already, some US banks would rather not take TBs maturing October 24 or 31 as collateral for loans and trades. The Hong Kong futures markets now only accept TBs with less than one-year maturity as margins for futures contracts with a discount (or haircut) of 3 percent to their value (against 1 percent previously). These are signs of losing confidence.

Frankly, damage to the economy is impossible to quantify. Quantitatively, it can really hurt. Experience of the 2011 debt-ceiling standoff near-miss provides an indication. That June, economists polled by the *Wall Street Journal* had estimated the third quarter of 2011 GDP to grow by 2.3 percent—the real outcome was 1.4 percent. This time we will have damage caused by both the shutdown and debt-ceiling standoff. Already Gallup's consumer confidence index has dropped as sharply over the past month as in 2011, which definitely hurts small business, household wealth, and stock market values, with serious ramifications for lending and economic recovery.

This time (not unlike August 2, 2011), Congress has again strayed to the edge. The further along the road the impasse goes, funding gets tighter while the need for cash grows more urgent. And the drag on the economy intensifies. After all, the third quarter of 2013 growth was only 2 percent, and inflation is so low, the economy risks collapsing into deflation. Estimating the precise impact is difficult, but economic evidence is clear about the direction of the effects: A large and persistent financial shock brings in its wake a slower economy and higher unemployment than otherwise would be the case.

Analysts talk of a 90 percent probability that there won't be a default. If there is only a 10 percent chance of default, the problem shouldn't exist at all since it's the politicians' job to compromise off small probabilities! But if it does happen, the damage would be extremely adverse.

My guess is that by the time this column is published, the debt ceiling impasse will be history. As I write, there appears to be an emerging pact in the Senate to reopen government through January 15, 2014, and permit the Treasury to borrow normally until mid-February 2014 to ease the dual crisis. Postponement is just kicking the can down the road. It just buys time. Solves nothing.

What, Then, Are We to Do?

The debt ceiling was first introduced to make it easier to finance World War I (WWI). Before 1917, each new bond issue had to be approved. Since more borrowing does look profligate, voting became partisan—voting against the president of the "other" party became orthodoxy, as Obama did against Bush. Horse trading is the order of the day in dealmaking. Nothing unusual here.

But brinksmanship has since evolved to become counterproductive, even catastrophic. The 2011 debt ceiling fight did hurt the economy. Now, Republicans intimidated (insisting to trade off Obamacare for a deal), but the president is standing firm, and so far refuses to bow to "extortion." So policy uncertainty has become no better than in WWI, and this makes investors and businesses nervous and unhappy. This episode, if it does come to pass, will derail the fragile recovery in Europe, make worse the ongoing deceleration in emerging economies, and serve to remind us that the world remains seriously connected with the American economy.

Unlike economic risks, which is hard enough but which can be analyzed, political risks like this one is really difficult to handicap. We just don't know what's going to happen. It also reminds us of the risks emanating from overdependence on a single dominant reserve currency, and the urgent need for international monetary reform.

Postscript

As expected, by the October 17 deadline, US Congress passed the bill to (1) fund government so that it can reopen until January 15, 2014, (2) extend Treasury's borrowing authority to enable it to borrow beyond its current US$16.7 trillion debt ceiling until February 7, 2014, and (3) force Congress to commence negotiations for a long-term budget with a December 13 deadline. It was signed into law on early morning October 17. Rating agency Standard & Poor's estimated that the 16-day government shutdown cost the US economy US$24 billion, shaving at least 0.6 percentage point off the fourth quarter of 2013 GDP. The Dow Jones Industrial Index rose sharply (up over 600 points) over the past week amid optimism to resolve the impasse. Asian markets opened with a sigh of relief. So, the political process cycle resumes. Uncertainty returns. No one knows what's going to happen in the spring of 2014.

Barcelona, Spain
Lisbon, Portugal
Kuala Lumpur
October 2–17, 2013

Notes

1. First published on October 19, 2013.
2. Nicholas D Kristof, "Gang of 40," *International Herald Tribune* (October 11, 2013).
3. Paul Krugman, "The Boehner Bunglers," *International Herald Tribune* (October 8, 2013).

CHAPTER 43

US Growth Deficit: Too Loose, Too Long[1]

International Monetary Fund's (IMF) latest July update downgraded its fore-casts for the global economy, which will now expand by 3.4 percent in 2014, down from 3.7 percent made in April 2014.[2] Advanced economies (AEs) continue to struggle to return to normalcy five years after the financial crisis. It also reflects the difficulties emerging and developing economies (EDEs) are facing to raise productivity to sustain growth. Most significant was the 1.1 percentage points cut in US growth where a bad winter and inventory over-hang led to a now-revised 2.1 percent contraction in the first quarter of 2014, which was made good by a robust 4 percent growth in the second quarter of 2014. Growth for 2014 is now projected at 1.7 percent, rising to an optimistic 3 percent in 2015. Both AEs and EDEs have been weaker for longer, despite prolonged periods of very low interest rates and fiscal breaks to aid recovery. What's been intriguing of late is the destabilizing cross-country conflicts, big power standoffs, and some manner of sanctions imposed in Iraq and Syria, and Ukraine and Russia, as MH 17 was shot down. They pose potential threats to energy supplies as well as globalized business links and supply chains. Yet, energy markets have barely really blinked. Crude oil prices should have been more volatile. But Brent crude hovered in the region of US$106 per barrel until this week—where it was at the beginning of this year, indeed, where it started last year and even the year before. The fear (VIX S&P 500) index even fell to a low of 10. Oil prices seem generally unimpressed.

Growth Deficit

The Fed had since slashed US growth to 2.2 percent for 2014, down from nearly 3 percent in March. That's a big cut in three months. The move reflected revision to the 1 percent contraction in the first quarter of 2014, which has since turned even worse (−2.1 percent) with the July revision. So it's not surprising that the IMF now cuts US gross domestic product (GDP) growth to 1.7 percent. It's still on the high side. Near-zero interest rates have not paid off in either faster growth or more jobs. But they led to flat incomes for Americans who don't own stocks or San Francisco town houses. And, damaged savers and fixed-income pensioners.

Productivity was also down—in the past five years, average worker's output per hour rose by less than 1.3 percent annually, against 2.3 percent average over 20 years before the recession. In the first quarter of 2014, average pay and benefits per private-sector employee was up 1.7 percent, just about flat after adjusting for inflation. According to the US Congress's Joint Economic Committee, annual GDP growth over the 19 quarters of this recovery was 2.2 percent on the average, with total growth aggregating 11.1 percent. All post-1960 recoveries had averaged 4.1 percent, with growth totaling 21.1 percent (the Reagan expansion averaged 4.9 percent; total growth being 25.6 percent). This growth deficit represents incomes lost and jobs unfulfilled.

Transatlantic Gap

Still, the United States expanded faster than Europe. Over 2011–2013, US GDP rose a total of 6 percentage points more, or 4.5 percentage points more per capita. The growth gap can be traced to the resilience of US private consumer spending, reflecting the rapid fall in household debt made possible because of (1) ease in resolving non-recourse mortgages in the United States (where subprime mortgages are foreclosed and entire debt extinguished, even if home values came up short); and (2) fast bankruptcy proceedings, which readily resolved personal bankruptcy debts (whether on full recourse mortgages or small business debts). In Europe, bankruptcies take years to resolve, with terms of discharge often still remaining onerous. So, household debts are worked off much faster in the United States for consumers to start afresh.

According to Daniel Gros (of the Brussels-based Centre for European Policy Studies), the transatlantic growth gap should not be attributed to "excessive eurozone austerity or the excessive prudence of the European Central Bank. There are structural reasons,"[3] including cumbersome legal constraints that shackle debtors for years. Reform in Europe is long overdue.

Messy Jobs Status

US jobs jumped significantly at the end of the first half of 2014 and unemployment closed on a six-year low at 6.1 percent. Employment has now risen above a 200,000-pace for six straight months for the first time since the late 1990s. Americans out of work for more than six months—that is, long-term unemployed (LTU)—fell to 3.1 million (or about one-third of total unemployed) at end-June 2014, the smallest pool since February 2009. Labor force participation (LFP) rate (i.e., share of working-age Americans who are employed and those actively looking for work) was a steady 62.8 percent, a low struck in December (down from 66 percent in 2008).

Although job growth is headed in the right direction, the labor situation remains basically weak: (1) only 48 percent of adults are working full-time; (2) 2.4 million Americans have given up and dropped out of the workforce; (3) involuntary part-timers swelled to 7.5 million, against 4.4 million in 2007; (4) number of LTUs is still too high and the LFP rate, too low; and (5) nearly 91 million over age 16 aren't working. So, overall labor conditions have remained awkward. Since mid-2007, US population had risen by 17.2 million; the economy is still 10 million jobs shy of where they should be.

Why is this so? Because:

- More than 24 million working-age Americans are jobless, working part-time, or having left the workforce.
- Labor's share of national income has fallen to less than 60 percent (compared to 65 percent in 1980).
- There is insufficient capital renewal.
- The United States is going through the weakest post-recession recovery, with growth at half of what it was after four previous recessions.
- The US national job-machine is spluttering.

According to Harvard's Lawrence Summers, in 10 years, one in seven Americans (age 25 to 54) won't be working.[4] This poses a formidable challenge.

Return of Inflation

Inflation is back on Wall Street's agenda. Consumer prices rose 2.1 percent in May, the highest since October 2012. If inflation returns and stays, it could signal a stronger economy, which should be good for stocks and jobs. But it could also end the long bond rally that has kept prices up so far (and yields down). Further, it could also mean interest rates can rise earlier than expected, which is bad for home buyers, businesses, and holders of low-yielding bonds.

So far, the Fed is playing it cool. Chairperson Janet Yellen had indicated that the key benchmark of labor market tightening will be when wages rise. So far, that hasn't happened. But my Harvard teacher and mentor, Martin Feldstein, thinks the Fed is not being proactive enough. He contends that inflation is rising and can become a serious problem sooner than the Fed now recognizes, for three reasons: (1) prices are starting to pick up; (2) the low short-term unemployment (STU) rate is beginning to create wage and price pressure; and (3) as inflation exceeds 2 percent, the Fed may not be able to respond aggressively enough to contain it.[5] Indeed, the Fed is already cutting it too fine, risking falling behind the curve and misinterpreting the labor market slack, as inflation gathers steam.

What, Then, Are We to Do?

Global growth is slackening. Stubborn persistence of LTU is the defining feature of the post–financial crisis US economy. While STU has returned to pre-recession level of about 4 percent, it is the elevated LTU that has kept the overall jobless rate well above the 5.5 to 6 percent level. As I see it, LTU is the United States' number-one cyclical economic challenge: Policy needs to ensure it won't become structural or a sclerosis. The only way out is faster growth.

Technological shifts and globalization have left many US workers unfit for high-skilled jobs of the twenty-first century. These Americans—trapped in extended joblessness—will limit the nation's growth potential, strain its welfare resources, and create a dilemma for the Fed. For Chairperson Janet Yellen, wages could start rising among the STU, lifting inflation and forcing the Fed to raise rates earlier than it would wish.[6] For now, the Fed feels confident the job market still has significant slack for it to hold onto its near-zero rates until next year. The Fed rightly sees no immediate pressure from the wage-price spiral.

Furthermore, US banks are sitting on thick cushions of capital and liquidity. Any financial excesses can be better dealt with by using "macroprudential tools" (i.e., regulations designed to address specific imbalances, including imposing stiffer standards). Frankly, I think they are oversold. As of now, the Fed prefers them as a better first line of defense against bubbles than the blunt raising of interest rates. Better not to unsettle the recovery that has been so carefully nurtured thus far. However, this could prove too little, too late. My sense is that the Fed should err on the side of overprotecting against inflation, since Congress can't be relied on anymore to act proactively on the fiscal front to help do the job. Overall, the Fed could do better in growth and jobs by releasing the zero-bound rates, which are distorting decisions by the private sector on the efficient allocation of capital. It's time to let go.

Kuala Lumpur
August 6, 2014

Notes

1. First published on August 9, 2014.
2. International Monetary Fund (IMF), *World Economic Outlook Update: An Uneven Global Recovery Continues* (Washington, DC: World Bank, July 2014).
3. Daniel Gros, "The Transatlantic Growth Gap," *The Edge*, Kuala Lumpur (July 28, 2014).
4. Lawrence Summers, "The Economic Challenge: Creating Jobs," *Asian Wall Street Journal* (July 8, 2014).
5. Martin Feldstein, "Warning: Inflation Is Running Above 2%," *Asian Wall Street Journal*, Hong Kong (June 12, 2014).
6. Janet Yellen, chair, Federal Reserve Bank System, in a statement following its two-day board meeting on July 30, 2014, in Washington, DC.

The European Union and Eurozone: More Austerity

CHAPTER 44

Dark Clouds over Europe and the United States[1]

Within the past couple of weeks since mid-2011, the world has changed. From a world so used to the United States playing a key leadership role in shaping global economic affairs to one now going through a multi-speed recovery, with the emerging nations providing the main source of growth and opportunity. This is a very rapid change indeed in historical time. What happened?

First, the convergence of a series of events in Europe (contagion of the open-ended debt crisis jolted France and spread to Italy and Spain, forcing the European Central Bank [ECB] to buy their bonds) and in the United States (last-minute lifting of the debt ceiling in early 2011 exposed the dysfunctional US political system, and the Standard & Poor's [S&P] downgrade of the US credit rating) has led to a loss of confidence by markets across the Atlantic in the effectiveness of the political leadership in resolving key problems confronting the developed world.

Second, these events, combined with the coming together of poor economic outcomes involving the fragilities of recovery, have pushed the world into what the president of the World Bank called "a new danger zone," with no fresh solutions in sight.[2] Growth in leading world economies slowed for the fourth consecutive quarter, gaining just 0.2 percent in the second quarter of 2011 (0.3 percent in the first quarter of 2011) according to the Organisation for Economic Co-operation and Development (OECD). The slowdown was most marked in the euro-area: Germany slackened to 0.3 percent in the second quarter of 2011 (1.3 percent in the first quarter of 2011) and France stalled at zero after growing at 0.9 percent in the first quarter of 2011. The United States picked up to 0.3 percent (0.1 percent in the first quarter of 2011), while Japan contracted 0.3 percent in the second quarter of 2011 (−0.9 percent in the first quarter of 2011).

The Eurozone Stumbles

Looming large as a risk factor is Europe's long-running sovereign debt saga, which is pummeling US and European financial markets and business confidence. So far, Europe's woes and the market turmoil it stirred are worrisome. The S&P 500 fell close to 5 percent in the week ended August 20, extending losses of 15.4 percent over the previous three weeks, its worst streak of that length in 2½ years, and down 17.6 percent from its 2011 high. The situation in Europe has been dictating much of the global markets' recent movements. The eurozone's dominant service sector was effectively stagnant in August after two years of growth, while manufacturing activity, which drove much of the recovery in the bloc, shrank for the first time since September 2009.

Latest indicators add to signs the slowdown is spreading beyond the periphery and taking root in its core members, including Germany. The Flash Markit Eurozone Services Purchasing Managers' Index (PMI) fell to 51.5 in August (51.6 in July), its lowest level since September 2009. The PMI, which measures activity ranging from restaurants to banks, is still above "50," the mark dividing growth from contraction. However, PMI for manufacturing slid to 49.7—the first sub-50 reading since September 2009. Both services and manufacturing are struggling. Going forward, poor data show neither Germany nor France (together making up one-half the bloc's gross domestic product [GDP]) is going to be the locomotive. Indeed, the risks of "pushing" the region over the edge are significant. Germany faces an obvious slowdown and a possible lengthy stagnation.

European financial markets just came off a turbulent two weeks, with investors fearing the debt crisis could spread further if Europe's policy makers failed to implement institutional change and new structural supports for the currency bloc's finances. In the interim, the ECB has been picking up Italian and Spanish bonds to keep borrowing costs from soaring. The action has worked so far, but the ECB is only buying time and can't support markets indefinitely. So far, the rescue bill included €365 billion in official loans to Greece, Portugal, and Ireland; the creation of a €440 billion euro rescue fund; and €96 billion in bond buying by the ECB. Despite this, market volatility and uncertainty prevail. Europe is being forced into an endgame with three possible outcomes: (1) disorderly breakup—possible if the peripherals fail in their fiscal reform or can no longer withstand stagnation arising from austerity; (2) greater fiscal union in return for strict national fiscal discipline; and (3) creation of a more compact and more economically coherent eurozone against contagion. This implies some weaker members will take a "sabbatical" from the euro.

My own sense is that the endgame will be neither simple nor orderly. Politicians will likely opt for a weak variant of fiscal union. After more pain, a smaller and more robust euro could emerge and avoid the euro's demise. Nobel Laureate Professor Paul Krugman gives a "50 percent chance Greece would leave and 10 percent odds of Italy following."[3]

The United States Slides

Recent data disclosures and revisions showed that the 2008 recession was deeper than first thought, and the subsequent recovery flatter. The outcome: GDP has yet to regain its pre-recession peak. Worse, the feeble recovery appears to be petering out. Over the past year, US output has grown a mere 1.6 percent, well below what most economists consider to be the United States' underlying growth rate, a pace that has been in the past almost always followed by recession. Over the past six months, the United States has managed to eke out an annualized growth of only 0.8 percent.

This was completely unexpected. For months, the Fed had dismissed the economy's poor performance as a transitory reaction to Japan's natural disaster and oil price increases driven by the Middle East turmoil. They now admit much stiffer headwinds are restraining the recovery, enough to keep growth painfully slow. Recent sentiment surveys and business activity indicators are consistent with expectations of a marked slowdown in US growth. Fiscal austerity will now prove to be a drag on growth for years. Housing isn't coming back quickly. Households are still trying to rid themselves of debt in the face of eroding wealth. Old relationships that used to drive recoveries seem unlikely to have the pull they used to have. Historically, consumers' confidence had tended to rebound after unemployment peaked. This time, it didn't happen. Unemployment peaked in October 2009 at 10.1 percent but confidence kept on sinking. The University of Michigan's index fell in early August 2011 to its lowest level since 1980. Thrown in is concern about the impact of the wild stock market on consumer spending. Indeed, equity volatility is having a negative impact on consumer psychology at a time of already weakening spending.

Three main reasons underlie why the Fed made the recent commitment to keep short-term interest rates near zero through mid-2013: (1) cuts all around to US growth forecasts for the second half of 2011 and 2012; (2) drop in oil and commodity prices, plus lower expectations on the pace of recovery, which led to growing confidence inflation will stabilize; and (3) rise in downside risks to growth in the face of deep concern about Europe's ability to resolve its sovereign debt problems. The Fed's intention is at least to keep financial conditions easy for the next 18 months. Also, it helps to ensure the slowly growing economy would not lapse into recession, even though it's already too close to the line; any shock could knock it into negative territory.

Productivity: The Critical Key

Productivity in the United States has been weakening. In the second quarter of 2011, nonfarm business labor productivity fell 0.3 percent, the second straight quarterly drop. It rose only 0.8 percent from the second quarter of 2010. Over the past year, hourly wages have risen faster than productivity. This keeps the labor market sluggish and threatens potential recovery. It also means an erosion of living standards over the long haul. But, these numbers overstate productivity growth because of four factors:

1. Upward-bias in the data—for example, the United States spends the most on health care per capita in the world, yet without superior outcomes.
2. Government spending on military and domestic security has risen sharply, yet it doesn't deliver useful goods and services that raise living standards.
3. Labor force participation has fallen for years. Taking lower-paying jobs out of the mix raises productivity but does not create higher value-added jobs.
4. Off-shoring by US companies, to China, for example, doesn't enhance American productivity.

Overall, they just overstate productivity. So, the United States, like Europe, needs to actually raise productivity at the ground level if they are to really grow and reduce debt over the long-term. The next wave of innovation will probably rely on the world's current pool of scientific leaders—most of whom are still US-based.

US Deficit Is Too Large

The US budget deficit is now 9.1 percent of GDP. That's high by any standard. According to the impartial US Congressional Budget Office (CBO), even after returning to full employment, the deficit will remain so large its debt-to-GDP will rise to 190 percent by 2035! What happened? This deficit was 3.2 percent in 2008; it rose to 8.9 percent in 2010, pushing the debt/GDP ratio from 40 percent to 62 percent in 2010.

This 5.7 percent of GDP rise in the deficit came about because of (1) a fall of 2.6 percent of GDP in revenue (from 17.5 percent to 14.9 percent of GDP), and (2) a rise of 3.1 percent of GDP in spending (from 20.7 percent to 23.8 percent of GDP). According to the CBO, less than one-half of the rise in the deficit was caused by the downturn of 2008–2010.

Because of this cyclical decline, revenue collections were lower and outlays higher (due to higher unemployment benefits and transfers to help those adversely affected). They, in turn, raise total demand and, thus, help to stabilize the economy. These are called "automatic stabilizers." In addition, the budget deficit also worsened because, even at full-employment, revenues would still fall and spending rise. So, the Great Recession did its damage.

Looking ahead, the Obama administration's budget proposals would add (according to CBO) US$3.8 trillion to the national debt between 2010 and 2020. This would raise the debt/GDP ratio to 90 percent, reflecting limited higher spending, weaker revenues from middle and lower income taxpayers, offset in part by higher taxes on the rich. Even so, these are based on conservative assumptions regarding military spending, no new programs, and lower discretionary spending in "real" terms. No doubt, actual fiscal consolidation would imply much more spending cuts and higher revenues.

According to Harvard's Professor Martin Feldstein, increased revenues can only come about, without raising marginal tax rates, through what he calls cuts in "tax expenditures," that is, reforming tax deductions (e.g., cutting farm subsidies, and eliminating deductions for ethanol production). Such a "balanced approach" to resolve the growing fiscal deficit will be hard to come by given the political paralysis in Washington, DC. Worse, the poisonous politics of the past two months has created a new sort of uncertainty. The Tea Partiers' (Tea Party) refusal to compromise can, at worse, kill off the recovery.

The only institution with power to avert danger is the Fed. But printing money can be counterproductive. Fiscal measures are the preferred way to go at this time. Even so, US fiscal problems will mount beyond 2020 because of the rising cost of Social Security and Medicare benefits. No doubt, fundamental reform is still needed for the long-term health of the US economy.

What, Then, Are We to Do?

The crisis we now face is one of confidence, starting with the markets across both sides of the Atlantic and in Japan. This lack of confidence reflected an accumulation of discouraging news, including feeble economic data in the United States and Europe, and signs that European banks are not so stable. The global rout seems to have its roots in free-floating anxiety about US dysfunctional politics and about euro-land's economic and financial stability. Confidence is indeed shaky, already spreading to businesses and consumers, raising risks any fresh shock could be enough to push US and European economies into recession. Business optimism, at best, is "softish." Consumers are still deleveraging—that is, unwinding their debts. Unfortunately, this general lack of confidence in global economic prospects could become a self-fulfilling prophecy.

In the end, it's all about politics. The French philosopher Blaise Pascal contends (wisely, I think) that politics have incentives that economics cannot understand. To act, politicians need consensus, which often does not emerge until the costs of inaction become highly visible. By then, it is often too late to avoid a much worse outcome. So, the demand for global leadership has never been greater. But, none is forthcoming—not for the United States, not from Europe, certainly not from Germany and France, or Britain. The world is adrift. Unfortunately, it will continue to drift in the coming months, even years. Voters on both sides of the Atlantic need to demand more from their leaders than "continued austerity on autopilot." After all, in politics, leadership is the art of making the impossible possible.

Kuala Lumpur
August 26, 2011

Notes

1. First published on August 27, 2011, as "Dark Clouds over US and Europe."
2. Robert Zoellick, speaking at the Asia Society in Sydney, Australia, on August 15, 2011.
3. Paul Krugman, at an interview in Stockholm, Sweden, on August 18, 2011.

CHAPTER 45

ECB and Fed Clear Way to Act[1]

August was a good month for stock markets despite "sell in May and go away": US equity prices rose by 4 percent; European markets were up even more—6 percent, quite at odds with economic fundamentals. Traditionally, September marks the end of summer holidays, expecting to kick off activity to high gear. But the coming days and weeks will be bristling with events, including decision time for the Federal Reserve Bank (Fed) and the European Central Bank (ECB).

As I write, the ECB's governing council is set to meet on September 6 to decide on details underlying its president's statement last July that the euro was irreversible and the ECB is "ready to do whatever it takes to preserve the euro. And believe me, it will be enough,"[2] words which encouraged the latest rally. The euro rose more than 4 percent as investors gained confidence that ECB would rescue troubled eurozone economies, and would soon start buying Spanish and Italian bonds, where nations have seen borrowing costs rise to become unsustainable. At the same time, investors have also weighed in to possible bond buying (expecting more quantitative easing—QE3) by the Fed, ahead of its policy meeting, which concludes on September 13. In the event both central banks decide to ease, the euro–US dollar exchange rate would move to reflect which central bank is perceived in the market as more aggressive. This has already set the options market moving.

Weakness Dogs the World

Latest estimates point to a weakening global economy rising at an annualized rate of 2.8 percent in the second quarter of 2012—slowest pace since end-2009. Economies are now slackening in sync. It's perturbing as the weakness spreads more widely and deeply, affecting rich nations as well as most emerging economies.

The European Union

At the epicenter is the eurozone, where gross domestic product (GDP) shrank at an annualized 0.7 percent in the second quarter of 2012, leaving the area's GDP value 0.4 percent smaller than a year earlier. Latest indications point to it sliding ever deeper into the abyss. The Markit gauge of eurowide manufacturing activity remains firmly in decline, holding for 13 months below "50," indicating contraction.

European manufacturers are feeling the impact of the crisis and the tough austerity that has undermined exports, consumer demand, and investor sentiment. Eurozone business and consumer confidence fell to a three-year low and inflation accelerated to 2.6 percent in August. Jobless rate remained in July at a record 11.3 percent (more than 18 million are unemployed). They will act to drag the zone back into recession with a further fall expected in GDP in the third quarter of 2012. Moody's has since downgraded the European Union's (EU) Aaa rating outlook to negative: reflecting a deterioration in the creditworthiness of EU member states.

Activity in Spain and Italy, already in recession, fell again in August. The bright spark has always been Germany's continuing strength. Its economy, which accounts for a quarter of the eurozone's GDP, rose by 0.3 percent in the second quarter of 2012 but its light is dimming. German business activity in August fell at its fastest clip in over three years. The outlook is for Germany possibly even falling into a technical recession in late 2012. France is not faring any better. Its GDP was flat in the second quarter of 2012, the third quarter without growth. Unemployment has risen to three million, the highest in 13 years. Looks like the "French dream," which the new president promised to reawaken, is fast becoming an illusion. Together, the EU's two largest nations account for more than one-half of the eurozone's GDP, which the ECB now expects to fall 0.4 percent in 2012. The dire situation in the EU will add pressure on the ECB to help shore-up economic conditions with more aggressive monetary easing.

Japan

The eurozone's troubles are also hurting other rich nations. Stepped up rebuilding construction works raised Japanese GDP by 5.5 percent in the first quarter of 2012 but it slackened to 1.4 percent in the second quarter of 2012. Exports to EU fell by 25 percent in the year ended July 2012.

The outlook for exports is downbeat. Prospects are for Japan to slow down significantly, reflecting poor global demand and soft consumer spending. Japan continues to struggle to adjust to a strong yen and weak exports. Manufacturing activity contracted in August, hovering at its lowest in 16 months, a sign that the economy could contract in the third quarter of 2012.

The United States

Across the Atlantic, the United States is doing somewhat better, with the second quarter of 2012 GDP rising 1.7 percent, against 2 percent in the first quarter of 2012 and 4.1 percent in the fourth quarter of 2011. But overall growth has been tepid, with a stagnant labor market. Unemployment has exceeded 8 percent since February 2009. Manufacturing, a pillar of growth in early recovery, is fast losing steam as global demand softens and family budgets remain strained. Signs of housing picking up are modest. Activity in the services sector, however, stabilized in August. Economists point to a slight pickup in growth to 1.8 percent in the third quarter of 2012 and 2.1 percent in the fourth quarter of 2012. Growth isn't strong enough to reduce unemployment substantially; most expect it to settle at 8.1 percent by end-2012.

Furthermore, there are risks from the political stalemate over the looming "fiscal cliff" (by January 1, 2013, a series of tax cuts will expire along with the temporary payroll tax; at the same time, "sequestration" kicks in to cut spending across the board), which would shrink the budget deficit to 4 percent of GDP (from 7.3 percent now). While helping to regain its fiscal footing, the impact of "falling off the cliff" can be severe: The bipartisan US Congressional Budget Office estimated that GDP would shrink 2.9 percent in the first half of 2013. The election is expected to break the political logjam but there is no guarantee—anything can happen, including an inconclusive mixed verdict.

BRICS

The impact on emerging nations has been contagious. Among the BRICS (Brazil, Russia, India, China, and South Africa), Brazil struggles to revive its once-booming growth; GDP rose by 1.6 percent in the second quarter of 2012 (0.4 percent in the first quarter of 2012). For the year, GDP growth will be still anemic (just 2 percent). As new stimulus measures kick in, in the face of a nation gearing up to host the 2014 World Cup and 2016 Olympics, growth will pick up toward year-end. But a wider slowdown in Latin America is underway as Chinese demand for commodities continues to slacken.

China

There is a broader slowdown of growth in China and elsewhere in Asia. Chinese GDP rose by 7.6 percent in the second quarter of 2012 (down from 8.1 percent in the first quarter of 2012), the slowest since the financial crisis. Index of manufacturing activity recorded its largest drop in nine months, hit in August by a steep fall in export orders reflecting slowing demand in Europe and the United States, and dragged down by stagnant real estate investment and inability of consumption to absorb the slack. Industrial production rose only 9.2 percent in the year ended July 2012 (up 14 percent a year ago). Shanghai stock market fell to a three-year low.

On a more positive note, consumption did rise in the first half of 2012 to account for 57 percent of GDP growth, while the share of investment growth fell, suggesting some progress in rebalancing the economy. Expectations are for growth to pick up in the second half of 2012 to reach 8 percent for 2012 as a whole, but this will require stronger stimulus, including more aggressive monetary and fiscal policy easing. Indeed, there is growing pressure to do more in support as China embarks on a once-a-decade leadership change.

Other Asia

Slowdown in China—a key driver in Asian growth—has had a knock-on effect around the region, with Australia (a major supplier of energy commodities) heavily impacted. Manufacturing in South Korea, Taiwan, and Vietnam, whose exports have been hit hard by weakening foreign demand, continued to shrink in August. In India and Indonesia, manufacturing had continued to expand but at a slackening pace, again reflecting falling global demand (including China). The Indian economy rose 5.5 percent in the second quarter of 2012, languishing at around its lowest in three years, with manufacturing now at a near standstill. However, the Bombay stock exchange (Sensex) is up 14 percent so far this year, and private consumption (68 percent of GDP) remains resilient—keeps the economy humming along. Overall, the outlook for Asia does not look too good. This raises pressure on governments to step up efforts to support growth.

Draghi's Dilemma

Many regard the ECB as euro's ultimate protector—it has the firepower to act decisively and the independence to do so. But there's a wrinkle—the Bundesbank (German central bank) is against bond buying because (1) it's illegal (the ECB is banned from financing governments); (2) it makes the euro a soft currency area with high inflation; and (3) it can become addictive, like a drug. ECB president Mario Draghi understands this well. He also knows the Germans don't have the votes. But, they can make life hard for him. So, in August, he set strict conditions for this purpose:

- Nations seeking help should first apply to the bailout fund.
- They should commit to reforms.
- Bailout fund should buy only long-term bonds at primary issue, to bring down borrowing cost.

Only then would the ECB deploy its firepower to buy short one- to three-year sovereign bonds in secondary markets without limit, similar to conventional open market operations. But there can be no monetary impact as purchases will be sterilized (offset in full by taking an equal amount out of circulation). No printing of money.

There are risks: Bonds purchased could be of a nation that eventually exits the euro, and Germany's constitutional court could outlaw its bailout fund on September 12. Be that as it may, in practice, the ECB acts always as a balance between its power to print money and its narrow legal mandate, between its independence and the need for political expediency. This dilemma requires unique leadership skills to resolve.

Bernanke's Barrel Roll

US Fed Chairman Ben Bernanke is feeling the pressure from both sides as he maneuvers his course of action consistent with the direction of flight. Many say he should just stand pat after cutting short-term interest rates to near barebones and buying more than US$2 trillion of long-term bonds since the crisis. However, just as many say he should be proactive and be more aggressive—his job is not yet done in the face of hardly any inflation at a time of continuing high unemployment.

In his highly anticipated speech at Jackson Hole (Wyoming) last Friday (September 7), Bernanke defended the unconventional policies (UCP) the Fed undertook since 2008, arguing that they bolstered growth while reducing the risk of deflation. Fed working models showed these UCP helped raise output 3 percent higher and created two million new jobs. Even so, current unemployment at 8.3 percent is at least 2 percentage points higher than that "deemed" should have been. This is of concern because: (1) the Fed's mandate is to keep unemployment as low as possible; (2) it brings great human suffering and incurs much human resource waste; and (3) persistent unemployment wreaks lasting damage onto the economy. From this perspective, there is some urgency for additional economic support.

Bernanke concluded:

> *Now, with several years of experience with non-traditional policies both in the United States and in other advanced economies, we know more about how such policies work. It seems clear, based on this experience, that such policies can be effective, and that, in their absence, the 2007–2009 recession would have been deeper and the current recovery would have been slower than has actually occurred. As we assess the benefits and costs of alternative policy approaches, ... Taking due*

account of the uncertainties and limits of its policy tools, the Federal Reserve will provide additional policy accommodation as needed to promote a stronger economic recovery and sustained improvements in labor market conditions.[3]

The underlying problem facing the United States is still too-slow growth, brought about by too-weak demand. It's not a jobless recovery; it's simply no recovery!

Nevertheless, it is still puzzling to me why after four years of super-low interest rates and extraordinarily large money pumping, the Fed hadn't achieved more to spur the slow-moving economy. What's holding the economy back that the Fed can't fix? As I see it, key problems to its effectiveness lie in (1) households, being burdened with huge debt, aren't responding to low interest rates as an incentive to spend; (2) the lack of demand, which is causing the high unemployment; and (3) skills mismatch, which can't be resolved with easy and cheap money.

What, Then, Are We to Do?

The world is in a bad shape. Lack of demand and lack of confidence remain the key problems. Leaders have to fix them. It's true the ECB won't be able to fix the euro, which is essentially a political problem; but it can buy time for politicians to introduce reforms. Bernanke is stuck with political gridlock and a coming presidential election.

As I read it, the crises in Europe and the United States have to get far worse before politicians feel they are painted into a corner and have no choice but to take radical action. Before then, either they can't or they won't. In the meantime, Draghi and Bernanke must act to stabilize the situation and buy time. You can only do so much. Like it or not, that's life!

Kuala Lumpur
September 6, 2012

Notes

1. First published on September 8, 2012, as "FED & ECB Clear Way to Act."
2. Mario Draghi, speaking at a Conference in London on July 27, 2012, one week ahead of the European Central Bank's next policy meeting.
3. Ben Bernanke, in a speech in Jackson Hole, Wyoming, organized by the Federal Reserve Bank of Kansas City on September 7, 2012.

CHAPTER 46

Eurozone Growth Can't Move beyond First Gear but Needs to Keep Deflation at Bay[1]

Not unlike most forecasters (including World Bank, Asian Development Bank, Organisation for Economic Co-operation and Development, and US Fed), the International Monetary Fund's (IMF) midyear update tells the same story of consistent overestimations since 2009, in a long line of serial misjudgments.[2] It blames unanticipated factors for the inaccuracies, never its outdated models. For now: Global growth is expected to rebound from the second quarter of 2014 to register a marked-down rise of 3.4 percent for 2014 as a whole; projection for 2015 remains at 4 percent. Similarly, growth in the eurozone is "expected to strengthen to 1.1 percent in 2014 and 1.5 percent in 2015."[3] Still too optimistic, I feel, given the prospective conditions. Today, we know better.

Definite Weakening

As I write, evidence is building that the conflict in Ukraine and the US/European Union (EU) sanctions and Russia's countersanctions are undermining the eurozone/EU recovery that President Mario Draghi of the European Central Bank (ECB) has already judged to be fragile at best. Chronically deficient demand is definitely holding back EU growth. A clear sign came on August 6, 2014, when the Italian economy fell back into recession, with gross domestic product (GDP) down by 0.2 percent in the second quarter of 2014 (–0.1 percent in the first quarter of 2014). Seriously, Italy never emerged from recession in practice—in the past 12 quarters, it had only one real growth quarter. The economy is today more than 9 percent below its pre-crisis peak, and when adjusted for inflation, its GDP is of the same size as it was in 2000. Italian youth unemployment now exceeds 40 percent and its sovereign debt, 133 percent of end-2013 GDP.

Last week, EuroStat signaled that eurozone GDP was flat in the second quarter of 2014 (+0.8 percent in the first quarter of 2014) and remains at 2.4 percent below its pre-crisis peak, leaving it vulnerable to outside shocks. In Germany—the EU's strongest economy—GDP shrank 0.2 percent from the first quarter of 2014; business confidence is dropping for the third straight month; the DAX share index is down 9.3 percent from its July 3 record high; and inflation stands at a low 0.8 percent. Moreover, France's economy stagnated for a second straight quarter, with manufacturing activity contracting at the fastest pace so far this year. The eurozone's three largest economies, accounting for two-thirds of the region's €9.6 trillion GDP, are among the worst performing. Indeed, unemployment was held at 11.5 percent in June, still close to the record high. So, growth in Europe continues to struggle to gain momentum. Also, Greece, Ireland, Portugal and Spain will have a difficult enough time keeping their heads above water; add deflation to the outlook, and Europe is in for a real tough time ahead.

Indeed, it still remains unclear to me whether the eurozone really did emerge from recession, despite experiencing four consecutive quarters of growth, albeit these have been weak and uneven and accompanied by only a slight improvement in jobs. The Euro Area Business Cycle Dating Committee of the Centre for Economic Policy Research has intimated that the eurozone may be just in a "recession pause," and warned that the contraction that first began in late 2011 may well resume. This Committee officially dates the "peaks and troughs" of economic activity in the same way as the US National Bureau of Economic Research's Business Cycle Dating Committee, placing more weight on job outcomes. It is noteworthy that the Committee's judgment has since prompted the ECB to introduce a package of measures on June 5, aimed at boosting growth and inflation. It would now appear that these stimuli might be too timid since the situation has worsened. Most economists think that the ECB's case for QEII (second round of quantitative easing) has now become more compelling.

"Lowflation" to Deflation

Latest data suggest inflationary pressures in the eurozone remain subdued. Inflation is falling in the year to July (0.4 percent), the lowest in more than four years. It had fallen to 0.5 percent in May and June from 0.7 percent in April, taking it further below the ECB's target of close to 2 percent. As I understand it from my euro-friends, the ECB's most recent projections have inflation undershooting this rate even at the end of 2016! Further, in early

August 2014, Germany's 10-year breakeven rate (a measure of inflationary expectations) fell to 1.27 percent, the lowest since 2012.

To be fair, core inflation (i.e., excluding food and energy prices) is no longer falling. But, at 0.8 percent in July, even this measure is still far too low. Besides, the conflict in Ukraine and the Gaza/Israel and Syria–Iraq wars are undermining recovery. Their impact is causing concerns among large European firms (including Anheuser-Busch Inbev NV and Siemens AG). The turmoil is beginning to hurt business and making Draghi's life increasingly more uncomfortable.

The June 5 stimulative measures (bringing lending rate down to a new low of just 0.15 percent, moving to negative deposits rates at the ECB, and extending cheap long-term refinancing to boost targeted bank lending) now appears to be "too little, too late."[4] So far, they don't really amount to much. The IMF's Christine Lagarde speaks of deflation as an ogre that must be fought decisively.

At this time, with recovery so very fragile and the macroeconomic situation so fluid, the major worry has been the possibility of a plunge to deflation, or falling prices—a serious twist that acts to deter consumers and businesses from spending, with the expectation that they can wait for prices to fall further and buy more cheaply later. This would bring down demand and make businesses postpone investment outlays, thereby hurting jobs and setting in motion a vicious cycle that can choke-off growth. History has shown that it is notoriously difficult to reverse deflation once the spiral takes hold (Japan is a living example). "Lowflation" is already hurting eurozone debtors since incomes are rising more slowly (if any) than expected when they first borrowed. As this mutates into deflation, the real burden of debtors rises when prices fall. Overall effects are particularly pernicious in the eurozone where private and public debt levels in most nations are perilously high.

QE as Last Resort

The case for quantitative easing (QE) now in the eurozone is especially compelling. QE—creating money by the central bank to buy financial assets to spread the monies around—is already orthodox practice. It's being used in the United States and Japan and the United Kingdom (until 2012). Already, Cyprus, Ireland, Portugal, Spain, and Greece have recorded wage declines in the first quarter of 2014. Yet, the ECB will only use it as a last-resort measure, even though broad money supply rose this year by only about 1 percent. Why? Because doubts surround the efficacy of QE: (1) banks dominate in providing credit in the eurozone, not bond markets, which are not big and deep enough, and where asset-backed securities badly need reform—whereas mature and deep US bond markets best meet US needs; and (2) small businesses require direct access to credit, which QE can't meet, in order to galvanize recovery in the peripheral. Besides, Germany worries QE makes less creditworthy members forsake badly needed reforms.

Of course, these risks are real. Still, the IMF repeatedly pushes the ECB to be ready for QE to "boost confidence, improve corporate and household balance sheets, and stimulate bank lending."[5] But, the eurozone did "cross the Rubicon" in September 2012, which then saved the euro from the fury of market speculation. The ECB has since left rates on hold with no new initiatives in early August 2014. It certainly needs to do much more.

What, Then, Are We to Do?

Europe is haunted by what economist Mohamed El-Erian calls the "One-Percent Troika": enrichment of the 1 percent of its wealthiest; years of anemic 1 percent growth; and inflation hovering around 1 percent.[6] The longer they persist, the recovery gets more fragile and more uneven in the face of structurally high unemployment, destabilizing high youth jobless-ness, and worsening high debt burden. This Troika signals a call for urgent action to get on with a pro-growth agenda. The mild stability the eurozone now enjoys is illusionary. Sure, political fears in Berlin are real. But I think the "bigger fear" lies in the eurozone continuing to limp along, mired in a deep rut of mass unemployment, weak consumer prices, and disincen-tives to invest—all eroding its growth potential in the face of unsustainable high debt.

For once, the IMF's call is right on—it's time to bring on QE before deflation engulfs Europe. But easy money alone is not enough. The new numbers are a wake-up call to the "big 3" to lead and go for real reforms to push private investment and hiring. The ECB has to do whatever it takes, as Draghi had promised. It just hasn't done enough to secure a healthy recovery.

Kuala Lumpur
August 21, 2014

Notes

1. First published on August 23, 2014.
2. International Monetary Fund (IMF), *World Economic Outlook Update* (Washington, DC: IMF, July 2014).

3. Ibid., p. 3.
4. European Central Bank (ECB), at a press conference announcing ECB's series of new measures to keep ultra-low inflation from becoming embedded and derailing the eurozone's fragile recovery, in Frankfurt on June 5, 2014.
5. International Monetary Fund (IMF), in a commentary by Richard Barley, published in the *Asian Wall Street Journal* (June 25, 2014).
6. Mohamed El-Erian, "Economic Problems Haunt Europe," *Asian Wall Street Journal* (June 26, 2014).

CHAPTER 47

PIIGS Can't Fly: The Trouble with Greece[1]

On my way back to Kuala Lumpur after attending Asia Vision 21: Values, Conflicts and Change in Asia, organized by Harvard's Asia Centre and Harvard Kennedy School's Ash Centre, I could not help but feel sorry for the people of Greece, given the predicament they are now in. Greece's problems are well known. My Harvard teacher, Martin Feldstein, had in late April 2010 judged Greece to be already insolvent and "at that point, will default," or, more politely in negotiated default.[2] This can take many forms, including an "organized restructuring of the existing debt, swapping new debt with lower principal and interest for existing bonds." That's certainly one way to go, where everyone (including creditors) shares in the pain.

Over the February Chinese New Year holidays, the debt "death trap" that engulfed Greece was all over the place. In Chapter 76, "The Kiss of Debt," I discuss Greece's dilemma and argue that Greece might have been able to avoid the outcome if it were not in the eurozone and had its own currency, the drachma, back. Greece was not alone in this. Together with the other eurozone PIIGS (Portugal, Italy, Ireland, Greece, and Spain), these so-called Club-Med members of the European Union (EU) share some common traits: weak fiscal and debt positions; weak exports; weak balance of payments; and weak productivity (too high wages) caught in a zone with a strong euro, which made them all the more uncompetitive.

As I see it, they have only one way to go to restore competitiveness—fiscal retrenchment (i.e., restructuring of its fiscal affairs through austerity—cutting spending and raising more revenue) and structural economic and labor reform. But the PIIGS don't have a track record of fiscal discipline. Greece, for example, lacks the economic governance of the EU and fiscal discipline of the Germans. Yet, it has to make the most of a weak hand at a three-way poker involving the EU, capital markets, and potential social unrest at home. I then concluded: "In my view, they can best do this under

287

an International Monetary Fund [IMF] program and not in the shadow of the EU and the European Central Bank [ECB] without smelling like a bailout. The IMF gives them the best option to re-establish lost policy credibility." As events unfolded, I was in the ballpark. Indeed, many of the eurozone's 16-member governments had opposed IMF involvement because it reflected badly on the European Union's inability to resolve its own internal problems.

Desperate Times, Desperate Measures

Early this week, the EU and IMF proposed a three-year €110 billion deal (about one-third of Greece's debt) that will extract huge sacrifices from the Greek people. As I understand it, the IMF leads the rescue by providing €30 billion, Germany €22 billion, France €17 billion, the rest from the remaining 13 EU members. In return, the bitter medicine for the Greeks will include (1) deep cuts in the fiscal deficit from 13.6 percent of GDP to comply with the EU limit of 3 percent by 2014; (2) reduction in public debt, topping at 150 percent of gross domestic product (GDP) in 2013 to 144 percent in 2014 and progressively lower thereafter; and (3) stiff austerity with a combination of pay and budget cuts and tax increases. The package needs EU approval this weekend.

Essentially, the EU and IMF have given Greece only 12 to 18 months to show it can reform itself. Then, it's back to the markets for more cash. This is tough by any standard. Especially when the package will bring about cumulatively 8 percent fall in GDP. It is worth noting that (1) the rescue involves no debt restructuring, which makes fiscal adjustment very onerous for the Greeks; and (2) the ECB will offer a lifeline to assist Greek banks with liquidity through suspending the minimum credit rating for Greek government-backed assets as collateral.

Debt Jitters Spread

As I had expected, the EU (especially France and Spain) is reported to have fought hard to keep the IMF out of the deal, but ended up endorsing a set of measures that bears the IMF's imprimatur—austerity. The IMF never learns. You can't cut and grow. This was deliberate, intended to persuade financial markets that Greece has a chance (I think, slim) of succeeding. Nevertheless, market reaction since has been swift and severe across the board. By Thursday (May 6), the US dollar had strengthened to a series of 12-month highs—the euro dropped to a 14-month low (below US$1.27) and falling, and the yen to 93.3 (London close); the euro had depreciated 12 percent against US dollar this year.

As optimism over economic recovery in the United States contrasted with doubts about successful resolution of the Greek debt crisis, sell-off in Asian equity accelerated in Europe and the United States. European stocks tumbled to three-month lows, while bond markets of the weaker eurozone members fell as loss of confidence rattled investors across all asset classes. Since Tuesday, the Dow (DJIA) fell 3 percent and the FTSE Eurofirst 300 index closed 4.5 percent lower, while Asian stocks were mostly lower, with the Shanghai index down 4 percent. The VIX S&P 500 index (a gauge of expected equity market volatility) rose to 25, the highest one-day spike since October 2008. It continues to stay elevated, reflecting trading on event risk.

The Risks

Overall, the Greece debacle casts a long shadow over market sentiment. Many risks still remain. Topmost is fear of contagion. Worry is centered on the other PIIGS, notably Portugal and Spain, since they may also need to be rescued. I have seen estimates of the total size of a possible liquidity backstop for the PIIGS totaling in the region of €500–1,000 billion. Bear in mind they are all facing interest rate increases at a time when they can least afford them. The private sector in many of them is simply not viable at rising higher rates. Last week, Spain joined Greece and Portugal in being downgraded by Standard & Poor's (S&P), the credit rating agency.

While Spain's credit rating remains well above Greece's junk status (BB+) and ahead of Portugal's A−, its fall to AA was a severe blow. After all, Spain's budget deficit stands at 8.9 percent of GDP and Portugal, 7.6 percent; in terms of public debt to GDP, Spain's ratio is 60 percent and Portugal, 82 percent.

My own sense is that it will not be easy for Spain and Portugal to avoid going to the IMF or EU for loans, as they both have deteriorating public finances and rather weak economies. The only way out for them is to get international help early. It is now an issue of market psychology. I am convinced that if the EU (especially Germany) had sealed Greece's deal in February, the rescue package would have been more cost effective.

By now, the vicious cycle at play should be familiar:

1. **The country's financial situation deteriorates**. Then, its debt is downgraded, which, in turn, triggers a sharp rise in market borrowing rates. That leads to further financial deterioration.
2. **The proposed package looks tight**. Market estimates are that Greece will need at least €150 billion to have a reasonable chance of success. The only certainty so far is its ability to meet the €8.5 billion bond payment in two weeks. To assume that Greece will do well enough

by end-2011 to be able to borrow from the capital markets is too optimistic. Bringing its budget deficit target down to 4.9 percent in 2013
will require, I think, €50 billion over three years. In addition, past debt
has to be serviced and Greece has another €70 billion to repay by
mid-2013. Thus, such financing already takes up €120 billion. There
is simply no way around the arithmetic implied by the scale and urgency of the deficit reduction, debt servicing, and the accompanying
economic decline. I am not surprised the market is skeptical.

3. **Fiscal consolidation is tough; but without it, the pain inflicted could
   make the burden very painful.** Burden sharing is critical. The political consequences should not be underestimated. It is incredible that
   the rescue involves no haircuts and no debt restructuring. This package can be likened to what the IMF did to Latin America in the 1980s,
   which led to a lost decade. Without debt restructuring, the beneficiaries will be foreign creditors who get away fully paid (no haircut). The
   risks make it well-nigh impossible for Greece to return to the market
   for more loans later on.

4. **The package calls for very demanding austerity and sacrifice.** In
   Greece, the past two days of workers' protests and pending strikes reflect very real risks. As a result, markets are in a panic mode, draining
   bond markets of liquidity and with forced sales because of sovereign
   debt downgrades.

The climate of confidence has definitely changed for the worse. It is
unclear whether the Greek government—facing angry unions and young
unemployed workers—can push through and maintain the austerity steps it
promised. It is also unclear if the uncompetitive Greek economy, mired by
recession still, can survive the sacrifices meted out while remaining in the
eurozone. It remains unclear how the political tensions within and among
the rich eurozone countries on handling the debt crisis will play out. There
is a sense that Germany, in particular, does not like any bailout. What is
clear is that the Greeks are ill-prepared for a long period of potentially
breathtaking austerity, devoid of social justice. Without support of the public, who are already outraged at corrupt politicians (whom they hold accountable for the crisis), the rescue is doomed to fail.

Headlines Miss Woods for the Trees

Why the mess? Most headlines in recent days were centered on Greece's
high debt as the villain—a profligate government who mismanaged the
nation's finances. This is certainly part of the story. But the Greek tragedy
has its roots in Greece being a member of the eurozone. Prior to the global

recession, the state of Greece's finances wasn't so bad. Its budget deficits and debt levels were high but manageable. It attracted its share of capital inflows on the belief that bonds of Greece (as a member of the EU) were safe investments. The 2007–2008 crises changed all that. With easy money fast disappearing in the face of falling revenues and rising costs and a good life, Greece soon became uncompetitive and its economic situation worsened. As they say, the rest is history.

Unfortunately, as a member of the eurozone, Greece had to give up its own currency (and adopted the euro in its place) and control over interest rates. The only way out for Greece is to make drastic budget cuts (i.e., deflate)—which can be very painful—to become more competitive. Unlike non-euro nations, Greece could not adjust by depreciating its own exchange rate (since it doesn't have its own currency, anymore), and the euro (controlled in practice by Germany) was not about to inflate. Its finances became precarious. So much so, its bonds were downgraded to junk status. This simply meant that the euro value of Greece's GDP is unlikely to revert to its 2008 level until 2017, according to Standard & Poor's, the rating agency. Greece simply is unable to grow out of its troubles. The concern is the European Union has no reliable financial mechanism to help members in trouble to adjust.

This is precisely what euro-skeptics like Professors Martin Feldstein and Princeton's Paul Krugman (Nobel laureate 2008) feared, bringing with it a crisis that can undermine EU as a monetary union without political union.[3] Indeed, without its own currency, there was no market signal to warn Greece that its deficits and debt reached unacceptable levels. Euro-skeptics remain convinced that the European Union's problems are anything but over. Maybe, a real default is what is needed to test the European Union as a viable political and economic union.

What, Then, Are We to Do?

The Greek tragedy should be instructive. For regionalists in Asia in a hurry to emulate the European Union and push for monetary union—however loose—recent experience offers valuable lessons. Among the necessary conditions are (1) allowance for a crisis resolution mechanism, (2) provision of effective fiscal policy coordination, and (3) arrangements for a reliable mechanism to reduce intraregional imbalances. These point to the need for strong, disciplined support and ready access to sufficient funds to cushion off adjustments among problem members.

The endgame is obvious: Avoid, at all costs, giving up degrees of freedom you already have in policy adjustments, without sacrificing safeguards needed to protect national interests. Governments need flexibility to act quickly and with clarity in times of crisis. Krugman is right on what he thought Greece did wrong in joining the EU: Greece denied itself the ability to do some "bad things" (like printing money), but also denied itself the ability to respond flexibly to events.

Cambridge, Massachusetts
Kuala Lumpur
May 7, 2010

Notes

1. First published on May 8, 2010, as "PIIGS Can't Fly: The Greek Tragedy."
2. Martin Feldstein, "Why Greece Will Default," *The Star*, Kuala Lumpur (May 1, 2010).
3. Ibid.; Paul Krugman, "When Crisis Hits," *International Herald Tribune* (May 4, 2010).

CHAPTER 48

Greece Is Bankrupt[1]

Arose by any other name would smell as sweet. In the case of Greece, default by any other name just stinks! The plain truth: Greece is bankrupt. Greece's sovereign debt crisis deepens daily as the gap in reality widens between politically driven "in-denial" views of European Union (EU) leadership and marketplace views as reflected in five-year Greek bonds trading at a yield close to 20 percent; Standard & Poor's cutting Greece's rating to triple-C (the lowest credit rating ever); and the highest premiums payable on credit default swaps (CDSs)—used as insurance to protect investors against defaults—on Greek debt. Probability of default by Greece over the next five years has jumped to 86 percent. Today, a CDS will cost US$2 million annually to insure US$10 million debt over five years. Markets have indicated for some time that Greece suffers from a condition of bankruptcy rather than a crisis of liquidity (i.e., cash-short). This simply means Greece cannot survive without significant debt relief and restructuring, combined with an overhaul of the ways its government collects revenue and expends. In essence, Greece has two major problems: It has too much debt and it cannot grow. I am afraid more and more of the European Union will get contaminated.

The Greek Illusion

Greece should not have been into the euro in the first place. It failed to join in 1999 because it did not meet the fiscal criteria. When it did so in 2001, it was through "phony" budget numbers. As Roger Cohen tweeted: "Europe's bold monetary union required an Athenian imprimatur to be fully European. So everyone turned a blind eye."[2] But Greece has had an awful history. The 1912–1913 war wrested northern Greece from Ottoman control. Then came the massive exchange of 1923, where 400,000 Muslims were forced from Greece to Turkey and 1.2 million Greek Orthodox Christians, from Turkey to Greece. A military dictatorship followed in the 1930s; brutal

German occupation in 1941–1944; and a civil war in late 1940s. There was the rightist dictatorship of 1967–1974, not to mention the ongoing conflict with Turkey over Cyprus. In *Twice a Stranger*, Bruce Clark wrote of Greece as a society: where blood ties are far more important than loyalty to the state or to business partners.[3]

It would appear the EU membership provided some balm to Greek wounds. It detoxifies history. So Greece took to the EU as a passport to live on the never-never. The bottom line: A monetary union among divergent economies without fiscal or political union support has no convincing historical precedent. For a while, the easy-money, easy-lifestyle allowed everyone to overlook peripheral economies like Greece becoming uncompetitive with the euro (with no drachma to devalue) and not showing any signs of "converging" (closing the gulf between strong and weak nations within the EU), but amassing unsustainable deficits and debt. Greece remains a nation suspicious of outsiders and a place where state structures command scant loyalty. This does not bode well. We now see a Greece resentful of deep spending cuts, and of the sale of state assets meted out by technocrats from outside. They feel the poor and unemployed are paying for the errors of politicians, and a globalized system that punishes those left behind. Strikes and violence are a measure of a EU that now leaves most Greeks unmoved by the achievements of European integration.

Greece Is Insolvent

It is true a sovereign state, unlike a firm, has the power to tax. In theory, it can tax itself out of trouble. But there is a limit on how far it can tax before it becomes politically and socially unsustainable. Already, Greece has a debt/gross domestic product (GDP) ratio of 143 percent in 2010, rising to 150 percent this year. It is too high to convince creditors to continue lending. In practice, the market expects Greece to reduce its debt ratio considerably before it can borrow again. This means it has to create a primary budget surplus (revenue less noninterest expenditure) in excess of 8 percent of GDP to be creditworthy again. Among advanced nations, none (except oil-rich Norway) has managed to attain a durable primary surplus exceeding 6 percent of GDP.

Greece is insolvent. This is a dire situation. Government bonds serve as a reference asset by setting the "riskless" rate of interest. So any doubts about its value can cause turmoil. Indeed, solvency of the Greek financial system is at risk. So are other European financial institutions. Equally vital is contagion—with its sights set firmly on other debt-distressed nations, notably Ireland, Portugal, Spain, and Italy. But it doesn't stop there. Top Europeans have warned contagion to EU members could spark off a crisis bigger than the Lehman Brothers collapse in September 2008. So, it is not difficult to understand the hard line taken by the European Central Bank (ECB) aimed primarily to protect European banks, which needs time to strengthen their capital base. For obvious reasons, it has rejected any sort of restructuring of debt, raising the specter of a chain reaction, and threatening to punish any restructuring (renegotiation of the terms of maturing debt) by cutting banks' access to liquidity.

Moreover, credit rating agencies would deem any such action as a default (i.e., nonpayment of due debt). With Greece insolvent, the European Union has taken the narrow road of beefing up the financing for Greece (which can't refinance itself in the market), while using moral suasion to persuade private creditors to roll over their bonds. It is buying breathing space. More denial doesn't work—it just prolongs the agony.

The Macroeconomics

What's happening to Greece is distressful. Over the past 12 months, the number of unemployed rose by close to 40 percent. Unemployment rate was above 16 percent—among youths, it's a devastating 42 percent. International Monetary Fund's (IMF) estimates showed its GDP contracted by 2 percent in 2009 and 4.5 percent in 2010 and will shrink by 3 to 4 percent this year.

Despite severe fiscal austerity, its budget deficit will improve only slowly: from −15.4 percent of GDP in 2009 to −9 percent in 2010 and −7.5 percent this year (and estimated at −6.2 percent in 2012). That's a long way to surplus! Greece has become so uncompetitive that its current balance of payments deficit was −11 percent of GDP in 2009, −10.5 percent in 2010, and optimistically estimated at −8.2 percent this year (and at −7.2 percent in 2012). Truly, Greece is in "intensive care"—a solvency crisis—not just caught in a short-term cash crunch (yes, it also does not have cash to meet its next debt payment before July 15). Even at today's low interest rates, Greece's government interest payments alone amounted to 6.7 percent of GDP, against 4.8 percent for Italy and considerably higher than all other major European nations and the United States (2.9 percent). Even Portugal's ratio is lower at 4.2 percent.

Political Solution: Slash and Burn Won't Work

What Greece needs is deep economic reforms or fiscal transfers from the EU, which will help address deepening market concerns about sustainability of its huge debts. Without these, the crisis will simply be deferred. The message is clear: Greece's debt load at €350 billion, or 150 percent of its expected economic output this year, is simply too large for the EU troika's (plus the ECB and IMF) strategy to succeed. Athens had accepted a package of €110 billion of EU/IMF loans in May 2010. But it now needs a second bailout of a similar size to meet financial obligations until end-2014 when it hopes to move seamlessly into the new European Stability Mechanism (ESM) bailout fund (which takes effect in 2013) to prop up fiscal miscreants.

Latest drawdown involves release of a vital €12 billion very soon but carries a proviso that Parliament passes on June 29 (which it did with a slim majority) €28.6 billion in spending cuts and tax increases as well as €50 billion from privatization of state assets, in addition to continuing existing austerity policies. That's not all. The new plan calls for private creditors' participation on a voluntary basis (meeting ECB's insistence to avoid even a hint of default) or a "Vienna Plus," a reference to the 2009 Vienna initiative where banks agreed to maintain their exposure to Eastern Europe.

For Greece, the brutal austerity plans call for enormous sacrifices; indeed, there is no end to their agonies. Today, the situation at Syntagma Square and in front of Parliament is getting more strained, angry, and confused, surrounded by riot police and clouds of teargas. The people are becoming frustrated at being always at the receiving end.

On the German side, however, voters are aghast at the prospect of a second bailout, which they regard as pouring good money after bad. Germans consider the Greek government as corrupt; its tax system operates on voluntarism; state railroad's payroll is four times larger than its ticket sales; many workers retire with full state pension at age 45; and so on. Be that as it may, the IMF in particular needs to learn from lessons of the Asian currency crisis, where it has since acknowledged its prescriptions at the time made matters worse in Indonesia, Thailand, and the Philippines, in the name of unleashing market forces to force adjustment and ignoring the adverse social and political impact of their policies. I see them repeating the same mistakes again in Greece, paying too little heed to human suffering and adverse social impact to protect private sector creditors, and pushing the endgame at breakneck pace. Germany's insistence to get private creditors to share in the burden is a good soft step forward. Even so, the IMF seems too harsh.

Few Options Left

The fact remains that Greece was outstandingly egregious in its fiscal profligacy and its lack of prudent economic governance. But Greece was not the only European economy that was living beyond its means and being pumped with ill-conceived loans mainly from German and French banks. Greece is today insolvent. The EU's solution addresses only immediate funding needs, without offering a credible long-term resolution. It's just a stopgap. Frankly, Greece's policy options are limited: either a default, partial haircut (creditors taking losses on their investments), or a guarantee on Greek debt. Bear in mind that Germany remains the biggest beneficiary of the eurozone experiment. In 2010, Germany recorded a US$185 billion balance of payments surplus or 5.6 percent of GDP. No doubt, the EU has since pledged to stabilize the eurozone economy, vowing to stave off a Greek default, and the ECB has categorically ruled out debt restructuring.

That leaves Greece with only deflation, a lot of it. As I see it, this will not work. First, in a democratic Greece, people are clearly not in the mood for deeper spending cuts and more austerity. Policies can be adopted but they can fail. Second, deflation had already made Greece's debt problem worse—the debt is too large and the economy won't grow with continuing austerity. It can't just deflate its way to solvency.

What, Then, Are We to Do?

The better option left is debt guarantee. Issuing guarantees (preferably partially backed by Greek assets) could help persuade creditors to exchange debt for new debt with longer maturities, effectively giving Athens more time to repay. As of now, only 27 percent of Greek debt is held by banks, 30 percent by ECB/EU/IMF, and 43 percent by other privates. Banks are already quietly resisting voluntary rolling over unless offered incentives. EU has preferred to use moral suasion, but also resisted haircuts.

Mr. Axel Weber, former Bundesbank governor, has since weighed in: "At some point you've got to cut your losses and restart the system," drawing parallels between guarantee for Greek debt and steps taken by Germany and others during the financial crisis to backstop troubled banks.[4] The Greek problem "is a deep-rooted fiscal and structural problem that probably needs more than a 30-year time horizon to solve. . . . The measures Europe needs to adopt are much more profound than just short-term liquidity funds."[5]

That, of course, raises the issue of moral hazard. The European Union has since pledged to stabilize the eurozone, and stave off a Greek default in exchange for continuing Greek deflation and voluntary creditors' rollover. Getting banks to share in the burden remains problematic. But, a narrow policy option is taken. It's another muddle-through created in response to politics. It offers no long-term way for Greece to resume growth. I am told the political mood in Greece improves automatically in July and August as the urbans head en masse for family villages in the islands and mountains. Surely, for a little while, human woes will be eased by exposure to the beauty of the Aegean.

Kuala Lumpur
June 30, 2011

Notes

1. First published on July 2, 2011.
2. Roger Cohen, "The Great Greek Illusion," *International Herald Tribune* (June 21, 2011).
3. Bruce Clark, *Twice a Stranger* (Cambridge, MA: Harvard University Press, 2009).
4. Axel Weber, former president of Deutsche Bundesbank (Germany's central bank), in an interview in Frankfurt on June 24, 2011.
5. Ibid.

CHAPTER 49

Greek Bailout Mark II: It's a Default[1]

The European debt crisis has evolved rather quickly since I wrote Chapter 48, "Greece Is Bankrupt." European leadership was clearly in denial. The crisis has lurched from one "scare" to another. First, it was Greece, then Ireland, then Portugal, and then back to Greece. On each occasion, European politicians muddled through, dithering to buy time with half-baked solutions: more kicking the can down the road. By last week, predictably, the crisis came home to roost. Financial markets in desperation turned on Italy, the eurozone's third largest economy, with the biggest sovereign debt market in Europe. It has €1.9 trillion of sovereign debt outstanding (120 percent of its GDP), three times as much as Greece, Ireland, and Portugal combined. The situation has become just too serious, if contagion was allowed to fully play out. It was a reality check, a time to act as it threatened both European integration and the global recovery. So, on July 21, an emergency summit of European leaders of the 17-nation euro-currency area agreed to a second Greek bailout (Mark II), comprising two key elements: (1) the debt exchange (holders of €135 billion in Greek debt maturing up to 2020 will voluntarily accept new bonds of up to 15–30 years); and (2) new loans of €109 billion (through its bailout fund and the IMF). Overall, Greek debt would fall by €26 billion from its total outstanding of €350 billion. No big deal, really.

Contagion: Italy and Spain

By mid-July, the Greek debt drama had become a full-blown eurozone crisis. Policy makers' efforts to insulate other countries from a Greek default, notably Italy and Spain, have failed. Markets panicked because of disenchantment over sloppy European policy making. For the first time,

I think, investors became aware of the chains of contagion and are only now beginning to really think about them.

The situation in Italy is serious. At US$262 billion, total sovereign claims by international banks on Italy exceeded their combined sovereign exposures to Greece, Ireland, Portugal, and Spain, which totaled US$226 billion. European banks account for 90 percent of international banks' exposure to Italy and 84 percent of sovereign exposure, with French and German banks being the most exposed. Italy and Spain together have €6.3 trillion of public and private debt between them. Reflecting growing market unease, the yield on Italy's 10-year government bonds had risen to 5.6 percent on July 20, and Spain's, to 6 percent, against 2.76 percent on German comparable bunds, the widest spread ever in the euro-era.

Italy and Spain face different challenges. **Spain** has a high budget deficit (9.2 percent of GDP in 2010, down from 11.1 percent in 2009)—the target being to take it down to 6 percent in 2011, which assumes high implementation risks. Its debt-to-GDP ratio (at 64 percent in 2011) is lower than the average for the eurozone. The economy is only gradually recovering, led by exports. But Spain suffers from chronic unemployment (21 percent, with youth unemployment at 45 percent), weak productivity growth, and a dysfunctional labor market. It must also restructure its savings banks. Spain needs to continue with reforms; efforts to repair its economy are far from complete and risks remain considerable.

Italy has a low budget deficit (4.6 percent of GDP) and hasn't had to prop up its banks. But its economy has barely expanded in a decade, and its debt-to-GDP ratio of 119 percent in 2010 was second only to Greece's. Italy suffers from sluggish growth, weak productivity, and falling competitiveness. Its weaknesses reflect labor market rigidities and low efficiency. The main downside risk comes from turmoil in the eurozone periphery. Another decade of stagnation also poses a major risk. But both Spain and Italy are not insolvent, unlike Greece. The economies are not growing and need to be more competitive. The average maturity of their debt is a reasonable 6 to 7 years. But the psychological damage already done to Europe's bond market cannot be readily undone.

The Deal: Europeanization of Greek Debt

The new bailout deal sought to ring-fence Greece by declaring: Greece is in a uniquely grave situation in the eurozone; this is the reason why it requires an exceptional solution, implying it's not to be repeated. Most don't believe it. But to its credit, the new deal cuts new ground, in addition to bringing in much-needed extra cash—€109 billion, plus a contribution by private bondholders of up to €50 billion by mid-2014. For the first time, the new framework included solvent counterparties and adequate collateral. For investors, there is nothing like having Europe as the new counterparty instead of Greece.

This Europeanization of the Greek debt lends some credibility to the program. Other new features include: (1) reduction in interest rates to about 3.5 percent (4.5 to 5.8 percent now) and extension of maturities to 15 years (from 7½ years), to be also offered to Ireland and Portugal; (2) the European Financial Stability Facility (EFSF), its rescue vehicle, will be allowed to buy bonds in the secondary market, extend precautionary credit lines before states are shut out of credit markets, and lend to help recapitalize banks; and (3) buy collateral for use in the bond exchange, where investors are given four options to accept new bonds carrying differing risk profiles, worth less than their original holdings. The Institute of International Finance (IIF), the industry trade group that negotiated for the banks, insurance funds, and other investors, had estimated that one-half of the €135 billion to be exchanged will be for new bonds at 20 percent discount, giving a savings of €13.5 billion off the Greek debt load. Of the €109 billion from the new bailout (together with the IMF), €35 billion will be used to buy collateral to serve as insurance against the new bonds in exchange, while €20 billion will go to buying Greek debt at a discount in the secondary market and then retiring it, giving another savings of €12.6 billion on the Greek debt stock.

Impact of Default

Once again, the evolving crisis was a step ahead of the politicians. There were fears that Italy and Spain could well trip into double-dip recession as global growth falters, threatening the debt dynamics of both countries. This time, the IMF weighed in with serious talk of contagion with widespread knock-on effects worldwide. Fear finally struck, forcing Germany and France to act, this time more seriously. The first reactions came from the credit rating agencies. Moody's downgraded Greece's rating three notches deeper into junk territory: to Ca, its second-lowest (from Caa1), short of a straight default. Similarly, Fitch Ratings and Standard & Poor's have cut Greece's rating to CCC. They have since downgraded it further. They are all expected to state Greece is in default when it begins to exchange its bonds in August for new, long-dated debt (up to 30 years) at a loss to investors (estimated at 21 percent of their bond holdings). The rating agencies would likely consider this debt exchange a "credit event," but only for a limited period, I think. Greece's financial outlook thereafter will depend on whether the country would likely recover or default again. History is unkind: Sovereigns that default often falter again.

What is also clear now is the new bailout would not do much to reduce Greece's huge stock of sovereign debt. At best, the fall in its debt stock will represent 12 percent of Greece's GDP. Over the medium term, Greece continues to face solvency challenges. Its stock of debt will still be well in excess of 130 percent of GDP and will face significant implementation risks to financial and economic reform. No doubt the latest bailout benefited the entire eurozone by containing near-term contagion risks, which otherwise would engulf Europe. It did manage to provide, for the time being, some confidence to investors in Ireland, Portugal, Spain, and Italy that it's not going to be a downward spiral. But the latest wave of post-bailout warnings have reignited concerns of contagion risks and revived investor caution. Still, the bailout doesn't address the very core fiscal problems across the eurozone. This is not a comprehensive solution. It shifted additional risks toward contributing members with stronger finances and their taxpayers, as well as private investors, and reduces incentives for governments to keep their fiscal affairs under strict check. This worries the Germans, as it weakens the foundation of currency union based on fiscal self-discipline. Moreover, the EFSF—now given more authority to intervene preemptively before a State gets bankrupt—didn't get more funds. German backlash appears to be also growing.

While the market appears to be moving beyond solvency to looking at potential threat to the eurozone as a whole, the elements needed to fight systemic failure are not present. At best, the deal reflected a courageous effort but fell short of addressing underlying issues, leading to fears that Greece-like crisis situations could still flare up, spreading this time deep into the eurozone's core.

Growing Pains

The excitement of the bailout blanked out an even bigger challenge that could further destabilize the eurozone—sluggish growth. The July Markit Purchasing Managers' Index came in at 50.8, the lowest since August 2009 and close enough to the 50 mark that divides expansion from contraction. And, it was way below the consensus forecast. Both manufacturing and services slackened. Germany and France expanded at the slowest pace in two years in the face of a eurozone that's displaying signs it is already contracting. Looking ahead, earlier expectations of a second half of 2011 pickup now remains doubtful. Lower GDP growth will require fiscal stimulus to fix, at a time of growing fiscal consolidation that threatens a downward spiral.

At this time, the eurozone needs policies to restart growth, especially around the periphery. Without growth, economic reform and budget restraints only exacerbate political backlash and social tensions. This makes it well-nigh impossible to restore debt sustainability. Germany may have to delay its austerity program without becoming a fiscal drag. This trade-off between growth and austerity is real.

What, Then, Are We to Do?

The IMF studies show that cutting a country's budget deficit by 3 percentage points of GDP would reduce real output growth by 2 percentage points and raise the unemployment rate by 1 percentage point. History suggests growth and austerity just do not mix. In practical terms, it is harder for politicians to stimulate growth than cut debt. Reform takes time to yield results. And, markets are fickle. In the event the market switches focus from high-debt to low-growth economies, a crisis can easily evolve to enter a new phase—one that could help businesses invest and employ rather than a premature swing of the fiscal axe.

Timing is critical. It now appears timely for the United States and Europe to shift priorities. They can't just wait forever to rein in their debts. Sure, they need credible plans over the medium term for deficit reduction. More austerity now won't get growth going. The surest way to build confidence is to get recovery onto a sustainable path—only growth can do that. Without it, the risk of a double-dip recession increases. Latest warnings from the financial markets in Europe and Wall Street send the same message: Get your acts together and grow. This needs statesmanship. The status quo is just not good enough, anymore.

Kuala Lumpur
July 29, 2011

Note

1. First published on July 30, 2011.

CHAPTER 50

Greece and Eurozone: Austerity Fatigue[1]

Europe is obsessed with austerity—determined to cut deep into public spending to pare the debt. So is the Tea Party and Republicans in the United States. As if to prove the point, 25 of the 27 European Union (EU) members have agreed to a new "fiscal compact," which obliges each of them never to have an underlying budget deficit (after adjusting for debt disbursements and the business cycle) of more than 0.5 percent of gross domestic product (GDP). The United States ran a deficit close to 8 percent of GDP in 2011.

With the EU flirting with recession (indeed Greece, Portugal, Belgium, Italy, and the Netherlands are already in recession—defined as two consecutive quarters of GDP declines), it is legitimate to ask: Is austerity becoming self-defeating? The example of Greece is real. In exchange for more bailout monies to keep the nation afloat (a second tranche of €130 billion is now needed) from the troika, viz. EU, European Central Bank (ECB), and the International Monetary Fund (IMF), Greece was forced to adopt still more severe austerity programs amid intense social unrest and destructive rioting. Greece's GDP had slumped 7 percent in 2011—its fifth year in recession, coming this time after harsh austerity measures imposed in September 2011.

Contributing to the malaise has been deteriorating business and consumer confidence as unemployment (already at 21 percent) keeps rising, and mounting fears over "Grexit," Greece's exit from the eurozone. Standard & Poor's insightful justification for its downgrades: We believe that a reform process based on a pillar of fiscal austerity alone risks becoming self-defeating, as domestic demand falls in line with consumers' rising concerns about job security and disposable incomes, eroding national tax revenues.

The Eurozone

The fourth quarter of 2011 wasn't good for the eurozone. Economic activity fell across much of debt-plagued Europe, with declines in output stretching from downtrodden Greece to mighty Germany. The eurozone's 17-nation economy contracted in the fourth quarter of 2011 for the first time in 2½ years: GDP fell 0.3 percent over the previous quarter as the region's debt crisis undermined confidence and forced governments from Portugal to Spain and Italy to Greece to sharpen budget cuts. That translates to an annual decline of 1.3 percent after seasonal adjustments. But for 2011 as a whole, eurozone's GDP rose by 1.5 percent, down from 2.0 percent in 2010. For 2012, economists expect the euro bloc to decline moderately—at best, to barely expand. The ECB has since forecast a mere 1.1 percent growth in 2013. No doubt, it will still flirt with a mild recession. The drag is coming from a stricken debt-laden south, epitomized by a slumping Italy. The eurozone is facing its second recession in three years. Moody's cut the ratings of six of the region's members (including Italy and Spain) and warned that it could cut the triple-A ratings of France, United Kingdom, and Austria, saying policy makers haven't done enough to restore investor confidence, and citing "a number of specific credit pressures that would exacerbate the susceptibility of the sovereign balance sheets." The outlook is for another contraction of activity in the first quarter of 2012, signaling a technical recession in the eurozone. Clearly, fiscal austerity has begun to bite. As I see it, faltering in the eurozone, which accounts for one-fifth of global GDP, could even work to derail the already fragile global recovery.

Germany, Europe's largest economy, despite the fourth quarter of 2011 contraction (–0.2 percent, slackening from +0.6 percent in the previous three months), still grew 3 percent for 2011 as a whole, the second straight year of 3 percent or higher. Indications are that it is taking a "growth pause" and likely to expand again this quarter, albeit at a very slow pace. Record low unemployment should boost consumer spending, and its exports should benefit from the weaker euro and continuing fast growth in Asia. But France's (Europe's second largest) GDP unexpectedly rose 0.2 percent in the fourth quarter of 2011, confounding the median forecast for a 0.2 percent contraction. Finland's GDP posted +0.7 percent in the fourth quarter of 2011. The exception in the "north" was the Netherlands, which dipped into recession, following a third quarter 2011 fall of 0.4 percent (its second recession in three years). Otherwise, it's clear there is wide regional divergence.

The "south" economies are in recession. The Italian and Dutch economies both contracted 0.7 percent in the fourth quarter of 2011, with Italy entering its fourth recession since 2001. Greece and Spain, Belgium, and Portugal also reported GDP declines. All these countries have taken drastic measures to reduce debt by cutting spending and raising taxes.

But this effort is hampered by shrinking economies, which drain public coffers of tax receipts and raise social spending. For the wealthy economies, such as Germany and the Netherlands, weaknesses at home would dampen public willingness to further support Greece and others with bailouts. The fourth quarter of 2011 was very weak. Latest survey and hard data point to tentative signs of stabilization in economic activity but at a very low level. According to the ECB, "The outlook remains subject to high uncertainty and downside risks." However, the 2012 inflation projection was raised to a mild 1.9 percent.

The Greece "Lock-in"

Greece fell deeper into recession as 2011 ended, showing up the dev-astating toll of two years of severe austerity even before the now-harsh budget cuts take hold in the months ahead. Its GDP contracted 7 percent, against a forecast of 5 percent, reflecting an accelerating contraction since the third quarter. Manufacturing fell 15.5 percent in December 2011 from a year before. Things will get worse: The economy is in a free fall—it can even contract by more than 4–5 percent this year. Greece's sinking economy has overshadowed talks with the troika for a second bailout, who are setting preconditions involving still more fiscal tight-ening, including more wage and pension cuts. Already, last September, austerity measures implemented included higher excise taxes along with new taxes on property and incomes. Consumer confidence has since fallen to record lows.

Last week, Greek businesses and households learned that they now face even hasher doses of hardship to secure a critical second lifeline to avert a catastrophic first-ever debt default on March 20, when €14.5 billion of bonds became due. The new cutbacks will further hit the economy hard, since they will weigh heavily on private consumption (70 percent of GDP). The new deal would slash private minimum wage by 22 percent, abolish another 15,000 public-sector jobs, with further pension cuts, and cuts of more than €3 billion in fresh spending.

This had led to widespread strikes and vicious riots and more are in the pipeline from business and trade groups and unions. With nearly one-half of the workforce aged 15 to 24 years old now without a job, the outlook doesn't look good. Unemployment soared to 20.9 percent, compared with 18.2 percent in October 2011. Let's face it. Greece has been living beyond its means, engaged in a kind of accidental experiment in Keynesianism on steroids. Between 2000 and 2008, Greece's private-sector labor costs rose 62 percent, against 12 percent in Germany. It is clear that the Greeks have enjoyed a prosperity that's borrowed, rather than earned.

Unlocking the Greek Bailout

After an epic effort to pass a deeply unpopular austerity package, Greece faces more hurdles amid intensely popular opposition, provoking much looting and burning in Athens. As I see it, the city is filled with a broad sense of dilapidation. Yet, a suspicious EU is worried about whether the entire program, especially the drastic cuts, will actually come to pass.

This lack of trust is not without basis. So far, Greece has overpromised and underdelivered. Already, it had failed to make good cuts of 30,000 public employees promised in 2010. In particular, the EU appears worried whether there is political will to follow through on reforms. I understand the prime minister as well as the leader of the conservatives have given written undertakings to stand by the conditions of both bailout packages after the elections, probably in April. Weary of broken Greek promises, the EU is known to have also demanded: (1) closure of the €325 million gap in shortfalls in austerity cuts so far; (2) clinching €107 billion in voluntary bond-swaps for debt relief (haircut) from private bondholders, who stand to lose more than 70 percent of their economic value; (3) revitalization of the stalled privatization drive; and (4) restoration of Greece's debt-reduction goal, which would only fall to 129 percent of GDP by 2020, missing the 120 percent (now 120.5 percent) target set as a condition at the first bailout, from 164 percent today.

Meanwhile, the IMF has concluded that the haircut for private bond-holders would not be sufficient to return Greece to sustained financial stability. While I can appreciate the IMF's concerns, this is being resisted fiercely, fearing other debt-distressed nations would press for equal treatment. Moreover, strengthening the firewall against contagion with enlarged IMF resources has yet to occur, and the European Financial Stability Facility (EFSF) also has not been enlarged. All these just add more uncertainty, and growth prospects are simply still too opaque. Indeed, rating downgrades by Standard & Poor's in January and by Moody's recently inject unwelcome tension among EU members.

On the macroeconomic front, in the absence of higher inflation in the surplus eurozone "north," economic adjustment would simply make the crisis nations deflate, with accompanying falls in production costs. In practice, this implies more unemployment and social distress. This leaves open the question if the current strategy of combining austerity and deflation makes good sense. It only explains why this massive cloud of uncertainty overhangs the eurozone.

What's worrisome is that no one worries about how to sustain economic recovery. Fiscal austerity, which is supposed to limit the rise in public debt, has depressed economic activity, making it well-nigh impossible to achieve urgently needed reductions in private debt. For all the moralizing about the evils of borrowing, Europeans aren't making progress against excessive debt and at addressing its dual problems of too little growth (if at all) and too much debt.

Politics beyond Borders

The eurozone is debilitated by the goings-on of two years of desperate politicians' debates, official negotiations, union strikes, and angry mobs taking to the streets. That was the state of play early this week, as I travel to Manila—still talking to corral support for the bailout. Make no mistake, the real paymasters are in Berlin. It may look like they have Athens by the throat, but Greeks know the event of a default (chaotic at best) would be disastrous for Europe, provoking wider contagion. It's a face-off. But growing social tensions make things more difficult.

Greece and the EU finally concluded a deal on Tuesday. This was not unexpected but leaves much doubt about the future. Fitch downgraded Greece to a low C. The ball is now in Greece's court as austerity deepens. Greece is unhappy it is subject to heightened external control and scrutiny, including monies placed in blocked accounts and priority given to debt servicing over other spending. It's clear the deal poses high implementation risks. Indeed, there is already talk of a third bailout, a politically toxic prospect. Crisis economies need time and resources to resolve, restructure, readjust, and reform to regain lost competitiveness in order to grow again. But this won't happen without easing tension between narrow national politics and tightened European surveillance. Harvard's Dani Rodrik puts it best:

> *The US and the EU, now burdened by high debt and low growth— and therefore pre-occupied with domestic concerns—are no longer able to set global rules and expect others to fall into line. . . . As a result, global leadership and cooperation will remain in limited supply, requiring a carefully calibrated response to the world economy's governance—specifically, a thinner set of rules that recognizes the diversity of national circumstances and demands for policy autonomy.*[2]

What, Then, Are We to Do?

How do we resolve this tension between European and national politics? The eurozone crisis typifies such tension at work in the politics beyond borders over sovereignty, creating massive uncertainties that markets don't really know how to interpret or nations know how to cope with. So long as there is a lack of global leadership, real cooperation won't come easy. Despite the Greek deal, expect Europe to continue to grope some more—its programs will remain accident prone, given much harsher austerity. No one-size-fits-all solution can last.

Eurozone members share many common interests, but also differ on many key issues. For example: Slovakia's average income is two-thirds of Greece; yet, it is now being asked to borrow to lend to Greece. Is this not hubris? Has the European project gone too fast and too far? I wonder.

Manila, the Philippines
Kuala Lumpur
February 23, 2012

Notes

1. First published on February 25, 2012, as "Eurozone & Greece: Austerity Fatigue."
2. Dani Rodrik, "Leaderless Global Governance," *The Edge,* Kuala Lumpur (January 23, 2012).

CHAPTER 51

Greece: More Aid Needed to Save the Austerity-Fatigued[1]

After much consternation and anxiety over the Greek bailout, Europe authorized its bailout fund, the European Financial Stability Facility (EFSF), in early March 2012 to raise monies for Greece's bond-swap exchange, the next step before final approval of the second €130 billion aid package on March 9 (first lifeline of €110 billion was in May 2010). The drawdown is expected "at the latest" by March 20, the €14.5 billion bond redemption date. The long-awaited debt restructuring won't be "voluntary," so legal challenges can be expected. But, in practice, bondholders understand the framework and are prepared for the losses (haircuts of as much as 75 percent of their value). By the March 8 deadline, most would have participated. Progress toward wrapping up the bailout came amid signs the crisis was easing. The European Central Bank (ECB) had since pumped €1 trillion into the financial system, pushing the risk premium between Italian and German bonds to the lowest in six months.

Greek authorities now have to deliver. Their hardest tasks include cutting 150,000 public sector jobs by 2015 and tackling unpaid taxes (€60 billion yet to collect). The IMF warned the probability of a sharp slowdown has eased, but risks to world growth remain squarely to the downside.

The outlook is worsening. Unemployment in the eurozone rose to a record 10.7 percent in January, leaving nearly 17 million unemployed. Its manufacturing sector contracted for the seventh month in February. This hasn't taken pressure off consumer prices, which rose to 2.7 percent in February, above the 2 percent target. The economy remains depressed (GDP fell 0.3 percent in the fourth quarter of 2011), and the key concern is the socially unacceptable size of unemployed, and because of the damage to growth. Emerging stagflation presents a dilemma: Rising prices require tight monetary policy, which worsens the downturn, and steps to boost the economy with easy money fuels inflation. The eurozone isn't quite there yet, since wages remain damped. The ECB's real problem lies in the widening gulf between the prosperous "north" and the fragile "south," complicating efforts at addressing the crisis with just a single interest rate tool. In January 2012, Austria's unemployment was 4 percent and Germany's 5.8 percent. The Spanish rate rose to 23.3 percent, while it was 19.9 percent in Greece; Italian unemployment is at an 11-year high of 8.7 percent. It's a similar trend with manufacturing activity in Germany, Austria, and the Netherlands expanding, while contracting in Greece, Spain, and Italy. The flow of ECB funds had lowered borrowing costs but could trigger more inflation, especially in Germany, creating asset bubbles in rate-sensitive sectors like housing.

Fleeting Relief

Greeks on the street are not impressed. They see no end to their troubles: They don't want to kill us but keep us down on our knees so we can keep paying them indefinitely—that's what is heard on TV, amid lingering clouds of teargas, surrounded by façades smashed-in by riots last week. Politicians were dubbed thieves, vagabonds, and traitors by angry mobs. Many doubt the added austerity measures will actually be implemented. Others are worried about the fine print—Greece could relinquish fundamental parts of its sovereignty to foreign lenders, bent on saving the banks more than Greece and its citizens: (1) it abdicates national assets to lenders; (2) lenders can seize its gold reserves; and (3) new bond terms are more favorable to lenders.

To the public, the logic of the new deal escapes them: Banks took off €105 billion, but Greece has to take on €130 billion in new loans. Why do Greeks want that? What's important is that these new measures will place Greece (already five years without growth) deeper into recession. For Fitch and Standard & Poor's, Greece has already technically defaulted. Harvard's Kenneth Rogoff (of *This Time Is Different: Eight Centuries of Financial Folly* fame) said: "I am amazed by the short-term psychology in the market . . . the idea that it's over is an illusion . . . I don't think we're anywhere near the endgame."[2] Greece's current predicament highlights the futility of the recent response:

1. Austerity has led to further economic contraction—the IMF estimated its economy fell 7 percent in 2011 and by 4.5 percent in 2012.
2. Despite haircuts, the IMF doesn't think Greece's debt of 120.5 percent by 2020 is sustainable.
3. The firewall ring-fence is inadequate to fight off contagion.
4. Lessons from US QE (quantitative easing) point to its impact being too long-term, and any "lifting" of markets would be temporary.
5. The provision of aid in "drips" with tightening conditions threatens to destabilize domestic politics and markets.

For the eurozone, making Greece a template has its dangers. Worried, the big risk is for investors to dump European sovereign bonds, leading to new consequences. Italy is vulnerable; for it to be sustainable, its economy needs to grow 5 percent annually with an interest rate not exceeding 3.6 percent. During its most recent boom (2002–2003), Italy's GDP rose on average 3.6 percent per annum; interest (10-year bonds) most recently improved to about 5 percent. Even with optimism, Italy and others like it might muddle through at best. If not, they are all in for a very bumpy ride.

Sins of the "Father"

It was Socrates who said that all evil is due to a lack of knowledge. But for Greece, their problems' causes stare them straight in the face. The main culprits are the Greeks themselves—with their ineffective, incompetent, and corrupt political establishment. Transparency International's corruption index ranks Greece 80th in the world; in September 2011, the Greek treasury carried out only 31 of 75 tax audits promised for the whole year. Although 750,000 (15 percent of workforce) have lost their jobs since the crisis, few came from the public sector (which employs one in four Greeks).

Europe had failed in its responsibilities, too: (1) it procrastinated, only to produce an unrealistic program, which foresaw Greece returning to the markets by 2013; instead, it will take many years; (2) it incoherently responded to the solvency crisis; the Germans and French assumed wrongly that Greece was solvent and what it needed was liquidity—it lent it billions and made the situation worse; (3) it set wrong priorities—the IMF diagnosed a twin problem of weak public finance and severe loss of competitiveness; but policy makers focused on the former in the hope that structural reforms would solve the latter; (4) it did nothing to stimulate growth; and (5) it was indifferent to fair burden sharing—as a political entity with strong social justice aims, it didn't make sense for the European Union (EU) to insist on cutting the minimum wage without making a real commitment on tax evasion. As I see it, overall, Europe "sinned" for its initially late, badly designed, unbalanced, and inequitable package of measures.

G-20 and EU Summit

At the February 26, 2012, weekend meeting in Mexico City, G-20 finance ministers forged a robust consensus[3] that the rest of the world would not stump up more money for the IMF until the eurozone acted more credibly to help itself. So, the "euro-area countries will reassess the strength of their support facilities in March." This review was taken against the backdrop of a "modest global recovery. . . . Nevertheless, growth expectations for 2012 are moderate and downside risks continue to be high." Succumbing to global pressure, European leaders agreed to push forward the funding of its permanent bailout fund. The aim is to line up US$2 trillion in firepower from existing and new funds (possibly by April), comprising a €750 billion European war chest (hopefully by combining the old and new funds) and US$500–600 billion in new IMF resources (on top of current funds of US$385 billion), giving enough cheap money to fuel growth and prevent contagion. It crucially needs German support. For the first time, EU leaders were engaged in finding the right balance between budget austerity and reviving lost growth. It is refreshing for these leaders to use the newfound breathing space to focus on structural reforms. "For too long, our crisis management has erred too far towards austerity," admitted the European Parliament President Martin Schulz after the meeting. Even German Chancellor Angela Merkel now appears prepared to "work on improving competitiveness, growth, and employment."

Asia's Lessons

It is clear Europe still faces an economic crisis (indeed, a dual crisis of "debt" and "growth") that has been deepened by collateral damage. Fiscal policy was being tightened too heavy-handedly and too rapidly. So much so that fiscal virtue has become an economic vice. This reminds me of the tough experience of Asia during the 1997–1998 currency crisis. At its deepest point in 1998, worse than Greece, I think, GDP in ASEAN-5 (Indonesia, Malaysia, the Philippines, Thailand, and Vietnam) fell by 8.3 percent, and in South Korea, down by 5.7 percent. Various IMF bailouts came with conventional austerity measures, involving deep cuts and structural reforms. Within two years, ASEAN-5's external balance turned from a deficit (4 percent of GDP) to a surplus of 6.8 percent; for South Korea, the turnaround was to a surplus of 8.6 percent, from –2.8 percent of GDP. By then, the GDP in these economies had returned to precrisis peaks. For the next 10 years, ASEAN-5 expanded annually at 5 percent on the average, and South Korea, 5.5 percent.

They all managed to endure and to expand despite the odds because (1) they took the pain and suffered the humiliation; (2) they devalued big-time (by 28 percent in South Korea, 37 percent each in Thailand, Malaysia, and Philippines, and 80 percent in Indonesia); (3) some even adopted unconventional measures (including exchange control); and (4) they restructured banking and undertook fiscal reforms—including programs from corporate governance to privatization, and from spending cuts to business debt restructuring. They fought the IMF all the way to ensure programs fitted their circumstance. In the end, they emerged more competitive. The trick: purposeful restructuring and sensible reform—that's the austerity that works in Asia. This can't be repeated in the eurozone because it needs strong political will to pull off. Certainly, devaluation is off the table for them. Yale's Stephen Roach thinks austerity can work for the eurozone: "But its success or failure ultimately boils down to power politics—namely, a resolution of the tension between short-term palliatives and the commitment to a long-term strategy. That's where the battle still rages in the West."[4]

No Pound of Flesh

I sense German intransigence and insistence on even more intense and self-defeating austerity has pushed Greece to the brink of no return. Why condemn the Greeks to misery as punishment for past profligacy? There was a time after World War II when the Allies—conscious of the disastrous impact of German reparations after World War I—did not insist on their pound of flesh: The entire Nazi public debt (600 percent of German GDP) was written off. So was the bulk of the disastrous Weimar period debt. In addition, the Germans received billions in Marshall Plan aid. The Germans did not have to pay for the sins of the father.

Similarly, the Germans did not condemn East Germans after 1989 to severe austerity to remedy its communist experiment. It generously exchanged the worthless ostmarks at one-for-one for deutschemarks, and pumped more than a trillion euros to help it reconstruct. As a result, we have today a strong Germany. I am reminded of Edmund Burke's wise remarks on the perversity of harsh British policy on its American colonies: The question with me is not whether you have the right to render your people miserable but whether it is not in your interest to make them happy. Germany is certainly in a position to do right by Greece.

What, Then, Are We to Do?

Without a return to growth, many peripheral European nations risk the same spiral of depression as Greece. They badly need growth-enhancing measures, including market deregulation and labor flexibility to unleash and lift trapped "animal spirits." Germany should stimulate and act as the region's locomotive. Its economy is outcompeting and outexporting the rest. It has to actively support the expansion of demand. Europe needs to be bolder; it needed to mutualize eurozone members' debts above 60 percent of GDP. Despite the bailout, Greece still remains in the hole. I think it urgently needs a massive helping hand to survive—the infusion of investment funds for modernization and infrastructure expansion, in the spirit of the Marshall Plan. I am reminded of the book written some 20 years ago by two old friends, Paul Volcker (former chairman of US Fed) and Toyoo Gyohten (former head of Japan's Ministry of Finance), *Changing Fortunes*,[5] where they cynically discussed the double standard of crisis resolution: "When the IMF consults with a poor and weak country, the country gets in line. When it consults with a strong country, the Fund gets in line." Unfortunately, Germany just won't get in line.

Kuala Lumpur
March 8, 2012

Notes

1. First published on March 10, 2012, as "More Aid Needed to Save Austerity Fatigue Greece."
2. Carmen M. Reinhart and Kenneth Rogoff, *This Time Is Different: Eight Centuries of Financial Folly* (Princeton, NJ: Princeton University Press, 2009).
3. G-20 Meeting of Finance Ministers and Central Bank Governors in Mexico City, February 25–26, 2012. Communiqué of February 26, 2012.
4. Stephen Roach, "Asia's Take on Austerity," *The Edge*, Kuala Lumpur (March 5, 2012).
5. Paul Volcker and Toyoo Gyohten, *Changing Fortunes: The World's Money and the Threat to American Leadership* (New York: Times Books, 1992).

CHAPTER 52

New Euro Deal: Not the Whole Bazooka[1]

The euro "Merkozy" Plan agreed to and announced in Paris by Chancellor Angela Merkel and French President Nicolas Sarkozy on December 5, 2011, targeting deeper euro-integration was a step in the right direction—but did not offer the big bazooka that could really ease market tension. It's only part of the solution Europe badly needed—it's not even the solution markets are waiting for. So far, wanting "more Europe" has come slowly and grudgingly, but crucially, lacked proper leadership to deal with a truly systemic crisis.

What's paralyzing the eurozone is a flaw buried deep within the monetary union's structure—what an old European friend rightly identified as: the unresolved conflict between the needs of the euro and the independence of its members. Put differently, the link between joint liability of debts and good behavior is missing. Looking back, all those wasted years of skirting the underlying problems, causing rising budget deficits, and building massive debt exploded in late 2009, when Greece first toppled into crisis.

The eurozone tried to stanch the problem with a bailout in May 2010 to no avail because Greece is bankrupt, and did nothing to squelch contagion. By the summer of 2011, Ireland and Portugal had collapsed into bailouts as well, with Italy and Spain now at risk of default. Leaders had pressured countries into gut-wrenching austerity and reform arrangements to stabilize their debt and cut deficits in the hope of rebuilding investor confidence. That strategy failed. Other agreements have also drifted. The second Greece bailout in July 2011 came to naught, while the plan to boost the firepower of the European Financial Stability Facility (EFSF) has since faltered. Frustration is building. It culminated in the week of December 5 summit, with high hopes to marshal the might of the entire eurozone—a US\$13 trillion economy—to provide an extinguisher powerful enough to put out the debt fire. But all it did was inject more painkillers; it was not the cure.

The Deal

The new deal bears the hallmarks of yet another in the series of half-measures that doesn't address increasingly vulnerable banks, or go far enough to instill confidence in the eurozone's battered debt markets; it certainly didn't convince Standard & Poor's (S&P) from putting the debt of 15 European economies, including Germany, on negative credit watch, and Moody's from cutting the credit ratings of France's top three banks. Sure, there had been progress but not enough to provide a defining resolution. Leaders were flirting with risk as Europe goes into recession. We have seen this movie before. The deal involves a promise by everyone to be a little more German about their spending and debt. The consensus now is that the 17-nation eurozone bloc's GDP growth will contract by up to 1 percent in 2012, sharply below 2011's already poor growth of 1 percent. There was little in the deal to address the drastic loss of investor confidence. Eurozone borrowing costs have resumed rising this week. Stock markets have retreated after an initial relief rally as optimism faded. The euro had since sunk below US$1.30, some 12 percent from its peak in May. The new "comprehensive" set of measures making up the eurozone's "fiscal compact" failed to calm markets; the compact included the following:

- Constitutional amendment to balance the fiscal budget. The European Union's (EU) Court of Justice would verify that each country had a compliant debt brake in its laws, but with no oversight from Brussels.
- The new "stability union" will adopt the "golden rule" to ensure structural deficits (i.e., adjusted for boom and bust of economic cycles) below 0.5 percent of GDP. For breaching the 3 percent of GDP deficit limit, nations will suffer "automatic consequences," unless member states vote to block them.
- The €500 billion European Stability Mechanism (ESM) to replace the existing bailout fund (EFSF) will be set up in March 2012 (instead of 2013).
- A €200 billion contribution to the International Monetary Fund (IMF) for on-lending will enhance the firepower of ESM to help Europe.
- No more "hair-cuts" for private holders of dodgy eurozone sovereign debts.
- New treaty to change the EU's foundational pacts. With the United Kingdom's rejection, 17 euro countries and up to 9 of 10 EU nations not using the euro will form a separate pact outside the EU structure.

Prior to the summit, the European Central Bank (ECB) took two decisive steps to shore up the eurozone: cutting interest rate to a record low of

1 percent to soften the looming recession, and crucially extending longer-term liquidity to Europe's cash-starved banks. Reserve ratios were also lowered. But the ECB managed to avoid mounting pressure to buy more troubled States' bonds. As I see it, on the moral hazard side, there are no multitrillion bailout funds and no promise by the ECB to become lender of last resort to monetize everyone's debt, at least for now.

However, the use of the European Court of Justice as final arbiter of rectitude is far from persuasive. Much of the new deal is reflective of the failed "stability and growth pact" that was around when the euro was launched, and which both Germany and France breached shortly thereafter. Such rules will inevitably be broken, because when it comes to fundamental rights to tax and spend, governments will always follow the dictates of national electorates rather than Brussels. No court has the political legitimacy to confront Italian or French unions when there is social unrest in the streets over budget cuts; the court won't (and doesn't) have the stomach to enforce its decisions. When German rectitude faces Italian or Spanish politics, we know who will get the upper hand.

Yet, for me, the irony is that the European Union had already agreed less than three months ago to rules that do much of what the new deal is now seeking to accomplish. They did so without having to endure the ordeal of changing EU treaties. The "six-pack" arrangements were approved after nearly a year of tortuous negotiations. In broad strokes, they would have already established the framework of a more integrated EU.

Tough Sell with No Growth

How to revive confidence? The big problem lies in economic growth, or the lack of it. Most Europeans (who are Keynesians) still believe in the direct linkage between spending and economic growth. So, the balanced budget requirement will work only with tax increases eternally matching higher spending. This implies a "long-term austerity gap." As of now, Europe needs major spending cuts and fiscal reform. But politicians outside Germany are hoping the ECB will eventually come to the rescue. At present, the ECB stands firm and won't play ball. So the political pressure mounts. The new deal simply means continued austerity in the eurozone's periphery without any offsetting impact of devaluation or stimulus at the core. Unemployment—already at 10.3 percent—will continue to rise, placing pressure on households (and youths—in Spain, youth unemployment rate now approaches 50 percent), governments, and banks. Anti-European sentiment will continue to grow, and populist parties will prosper. Violence and social unrest will prevail.

Unfortunately, the new deal has no place for institutional changes to avert such a scenario. I am afraid if such changes are politically not possible, then the euro is doomed. It's just a matter of time. As the post-2008 record shows, the biggest deficit in Europe these days is in ideas to spur growth and in the lack of political will to enact them. Already, in France, its Socialist Party presidential candidate is picking up on this undue emphasis on austerity, stressing Europe's need for growth to get out of the crisis: If there is no growth, none of the objectives will be reached. Alas, Europe's present leadership seems to have no stomach for this option. So I am afraid we are stuck with more summit sequels and the certainty of more uncertainty. Investors' confidence will not return.

Not Enough Firepower

The eurozone firewall still looks inadequate. As of now, plans to leverage the EFSF are mired in technical details. The combined size of EFSF and ESM is capped at an insufficient €500 billion. An infusion of €200 billion through the IMF is not game changing. Even so, this measure is controversial. The ECB has indicated that earmarking is illegal. Moreover, the IMF's shareholders aren't uniformly keen about directing cash to rich Europe. The United States has parliamentary problems; so do Germany, Austria, Czech Republic, Poland, and Ireland, not to mention Holland and Finland. Pressure by S&P to downgrade, and by Moody's, including denying the likes of France AAA rating, has been priced into some markets. Nevertheless, there is still potential to shake prices. Further definite downgrades will take another leg down. Moreover, the eurozone is facing significant risk of a recession in 2012 and a credit crunch. Another shock may be needed to get European politicians to all read from the same page.

Already, the eurozone also faces imminent acute funding problems. Member states need to repay over US$1.2 trillion of debt in 2012, mostly due in the first half-year. In addition, European banks, heavily dependent on State largesse, have US$665 billion of debt coming due by June 2012. On Germany's insistence, the ECB won't be allowed to unleash US-style quantitative easing or heavily buy up bonds or even issue eurozone bonds, which I consider critical. Many believe Germany will eventually relent. Its chancellor has political problems. So, the eurozone's big test still lies ahead. One thing is clear. The market is weighing in. So long as Spanish/Italian bonds cost more than 6 percent, the crisis is not fixed; confidence has not yet returned. The refinancing calendar of Europe's sovereigns is onerous. Pressure will continue to be daunting as long as the ECB is not the lender of last resort.

The real problem is that Europe's banks remain locked out of traditional funding markets, leaving them reliant on the ECB, which is playing it cool. Faced with a funding freeze, banks will shrink their balance sheets and strangle growth by not lending. The situation is serious. Eurozone banks can't raise cash and won't lend to each other because of counterparty risks. On top of it all, the results of last week's "stress tests" suggested Europe's banks are short of €115 billion (up from €106 billion in October). No one knows who is really solvent, anymore.

Drag on Asia

For Asia, the growing uncertainty is killing. The series of sequels following each European summit leaves a trail of deals, but not the cure. Investors are growing more nervous in the face of rising risk of recession. As the economic outlook for Europe worsens, Asia's exporters will experience and expect continued weakening demand. Most exposed will be trading hubs like South Korea, Hong Kong, Taiwan, and Singapore. In 2010, Korea's exports were equal to 45 percent of its GDP, with Europe as its second largest importer. But regional powerhouses China, Japan, and India are also taking a hit. China is most exposed. Exports accounted for 36 percent of GDP in 2010, and Europe is its biggest destination (19 percent). So far, their own huge domestic market has shielded them from Europe's lack of growth, more than their smaller neighbors.

Export focus also matters. European slowdown is already affecting services exports from Hong Kong and Singapore. More cautious consumers in Europe undermine demand for Korean and Taiwanese consumer electronics. China's dominance at the lower end of the value chain is largely immune to shifts in the economic cycle. But what's most worrisome is the continuing kick-the-can-down-the-road attitude of Europeans leaders, which works to prolong the crisis, and translates into reduced investment and employment in manufacturing capacity. The longer the crisis is left unresolved, the worse the impact on Asia.

What, Then, Are We to Do?

I well recall Lord Keynes wrote in 1921: About these matters—the prospect of a European War, the price of copper 20 years hence—there is no scientific basis on which to form any calculable probability whatever. We simply do not know. And Keynes is right. While the euro enjoys widespread support, spending more money to save it doesn't. Germans resent seeing their hard-earned cash diverted to rescue Greeks, perceived by them to be irresponsible. Recent polls show that more than 50 percent of Germans reject euro-bonds, and 59 percent oppose further bailouts. We are now stuck with the classic dilemma—with austerity politics bringing no growth and no framework for common financing, continuing political intransigence has left politicians with the option to continue kicking the can down the road.

Like Keynes, we just don't know how and how far eurozone politicians will go toward assuming joint liability for debts (euro bonds). At some point, Europeans have to make the fateful choice between national sovereignty and the euro's well-being. Time is of the essence for a real breakthrough. In his recent book, Harvard's psychologist Steven Pinker argued that mankind is becoming steadily less warlike and predicted words to this effect: that today we may be living in the most peaceable era in human history.[2] For now, Pinker offers comfort that although the risk of another severe crisis is real, the world won't go to war over it—he is right.

Kuala Lumpur
December 15, 2011

Notes

1. First published on December 17, 2011.
2. Steven Pinker, *The Better Angels of Our Nature: Why Violence Has Declined* (New York: Viking, 2011).

CHAPTER 53

European Union: Favoring Growth Against More Austerity[1]

The world's US$80 trillion economy is split 50–50 between advanced economies (AEs) and developing countries (DCs). Since the financial crisis, AEs struggled to stay afloat. In 2012, they will grow a meager 1.4 percent according to the International Monetary Fund (IMF). Most of Europe is in recession (two consecutive quarters of shrinking growth); the United States isn't doing better than expected (+2.1 percent); and Japan is driving hard to grow 2 percent.

Although DCs have done better, they are already slowing down. Emerging Asia (excluding Japan) remains the driving force as growth slackens to 6.8 percent this year, with China rising by 8.2 percent, and India, 7 percent. Just when the world economy might be turning the corner, along come Spain and United Kingdom slipping into recession, joining Belgium, Czech Republic, Italy, and the Netherlands. Mighty Germany may even be in recession in the second quarter of 2012. Then last week, it was the Dutch's turn to realize the difficulties in pushing for more austerity, placing its AAA credit rating at risk. Spain is the next domino, struggling with continuing budget deficits, very high unemployment, and a very angry public.

The problem with Europe is not the debt crisis; it's the lack of growth. The dilemma is plain: Cutting spending risks deepening the slump, widening the deficit with no prospect of growth, resulting in more street protests; however, any easing of austerity leaves the deficit wide open, triggering a crisis of confidence, making debt servicing more difficult. Europe accounts for about 20 percent of the world economy, roughly the size of the United States. Its 27 European Union (EU) members are collectively the world's largest importer. Their banks have global operations. They matter. The weaker feeble Europe becomes, the more it drags down the global economy. With unemployment at 10.9 percent (17.4 million), there are growing pressures for protectionism, and for less political cohesion and more social unrest.

The Pain

A fierce battle has developed over the best strategy to resolve European woes—austerity or growth—as the eurozone hovers on the brink of its second recession in three years. It just can't cut and grow. Growth advocates say more coordinated fiscal consolidation only backfires and exacerbates economic contraction, since less government spending reduces jobs and shrinks consumer spending and investment; swells the ranks of the unemployed; and makes it more difficult to reduce deficits, thereby risking pushing the economy into a self-defeating vicious cycle. So, government has to relent efforts to reduce deficits now when the global economy is still weak. The "austerians" contend that cutting spending is vital to build credibility and create confidence for healthy growth to come.

Bailouts of Greece, Ireland, and Portugal were accompanied by unpopular budget cuts and structural reforms, consistent with the German-driven pact that forces balanced budgets in law. Eurostat (the EU's statistical agency) had indicated (1) deep cuts can help to reduce deficits; (2) however, overall debts continue to rise—up to its highest at 87.2 percent of GDP by end-2011 (85.3 percent in 2010). The pain is huge in Greece: GDP fell 7 percent in 2011 (fifth year in recession); 25 percent of its 1 million companies had folded and 300,000 more still don't pay workers on time. Its devastation is the most severe in Europe in peacetime. Spain has since gone into recession (second since 2009), threatening deeper unemployment, already at 24.4 percent in the first quarter of 2012, with 5.6 million out of work (52 percent of youths never held a job, with no prospect of getting one soon). Standard & Poor's slashed its sovereign rating two notches to BBB+. The vicious cycle of austerity plunges any nation into a self-defeating deeper hole. This can't go on—and then Holland comes into the fold. Like Germans, the Dutch regard hard work and fiscal discipline as hallmarks of success. In one twist last week, the Dutch refused to "let pensioners bleed because of orders from the EU."[2] The pain deepens.

"Growth Compact"

More and more politicians argue that austerity is now Europe's real problem. The IMF and European Central Bank (ECB) seem to agree. "Europe needs a growth compact," said ECB's President Mario Draghi.[3] The IMF has since called for a pullback, warning nations to avoid "excessive heavy front-loading," and called for gradual budget reductions or face a "full-blown panic."[4] What is there to replace austerity? The growth crowd comprises mainly US economists, including Harvard's Lawrence Summers, Nobel Laureates Paul Krugman and Joseph Stiglitz, academic Brad DeLong, and lately, the Italian prime minister and French socialist presidential candidate Francois Hollande. The debt scourges are led by German Chancellor Angela Merkel, French President Nicolas Sarkozy, and the European Commission. The predicament facing Europe is acute. For decades, politicians derived their legitimacy from assurances to delivering jobs, decent wages, and enough growth to sustain the welfare state. That is now gone. The recent defeat of the Dutch government (a staunch German ally) signals the reality of a need for strategic change. The "fierce" French and Greek elections on May 9 also reflect this need for European leaders to move away from years of denial: "Budgeting responsibility? Yes. Austerity for life? No. Germany must realize that it is growth that will allow us to solve a big part of our problems."[5] Mr. Hollande's camp[6] speaks nebulously about "the reorientation of European spending toward productive enterprise," and the launch of infrastructure projects through the creation of "project bonds." He talks of reorienting ECB to "favor growth and employment."

The real snag is that governments have vastly different views of how to promote growth, but with no practical mechanisms to implement. Sure, both sides agree on structural reforms to boost potential growth by (1) removing barriers within the single market and (2) making labor laws more flexible. But they differ mostly about the pace of debt reduction. Many feel what's being done now depresses revenue, thereby making governments miss fiscal targets. The ECB has since admitted that austerity has taken a higher-than-expected toll. The "growth compact" it advocated in December 2011 would focus on structural reforms and boost competitiveness. Realistically, expect the ECB to act in a reactive rather than a proactive way, because austerity is already hardwired into eurozone structures. Yet, the German chancellor has since called to bolster the European Investment Bank (EIB) and to use EU infrastructural funds to spur growth, agreeing that austerity alone is not the whole answer: "We need growth in the form of sustainable initiatives, not simply economic stimulus that just raises public debt."[7]

This opens the door for compromise, when needed. I sense the ECB was taken aback by latest signs of weakness reflecting "prevailing uncertainty," and by fears over future strategy triggered by the French election and the Dutch government's collapse. Germany, Europe's largest economy, has championed debt reduction as key to ending the region's crisis. Its debt burden will fall below 79 percent this 2012, while it rises to 89 percent in France, Europe's No. 2 economy. German unemployment is down to 6.7 percent, against 9.6 percent in France, which is expected to balance its budget by 2016. So, the debate is shifting, admits Hollande: ". . . the President of European Council said he's ready for changes . . . there is no magic formula. . . ."[8] The recent call to raise the capital of the EIB to leverage total investment outlays of €180 billion was a positive move.

Economic Suicide

The *New York Times* recently reported on growing suicides in Europe: people taking their own lives in despair. As an economist, as much as the stories are heartbreaking, I am more worried about the macroeconomic suicide being committed by European leaders. It is now clear Europe's harsh austerity programs have pushed economies even deeper into depression-like conditions; and even healthy ones face a series of "electoral" setbacks. "All the reforms we have put in place are not creating growth; they are deflationary," said the Italian prime minister.[9] While there is growing consensus on the need for new growth policies, it is far from obvious how to get there. The dilemma is this: Borrowing more to finance growth could stir up the financial markets. One radical way out is to issue common European debt (euro-bonds); this still remains sensitive. But, Germany could turn around and surprise. Of course, Germany could ease its own drive on austerity and do more to encourage domestic consumption. However, what we are actually seeing so far is complete inflexibility. In a nutshell, you need growth and job creation, or else debt reduction doesn't work. That's reality. For Professor Paul Krugman,[10] the solution lies in more expansionary monetary policy—even at the cost of higher inflation; Europe also needs more expansionary fiscal policies in Germany to offset austerity in Spain, and so on, rather than reinforcing it.

Even with such policies, peripheral nations still face years of hardship; but at least there is hope. Joseph Stiglitz[11] is more emphatic: "There has never been any successful austerity program in any large country . . . I think Europe is heading to a suicide." He added, "austerity combined with the constraints of the euro are a lethal combination . . . leading to high levels of unemployment that will be politically unacceptable and will make deficits worse . . . destroying human capital and creating alienated young people."

Three-Pole Global Economy

Political uncertainty in France and Holland, until now safe from contagion, has stoked renewed fears a more serious eurozone crisis is about to break out again. Fitch has expressed doubts about Netherlands' Aaa status, reducing the real European core to just Germany, Finland, and Luxembourg. Then there are possible leadership changes in France, China, and the United States. This underscores rising political risk in looking forward. It has not ended yet. The EU's overall index of economic confidence for April fell to its lowest level since end-2009, suggesting continuing contraction in the second quarter of 2012. A weaker Europe is not good for the world because of damaged confidence, lower imports, and less credit flows. The latest

SWIFT[12] (Society for Worldwide Interbank Financial Telecommunication) estimates show GDP in the rich Organisation for Economic Co-operation and Development (OECD) picking up to grow by 2.3 percent in the second quarter of 2012 (2 percent in the second quarter of 2011), sustaining the rate of the first quarter of 2012. Since then, there is added political uncertainty as nations, big (United Kingdom, Netherlands, Italy, and possibly Germany and France) and small (Spain, Ireland, and Greece) are caught in recession.

The outlook is all too uncertain. The reality is that US (first pole) growth has cooled, as businesses cut back on investments and restocked shelves at a more moderate pace. Labor markets are showing early signs of fatigue while consumer spending appears to be softening. The Fed stands pat as US growth appears just firm enough to weaken the case for QE3 (new quantitative easing). With European (second pole) prospects still up in the air in the face of widespread May Day protests, Asia continues to grow (with soft landing in China)—but the IMF, Asian Development Bank, and US-based Institute of International Finance have all cautioned against renewed European slowdown. The third Asian pole has ably carried the global economy thus far. Going forward, growth in emerging Asia remains fragile, underscoring the continued impact of Europe's crisis and weak demand from the United States and China. Fiscal contraction reduces incomes, limiting the capacity to repay debts. Economists have since scaled back expectations in China, India, and Indonesia.

What, Then, Are We to Do?

When you have Germany, the United Kingdom, Italy, France, and the Netherlands under austerity, it's like a joint undertaking in fiscal consolidation; the economic consequences are bound to be dire. European efforts to contain the crisis have fallen short again. May Day anti-austerity rallies call for a strategic change in course. The bottom line: Policy reversals seem unlikely soon; the tone will change but not the content. It is hard to avoid a sense of despair. What's worrisome is that leaders seem determined to drive Europe off the cliff, and the world will pay the price. That's a real shame. If they persist to meet fiscal targets, investors are likely to punish them because they ignore growth. However, if they ease austerity, the markets—concerned about long-term sustainability—will make them pay in terms of higher costs for their bond issues. They are damned if they do, and damned if they don't. As I see it, only if growth is restored can the eurozone endure. Europe has for years talked about growth, but did nothing! The time to act is now. The world is watching.

Kuala Lumpur
May 3, 2012

Notes

1. First published on May 5, 2012.
2. Mark Rutte, Dutch prime minister, before his government collapsed, on April 23, 2012.
3. Mario Draghi, president, European Central Bank, speaking to the European Parliament's Committee on Economic and Monetary Affairs in Brussels on April 25, 2012.
4. Christine Lagarde, managing director of the International Monetary Fund, outlining risks for the global economy in Washington, DC, on April 18, 2012.
5. François Hollande, French presidential candidate, speaking on France 2 TV in Paris on April 26, 2012.
6. Michel Sapin, chief economic adviser to Mr. Hollande, speaking in Paris on April 26, 2012, in support of Mr. Hollande's presidential runoff.
7. Angela Merkel, German chancellor, called to bolster the capabilities of the European Investment Bank in Berlin on April 29, 2012.
8. Hollande.
9. Mario Monti, Italian prime minister, speaking at a business conference in Bussels on April 24, 2012.
10. Paul Krugman, "Europe's Economic Suicide," *New York Times* (April 16, 2012).
11. Joseph Stiglitz, "Europe Headed Towards Suicide on Austerity," told reporters in Vienna on April 26, 2012.
12. Andre Boico, managing director of SWIFT (Society for Worldwide Interbank Financial Telecommunication, which operates the global messaging service for financial institutions), releasing the SWIFT Index (based on payments traffic sent through its network by banks—some 5 billion messages are sent globally a year) on April 24, 2012, in Singapore.

CHAPTER 54

European Union: A Summer of Discontent[1]

Brussels is known for its fickle weather. I have written repeatedly on the prospect of the eurozone witnessing more winters so long as politicians (and politics will decide Europe's fate) avoid addressing its underlying problems. For a little while, the crisis enjoyed a hint of summer when the European Central Bank (ECB) injected more than €1 trillion in short-term money into Europe's banks. Alas, it has now returned to a wintry gloom as new storm clouds have begun to blow from Spain and Italy. Yields on Spanish bonds have risen dangerously, with Italian ones close behind. Like Spain, Italy is already in recession and will miss its deficit target this year. The big surprise has been the Netherlands, which, too, will miss its fiscal target. So will France and Greece.

A chance for change happened on May 6, 2012. France elected a new president with an alternative economic strategy to the "unexpurgated diet" of austerity, demanding that the European Union (EU) treaty limiting debt be expanded to include measures to stimulate economic growth. Despite many years of belt tightening, growth in Europe has stagnated and a record 11 percent of its labor force is still out of work. In France, 10 percent are unemployed; competitiveness is sliding and labor costs are among the highest in Europe. France has since lost its Aaa rating. On the same day, the Greeks delivered their verdict on the bailout: Nearly 70 percent of the electorate voted against the "barbarous" austerity rescue policies and signaled the depth of their anger over the political establishment and its parasitic political system fueled by patronage and cronyism and corruption. Greece did make big inroads into its deficit: Between 2010 and 2011, 6 percentage points were cut off the budget through sharp tax increases and painful budget cuts. By the end of 2012, Greece will have lost 20 percent of its pre-crisis gross domestic product (GDP). Unemployment stands at 21 percent. The euro has since sunk to hit its lowest level since January 2012 against the US$ (1.2845). Investor confidence dropped to its lowest level in three years as the deepening crisis stoked anxiety in Asia and the United States; stock markets plummeted throughout Asia.

Austerity Backlash

The anti-austerity wave that voted in a new French president and pulverized the Greek government has had broad resonance that can't be ignored. France and Greece aren't the only ones revolting against austerity. In Britain, the ruling party suffered heavy losses in local elections as voters vented anger against severe spending and welfare cuts. In Italy, voter discontent with harsh fiscal restraints has given rising support to angry protests. Even in Germany, state elections this week in May 2012 repudiated tough austerity. The Netherlands government fell on too much budget cuts. All these can destabilize an already fragile euro-area and worsen recession in larger nations like the United Kingdom, Italy, and Spain. Besides, there appears to be a growing disconnect between public support for the euro and public anger on the harsh austerity prescribed to save it. The new sentiment is best expressed by a Greek parliamentarian: "We want to stay in the eurozone so we can change its policies, because they are unfair to people. But we won't stay if Europe gives us no choice but austerity."[2] Even German Chancellor Merkel was reconciliatory on May 7: "We are talking about two sides of the same coin. Progress is achievable only via solid finances plus growth."[3]

France Fumbles

Unlike its robust German neighbor, the French economy remains moribund. The Bank of France expects no growth in the second quarter of 2012, marking two quarters running of stagnation (+1.7 percent GDP growth in 2011 and +0.2 percent in the fourth quarter of 2011). Unemployment has risen above 10 percent, more layoffs are due from corporates, and government spends the equivalent of 57 percent of its GDP, the highest in Europe.

In France, the state's strong role in public life remains broadly cherished. Nevertheless, the need is being acknowledged to reduce its huge $2.2 trillion public debt (90 percent of GDP). Already, Brussels had raised a red flag on France's budget deficit next year—at 4.2 percent of GDP, exceeding the EU's target of 3 percent; for this year, it is expected to reach its 4.5 percent target. Voters rejected the severe austerity not just because it's painful at a time of high unemployment and deep social discontent, but more so because it isn't working. François Hollande (the new president) had pledged to create 150,000 state-subsidized jobs for youth (unemployment at 22 percent) and reform the swamped pension system by rolling back the retirement age to 60 from 62. To lower unemployment, France also has to address crucial social conflict. It is a platform made for France's 99 percent: There need to be signs of fairness and of equal treatment across society. The young's outrage reflected a national discontent best expressed in a wildly popular pamphlet by a World War II (WWII) resistance fighter, Stephane Hassel, "Indignez-Vous!" ("Time for Outrage"), calling on young people to revolt in a peaceful insurrection against injustice, mass consumption, and the endless competition of all against all.

Greece Crumbles

Elections in Greece reflected a widespread cry of rage. The economy will have shrunk by a fifth since 2008; its GDP will fall 4.7 percent this year (–6.2 percent in the first quarter of 2012), with no signs of recovery and youth unemployment topping 50 percent. Overall, unemployment spiked to a record 21 percent; more than 100,000 small businesses have closed; and wages and pensions have been badly cut. Homelessness is on the rise, and suicides had jumped 40 percent in the past two years. Its budget deficit, despite stringent efforts to consolidate, will reach 7.3 percent of GDP, and increase to 8.4 percent in 2013; by then, its debt/GDP ratio will rise to 168 percent. Complains a typical 45-year-old schoolteacher (Evgenia Vogiatzi, a lifelong socialist) in Athens: "I've had my salary cut 30 percent. I am paying taxes through the nose, and they are talking about more cuts. If that is what it takes to stay in Europe, I don't want Europe."

Greece will run out of money this summer. Citigroup has placed the odds of a Greek euro exit at 50–75 percent over the next 12–18 months. People with no prospects are beginning to feel they have nothing to lose by leaving the euro. The long-speculated Greek default and euro exit just won't go away. A "Grexit" (abbreviation for *Greece exit*) will surely test the firewalls. Also, there will be contagion. All these prolong market uncertainty.

Spain Stumbles

Spain remains a bigger problem because of its size. Like Greece, Spain has endured austerity that pushed unemployment to 25 percent and led to a severe recession (GDP of –1.8 percent in 2012). Pensions are slashed, government workers fired, and taxes hiked. It still has a budget shortfall of 6.4 percent of GDP in 2012 (EU target, 5.3 percent). It struggles to live with austerity and rebuild its banking sector following the housing bubble collapse. Resentment is growing against politicians and beneficiaries of bank bailouts. Spain will succumb to corrosion, not collapse. More serious, Spain faces being shut out of financial markets.

Berlin Scrambles

Like it or not, the Germans—keeper of fiscal rectitude—will need to shift policy to do more for growth. The cry of rage cannot be ignored. Germany needs to compromise. There is a range of pro-growth policies on the table, including the creation of a public investment bank and tax breaks for small businesses, incentives for enterprises to retain workers and for new hires, and deployment of EU financial institutions to ease the crisis and under-write infrastructure projects. The presidents of Germany and France have since pledged to forge a joint approach on a growth pact in time for the European Union Summit in June.

Stiffest Test Ever

Europe is in a mess. Growth has been falling back for decades. In the 1970s, GDP growth averaged 3.2 percent annually; in the 1980s, 2.5 percent; in the 1990s, 2.2 percent, and in the 2000s, 1.2 percent. The 2008 crash was bad for most, but Europe continued to slide. This year, it will hardly grow—at best an anemic 0.5–1 percent. While the US share of global GDP was held steady at 26 percent for two generations, the EU's share has since dropped to 26 percent, from 35 percent in 1970. The odd man out is Germany. Joblessness is down to 6.7 percent; the budget deficit is heading to zero; and Germany's debt/GDP ratio held at a steady 76 percent.

Within the EU, there is definitely austerity fatigue. You just can't cut and grow. Austerity begets more austerity. The International Monetary Fund (IMF) studies showed that the debt/GDP ratio will rise (not fall) in every year from 2008–2013 in Ireland, Italy, Spain, and Portugal. Because of severe debt restructuring, the ratio in Greece fell briefly. More scary are the unemployment numbers: Among youth (15–25 years), those without a job represented 51 percent in Greece and Spain, 36 percent in Portugal and Italy, and 30 percent in Ireland. France fares better, but the situation is dire: One in five youths is unemployed. Politically, eight leaders were swept from office in the past year. The economic outlook is poor. GDP will shrink in Greece, Italy, Portugal, and Spain. With luck, it will stagnate in France and Ireland. Optimistically, as a whole, they can be expected to grow just 0.5–1.0 percent in 2013. This is politically unacceptable.

Austerity Rebuked

The French and Greek elections sent a common message that voters won't stomach tough austerity anymore. So change must happen: a better bal-ance of austerity and growth, perhaps. The president of the Deutsche

Bundesbank (Germany's Central Bank)[4] has insisted (1) monetary policy has reached its limits; (2) the fiscal "compact" precludes discretionary fiscal policy; and (3) the currency union lacks fiscal solidarity. How, then, to square the circle to restore confidence, as more economies plunge deeper into recession? For the Germans, this leaves only structural reform—what they now call growth policy. Growth proponents say such reforms don't offer a swift return to growth. It took the 1980s Thatcher reforms more than a decade to derive benefit for the United Kingdom. Nobel Laureate Joseph Stiglitz[5] contends that there is no example of a large economy (Europe is the world's largest) recovering as a result of austerity. Also, Professor Paul De Grauwe[6] has stressed that the current adjustment process is asymmetric: countries in difficulties disinflate, but those in a strong position don't inflate (e.g., Germany). That's the crux of the problem.

Growth Pact

But, all is not lost. Stiglitz suggested two ways[7] to grow: (1) nations like Germany with fiscal room to maneuver should use it to push for more investment to enhance growth, with positive spillover for Europe—the balanced expansion of taxes and spending can stimulate growth; (2) Europe as a whole is still in good fiscal shape. The whole is more than the sum of its parts. Europe has much capacity to borrow and recycle (especially ECB) by on-lending to promote growth and jobs.

It all depends on Germany. It could become the locomotive to the rest of Europe, spurred by very low borrowing costs. Coupled with a sharp fall in the euro (say, by 15–20 percent), the German economy can lift off, enhancing economic prospects for the eurozone. It has been argued that a cheap currency, by giving an artificial boost to competitiveness, is more palatable than austerity. To really help struggling euro-nations, the ferocity of fiscal contraction needs to be lessened by slowing down budget adjustment, while finding a realistic and credible path to budget balance. Start by pushing back fiscal targets; for example, allow Spain to meet its goal in 2014 (not 2013).

Furthermore, there are already institutions within Europe, such as the European Investment Bank (EIB), that could help finance the much-needed investment, including giving the EIB more clout (new capital injection) and allowing it to issue "project bonds" to fund new energy technology and infrastructure, and small business expansions (to offset credit denial by banks). Then, the structural funds within EU can be deployed as growth stimuli. Finally, create new financial capabilities to promote for growth and jobs. There is no need to reject the budget compact. Just add on growth stimulus measures as a companion. This is one way to avert the vicious cycle of recession and austerity.

What, Then, Are We to Do?

The pain in Europe is self-inflicted and quite unnecessary, especially the suffering of the poor and the young. Relentless austerity is not working. Fortunately, there are serious alternatives to austerity economics. It was Keynesian Sir Roy Harrod who gave an erudite refutation in the 1950s titled: Are the hardships really necessary? Controlling deficits is important. But sharp reductions in public spending as the one-size-fits-all answer to Europe's problems is dangerous. It stalls recovery; worse, it wreaks havoc on human lives. Social discontent and grim numbers and a poor outlook prove that. Surely, voters in Europe have figured it out. Nations must be allowed to grow. According to Mr. Hollande: "People need to see that while the collective effort may be long and difficult, it's going to be fair and involve everyone."[8] But all eyes now are on Greece and Spain. Europe's voters know what to do with leaders who don't, or won't, meet their expectations. And Europe is running out of time.

Kuala Lumpur
May 17, 2012

Notes

1. First published on May 19, 2012.
2. Alexis Tsipras, head of left-wing coalition Syriza, after almost quadrupling its share of Greek votes, in Athens on May 7, 2012.
3. Angela Merkel, in welcoming the election of the new French president, Mr. François Hollande, in Berlin on May 7, 2012.
4. Jens Weidmaan, "Monetary Policy Is No Panacea for Europe's Ills," *Financial Times* (May 2, 2012).
5. Joseph Stiglitz, "After Austerity," *The Edge*, Kuala Lumpur (May 14, 2012).
6. Paul De Grauwe, of London School of Economics, stated in a privately circulated note in London on May 4, 2012.
7. Stiglitz.
8. François Hollande, at an interview with *Time* in Paris on May 18, 2012.

CHAPTER 55

European Union: Draghi's Bumblebee[1]

Mario Draghi, president of the European Central Bank (ECB), can be forgiven since he is neither English nor an entomologist when he compared euro's growing pains with the impossibility of flight by the bumblebee. The ECB president was reported to have said:

> *The euro is like a bumblebee. This is a mystery of nature because it shouldn't fly but instead it does. So the euro was a bumblebee that flew very well for several years. And now—and I think people ask 'how come?'—probably there was something in the atmosphere, in the air, that made the bumblebee fly. Now something must have changed in the air, and we know what after the financial crisis. The bumblebee would have to graduate to a real bee. And that's what it's doing.*[2]

But it was his pledge to help in this transformation that attracted market interest: "The ECB is willing to do whatever it takes to preserve the euro and believe me, it will be enough."[3]

Unlike politicians, markets do give deference to the ECB since it can match bold words with actions because of its powers to print unlimited euros. As to be expected, the very next day, Italian and Spanish bonds strengthened (Spanish 10-year bond yield fell below 7 percent, and Italian bonds, down to 6.03 percent); and the benchmark index for Italian stocks closed 5.6 percent higher, and Spanish, up 6.1 percent.

Euro Does Not Fly

Dr. Draghi's credibility was tested after the ECB's recent meeting when he failed to deliver and soured market sentiment, in the face of German opposition to ECB's further purchases of sovereign debt, pushing Spanish 10-year bond yield back to 7.13 percent, and Italian, to 6.3 percent. The euro hit as low as 1.214 against US dollar. Safe-haven German bunds, however, rallied, with 10-year yield at 1.25 percent. So, it does appear Draghi's bumblebee couldn't fly after all—even though scientifically, it is established bumblebees can fly—but does not include a metamorphosis into some "real" bee. Be that as it may, it is unclear if the ECB will ever be transformed into a true central bank—whether it can be eventually joined up in a currency, fiscal, and banking union, which the eurozone badly needs to have if it were to overcome structural weaknesses in the current arrangement.

Dr. Draghi is right in pointing out that the growing gap in interest rates within the eurozone (with Greece paying 25 percent for two-year money despite rock-bottom ECB reference rates) reflects a malfunction in the transmission mechanism of monetary policy. Draghi labeled this "financial-market fragmentation," which is threatening to undermine the euro as banks in one nation try to avoid dealing with banks in another. Until 2011, 60 percent of money-market loans were made across borders. Today, it's only 40 percent and falling. So long as this persists, the eurozone will remain crisis prone.

Europe Limps into the Third Quarter of 2012

Europe is now looking worse as the United States moves sideways. Unemployment in the eurozone hit 11.2 percent in June, the highest ever, bringing the total jobless to 17.8 million, which further weakens consumer spending. But it hides vast divergences: from a low of 4.5 percent in Austria to a high of 24.8 percent in Spain, where a shrinking economy makes it even more difficult to service its debt. Eurozone activity fell to its steepest point in July in more than three years, while export orders plunged despite a weakening euro. The French economy contracted in the second quarter of 2012 and is likely to slip into recession in the third quarter of 2012. Italy, the eurozone's third-largest economy, is wallowing in recession, contracting further in the second quarter of 2012, its fourth straight quarterly decline. Spain's recession also worsened in the second quarter of 2012. In one of the starkest signs yet, German manufacturers suffered the largest fall in new export orders, indicating that Europe's powerhouse is now flagging. Manufacturing activity in both Germany and France fell at the fastest rate in more than three years.

Overall, economic sentiment in the eurozone fell to near a three-year low in July as the bloc's economy deepened its slump and businesses became more pessimistic. Confidence had continued to fall, suggesting the slump is extending into the third quarter of 2012 as policy makers struggled to tame the euro and growth crises. Clearly, all macroeconomic indicators are pointing south: The gauge of sentiment among European manufacturers fell to –15 in June; the services confidence indicator dropped to –8.5, while the gauge of consumer sentiment slipped to –21.5. So much so Moody's put a negative outlook on triple-A-rated Germany, and borrowing costs from Spain to Italy surged to record highs, threatening the euro's survival. The euro had since depreciated 7.4 percent against the US dollar in the past three months. With continuing fiscal austerity and debt reduction, eurozone as a whole is struggling—amid its second recession in four years. The International Monetary Fund (IMF) has since cut its eurozone growth forecast for 2013 to 0.7 percent, expecting gross domestic product (GDP) to fall 0.3 percent in 2012.

Rising unemployment and growing pessimism about the future are grim evidence of how far the eurozone crisis is affecting ordinary people and the wider economy. Government spending cuts and tax increases aimed at stemming rising debt levels have combined with poor consumer and business confidence to spark widespread slowdown across the bloc. Already more than half-a-dozen eurozone nations are in recession. Expectations are for more nations to need a bailout. What's worrisome is Germany's weakening retail sales, which fell for the third straight month in June.

Consumers all over are retrenching as prospects sour. Europeans are trading down to cheaper groceries, buying fewer big-ticket items, and searching more for bargains online. The mood has also deteriorated in France, where it is caught between trying to revive growth with major infrastructure spending and meeting EU rules to bring down the budget deficit. Private investors in France and Germany are holding back. Consumers prefer to save for the next rainy day. Eurozone investor sentiment fell for the fifth straight month in August, amid ongoing worries about the bloc still in crisis. So long as the risk of a eurozone collapse remains a real possibility, private spending will not be forthcoming. Delay has become Europe's worst enemy.

US Economy Cools

The US expanded in the second quarter of 2012 at its slowest pace at a time when weakened labor market conditions prompted consumers to cut back on their spending. GDP rose by 1.5 percent, against 1.9 percent in the first quarter of 2012 (and 4.1 percent in the fourth quarter of 2011) as businesses became more cautious about spending and hiring as the economy lost more steam. Uncertainty and joblessness persist. Unemployment edged up to 8.3 percent, although the private economy created 172,000 jobs in June. The slowing economy raises the possibility that any sudden shock—including a major escalation of the eurozone crisis—could push the economy back into recession. Meanwhile, the US Midwestern drought could slow down growth further and raise food prices, which makes consumers stingier. Since then, big retailers had reported healthier sales in July despite private efforts to save more. House prices appear to have begun to turn up, and recent house construction expansion looks sustainable. Automakers are also selling more. Of late, with interest rates so low, bank lending is rising lustily. But it's not enough. Manufacturing new orders have since slowed. More than one-half of the counties in the United States are deemed disaster areas as the drought spreads. Overall, 5.2 million are still out of work for six months or more, and still looking. At July's rate of job growth, it will take more than eight years to get back to full employment. So, it's not surprising the Fed recently signaled its readiness to spur the anemic expansion: "as needed to promote a strong recovery and sustained improvement in labor market conditions." Frankly, the Fed has used up most of its bullets. What's really needed is fresh fiscal accommodation, which it is unlikely to get in an election year. That's politics. Overall, the outlook for the rest of the year is not encouraging—third-quarter 2012 could be weaker than the first half of 2012 amid slackening demand; US$ strengthening will make it harder for exporters, and considering businesses have been stockpiling inventory in the face of sluggish consumption. Fed initiatives can only help. But markets are eager for quick and forceful action and easily get disappointed if either doesn't deliver what's expected.

Sticky Spell for Asia

This time around, emerging markets can no longer be relied on to pick up the slack. Every major economic region is slackening in sync. At the last recession, China and India in particular provided strong support to shore up world demand. This will no longer happen, as these nations face familiar problems of their own. In Asia, there are growing signs of slowdown almost everywhere. In China, slackening in manufacturing growth in July added to the broader ramp-down in the region. Manufacturing growth in India slowed significantly in July, reflecting largely political paralysis while South Korea, Taiwan, and Vietnam experienced similar industrial contraction. In South Korea (Asia's fourth largest economy), exports in July fell to its lowest in nearly three years and manufacturing activity shrank at its sharpest pace. The story is similar in Taiwan and Vietnam, where the slowdown is compounded by poor domestic demand. Indonesia, Southeast Asia's largest economy, experienced a pickup in manufacturing activity, but weak external demand widened its trade deficit significantly. GDP rose 6.4 percent in the second quarter of 2012 with robust domestic demand driving growth, led by the increasingly affluent middle class.

In July, China reported its slowest growth at 7.6 percent in the second quarter of 2012, struggling to grow 8 percent for the whole year. For 2012, growth in Asia (outside Japan) would be 7.1 percent. The outlook has gotten weaker. While slackening global demand was crimping exports, it also helped to bring down rising oil and food costs, easing inflationary pressures.

In Southeast Asia, domestic demand and reconstruction should keep growth robust, with a strong rebound in Thailand and healthy expansion in the Philippines, Malaysia, and Indonesia. What's important, Asia has sufficient policy space to conduct easier monetary and fiscal policies to provide the needed stimulus.

China Stabilizes

Emerging nations should do reasonably well. The IMF reckons emerging Asia will grow 7 percent in 2012, against 7.8 percent in 2011. Europe's recession had significant impact—it sapped demand for its manufacturing exports and restrained price for its commodities. Russia, Brazil, and South Africa are notable casualties. Fortunately, big emerging nations have scope to respond; most have restructured—their banks are well capitalized and central banks are well stocked with foreign reserves. A hard landing in these nations looks unlikely.

Nevertheless, there is no returning to past decades' unsustainable high growth. China, for one, doesn't want it. It is rebalancing and moving to adopt a slower growth model led by consumers. When the dust settles, China will emerge as the "new normal." In its recent monetary policy report for the second quarter of 2012, the People's Bank of China (its central bank) talks of stabilizing economic growth as top priority in balancing its three objectives: maintaining steady and relatively fast growth, adjusting the economic structure, and managing inflation. It sees the global slowdown ("It will remain relatively weak for an extended period") as the biggest risk to the Chinese economy and it may need to take measures to boost growth. The report concluded: The tasks of restructuring the domestic economy and expanding domestic demand remain huge, and domestic growth drivers still need to be strengthened. It is clear China is determined to stimulate, if necessary, by spending more on urban social infrastructure and low-income housing.

What, Then, Are We to Do?

The outlook for the rest of the year is darkening. The headwinds from a stagnating Europe are real and worrisome. The United States runs the risk of being "forced" into contraction in 2013. As I see it, there is serious concern over a looming crisis. Emerging nations face not just the risk of a cyclical downturn, but also the risk of a "new normal" of slackened growth over the longer term. How can they cope? Economically, these can be dealt with in relative ease, given the vast policy space they now have. Nations with large domestic markets and a prosperous middle-class will cope better.

Socially and politically, these risks are much more difficult to manage. More serious are growing tensions within the eurozone arising from further fiscal consolidation and forced compliance with much stricter terms of severe budget cuts and tax increases in the face of rising unemployment with its attendant potential for social upheaval. Political uncertainty will surely feed back into the economy, which will further deteriorate; and so the vicious cycle continues. Painted into a corner, politicians can be shocked into action—perhaps by a serious euro-wide bank-run or a chaotic Greek exit. Maybe this is not such a bad thing.

Kuala Lumpur
August 9, 2012

Notes

1. First published on August 11, 2012, as "Draghi's Bumblebee."
2. Mario Draghi, the European Central Bank chief, speaking at a conference in London on July 27, 2012.
3. Ibid.

CHAPTER 56

Cyprus's Bailout Turns Bail-In[1]

Cyprus blinked! A bailout designed to rescue Cyprus and keep it in the 17-nation eurozone badly backfired a fortnight ago toward the third week of March 2013. The European deal agreed to in the wee hours of March 16 in fact "bailed-in" all bank-insured and uninsured depositors alike of this Mediterranean midget (population: 800,000), with a gross domestic product (GDP) of only €18 billion—equivalent to less than 0.2 percent of eurozone's total output. The 9.9 percent tax levied on deposits exceeding €100,000 (European Union [EU] guarantee threshold) alienated Russia (one-third of total deposits held by its businesses and banks). The 6.75 percent tax on guaranteed deposits sparked such outrage that even when later sweetened with an exemption for deposits below €20,000, the rescue was voted down 36–0 by Parliament on March 19.

Cyprus may be bankrupt, but this was a messy deal. Eight months after the European Central Bank (ECB) had managed to restore some semblance of stability by promising "to do whatever it takes" to save the euro, the risk of exit by a euro member returned. Indeed, it raised the chances of bank runs—if Cyprus can grab your savings, why not Italy or Spain? It just reflects the lack of real progress toward a durable solution to euro's woes. I think it's wrong for the eurozone to even consider letting tiny Cyprus slide out so easily. Euro's stability must rest on its irreversibility. Already, eurozone is in recession. Protest parties are getting more popular and more aggressive again. The real surprise was the International Monetary Fund's (IMF) support for a haircut on guaranteed deposits—a sure sign of double standards. The Institute of International Finance (IIF), representing the world's largest banks, calls the move an incredibly dangerous precedent, in that it broke with practices that depositors' savings were guaranteed. In so doing, eurozone breaks its own financial system's last great taboo. The consequences can be toxic.

Cyprus Is Unique

I well recall in the early stages of the European crisis, eurozone's preferred solution was to lend governments money to bail out holders of financial assets (e.g., bank bonds), thus passing the burden to future generations of taxpayers (moral hazard). Over time, as the debt burden ballooned and public finances became less sustainable, this approach softened. In Greece, part of the burden was shifted to private holders of government bonds. In Spain, Ireland, and Netherlands, losses were inflicted on junior bondholders. On each occasion, alarms were raised that imposing losses on investors could trigger contagion. But each time, the euro survived.

Now, eurozone has gone one step further by imposing losses on depositors, with the familiar warnings of impending doom. It is said Cyprus is unique because its debt (comprising mainly large bank deposits) is overwhelming. Combined assets of its two largest banks totaled €85 billion (or five times GDP), with total deposits of €58 billion at the end of 2010. To get a sense of what this means relative to the US size, total deposits with these two banks alone would translate to the equivalent of US$45 trillion (actual deposits with all US banks totaled only about US$9 trillion).

In a sense, Cyprus had become two banks with a country attached! This business model cannot survive. Even after the severe haircut on large depositors, Cyprus still requires a €10 billion bailout, equivalent to 60 percent of GDP. Cypriot banks are overwhelmingly deposit-funded, invested mainly in Greece. The nation is bankrupt. Its debt (including bank liabilities) would hit 145 percent of GDP. The choice was really between hitting big depositors or hitting eurozone taxpayers. For Germany and the IMF, the choice is obvious. Cypriot politics, too, played a role—it feared scaring away offshore cash that has flowed in to take advantage of its weak money-laundering enforcement. Basically, Cyprus is a place where people (especially Russians) hide their wealth from both taxmen and regulators. Then there is the delicate gap in trust and political cultures between northern and southern Europe. This lack of convergence keeps holding it back.

A Bitter Deal

With a failed deal at home, the EU and IMF stepped up pressure on Cyprus to seal a bailout worth €10 billion, provided it raised another €5.8 billion through reworking the bank levy to shelter all depositors below €100,000 each (EU threshold for deposit guarantee). The ECB's emergency funding for Cyprus expired on March 25—first-time ECB publicly declared the removal of a member state's banks from emergency lending support by the euro-system (i.e., the ECB and eurozone's 17 central banks). With its two largest banks already insolvent, Cyprus's financial system would collapse without continuing access to euro-central bank funding, threatening its euro-membership. Cyprus was left with Hobson's choice. In the end, it clinched a last-ditch deal that would unlock €10 billion of troika money (EU, ECB, and IMF) in exchange for: (1) imposition of steep losses on uninsured depositors (including wealthy Russians); (2) closure of Cyprus's second largest bank to avoid a financial meltdown; (3) protection for guaranteed deposits (up to €100,000 each); radically restructure its largest bank (Bank of Cyprus), recapitalizing it at 9 percent through a deposit/equity conversion; freezing temporarily uninsured deposits at Bank of Cyprus; and strict (again temporary) controls on money transfers and withdrawals and on capital transactions to prevent bank runs.

As I see it, the deal averts calamity of a disorderly default and a euro exit but at a high price—indeed, the terms of this deal appear tougher than even the original proposal, which clearly breached the spirit of EU's mandated deposit guarantee, rejected by Parliament. No doubt, it dealt a severe blow on Cyprus as an offshore financial center. Drastic shrinking of the financial sector (18 percent of GDP) will have a profound impact on the domestic economy, predicted to contract by up to 10 percent in 2013. Like Greece, Cyprus will suffer a massive implosion without being able to devalue. This could prove intolerable. Given the scale of the shock, the troika has indicated readiness to allow Cyprus more time (until 2018) to bring its budget to surplus. Small wonder. The main downside risk rests on the severe loss of confidence, very likely needing further bailouts to help rebuild its economy. Cyprus is expected to enter the same downward spiral that led other bailed-out economies (Greece and Portugal) to shrink dramatically, while strict money controls in and out would further restrain economic activity. In all, Cyprus faces an immediately painful, deep recession and years of hardship.

It has now become clear that the haircut on unsecured depositors can be as much as 60 percent: 37.5 percent to be converted into bank shares, and another 22.5 percent to be temporarily frozen to facilitate real bank recapitalization. But the remaining 40 percent of deposits exceeding €100,000 each will be temporarily frozen to ensure the bank remains liquid; it will attract interest at 10 percent above current levels. This "bail-in" won't apply to Bank of Cyprus depositors below the €100,000 threshold. Realistically, winding up or restructuring a bank takes lots of time. In practice, deposits and other liabilities are converted into claims on the bank's assets. Liquidators sell the assets and repay claims piecemeal. Bank of Credit and Commerce International (BCCI) collapsed amid fraud in 1991. After two decades, creditors received an average of 80 percent of their claims. Iceland's big banks collapsed in 2008. They are still paying off creditors. Its major bank (LBI hf) is likely to complete payments by 2017. Make no mistake, it's a long haul.

Cyprus Euro Not the Euro

For the first time, the euro-bailout was accompanied by capital controls to avert bank runs and potential economic collapse. Two types of controls were instituted: curbs on domestic transactions (limits on cash withdrawals, cashing checks, card payments, redeeming time deposits, etc.), and cross-border capital flows (limits on cash takeouts and transfers, on funds for studying abroad and travel, etc.). These are safeguard measures to preserve systemic stability. Experience has been that money curbs are easy to impose but tough to lift. True, some of these controls are now being eased to soften the blow. It will take time. Iceland still maintains capital controls five years after its crisis.

The key rests on rebuilding confidence. This is tough. It is also true Cyprus faces a run on its banks, not on its currency. Yet, capital controls create in reality two euros. Common currency is based on the concept that the euro held in one country is the same euro everywhere else. When this trust is broken (as in Cyprus), the Cypriot euro isn't the same as the Greek or German euro; it has since become second class. That's reality. Euros trapped on the island are less valuable than euros that can be freely spent anywhere. Even now, insured depositors are wondering whether they will be better off keeping their savings away from the banks and Cyprus in the event controls are ever lifted.

The eurozone has now entered risky territory. Capital controls run counter to EU's guarantee of free capital movement across borders. In a sense, Cyprus had "withdrawn" from the euro once it imposed capital controls. After all, depositors elsewhere in Europe, too, could someday face strictures on capital movements. It brings home the reality of convertibility risk within eurozone. Economists polled recently stated that this represents a uniquely bad deal for the euro's future. Further, the majority singled out Spain and Slovenia, and possibly Italy, as the next likeliest candidates for a bailout. A handful cited Malta, France, and again, Portugal. It's clear this bailout won't be the last.

What, Then, Are We to Do?

The *Financial Times* of London summed up the underlying issue best on March 27 following the Brussels-Nicosia deal: "Eurozone shifts burden of risk from taxpayers to investors." Yes, it's the first euro-bailout to impose losses on bank deposits. The March 25 deal, including restructuring of Cyprus's two largest and baddest banks, would save EU taxpayers some €7 billion. Is this the new rescue template? Jeroen Dijsselbloem, Dutch finance minister and Eurogroup Chairman, stated (with words to this effect):

You took the risks, now you pay for your thrills; no more moral hazard. He later backtracked to emphasize, "Cyprus is a specific case with exceptional challenges which required the bail-in measures . . . macroeconomic adjustment programs are tailor-made to the situation of the country concerned and no models or templates are used."[2]

Be that as it may, it raises a fundamental economic issue: How much of a precedent has been set for future EU bailouts? How much of the Brussels deal reflected German politics? (Chancellor Angela Merkel faces an election and doesn't want to tell Germans they had to rescue the huge deposits of Russian oligarchs.) Where does this leave depositors once the politics is over? But there will always be politics. Mind you, depositors don't run banks; they really have no say. The forced transfer of large deposits into bank equity is unfortunate collective punishment. It is a stark reminder that banks do fail, and uninsured deposits are subject to the limits of government patronage in the face of moral hazard.

The rules of capital restructuring start with equity taking the first loss, then bondholders and other creditors, with unsecured deposits the last to suffer. Since the crisis, the United States and Europe have handled bad banks by sheltering creditors and depositors from the consequences of their risk, taking ways that enabled them to take on more and sillier risks with moral hazard. When unsecured deposits were hit in Cyprus, a line had been crossed. Yet, of the 147 banking crises since 1970 tracked by the IMF, none inflicted losses on all depositors, irrespective of the amounts they held and the banks they saved with. Now, depositors in Spain and Italy have every reason to worry about sudden raids on their savings. In the end, banks will need to hold a layer of loss-absorbing senior debt, designed to spare all depositors, in all but the last resort. Here, the Volcker Rule (which bars deposit-taking banks from trading—that is, taking undue risks, with their own capital) can act to reduce risk-taking by deposit takers. In the final analysis, protection of depositors—secured and unsecured—can only come about with the creation of a proper banking union and some form of mutualization of sovereign debt. There is just no other way.

Kuala Lumpur
April 4, 2013

Notes

1. First published on April 6, 2013.
2. Jeroen Dijsselbloem, Dutch Finance Minister, at an interview with the *Financial Times* of London on March 27, 2012, in London, followed by a later statement of clarification.

PART V

Japan: Dead On but Not Deadened

CHAPTER 57

Japan in Deep Hibernation[1]

I am privileged to be associated with the Asian Economic Panel (AEP), first convened in 2002 on the initiative of the Centre for International Development at Harvard University, Keio University, and the Korea Institute for International Economic Policy. This forum promotes quality analysis of key economic issues in Asia, and offers creative solutions by drawing on the collective wisdom of worldwide economists. The prime movers are Professor Jeffrey Sachs and Professor Eisuke Sakakibara. When Jeffrey moved to Columbia, his new Earth Institute replaced Harvard. Brookings has since come on board.

The AEP last met at Keio University (Tokyo) on September 11, 2010. Observations on what's happening in Japan by Professor Naoyuki Yoshino, a respected insider from Keio with deep knowledge of official thinking, were insightful. He is optimistic that Japanese economic activity will gradually improve, shake off deflation, and return to steady nominal growth since the bubble burst in 1990.

Sure, the economy is stuck with deflation; public debt is rising, population is aging, and Japan still has to define and find its "proper place" in the world. But Japan is unique. Contrary to conventional wisdom, it is simplistic to say all Japan needed is a strong leader with guts to do what everyone knows has to be done. Yes, Japan's leaders have so far vascillated and shirked hard choices. To be fair, solutions are far from obvious. A visitor to Tokyo sees no outward signs of crisis. However, lots of political intrigue is evident. Politicians and policy makers have bickered and schemed, but have chosen to leave things as they are. The September 10, 2010, set of disappointing "stimulus" measures by the Kan administration reflects recognition of the complex web of bureaucratic intrigue and the public's deep ambivalence about what is wrong and how to fix it. There are no magic solutions.

Sleepwalking in Slow Motion

Since the bubble burst in 1990, Japan experienced three bouts of negative growth dips (1993, 1998, and 2002), with nominal gross domestic product (GDP) falling faster than real (price adjusted) GDP, reflecting deflation—the so-called first "lost decade," 1990 to 2000. In 2001, growth recovered but only gradually—since averaging 2 percent a year, with nominal income slackening (about 1 percent per annum). This trend was interrupted by the global crisis when GDP fell by 0.7 percent in 2008 and –6 percent in 2009. So, after two decades of virtual stagnation, nominal GDP today is at the same level as in 1992. Growth in 2010 is expected at 1.7 percent (second quarter of 2010 growth has been revised to an annualized 1.6 percent against just 0.4 percent earlier).

To put this in perspective, the world is expected to grow by 2.5 percent in 2010, with advanced economies recovering at an average 0.6 percent (with less than 1 percent each in the United States and eurozone), compared with 7 percent in developing Asia; 8.5 percent in China, 6.5 percent in India, and 3.7 percent in ASEAN-5 (Indonesia, Malaysia, the Philippines, Thailand, and Vietnam). But the outlook for global growth will likely get worse. Once heralded as the unchallenged economic giant of Asia, Japan is today a pale reflection of its old self. Although recovering, the vital signs are weak in the face of faltering global growth and a high yen. There is widespread concern that its fragile recovery could soon run out of steam as key export markets in Asia contract and the strong yen exerts new pressure on its exporters.

Already, corporate capital spending slipped in the second quarter of 2010, even though inventory surged. Such spending, accounting for 16 percent of GDP, is likely to moderate. Official data showed businesses becoming nervous about the outlook even before the yen's continuing gain and as share prices tumble. Japan has emerged as a key beneficiary of global recovery, helped by its proximity to Asia's fast-moving economies and its companies' large presence in the region, especially China. In first quarter of 2010, Asia accounted for 55 percent of Japan's exports (26 percent for the United States and 23 percent for Europe). This has heightened anxiety since Japan ceded ground to China as the world's second-largest economy.

Other indicators point to more of the same: (1) private consumption spending (60 percent of GDP) was flat in the second quarter of 2010; as a result, domestic demand subtracted 0.2 percentage point from GDP growth; (2) contribution to GDP from external demand (exports less imports) added only 0.3 percentage point in the second quarter of 2010 (0.6 percentage point in the first quarter of 2010), reflecting softening of global demand, including from Asia; (3) weak job market weighed in on consumer sentiment in June; unemployment hit a 7-month high at 5.3 percent; and (4) deflation continued to drag on recovery.

Persistent price falls encourage consumers to postpone purchases, waiting for prices to fall further; they also hurt business investment by weighing in on firms' bottom line and raising real borrowing costs. The GDP deflator (the broadest measure of prices) was –1.8 percent in the second quarter of 2010 against –2.8 percent in the first quarter of 2010. It continues to underscore how deeply entrenched deflation really is. As I see it, risk of protracted deflation is rising, given the strong yen. It looks like Japan will remain in deep sleep for a while longer.

New Stimulus

Clouding the outlook for deflation, exports, and competition is the recent strengthening of the yen. Dollar-yen fell in mid-September to 84.72, its lowest since July 1995. No wonder the Japanese economy doesn't instill confidence. It continues to wage a losing battle against deflation; population is aging (and in decline); and government is struggling with a mountain of debt. Yet, the yen has strengthened steadily and is now at its highest in 15 years. Most economists, including Yoshino, think Japan is in a lull but the risk of going into a double-dip remains low.

Amid strong calls for government and Bank of Japan (BoJ) to do more to support growth and ease business concerns facing a bleak future, is the unmistakable and urgent need for them to take strong supply-side and tax measures to encourage companies to grow. In response, on September 10, 2010, the Kan administration unveiled a ¥915 billion stimulus package to ward off dangers of double-dip recession in the face of increasing downside risks from a strong yen and slowing global demand. The measures comprised: (1) about US$10 billion of fiscal stimulus offering support for jobs, investment, consumer spending, disaster prevention, and deregulation; these efforts are expected to boost GDP by 0.3 percentage point and create 200,000 new jobs; and (2) a ¥10 trillion top-up (to ¥30 trillion) from Bank of Japan (BoJ) of soft loans at 1 percent for local banks to help bolster their lending. Not surprisingly, the impact felt like water off a duck's back since what the market wanted was strong supply-side stimulus; after all, the banks are already so flush with funds and so risk-averse that more funding doesn't help.

¥ Intervention

A week later (September 15, 2010) in a measure that took the market off-guard, Japan broke international convention and intervened directly to weaken the yen for the first time in six years. The impact was swift when selling orders hit the market early as US$ fell to a new low of 82.57 yen. It hits 1 yen higher and was trading up 1.6 percent on the day at 84.50 yen. It closed midday in New York at 85.59. Effects have already begun to fade with the rate at 84.91 (Tokyo) on September 22. Historically, Japan has not intervened since March 2004 after a 15-month, ¥35 trillion (US$422 billion) selling spree aimed at stopping the strong yen from railroading economic recovery.

However, the yen rose to its highest since 1995 in the face of surging carry-trade business made possible by low US$ interest rates, bringing the yen closer to its record peak of 79.75 set in 1995. Japan is not alone in this. The Swiss National Bank intervened to hold the Swiss franc (SF) down against the euro in a move in March 2009 as part of a package to fight off deflation risks. The euro has since fallen 12 percent this year. Similarly, the strengthening yen is of concern to Japan's neighbors in the face of a weakening US dollar. Prior to the intervention, the US dollar fell 4.2 percent against the Singapore dollar so far this year. It has also fallen against other Asian currencies—down 8.7 percent against Malaysian ringgit, 6.6 percent against Thai baht, 4.4 percent against Indonesia's rupiah, and 3.4 percent against Philippino peso. Asian authorities worry swift and sharp rises in their currencies can become destabilizing. It also makes their exports less competitive. But it's anti-inflationary. In comparison, the US dollar had devalued by nearly 10 percent against the yen.

As I see it, Japan is fighting fundamentals. Like the SF, the yen has strengthened because the market doesn't like the US dollar (with its weak economy and high deficits) or the euro (so crisis stricken). Swiss intervention could not hold back bags of monies flowing in for safety. Similarly, its own 2003–2004 experience points to only slowing down the yen's rise. However, this time Japan may have an advantage. Deflation (near-zero interest rate) means its interest rates are still too high; hence, more QE (quantitative easing). Printing money to buy US dollar has a similar impact, by allowing US$23.5 billion through intervention to remain in the market. Japan may not be able to hold back the yen's rise. But the side effects make it worthwhile.

Deflation, Status Quo, and Recovery

For Japan, deflation remains a constant worry. Make no mistake, deflation is becoming more alarming. Prices in Tokyo (a leading indicator) fell again in June. Nationwide core deflation (excluding food and energy) was 1.2 percent, the sharpest fall since 1971. Yen strength is asphyxiating exporters and feeding (through imports) a self-reinforcing spiral of lower prices and wages. This process raises the real burden of private debt; public debt-to-GDP ratio is a whopping 190 percent.

Yet, bond yields are stubbornly low and living standards high. This is not sustainable for three reasons: (1) as expectations of deflation become entrenched (35 percent of Japanese expect prices to be the same or lower in five years' time), consumption will be depressed; (2) as Japan ages, savings will run down, and less monies will be invested in Japanese Government Bonds (government bonds). Even with savings rate maintained, gross debt will exceed gross household savings by 2015. Already six persons of working age supported one retiree in 1990. By 2025, the ratio will fall to two. That's a harsh reality check; and (3) Japan can't count on export-led growth.

Without a much stronger economy, tax revenue is insufficient to reduce rising debt (borrowing exceeds revenue for the first time in the 2010 budget). Getting out means structural reforms to raise productivity, fiscal tax restructuring, and strong monetary stimulus. Politicians prevaricate bold moves. BoJ argues there's only so much it can do: QE can't resolve a problem it can't fix. In the end, Japan is still stuck with the status quo.

What, Then, Are We to Do?

Two obstacles promote inaction: (1) many perceive these problems to be not as serious as portrayed. At the AEP, Professor Sakakibara said, "We should enjoy mild deflation, rather than to deplore deflation as a disease." Japanese are reluctant to give up what they have got: low unemployment, a pacifist constitution, a homogeneous, equitable society, and high living standards; and (2) these problems are not so easy to resolve—the public is divided on what's really wrong and how to fix it.

Take raising sales tax (now just 5 percent). It has a troubled record. When it was raised from 3 percent in 1997, retail sales fell for the next seven years. The real problem is that the Japanese want US tax rates with Swedish levels of welfare. Nice thought. At the Jackson Hole Conference organized by the Federal Reserve Bank of Kansas City in September, Fed Chairman Ben Bernanke concluded: Central bankers alone cannot solve the world's economic problems. Now, over to the politicians.

Tokyo, Japan
Kuala Lumpur
September 23, 2010

Note

1. First published on September 25, 2010.

CHAPTER 58

3-11: The Tohoku Disasters One Year On[1]

I arrived in Kyoto on the JR-West fast "haruka" train from Osaka's Kansai on a cold 8°C morning of March 9, 2012, to attend the Harvard Alumni Association's gathering of Asia Pacific Club Leaders as president of the Harvard Club of Malaysia, leading a delegation of four. It's more than 25 years since I was last in Kyoto, Japan's capital in 794 (many residents believe it is still the capital, since the Emperor never officially declared that he has taken up residence in Tokyo). Besides being famous for historic monuments and gardens, I am always intrigued by the traditional Japanese Kabuki—the legendary theater of acting, dancing, and singing of unusual eccentricity and social dancing—which was founded in Kyoto around 1603. The earliest performance of Kabuki had no significant plot, often disdained as gaudy and cacophonous, but equally lauded as colorful and beautiful. But I love it. For a while at least, I can again breathe and smell the birthplace of Kabuki.

Japan Remembers

March 11, 2012, marked one year since the massive earthquake and tsunami struck parts of the Tohoku (Japan's northeast) region. The catastrophe—the worst political and humanitarian crisis faced since the end of World War II—left nearly 20,000 confirmed dead or missing, while nearly 344,000 had to be evacuated. The magnitude-9 earthquake (that struck at 2.46 p.m. on March 11, 2011) triggered a tsunami 39 m (128 feet) tall at its highest point, which crippled the Fukushima Dai-ichi nuclear plant and laid waste to entire towns as it came ashore along hundreds of kilometers of Japan's Pacific coastline. An emergency was declared and a 20-kilometer no-go-zone around the plant established.

355

So far, less than 10 percent of the 22.5 million tons of debris left by the tsunami has been cleared. This triple-accident has had a tremendous impact on agriculture, fisheries, manufacturing, and tourism. Vast areas around Fukushima city, with a population of one million, were contaminated as much as 1,000 times the level of background radiation from before the accident.

As I understand it, anxious local residents are dismayed, frustrated that recovery is still only taking baby steps. Already, many worry that memories of the related disasters are starting to wear thin. The three disasters destroyed more than 370,000 buildings and damaged roads at nearly 4,000 points. The total damage is estimated at ¥16.9 trillion (US$195 billion). As reported in the *Japan Times*,[2] in his book, *Lessons from the Disaster*, which includes analyses by a number of experts, Keio University Professor Heizo Takenaka pointed out that the government had "failed to act promptly," especially in aiding shattered municipalities because of intense political bickering, thereby preventing works to "reinvent the region's agriculture and creating eco-friendly new coastal municipalities."

To be fair, there is much to applaud in its reconstruction efforts—according to government sources, most of the tsunami zone's roads have been fixed, and landscape once strewn with debris is lined now with tidy plots and a growing number of restored buildings. Several supply chains are back in business and many of the devastated fishing ports are now in service. But the story of towns around the nuclear plant is a painful reminder that this was no ordinary disaster.

The Fourth Disaster

As I visit, I sense most Japanese I spoke with are increasingly disillusioned about the political establishment's ability to tell the truth and rise to the occasion on 3-11 and thereafter, including a deep lack of trust. Philip Brasor,[3] writing in the *Japan Times,* talks of his encounter with A. Yasutomi's recent book, *Genputsu Kiki to Todai Waho,* which irreverently analyzes the "parlance of the University of Tokyo" as it was used to couch public statements in optimistic language, avoiding commitment of what had actually happened, on the presumption that the listener is incapable of handling the truth. They won't call a dangerous thing, dangerous.

As a result, Yasutomi observed people learn to mistrust those in authority, so much so that even when they did tell the truth, people couldn't tell. They just assumed they were lying. So it is not surprising that a recent survey found 94 percent of Fukushima residents didn't believe its prime minister when he said in December 2011 that the nuclear crisis was contained. Or, 80 percent didn't believe reconstruction activities were "making things better." The public lack of confidence in the ability of their leaders to help them was considered by one Japanese commentator as the "fourth disaster" of March 11.

Tea at Entokuin

Nearby Kyoto city center is Kodaiji Temple. The Harvard group visited Entokuin, a subtemple there known to have elegant gardens of the Momoyama period. We entered through the main "Nagayamon" gate designed in the style of a samurai house. Inside, along the walls are four fantastic panel paintings by the renowned Japanese painter, Hasegawa Touhaku: "Sansuizu-husuma," a landscape of his hometown; "Hakuryu," a white dragon; "Setugetuka" (snow and moon and cherry blossoms), signifying natural beauty; and "Syoutikubai" (pine tree and bamboo and plum-blossoms) for good luck.

The North Garden of the house is sheer elegance. The Kobori Enshuu is of Zen style, built in 1605 by Nene, Kitano Mandokoro (wife of Toyotomi Hideyoshi, the shogun), to mourn her husband. Spread around the side of Entokuin are many big natural stones donated by numerous samurais to honor the shogun. We sat down (cross-legged) in the tearoom of Entokuin to enjoy the Zen garden, portraying in the cold wind naked cherry blossom trees against lush green spring trees with lots and lots of large stones sitting harmoniously on a vast carpet of white-gray stone pebbles so arranged to symbolize ripples of flowing water in the foreground.

As we waited for the tea ceremony (*sado*: the way of the tea), the clock struck 2.46 p.m.—the moment to join the emperor and the nation, amid makeshift altars in disaster-flattened neighborhoods, to a minute's silence to pay respects and remember the victims of 3-11. We did so fully aware their impact extended far beyond: both physically and through changed outlook on life through much soul searching, from a 30,000 anti-nuclear rally in Tokyo, and from across Hokkaido all the way to Kyushu, Shikoku, and distant Okinawa. Some trains even stopped to allow people time to pray and reflect. Tea and sweets ended a perfect, solemn day of remembrance.

Digital Archive

Harvard's Reischauer Institute (HRI) of Japanese Studies faculty has since March 11 mobilized to develop the Digital Archive (DA).[4] As HRI's T. Gilman puts it, it's a long-term effort to record and archive the electronic communications after, and in response to, the disaster. Clearly, the Tohoku disasters have provoked a global barrage of online blogs, tweets, audio recordings, photographs, videos, news, new websites, articles, and other digital documentations and communications.

Global interactions online have provided instantaneous updates and reactions way beyond the mass media and outside official control. Yet, 3-11 is ongoing, and a comprehensive digital record will become indispensable for future history. I am told the DA intends to become an "active, dynamic, ever-expanding public space," not a mere repository. Gilman says, its innovation involves a rich interface that will enable users to curate personalized recollections and submit their own digital materials. It uses an open-source platform, Zeega, which allows users to compile their own collections, provide commentary, and "tag" them with their own key words, with the option of whether to make their collections public.

The DA project stretches beyond Harvard and its immediate institutional community. It features (1) a personal testimonial page about the disasters and encourages shared experiences; (2) outreach initiatives through active Japanese and English presence in the social media, Twitter, and Facebook; and (3) content partnerships ranging from the US Library of Congress to Japan's National Diet Library (with Yahoo Japan overseeing the project) as well as to local-level organizations in the disaster-affected regions. The amazing thing is that these partnerships link archiving organizations around the world to collaborate and move beyond conventional models to truly bring historical preservation to the digital age.

Economy Grapples with Aftermath

After a year, the disasters' impact continues to reverberate throughout Japan. In Tohoku, nearly 350,000 are displaced from their homes, with many living in cramped temporary housing, the majority jobless, some without hope, others worried their areas would be declared uninhabitable, as they all face an uncertain future. Amid concerns about Japan's nuclear future, the accident has sharply reduced Japan's energy-supply capabilities, making the Japanese even more energy-saving conscious, a trend that could weigh on the national economy for decades. Through it all, the Japanese earned the Harvard group's admiration for their composure, discipline, and resilience in the face of adversity, while its companies impressed with the speed with which they bounced back. As a result, the economy looks set to return to predisaster levels in the second half of 2012, with the help of US$250 billion (about Portugal's gross domestic product [GDP]) set aside for rebuilding the region.

The economy now appears to be on the recovery track because of rising reconstruction spending and incentives to purchase fuel-efficient cars. Japan's core machinery orders rose rapidly in January 2012, reflecting ongoing rebuilding activity supporting the fragile economy. The weakening yen is also looking up. Manufacturers, however, turned more pessimistic about business conditions in the first quarter of 2012, but expect sentiments to improve in the second quarter of 2012 with the yen now off record highs, and signs of sustained reconstruction spending.

Bank of Japan's (BoJ) Tankan sentiment survey is expected to turn more positive in April. Revisions last week showed GDP in the fourth quarter of 2011 contracting by only 0.7 percent (–2.3 percent earlier) because of higher capital spending (up 4.8 percent). Prospects for the first quarter of 2012 have begun to look brighter. Both the International Monetary Fund and the World Bank now place growth in Japan in the region of 2 percent in 2012, somewhat better than a month ago (against Asian Development Bank's 2.5 percent). Overall activity appears to be improving.

What, Then, Are We to Do?

Watching them up close, the Japanese are a resolutely resilient society. The catastrophic destruction last March had also led to widespread radioactive contamination of life, landscape, and livelihoods. This has rightly prompted a radical rethink on the quality of life. Article One of the Basic Law for Reconstruction from the East Japan Great Earthquake says the government must push reconstruction efforts smoothly and promptly in order to "realize the rebirth of Japan full of vitality."

As it turns out, reconstruction spending is now upping the GDP, but what about raising the quality of life? With landscape as the true life-enhancing resource, the lesson is to ensure the land retains its beauty, tranquility, diversity, and accessibility. Surely, Japan must learn not to neglect the safety and integrity of the people and the land. So, there is a need to rethink and reprioritize development goals—Tohoku land must be given back to its rightful owners. People should not simply be silent victims. Many Japanese believe they have lost their national spirit. In a rudderless nation, it is not surprising for people to feel nostalgic for the return of institutions that helped to produce leaders of the 1868 Meiji Restoration. As activist Mitsuko Shimomura (like many Japanese youth who are fed up with Japan's drift) acidly puts it (words to this effect): She wants to put some spine back into the Japanese people.

I know the Japanese well enough to appreciate the notion that for men, shirogohan (white rice) is the wife, while ramen is the eternal mistress. However far he strays, a man will eventually come home for his home-cooked white rice. But the rest of the time, his thoughts are with his ramen noodles. Japan continues to struggle to meet the competitive challenge, especially in high-tech and autos. It has to spend time marshalling to lift its animal spirits to stay astride the green technology frontier. Japan can always rely on its "rice" wife (traditional exports), but it needs to spend time with its "ramen" mistress (high-tech) to aggressively spin more investments in green IT for long-term survival.

Kyoto, Japan
Kuala Lumpur
March 22, 2012

Notes

1. First published on March 24, 2012.
2. "A Year On, Tohoku Stuck in Limbo," *Japan Times* (March 11, 2012), pp. 1 and 4.
3. Philip Brasor, "Public Wary of Official Optimism," *Japan Times* (March 11, 2012), p. 16.
4. Harvard University, Edwin O. Reischauer Institute of Japanese Studies, *Reischauer Reports*, vol. 16 (November 1, 2011), pp. 6–7.

CHAPTER 59

Japan Picks Up the Pieces[1]

A ttended the global think-tank Asian Economic Panel (Columbia University) meeting recently in Tokyo hosted by Keio University. Research papers centered on Asia covering a range of topics were considered—from income distribution and wealth polarization, to business cycles and myths about China's high-tech exports, to multinationals' energy efficiency in manufacturing, to fresh approaches in financing disaster reconstruction projects. Its timing accorded an opportunity to be updated on what's happening to Japan, just prior to the October 2012 Intermeet gathering of the International Monetary Fund (IMF) and World Bank stakeholders in Tokyo. After all, Keio University advises the Ministry of Finance (MOF) and Bank of Japan (BoJ) on economic affairs; this special access provides its professors with unique insights, which enrich perspectives on Japan during meeting interactions.

IMF Updates

The October 2012 *World Economic Outlook* (WEO 2012) of the IMF paints an already familiar picture:

> *Recovery continues but it has weakened . . . (and) suffered new setbacks, with uncertainty weighing heavily on the outlook. . . . Those forces pulling growth down in advanced economies are fiscal consolidation . . . (which is holding back demand) and a still weak financial system. . . . Policies have not built confidence. Tail risks, such as those relating to the viability of the euro area or major US fiscal policy mistakes, continue to pre-occupy investors. Low growth and uncertainty are affecting emerging markets through both trade and financial channels, adding to home-grown weaknesses. . . . Forecasts for 2013 growth have been revised from 2 percent down to 1.5 percent for advanced economies, and from 6 percent down to 5.6 percent for emerging and developing economies.[2]*

These predictions are optimistic. WEO 2012 sees growth in Asia moderating further to 5.5 percent in 2012, reflecting weaker external demand and soft landing of domestic demand in China and India. Outlook is for a modest pickup on the back of recent policy easing and limited fiscal stimulus. As I see it, the global economy is unlikely to have hit bottom because complexities of the ongoing slowdown are too multifaceted, making firm assertions well-nigh impossible at this time. Current sentiment points to Asian growth being unlikely to pick up in the second half of 2012. Indeed, there is a 10 to 15 percent chance for growth to fall below 4 percent in 2013, back to after the 2009 Lehman shock. Risks on the outlook remain tilted to the downside.

The IMF estimated growth in China will soften to 7.25 percent this year and then bounce back to 8.25 percent in 2013 on the strength of domestic demand. Depressive impact of the eurozone on China (and India), I feel, remains underestimated given its direct impact on the rest of the world will, in turn, weigh heavily indirectly in a backward loop with broad disruptive effects on growth in China (and India). Sure, China has plans to stimulate but with stable growth as its aim. There is also uncertainty on what the new leadership can do politically, given the serious spate with Japan over disputed territories—an issue deeply rooted in history and strongly implanted in the Chinese psyche.

Growth in India is expected at 5 to 6 percent in 2012–2013, the downgrade reflecting poor business sentiment and investment. ASEAN-5 (Malaysia, Thailand, Indonesia, Vietnam, and Philippines) economies will be modestly weaker in 2012 except for Thailand, where growth has bounced back with reconstruction. Overall, growth will pick up to 5.25 percent in 2013. ASEAN-5's exports to China and India fell faster recently than in previous crises. Then there is the poor outlook in Europe and the United States, feeding on fears that lack of progress in reforms and austerity fatigue will fan severe external headwinds to weaken momentum further in regional economies. Worries that demand will remain deficient will act as a powerful downdrag on global growth. Two-thirds of Asia's exports are linked to demand from the United States and Europe.

Japan's Outlook

WEO 2012 expects growth in Japan to reach 2.25 percent in 2012, reflecting mainly reconstruction activity and some rebound of manufacturing in the first half of 2012 following supply shocks associated with the March 2011 earthquake and tsunami and the October 2011 Thai floods. As effects of these factors fade, growth will moderate to 1 to 1.25 percent in 2013. I see this as optimistic, considering the recent flare-up in its long-standing territorial dispute with China, which has become a serious new threat to Japan's outlook, broader regional growth, and multinationals' global supply chain. The spreading paralysis has since led BoJ to downgrade its growth assessment for the rest of the year (–0.31 percent in the third quarter of 2012 against +0.7 percent in the second quarter of 2012), citing "uncertainty about the external economic prospects affecting its exports." This has cast a damper over everything from Japan's output growth to China's employment outlook to the supply of auto and electronic parts around the world. In turn, this undermines growth in other trade-dependent economies, especially South Korea, Taiwan, Malaysia, and Indonesia. Put together, these could put a kink in the supply chains from basic commodities to parts, which, in turn, could lead to shortages of finished goods and, possibly, spur global inflation. There is concern that this chill could turn into a freeze, spreading all over Asia.

So far, the immediate impact has been on Japanese car sales in China (plummeted 50 percent in September), while Chinese tourists' cancellations have significantly affected services activity in Japan. Many Japanese businesses in China are already taking a breather. My assessment is things can only get worse. Upcoming once-in-a-decade leadership change in China and the already complex shake-up in Japan's fragile government can complicate the outlook. Japan is already reassessing its exposure to China and is seriously considering cutbacks, which will show up in lower foreign direct investment, warts and all. Japanese firms in China employ 1.5 million to 2 million in 2011, where employment is closely linked with social stability.

Japanese politics is as complicated as it is complex. To keep the growth momentum, Japan's cabinet approved on Monday, October 29, 2012, a ¥423 billion economic stimulus package (double the original size expected), which could boost gross domestic product (GDP) by 0.1 percentage point. But domestic demand remains weak; most economists expect growth in the second half of 2012 to contract until the end of the year. That's why BOJ eased policy early this week (raising its asset purchases to ¥91 trillion and introducing a new facility to stimulate bank loans), likely to further weaken the yen to arrest its fast-rising trade deficit.

But Japan has three other serious problems to resolve, as follows:

Its Own Fiscal Cliff

Like the United States, Japan faces its own version of the "fiscal cliff" as its complex political wrangling has created problems in raising its debt ceiling, giving rise to concerns of a possible government shutdown and serious disruptions in the bond market. What is required is legislation to approve the issue of new bonds to finance 40 percent of this year's budget. Without it, political gridlock will involve government running out of cash to pay for allocated spending. This is the same kind of shutdown that hit the United States in 1995. Already, the government is planning to suspend bond offerings if the new bill is not passed by end-November; that will be its first cancellation ever for 2-year bond tenders, and the first for 10-year bonds in 25 years. This impasse will result in a lack of fresh supply of Japanese government bonds (JGBs), leading to a rush for existing bonds, putting downward pressure on JGB yields (which varies inversely with the rising price). This could erode confidence in the JGB market and risk a ratings downgrade, and possibly trigger potential sales by foreign investors (who hold less than 10 percent of outstanding JGBs, which they regard as a haven). This is most serious.

Deflation

Japan faces rising pressure to continue easing policies in the face of political gridlock and rising pessimism among manufacturers, intensifying calls for more aggressive action to end deflation and revive growth. BoJ's Tankan corporate survey indicated that business sentiment remains pessimistic, reflecting concerns about the yen's continuing strength and looking to more easing measures to meet such concerns. The index is calculated by subtracting the percentage of companies saying business conditions are bad from those saying they are good. Japan's absence of concrete reform plans is contributing to deflation and sluggish growth through discouraging spending by the public and businesses amid concerns over future fiscal developments.

A host of factors are threatening recovery: (1) concerns over reliable electricity supply; (2) strength of the yen in the face of fast-rising trade deficits; (3) sovereign risks looming large in investors' minds, with state debt rising to 237 percent of GDP; and (4) political and economic uncertainties weighing heavily over longer-term prospects. As I see it, Japan faces the classic policy dilemma in tackling the problem of strong yen (at a time of weak external demand and ongoing deflation) by trying to ease monetary policy to weaken the yen, thereby raising the price of bonds (which, in effect, leads to a rise in interest rates). The yen has already fallen 2.4 percent against the US dollar in October. This time around, BoJ took pains to emphasize its shared commitment "with the government on ending deflation."

Unfolding Demographic Disaster

Doubling the consumption tax isn't enough to solve Japan's fiscal problem. Its demographics have made social security programs unviable. Japan's National Institute of Population and Social Security Research forecasted that by 2060, it would have lost nearly one-third of the 2010 population (128 million), and just one-half of this smaller population will be between 15 and

65 years old. By 2050, Japan "will be the oldest society ever known," with a median age of 52 years.

Over the next decade, Japan's aging population will bring GDP down by 1 percentage point every year. This shrinking workforce is most serious. To resolve this, Japan has to (1) raise birthrate sharply; (2) open up to a new wave of immigrants; and (3) unleash the energy and talent of its female workforce (only 65 percent of women with college degrees are working).

Option (1) is not practical—it just won't happen fast enough. Japan's birthrate has fallen to 1.37 children per female, too low to stabilize the population. Option (2) makes policy sense. But given the poor track record of this long-insular society to immigration, this is expecting too much. In any case, it will be inadequate given the huge demographic challenge (foreigners make up less than 2 percent of population). The United Nations had estimated Japan would need annual inflows of 610,000 immigrants until 2050 to maintain the ratio in its working population. This is just too massive for Japan. Option (3) is viable, provided bold steps are taken first to create the right work environment for women. Recent studies show that raising the female labor force participation rate (LFPR) to parity with men would add 8 to 9 million workers, virtually replacing the fall in the projected workforce and boost GDP growth by 15 percent. That's powerful. The Organisation for Economic Co-operation and Development's (the rich nations' club) experience has been that nations with higher female LFPR also have higher birthrates.

In the end, it simply means bringing about a better work–life balance that benefits both males and females, in the face of readily available and easily affordable child care. Japan's female university enrolment rate already exceeds men since 2009. Women do work, but the culture of long hours on the job and the custom of post-work socializing has tended to conflict with motherhood, giving them less stable employment and reducing their chances for advancement. Beyond cultural obstacles, innovative ways are needed to raise the odds to attract more females to work. This presents a really huge challenge.

What, Then, Are We to Do?

I sense in Tokyo that the Japanese have lost the spark of "Japan as No.1," the 1979 bestseller by Harvard's Ezra Vogel. The younger generation, its expectations sapped by two decades of deflation, "doesn't have the excitement about doing things better," Vogel told me when we last met in Tokyo: Sure, "they still have a comfortable life, but the political system is an absolute mess." Japan has already lost its electronics crown and tech edge to its neighbors. Japanese have become more inward looking, more risk averse, and less ambitious. There is a sense that they are unprepared to be a tough competitive player in the global world.

Indeed, I feel that Japan is not just in a prolonged slump, but in an inescapable decline—it's shrinking, aging, and stuck in protracted gloom. Even the old faithful is losing faith in ailing Japan. My friend Ezra has since turned much of his attention to China.

Tokyo, Japan
Kuala Lumpur
November 1, 2012

Notes

1. First published on November 3, 2012.
2. International Monetary Fund (IMF), *World Economic Outlook: Coping with High Debt and Sluggish Growth* (Washington, DC: IMF, October 2012), pp. 6–7.

CHAPTER 60

Abenomics: Japan Comes Alive Again[1]

Abenomics is the aggressive management blend of monetary and fiscal stimuli to reflate Japan's stagnant economy, according to Prime Minister Shinzo Abe. Consequently, the yen weakened considerably, notching 23 weeks of back-to-back falls against the US dollar, completing the longest losing streak in 24 years. The sell-off brought it within striking distance of ¥100 = US$1, a level not seen since 2009. The US dollar has since climbed 25 percent, and €, 9 to 10 percent against ¥ since mid-April. Worries are that yen can move to within 110. This has led to a growing chorus of emerging nations (including China, Russia, Colombia, and Thailand), expressing alarm over the prospect of "currency wars."

Indeed, many nations around the world are vying to keep their currencies weak as well, through "macroprudential" means, including limited interventions. So much so the Moscow G-20 meeting in February 2013 had to reaffirm that economic stimulus policies should be aimed at lifting domestic growth and not target the exchange rate.

The Asian Shadow Financial Regulatory Committee[2] (of which I am a member) recommended at its April 18 meeting at Shanghai's Fudan University that (1) Asian economies, particularly those in Northeast Asia, should refrain from competitive devaluation and protectionist policies, which would have a negative impact on world trade flows; (2) Bank of Japan should be considerate, cautious, and transparent in undertaking further quantitative easing, by not targeting a weak yen and taking into account the concern of others; and (3) the International Monetary Fund (IMF), and, in particular, Asian Development Bank (ADB), needs to closely monitor international financial flows and strengthen its surveillance framework for macroeconomic policies of nations, so that it will be more effective in promoting global monetary stability.

The Three Arrows

The perspective: Japan's gross domestic product (GDP) today is still 3 percent below its prerecession peak. Deflation is persistent and deeply entrenched. Wages and prices have continued to fall. There has been no growth in the past 15 years and the economic outlook remains poor. Abe's three arrows remedy is centered on: first, aggressive monetary easing; second, more fiscal spending; and third, a growth strategy to induce private investment through structural overhaul to revive business "animal spirits" as follows.

Bank of Japan (BoJ)

The BoJ will launch quantitative and qualitative monetary easing (QQE or Q^2) to significantly raise the size (up to ¥70 trillion a year) of its easing package; shed its long aversion to buying longer-term bonds (up to 40 years), including abolishing its self-imposed cap on the amount of Japanese government bonds (JGB) it can buy; and ramp up its purchases of instruments linked to stocks and mortgages.

Its aim is to achieve an inflation target of 2 percent within two years (now extended to three years) and undo 15 years of nagging deflation. To create 2 percent inflation, BoJ will need to double the monetary base (money in circulation plus bank reserves at BoJ); double BoJ's holdings of JGB; and double the average maturities of bonds it buys to seven years. Consequently, this huge flood of money creation would weaken the yen. BoJ's open-ended bond buying would inject US$1.4 trillion into the economy, a radical gamble that sent yen bond yields to record new lows, but the Nikkei Stock Average was up 12.3 percent in April (+60 percent since mid-November 2012).

BoJ first tried quantitative easing to end deflation in 2002. It didn't work. Traditional view at BoJ has always been that monetary policy cannot raise inflation. The idea of deliberately targeting inflation was first pushed by Nobel Laureate Paul Krugman. While many endorsed the view (reminiscent of Milton Friedman's belief that central banks can create money and, hence, inflation), including the Fed, no central bank was courageous enough to test the theory until now by making it an explicit policy.

Conventional wisdom suggests that the critical factor in ending deflation is confidence, or Keynes's "animal spirits," which can only come with market-based reforms to incentivize and lift firms to invest on promise of future profits.

Fiscal Pump-Priming

To kick-start growth, Japan passed its second-largest-ever supplementary budget worth ¥13.1 trillion, focused mainly on infrastructure and public works spending to create thousands of jobs. This stimulus is expected to boost GDP by 2 percentage points. It seeks to create private demand.

Structural Reform

This third arrow aims at restructuring the economy, making it more "open and innovative" to raise productivity (now lower than South Korea); raise labor-force participation by women (48 percent, well below Europe and the United States), bearing in mind its 127 million population will shrink to 108 million by 2050; and push deregulation (too much red tape within a cumbersome bureaucracy).

This strategy is intended to maximize Japan's economic potential. Its labor market is notoriously sclerotic. The way out is to embrace the competition of freer trade—by joining the Trans-Pacific Partnership (TPP). This will be tough because it means dumping rules protecting dairy and rice farmers, and bringing in competitors to make them more efficient and profitable. Also, it helps free consumers and businesses from the shackles of protectionism and excessive regulation in healthcare, utilities, and farming. Government also needs to embrace the Internet and digital technology across most sectors. Just as crucial is to promote foreign direct investment, for which Japan receives a mere trickle, depriving it of innovation. Further, government needs to fully leverage relatively untapped human resources (young, elderly, and women), including raising the nation's lagging English-language ability, and set out an energy policy.

With the recent improved corporate sentiment and windfalls from a weaker yen, businesses are expected to raise wages to boost consumer spending and offset price rises as BoJ's reflation efforts take hold.

Takahashi-nomics

Peter Tasker's recent piece with the *Financial Times* of London on Japan's last successful reflation in the 1930s offers a valuable lesson.[3] Korekiyo Takahashi, finance minister from 1931 to 1936, took Japan off the gold standard. Through a combination of fiscal stimulus, monetary easing, and ¥ depreciation, Takahashi brilliantly saved Japan from the world depression, according to Fed Chairman Bernanke. GDP rose 60 percent, and consumer prices, 18 percent; debt/GDP stabilized and stock price doubled.

Unfortunately, Takahashi was assassinated by rogue army officers, enraged by his "exit strategy" of cutting military spending. Inflation subsequently soared under the irresponsible militants. The lesson points to reflation taking hold only if policy makers were determined. Also, firing one arrow isn't enough (as the United Kingdom's experience showed). To sustain recovery in Japan, all three arrows need to be fired simultaneously. A clear exit strategy is also needed.

The Risks

Japan's situation is peculiar. Expectations of deflation are well entrenched. Classical economics argues consumers welcome deflation because it increases their purchasing power and people hunt for bargains in earnest only when they worry prices will rise. In Japan, purchasing power has been falling faster than prices—average earnings are down 12.2 percent since 1997, while "core" (excluding food and fuel) consumer prices fell 6.8 percent. In a weird way, finding ways to spend less has become a habit. Most Japanese do maintain their lifestyles with falling prices. It also meant government could easily borrow at ludicrously low rates—less than 1 percent for 10-year debt.

Over time, however, deflation becomes corrosive; it suppresses growth and penalizes the young. Government's job is to break the grip of this long deflation, which was exacerbated by the yen's rise against US dollar of more than 25 percent since 2009. Cheap imports led to further deflation. This time, Q^2 easing will inject huge sums into banks; their conundrum is what to do with all this cash. For this to work, it has to lend out to facilitate growth. But caught in deflation, companies prefer to pay down debt and won't invest. Banks are thus stuck with lots of money, which they place either with BoJ or invest in JGB or abroad. Japan experimented with Q^2 easing as far back as 2001. In 2002, Japan's monetary base rose 18 percent but bank lending fell! BoJ further raised annual JGB purchases to ¥14.4 trillion, but deflation persisted. US experience helps illustrate the challenge. From September 2008 to March 2013, the Fed expanded monetary base by 247 percent; but money supply rose only 34 percent!

There are other risks:

1. BoJ's Q^2 policy will artificially depress JGB yields (particularly at the longer end). This encourages the move into equities, real estate, or loans, spurring broader economic activity and investment. However, it is likely prices will rise before wages. This leaves consumers scrambling to keep living standards, ultimately working to depress activity. The ¥ is likely to weaken, raising costs of imports, including fuel and vital commodities. This increases the risk of "bad" inflation and "bad" yen-weakening consequences.

2. It leaves BoJ heavily exposed to JGB. Japan now joins the easy-money party; once inflation sets in, interest rates will rise—bond prices will fall and cause instability. BoJ has to worry soon about this.

3. It could trigger a currency war, a zero-sum game; exports gained are somebody else's loss.

4. Q^2 artificially depresses yields, triggering off capital outflows to seek higher yielding, high-quality risky assets, which led French, Dutch,

Austrian, and Belgian bond yields to all fall to record lows last week. Yields on 10-year German bunds (at 1.35 percent) are 2.4× JGB return, and US Treasuries (1.9 percent), 3.4×. Falling ¥ surcharges the returns. In ¥ terms, eurozone bonds yielded 9 to 10 percent so far this year.

5. Asset bubbles are possible in any of Japan's markets, including abroad. Large flows of cheap Q^2 funds into the region (in search of higher returns) and cheap credit has pushed asset prices and risks higher. The reaction of Japan's insurance and pension funds, which hold 35 percent of JGB, is crucial. A 5 percent shift could lead to US$100 billion in additional demand for the United States and German fixed-income securities. BoJ's massive JGB purchases have crowded them out. Prospect of such a massive global asset reallocation also depends on where the yen goes from now.

6. There is a possible backlash from Japan's growing legions of pensioners wanting to protect their wealth and fixed incomes from being eroded by inflation. Japan sits on the world's largest pool of savings: US$9 trillion held in cash and bank deposits against US$7.8 trillion in the United States, which has more than twice the population. Today, only 11 percent of Japanese financial assets are invested in equities and mutual funds (45 percent in the United States, and 22 percent in Europe).

7. Printing money will eventually boost interest rates. Already, debt servicing (even at a 0.5 percent cost) swallows one-quarter of Japan's budget. If inflation reaches 2 percent, the higher cost of government funding (at 2.5 percent) will take up virtually the entire budget. Moreover, at quintupled interest rates, GDP will have to grow 6.25 percent (4.25 percent in real terms) to keep the debt/GDP ratio (already 250 percent by end-2014) from rising.

This will not happen. But, then, there is calamity for banks that carry JGB in their books, totaling 80 percent of GDP. As in 1990s, they will need to be bailed out, bigtime! The effects can be mind-boggling.

What, Then, Are We to Do?

Tokyo's aggressive Q^2 strategy holds frightening implications. Governor Kuroda has pledged that "our stance is to take all the policy measures imaginable"[4] to achieve the inflation target in two years, an overly ambitious timeframe. This has in recent days been extended to three years (by 2016). Many Asians view Q^2 as a deliberate attempt to beggar-thy-neighbor, risking irreparable retaliation. So far, it's mere wait-and-see from its Northeast Asian neighbors.

Japan's Achilles' heel remains the weak ¥. IMF has since warned policy makers to guard against the risk of overheating in managing the huge capital flows and a weak ¥. Already, many Asian stock markets have seen record highs; property prices in some nations have been red-hot. Financial imbalances are emerging and asset prices soaring.

Frankly, Japan's problem is not its strong currency. Its corporate culture prevents it from creating innovative, competitive products. Japan, which is highly integrated into the global economy, is a price taker for tradable goods. Debasing its currency provides only short-term relief. In the global market, competition is not confined to price—it must compete on value. That's why the policy targets matter. Japan will need to convince its neighbors that the weakening yen will not be overdone: BoJ will soon find the right balance to pursue its inflation goal. Indeed, Japan's challenge is to move from its old "deflation" comfort zone to a new equilibrium based on mild inflation and a stable yen. Overtime, its policy shift has to be credible and credibly contained, anchored to a credible exit. Shooting all three arrows simultaneously as BoJ stabilizes the yen offers Japan the best opportunity to avoid a third lost decade and contribute once again to world growth.

Shanghai, China
Kuala Lumpur
May 2, 2013

Notes

1. First published on May 4, 2013, as "Abenomics & Currency Wars."
2. Asian Shadow Financial Regulatory Committee. Communiqué issued at Fudan University in Shanghai, China, on April 19, 2013.
3. Peter Tasker, "Japan and Britain Must Lead Way to a Reflated Economy," *Financial Times* (April 4, 2013).
4. Haruhiko Kuroda, governor, Bank of Japan, stated that the bank will use all options available to achieve its 2 percent inflation target, reinforcing expectations of bold monetary stimulus ahead of his first policy-setting meeting on April 4, 2013, in Tokyo.

CHAPTER 61

Abenomics Hitting Speed Bumps[1]

Five woes led to the rise of Abenomics: (1) severe side effects of the 1997 and 2008 global financial crises, which resulted in the United States, eurozone, and Japan each struggling with its own version of recession, and then, a jobless slow recovery; (2) the crises were multifaceted, involving property bubbles, easy money, unprecedented shifts in demography, and widespread impact of advances in ICT (information and communication technology) that revolutionized the workplace and marketplace; (3) series of natural disasters and incidents; (4) overvaluation of the yen; and (5) "reactive" expansionary macroeconomic policies reflecting mostly "denial" and avoidance of "reform" in advanced economies.

Once elected prime minster in December 2012, Mr. Abe launched his own eponymous "three arrows" revival program comprising (1) "bold," easy monetary policies; (2) "flexible," expansionary fiscal policies; and (3) investment-enhancing structural reforms. Chapter 60, "Abenomics: Japan Comes Alive Again," provides fuller details.

In six months, the Nikkei Stock index rose 57 percent, while the yen fell some 20 percent against the US dollar. After a correction last May, the index continued to climb (now up 16 percent from a year ago). What's clear is that Abenomics had spectacular initial success in changing the nation's mood and business sentiment. Since April 2014, however, its magic has begun to fade because of re-recognition of uncertainty over its long-run prospects. Abenomics today remains very much a promise of structural reforms yet to be fulfilled.

Impact

The Japanese economy since 2013 has been powered by consistently massive monetary stimulus and significant new public spending to end deflation. There is consensus that the first two arrows are right on course, while the third is still in flight—so far in hesitant, small steps. Ultra-easy monetary quantitative and qualitative easing (QQE or Q²) policy introduced in April 2013 pledged to double base money through aggressive asset purchases to raise consumer inflation to 2 percent in three years. As a result, the Bank of Japan's (BoJ) balance sheet expanded to reach 52 percent of gross domestic product (GDP) at end-May 2014 (against 25 percent for the US Federal Reserve). BoJ is today the largest holder of government bonds (20.1 percent of the total), ahead of the insurance companies.

Continuing fiscal expansion has kept the government's debt high—exceeding 200 percent of GDP. Total GDP rose 1.8 percent in 2013, about what the United States was doing but well ahead of the eurozone. Growth in the first quarter of 2014 rose unexpectedly fast at an annualized rate of 6.7 percent—marking the sixth straight quarterly expansion, mainly due to a surge in private capital spending and a one-time consumption splurge ahead of the tax hike in April. Growth in the second quarter of 2014 will likely slacken to contract by 4.2 percent. Overall, the economy will expand on track in an effort to meet the 2 percent inflation target for the year. The first two arrows did succeed in raising growth over the past year and in pushing inflation to about 1.3 percent, from a 15-year average deflation of 0.3 percent.

Speed Bumps

It has been a year since Abe pledged to provide details of his third arrow proposals to reform Japan. The draft blueprint, "Strategy for Reviving Japan," announced last week comprises the following:

1. A corporate tax cut to below 30 percent over a few years (from 36 percent now).
2. A corporate governance code for listed companies.
3. Revamp of the giant US$1.26 trillion public pension fund expected to boost returns.
4. Focus on Japan's population decline to 87 million by 2060 (from 127 million) with proposals to spur more women to enter the workforce, including after-school programs for kids, more day-care centers, and new tax and pension rules to favor stay-at-home wives.
5. Calls to admit foreign workers in designated industries on "training visas" and to attract foreign housekeepers.
6. "White-collar exemption" to revamp labor rules for professionals, including changes to allow companies to shed unneeded workers more easily.
7. Creation of "special economic zones" (SEZs) with authority to cut redtape involving wide-ranging issues, including agriculture land ownership and management.

Other initiatives include promotion of clean energy, robotic technology, and tourism. This is Abe's second attempt to revive the nation's animal spirits. It falls short of expectations—still chipping around the edges of Japan's economic foundations, but in the right direction. The plan does lack crucial details such as size and timing. The cut in corporate tax gives no indication of the new rate (the Organisation for Economic Co-operation and Development's average is 29 percent) or when it will get there or what offsetting tax increases will be needed. Too much is left to be resolved in the new SEZs—this will take years to sort out.

Most of the ideas are a mishmash and they shy away from serious speed bumps—that is, difficult-to-accomplish reforms with a larger economic pay-off, such as the broader opening up of immigration; innovative ideas to tackle female underemployment and raise the status of women vis-a-vis men, with ample legal protection; and critical labor law reform.

Badly needed is civil service reform. Japan is notorious for the short life expectancy of governments—so bureaucrats operate with little threat of political oversight. Also problematic is the practice of "amakudari" (descent from heaven, literally) in which bureaucrats retire to assume top positions in industries they had regulated—making them reluctant to "rock the boat" onto which they are expected to head. In the end, that's what the third arrow is really all about—to make the economy reformable and fixable. As I see it, broader reform is critical to create new efficiencies in the economy.

Wages and Growth

After a year of Abenomics, growth, profits, and even inflation is ticking up. Will wages and consumption follow? Wage increase is critical, so much so Abe is practically begging employers to boost pay. By now, most wage negotiations (only 10 percent of workers is unionized) are completed and both big and small firms are raising wages, but not by much. Labor cash earnings (wages plus bonuses) rose 0.7 percent year-on-year this March, which is not in keeping with inflation created by the weak yen. So real earnings fell by 1.3 percent before the 3 percentage points consumption tax hike—denting further purchasing power.

Productivity is at the core of Abenomics. Rigid labor laws and falling productivity make it difficult for employers to raise wages—overall, the economy is estimated to be already overstaffed by 5 percent. Hence, the need for labor reforms focused on raising productivity. Former BoJ Governor Shirakawa[2] recently observed that monetary policy has limited impact in restoring economic recovery. The main problem with the Japanese economy is not deflation, but demographics. After all, prolonged stagnation has reduced potential GDP growth to less than 0.5 percent (4 percent in 1980s) against 2 percent in the United States and 1 percent in struggling Europe. Reforms need to attack deep structural problems, including demographic and labor imbalances. This productivity gap explains why monetary expansion won't boost wages, which Abe badly wants. He needs to promote greater competition to stimulate productivity gains. He needs deep reforms, wholesale.

What, Then, Are We to Do?

Japan is not out of the woods yet. Businesses are still cautious about prospective economic conditions. They do see "green shoots" but are worried about their sustainability and Abe's ability to reform sufficiently fast to root out long-standing traditional practices that have defined business culture but that are now blamed for its protracted slump. There is widespread impatience with the government's pace and commitment to cut red tape, and foster enough confidence for businesses to invest.

BoJ Governor Haruhiko Kuroda is right: "Implementation is key, and implementation should be swift. The major work is done by the government and the private sector."[3] I was in Seoul recently. It's notable that even as the Korean won had appreciated close to 9 percent against the US dollar, South Korea maintained its economic resilience and held its own in the world markets in the face of Abe's use of significant yen devaluation to remain competitive.

Abe's third arrow isn't shooting straight—it remains unsatisfyingly off-target. It hasn't inspired enthusiasm with half-measures. Abe is tinkering and acting at too-slow, typical "Japanese speed," indeed, "at slow-mover disadvantage"! He needs to spend the vast political capital he has since garnered on "big-bang" reforms.

Kuala Lumpur
June 26, 2014

Notes

1. First published on June 28, 2014.
2. Masaaki Shirakawa, former governor, Bank of Japan, at a lecture at the Tuck School of Business at Dartmouth College, Hanover, New Hampshire, on May 13, 2014.
3. Haruhiko Kuroda, governor, Bank of Japan, in an interview with the *Wall Street Journal* in Tokyo on May 25, 2014.

The International Financial System

PART VI

The International Financial System

CHAPTER 62

So, the Gold Bug Still Bugs You[1]

Keynes called it a "barbaric relic" in 1924. Scarce, attractive, malleable, and immune to corrosion—gold used to be ideal money before the advent of modern paper money. Today, just like diamonds, gold is also a girl's best friend. In Asia, it is the masses' darling. Most Asians are showered with gold when they are born; gold is figuratively given away at every Chinese New Year; Asians are blessed with it when they get married; and even when they die—gold paper is burnt to accompany them to wherever. Money aside, gold plays an important part in the social lives of most people in Asia.

Monetary Gold

Britain went off the gold standard in September 1931 in the midst of the Great Depression (1929–1932). Two groups of European "gold bloc" nations (including Germany and France) held on, and did not abandon the gold link until 1936. By then, rigid adherence to the gold standard had made the Great Depression worse. Between 1934 and 1940, some US$16 billion of gold flowed into the United States, giving it three-quarters of global official gold holdings. By the end of World War II (WWII), it was clear that the US dollar was as good as gold. Indeed, it was even better since US$ holdings earned a regular return.

After WWII, the Bretton Woods system was put into place. The original system worked well for 25 years mainly because the US dollar was convertible into gold at a fixed price (US$35 an ounce). The International Monetary Fund (IMF) served as administrator for this gold-anchored monetary system of fixed (but adjustable) exchange rates among currencies. However, in August 1971, President Richard Nixon closed the vestigial gold window and the world went off this gold-exchange standard.

So, for the past 38 years, the world has been engaged in an experimental monetary system based essentially on a single reserve (US$) with no link to gold. This new arrangement of flexible (and managed) exchange

379

rates worked flauntingly in the early years of the 1970s; and passably well in the next two decades. Lately, however, the dollar exchange standard has been blamed for everything from promoting global imbalances to the recent economic crisis—and a future of rampant inflation yet to come. For more details, refer to Chapter 67, "The Dollar Quagmire."

The gold bugs are having a field day since. A Canadian gold-watcher friend talks enthusiastically of: gold being the only currency central banks can't print; and gold as an attractive new pillar of the global monetary system since it is not beholden to national politics, nor dependent on the whims of any central bank.

The World Running out of Gold?

The continuing interest in gold by commodity investors, central bankers, savers, speculators, and consumers makes it unique among commodities. Indeed, contrary to recent talk of "peak gold," the world is not running out of gold. Rising prices and faltering mines do not imply scarcity. Gold is constantly mined, bought, held, and sold. Every year, over four times as much gold is mined and over twice as much recycled as is needed by industry. Contrast this with, say, oil. Annual crude oil supply more or less matches demand. Global oil stockpiles satisfy up to 40 days of crude demand. The World Gold Council estimated that gold above ground today amounted to 163,000 tonnes. They would last 375 years or nearly 3,000 times longer. Of this, holdings by central banks, the IMF, and governments (i.e., monetary gold) aggregated about 25,000 tonnes (15 percent of global), of which the largest hoard is in the United States, 8,100 tonnes. China, world's largest gold producer, holds only 1,054 tonnes (up 76 percent since 2003).

Even so, the very threat of any scarcity triggers off substitution. The 1970 price spike boosted porcelain in dentistry. Jewelry demand may possibly be more price inelastic. But that's also a matter of fashion, as the recent slide in sales suggests. What's more, psychology rather than supply and demand, remains critical.

Man's Addiction to Gold

Gold and its mystique are deeply rooted in the human psyche. What's clear is the absence of any rationale to tie money to gold; it is an anachronism of our modern world. Why hold gold, then? The context is revealing. The US dollar bill (its current basic design was from 1957) has since lost 87 percent of its purchasing power against the US consumer price index (CPI) (average annual rate of 4 percent, against 2 percent in Europe). According to Harvard historian Professor Niall Ferguson,[2] if you had exchanged US$1,000 of savings for gold before the window was slammed shut in 1971, you would have received 26.6 troy oz. of gold. Sold at even US$1,000/oz., the savings would have been worth US$26,596 today! But that's history.

Is gold a good store of value? No. On the surface, it seems so. Look at the facts. In 1980, gold price was US$400. By 1990, the US CPI had risen more than 60 percent, but the gold price stayed at US$400. By 2000, the gold price fell back to US$300, while the CPI more than doubled! Even when the gold price peaked to US$850 in 2008, it fell back quickly in the face of falling demand. So, over 20 years, the gold price had failed to keep up with the rise in the CPI. When investors are scared—about inflation, political turmoil, financial crises, deflation—they run for cover to gold, which price trend has been tracked and labeled the "index of anxiety." But, clear as day, when things calm down, gold price always retracts.

Is gold a good hedge against the weak US dollar? Again, no. History shows gold does not hold its value against the euro or yen when the US dollar depreciates. In 1980, US$1 = Yen 200. And, 25 years later, US$1 = Yen 110. The gold price had remained during this period at about the 1980 level—that is, US$400. So holding gold did not offset the fall in the value of the US dollar.

Surely, there is more to just "flight to safety" in gold. Recent experience shows that gold had performed well. Admittedly, gold is no slouch; it can have legs. But the future is changing. In 2009, the gold price averaged US$972, 10 percent higher than what the London Bullion Market Association (LBMA) analysts and traders had predicted early in 2009. The median forecast for 2010 is an average US$1,100. Gold reached a record US$1,226 on December 3, 2009—best ever since 1948; by year-end, it was US$1,096. Gold stood at US$1,121 when I last checked (i.e., on January 12, 2010). So gold did have a good run in 2009—up by about 35 percent to its all-time high.

Gold Is Looking Less Barbaric?

Several reasons account for the bullion's price rally. They also suggest gold to be a high-risk and highly volatile investment as an asset class with other commodities. First, there has been (and still is) unprecedented investor interest, prompted by continuing uncertainties of all sorts, including doubts about US dollar's long-term role as a reserve currency. Second, there has been a shift by many central banks to be net buyers of gold (net sellers since 1988). Recent buying by China and India excites the market. Third, there are worries that continuing government stimuli to counter the credit crunch could well be inflating another round of asset price bubble. I already hear LBMA traders complaining that gold is trading above "fair value," as reflected by the current state of the fragile and anemic global economy. Fourth, rising sovereign risk (United Arab Emirates, Greece, Ireland, and Spain) is raising doubts about the political will of the United States and European governments in putting a credible backstop on the "too-big-to-save" financial system. Fifth, rapid changes have taken place in the mechanics of investing in gold (including more complex modes of investing in gold-mining stocks and exchange-traded funds—ETFs) to effectively own gold without the hassle of actually owning physical gold. Sixth, there is the ever-present herding behavior and "momentum trading" by ever-bullish traders, reaching for new highs. Overhanging the market is the unraveling of the US dollar–funded carry-trade. Finally, instability of the current gold-free international monetary system poses new risks of price volatility that cannot be readily identified nor easily explained. Last year's financial implosion had led to great loss of confidence in paper assets. There is now a definite shift to holding tangible assets.

Gold's Uncertain Future

I don't see how gold can become a really sexy investment. Over its very long run since 1971, the yield on gold averaged 2 percent annually. Stocks were up 8 percent per annum by contrast. I do know some who look at buying gold as an insurance policy. As I see it, investors in gold are in it for the excitement of making money. The recent increasing involvement of commodity traders and private investors in gold points to continuing volatility and speculation. So, expect boom-and-bust-like movements in gold prices. The new players providing any element of stability are the rich emerging countries' central banks, who are essentially long-term players. If nothing else, they have staying power. The IMF will remain, in the short run at least, a net seller through its limited gold sales program (403.3 tonnes).

What, Then, Are We to Do?

In the end, I share the views of my Harvard teacher and mentor, Martin Feldstein,[3] and the ever-pessimistic Columbia Professor Nouriel Roubini[4] that gold is just not a good hedge, period. It must be remembered that gold really has no intrinsic value. It is sterile. Hence, there is the ever-present danger and risk of constant downside corrections. Indeed, I can see gold going back to previous peaks of US\$750–800 with ease. So if you want to hold some gold, there is no reason why you should do it in a rush—gold bug or not.

Kuala Lumpur
January 14, 2010

Notes

1. First published on January 16, 2010.
2. Niall Ferguson, *The Ascent of Money: A Financial History of the World* (New York: Penguin Press, 2008), p. 63.
3. Martin Feldstein, "Is Gold a Good Hedge?," a commentary published in *The Star*, Malaysia (December 30, 2009).
4. Nouriel Roubini, "The Gold Bubble and Bugs," a commentary published in *The Edge*, Malaysia (December 21, 2009).

CHAPTER 63

Man's Addiction to Gold[1]

I am not a gold bug. Gold is an artifact from early history. So much so, it is deeply rooted in the collective human consciousness. The last time I wrote about it was more than two years ago on January 16, 2010 (Chapter 62, "So, the Gold Bug Still Bugs You"). Then, as now, I am not the most optimistic about gold as an investment. But I am a realist. Over the past 50 years, capital gain on gold averaged 2 to 5 percent annually over each decade. Stocks were a better investment—about double to three times the gold "yield." This is not surprising, since gold has no real intrinsic value. It is sterile, making it difficult to value—one can't assign a credible price-earnings ratio (PE).

So long as there is love, lust, and guilt, there is a demand for this "barbaric relic" (Lord John Maynard Keynes). But in this uncertain world, many see it as a sexy investment. That's why gold scams thrive. It is still scarce, readily malleable, and will always command a price. Since the summer, even the darnedest optimist got worried as prices lurched down to US$1,500 a troy ounce (from a September 2011 high of just above US$1,900), wondering whether the decade-long bull-run had ended. No longer. Since US Fed launched its third quantitative easing (QE3) in mid-September 2012, gold has yet to catch its breath, rising 12.5 percent by October 6 to its highest level in nearly a year at US$1,795 per troy ounce. As reported, in terms of euro and Swiss franc, gold hit an all-time high this first week of October.

Sentiment in favor of gold has turned. Since the magic trio (US Fed, European Central Bank, and Bank of Japan) decided to create indefinite flows of liquidity (dubbed "QE infinity," i.e., they generate new streams of US dollars and € with no limit), gold investors have refocused their attention, based on fears of competitive devaluation, currency debasement, and prospect of soaring inflation. Bill Gross of PIMCO (the world's largest bond fund manager) warned: If the United States failed to put its finances in good order, "bonds would be burnt to a crisp (since yields will rise, implying a sharp fall in bond prices) and stocks would certainly be singed." He concluded: "Only gold and real assets could thrive."[2] That's a clean dose of reality! Today, gold is a safe haven, a hedge, and a speculative play. Whatever it is, gold has reached near-mythical status.

Gold Standard

To understand the role of gold in the international monetary system (IMS), it is important to appreciate its evolution since the nineteenth century. Under bimetallism (1815–1873), gold and silver served as basic reserve assets with France and the United States managing the system. Price ratio of gold and silver was fixed around 15:1, providing a fixed-anchor exchange between nations on the gold and silver standards. But from 1862 to 1870, the United States left the gold standard (GS) after experiencing persistent inflation as gold flowed in following trade surpluses.

In the 1870s, France and Germany went to war, so both left GS, thereby ending bimetallism. Deflation set in as nations moved to GS, creating excess demand for gold (i.e., tight money) until 1896, when rising gold supplies following discovery of gold in South Africa exposed the world once again to inflation. By 1914, Europe went off GS in order to fund deficit spending. So, gold flowed into the United States and the newly created Fed (Federal Reserve, US central bank) monetized the gold, forcing its price to double, followed by inflation.

From 1914 to 1924, the United States was the only major nation left on GS. US gross domestic product (GDP) was then equal to that of the United Kingdom, Germany, and France combined. And so, other economies began to base their currencies on US dollar rather than on gold. Germany went back to GS in 1924 to contain hyperinflation; the United Kingdom followed suit in 1925, and France in 1926. So the world returned to GS. Just as in 1914, when nations went off GS and created inflation, this time their return to GS created excess gold demand, thereby causing deflation—leading eventually to the Great Depression (1929–1932). Once again, the United Kingdom went off GS in 1931 and the United States in 1933. The US dollar devalued and the United States went back to GS in 1934 (and raised the gold price), and France followed in 1936. By 1937, gold became overvalued, causing a US dollar shortage that lasted until 1948.

US$ Standard

The 1936 Tripartite Monetary Agreement established the new US dollar–gold standard, and the US dollar became the only currency anchored to gold. The United States held 70 percent of world's gold by 1948. This system lasted until 1971, when President Richard Nixon took the US dollar off gold in August. The world then moved to a regime of flexible exchange rates for a brief period, with the US dollar as the main intervention currency. For the first time, the world moved to a pure US dollar standard (ignoring gold) by December 1971.

But the real challenge was that this only works if the main "reserve currency" nation stays rooted in monetary discipline. Not unexpectedly, the United States subsequently pursued a monetary policy that was too loose and hence inflationary. In February 1973, US$ devalued once more. Since then, more and more US dollars started flowing abroad and the euro-dollar market was born.

Eventually, to counter the weakening US dollar, the deutschemark assumed European leadership. By June 1973, the International Monetary Fund (IMF) moved the world to a regime of floating exchange rates to put a lid on inflation. The United States and Europe struggled to manage flexible exchange rates in the midst of facing the most inflationary peacetime monetary policies: US inflation in the 1970s rose to 13 to 14 percent per annum and the price of gold shot up above US$50 per troy ounce in February 1980.

Fear that the United States has lost its monetary discipline and US dollar would continue to depreciate forced Europeans to act decisively to counter US dollar weakness and maintain price stability, by launching the European Monetary System (EMS) in 1978. It severed the world economy into two parts. Gold stocks in Europe were nearly double that of the United States. By 1985, the Plaza Accord moved the world's exchange rate regime to a managed US dollar system of floating relative to European currencies. In the process, Japan was "forced" to appreciate the yen against US$. Unlike what Nobel Economics Laureate Milton Friedman had predicted, that nations don't need reserves under flexible exchange rates, economies in practice are needing more and more reserves today under a floating exchange regime than they ever needed under fixed exchange rates.

Gold and SDRs

So much for the past. In the twenty-first century, US dollar remains the world's predominant reserve currency as the euro is seen to struggle for survival. Today, it's just too feeble and unstable to pose a major threat to the US dollar's reserve currency role. RMB (renminbi) or yuan of China (world's second largest economy) will certainly take many years to become truly convertible, let alone assume the role of a proper reserve currency.

The Special Drawing Rights (SDRs) are a "book facility" created by the IMF in 1968 (i.e., providing a unit of account in its books) to act as a new reserve asset to deemphasize gold. Despite much promotion, SDRs have remained a "wallflower" of IMS. It was initially given a gold guarantee, which would have benefited it today. But, this was "stripped" in the early 1970s when the price of gold soared. With high hopes for SDRs, the IMF and the United States sold off part of their gold holdings. Others, however, held on to eventually reap huge unrealized capital gains when the price of gold rose in the late 1970s. A few nations (notably, Holland and Canada) sold gold to help finance their large budget deficits. By and large, gold holdings of all central banks were maintained (at around 1 billion ounces). Despite attempts to demonetize it, gold has maintained its allure. The mystique of gold is intact. It just won't go away.

Future of Gold

Officially, the superpower of the day plays the central role in IMS. This has been true going back to the Roman denarius, Islamic dinar, and so on, as it has for the familiar pound sterling in the nineteenth century and US dollar in the twentieth century until today. Indeed, the superpower holds the veto over the future of IMS. We saw this at Bretton Woods (BW) in 1944, when the "desired" creation of a world currency ("Unitas" proposed by the United States, and "Bancor" by the United Kingdom) fell prey to nationalist self-interest. As I see it, BW did not create a new IMS; it merely kept what was in place since 1934.

To be fair, BW did create the IMF and World Bank to independently manage the IMS anchored on US dollar. It gave the US dollar a new supranational status and a new legitimacy. I agree with my friend, Nobel Laureate Robert Mundell,[3] that in today's world, neither the United States nor European Union nor China will ever "fix their respective currencies to gold. More likely, gold will be deployed at some point (maybe in 10 to 15 years) when it has been banalized among central bankers, and they are not so timid to speak about its use as an asset that can circulate between central banks. Not necessarily at a fixed price, but at market price."[4] Like it or not, the world stock of gold is going to continue to be regarded as a reserve asset. It can't be wished away. If nothing else, it will remain to act as a useful warning signal on inflation.

Gold is here to stay. It's going to be part of the structure of IMS in the twenty-first century. But not in the way as it had been historically as the centerpiece of GS. That's the unique part of its history. Even "gold bug" French President Charles de Gaulle admitted that "the gold exchange standard no longer corresponds to present realities."[5] But he maintained that a true IMS should act on "an undisputable monetary basis bearing the mark of no particular country." He meant gold. Gold's role as an alternative currency will evolve and its price will reflect inflationary expectations. As of now, I don't see gold price collapsing since real interest rates (adjusted for inflation) are already set by the US Fed to hold until 2015.

But why this obsession with gold? Some believe tying money to gold prevents its overissue. That's not true. Historically, declaring a gold parity for currency has certainly not prevented governments from overissuing currencies and experiencing price inflation. Again, others believe gold provides the discipline governments need to maintain price stability. Certainly not. History is full of instances where mercantilist excesses led to inflation at home and deflation overseas, and vice versa. Yet, there are those who believe gold provides a sustainable form of settlement for international payments. Not true. Growth of international commerce requires flexible access to an adequate money supply to meet its needs—gold does not meet this need in any stable way. Also, many believe gold serves as a good store of value. Again, no. Because it is sterile, it is not a good store of value compared with other assets. According to billionaire Warren Buffett,[6] US$100 invested in gold in 1965 is worth US$4,455 at the end of 2011; this same amount invested in S&P 500 stocks is worth US$6,072 after the same 46 years.

What, Then, Are We to Do?

Gold is limited. Since old Egyptian days, the stock of gold in the world totaled less than 170,000 tons, worth US$9.5 trillion at today's price. About one-third is parked in vaults of central banks; close to one-half is in jewelry and ornaments; the rest is in speculative hands. According to the World Gold Council, two-thirds of today's flow of gold ends up in China (26 percent) and India (40 percent). In India, it's almost all in jewelry, whereas in China, it's part jewelry, part investment. Indian households hold the largest stock of gold in the world (18,000 tons or 11 percent of world stock). At today's prices, that's worth US$1 trillion, or more than 50 percent of India's GDP. Up to 8 percent of India's household savings is held in gold. So, India's obsession with gold reflects a unique fascination, not unlike in other parts of Asia. That's why Asians are often the target of bogus gold schemes and scams. We see this in Malaysia and Singapore, where investors flock, only to be cheated wholesale by so-called gold guarantee schemes that are clearly designed to defraud and sure to collapse—simply because monies collected are unscrupulously invested in high-risk, "get-rich" ventures that are fraudulent from the start and doomed to failure every time. My advice: Avoid investing in any of them at all cost!

Central banks will keep on printing money, having created US$9 trillion since the financial crisis. Inflationary expectations will evolve in time, off and on. And with it, occasional outbreaks in price of gold, leading to bond sales that drive up interest rates. Use of gold for monetary purposes is an anachronism, capable of causing terrible damage because it is so utterly inappropriate in today's world. Yet, the reality is that the world will not be able to find genuine financial stability until it comes to terms with and accommodates the dominant position gold now holds in Asian economic life.

Kuala Lumpur
October 18, 2012

Notes

1. First published on October 20, 2012.
2. Bill Gross, as quoted by Jack Farchy, in "Investors Make Swift Grab for Gold," in the *Financial Times* of London (October 6, 2012).
3. Robert Mundell, "The International Monetary System in the 21st Century: Could Gold Make a Comeback?," lecture at Saint Vincent College, Letrobe, Pennsylvania, March 12, 1997.
4. Ibid., p. 10.
5. Charles de Gaulle, president of France, "On the Gold Standard," excerpts from remarks by President de Gaulle, *New York Times*, February 5, 1965, p. 12.
6. Warren Buffett, "Why Stocks Beat Gold and Bonds," *Fortune*, New York (February 27, 2012), p. 44.

CHAPTER 64

In Search of Gold at Bretton Woods: Lust for Gold Not Paying Off[1]

Bretton Woods, New Hampshire, USA—that's where it all began in July 1944, where 730 delegates from 44 nations gathered to conclude the final Articles of Agreement of the International Monetary Conference (IMC). It established the new international monetary system, tying the value of countries' currencies to the US dollar, which was convertible into gold at a fixed price (US$35 per troy ounce). The United States then held 70 percent of the world's gold. The IMC also set up: (1) the International Monetary Fund (IMF) to administer this gold-anchored monetary system of fixed exchange rates among currencies; and (2) the International Bank for Reconstruction and Development (IRBD or World Bank) to provide long-term loans, especially to underdeveloped countries.

Ironically, the IMF should have been called a *bank* (because it lends short-term "working capital" to nations with temporary payments deficits to enable them to adjust), whereas the World Bank should have been called a *fund* (since it makes long-term loans up to 30 years to assist nations to build physical and social infrastructure). It is said that the IMC was more important than the Treaty of Versailles, which ended World War I, but crippled the German economy. This time it established the economic base, which led to global prosperity after World War II—rebuilt the German economy and stabilized Europe for the first time in centuries (through the massive US Marshall Plan). It was the first time the victor of a major war helped rebuild a defeated nation!

Back to New England

I just made a nostalgic return drive through New England, whose colorful foliage first charmed me as a student at Harvard in the fall of 1969, and which I have since lost touch with. I am reminded of the American writer John Steinbeck's similar road trip five decades ago, which he published in his memoir of the jaunt in 1962: *Travels with Charley: In Search of America*[2] (his pet poodle). Like him, I drove through the highways of New England just as fall foliage was coming past its peak, seeking (but not always finding) that fabled place where "the trees burst into color . . . reds and yellows you can't believe." I started from my daughter's home in Westerly, Rhode Island (RI), which shares a border with Connecticut, and cut north through Rhode Island's capital of Providence, and then westward, moving through beautiful southern New Hampshire, to the hip-town of Woodstock in Vermont, staying at the Woodstock Inn, which dates back to 1793.

Its southern flank, full of bucolic vistas and winding backroads in between, provides the most fabulous scenic drive, with breathtaking foliage color only available in this Green Mountain State. It's off the next day further north to Bretton Woods, high up in the White Mountain Forest of New Hampshire, best known for its majestic peaks and picturesque lakes, rivers, and ponds.

Bretton Woods Accord

For me, it was the stay at the Mount Washington Hotel where the 1944 IMC was held that brought it all back. I spent time at the historic Gold Room, where Harry D. White (United States) and Lord John Maynard Keynes (United Kingdom) did much of the talking and horse-trading, but to no avail. National self-interest finally prevailed—the US dollar assumed a new suprainternational status. On the door hangs the plaque: "In this Room the Articles of Agreement Setting Up the International Monetary Fund was signed in July 1944." On an adjacent wall was displayed a photo of Henry Morgenthau Jr., secretary to the US Treasury, signing the Bretton Woods Accord. There are also pictures of Keynes, White, Dean Acheson, and S. Stepanov, chairman of the USSR delegation. It is amazing that a hotel with only 200 rooms could accommodate close to 1,000 delegates!

Back to Harvard

The journey continues to take me south to historic North Conway and then westward across the massive state of Maine via the I-95 highway and the arching Piscataqua River Bridge, passing by Bangor, its capital. Then to "downtown" Bar Harbor on Mount Desert Island, which hosts the fabulous Arcadia National Park. Its 27-mile scenic "Park Loop" drive was breathtaking. Backtracking Route 3 led me southwestward toward Deer Island, which earned Steinbeck's relentless praise.

Retracing his drive to picturesque Stonington to try out Steinbeck's boast that "Maine's lobsters are the best in the world," I must admit he was spot-on after chewing this spiny crustacean at the Fisherman's Friend eatery at this harbor. Thereafter, the drive takes me along the broken, rocky coastline on Route 1, south toward Portland and then to Portsmouth. But fall is still here, with yellows and oranges scattered with bright reds and some blues lining the way. Driving farther south on I-95 all the way to Boston was uneventful enough, as I concluded this unusual journey in Boston and on to the Charles at Harvard Square, as I settled in to prepare for my two-day meeting of Harvard's Graduate School Alumni Association Council at the end of the first week of November. Yes, it was great to be back at Harvard.

Gold

Bretton Woods made me look back on gold. I am one of those who believe gold has no future. It's just an anachronism of our modern world, although I won't go so far as Keynes, who called it a "barbaric relic." It simply has no intrinsic value. I had written twice why this is so (Chapter 62, "So, The Gold Bug Still Bugs You," and Chapter 63, "Man's Addiction to Gold"). Nevertheless, the Bretton Woods system based on gold lasted for 27 years, until President Richard Nixon closed the gold window and took the world off the gold-exchange standard.

Events thereafter turned out that the US dollar is not as good as gold. Even so, the world struggled for the next 42 years on an arrangement of flexible (but managed) exchange rates with no link whatsoever to gold. In return, there were occasional crises of confidence, but the world always survived, although the US dollar was blamed for much of the world's ills—from promoting persistent global payments imbalances to being a major cause of the recent Great Recession and the last financial crisis. For details, read Chapter 67, "The Dollar Quagmire." Nevertheless, gold continued to maintain its allure despite attempts to demonetize it. Gold's mystique remains intact. It just won't go away, even though the superpower of the day still calls the tune.

Goldbuggism

For goldbugs, or what economics Nobel Laureate Paul Krugman[3] calls "goldbuggism," 2013 has been a dud year so far. Frankly, gold's behavior over the decades has not been easy to define. It's "somewhat of a chameleon."

Fans see it as mostly a hedge against inflation, sometimes as protection against poor economic performance, at other times, a haven when the US dollar is deliberately debased (decline in value). Gold plays different roles at different times. In the early 2000s, gold behaved like other base commodities (such as copper and oil), surging ahead amid fast-rising demand from emerging markets and a weak US dollar. In 2008, it offered protection when other asset classes fell in troubled times. Gold is still up 68 percent since Lehman's collapse on September 15, 2008. Today, a few still believe it acts as a hedge against potential interest rate hikes, slowing economic performance, and irrational fears and panics. This is happening simply because no one knows how to really value gold. Unlike common stocks (which give dividends and have earnings growth) or bonds (which pay interest), gold doesn't provide an income flow. Let's face it. In the end, gold is worth what the investor is prepared to pay. Gold closed at US$272 an ounce at end-2000; by August 2011, its price was up sevenfold. This drives investors crazy.

Gold Disappoints

The gold rush appears to be over—this year, gold is on track to record its first yearly fall in 13 years. It closed on November 8 at US$1,292 an ounce, down 22 percent for 2013 (–30 percent since its peak on August 22, 2011). All's gone wrong for goldbugs. Indeed everything they wanted gold to do fell flat. According to the *Wall Street Journal*,[4] large-cap US stocks were up significantly (S&P 500 has since returned 25 percent); small-cap stocks did even better (Russell 2000, up 30 percent). Even US bonds, reflecting the threat of rate increases, fell only 1.1 percent so far this year, leaving gold licking its wounds. As a hedge against inflation, gold performed just as poorly. The much-rumored and much-anticipated inflation to have followed the massive QE (quantitative easing) injection of monies into the United States and the world (up at least US$3 trillion) never came—US consumer prices rose only 1.2 percent for year ended September 2013. Over longer periods, gold also failed to keep up with prices. For two decades in the 1980s and 1990s, price of gold fell by 46 percent to less than US$290 an ounce, as consumer prices doubled. Today, gold is still below its 1980 inflation-adjusted peak price, estimated at more than US$2,300.

Conventional Wisdom Is Wrong

Conventional wisdom has it that demand for gold varies directly with flows in disposable income. So, economic slowdown in China and India will reduce demand for the metal. As Chinese and Indians will have less disposable income, they will cut spending on luxuries like gold and jewelry. Conventional wisdom is probably wrong on China and India, where people purchase gold jewelry for adornment and invest in bullion for appreciation as a store of value. Unlike the West, Chinese and Indians instinctively turn to gold as a financial refuge in times of social and political uncertainty and turmoil.

With this mind-set, any softening of growth in China will lead to a weaker yuan (or renminbi, the Chinese currency) and a rise in political instability, so that demand for gold will accelerate as a way of preserving wealth. China's gold purchases more than doubled from a year earlier in the second quarter of 2013, or 20 percent higher than in the first quarter of 2013. They could reach a record 1,000 tonnes this year and will overtake India to become the world's number-one buyer.

However, India's consumption this year will be lower than last year's 860 tonnes as the government's curbs on imports begin to bite. Diwali is the biggest gold-buying occasion in India; this year, very weak gold purchases at a time of traditionally strong demand indicated that official restrictions are indeed working, as would the US Fed's anticipated move to taper its bond-buying program. Unlike India, China's gold consumption has reached a new high, powered by "da-ma" (literally, "big-mama") oversight, a group of middle-aged women who keep a tight grip on the family purse and an eagle-eye on gold prices at retail outlets. They even help stabilize prices, indeed, setting a floor at times of crisis. They also ensure retail prices remain at close to world prices, unlike India, where 8 to 10 percent premium above the global price is not uncommon. Overall, China and India remain the driving force for gold purchases; together with Vietnam and Indonesia, they account for 60 percent of world consumption against 35 percent ten years ago.

Bitcoin—Digital Gold?

Bitcoin is strange. This cult digital currency, invented in 2009, is pure computerized money. It exists only as strings of digital code. Some explanation is in order. Unlike normal money, which is created and regulated through monetary policy by central banks, bitcoin is created by computer geeks—using similar technology as discredited Napster (which started in 1999, allowing individuals to swap music files among themselves to the exclusion of the record labels) and shut down by legal suits in 2001. Instead, bitcoin is determined by clever algorithms. That is, new bitcoins are mined—users can acquire them by letting their computers compete to solve complex mathematical problems; "winners" get virtual cash, in the form of a string of numbers. Owners regard them as digital gold simply because their purchasing power is protected by a hard limit (21 million) on the number of coins that can exist, currently about 12 million.

Early this year, a unit of bitcoin cost around US$15; by mid-April, it had risen to US$179, valuing bitcoins in circulation at about US$2 billion. It has become a hot commodity, creating a bubble inflated by social media, cheap cash in search of high return, and unsettled investors from repeated crises. Not surprising, bitcoin went through a sharp correction in April 2013 (at one point losing 50 percent of its value), before recovering sharply. By November 5, its price rose to a record US$252.61 on the leading Tokyo-based Mt. Gox exchange.

Bitcoin has survived because it (1) acts as a store of value; (2) has a unique digital signature, making it almost impossible to forge; (3) is used in Silk Road, a marketplace hidden in the web (Tor network) to settle transactions (through BitPay); (4) is anonymous and untraceable; and (5) effectively promotes e-commerce (especially business-to-business because of its low transaction costs). But bitcoin's success has attracted growing regulatory scrutiny. Already, lawsuits are growing, including recent bankruptcy filing of the CoinLab mining unit, Alydian Inc. ("Bitcoin business incubator").

Lack of regulatory oversight is challenging law enforcement's ability to keep tabs on the criminal underworld. It is difficult to ascertain how much of the US$2.4 billion bitcoin market is tied to crime. I believe most of bitcoin transactions are legal since it does have legitimate uses; also, it can be bought and sold on online exchanges, similar to a stock market. Will bitcoin go the Napster way? We will have to wait and see.

What, Then, Are We to Do?

Most economists, including Krugman, agree that gold has been anything but a safe investment. Nevertheless, gold has survived as acknowledged even by Keynes because gold has become part of the apparatus of conservatism and is one of the matters that we cannot expect to see handled without prejudice. And so it remains to this day. Dr. Doom (Columbia's Professor Nouriel Roubini) has since predicted that "gold prices are likely to move much lower, toward US$1,000 by 2015."[5]

His six reasons do make good sense: (1) gold prices only rise in times of crises; (2) gold performs best in the midst of high inflation; there is little inflation now and it is likely to remain so; (3) gold gives no income; (4) gold prices rise when interest rates adjusted for inflation become negative; (5) many highly indebted nations also own large stocks of gold; to keep their credit rating, they will be increasingly tempted to sell gold reserves (as did Cyprus; Italy and France may similarly be tempted); and (6) gold price is political—the conservative far-right fringe is unlikely to have it their way to return to the gold standard; this together with the inability to use gold as a currency means gold will remain impotent.

So gold price will continue to gyrate and bump along. I believe the gold rush is over. To breathe new life into gold, the World Gold Council (WGC) is on the offensive to woo the new generation, campaigning through "Love Gold," including giving low-interest, long-term loans to independent gold jewelers to create, distribute, and market new images of gold, using social media. WGC places special focus by directing more firepower behind its efforts especially in China and India. Good luck!

Boston, MA, USA
Kuala Lumpur
November 13, 2013

Notes

1. First published on November 16, 2013.
2. John Steinbeck, *Travels with Charley: In Search of America* (New York: Viking Press, 1962).
3. Paul Krugman, "Lust for Gold," *International Herald Tribune* (April 11, 2013).
4. Joe Light, "What's Next for Gold," *Wall Street Journal* (November 2, 2013).
5. Nouriel Roubini, "After the Gold Rush," a commentary in *The Edge*, Malaysia (June 10, 2013).

CHAPTER 65

What's Wrong with the International Monetary System?[1]

US President Lyndon Johnson stated in 1968: "To the average citizen, the balance of payments, the strength of the US$, and the international monetary system are meaningless phrases. They seem to have little relevance to our daily lives. Yet, their consequences touch us all—consumer and captain of industry, worker, farmer and financier."[2] It does not matter whether international financial arrangements are working well or not; but it gets even more evident when they are not. While not all would argue there is no life left in the international monetary system (IMS), almost all would agree the current system contains inherent contradictions, which lead to frequent breakdowns.

Basic Principles

Four basic principles underlie the IMS:

1. A country's sovereign right to regulate internal demand to maintain stable conditions at home in terms of employment and domestic prices.
2. Free international movement of goods and capital (substantial progress has been made in meeting this goal).
3. A system of mixed exchange rate regimes—from fixed exchange rate (e.g., China) to flexible exchange rate (e.g., US dollar, pound, and euro) to degrees of managed floats (e.g., yen and the ringgit).
4. A nation's right to hold international reserves in the form of gold, US$, and other major currencies.

In addition, lines of credit are available from the International Monetary Fund (IMF). The reserves available and potentially obtainable set a limit on the cumulative size of a country's balance of payments (BOP) deficit, thus acting as a BOP constraint in domestic policy making. But there is no such corresponding limit for surplus nations. The system is asymmetrical; it punishes those in deficit and lets the surplus nations alone.

Most countries experience some trade-off between unemployment and price stability. As unemployment is lowered by policies to expand demand (as with the US stimulative packages), the higher is the price that has to be paid in rising inflation. The trade-off varies over time and from country to country. The rationale behind this relationship centers on the tendency for money-wage increases to outstrip rises in productivity even under conditions of high unemployment. The current state of a jobless growth in the United States with low inflation in the face of continuing high unutilized capacity shows no trade-off at this time. But as demand picks up and as growth picks up and unemployment trends down, inflation is bound to creep up.

What's Wrong?

First, there is the adjustment problem. The present IMS has no reliable mechanism to eliminate BOP disequilibrium (i.e., international payments imbalances). This is fundamental. There are three possible ways of correcting a payments deficit: use of trade and capital controls; adjustment of exchange rate; and government policies working through internal changes in income and prices. All three go against the three principles underlying the system. So, when a country experiences a deficit, there is no assurance the deficit will be eliminated before its reserves are used up; or depending on the extent to which market forces are allowed to sufficiently depreciate the currency; or whether domestic policies are tightened enough to reduce demand.

Second, there is the problem of the exchange rate, which usually doesn't react fast enough to correct imbalances. Destabilizing capital flows exacerbate the problem. The IMS is also subject to massive (especially speculative) flows of funds, which could complicate BOP adjustment. The flooding of cheap US$ funds into emerging markets following QE2 (second phase of Fed's quantitative easing) has led to capital controls and managed exchange rates limiting their appreciation. Of late, the size of speculative flows has become too large for even the larger emerging markets to cope. This is not the end. In the event QE2 exits, the impact of large capital withdrawals on the exchange rate can be just as destabilizing.

Third, there is the problem of liquidity. The system has no arrangement to generate, in an orderly and predictable way, increases in foreign reserves that are needed to meet demands of growing world trade. The creation of Special Drawing Rights (SDRs) in the IMF, as and when needed, is supposed to do the job, but in practice, increases in SDRs have been few and far between. By chance, the Fed's recent expansionary program, including

QE2, is now overdoing the job; indeed, these capital flows have become too large for orderly adjustment to take place.

Finally, there is the confidence problem. The system allows persistently large surplus nations to do virtually whatever they please in postponing real adjustment. Today, about two-thirds of global reserves is held in US$-denominated assets (especially Treasuries). China's international reserves today amounted to about US$3.1 trillion, of which US$1.15 trillion is invested in US$. It has been estimated that Italy's entire sovereign debt (principal plus interest until 2062) totaled US$3 trillion. In terms of oil, China's reserves can buy 25 billion barrels of Brent crude, equivalent to 13 years of its net oil imports. Indeed, it could pay for the entire Nikkei 225 list of companies, with US$30 billion in change. That's how big China's reserves are.

True, the Bretton Woods (BW) system has served the world economy reasonably well. In a sense, the system operated well in the 1950s and 1960s, but on borrowed time. The "tearless deficits" during this period left a legacy of a large and growing "overhang" of foreign dollar holdings, which frequently threatens a confidence crisis. Persistent US deficits had since led to a diminution in the quality of the US dollar in the eyes of most foreign holders. Global payments imbalances require coordinated global action to resolve. This is hard to come by.

Of the four problem areas, I think the matter of speculative and exchange rate instability is serious. This involves two aspects: (1) threat imposed by the "overhang" of convertible claims against the reserve currencies (especially US$) where such claims are today touching 15 percent of global gross domestic product (GDP) (6 percent, 10 years ago); and (2) danger of private speculative runs against currencies under pressure, especially US$. They are interrelated. To top it all, the IMF practice of allowing nations to choose their own exchange rate regimes didn't help the adjustment process. Fixed exchange rates operated uneasily alongside flexible exchange rates, including managed floats and permutations of these two major regimes, in the hope that somehow policies would be coordinated to converge and foster imbalances adjustment. Nothing like it will ever happen as each regime did its own thing to protect its national interest.

And so, until today, the four problems of adjustment, exchange rate, liquidity, and confidence underlying the IMS have persisted. One thing is clear: There is no political will to reform. The United States, for which reform means the diminution of the dollar's global role, is lukewarm. And Europe is distracted more than ever with protecting the status of the euro and the EU's sovereign debt crisis. France, as chair of G-20, wants to find an IMS that more accurately reflects the new structure of the world economy. But the major emerging nations, especially the BRICS (Brazil, Russia, India, China, and South Africa), want to move away from a virtual one-reserve regime to one based on multiple reserve currencies.

Are Payments Deficits Good or Bad?

For most, payments deficits are instinctively bad. But think about it. After all, the purpose of international trade is to obtain goods and services from abroad at less than can be produced (or that are not available) at home. Imports are the benefits of trade. A trade deficit means more goods and services are being received from abroad than are being given up. Surely that's good—from the deficit nation's point of view. But this deficit has to be financed. So, the nation either loses reserves (uses savings) or borrows (living on credit), and this may prove uncomfortable as the deficit persists. In the end, the deficit country has to take corrective actions, such as deflationary domestic policies (austerity measures), exchange controls, or devaluing its currency. All of them conflict with one or more of its domestic economic goals. There is a cost to adjust.

The soft solution is to use reserves: Its function is to render exchange rate stability compatible with freedom for individual nations to pursue national economic goals. While drawing down reserves or borrowing may reduce the conflict of objectives, it nevertheless increases the potential for future conflict. That's exactly what's happening in the United States. It has run persistent deficits for so long that its debt is now too high (close to 100 percent of GDP) and its liabilities to nations accumulating US$ reserves (especially China and Japan) have grown so large that it can trigger off a confidence run on the US$. This has proved inconvenient at a time when the United States continues to need expansionary policies to bring down its high unemployment.

Surplus nations have the opposite problem since these surpluses are inflationary and reflect an inefficient utilization of reserves in the form of involuntary foreign lending. It can be viewed as the mere hoarding of resources that might have enhanced future output and welfare if added onto domestic investments instead. To sum up, today's mixed exchange rate regimes provide no mechanism for systematic and effective BOP adjustment that does not conflict with major goals of public policy.

IMS Reform

Reform of the IMS is clearly needed. Vladimir Lenin, founder of the Russian Communist Party and first head of the Soviet Union, is often attributed to have said: "The surest way to destroy the capitalist system (is) to debauch its currency." There is truth in it. The IMS is at the heart of the world economy. When rules of the global monetary game are unclear, inadequate, some even obsolete, nations find it difficult to play; indeed, some may exploit them to their advantage. This undermines the very fabric of the IMS.

Some history: In 1944, BW gave birth to the IMF and today's US$-centered IMS. The BW conference was dominated by two strong-willed economists, Harry D. White (United States) and John Maynard Keynes (United Kingdom).

The United Kingdom wanted a system in which global liquidity is regulated by a multilateral agency (IMF), while the United States (for self-interest) preferred a US$-based system. Because of its enormous political power, the United States got its way. Keynes, for all his intellect and persuasiveness, failed to (1) endow the IMF with the power to create a new global reserve unit as an alternative to the US dollar; and (2) secure a global regime that forces surplus as well as deficit nations, and the issuer of the reserve currency as well as its users, to adjust. It's a pity, as Keynes's failures haunt us to this day. Nations with chronic surpluses (Germany, China, and Japan), and the United States as dominant supplier of US$ reserves, do not face the same pressures to adjust their imbalances as do deficit countries that are often bullied to do so.

What, Then, Are We to Do?

In my view, what is needed is a tripolar IMS organized around the US$, €, and RMB (China's yuan). Let's face it, neither the € nor the RMB are in any position today to challenge the US$. The world will be better off with a viable alternative to the US$. Their interplay forces on the reserve currencies a market discipline earlier and more consistently. This way, central banks seeking to accumulate reserves will have a choice, so that the United States no longer has "so much rope with which to hang itself" (so says my friend, Barry Eichengreen). Another view is to transform the IMF's SDRs into an international reserve currency. The trouble is the SDR is not market tradable. To be an effective international reserve currency, the IMF will have to be accorded the role of a world central bank. This is unlikely—indeed, a nonstarter—as it was in the BW days.

At the recent G-20 finance ministers meeting in Paris, all central bankers acknowledged that global imbalances remain a critical problem, and that a solution will involve policy coordination. Yet, each played down its own role. Until a solution is found, the accumulation of foreign exchange reserves becomes a powerful instrument of self-insurance. There is no political will to reform—only the will to congregate and obfuscate. In the BW days, the might of the United States called the day. Today, it's nobody's call. So nothing is done. Just kick the can down the road. What a pity.

Kuala Lumpur
May 6, 2011

Notes

1. First published on May 7, 2011.
2. Lyndon Johnson, US president, in his Balance of Payments statement on January 1, 1968, in Washington, DC, 2009.

CHAPTER 66

US Dollar: Cracking at the Seams[1]

My previous chapter dealt with the international monetary system (IMS): why the world monetary order is in disorder, and why free movement of capital underpinning the IMS is increasingly being challenged. This chapter concerns the basic anchor of the IMS—reserve currency role of the US dollar—and why it will give way to rapidly rising pressures toward multipolarity, that is, the concurrent pulling of forces emanating from more than two growth centers. According to the new World Bank report,[2] "Global Development Horizons 2011—Multipolarity: The New Global Economy," the World Bank expects the newly emerging BRIIKs (Brazil, Russia, India, Indonesia, and Korea) to join the ranks of China as new drivers of growth toward a multipolar world by 2025. It expects US$ to lose its solitary dominance in the global economy by 2025 as the euro and renmimbi (RMB) established themselves on an equal footing. Today, none of them has a currency that is used for reserve accumulation, invoicing, or exchange rate anchor. The status quo remains centered on the US dollar. But change is in the air. In 1991, G-3 (the United States, eurozone, and Japan) accounted for 49 percent of world trade, and the BRIICKs (including China) only 9 percent. By 2010, G-3's share had fallen to 29 percent, while BRIICKs' share rose beyond 30 percent. Without doubt, the postwar structure reflecting the dominant position of advanced nations is in the midst of fundamental change. Globalization and rapid growth in emerging market economies (EMEs) are bound to translate into greater global economic power. It's just a matter of time.

Multipolarity

We are witnessing the cracking of global institutions created in 1945, still unadjusted to the growing weight of the EMEs, reflecting reluctance by the United States and eurozone to come to terms with a world they no longer dominate. It is also a manifestation of uneasiness in China, India, and Brazil that management of their domestic economy, long the jurisdiction of internal prerogative, now matters to the rest of the world. This is understandable. The founding of the Bretton Woods institutions (International Monetary Fund [IMF] and World Bank) after devastation of the Great Depression and World War II (WWII) set in motion an era of stability at a time the United States was unchallenged as the dominant global economy. In international finance, this postwar order began to fall apart in the 1970s as the US economy floundered, the dollar tanked, Europe was rebuilt, and Japan asserted itself.

The beginning of a trend toward multipolarism was, however, interrupted in the 1980s and 1990s with the collapse of the Soviet Union, eurozone's indigestion in swallowing a reunited Germany, and the Asian currency crisis. The United States was thrust into the forefront to lead. But, the homemade US financial crisis in the 2000s, in the face of rapidly rising EMEs, brought the era of US dominance to an end. Yet, neither the United States, eurozone, nor China has the capacity and clout to manage global problems. Happily, G-20 came along to replace G-7, stumbling onto a mutually beneficial cooperation. Professor Barry Eichengreen's reference in history of another scenario is scary: "The decades following World War I were marked by the inability of rising or declining powers to stabilize the world economy or create functioning global institutions; the result was the Great Depression and WWII."[3]

A definite shift is taking place, driven by the rising power of the emerging six-nation BRIICK, together representing more than one-half of global growth in 14 years. According to the World Bank report,[4] EMEs will grow at an average of 4.7 percent per annum between 2011 and 2025, more than double the rate of the advanced nations (2.3 percent per annum). The implications are far reaching: Balance of global growth and investment will shift to the EMEs; this shift will lead to boosts in investment flows to nations, driving global growth, with a significant rise in cross-border mergers and acquisitions, and a changing corporate landscape where established multinationals will largely be absent; a new IMS will gradually evolve, displacing the US dollar as the world's main reserve currency by 2025. The euro and the RMB (renminbi, China's currency) will establish themselves on an equal footing in a new "multicurrency" monetary system; the euro is the most credible rival to the US dollar: "Its status is poised to expand provided the euro can successfully overcome sovereign debt crisis currently faced by some member countries and can avoid moral hazard problems associated with bailouts within the European Union"; the rising role (and internationalizing) of the RMB should "resolve the disparity between China's growing economic strength on the global stage and its heavy reliance on foreign currencies"; and the transition will happen gradually.

At no time in modern history have so many EMEs been at the forefront of an evolving multipolar economic system.

A Strong US Dollar: A Delusion

The US dollar is the reserve currency. This refers to its use by foreign central banks and governments as part of their international reserves. This role, combined with widespread use of the US dollar as a medium of exchange (transactions and settlement vehicle), a standard of measurement (unit of account), and a store of value (method of holding wealth), has given rise to the key currency status of the US dollar. For these reasons, the United States serves as world banker. None of these roles were planned. It just evolved since it met various needs of foreign official institutions and foreign private parties more effectively than any alternative could (at one time gold, then the pound sterling, also yen and deutsche mark). Many of the reasons for the use of US dollar by official and private parties are the same. However, the aims of the two users need not always coincide. If the US dollar role as a reserve currency was terminated, its use by private traders and institutions would most likely remain, perhaps even stronger. The wheels of commerce keep turning. The role of the United States serving as world banker remains relevant.

It is a long-standing tradition for the US Treasury to favor a strong US dollar. The US Fed has no say, since it is outside its purview of fighting inflation and unemployment. The exchange rate is just another price. The price of the US dollar relative to other currencies is determined in the market, and not under the control of anyone. Increase in demand for US dollar or reduction in its supply strengthens the US dollar. Lower demand and increased supply will weaken the US dollar. A strong US dollar is not always good.

It depends on what causes it to strengthen: If it is raising productivity or innovation, that's good. But in an economy struggling to grow and to create more jobs, a strong US dollar is not so desirable. A weak dollar means goods are cheaper relative to foreign goods; it stimulates exports and reduces imports. Foreign goods get more expensive but more US jobs are created. At this time, the United States is better off with a weak dollar. Strangely, most politicians think it's desirable for the US dollar to weaken only against one currency, the RMB. US Congress routinely bashes China for not weakening the US dollar enough. Indeed, a fall in the value of the US dollar against all currencies would help the United States even more. Yet, in the next breath, the same Congress wants the dollar to be strong. This delusion just won't go away. They are like failed dieters who talk earnestly about healthy living while eating a chocolate donut.

The US dollar isn't going anywhere. It is not about to be replaced any-time soon. The only dangers are (1) reckless US mismanagement giving rise to chronic inflation (or deflation if QE2 exit is not well handled), which is implausible; and (2) US budget deficits running out of control; outright debt default is far-fetched. Mark Twain once responded to accounts of his ill health: Reports of my death are greatly exaggerated. He might well have re-ferred to the US dollar. For the moment, the patient is stable, external symp-toms notwithstanding. But there will be grounds for worry if he doesn't commit to a healthier lifestyle.

The Euro and the RMB

Today, the US dollar faces growing competition in the global currency space. The serious contender is the euro (€), which has gained ground as a cur-rency in which goods are invoiced and official reserves held. Nevertheless, share of reserves held in US$ remains well over double the share held in euros: US$ share did fall from 71 percent in 2000 to 67 percent in 2005 and 62 percent in 2009; euro's share rose from 24 percent in 2005 to more than 27 percent in 2009. In terms of global forex, the US$ market turns over US$3.5 trillion daily, more than double that in euros. But US$ share of the market fell from 45 percent in 2001 to 42 percent in 2010. Euro's capital markets are somewhat less comparable in depth and liquidity against the US dollar's, and the eurozone economy is roughly the same size as that of the United States. Events since 2008 have shaken faith in US financial markets. But the banking crisis and its economic fallout is a transatlantic affair. Con-tinuing euro bailouts is a sign the old continent is not much safer than the United States. Worried savers may still sleep better with US$ under their pillow. So for the euro, it's going to be a long haul.

The sheer dynamism of China and globalization of its corporations and banks will propel the RMB to assume a greater international role. The RMB can become a global settlement currency soon enough. It has made good progress signing currency swaps with more central banks. The issuance of RMB-denominated bonds is actively promoted; RMB offshore deposits in Hong Kong (to top RMB1 trillion by year-end) are rising rapidly; and offshore RMB trading will expand beyond Hong Kong. But with the under-valued exchange rate, an asymmetry in settlement has arisen—foreign importers are reluctant to settle in RMB while foreign exporters are glad to do so. In the end, success at internationalizing the RMB depends on the pace it liberalizes the capital account. The problem lies in speculative capital flows aimed at profiting from arbitrage. Capital controls remain as China's last line of defense against "hot" money inflows. Its policy continues to encourage nonresidents to hold more RMBs and RMB-denominated assets.

The sequencing of policy adjustments remains critical as China moves forward. The road ahead is going to be bumpy.

Policies Coordination

By 2025, the World Bank's[5] best bet is the emergence of a multipolar world centered on the US dollar, €, and RMB. A world supported by the likelihood that the United States, eurozone, and China will constitute the three major "growth poles" by then. They would provide stimulus to other nations through expanding trade, finance, and technology transfers, which in turn creates international demand for their currencies. Already, private investment inflows into EMEs are expected at US$1.04 trillion in 2011 (mainly to China) against US$990 billion in 2010 and US$640 billion in 2009. Inherent in this shift is rising competition among them, which is real. This is bound to create situations of potential conflict, which can exact a heavy toll on global financial markets and growth. This calls for workable mechanisms to strengthen policy coordination across the major growth poles, in particular. This is critical in reducing risks of political and economic instability. In the recent crisis, G-20 was able to pick low-lying fruits, managing realignment of macroeconomic policies aimed at generally common objectives—to get out of recession and to rebuild financial systems. In today's world, shifts in policy coordination will be increasingly toward more politically sensitive domestic fiscal and monetary and exchange rate policies. Also, there are interests of the least developed countries (LDCs) to be safeguarded against pressures accompanying transition to a multipolar order.

What, Then, Are We to Do?

Against the backdrop of the tragic earthquakes and tsunami that hit Japan, the political turmoil of "Arab Spring" gripping much of Middle East and North Africa (MENA), and growing uncertainties emanating from eurozone sovereign debt crisis, global growth remains at subpar this year with high unemployment, and rising inflation in the EMEs and LDCs. This calls for building confidence and promoting investment to boost productivity and create jobs to absorb the large pool of youth in MENA, in particular. The LDCs and MENA nations are heavily dependent on external demand for growth. Aid and technical assistance have the ability to cushion adjustments as they adapt in the transition process.

According to the World Bank: "It is also critical that major developed economies and EMEs simultaneously craft policies that are mindful of the growing interdependency associated with the increasing presence of developing economies on the global stage and leverage such interdependency to derive closer international cooperation and prosperity worldwide."[6] We really have to work on this.

Kuala Lumpur
June 2, 2011

Notes

1. First published on June 4, 2011.
2. World Bank, *Global Development Horizons 2011—Multipolarity: The New Global Economy* (Washington, DC: World Bank, May 2011), pp. 7, 13.
3. Barry Eichengreen, reported to have said at a symposium at the Bank of Finland on May 14, 2011.
4. World Bank, pp. xi–xii, 7–9.
5. Ibid., 2, p. xii.
6. Ibid., 2, p. 10.

CHAPTER 67

The Dollar Quagmire[1]

Once in a while, we have good reason to feel unhappy with the United States dollar (US dollar). Like now. Many feel let down. Not only did the US bring down the global economy, whatever wealth there was left in US dollar was subject to significant diminution. After peaking in 2002, the trade-weighted US dollar has depreciated ever since. Sure, the US dollar has since been given a temporary lift on its safe-haven status. As things stand today, it's just a matter of time before the US dollar, as it begins to further weaken, to once again take its toll against strong headwinds. So, we are all caught in a strange quagmire. Strange, because ever since I was little, the US dollar—known in Cantonese as *mei-kum* or American gold—is now anything but. A quagmire, on account of feeling caught in a trap: In good times, you feel safe holding onto *mei-kum*. When things turn sour, you can't (as a group) get out of US dollar assets fast enough, without "cutting your nose to spite your face." How did we get here? Some history is helpful.

US Dollar as Anchor and Reserves

After World War II (WWII), the US financial system was the only one kept intact. There was runaway inflation, widespread currency restrictions, rationing, and price control in Europe, Japan, and most other countries. The American economy was the strongest then, and US dollar was very much in demand. For the United States, winning the war didn't hurt. And so, under the Bretton Woods Accord of 1944, every nation pegged to the US dollar. But the US dollar was not required to have a formal exchange rate peg—except for the residual tie to gold. Hence, *mei-kum*.

Soon, one thing led to another, and the US dollar became a natural monopoly—mainly because of economies of scale. The more nations dealt in US dollar, the cheaper and more convenient it was to deal in US dollar. Before you knew it, the US dollar became the textbook anchor and reserve currency (alongside the pound sterling—which even before WWII

411

was already a reserve currency, but was devastated by war). To do this well, the US price level has to be kept stable and expected to remain so. To complement this role, the US dollar met what has now come to be known as Kenen's rule of international money:[2] A reserve currency must have the ability to facilitate as (1) a medium of exchange; (2) a store of value; (3) a unit of account; and (4) a standard of deferred payment for international transactions (e.g., bonds). The US dollar and the dollar exchange standard have been so from 1945 into the new millennium.

The Bretton Woods System

There is more. The dollar standard is supposed to work within the Bretton Woods–designed international monetary system, based on four main principles: (1) right of each nation to manage internal demand to meet the objective of growth with price stability; (2) exchange rate convertibility in the face of free movement of goods, services, and capital as a means to achieve efficient use of resources; (3) international trade to be conducted on an adjustable-peg exchange rate regime, with provision for material changes in the event of structural imbalances; and (4) countries holding own-reserves but given a line-of-credit by the International Monetary Fund (IMF).

However, the system began to unravel in the late 1960s. The Special Drawing Rights (SDRs) were created by the IMF in 1969 as a new international reserve asset to supplement existing reserves. Former US President Richard Nixon closed the "gold window" in 1971. By 1973, US$ parities were abandoned and currencies moved to nonpar floating. High and variable inflation in the 1970s and 1980s eroded the US dollar's usefulness as the anchor. The euro only came into its own in the late 1990s.

Despite the changes and more flexibility in exchange rate regimes, the overall basic structure of the international monetary system (IMS) had remained essentially the same. So, it still faced three underlying difficulties: (1) no reliable mechanism to correct international payments imbalances; (2) it is subject to destabilizing speculative bouts; and (3) no orderly arrangement to generate, in a predictable way, new reserves to meet demands of a growing world economy. Hence, you now see the mess we are in today. Clearly, the IMS is in need of real reform.

Are Payments Surpluses Good or Bad?

Simply put, the system works as follows: A nation with a payments deficit means that it is importing (spending) more than it exports (earns). It settles this by losing reserves or borrows to cover it (i.e., living off its savings or on credit). Often, it has to deflate or slow down or devalue (or some combination), which brings about a dilemma in the form of conflict of policy objectives. In other words, any adjustment comes at a cost. But one thing is certain, continuing deficits are not sustainable (e.g., the United States). Similarly, a payments surplus nation exports too much (saves). To adjust, it has to inflate, push growth, or revalue—each of which (or a combination thereof) also comes at a cost. Like persistent deficits, continuing surpluses (e.g., Japan and China) are also not sustainable. For the world system to get back into balance, both surplus and deficit countries have to adjust—that is, the surplus nation has to expand and the deficit nation, contract. But, in practice—unlike the gold standard—the Bretton Woods system has no reliable mechanism to make both of them adjust. And, both parties often find adjustment inconvenient and just too costly. Hence, this often precipitates in a crisis that forces adjustment at a time that is usually suboptimal.

To most, deficits are bad. Why? After all, the idea of trade is to obtain goods and services from abroad that cost less than they can be produced at home. Imports are the fruits of foreign trade. So, an excess of imports has to be good—for the deficit nation, most certainly. But that's just part of the story because the excess of imports over exports has to be paid for, resulting in having less reserves or using up borrowing power—either may not be convenient, indeed, not the most comfortable. And, adjustments can be costly in economic terms, whether in slowing down the economy or having to devalue its currency. Similarly, surpluses may sound good but are actually not. It can be inflationary and represent an inefficient use of resources. For the surplus country, the saving reflects the mere hoarding of resources, which otherwise could be invested to enhance future output and welfare. Adjustment back to equilibrium here can be just as costly in terms of having to revalue its currency or stimulate spending.

US Dollar Reserves

So the world is driven into the dollar trap. Like it or not, countries especially in Asia have been accumulating reserves. As at the end of the first quarter of 2009, these reserves totaled US$6.5 trillion, close to one-half of US gross domestic product (GDP): 65 percent is held in US dollar, 26 percent in euros (€), 4 percent in British pounds (£), and 3 percent in Japanese yen (¥). Indeed, up to three-quarters of all reserves are in the hands of emerging nations. China alone holds one-third of the global stash, or US$2.2 trillion (i.e., more than one-half of its own GDP). Of these, some 35 percent remains invested in US Treasuries. Realistically, Asia, especially China, is hooked on the US dollar. It is worth noting that about 70 percent of world trade is invoiced in US dollar. Is there room to diversify into euros? or SDRs?

The Euro

Adam Posen's new book, *The Euro at Ten: The Next Global Currency?*, made the interesting observation that despite the recent US induced currency melt-down and global recession, the consequent "flight to safety of world savings was to US Treasuries, and not noticeably to the euro."[3] There are four reasons for this: (1) European banking and capital markets are not as sophisti-cated and are more fragmented; (2) eurozone lacks correct rules and tools of governance; (3) euro has yet to become an effective anchor of regional stability; and (4) euro appears likely to become more and more a regional currency. Sure, euro is now a credible currency. But the commitment of euro governments to run up large payments deficits (in order to issue more euros) is questionable. Besides, the euro appears overvalued today.

Special Drawing Rights (SDRs)

For Paul Krugman, SDRs "aren't real money." They are units of account at the IMF whose value is set by a basket of US dollar, €, ¥, and £ (44 percent weight assigned to US dollar). In practice, it is possible to buy IMF bonds that are linked to the SDR to diversify away from the US dollar. Brazil, Russia, and China have indicated their interest to invest in such SDR bonds. However, these bonds can only be traded among central banks, in which case a nation will be better off by directly raising its holdings of €, £, and ¥ to reflect their SDR weighting. However, any move to do so in a significant way could prove counterproductive. I am sure new and innovative ways will be designed to enhance the stature and role of the SDR. But I am not optimistic about its future at this time, despite strong support from China and Russia in particular. SDRs today account for less than 1 percent of world reserves. Lots more work needs to be done.

New Realities for China

China is a big part of this dollar trap. Indeed, the stakes are high. It holds one-third of world reserves; two-thirds of its holdings are in US dollar assets in the face of world reserves that are also two-thirds invested in US dollar assets. By 2010, China is expected to overtake Japan as the world's second largest economy. By end-2009, China looks certain to overtake Germany as the world's second largest trading nation. Sure, the US dollar system is flawed. Yet, China cannot have unrealistic expectations. After all, the US dollar did not replace £ for 50 years after the US economy had overtaken the United Kingdom. Today, US GDP is three times as big as China, and US total trade is still way larger. Moreover, more than 70 percent of world trade is conducted in US dollar. So China has a way to go.

Be that as it may, China has emerged in a changed world since end-2007. The phenomenon of prolonged, persistent payments surpluses has to be a thing of the past. What is now urgently needed is a reliable international mechanism to correct fundamental imbalances in both deficit and surplus nations. I can't see a system as being stable in which only Asia and Germany save. Of course, Americans have already begun to save, too. But very slowly, if at all. Similarly, stability won't come easy where mere exchange rate revaluation on the part of those with surpluses can—as if by a magic stroke of the pen—resolve the spendthrift ways of those with persistent deficits. Recent experience suggests the rules of the game need to be changed. Indeed, new economic realities are already changing the costs and benefits of being a reserve currency.

China's Global Role

As I see it, China will have to assume new responsibilities to help resolve the US$ trap. To begin with, it will need to internationalize the renminbi (RMB), China's currency. This will help facilitate its use as a reserve currency; however, it must meet Kenen's rule. Also, it means moving—over time—toward capital account convertibility. Sooner rather than later. Recent initiatives to invoice and settle trade in RMB between Hong Kong and the five big trading cities (including Shanghai and Guangzhou), will naturally expand. Similarly, the series of currency swap arrangements (totaling US$650 million) with ASEAN, South Korea, Argentina, and Brazil form part of the same process. The intention is to support and widen the settlement of more and more inter- and intra-Asian trade in RMB and other local currencies. These are necessary first steps. To succeed, complementary initiatives to open up, broaden, and deepen the banking and capital markets of China will be required.

What, Then, Are We to Do?

I believe there is merit in China's proposal for a super-sovereign reserve currency based on IMF's SDR—as a move away from reliance on currency of a single sovereign nation, no matter how strong. Support by India and Russia of an IMF-issued SDR-based fund is promising. Realistically, it's extremely unlikely that the US dollar will be replaced as a reserve currency anytime soon.

Nevertheless, the world needs to move innovatively and act boldly. In the short run, an expanded SDR will be needed, evolving step by step into a real-time trading and settlement currency in world markets. Presumably, the RMB will be included at some time in the SDR basket. In the final analysis, what is called for is a workable package deal—a realistic attempt at comprehensive reform of the entire IMS. Present piecemeal efforts won't do. A really new (not just improved) Bretton Woods has to emerge. I don't see how the US dollar trap can be satisfactorily resolved otherwise. This has to be a long-term commitment. To do otherwise is foolhardy. But the United States won't like it. Indeed, the United States won't do it.

Kuala Lumpur
August 6, 2009

Notes

1. First published on August 8, 2009.
2. Peter Kenen, "The Role of the Dollar as an International Currency," Group of Thirty Occasional Papers, No. 13, New York, 1983.
3. Adam S. Posen, *The Euro at Ten: The Next Global Currency?* (Washington, DC: Peterson Institute for International Economics, 2009). This new book was referred to by Tony Barber in Brussels Blog, and published under "More Comment On-line" in the *Financial Times* of London on April 30, 2009.
4. Paul Krugman, "China's Dollar Trap," *International Herald Tribune*, New York (April 2, 2009).

CHAPTER 68

The "Trilemma" of Capital Controls[1]

Chapter 65 examined principles underlying the international monetary system (IMS) as we know it today. I also explained why the IMS isn't working and what's really wrong with it. In this chapter, I want to dwell on one of these principles, namely, the free international movement of goods, services, and capital. We have since come a long way in freeing the movement of goods and services. As a result, currencies of many emerging nations are today readily convertible for current transactions of the balance of payments (BOP). Unfortunately, failure at the Doha Round to further liberalize trade is a setback.

Convertibility on capital transactions remains an issue. First, some history: In the intermediate years after World War II (WWII), controls on capital movements were common. Unlike today's controls directed at slowing down massive inflows of capital, however, these postwar controls mainly aimed at slowing down outflows. After the United Kingdom lifted exchange controls under Margaret Thatcher in 1979, more governments have come to allow freer movement of money into and out of their economies. While increasingly free capital flows can help spur economic growth by enabling the flow of more productive investment, the growing volume of inflows into emerging nations has raised concerns. Today, capital controls refer to taxes or other administrative measures meant to regulate those flows.

Exchange control directly violates one of the precepts upon which the IMS is predicated: The world economy relies primarily upon decentralized decision making by billions of individuals and businesses responding to market forces. Government, to be sure, is responsible for influencing these market forces consistent with national objectives, but always without attempting to direct and interfere with individual transactions. The Bretton Woods Accord set up the IMS in 1945 based on this principle, and changes made over the years have kept faith with it. Of course, as a matter of practical expediency, in the transition to free capital movements, countries in (what the International Monetary Fund [IMF] calls) fundamental BOP disequilibrium, that is, with persistent payments imbalances, could temporarily impose exchange controls (previously called Article XIV nations) to enable them to better adjust under IMF supervision.

The French Connection

Ironically, it was the French socialists who brought global financial liberalization home to the IMF. According to Harvard's Rawi Abdelal,[2] when capital flight forced socialist French President François Mitterand to abort his program in 1983, this event set in motion developments that ultimately enshrined free capital movements as a global objective. It started first in the European Union (EU) in late 1980s, then on to the Organisation for Economic Co-operation and Development (OECD), and eventually, at the IMF under French socialist Managing Director Michel Camdessus (governor, Bank of France, under Mitterand). Paradoxically, it was again a French socialist, recently resigned IMF Managing Director Dominique Strauss-Kahn (now in a New York prison), who distanced the IMF from its long-standing tenet on free capital movements. Speaking in Asia in January 2010, he said: "Capital controls can also play a role, particularly where the surge in capital flows is expected to be temporary or where exchange rate over-shoot is a real danger. . . . As long as it's temporary, it may be the only way."[3]

The "Trilemma"

Capital will go where it finds the best returns. In the past year, it's Asia. Also, Latin America. Recipients of large capital inflows have begun to fret about their impact and on how to "manage" them. Indeed, emerging markets states seek some measure of protection against the new flows of cheap and easy money generated in the United States, Europe, and Japan. The massive inflows (estimated by IMF early this year at over US$1 trillion in 2011, against a high of US$1.3 trillion in 2007) have raised the chances of trade and currency conflicts. A long list of emerging nations including from Indonesia, Thailand, South Korea, Taiwan, Philippines, India, and China to Turkey to Chile, Mexico, and Brazil have already imposed capital controls, motivated simply to curb "hot money" that threatens to distort their economies, drive up demand and exert undue pressure on their currencies, and pose dangers of asset bubbles.

In China, besides monetary moves, exporters are allowed to hold more US$ offshore—a negative capital control to keep foreign monies out, rather than a loosening of capital controls. Malaysia announced on May 18, 2011, more liberal capital measures to promote large investments abroad. In South Korea, a levy was imposed on foreign currency debt held by banks; while in Brazil, the tax on capital inflows was tripled to 6 percent. Indonesia sets a minimum one-month holding period for investors of its bonds, and India imposed a capital gains tax on all stock trades.

Nations face an economic choice—often two out of three (trilemma): fixed exchange rate, freedom to set monetary policy, and free flow of capital. Having all three is impossible, only any two of the three. In the United States, it has long had free capital flows and the right to set monetary policy. So, it is forced to live with currency fluctuations. The same orthodoxy is imposed by IMF on the world. The case of Japan in the late 1980s (Plaza Accord 1985 and Louvre Accord 1987) is classic. However, the IMF faces problems imposing it on China, which prefers to give up free flow of capital; it likes very much for China to be like the United States.

"Smoke, but Do Not Inhale"

Notwithstanding the blaring narrative about peaking in global growth, sovereign debt risks in Europe, fiscal austerity, and "unusually uncertain" outlook for the US economy, many emerging nations continue to be saddled with massive capital inflows, which, if left unchecked, could make some of them self-destruct. Although these factors are worrisome, fortunately many of them have built up enough fat. Consider their massive foreign reserves—totaling more than US$7 trillion, exceeding 10 percent of global gross domestic product (GDP). These reserves will be used as emerging nations move gradually to adjust to face the structurally impaired consumer demand in the West. This reminds me of *Financial Times*'s writer, Martin Wolf, who observed in a July 29, 2010, column that emerging markets "smoke but do not inhale" global capital. While emerging nations welcome capital inflows (smoke it), they are concerned about speculation, quick exit and reversals, and large net inflows (inhaling is bad for health). This is reflected in their preference to intervene in the forex markets and to recycle the monies (through current BOP accounts and capital flows) into foreign exchange reserves. Preventing capital inflows from reaching the real economy has been their best insurance against the impact of rising currencies on competiveness, inflation, and stoking domestic demand.

Conventional wisdom has it that a nation's reserves are adequate if they are (1) equivalent to three months' imports; and (2) equal to or exceed short-term debt. Most emerging nations easily pass these rules of thumb. China's reserves (at US$3.15 trillion) far exceeded its short-term debt. The reserves-to-debt ratio of Russia, India, and Brazil also points to large excesses. Saudi Arabia and Algeria have reserves that cover more than two years of imports; Brazil, a year; and India, nine months. Their robust financial health augurs well for the future. After successfully weathering one of the worst financial crises in history, growth in 2011 and 2012 will slacken—saving less and spending more. This policy switch comes at a time when emerging nations recognize that future growth rests in their own hands, and not on the fortunes (or lack of it) of the much-indebted West. Although forced to "smoke" massive inflows (including collateral smoke), they should heed Professor Joseph Stiglitz's (Nobel laureate in economics 2001) advice: "Now that the IMF has blessed such interventions . . . (exchange control) should be a key part of any system to ensure financial stability; resorting to them only as a last resort is a recipe for continued instability . . . it is best if countries use a portfolio of them as management tools."[4]

Controls Stir Debate

At its 1997 annual meetings in Hong Kong, the IMF tried to push deep into capital market liberalization. The timing was bad as the East Asia crisis was just brewing. The crisis exploded soon enough in a region of high savings with little need for more capital inflows. The crisis showed that free and unfettered markets are "neither efficient nor stable" (Stiglitz).[5] Studies have shown that capital controls have helped small nations (e.g., Iceland) to manage. The far-reaching surge of cheap and loose money from the United States, Europe, and Japan into emerging markets had loomed so large that even finance ministers and central bank governors, who are ideologically adverse to intervention, now believe they have no choice but to do so. Hence, the change of stance at the IMF. At its April 2011 meetings, the IMF's "guidelines" on managing capital inflows was rebuffed by most emerging nations as an attempt to restrain them, rather than help. As a result, they were delayed for further study. The IMF's recent reversal of its long-standing opposition to limits on free capital flows was based on the compelling need by emerging markets to curb surging inflows, which they recognize can fuel asset bubbles and inflation (e.g., China, India, and Brazil) and hurt exporters by driving currency value higher. The IMF wanted nations to use exchange controls as a last resort, after they had used other tools, including interest rates, currency values, and fiscal adjustments. But emerging nations objected vehemently, viewing the proposals as hamstringing their policies. Brazil's finance minister called capital controls "self-defense" measures. Ironically, some major advanced countries most responsible for the global crisis and that have yet to resolve their own problems are most eager to prescribe "codes of conduct to the rest of the world including countries that have become over-burdened by the spill-over effects of policies adopted by them."[6]

Who's to Blame?

The controversy is centered on "blame." Emerging nations blame the United States: as a fountain of excess cheap capital because it is holding short-term interest rates near zero and pumping money into the economy by buying government bonds (quantitative easing). Developed countries led by the United States blame China's policy for tightly controlling its currency value, driving "capital into economies with freer exchanges." The IMF has a tough sell to establish a shared understanding around the use of capital controls. It tries to create a "comfort zone," which nobody wants because there is nothing comforting about being judged negatively at the IMF's annual review if they did not follow the rules. Nations need all the tools at their disposal to prevent financial crises and mitigate massive capital flows. Controls may not always be the first-best response, but they are easy to understand and implement, and have a strong "announcement" impact.

There are of course many pitfalls to controls. Most important is the danger from a self-feeding system of continuing tightening of controls. There is Professor Cohen's Iron Law of Economic Controls:[7] To be effective, controls must reproduce at a rate faster than that at which means are found for avoiding them. Moreover, a partial system of controls would readily breakdown as funds flowed through uncontrolled channels—spurred by fear of still further controls. In the end, a complete system of controls is required. Any policy of attempting to "muddle through" via adopting certain controls only reduces and distorts the volume of international trade and investment. Controls can breed revival of a brand of mercantilism, which cannot be for the global good.

What, Then, Are We to Do?

Any shake-up of conventional wisdom and comfortable modes of behavior is bound to pose a challenge. John Maynard Keynes is known to have said something to this effect: What used to be heresy (restrictions on capital flows) is now endorsed as orthodoxy. That happened in 1945 at the dawn of the Bretton Woods era. More than 65 years later, it is ironic that we need a similar shift in mind-set to effectively meet the challenge.

Kuala Lumpur
May 20, 2011

Notes

1. First published on May 21, 2011.
2. Rawi Abdelal, *Capital Rules: The Construction of Global Finance* (Cambridge, MA: Harvard University Press, 2007).
3. Dominique Strauss-Kahn, speaking at the Asian Financial Forum in Hong Kong on January 20, 2010.
4. Joseph Stiglitz, "The IMF's Switch in Time," published in *The Edge*, Malaysia (May 14, 2011).
5. Ibid.
6. Guido Mantega, Minister of Finance, Brazil, in remarks at the IMF's Policy-Steering Committee Meeting in the Spring of 2011 in Washington on April 16, 2011.
7. Benjamin J. Cohen, "Capital Controls and the US Balance of Payments," *American Economic Review* 55, no. 1 (1965): 172–176.

CHAPTER 69

Burgernomics and the Ringgit[1]

I am often asked: What is per-capita PPP income? What does US$5,000 income at PPP prices mean? Off-and-on, the term *PPP* intrudes into our lives via TV news, newspapers, and economic reports. *PPP* stands for purchasing power parity—a theory in economics first developed by Swedish economist Gustav Cassel after World War I (WWI). Simply put, this doctrine states that the exchange rate is determined by the relative purchasing power of any two currencies. The common sense of this is that the same amount of money should purchase the same product in any two countries (whence the term purchasing power parity). That is, the purchasing power of money, expressed in one currency, should change pari-passu in different countries. If US$5 buys a cup of Starbucks coffee in New York and the actual cost of the same Starbucks coffee in Kuala Lumpur is RM12, then the exchange rate should be US$1 = RM2.40 according to PPP. But the actual real-life exchange rate is close to RM3.60, or 33 percent cheaper.

PPP in Today's World

Is PPP relevant? To answer, we need to backtrack. During WWI, trade had been disrupted between allies and halted with enemies. When trade resumed after the war, a choice of new exchange rates was required. Any return to prewar rates would not make practical sense since countries had experienced significant differing rates of inflation because of the disruption of war. Let's say before the war, US$1 = 30FF (French franc). Since then, the price level in France had risen (say) 20 times, and in the United States, doubled. Prices in France had thus risen 10 times more than in the United States; so the new exchange rate should be US$1 = 300FF based on PPP (i.e., exchange rate determined by relative purchasing power of the two currencies). Thus, the PPP served as a useful guide at a time of major international turbulence. It was also practical to use and easy to understand. But it's also too simplistic and even unrealistic. The world is not perfect. It's also complicated. Many nontrading factors and too many other considerations do come into play in determining an exchange rate.

Today, the world has become even more imperfect and much more complex. Adjustment to stability (if ever) is far from instantaneous. Often, it involves a complicated web of geopolitical considerations, which work to derail the timing of an often long process. Recent developments have led to widespread structural disruptions not seen since the 1930s. As a result, the market price discovery mechanisms we have taken so much for granted no longer function as a reliable guide for decision making. Exchange rates, interest rates, retail prices, and the range of other price indices have become too "manipulated" to make good economic sense, in the face of an eco-system that has now become neither capitalist nor communist. It is in times like this that we look for simple, practical benchmarks that can offer sensible guides to help us manage the myriad risks that just won't go away.

The Big Mac Index

In today's globalized world, we encounter difficulties in assessing the value of currencies. It is often asked: Is it true the ringgit is undervalued? Why is the US dollar still so strong? How much basis-in-fact is there? The *Economist* magazine publishes annually its Big Mac index. The latest appeared in this week's (July 18, 2009) issue. It calls this index a "light-hearted guide to valuing currencies, provides some clues."[2] Interestingly enough, it is based on the PPP theory and uses the Big Mac hamburger as the benchmark product, since it is standardized and sold in more or less the same form worldwide. A Big Mac in New York tastes the same as the Big Mac in Malaysia—it is supposed to, anyway. Comparison of the purchase price of this "common" burger in domestic currencies against the US dollar price would yield a PPP exchange rate between any currency and the US dollar. In this way, the rate of exchange that leaves the Big Mac costing the same in US dollars anywhere in the world provides a "fair value," or PPP benchmark. For example, you actually pay US$3.57 for a Big Mac in the United States; in the United Kingdom, it costs £2.29 or equivalent to US$3.69 converted at the current market exchange rate. The implied PPP exchange rate is therefore £1 = US$1.56, compared with the actual market rate of £1 = US$1.61. That's close enough to fair value. But this is not always the case.

Value of the Ringgit

Take Malaysia: According to this index, the Big Mac costs RM6.77 or only US$1.88 (converted at current market exchange rate), which is about half its price in the United States (US$3.57). This means that the ringgit has a much higher purchasing power in Malaysia than in the United States! Look at this another way: The implied PPP exchange rate is US$1 = RM1.90. But the actual market exchange rate is closer to RM3.60. Nearly double! Based on PPP, the ringgit is undervalued by 47 percent.

By the same token, the index showed the Chinese RMB is similarly undervalued: by 49 percent, Thai baht by 47 percent, Indonesia rupiah by 43 percent, Hong Kong dollar by 52 percent, Taiwan dollar by 37 percent, the Philippine peso by 25 percent, Singapore dollar by 19 percent. It would appear that the currencies of China and Hong Kong and those of most emerging ASEAN economies are significantly undervalued by 40 to 50 percent against the US dollar. At the other spectrum, most major European currencies appear substantially overvalued vis-à-vis the US dollar: euro by 29 percent, Swiss franc by 68 percent, and Scandinavian currencies by 40 to 70 percent. However, like the British pound, the Japanese yen and Australian dollar are close enough to fair value on this basis. These are interesting comparative numbers.

Malaysia's 2008 per-capita income (at current market prices) was placed at US$7,738. On a PPP basis, the International Monetary Fund (IMF) estimated this income's purchasing power to be in the region of US$14,000. A word of caution, however: The PPP is subject to many flaws. Indeed, many economists regard it as quite irrelevant these days. Why is this so?

PPP as a Guide

For one thing, costing of the burger includes many local inputs (e.g., wages, rent, and advertising), which tend to be lowest in the poorest countries. Perhaps that is why the Big Mac is so overpriced in Europe. Worse, the outcome will be different for different single standardized products used. To be really helpful, we will need a representative basket of goods and services (not just the Big Mac alone).

Price indices, however, include many goods and services that do not enter into international trade. Moreover, the jury is still out on whether the exchange rate moves in response to price changes or the other way around. The causal relationship is very unclear. The PPP works from a base rate, the legitimacy of which can be in doubt. Most important, it overlooks the often-volatile supply and demand of foreign exchange arising from non-trade sources: long- and short-term foreign investment, loan flows, transfers, and other speculative movements of capital. Finally, in our imperfect world, government interventions (e.g., exchange control, trade restrictions, and taxes) do affect the purchasing power of currencies.

Nevertheless, PPP remains in use simply because it is readily understood, has an unusually simple construct, and is very transparent. It appears to be more useful during periods of marked changes (especially in rates of inflation). Also, it acts as a more reliable guide in times of exchange rate misalignments among nations with similar levels of income. Be that as it may, the latest Big Mac index points to interesting trends: Major European currencies appear grossly overvalued vis-à-vis the US$, and many Asian currencies, overly undervalued. Or is it that the base currency—the US dollar— is way overvalued?

You can't tell from the PPP exchange rates. Nevertheless, the theory can serve as a crude approximation. But, it cannot offer a satisfactory explanation of today's exchange rates. Professor Gottfried von Haberler, my teacher and mentor at Harvard and a guru on exchange rates, used to say: After all, in the final analysis, people value currencies for what they will buy.

The Japanese Lesson

In Asia, the Chinese RMB (renminbi) is often singled out as grossly undervalued (the PPP also shows this). Strong pressures to revalue have come from the United States and the IMF. However, these have eased with the recent global meltdown. The Japanese experience over three decades ago and earlier offers a valuable lesson in history. From the 1980s into the mid-1990s, Japan-bashing was in vogue in the United States, much as China-bashing was in the Bush years.

Back then, Japan's large bilateral trade surplus led the United States to continually threaten it with trade sanctions. Consequently, "voluntary" export restraints were put into place and the yen was allowed to appreciate. It did so all the way from US$1 = ¥360 in 1971 to touch ¥80 in April 1985. This unhinged the Japanese financial system and induced the bubble in stock and land prices in the late 1980s, which eventually collapsed in 1991. This resulted in Japan's unrelenting deflationary slump of the 1990s—known now as the "lost" decade. Japan has yet to fully recover and remains today in a zero-interest liquidity trap. The Bank of Japan has failed to reignite economic growth. The recent financial meltdown and global recession have not made matters any better. Yet, Japan's trade surplus as a share of GNP has not been reduced in any significant way.

What, Then, Are We to Do?

Of course, the world has since changed dramatically. Nonetheless, in my view, any renewed pressures to force a revaluation of the RMB at this time will run the risk of (1) possibly sending China into a similar deflationary slump that hit Japan during the 1990s, and (2) destabilizing its currency to the detriment of global growth recovery. The state of the world economy remains delicate. It calls for prudence. In the final analysis, I don't see how the US trade deficit can be bridged by simply revaluing China's exchange rate. The key must lie in increased US national savings and improved productivity. This won't be easy given the current weak US economy.

Kuala Lumpur
July 24, 2009

Notes

1. First published on July 25, 2009.
2. "Cheesed off," *The Economist*, London (July 18, 2009).

CHAPTER 70

The Yuan Way to a New Monetary Order[1]

Chinese New Year has come and will soon go. The eurozone debt crisis is well past two years. Yet uncertainty persists. The World Bank's January 2012 "Global Economic Prospects" reports: "World economy has entered a very difficult phase characterized by significant downside risks and fragility . . . and as a result, forecasts have been significantly downgraded. . . . However, even achieving these much weaker outturns is very uncertain. . . . Overall, global economic conditions are fragile."[2] This week's International Monetary Fund (IMF) January 2012 *World Economic Outlook Update* says more of the same: "The global recovery is threatened by intensifying strains in the euro area and fragilities elsewhere."[3]

China, India, South Africa, and Brazil have entered a slowing phase. No country and no region can escape the consequences of a serious downturn. Nevertheless, growth in the East Asia and Pacific region (excluding Japan) is expected to slow down to about 7.8 percent in 2012 (8.4 percent in 2011) and stabilize in 2013. This reflects continuing strong domestic demand (evident in the third quarter of 2011 gross domestic product [GDP]), while exports will slow to about 2 percent due to Europe heading toward recession and sluggish rich Organisation for Economic Co-operation and Development's (OECD) demand.

The middle-income nations are, I think, in a good position to weather the global slowdown, with significant space available for fiscal relaxation, adequate room for interest rate easing, ample high reserves, and rather strong underpinning for domestic demand to rise. I see the modest easing in China's growth being counterbalanced by a pickup in GDP gains in 2013 over the rest of the region. Outside China, growth has slackened sharply to 4.8 percent in 2011 (6.9 percent in 2010), but is expected to strengthen in 2012, reaching 5.8 percent in 2013.

China

GDP growth in China, which accounts for 80 percent of the East Asia and Pacific region, had eased to about 9.1 percent in 2011 (10.4 percent in 2010), and is expected to slacken further to a still-robust 8.2 to 8.4 percent in 2012. World Bank projections point to growth moderating at 8.3 percent in 2013, in line with its longer-term potential GDP. Expansion is expected to emanate from domestic demand, with private spending and fixed capital outlays contributing most of the growth in 2012.

For China, the health of the global economy, and high-income Europe in particular, represents the key risk at this time. Domestic risks include property overheating, local government indebtedness, and bloating bank balance sheets. The fourth quarter of 2011 growth of 8.9 percent annoyed investors who are looking for indications either weak enough to justify further policy easing or strong enough to allay fears of a hard landing. Bear in mind the forecast growth for 2012 will be the weakest in a decade, and may cool further as exports slump.

The Chinese economy is buffeted by two very different forces: (1) slow global growth will hurt Chinese exports (especially to its largest trading partner, European Union), which rose by 7 percent in December 2011, and exporters foresee more trouble ahead, however; (2) analysts point to strong retail sales (up 18 percent in December 2011) reflecting rising wages and domestic spending, which represented about 52 percent of GDP estimated in the first quarter for 2012, higher than in 2009–2011.

China is counting on its massive effort to build low-income "social housing" to provide enough demand to keep the real-estate market from collapsing. It is unclear whether China can accelerate this program to build 36 million subsidized housing by 2015—enough to house all of Germany's households. But financial markets are anticipating worse news ahead. After all, the Shanghai Composite Index fell 21 percent in 2011. As the adage goes, stock analysts did forecast 10 of the past three recessions!

The Yuan

Appreciation of the yuan (renminbi) against the US$ in 2012 is expected to slow to about 3 percent, from +4.7 percent in 2011. The yuan closed at 6.3190 at end-2011, up about 8 percent compared with June 2010 (when China effectively ended its two-year-long peg to the US$) and has gained 30 percent since mid-2005 when it was last revalued. The slowdown reflects growing demand for the US$ amid uncertainty, lower growth, diminishing trade surplus, and growing US military presence in Asia, according to China's Centre for Forecasting Science[4] (of the Chinese Academy of

Sciences), which reports directly to the State Council, China's Cabinet. Much of it will be in the latter part of the year, as China is likely to keep the yuan relatively stable in the first half-year to allow time to assess the impact of goings-on in the eurozone. Dollars are pumped in via state banks, providing markets with a clear signal it will not allow the yuan to depreciate, while not in a hurry to let it appreciate, either. The yuan has since moved sideways.

Offshore Yuan

To make the yuan a true reserve currency, China has begun to liberalize currency controls and encourage an offshore yuan market in Hong Kong, creating an outlet for moving the currency across borders. However, foreign investors in China have been slow in using the yuan. In practice, it is still difficult to buy and sell yuan because of paperwork and bureaucracy. It is still easier to settle in US$, as it is the universal common practice. Its convenience outweighs the potential costs of any unfavorable move in the US$-yuan rate. Nonetheless, China is encouraging more businesses to use the yuan and more US banks to step up their yuan-settlement business. This market will grow as China diligently moves to internationalize its currency.

Encouraged by the authorities, a vibrant offshore yuan market has blossomed in Hong Kong. Beijing still controls the currency and how yuan bought in Hong Kong can be brought back to China. Yuan deposits in Hong Kong rose more than four times to 622.2 billion yuan (nearly US$100 billion) at end-September 2011 from a year earlier, according to the Hong Kong Monetary Authority, and now account for 10.4 percent of bank deposits. Growth in offshore yuan stalled in late 2011 as China slowed its currency appreciation against the dollar. Given Beijing's gradualist approach to reform, the market will soon revive.

An audience poll at the recent 2012 Asian Financial Forum in London indicated 63 percent believes full yuan convertibility is more than five years away. The very fact that London wants to be a yuan trading center now says a lot. Only 10 percent of China's international trade is settled in yuan, rising to 15 percent in 2012. It's still a small market in the global context. The yuan is used for just 0.29 percent of all global payments in November 2011, according to financial messaging network SWIFT. By comparison, the euro's share is about 40 percent.

Dim-Sum Bonds

A booming business in dim-sum bonds (offshore yuan-denominated bonds) followed, with companies including Caterpillar and McDonald's issuing such bonds. In September 2011, a spurt of capital flight toward "safe haven" assets in the US tied to the worsening debt crisis in Europe caused currencies of emerging nations to depreciate against the US$. In East Asia, modest declines were recorded compared with South Africa (the rand fell 22 percent) and Brazil (the real dropped 18 percent). Only the Indonesia rupiah (down 5.8 percent) and the Malaysia ringgit (fell 5.4 percent) come under some pressure. This event slowed the appreciation of the yuan and with it, trading in dim-sum bonds eased as investors were no longer in a hurry to invest. Over the medium term, most analysts expect this yuan market to grow in the face of its massive US$3.18 trillion in reserves, as China moves to build its international status. When dim-sum bonds started to hit the market in 2010, investors were enthusiastic, bidding up prices and driving down yields. But in the second half of 2011, the average price of investment-grade dim-sum bonds fell 3.3 percent, amid a broad flight toward quality spooked by eurozone turmoil and Chinese accounting scandals.

Bankers hope new entrants (private banks, commercial banks, mutual funds, and life insurers) will give the market more stability this year. They would add depth and breadth to the market, which tripled to 185 billion yuan (US$30 billion) in dim-sum bonds issued in 2011. Expectations are for such bond issuance to reach 240 billion yuan this year, as new issuers (including more foreign companies) join early adopters such as government entities and State-run banks. This offshore bond market has developed well over the past year. Investor diversification in both types and geographics is still evolving, which is key to the healthy growth of the market. Equally important, investors look to the continuing appreciation of the yuan. In addition, its average yield has risen to 3.8 percent (from 2.35 percent since mid-2011) and most now trade at higher yields than comparable US$ bonds. This rise in yields reflects expectation for (1) slower yuan appreciation; (2) increase in supply; and (3) investors' desire for a higher liquidity premium during market downturns. Overall, the dim-sum bond market is turning into a buyer's market.

Bilateral Arrangements

China is forging ahead in laying the groundwork to internationalize the yuan via bilateral arrangements with foreign companies, nations, and financial centers, particularly Hong Kong (mainly because it can fully control the terms of the market). More mainland-based financial institutions will be able to issue yuan-denominated bonds in Hong Kong. This is part of a broader effort, first started in July 2009 when it encouraged enterprises in Shanghai and Guangzhou province to use the yuan when settling trade with Hong Kong, Macau, and some foreign companies (for more details, see Chapter 135, "China: RMB Flexibility Not Enough"). The post-Christmas direct yuan–yen trade deal forms part of a wide-ranging currency arrangement between China and Japan to give the use of the yuan a big boost. After all, China is Japan's largest trading partner with 26.5 trillion yen in two-way transactions last year.

Encouraging direct settlement in bypassing the US dollar would reduce currency risks and trading costs. Also, Japan will buy up to US$10 billion in yuan bonds for its reserves even though it represents no more than 1 percent of Japan's US$1.3 trillion worth of reserves. And, it is now easier for companies to convert Chinese and Japanese funds directly into each other without an intermediate conversion to US dollar. About 60 percent of China–Japan trade is settled in US dollar, a well-established practice.

The package allows Japan-backed institutions to sell yuan bonds in the mainland (instead of Hong Kong), helping to open China's capital market. In recent weeks, China has taken new steps to promote the use of yuan overseas, including allowing foreign firms to invest yuan accumulated overseas in mainland China, and widening the People's Bank of China (its central bank) network of currency swaps with other central banks to enable their banks to supply yuan to their customers, including with Thailand, South Korea, and New Zealand, totaling 1.2 trillion yuan. It already has completed arrangements with the big ASEAN counterparts.

Barry Eichengreen (University of California at Berkeley) observed: "Japan appears to be acknowledging implicitly that there will be a single dominant Asian currency in the future and it won't be the yen."[5] But Harvard's Jeffrey Frankel is more down to earth: "This hastens a multi-currency world, but this is just one of 100 steps along the way."[6] China still has a way to go in: (1) getting the yuan fully convertible, (2) reducing exchange rate interventions, (3) liberalizing interest rates, and (4) reforming the banking system. In all, so the yuan can really trade freely.

What, Then, Are We to Do?

The China–Japan deal points the way, nudging the yuan toward the inevitable—becoming a reserve currency alongside now-discredited US dollar and euro. This is to be welcomed by all. China must realize a fully internationalized yuan should be free to float (and to appreciate)—part of its overall reform. Over the longer term, though, avoiding huge imbalances is good for everyone, not least China. While it is understandable for Chinese Prime Minister Wen Jiabao to label China today as "unstable, unbalanced, uncoordinated and ultimately unsustainable," opportunities to take advantage of new openings don't come often.

Alexander Gerschenkron, my professor at Harvard (in my view, the best economic historian of his time), points to economies like China as having "advantages in backwardness," including China's ability to weather shocks: high reserves, robust fiscal situation, and comfortable external position. I think Shakespeare's *Hamlet* sums it up best: If it be not now, yet it will come—the readiness is all. A grown-up yuan is good for China's welfare. It also means a more stable world economy, which benefits the United States. For China, there will never be enough cushion. Politicians need to seize the moment and act boldly. ASEAN will surely benefit if they do.

Kuala Lumpur
January 27, 2012

Notes

1. First published on January 28, 2012.
2. World Bank, *Global Economic Prospects: Uncertainties and Vulnerabilities*, vol. 4. (Washington, DC: World Bank, January 2012).
3. International Monetary Fund, *World Economic Outlook Update—Global Recovery Stalls, Downside Risks Intensify* (Washington, DC: IMF, January 24, 2012).
4. According to its director, Wang Shouyang, in a statement on January 19, 2012, in Beijing.
5. Professor Barry Eichengreen, commenting in Beijing on the meeting between China's President Hu Jintao and Japanese Prime Minister Yoshihiko Noda, at which several moves were made in promoting direct trading of their currencies, especially in enhancing the Chinese yuan as a more dominant currency in the global monetary system.
6. Professor Jeffrey Frankel, commenting in Beijing on the meeting between China's President Hu Jintao and Japanese Prime Minister Yoshihiko Noda, at which several moves were made in promoting direct trading of their currencies, especially in enhancing the Chinese yuan as a more dominant currency in the global monetary system.

CHAPTER 71

Why Tokyo Failed to Be Top-Tier IFC[1]

Asian Economic Panel (AEP), the premier economic forum dedicated to promote high-quality analysis on key economic issues and formulate the best practical solutions, came to Penang this third week of March 2013. AEP was first convened by Professor Jeff Sachs in April 2001 at Harvard's Center for International Development (now at the Earth Institute, Columbia University) in conjunction with Keio University and Korea Institute for International Economic Policy. This time, the 26th AEP brought together about 50 scholars from ASEAN, China, Japan, South Korea, Europe, and Australia.

As is traditional, thoughtful papers covering a wide range of topics ranging from innovation and knowledge to debt and budgets, from water and sustainable development to trade integration and financial centers, were presented and discussed. The discourse was highly technical and most stimulating. It was Australian Huw McKay's[2] presentation on why Tokyo failed to become a top-tier international financial center (IFC) that attracted much attention. To me, it offers many lessons for China on its arduous journey of discovery to transform the renminbi (RMB) or yuan in the markets into a global reserve currency and promote Shanghai as a top-flight IFC.

Tokyo Didn't Make It

According to McKay, Tokyo's bid to become a first-tier IFC was not successful because it was (1) never a superordinate goal of national policy; (2) unable to establish the yen as a competitive international vehicle currency; (3) able to acquire many of the needed characteristics (but not all), but did not do so quickly enough when it started liberalization and deregulation; and (4) a latecomer, and it became well-nigh impossible to catch up with the incumbents. McKay concluded that with more focused political will, Tokyo's bid would have been more compelling. So Tokyo had to settle with just being an important but not dominant IFC.

435

McKay took pains to point out that Tokyo made the vital error of not placing sufficient policy focus on yen trade invoicing. It failed to reach "critical mass in terms of nonresident demand for the yen as it was unable to denominate the majority of its own trade in its own currency, which meant it was not able to assume a full role as an international "vehicle currency"; instead, it remained dependent on US$ for a large proportion of its international transactions . . . (reaching only a) 40 percent share of yen denomination of its exports, alongside 20–25 percent share of yen denominated imports, resulting in Japan's onshore share of foreign exchange turnover to peak at 10.3 percent in 1995." This led to a "vicious cycle" of "underdevelopment of the yen, leading to low transactions volumes and on-going underdevelopment." So Tokyo missed the boat. But I do have sympathy for McKay's apologetic end: "Decisions were made at each time based upon visions of the future that were in the first instance both too cautious and too humble and in the second instance, both too cautious and too proud."

McKay presented well his case why Tokyo failed to become a top-tier IFC. The reasons are understandable and well researched. I note in particular his frequent reference to Professor Yoshino's Summarization of the Conclusions of the "Study Group on the Internationalization of Japan's Financial and Capital Markets" on which he was its chairman.[3] This reference is important and relevant since the summarization comprehensively covered the many specific measures that Tokyo readily needed to push: to internationalize Japan's financial and capital markets, including focusing on promoting investment in Japan's financial and capital markets by nonresidents; to strengthen linkages with Asia and its financial markets (including direct trading between yen and Asian currencies); to further improve attractiveness of Japanese markets, including IT and human resources development; and to develop multipolar market/financial structures in Japan. Professor Yoshino, however, admitted that five factors did Tokyo in: volatility of the yen; strict regulation and supervision after the bubble burst in end-1989; Japanese is not English; high cost of living; and high income/corporate tax.

Global Livable City

Both these documents comprehensively cover what Japan needed to do to become a first-rate IFC, and what Japan had failed to do to secure that position. While they do cover a lot of ground and the arguments are compelling in many respects, I think McKay's conclusions left behind vital gaps that needed to be bridged. Indeed, it listed only the necessary economic and financial conditions to be met. But these were not sufficient, in my view, to make Tokyo first-tier. What's really missing is that Tokyo must become a global livable city in order to make it to first-tier.

IFC depends critically on the free flow of human power and its ability to command expertise and software. Human resources will not become readily available unless the city is both global and livable to attract them. Being livable simply means it possesses the physical and social infrastructure as well as the range of amenities and facilities to attract not just people's expertise but also accommodate their demanding lifestyle and that of their families (first-class education, easy access to home food, etc.). These have proven time and again to be critical in making a first-tier IFC. London and New York are drawn by the long-established concentration of financial expertise and supporting services, by the English language, by business-friendly labor and tax laws, and by the buzz of London's and New York's highflying and quality living, if not by reasonable living costs.

The IFC works best when it reflects a nation's innate competitive advantages, including the city's ability to design and implement (without too much fuss) the right policies on regulation, tax, and immigration. On regulation, IFCs thrive because they are supported by a huge financial services industry, which also means huge risks for taxpayers. Recent experience in New York and London bears this out. The US Dodd–Frank Act and proposals by the United Kingdom's Vickers Commission go a long way to deal with this—separating a tightly regulated domestic financial system (the part that puts taxpayers at risk) from the more freewheeling IFC activities for volatile, ungrateful global capital. Tokyo still has a way to go in this regard. Many are still awaiting real structural reform of the Japanese financial system. By contrast, the thrust of many of Brussels's recent proposals looks harmful, including the proposed financial transaction tax.

On tax and immigration, lots of damage is being done, not just in Tokyo but also New York and London (its 50 percent tax rate is highest among the top-10 IFCs for high-net-worth individuals; Tokyo is not far behind). As for immigration policy, IFCs need to be able to lure a growing stream of young and newly minted financiers as well as experienced bankers. Tight limits on talented immigrants (including their extended families and immediate "helpers") damage Tokyo's prospects (as they now begin to do so also in London and New York) and, indeed, the prospects for all manner of overall Japanese business.

Wimbledon Effect

But London's position is unique among the competition. Its long, normal business day bridges the close of Asia's markets with New York's opening, making it easily the most convenient location for global business, especially global fund managers and traders (who thrive on 24/7 business hours). Indeed, financial trading attracts liquidity and expertise in a virtuous circle.

Besides the extensive use of English, London remains the ideal place to strike international deals because of its highly respected body of commercial law and experienced judges. Most of its growth of IFC businesses in the past 60 years has come from international banks choosing to do business in London: There are already more than 250 foreign banks, which together own more than 50 percent of British banking assets.

This "Wimbledon effect," in which the United Kingdom provides the "courts" but not necessarily the "best players," is particularly pronounced in trading and wholesale banking business. Today, about 40 percent of foreign currency turnover (against 5 percent in Tokyo), 46 percent of interest rate over-the-counter (OTC) derivatives deals (3 percent in Tokyo), and 18 percent of cross-border bank lending (9 percent in Tokyo) already take place in London. It also handles about 40 percent of the global trade in euros (much more than in all 17 eurozone nations combined). Together with New York, which now accounts for 68 percent of hedge-fund assets (Tokyo, 2 percent); 53 percent of private equity investment value (Tokyo, 1 percent); 47 percent of global fund management assets (Tokyo, 7 percent); and 32 percent of world exchange-traded derivatives contracts (Tokyo, 2 percent), they both dominate by far the entire global financial businesses. However, Tokyo is left far behind. Nevertheless, even the strongest incumbent is vulnerable to competition from fast-growing Hong Kong, Singapore, and Dubai.

Top Ranking

Above all, a top-tier IFC has to be the center of politics, business, administration, and fun (not just funds)—London has proved successful being one since the eleventh century; and New York has grown rapidly since World War II to become a dynamic, broad, and deep channel mobilizing worldwide savings and transforming them into productive initiatives the world over. In the end, IFC has to be synonymous with being the global city to live, work, deal, and trade.

According to the 2012 Global Power City Index (compiled by the Mori Memorial Foundation), which ranks world cities by political, economic, and cultural clout, the ranking is as follows: (1) New York; (2) London; (3) Paris; (4) Tokyo; (5) Singapore; (6) Berlin; (7) Seoul; and (8) Hong Kong.

But if ranked by the level of living comfort, as the Economist Intelligence Unit 2012 Livability Index did, rankings change dramatically as follows: (1) Melbourne; (2) Vienna; (3) Vancouver; (4) Toronto; (5) Calgary; (6) Sydney; (7) Helsinki; and (8) Perth. Tokyo is not among the top 10, which is unfair since it is a safe city to live, and has good public infrastructures, good food, and fascinating culture.

However, a new Global Liveable Cities Index (July 2012) has since emerged, compiled by researchers at the Asia Competitiveness Institute in

Singapore, covering 64 Asian, European, and US cities, based on a criteria list of five categories (each with equal weight): economic vibrancy and competitiveness; environmental friendliness and sustainability; domestic security and stability; social-cultural conditions; and public governance. This index attempts to integrate the aims of the first two indices into a cohesive whole. Global cities are ranked as follows: (1) Geneva; (2) Zurich; (3) Singapore; (4) Copenhagen; (5) Helsinki; (6) Luxembourg; (7) Stockholm; (8) Berlin; (9) Hong Kong; and (10) Auckland/Melbourne. Tokyo stays way below, still rather unfair, I think.

Also, IT connectedness is becoming increasingly important. The 2012 DHL Global Connectedness Index (which measures a nation's integration into the global economy via its trade, capital, IT, and people) ranked Tokyo way outside the top 10 (Singapore was ranked no. 2, and London, no. 6, with the Netherlands as no. 1).

What, Then, Are We to Do?

Becoming a top-notch IFC has now become highly political, as it is already emotional. Late last year, the governor of the Bank of France publicly "attacked" the supremacy of London because Britain, a member of European Union (EU) but not eurozone, should have captured by far the largest share of trading in euros.

He lamented that there was "no rationale for having the biggest financial center active in our currency or providing services in our economic union being an offshore center."[4] The mayor of London's response was swift: ". . . a naked attempt to steal London's financial crown." More objectively, global bankers do acknowledge that a strong British IFC has been good for Europe. After all, London has been a trading hub from when it was founded by Romans in AD43. But the global stage is changing.

The European Central Bank based in Frankfurt, is scheduled to become overall supervisor of banks in the eurozone; it will soon gain oversight throughout the EU, and so vitiate the function of the European Banking Authority now based in London. CEBR's (the economics consultancy) recent report suggested that London could lose its place as a top IFC in terms of total people employed in finance, to New York this year; and in 2015, London could fall to third place after Hong Kong (not Tokyo). The game goes on. What is clear is that Tokyo still has much, much more to do to become a globally livable and connected city before it can emerge to fight as a dominant top-tier IFC.

Penang and
Kuala Lumpur
March 22, 2013

Notes

1. First published on March 23, 2013.
2. Huw McKay, "Tokyo as an International Financial Centre: Why Did It Fail to Reach The Very Top Tier?" A paper presented at the Asian Economic Panel Meeting in Universiti Sains Malaysia, Penang, Malaysia, on March 19, 2013.
3. Naoyuki Yoshino, "Enhancing Japan's Status as an International Financial Center," chairman's summarization of the "Study Group on the Internationalization of Japan's Financial and Capital Markets," Tokyo, Japan, July 7, 2003.
4. Christian Noyer, governor, Bank of France, in a statement on November 9, 2012, in London, United Kingdom.

CHAPTER 72

At Risk: Beggar-Thy-Neighbor[1]

Almost everyone is for free trade. Protectionism is a no-no. And, gains made so far need to be consolidated, especially at this time of the Great Recession. Surely, no one wants to fuel a new era of protectionism as in the 1930s, put into place by the infamous US Smoot–Hawley tariffs of 1930.

At the November 2008 and April 2009 G-20 Summits, both rich and emerging economies promised to eschew new trade barriers and work hard to complete the Doha Round by end-2009. Yet within days of the November 2008 Summit, Russia, and India raised tariffs on cars and steel respectively. No progress has since been made on Doha.

This year, more protective tariffs were invoked—from European Union's preemptive penalties on imports of Chinese steel pipes and US ban on imports of Chinese poultry, to Italy's anti-dumping duties on Chinese and Vietnamese shoes. China has since retaliated with vigorous complaints to the World Trade Organization (WTO). It also initiated anti-dumping and anti-subsidy investigations into chicken parts and car components imports from the United States. The most recent irritant is US imposition of high tariffs on tire imports from China. This latest move needs to be viewed in the context of a string of ominously protectionist measures, starting with the set of "Buy America" provisions for public works in the Obama stimulative package.

Playing with Fire

The lessons of history are clear. Economic isolationism of the 1930s, epitomized by the US Smoot–Hawley Tariff Act of 1930, cruelly intensified the Great Depression. To be sure, the WTO and its multilateral trading rules are a bulwark against protection on that scale. With just-in-time delivery and far-reaching efficiently organized international supply chains, today's globalized world could be seriously disrupted by policies far less onerous than Smoot–Hawley. Even modest shifts from "openness" within the WTO rules can spark off enough to turn the current recession much nastier. With their exports faltering, the WTO rules do allow nations plenty of scope to be less keen on free and fair trade: After decades of tariff cuts, for example, many nations' tariffs have dropped below "bound" rate ceilings. On average, they could readily triple their import levies without breaking WTO rules.

I am almost certain President Barack Obama does not intend to start a trade war. Neither did President Herbert Hoover intend to pick one either; his political abdication made it possible. We all know once anti-trade passions are unleashed, they can readily spread out of control. Obama should not give any nation reason to conclude he is protectionist.

The Battle of Smoot–Hawley

Modern free trade began during the Great Depression, after the catastrophic Smoot–Hawley Tariff Act of 1930. This act increased nearly 900 US import duties. It was debated, passed, and signed as the world tumbled into the Great Depression. Its sponsors, Congressman W. Hawley and Senator R. Smoot, have now come to personify economic isolationism of the era. Despite strong near-unanimity among economists (including big names like Frank Taussiq, Paul Douglas, and Irving Fisher) against the act (unusual at a time when the profession was ideologically split on how best to deal with the macroeconomics of the ongoing Great Depression), President Hoover signed it, reportedly as a "shrewd play of tactical politics" by sharply raising the cost of imports. In so doing, he had hoped to increase the trade surplus. This, in turn, would force the rest of the world to adjust their overcapacity (instead of the United States), thereby minimizing US pain.

Of course, it later fell flat on his face. The tariffs ignited widespread beggar-thy-neighbor reaction around the world. The flow of global capital and goods and services collapsed. President Franklin D. Roosevelt rebuilt pro-trade consensus with a series of successes in the 1930s. It was not until the aftermath of World War II that John Maynard Keynes and Harry Dexter White and others who negotiated the Bretton Woods Accord also created the General Agreement on Tariffs and Trade (GATT), the predecessor of the WTO.

The New Protectionism

As I see it, what has evolved finds its parallel more with the 1970s. That's when nations responded to the first oil shock and other exogenous developments. Governments then, like now, increased domestic interventions, ranging from fiscal stimuli, subsidies to the most affected, and monetary easing, to labor and capital market restrictions. These spilled over into increasingly protective practices, including tariff barriers, buy-local initiatives "voluntary" export restraints, and "orderly" market arrangements.

These managed trade measures (dubbed the new protectionism) lasted well into the 1980s. They affected about one-half of global trade. The value of world trade shrank in 1976 and 1983, with anemic annual growth rates well below 5 percent in 1981 to 1987. There was deep and prolonged economic stagnation (global gross domestic product [GDP] was way under 3 percent in 1973 to 1975 and 1980 to 1983). This creeping protectionism led to complex regulatory barriers that emerged (slowly and insidiously) from bigger and more arbitrary government at home—an experience that many in the United States wish now to forget. Realistically, this 1930s- or 1970s-type of protectionism can become the big danger today. Avoiding it will require limits to government intervention. Also needed are well-functioning open markets that provide credible price discovery to promote stable growth.

The Many Faces of Protection

With weakened economies, growing popular skepticism of open markets will surely grow. Bear in mind that US presidents have not hesitated to use protectionist measures to suit their political ends: With consent of the US Congress, in 1983, President Ronald Reagan imposed a 49 percent tariff on Japanese motorcycles; in 1989, President George H. W. Bush extended Reagan-era steel import quotas; in 1995, President Bill Clinton threatened Japan with tariffs on luxury cars—only an eleventh-hour deal scrapped the tariff; and in 2002, President George W. Bush imposed up to a 30 percent tariff on imported steel—facing European retaliation, it was repealed in 2003.

All this, of course, is history. For years, US presidents have faced a China conundrum, confronting great difficulties in finding the right balance in getting China to practice "fair trade" without unleashing global protectionism. Realistically, for the United States, the US$16 billion wholesale tire market is no big deal. But flirting with protectionism can be dangerous, especially before the September G-20 Summit. China must fear the worst. If the United States and China can do it, why not others? Tit-for-tat retaliation can only ignite a global trade war. Fair enough, the United States did engineer G-20 to come out strongly for free trade at the September 2009 Summit: "We will fight protectionism. We are committed to bringing the Doha Round to a successful conclusion in 2010;"[2] and charged ministers to review and remain engaged on the progress of negotiations for further action at its next meeting in 2010.

The October International Monetary Fund (IMF)/World Bank 2009 meetings just ended in Istanbul did, however, reemphasize these commitments: "We affirm our collective responsibility to avoid protectionism in all its forms" (Financial Committee, IMF); and, "We urge members to avoid protectionist measures" (Development Committee, World Bank).

Fair-Weather Free Traders

The global trading system has many enemies. Like it or not, at this time, the man in the White House is counted as its main champion. World trade will shrink by some 12 percent in 2009. A recent report from World Trade Alliance (Geneva) claimed that, on average, a G-20 member has broken the no-protectionism pledge once every three days since it was made. Some of this, I am sure, is hyperbole. As economies weaken, there will be growing skepticism of open markets. We now see politicians from Washington, DC, to Beijing, to Paris, to Seoul, being pressed to help troubled industries, regardless of the consequences for trade.

The bailout of US carmakers represented a discriminatory subsidy. Chinese industries from textiles to steel are given handouts and rebates in the name of economic stimuli. Subsidies will beget more subsidies. France's President Nicolas Sarkozy even talks of Europe becoming an "industrial wasteland" if it does not prop up its manufacturers. They will also invite retaliation. All these come at a risky time. As I see it, protectionist actions in particular against China have been multiplying in recent months. Of late, global leaders as a group—sensing where such tit-for-tat can lead to—have stayed cool. Yet, new barriers have steadily been erected.

What, Then, Are We to Do?

Viewed in its totality, free traders like myself cannot but worry. What's needed is (1) credible political leadership, especially from the United States and China—at least they should avoid beggar-thy-neighbor politics; (2) at some point in time, hopefully sooner than later, President Obama must act firmly to show his anti-protection credentials; (3) serious conclusion of the Doha Round (as the G-20 said they would by year-end); (4) increased transparency (via WTO) to publicize new barriers of any kind—whether or not they are allowed under WTO rules, to avoid backsliding in particular; and (5) best of all, continued vigorous economic stimulus until recovery is stabilized and secure. There is nothing like boosting demand at home to reduce any temptation to hijack it from abroad. Protectionism in the 1930s flourished on the back of serious macroeconomic failures. Surely, we can't afford to have this happen again.

Kuala Lumpur
October 13, 2009

Notes

1. First published on October 31, 2009.
2. Group of 20 (G-20), "Leaders' Statement," G-20 Summit, Pittsburgh, Pennsylvania, September 24–25, 2009, para. 28.

CHAPTER 73

Currency Wars at a Time of Deficient Demand[1]

B razil's finance minister[2] said it all in the first week of October 2010: "We're in the midst of an international currency war, a general weakening of currency. This threatens us because it takes away our competitiveness." The International Monetary Fund (IMF) has since warned that widespread currency interventions could derail the fragile recovery. Many nations are engaged in deliberate policies to weaken their currencies. Further competitive devaluation will inflame global tensions. At a time of continuing deficient demand, this is not the time for the world's major currencies to face-off in what can only be described as an "ugly contest." By the third quarter of 2010, attention had shifted from deep woes engaging the eurozone to reemerging economic and fiscal fissures in the United States. This sudden reorientation of focus helped the euro reverse most of its springtime collapse, and saw the US dollar lose more luster. Then, there is the ever-strong yen. Japan is faced with a deep economic malaise and anxious to ease the burden on exporters. It is not surprising the third quarter of 2010 highlighted the standoff over which of the three most actively traded currencies has the lousiest outlook.

The euro hit a new low against the US dollar (1.1917) on June 7, and for the first half of 2010, it was 15 percent from where it started in 2010. But the euro rose 11.5 percent in the third quarter of 2010. Against the yen, the US dollar fell to a 15-year low (83.10 yen) in mid-September 2010. That prompted the unleashing of a US$20 billion blitz of yen selling, driving it off its high. The yen has since returned to its preintervention rate. The end result: The US dollar not only slid against the euro and the yen, but also fared worse against most emerging market currencies. When measured against a basket of major currencies, the US dollar sank to its lowest level since January 2010. By October 5, the ICE Dollar Index was below 78, against 88 in June 2010.

The "Grass Gets Crumpled"

This is not the first time for currency conflicts: 39 years ago (August 1971), the "Nixon shock" ended US dollar convertibility to gold; 25 years earlier (September 1985), the Plaza Accord devalued the US dollar notably against the yen. This time around, the target is the Chinese yuan. The East has a saying: When tigers fight or make love, the grass gets crumpled. The United States has pressed hard on China to revalue faster; the European Union (EU) and Australia have since raised the volume of their rhetoric on China. Meanwhile, others, including Japan, Australia, South Korea, Brazil, and Switzerland, have been intervening to hold their currencies down. Australia added to warn Europe against reviving protectionism masquerading as environmentalism. The situation can only get worse.

Already, the Institute of International Finance (IIF)[3]—representing 420 world's leading financial institutions, just revised upward its latest forecast for net inflows of capital into emerging markets, showing a sharp increase to US$825 billion for 2010—all in search of higher yields, thereby risking instability. Of course, the United States and European Union blame all this on China. But many emerging economies blame ultra-low interest rates in rich countries (reflecting aggressive quantitative easing [QE]) for diverting vast amounts of cheap funds to their domestic markets, creating a policy dilemma for most. Their economies are growing nicely in the face of rising inflation. This limits the use of interest rates to curb these funds inflows. Brazil, on October 4, doubled a tax on foreigners' purchases of local bonds. Australia and Indonesia kept their benchmark rates unchanged to ward off further inflows. The Philippines is expected to hold their rates. India and Thailand are considering new steps of protection.

The big problem remains: Globally, ad hoc currency interventions don't work. At its heart is the US dollar, trapped in a downward spiral as expectations of further monetary easing by the Fed (US Federal Reserve Bank) drags it lower. The global architecture is broken. But how best to move away from a system where the US dollar plays the role of a major reserve currency, and the United States sets global interest rates? It looks like the entire Asian sovereign community is suddenly buying euro and yen—so much so the Japanese on October 6 lowered the target for its key overnight rate to a range of zero to 0.1 percent. John Connally (Nixon's Secretary of the Treasury) said it best when he famously told Europeans that the "US dollar is our currency, but your problem." In the absence of currency adjustments, the Chinese response appears to be, in the words of *Financial Times*'s Martin Wolf: In effect, the United States is seeking to inflate China and China, to deflate the United States.[4] It's a stalemate. The grass continues to get crumpled. There is now, according to the IIF, an environment of unilateralism and bilateralism laced with isolation and parochialism. Somewhat exaggerated, but in essence, correct as I see it.

The Yuan Scapegoat

Reality check: First, the developed world suffers from chronic deficient demand. The IMF just cut its growth forecast. The six biggest high-income nations' (United States, Japan, Germany, France, United Kingdom, and Italy) gross domestic product (GDP) in the second quarter of 2010 is nowhere near what it was in the first quarter of 2008. They are operating up to 10 percent below potential; in the United States and eurozone, core inflation is only 1 percent. Deflation beckons. Those with trade deficits (the United States) and surpluses (Germany and Japan) alike all love to have export-led growth. In a zero-sum world, this can only happen if emerging nations shift to run huge current deficits. That's not about to happen.

Second, the vast accumulation of foreign reserves complicates any meaningful adjustment: Between January 1999 and May 2010, reserves reached US$8.4 trillion (up US$6.8 trillion since January 1999). China accounted for 30 percent of the world total, or equivalent to 50 percent of its own GDP. That's the big picture.

Until the early 1970s, currency rates were fixed under the Bretton Woods monetary system. It fell apart with the US-inspired inflation of the 1970s. So the world moved to floating rates. But most nations still chose to peg to the US dollar. With the euro, most of Europe moved to fixed exchange rates. Pegging offered the benefits of exchange rate stability, eliminating a source of uncertainty for investment and trade to flourish. One catch, though: Pegged nations give up monetary independence. In the US dollar-bloc, they yield to the Fed, and in the euro-bloc, the European Central Bank. This is what China did when its yuan was pegged to the US dollar. In exchange for the benefits of exchange-rate stability, it subcontracted much of its monetary discretion to the Fed. For more than a decade, this served the world economy well: Americans raised their living standards and millions of Chinese enjoyed prosperity.

For years, the United States had pressed the yuan to revalue in the name of reducing US trade deficit. What's not so obvious is that much of this deficit is intracompany trade—that is, US firms outsourcing production to China to stay globally competitive (US workers earn higher wages, and shareholders, higher profits). Beijing bent for a while in the middle of the last decade and adopted a crawling peg, allowing the yuan to revalue by 18 percent over time with little impact on US trade deficit. China repegged amid the financial panic in 2008. American clamor to revalue revived and the yuan relented and moved to greater "flexibility" in June 2010. Recently, the yuan reached its strongest since 1993—up 2 percent to 6.69 per US dollar but fell 10 percent against the euro. That's far too slow for the United States and Europeans.

The US trade deficit with China surged to US$268 billion in 2008, up from US$202 billion in 2005. Currency is but one factor influencing where firms manufacture. Furthermore, the United States no longer makes many of the goods China exports. So a shift in business out of China would more likely mean relocation to other low-cost Asian nations, rather than rebuild US capacity. The yuan has appreciated 55 percent against the dollar since 1994 when Beijing begun to overhaul its forex system. That bilateral imbalance is structural. As I see it, the only way the United States can fight off Chinese competitive challenges is to innovate and boost productivity at home.

Both the United States and the European Union now urge China to allow an orderly, significant, and broad-based appreciation of the yuan. I think China is right to resist these calls, not least because a large revaluation is likely to damage China's growth and basic restructuring plans—at a time when China's continuing expansionary "train" is pulling along growth in East Asia nicely, and to a lesser extent, the developed world as well. "The world has already become partially de-coupled," says Nobel Laureate Joseph Stiglitz. China has learned from past experience, including that of Japan, which bowed to similar US pressures in the 1980s and 1990s, revaluing the ¥ from 360 per US$ to a high of 80 in 1995. According to Stanford Professor R. McKinnon, one result was domestic deflation and its lost decades in growth. Meanwhile, Japan continues to run a trade surplus as imports fell with slower growth and cross-border prices adjusted. China helped lead the world out of recession, and the world needs that to continue.

What's China to Do?

The media want us to believe the biggest sinner in this game of beggar-thy-neighbor is China. But, in their own way, the United States, United Kingdom, and the EU are engaged in much the same thing. Massive QE has effectively created negative interest rates and debauched their currencies to boot with floods of liquidity. QE proved a highly effective way to devalue the dollar. Indeed, it is a much more powerful form of persuasion than the threat of tariffs. The very prospect of more QE can rattle China and most of Asia to submission.

But global imbalances that created the crisis have yet to be addressed by centering criticism on China. Indeed, reform of the international monetary architecture is needed to resolve the problem—with a global "clearing" organization acting independently among nations to manage "surpluses" and "deficits." This institution is intended to keep the world in balance. This won't happen.

Maybe the approach is wrong. I think the real problem is not the yuan's exchange rate but its inconvertibility and capital controls. As a result, the yuan's development has been stunted since private markets can't recycle the flow of dollars arising from continuing large surpluses. China's huge reserves represent a significant misallocation of global resources. Instead of letting these reserves find their optimum private investment use, China uses them to buy US Treasuries and bonds. Once made convertible, capital and trade flows will adjust through private markets rather than the People's Bank. That's how Germany recycles its surpluses. In this way, a one-time modest revaluation accompanied by convertibility can assist in the global adjustment process while avoiding the perils of a Japan-like deflation.

What, Then, Are We to Do?

Whether China is ready for convertibility of its yuan is a key question. All I can say is that stage-by-stage convertibility increases domestic pressures for China to further liberalize to develop its financial system, which in turn helps in global rebalancing. What's important is for China and the other surplus nations (Germany and Japan) to understand that their policies are not helping the United States to rebalance. Similarly, the United States and the European Union need to understand that the surplus nations simply can't adjust fast enough to suit them. Resolution requires realistic "grown-up" behavior on the part of core parties in this dispute to agree to global rebalancing with care and with determination. For a start, I see merit in the IIF's call for a new coordinated currency pact by the core parties to hammer out with haste an understanding to help rebalance the global economy. It needs a more sophisticated version of the 1985 Plaza Accord to include stronger commitments to medium-term fiscal stringency in the United States and structural reform in Europe. The world deserves more, not less.

Kuala Lumpur
October 7, 2010

Notes

1. First published on October 9, 2010.
2. Guido Mantega, minister of finance, Brazil, in a statement during an event in Sao Paulo, Brazil, on September 28, 2010.
3. Institute of International Finance (IIF), "Capital Flows to Emerging Market Economies," IIF Research Notes, October 4, 2010.
4. Martin Wolf, "Currencies Clash in New Age of Beggar-Thy-Neighbor," *Financial Times*, London (September 28, 2010).

CHAPTER 74

Tension over Exchange Rates[1]

Amid heightened fears over eurozone sovereign debt risks and increasing concerns about the health of the United States and eurozone economies, worried investors have flocked to the safety of haven currencies, especially the Swiss franc (CHF), and gold. While investors and speculators have since moved aggressively to buy gold, the switch from being large sellers to buying by a number of emerging nations' central banks (Mexico, Russia, South Korea, and Thailand) has helped propel the price of gold more than 25 percent higher this year, hitting a record US$1,920 a troy ounce earlier this month. At a time of high uncertainty in the face of the International Monetary Fund's (IMF) latest gloomy forecast of global growth, few central banks relish the prospect of a flood of international cash pushing their currencies higher. Massive overvaluation of their currencies poses an acute threat to their economic well-being, and carries the risk of deflation.

The Swiss Franc

Switzerland's national currency, the CHF, should be used to speculative attacks by now. So much so that in the 1970s, the Swiss National Bank (SNB) was forced to impose negative interest rates on foreign investors (who have to pay banks to accept their CHF deposits). And, it has been true in recent years, with the CHF rising by 43 percent against the euro since the start of 2010 until mid-August this year. There does not seem to be an alternative to the CHF as a safe haven at the moment. With what's going on in the United States, eurozone, and Japan, investors have lost faith in the world's two other haven currencies: US dollar and Japanese yen. This reflects the Fed's ultra-loose policy stance and the political fiscal impasse in the United States, which have scared away investments from the dollar. The prospect that Tokyo might once again intervene to limit the yen's strength has deterred speculators from betting on further gains from it. To be fair, the CHF has also benefited from recent signs that the Swiss economy, thanks in large part to its close ties to a resurgent Germany, is thriving.

But enough is enough. The SNB's surprise announcement on September 6 was that it would buy foreign currencies in "unlimited quantities" to combat a huge overvaluation of the CHF, and keep the franc–euro exchange rate above 1.20 with the "utmost determination." On August 9, the CHF reached a new record, touching near parity against the euro from 1.25 at the start of the year while the US$ sank to almost CHF0.70 (from 0.93). The impact so far has been positive: The euro rose 8.0 percent on that day and the 1.20 franc level has since stabilized. It was a gamble.

Of course, SNB had intervened before in 2009 and 2010, but in a limited way at a time when the euro was far stronger. But this time, with the nation's economy buckling under the currency's massive overvaluation, the risks of doing nothing were far greater. In July last year (2010), following a checkered history of frustrated attempts, SNB vowed it would not intervene again. By then, the central bank was already awash with foreign currency reserves. Worse, the CHF value of these reserves plunged as the currency strengthened. In 2010, SNB recorded a loss of CHF20 billion, and a further CHF10 billion in the first half of 2011. As a result, SNB came under severe political pressure for not paying the expected dividend. But exporters (to survive) also demanded further intervention to stop the continuing appreciation.

This time, SNB is up against a stubborn euro-debt crisis, which just won't go away. True, recent efforts have been credible. Indeed, the 1.20 francs looks defensible, even though the CHF remains overvalued. Fair value appears to be closer to 1.30–1.40. But inflation is low; still, the risk of asset-price bubbles remains. What's worrisome is that the SNB acted alone. For the European Central Bank (ECB), the danger lies in the SNB's eventual purchases of higher quality German and French eurozone government bonds with the intervention receipts, countering the ECB's own intervention in the bond market to help weaker members of Europe's monetary union, including Italy and Spain. This causes the spread between the yields of these bonds to widen, and piles further pressure on peripheral economies. Furthermore, unlimited Swiss buying of euro would push up its value, adding to deflationary pressures in the region.

The Devil's Trade-Off

As I see it, the Swiss really have no other options. The SNB has been attempting to drive down the CHF by intervening in the money markets but with little lasting effect. Indeed, the current massive overvaluation of the CHF poses an acute threat to the Swiss economy, where exports accounted for 35 percent of its gross domestic product (GDP). The new policy would help exports and help job security. As of now, there is no support from Europe to drive the euro higher. The SNB is caught in the "devil's trade-off," having to choose risking its balance sheet rather than risk mounting unemployment, deflation, and economic damage. The move is bound to cause distortions and tension over exchange rates globally.

New Haven: The "Nokkie"

The SNB's new policy stance has sent ripples through currency markets. In Europe, it drove the Norwegian krone (the Nokkie) to an eight-year high against the euro as investors sought out alternative safe havens. Since money funds must have a minimum exposure in Europe, with most European currencies discredited and quality bonds yielding next to nothing, the Nokkie became a principal beneficiary. It offers 3 percent return for three months' money-market holdings. Elsewhere, the Swedish krona also gained ground, rising to its strongest level against the euro since June after its central bank left its key interest rates unchanged, while signaling that the rate will only creep up. What's worrisome is that if there is continuing upward pressure on the Nokkie or the krona, their central banks would act, if needed, with taxes and exchange controls. With interest rates at or near zero and fiscal policy exhausted or ruled out politically in the most advanced nations, currencies remain one of the only policy tools left.

At a time of high uncertainty, investors are looking for havens. Apart from gold and some real assets, few countries would welcome fresh inflows, which can stir to overvalue currencies. Like it or not, speculative capital will still find China and Indonesia particularly attractive.

The Yen Resists the Pressure

SNB's placement of a "cap" to weaken the CHF has encouraged risk-averse investors who sought comfort in the franc to turn to the yen instead. So far, the yen has stayed below its record high reached in mid-August. But it remains well above the exporters' comfort level. Indeed, the Bank of Japan (BoJ) has signaled its readiness to ease policy to help as global growth falters. But so far, the authorities are happy just monitoring, and indications are they will resist pressure to be as bold as the Swiss, for three main reasons: (1) unlike CHF, the yen is not deemed to be particularly strong at this time—it's roughly in line with its 30-year average; (2) unlike the SNB, Japan is expected to respect the G-7's commitment to market-determined exchange rates; and (3) Japan's economy is five times the size of Switzerland and the yen trading volume makes defending a preset rate in the global markets well-nigh impractical.

Still, they have done so on three occasions over the past 12 months: a record ¥4.51 trillion sell-off on August 9 (surpassing the previous daily record of ¥2.13 trillion from September 2010). The operation briefly pushed the US$ to ¥80.25 (from ¥77.1), but the effects quickly waned and the dollar fell back to a record low of ¥75.9 on August 19. But, I gathered the Ministry of Finance (MOF) needed to meet three conditions for intervention: (1) the ¥/US$ rate has to be volatile; (2) a simultaneous easing by BoJ; and (3) intervention restricted to one day only. Given these constraints, it is no wonder MOF has failed to arrest the yen's underlying trend. In the end, I think the Japanese have learned to live with it—unlike the Swiss, who have the motivation and means to resist a strong currency.

Reprieve for the Yuan

I sense one of the first casualties of the failing global economic expansion is renewed pressure to further appreciate China's yuan. For China, August was a good month to adjust—strong exports, high inflation, and intense international pressure. As a result, the yuan appreciated against the US$ by more than 11 percent, up from an average of about 5 percent in the first seven months of the year. However, the surge had begun to fade in the first half of September. But with the US and eurozone economic outlook teetering in gloom, China's latest manufacturing performance had also weakened, reflecting falling overseas demand. This makes imposing additional currency pressure on exporters a no-go.

Meanwhile, inflation has stabilized. Crude oil and imported food prices have declined, reducing inflationary pressure and the incentive to further appreciate the yuan. Looks like September provided a period of some relief. But, make no mistake, the pressure is still there. The fading global recovery may have papered over the cracks. Pressure won't grind to a halt.

Return to Global Strife

Central banks instinctively try to ward off massive capital flows appreciating their currencies. There are similarities between what's happening today, highlighted by the recent defensive move by the SNB, and the tension over exchange rates at last year-end. It's an exercise in pushing the problem next door. This can be viewed as a consequence of recent Japanese action (Tokyo's repeated intervention to sell the yen). It threatens to start a chain of responses where every central bank tries to weaken its currency in the face of poor global economic prospects and growing uncertainty. So far, the tension has not risen to anything like last year's level. But with rising political pressure provoking resistance to currency appreciation, the potential for a fresh outbreak remains real. The Brazilian finance minister just repeated his warning last year that continuing loose US monetary policies could stoke a currency war.

With the euro under growing stress from sovereign debt problems, the market's focus is turning back to Japan (prompting a new plan to deal with a too-strong yen), to non-eurozone nations (Norway, Denmark, Sweden, and possibly the United Kingdom) and on to Asia (already the ringgit, rupiah, baht, and won are coming under pressure on concerns over uncertainty and capital flight). Similarly, Brazil's recent actions to limit currency appreciation highlights the dilemma faced by fast-growing economies (Turkey, Chile, and Russia) since allowing currency appreciation limits domestic overheating but also undermines competitiveness. This low-level currency war between emerging and advanced economies had further unsettled financial markets. Given the weak economic outlook, most governments would prefer to see their currencies weaken to help exports. The risk, as in the 1930s, is not just "beggar-thy-neighbor" devaluations but resort to a wide range of trade barriers as well. Globally coordinated policies under G-20 are preferred. But that's easier said than done.

What, Then, Are We to Do?

So, it is timely for the IMF's September 2011 *World Economic Outlook*[2] to warn of "severe repercussions" to the global economy as the United States and eurozone could face recession and a "lost decade" of growth (a replay of Japan in the 1990s) unless nations revamped economic policies. For the United States, this means less reliance on debt and putting its fiscal house in order. For the eurozone, firm resolution of the debt crisis, including strengthening its banking system. For China, increased reliance on domestic demand. And, for Brazil, cooling an overheating economy. This weekend, the G-20 is expected to take up global efforts to rebalance a world overwhelmed by heightened risks to growth and the deepening debt crisis. Focus is expected on the role of exchange rates in rebalancing growth, piling more pressure on China's yuan. Frankly, IMF meetings and G-20 gatherings don't have a track record of getting things done. I don't expect anything different this time. The outlook just doesn't look good.

Kuala Lumpur
September 22, 2011

Notes

1. First published on September 24, 2011.
2. International Monetary Fund (IMF), *World Economic Outlook—Slowing Growth, Rising Risks* (Washington, DC: IMF, September 2011).

CHAPTER 75

RMB: What's a Budding Currency to Do?[1]

China's yuan or RMB (renminbi) is brewing a storm of late. I was visiting Bangkok when news came that on the last Friday of February 2014 the usually predictable RMB took its biggest dive against US dollar since it was depegged in 2005. RMB had depreciated by nearly 1 percent over the past week—reversing a long-running trend of gradual, incremental appreciation against US dollar and other major currencies during the past eight years. The move caught the market by surprise—ending at US$1 = RMB6.1450 on Friday, down 1.5 percent since the beginning of the year. This is its lowest level in 10 months, a dramatic move for a currency that often barely budges and that only gained close on 3 percent for 2013 as a whole.

The slide added jitters among investors already anxious about the slackening Chinese economy and touched off concerns about a possible RMB sell-off in offshore markets. Certainly, it has rekindled uncertainty about the RMB exchange rate. Indeed, has China finally joined the currency war? Many have also expressed concern. Before too much is being read into RMB's fall, some perspective is in order.

US Dollar in 2013 and to Date

Between 2001 and 2008, the dollar index, which measures US$ against a basket of major currencies, fell more than 40 percent as the United States' long-standing "strong dollar" policy degenerated into a "hackneyed punchline." Since the collapse of the Bretton Woods monetary system in 1971, when the US dollar's convertibility into gold was rescinded, US dollar went through three-down cycles and two-up cycles, each with an average duration of about seven years. The US dollar has since gained nearly 11 percent from its 2011 low, and despite the euro's resilience—it was up 9 percent against the single European currency over the same period. In 2013, US dollar strengthened 26 percent against Indonesian rupiah, 24 percent against South African rand, 22 percent against Turkish lira, 15 percent against Indian rupee, 19 percent against Japanese yen, and 10 percent against Malaysian ringgit. However, US dollar weakened against euro (–4.2 percent), RMB (–2.9 percent), Swiss franc (–2.3 percent), and pound sterling (–2.3 percent). This year, the winter has been tough for US dollar bulls. The dollar index—after a slight bounce at the start of the year—has since given up its gains to trade near the January 1 level. Until end-February, US dollar has depreciated against yen (–3 percent), A$ (–1.3 percent), sterling (–0.85 percent) and euro (–0.06 percent). But it appreciated 4 percent against Canadian dollar, 2.15 percent against Korean won, 2.7 percent against Turkish lira, and 36 percent against Russian ruble. Ukraine has since become the wild card. As a result, a lot of people have already pared back risk. The impact on currency markets has been pervasive as people rushed to exit. There is now a lot more risk on the table.

China's Resolve

The currency wars first warned of in 2010 by Brazil's finance minister did not come to pass—at least not overtly. In fact, there has been sharp "competitive" depreciation in the currencies of many major emerging Asian nations (Indonesia, India, South Korea, Australia, and Malaysia), as well as some in Africa (e.g., South Africa), South America (Brazil and Mexico), and Europe (Turkey and Russia), not to mention Japan, which smacks of skirmishes as ultra-loose global monetary policy still reverberates through the markets. There wasn't much of a war so far.

Be that as it may, I sense two popular explanations for China's weakening exchange rate. The first alludes to China's worry about the strength of its currency—after all, RMB has risen 33 percent since it was revalued in 2005—the official view appears to be that RMB can now be as much as 10 to 15 percent overvalued for the past three years (as a result, labor costs have risen ahead of productivity) or at least close to the equilibrium level or its fair market value. Already, the strong RMB is hurting Chinese exporters' competitiveness (adjusted for inflation; RMB rose 18.5 percent against US$ from June 2010 to November 2013). Japanese products, for example, have become more competitive because of yen's plunge, as have those from emerging markets hit by sell-offs.

The second explanation rests on the popular saying, "One arrow, two vultures." The first vulture being speculators, reflecting People's Bank of China's (PBoC) repeated warnings of international currency speculators who trade RMB against US dollar as a one-way bet on appreciation. It is a no-brainer to borrow US dollar—as long as RMB appreciates, it is a sure thing! The other vulture stems from the activities of domestic "shadow" financiers offering attractive returns; their resource power is nourished by inflows of capital that gush through "a hundred holes" in China's nominally closed capital account.

It is easy to borrow US dollars at up to 3 percent annual interest and sell them for RMB in China, and then invest in "shadow" institutions at 10 to 12 percent or in underground "banks" for up to 20 percent. On top of this, there is arbitrage profit to be taken from RMB appreciation at the time of repayment. Such cross-border carry-trade (involves no forex hedge) has been robust and often done illegally through export overinvoicing. PBoC worries that shooting the arrow could trigger the very wave of "defaults" it hopes to avoid. All PBoC can expect is to ruffle sufficient feathers in shooting the arrow—unfortunately, not effectively enough. Good enough as a warning shot! Banks brought in US$76.3 billion in the onshore market in January 2014, the highest monthly amount on record. Indeed, inflows have been accelerating since mid-2013, when China's foreign exchange reserves rose by some US$510 million to US$3.8 trillion. That does provide a high level of comfort.

RMB Global Role

Overall, China's recent actions, in my view, serve notice that it is opening up a new front in its national battle to manage growing risks in a highly open and volatile financial system. To start with, PBoC has been unable to bring "shadow banking" to heel without triggering defaults among local government and state-owned enterprise (SOE) borrowers. By engineering a significant fall in RMB, it is reported that the authorities' aim is to (1) punish speculators; (2) restrain the huge capital inflows, especially "hot" money (estimated at US$150 billion in 2013); and (3) assume some control over capital flows that can generate inflationary pressures, which thwart efforts to reform the financial system and restructure the economy.

At the heart of the shift in the financial landscape is reform of the exchange rate system to one that is market-based in practice and where trading is not a one-way bet, where price discovery reflects the ups and downs of market forces interacting in an orderly manner within a wider trading band (up to 2 percent on either side instead of 1 percent at present). To be effective, reform is also needed to put into place market-based deposit rates—beginning with small steps in the new free-trade zones (FTZs). China had already scrapped controls on lending rates in July 2013. The intention is to make it easier for multinationals and domestic companies to manage, in particular, their foreign exchange, including ease to borrow and lend offshore.

As RMB evolves, its growing stature is visible on many fronts.

Trade and Payments Currency

China is the world's biggest trading nation. Reflecting this, RMB has since overtaken Swiss franc as the seventh-most-used currency (1.4 percent share) for payments worldwide (behind the US dollar, with a 39 percent global share, euro, sterling, yen, Canadian dollar, and Australian dollar). It has, in December 2013, overtaken euro to become the second-most-used currency in international trade finance. Bank of International Settlements reported that RMB is the ninth-most-traded currency in the world. In the past year, trading in derivatives tied to RMB has also soared—some US$250 billion of such contracts were traded in 2013.

Investment Currency

RMB is transforming to extend the yield curve for government bonds and create a broad-based capital market to serve the needs of global borrowers and investors. China's RMB-denominated debt market is already the biggest in emerging markets; it aims to stand alongside the US dollar and euro as the top three in the international bond market.

International Reserve Currency

Here, RMB has most ground to make up. It accounts for only 0.01 percent of world central bank reserves, compared with 60 percent in the US dollar and 25 percent in euro. But the influence of RMB on emerging currencies is already rising. Its main constraint is lack of capital account convertibility. Plans are in place to make RMB a convertible currency; it needs time.

What, Then, Are We to Do?

The recent RMB move is significant. It has to be viewed from China's broad perspective of exchange rate and financial reform. Surging capital inflows have complicated efforts to manage the economy, contributing to soaring property prices and injecting excess cash into the financial system. Showing that RMB is not a one-way bet will help cool the speculation somewhat. The weaker exchange rate wipes out several months of "unearned" profits from the "carry-trade" in holding RMB and hoping to pocket the extra interest from ever-rising appreciation. It also helps to deter borrowing offshore, risking currency mismatches.

But it's quite clear that PBoC cannot inflict enough pain to make such trades unwind completely. Hopefully, the lesson is learned—that carry-trades are no sure thing. PBoC's emphasis on not reading too much into RMB's fall is well taken. Currency will be allowed to go up and down; exchange rate volatility is normal. That's what an efficient forex market does. In a world of floating exchange rates, they are supposed to.

However, a policy dilemma arises because a weak currency raises the volume of bank liquidity and eases money market rates. That's what is happening now, as US dollars are being soaked up and as the consequential RMB funds flooding the market send short-term interest rates plummeting. But reform involving a shift from exports and fixed investment to consumption calls for continuing deleveraging of the economy, which means keeping interest rates high and liquidity tight.

A choice has to be made; it's a matter of prioritizing. For now, PBoC has to tackle rising financial risks and deterring hot-money inflows in the face of a 7.5 percent growth target, without losing sight of its longer-term goal of rebalancing the economy. That's what central bankers do best. Looking at 2014 as a whole, I expect RMB over time to resume to appreciate moderately, with the exchange rate settling in the region around US$1 = RMB6. There is an off chance it can close the year at 5.9! Realistically, it is not easy for investors to find outside China an economy with fast growth, high interest rates, and a steadily appreciating currency. So the bet is still on RMB.

Kuala Lumpur
March 6, 2014

Note

1. First published on March 8, 2014.

CHAPTER 76

The Kiss of Debt[1]

So the world managed to survive the deepest and longest recession since the Big One in early 1930s. It did so with extraordinary public policy support (fiscal and financial)—the price paid to stop the global economy from falling off the precipice. Two years later, ballooning fiscal deficits and rising public debt are raising investor anxiety about sovereign risk in many advanced economies. Ironically, the shoe is traditionally on the other foot coming out from deep recession. Sovereign risk concerns historically reflected profligacy in emerging market economies. In the past, Brazil, Mexico, Russia, and Argentina were notable examples of public debt defaults. Many others (Pakistan, Ukraine, and Iceland) were forced to restructure under threat of default. To a large extent, many emerging economies have changed their ways—tightening their fiscal belt, exporting more (some from new commodity resources), lowering debt-to-gross domestic product (GDP) ratio. Basically, implementing early fiscal consolidation (oftentimes forced on by promises of new credits).

This time, severe recession and recent financial crisis took a high toll on a good number of advanced economies in the eurozone—those with a history of fiscal problems, ignoring reforms in good times. Today, "biggies" like the United States, the United Kingdom, and Japan are made more vulnerable by weak economic (and jobless) recovery and an aging population—both likely to add to their debt woes, made worse by the monetization of fiscal deficits (printing money) and ready access to "costless" bank funds via quantitative easing (also printing money). Unless properly handled, their anemic economies could fall back into recession (double-dip) and even deflation (à la Japan), with often-disastrous impact on their longer-term growth prospects.

PIIGS Can't Fly

News over the Chinese New Year holidays was dominated largely by Greece—had it coming and, eventually, pressured by the market to bring on early fiscal reform. Together with other eurozone PIIGS (Portugal, Italy,

Ireland, and Spain)—these so-called Club Med members share common traits: weak fiscal and debt positions; weak exports; weak balance of payments; and weak productivity (too-high wages) caught in a zone with a strong euro, which made them all the more uncompetitive.

What is often not appreciated is that these PIIGS have limited policy options as part of the European Union (EU). For them, their exchange rate is a given. By adopting the euro, they cannot depreciate since they have no currencies of their own. And, the European Central Bank (ECB) is not about to weaken the euro for their sakes. They have only one way to go to restore competitiveness—fiscal retrenchment and structural reform. But the PIIGS don't have a track record of fiscal discipline. Greece, for example, lacks the economic governance of the EU. Yet, it has to make the most of a weak hand at three-way poker involving the EU, capital markets, and potential social unrest at home. If PIIGS fall apart, the European Commission (EC) falls apart.

In my view, they can best do this under an International Monetary Fund (IMF) program and not in the shadow of the EC and the ECB without smelling like a bailout. The IMF gives them the best option to reestablish lost policy credibility. Moreover, the euro is not a debt union (Europe is only halfway through creating a viable monetary union)—it has yet to have an emergency financial mechanism, if ever. I must agree with Professor Paul Krugman (2008 Nobel Laureate) that the euro was adopted ahead of the readiness of all constituent parts to effectively engage.

Harvard's Martin Feldstein had cautioned early in 1999 that divergent economies can't work under a single EU roof. Germany had demanded too much: (1) German aversion of debt, and (2) an authoritarian central bank (ECB) whose excessively tight policies have since aggravated the plight of the PIIGS. Of course, Germany had benefited greatly from the euro. At the same time, Greece and the other PIIGS enjoyed a free lunch as German interest rate pulled down everyone else's within the euro-bloc.

Now is payback time. Greece's ratio of debt-to-GDP is nearly twice Germany's and projected to hit 120 percent this year. Its moment of truth came for concealing a 13 percent budget deficit. Overall, even EU is not out of the woods. According to the EC, its public debt ratio could rise above 100 percent by 2014—that is, costing an entire year's output—unless firm action is taken to restore fiscal discipline. This ratio is expected at 84 percent this year (only 66 percent in 2007) and to rise to 89 percent in 2011. Ironically, nations aspiring to be members must meet a maximum 60 percent target!

US and Its AAA Rating

Very much like Europe, the United States is not out of the woods, either. The deep recession and financial crisis have devastated the state of its public finances. Indeed, the question in most observers' mind: Is the United

States at (or approaching) a tipping point with global investors? It's an issue that has become more burning with US President Barack Obama's 2010 federal budget envisaging a deficit of US$1.6 trillion, or 10.6 percent of GDP. By the end of 2009, public debt had reached US$5.8 trillion or 53 percent of GDP. This ratio is projected to reach 72 percent in 2013, unprecedented in US history except when at war.

Markets do have cause to worry. So do we, especially China with very large US$ reserves. But for Paul Krugman,[2] the reality isn't as bad as it sounds. First, the large deficit reflected countercyclical expansionary spending (not "runaway spending growth") to offset the impact of the worst recession in 80 years. It's already stimulating growth and supporting job creation. Second, sure there is a longer-term fiscal problem. But once sustainable growth returns, the administration needs to tackle the difficult task of budget reform. Third, there is no reason for panic. For him, what's the big deal with projections of interest payments on debt of 3.5 percent of GDP? That's what the United States paid under the elder President Bush. Fourth, the "scare tactics" are all politics.

To me, the real concern is whether the United States can stay the course and do what it takes to firmly establish a sustainable recovery, with priority centered on licking mass unemployment. This could even mean facing larger deficits now. That's what leadership is all about. Nevertheless, there is no denying the United States has structural fiscal problems. Serious enough for Moody's Investors Service to state following February 1's budget release: "Unless further measures are taken to reduce the budget deficit further or the economy rebounds more vigorously than expected, the federal financial picture as presented . . . will at some point put pressure on the Aaa government bond rating."[3] Quite obviously, this raises fresh concerns.

To be fair, under the Democrats in 2007, the public debt ratio was 36 percent and rose to 40 percent within a year. It's expected at 64 percent this year, 69 percent in 2011, and to go above 70 percent later this decade. Let's not forget Moody's ratings care more about balancing the budget. It seems to me that growth and job creation should matter more, just as how nations do the balancing counts. But, frankly, a rating downgrade would not be cataclysmic for the United States. In practice, borrowing costs will rise for all. This simply means further pressure on the deficit and debt.

Japan was marked down in 1998 when its debt ratio hit 115 percent. Stabilizing debt requires some combination of faster growth, higher taxes, and lower spending. The trouble is, Americans want lower taxes, more lavish social safety net, and the world's best-funded military machine—having all at the same time by simply piling on debt.

Sure, the United States has formidable strengths, which allow government to be profligate far longer than most. But reality is coming home to roost. World history over the past 30 years does suggest, as the popular saying goes: You never want a serious crisis to go to waste. The emerging

BRICs (Brazil, Russia, India, and China) needed a fiscal crisis to set them on the road to real economic reform and national resurgence. Maybe it's now the United States' turn. Obama's response so far is "First, growth." Let's hope his timing is right. Let's hope he is well committed to it.

Till Debt Do Us Part

Within G-7, there is a tacit understanding to resolving the dilemma of high employment and worsening public debt: to persevere in support of growth and job creation now (even at the expense of higher deficits); and then get the budget deficit down real hard as recovery gets firmly established. Among academics, this debate has split the profession. In Britain, Professor Tim Besley of the London School of Economics (LSE) and 19 mainly British co-signatories stated that "there is a compelling case" for an accelerated program of fiscal consolidation now. If it doesn't, economic stability is at stake, including a run on the pound. In response, two groups of prominent international economists, one led by Lord Layard of LSE (and nine others, including MIT's Nobel Laureate Robert Solow), and the other by Lord Skidelsky of Warwick (and 19 others, including Columbia University's Nobel Laureate Joseph Stiglitz), believe they are dead wrong and said so in the *Financial Times* on February 19, 2010. Essentially, the basic difference is centered on timing.

As I see it, the growth-now economists point to the growing weight of evidence for first priority on the restoration of robust growth. This makes sense given current high unemployment, debt not being out of control, and more private savings mobilized to finance the deficit (as in Japan). Moreover, an immediate accelerated fiscal cutback now would not produce offsetting private demand to "make a sustainable recovery more likely." Indeed, any sharp "reversal" shock can prove damaging to early firm recovery. For them, history is "littered with examples of premature withdrawal of government stimulus" gone wrong (United States in 1937 and Japan in 1997).

No Such Dilemma in Asia

Latest IMF estimates show fiscal deficits in advanced G-20 nations (A20Ns) averaging less than 2 percent of GDP before the crisis in 2007, rising sharply to 9.7 percent in 2009. For the emerging G-20 economies (E20Es), the comparable ratios were one of near balance in 2007 and in the region of 5 percent in 2009. Similarly, the public debt ratio of A20Ns is expected to rise to 114 percent of GDP by 2014, as against 78 percent in 2007. Comparable ratio of E20Es, at just over 40 percent in 2007, is likely to fall below

40 percent by 2014. Emerging economies with their more rapid growth and greater restraint in borrowing expect lesser buildup of debt. With the exception of Japan, most Asian economies (from India to China to Korea) approach the piling up of public debt with less hubris. Even China, with one of the world's largest stimulus programs (up to 12 percent of GDP in 2009), recorded a fiscal deficit of less than 5 percent of GDP in 2009; its debt ratio was less than 20 percent. Similarly, India's ratios were 6 percent and 22 percent, respectively. Malaysia's record is quite exemplary, with a fiscal deficit of 4.8 percent in 2008 and 7.4 percent in 2009 (expected to fall to 5.6 percent in 2010) in the face of substantial pump priming (up to 8 percent of GNP); its public debt ratio was 52 percent (foreign debt of 2 percent) in 2009.

Japan's case is rather curious. In 2009, its budget deficit was 10.5 percent of GDP, its public debt, 200 percent—twice the size of the economy. This huge debt reflected years of slow growth, numerous stimulus plans, an aging society, and the impact of global recession. Experts expect it to rise to 300 percent by 2020. Yet, it manages rather well. Japanese investors, including households, absorb 95 percent of this debt. Its long bonds yielded 7.1 percent in 1990; it's now 1.4 percent. The trick, I think, is high private savings in Japan. It's like government spending on behalf of its citizens, who prefer to save than consume. The important issue is investors' confidence that their debt will be serviced and new debt financed. Unlike Japan, a significant part of US debt is financed by foreign savings from China, Japan, Europe, and most of Asia. The inconvenient truth is this: The United States can easily and readily borrow as much as it wants until confidence evaporates—not unlike the US$.

What, Then, Are We to Do?

Much of Asia's confidence lies in its high rate of domestic savings—some even call this habit uniquely Asian. Malaysians save about one-third of their national income. Private savings in the United States until the crisis in 2007 was zero; it now saves 6 to 7 percent. Based on this confidence, Malaysia, for example, can rely on a sustainable stream of noninflationary finance. So long as development strategies for growth are creditably conceived and designed, the domestic savings will be there to fund such public programs to build capacity and generate sustainable growth. Indeed, it is legitimate to ask: Why are excess Malaysian savings used to fund US spending (through investment in US Treasuries)? More so when rates are so miserably low today. Surely, we do have worthwhile much higher-return investments that warrant the use of these excess savings domestically (beyond what's prudently needed to be set aside for the rainy day) to promote the public good.

The efficient allocation of scarce financial resources must form an integral part of Malaysia's New Economic Model. The trick lies in the quality of projects that the savings are mobilized to finance.

Kuala Lumpur
February 25, 2010

Notes

1. First published on February 27, 2010.
2. Paul Krugman, "Fiscal Scare Tactics," *International Herald Tribune*, New York (February 4, 2010).
3. Moody's Investors Service, New York. According to a February 2, 2010, assessment released in New York.

CHAPTER 77

This Obsession with Debt[1]

At Harvard, I really enjoyed graduate macroeconomics taught by Nobel Laureate Professor Wassily Leontief and Professor Martin Feldstein—in particular, the philosophies underlying different policy approaches by John Maynard Keynes, Friedrich Hayek, and Milton Friedman. Simply put, Hayek (the Austrian school ascendant in the nineteenth and early twentieth centuries) promoted the idea that the private sector should be left free to find its own balance in a downturn. The markets' resulting purging power served the United States well in the nineteenth century, when the economy emerged stronger after each recession. But, it was later taken too far in the mix of tight money and high taxes that led finally in the Great Depression. That's when the Keynesian idea of fiscal stimulus took root. In October 1932, Keynes made the case that depressions are caused by a spending deficit, which can only be made up by government spending. Because of "a lack of confidence," there is no assurance that excess funds will find its way into investment in new capital construction by public or private concerns. With global recession, the consensus made us all Keynesians—resorting to heavy government spending to resuscitate the economy was the answer to severe downturns. First cracks appeared with the outbreak of the fiscal crisis in Greece early in 2010. Critics argued government spending brought in diminishing returns, producing an anemic (jobless) recovery that benefited mainly special-interest groups.

In the United States, Fed Reserve Chairman Bernanke stood steadfast and let it be known more stimulus was needed. His monetary activism led to an open-ended commitment to pump as much money into the system as is required to push for maximum employment. He added that he was doing what Friedman would do. Milton Friedman (father of monetarism) advocated that the Great Depression was largely the result of a major contraction in money supply and could have been avoided had the Fed held money supply stable. There is now growing backlash against the Fed's new approach. As I read it, Keynes would not have supported big deficits during boom times, such as those that led eventually to the 2007–2008 crises.

Similarly, Friedman is unlikely to have backed the Fed's monetary activism in engineering economic expansion rather than merely cushioning the pain in downturns. So, systematic perversion of Keynes's and Friedman's thoughts has led to their falling out of favor once again.

"Confidence"

The greatest disagreement between Keynes and Hayek was over benefits of government spending financed by deficits. Keynes pointed out the public interest in a recession cannot rely on the private economy—he went so far as has been reported to have said: To spend less money than we should like to do is not patriotic. But Hayek argued: The existence of public debt on a large scale imposes frictions and obstacles to readjustment very much greater than that imposed by the existence of private debt. Simply put, no stimulus is needed.

Nevertheless, both agreed that this lack of confidence is simply destructive to any weakened economy. For Keynes, confidence will come by bridging this gap in aggregate demand. "Private economy" was the culprit that impeded a return to prosperity by hoarding savings. That is, the potentially pernicious consequences of an increase in demand for money being not met by a corresponding increase in the supply of money. Even Hayek agreed that hoarding is deflationary, and no one thinks deflation is in itself desirable. For Hayek, the way forward to building confidence, in the face of destructive Smoot–Hawley tariffs of 1930 protectionism, is for governments worldwide, led by the United States, to abolish all those restrictions on trade and the free movement of capital. Only expanded trade can rebuild confidence to enable the United States to pay off the public debt.

Growth versus Debt

With recovery, albeit anemic, attention is turned to exit (of stimulus) and fiscal consolidation (bringing down deficits and debt). After more than a decade of good times, the world awakens to face the reality of painful cuts and tax increases, which are now needed to restore sanity in public finances, battered by a combination of years of overspending and the effects of global crises. When recession set in in 2007, advanced nations' budget deficit averaged 1.1 percent of gross domestic product (GDP). By end-2010, this had exceeded 9 percent, according to the International Monetary Fund (IMF), as revenues plummeted and banks got bailed out, bigtime. Government gross debt will exceed 110 percent by 2015, against 73 percent of national income in 2007. This global rise in mounting debt will require nations to (1) reduce accumulating debt to bring down debt ratios; and (2) inject fiscal discipline to reduce deficits. This, warns the IMF, means: sizable and sometimes unprecedented efforts, as failing to do so would ultimately weaken the world's long-term growth prospects.

While this is all well and good, there are fundamental differences in policy on opposite sides of the Atlantic. Germany's Finance Minister Wolfgang Schauble puts it this way: "While US policy makers like to focus on short-term corrective measures, we take the longer view and are therefore, more preoccupied with the implications of excessive deficits and the dangers of high inflation."[2] Last week's Franco-German move to end wage indexation, raise retirement age, and lock in debt limits into national constitutions across the eurozone is bound to be provoking. In a public lecture, the infamous George Soros said: "Something has gone fundamentally wrong in Germany's attitude towards the European Union."[3] By not only insisting on strict fiscal discipline for weaker eurozone countries but also reducing its own fiscal deficit, Germany was in danger of setting in motion "a downward spiral."

Soros said this policy stance ignores a lesson from the 1930s Great Depression and so is "liable to push Europe into a period of prolonged stagnation or worse. That will in turn generate discontent and social unrest."[4] Much of this is already today's reality. President Obama's stance is different but clear: Secure a sustainable recovery first, while setting the stage for fiscal consolidation over the near medium-term. Growth is critical to success in reducing budget deficits. The US position is unique in that with US$ at the heart of the global financial system, it can afford to tighten fiscal policy only when expansion is invigorated. While the US fiscal deficit (10.7 percent of gross domestic product [GDP]) is larger than the eurozone, the Greek and Irish crises have prompted a flight to, rather than from, the US$ and US bonds. Indeed, there is no market pressure to adjust. So, while the United States recognizes it has to seriously tackle problems of fiscal deficit and high debt, there is an unwillingness to act politically.

Is Debt Too High?

Today's deficits, which are leading to ever-higher debt and servicing burdens, are plainly unsustainable. What level of public debt is appropriate? Conventional wisdom says a safe level in a rich economy is 60 percent of GDP—pitched at the limit enshrined in the Maastricht Treaty, which governs membership in the euro. That's before the crisis. As I see it, there is no empirical evidence to support this limit. Of course, the lower the better, since it is unlikely to crowd out private sector initiative. In the past, this limit was often bypassed anyway.

A recent study by Harvard's Kenneth Rogoff and Carmen Reinhart reported in the *Economist* finds that public debt burdens of less than 90 percent have scant impact on growth; but they see significant impact at higher levels.[5] No one size fits all. The United States, with the broadest and deepest bond market and dollar as reserve currency, surely will be able to carry a higher debt than any eurozone members. In the end, the right level of debt depends on the means used to get there, consistent with growth targets. Evidence shows that cuts in spending are more sustainable and friendlier to growth, whereas tax increases can harm growth. Taxes that do least harm to growth are on consumption and immobile assets (e.g., property). Green taxes also make good sense. But politics often point elsewhere, such as toward making the rich pay to clean the environment. In the United Kingdom and United States, the highest marginal income tax rates are possibly poised to rise. Good for populists—but it will not boost growth.

Debts Matter, but Assets Also Count

During the Great Depression, Keynes advocated spending: of any kind, private or public, whether on consumption or investment. The immediate aim was to urgently fill the void in demand. Hayek took exception, for it mattered to him the form spending took, since for him revival of investment was particularly desirable. Sure, once recovery comes on-stream, it does matter what the spending is on. Henry Morgenthau Jr., President Franklin Roosevelt's Treasury secretary, is said to have advised: You can do something about the railroads. You can do something about housing. Above all, you must do something to reassure business. . . . We want to see private business expand. We believe much of remaining unemployment will disappear as private capital funds are increasingly employed. History does suggest that the new respect for market confidence helped in the recovery following the double-dip recession in 1937–1938. So, the lesson for US Treasury Secretary Timothy Geithner is: Those who forget the past condemn us all to repeat it.

Come to think of it, fiscal consolidation is not just about deficits and debt. Depending on how they are incurred, assets are usually created. It is true we should not burden the future with unproductive debt. All societies have infrastructure assets—transport, energy, and water systems. They also have basic education, health, judicial, and defense systems. These systems provide a "public good," which is not usually provided by competitive markets. Surely, it does not make sense to slash infrastructure and utility investments and support for university teaching when borrowing can be had at absurdly low cost. Indeed, never has there been a better time to borrow than now, to productively build public assets. Such Keynesianism is worthy of support, especially in the face of large unused capacity. I think it is wrong to insist that solving the problem caused by debt can't be solved by piling on more debt. It's wise to look at net debt. Yale's Professor Robert Shiller argues there is "an arbitrage opportunity for governments to borrow massively at these low real interest rates, and invest in positive returning projects, such as infrastructures or education. . . . Moreover, unlike private firms, government can count as economic profits" on their investments with positive externalities (benefits that accrue to everyone).[6] Of course, unsustainable government consumption must be curbed. In my view, borrowing is no sin so long as they create productive assets. Assets created cannot be ignored when looking at debt.

What, Then, Are We to Do? The Keynesian Way

I should end on a lighter note. I well recall a fascination with Keynes's lesser-known short essay, written in 1930: "Economic Possibilities for Our Grandchildren."[7] While in the thick of the Great Depression, Keynes reminded us that "the long-run trend was inexorable growth." He then went on to predict: The standard of life in progressive countries 100 years hence will be between four and eight times as high as it is today. After 80 years, with all the disasters in between, the United States and Western Europe are already about five times richer. And still counting. In emerging nations, income growth in the past 30 years has been even more impressive. What's of concern is the quality of the sort of growth we are after in the end. Keynes acknowledged the insatiable desire of human beings to blindly pursue wealth. Recent events have shown, even with wealth, people still wanted to borrow more than they could repay. In the end, most would adjust, albeit grudgingly, to a life of plenty. It is in this future good life Keynes famously imagined economists could be thought of as: humble, competent people on a level with dentists. Economists have a way to go yet.

Kuala Lumpur
February 10, 2011

Notes

1. First published on February 12, 2011.
2. Wolfgang Schauble launched a forthright defence of Germany's economic policy in the *Financial Times* of London on June 24, 2010, to head off US charges that its austerity measures will choke off global economic recovery.

3. George Soros, public lecture at Humboldt University in Berlin, June 23, 2010.
4. Ibid.
5. Kenneth Rogoff and Carmen Reinhart, "Fiscal Tightening and Growth—A Good Squeeze," *Economist*, London (April 3, 2010), p. 67.
6. Robert Shiller, "Shorting Fiscal Consolidation," a commentary in *The Edge*, Malaysia (November 29, 2010).
7. John Maynard Keynes, "Economic Possibilities for Our Grandchildren," *Essays in Persuasion* (New York: W.W. Norton, 1963).

CHAPTER 78

The Tobin Tax Revisited[1]

For seven years in the 1990s (1994–2000), I served the United Nations in New York in two capacities, as: (1) chairman, Ad Hoc Inter-sessional Government Working Group of Experts on Finance, UN Commission on Sustainable Development (UNCSD), and (2) chairman, International Experts Group on Financial Issues, Agenda 21. The focus of my work was to (1) develop policies to secure ready access to external finance to fund sustainable development (including Official Development Assistance, Foreign Direct Investment, and low-interest debt); (2) advance new initiatives on domestic resource mobilization policies (including widespread use of the entire range of "green" taxes and charges, push subsidy reform, and encourage private financing); and (3) promote innovative national and international financial mechanisms for far-reaching resource mobilization.

Agenda 21: The Rio Declaration

Toward the end of the 1980s, the United Nations General Assembly called on the world to devise strategies to halt and reverse the effects of environmental degradation. And, to do so in the context of increased national and international efforts to promote sustainable and environmentally sound development in all countries. Agenda 21, adopted at the Rio Summit—United Nations Conference on Environment and Development (UNCED)—in mid-June 1992, was the international community's response. It represented a comprehensive program of action to be implemented into the twenty-first century in every area where human activity affects the environment. UNCED had then estimated the implementation of all activities under Agenda 21 to require additional external resources of no less than US$125 billion a year (in 1992 prices), or about 1 percent of the North's combined gross national product. In addition, governments and the private sector in the South would need to raise another US$500 billion a year to put their economies on a sustainable development path. That's the perspective. That was the deal, then. In the end, this proved to be too much.

Innovative Mechanisms

The initiatives of my Working Groups included focus on prospects of using innovative forms of international taxation and globally market-based instruments and mechanisms to raise new funds to support sustainable development. International taxes included charges on foreign exchange transactions (Tobin tax), levies on international air transport, and taxes on carbon. Reduction in military spending was vigorously promoted but strongly resisted. Each tax and measure had several variants, representing differing degrees of full-cost pricing with a varied range of implications for economic efficiency. Furthermore, each raises serious political issues. Also examined were internationally tradable CO_2 permits, including carbon offsets and the like (which have since become fashionable). These financial initiatives were each difficult to accept, adopt, and implement in the absence of any existing international framework. At the time, the very idea of the Tobin tax was not even acceptable, let alone being seriously discussed and considered.

Tobin Tax

In the wake of the recent turmoil in global financial markets and the great recession, a late August 2009 report drew my attention to news I thought I would not hear in my lifetime. After nearly 40 years, Lord Turner (the United Kingdom's chief financial regulator) supported the introduction of a Tobin tax—this time, a global tax on financial transactions. Such a tax could help meet growing concerns about the large size of banks and excesses in compensation. I first heard of the Tobin tax in 1972 (as a student at Harvard), when some of us visited Princeton to hear Nobel Laureate Professor James Tobin (Yale) speak at the Janeway Lectures in honor of Harvard economist Schumpeter: "The New Economics One Decade Older." On his list of measures to enhance the efficacy of macroeconomic policy was the idea of a currency transaction tax. He offered two main objectives: (1) to bring down foreign exchange volatility (through reducing speculative short-term expectations and risks); and (2) to promote autonomy of national macroeconomic policies.

The idea was anathema to central banks—to them "it sank like a rock," according to Tobin at the Lecture. Not surprisingly, the community of professional economists simply ignored it. The idea is often resurrected and mutated by currency crises, and has died out soon after each crisis. A source of recent interest (after the Asian currency crisis, 1997–1998) is its potential to generate vast revenue.

Indeed, Tobin even suggested in 1978—as a byproduct and not as its principal purpose—that in the event the probable necessity of having such a tax was implemented globally, its potentially huge revenue collection could be dedicated to multilateral purposes for the global good. Tobin often lamented that his critics seemed to miss what he considered a "beauty" property of the tax: that this simple, one-parameter tax would automatically penalize short-horizon round-trips while negligibly affecting the incentives for commodity trade and long-term capital investments. Tobin realized in 1995, when foreign exchange transactions reached US$1.5 trillion a day, that even a very modest 0.2 percent tax could yield up to US$700 billion a year. For Tobin, there will be difficult political problems in any international agreement under which sovereign nations levy a tax tailored to international specifications and turn over part or all of the revenues collected.

Global Tax on Financial Transactions

The Tobin tax was certainly ahead of its time. Indeed, most good ideas take years to be recognized. The eventual outcome of the Tobin tax is still uncertain; it remains controversial. In today's environment, much weight is put behind a broader version of the Tobin tax—the global tax on financial transactions (GTFT). At this time, in November 2009, it remains one of four to five options up for review. UK Prime Minister Gordon Brown (to reduce risky behavior of banks and fund future bank rescues) even pushed this tax for priority consideration at the recent November G-20 Finance Ministers' gathering at St. Andrews. Germany and France reaffirmed their support.

Others included the outspoken German Finance Minister Peer Steinbrück (to ensure equitable burden-sharing), the Finance Ministers of Brazil and Egypt (to help developing nations during financial crises), the International Monetary Fund (IMF)—lately more lukewarm (to prefinance a bailout fund), and economists including John Williamson, Stanley Fischer, Dani Rodrik, and the US Economic Policy Institute (to raise US$100–$150 billion a year to "recoup" from the US financial services industry). Professor Tobin would be pleased that the proposal is finally being seriously evaluated.

To Tobin or Not to Tobin

Benefits

Three justifications come to mind: (1) to raise revenue for multilateral development (to partly offset the amount of damage the recent financial crisis had inflicted)—to be shared between nations and multilateral institutions in a manner that renders the tax attractive to all; (2) to reduce excessive destabilizing volatility in financial markets, which have often demonstrated to have functioned less optimally—to at least get the financial industry ("Wall Street") to bear its share of the burden in getting "Main Street" to bail it out; and (3) to enhance independence of action taken by monetary and fiscal policy makers in defending the integrity and solvency of the global financial system; recent developments have demonstrated again the very significant political and economic costs exacted by financial crises.

The September 2009 G-20 Summit in Pittsburgh weighed in on this global tax—to at least evaluate how the financial system could make a "fair and substantial" contribution toward paying for the burden associated with massive government intervention thus far to repair the global financial system. In the end, to protect taxpayers from future bailouts, there should be no "free-ride." Of course, the revenue prospects for host nations and multilaterals can be staggering. Today, based on a very low tax rate of 0.05 percent, and depending on how wide the financial transactions are defined to capture, a yield of up to US$1 trillion a year (or less than 2 percent of world gross domestic product) is feasible. But raising revenue should not be the primary concern. Nor should it outweigh other aspects of the tax, namely adverse market impact, distortionary effects, and systematic regulatory risks.

Reservations

Three important reservations in implementing and enforcing the GTFT include (1) political feasibility—to the extent feasibility of the tax depends on whether nations want to participate, the key issue remains political will: Why should they support? As demonstrated at the recent St. Andrew's gathering, the US Treasury secretary was reported to have stated that such a "day-by-day" tax on speculation was "not something we're prepared to support"; Russia, Canada, and the European Central Bank are also not keen on this idea; (2) market migration—geographical coverage is unlikely to be complete because of leakages through tax havens, and so on; and (3) asset substitution—the more limited its coverage, the greater the omission and substitution effects; should derivatives be also included? As a practical matter, the GTFT should not create a supernational taxation power. Instead, government will levy it nationally. Even British Prime Minister Gordon Brown took particular care to advocate the need for global coordination and cooperation with existing multinational agencies (IMF and World Bank).

What, Then, Are We to Do?

As I see it, the latest variant of the Tobin tax (i.e., the GTFT) is an idea deserving careful analysis and serious political consideration. Realistically, Tobin's idea is still very much a rough diamond—it needs to be thrashed out more fully and then polished so that it will be both technically foolproof and politically attractive enough. More spadework must be undertaken before we can expect the international community to develop the needed confidence, and an appetite for it. At the same time, powerful forces are at work against its adoption, with attractive options available for compromise. In the end, it is still possible this levy could be put back on the shelves, as it was in the 1970s and 1990s. Will it remain a curiosity of economic history?

Kuala Lumpur
November 12, 2009

Note

1. First published on November 14, 2009.

CHAPTER 79

Dubai: Or Is It Bye-Bye?[1]

After two difficult years, most come away with the thought that financial markets the world over should have stabilized. Sure, the extraordinary steps taken to stop the panic resulted in flooding the global system with trillions of US dollar liquidity. In all, governments had spent, lent, or guaranteed close to US$12 trillion, and central banks held interest rates to near zero to end the financial crisis. Even so, as to be expected, most of the previous excesses were never quite worked off. They can't just make all these excesses go away—no thanks to continuing flows of cheap money around the world. So, we should not be surprised to see overleveraged Dubai stumble toward the end of November 2009. Inevitably, it had to cut its debt burden down to size. Around the world, financial markets quivered. Investors—mainly banks—found themselves in a flare-up they feared would happen, but had hoped would not.

Dubai's Caustic Lesson

The problems of Dubai are already well known. A property play that turned into a bubble that burst. The boom was fueled by easy credit, a poorly regulated market overrun by speculators, and cheered on by a go-go Dubai during the heyday of the prefinancial crisis. Since then, residential real estate prices have slumped by nearly 50 percent. Across the United Arab Emirates (UAE), it has been reported that some US$450 billion of construction work had been scrapped. It all culminated in the recent announcement by Dubai World, the UAE's largest state-owned conglomerate, to impose a six-month standstill on debt repayments. Because Dubai is not rich in oil, it borrowed heavily to fund its grand ambitions.

Nakheel, a government-sponsored developer, used part of these funds to develop the Palm Islands and other spectacular land reclamation projects. On December 14, 2009, Nakheel is due to repay US$3.52 billion to holders of its Islamic "sukuk" bond. This is part of the US$26 billion debt that its parent, Dubai World, is seeking to restructure. In all, Dubai's sovereign and its state-controlled companies' debt could reach US$80 billion, in excess of the size of its gross domestic product (GDP) (nobody knows for sure). Viewed in perspective, Dubai makes up less than 0.1 percent of the global economy, and the UAE, just 0.4 percent of outstanding global cross-border lending.

What caught investors "feeling wrong and wrong-footed" were reports that (1) Dubai's ruler had only weeks earlier assured investors that enough funds would be raised to meet "current and future obligations"; (2) the emirate had only hours earlier raised US$5 billion from two state-controlled banks in Abu Dhabi, having raised US$10 billion from this neighbor in February; and (3) banks in particular felt sure that the emirate would make good on publicly traded papers (particularly Nakheel's sukuk) rather than lose face and damage the reputation of the Gulf as a business and financial hub. So, investors can no longer take the "UAE umbrella" for granted—in the end, there are widely reported hints that it may still "pick and choose when and whom to assist."

Over the past year, moral hazard appears to be firmly embedded throughout the global financial system. So for bankers, Dubai offers an expensive lesson. Most had expected the government to stand behind its "ward" (Dubai World). In the wake of the Dubai debacle, it looks like Dubai is set to make investors share the pain, rather than foster moral hazard. Indeed, lenders are still reeling from the spectacular Saudi defaults not so very long ago. Fair enough, Dubai World was technically not government backed. But investors had perceived it to be so and acted accordingly. Dubai's repudiation of such an implicit guarantee leaves a bitter taste in the mouth of most investors—something they are unlikely to forget any time soon.

Tail Risk Resurfaces

Credit worries are back. Two years ago, few investors would worry about "fat-tail" risk. This refers to the occurrence of seemingly remote risky events, carrying with it blotted (hence, fat) devastation. The rest is history. But the lesson is not easily unlearned. Indeed, the mere sound of a crack can get everyone running for cover. Little wonder for the knee-jerk reactions to recent developments: from the sharp rise in risk premium for Greek bonds and Turkish as well as Hungarian credit default swaps (following their profound budget mess) to the Dubai debacle when investors fled from risks. Wall Street tells us government debt is "risk free." Don't you believe it. History is littered with sovereign defaults. The charade continues. This week, in early December 2009, reality came home to roost. Greece's and Spain's sovereign credit ratings were downgraded. Even the United Kingdom and United

States are not spared. Moody's ratings for them were set apart from other top-rated sovereigns, calling them "resilient" and not "resistant" (a label kept for Germany, France, and Canada). In Dubai, lack of confidence continued to spread—Tuesday's (December 8) tumble in Dubai's stocks wiped out its whole year's gain; Moody's downgraded six Dubai government-controlled companies, citing lack of government support. The carnage goes on.

The moral of the Dubai saga is clear and twofold:

1. Nasty fiscal shocks are not confined to just emerging nations; markets soon realized that debt fundamentals in Dubai are no different from those in developed nations, even the United Kingdom and United States. Indeed, the line between emerging and developed is increasingly blurred.
2. The rush to judgment that stability has returned is premature; fundamental imbalances created during the crises (e.g., excess leverage) have yet to disappear. Beneath it all, huge vulnerabilities remain.

The Dubai saga is a welcome wake-up call.

Sukuk's Dilemma

No doubt, the problems of Dubai will have a chilling impact on the market for sukuk (Islamic) bonds. These are a class of financial instruments that complies with Islamic investment principles, which prohibit the payment of interest (ironically, bonds theoretically are associated with interest payments). In the past decade, the market for such US dollar–denominated debt-like instruments has gained popularity. This year, US$19 billion was raised in the international sukuk market—it peaked in 2007 with US$25 billion. The range of issuers, investors, and instruments has since widened and deepened. About a month ago, General Electric's financing arm became the first Western industrial company to issue a sukuk bond, for US$500 million. It attracted a new source of investors.

The debt standstill sought by Nakheel has thrown a spanner in the works. And so close to repayment date of December 14. In the past week, activity in sukuk bonds came to a virtual standstill in the face of its potentially biggest default. By any standard, sukuks are small potatoes in the bond world. Less than US$1 trillion of such-like debt is outstanding—smaller than the amount of new bonds sold by nonfinancial institutions this year alone. Nevertheless, it's a big deal since it is now unclear how sukuks can be restructured; it will be a test case for how well investors are protected, because these are viewed as quasi-sovereign credit (i.e., akin to government debt). There have been at least two defaults so far—one in Kuwait and the other in the United States by a small oil and gas company. At issue is whether investors can take possession of the underlying assets or are simply entitled to the assets' cash flow. There are no precedents in the Dubai courts. Further, sukuks are structured to comply with Islamic law but created under English law. Further complications can arise since Nakheel's assets are situated in the UAE. Moreover, investors have the benefit of Dubai World's guarantee, which enforcement is subject to some local law issues.

Be that as it may, the episode looks likely to be long drawn out. Bankruptcy in the UAE does allow for a protective moratorium, which can be a two-edged sword. Whatever the outcome, Dubai's action has done the sukuk market a great disservice. While Islamic finance wasn't at the root of Dubai World's problems, investor reaction so far in the face of delicate markets and an uncertain global recovery makes people nervous about the future. At the very least, short-term activity in sukuk will remain stalled. Credibility in the manner restructuring is being handled will determine the future. Indeed, investors are fast learning that no matter how buoyant potentials look, resources are not limitless.

Looking Past the Sandstorm

As it now stands, the Gulf markets are soft and under continuing pressure. To be fair, the structural underpinnings of these markets need to be viewed in perspective over the longer term. Lest it's forgotten, Dubai's hydrocarbon-rich neighbors—Saudi Arabia, Kuwait, Qatar, and Abu Dhabi—command two-thirds of the world's oil and 45 percent of gas reserves. Debt levels are very low and high oil prices have enabled them to accumulate more than US$1 trillion in reserves. A few key elements set the stage: These Gulf nations (1) need some US$2 trillion in infrastructure spending to diversify from oil. This fiscal spending can be financed out of current reserves (viable even at US$40 oil price); (2) offer strong benefits viz. no taxation, cheap feedstock, and virtually free land; (3) give rates of return on equity hovering historically around 25 percent, as against 10 to 15 percent in other emerging markets; and (4) provide access to low-cost funds made possible by accommodative monetary policy, with Gulf currencies pegged to the US dollar.

As with any market, risks loom large—it is always possible for oil prices to fall below US$40; geopolitical risks don't lend readily to being well managed; and opaque family groups dominate markets that are not really transparent. But these oil-rich nations are known to be basically conservative. No doubt, the Dubai excesses present lessons to be learned. Throughout history, nations have defaulted and lived to fight again, and succeed—even prosper.

What, Then, Are We to Do?

To regain confidence, a number of things need fixing: (1) call for fiscal transparency; (2) opaque family business groups need to heed the lessons of the Korean chaebols; and (3) clarity on the roadmap to government prudence over the longer term. This includes a credible plan on debt management once global recovery becomes sustainable. Dubai teaches an important lesson. Unpredictable, unsustainable, unclear, and uncertain policies are a no-no.

Kuala Lumpur
December 10, 2009

Note

1. First published on December 12, 2009.

CHAPTER 80

Whatever Volcker Wants, Volcker Gets?[1]

I first met Paul Volcker, 82, in the summer of 1986. He was then chairman, US Federal Reserve System (Fed). I was a rookie Fellow of the Eisenhower Exchange Program, the chairman of which was President Gerald Ford. Volcker was well known to me as the towering central banker (at 6 feet 7 inches, I'm not sure if he is the tallest economist around; late Harvard Professor Ken Galbraith was about there). He was better known as the daring but brutal inflation fighter of the late 1970s and early 1980s, at great cost in lost output and jobs. He was kind to me when I visited him in his office; he even gave me lunch. He was impressive and friendly and had time for a visitor (and fellow Harvard alumnus) who was completely at awe with what he does. We spent four hours together. We have since been in contact, off and on.

The Volcker Rule

Volcker is now back at center stage, after retiring from the Fed for some 20 years (me, for 16 years as I write). This time, introduced as the "tall guy behind me," President Barack Obama proposed a "simple and commonsense reform, which we are calling the 'Volcker Rule.'" Essentially, the new bank reforms would ban proprietary trading and prevent banks from "owning, investing in and sponsoring" hedge funds or private equity ventures. The proposals are intended to curb the size and spread of the biggest US banks. Volcker had pushed hard for such a version of the separation between commercial and investment banking, first brought into being by the Glass-Steagall Act of 1933, soon after the Great Depression. He considered this to be key in resolving the problem of banks getting "too big to fail" (TBTF). Indeed, it challenges the status quo that institutionalizes moral hazard and exposes governments to constant bailouts at taxpayers' expense. Volcker wants to limit this guarantee. His proposal was first mooted more than a year ago.

The Mayor and the Gunslinger

The Volcker Rule (VR) can be likened to separating a prosperous cowboy town's operations into the mundane mayor-like activities (safe and less-risky but unexciting) and the gunslinger-like operations (indulging in taking undue risks and speculation, such as credit default swaps [CDSs]), including proprietary trading for own profit, quite unrelated to serving their customers. The VR would provide government backing to the unexciting but safe town-mayors, but not to the speculative gunslingers. Thus, getting banks out of the gunslinger's business would eliminate the likes of Bear Stearns and Lehman Brothers from holding government hostage—a moral hazard every time. These gunslingers should be allowed to fail. Volcker rationalized that governments shelter banks because providing credit is critical to economic growth. As such, banks should be prevented from taking advantage of the safety net to make risky investments. For Volcker, banks are there to serve the public, and that's what they should do. Other activities can create conflicts of interest. They create unnecessary risks.

Wide-Ranging Support

Once called "big nanny" by Walter Wriston (chairman of Citicorp in the 1970s and 1980s), Volcker has a towering reputation worldwide. "He is brilliant, eminently logical, and steadfastly devoted to his work," said David Rockefeller (Volcker's boss in the late 1950s). According to an old friend, Gerry Corrigan (New York Fed president when Volcker was Fed chief), whenever Volcker was criticized, he never "flinched" simply because "he's a man of utter conviction and absolute integrity." That's why Volcker's ideas are widely respected. European Central Bank President Jean-Claude Trichet offered qualified support: It goes "in the same direction of our own position."[2] Along the way, he picked up other allies—notably John Reed (former chairman, Citicorp) and Stanley Fischer (ex-first deputy managing director, International Monetary Fund [IMF]). Support has also come from the chairman of the Financial Stability Board, the new president of the Swiss National Bank, and the French minister of Finance: "It is a very, very good step forward."

Mervyn King (governor, Bank of England) had been an early campaigner of a similar proposal to resolve the TBTF problem: "After you ring-fence retail deposits, the statement that no one else get bailed out becomes credible. . . . That is the argument for trying to create firewalls."[3] His version goes further than Volcker's: He wants government to break up the big banks into "utilities" and "casinos"—the former are safe, the latter to live and die in the markets. There is, of course, support from Professor Joseph Stiglitz (2001 Nobel Laureate in economics): "Banks that are too big to fail are too big to exist. . . . That means breaking up too-important-to-fail (or too-complex-to-fix) institutions."[4] The latest being Harvard Professor Niall Ferguson: "So far, there is only one credible proposal." Since then, George Soros has also come on board. (Postscript: As have five former US Treasury secretaries who have served both Republican and Democrat presidents, calling on Congress on February 22, 2010, to implement the VR to limit the size and trading of banks.)[5]

Deciphering the Volcker Rule

The United States desperately needs financial reform. Ironically, as a result of massive government support, banks as a whole are now doing reasonably well. This contrast of strong finance and a weak jobless economy in the early stages of recovery makes the politics of reform easy to understand. But, unemployment looms large. Voters in the United States feel betrayed by the banks and want to feel their anger has been heard. Yet, voters cannot be sold on technicalities. The VR has concerns in controversial technicalities. The best insight I have read in deciphering the VR is provided by two of (what I consider) London *Financial Times*'s best economic columnists, Martin Wolf and John Gapper. I have respect for Wolf, whom I have met occasionally at seminars run by Harvard's Martin Feldstein at the National Bureau of Economic Research. Wolf raises three pertinent questions: Are Volcker's proposals desirable, workable, and relevant?[6]

1. *Desirable?* Of course. Surely, banks should not be allowed to exploit the government's "guarantee" to make speculative investments with little economic benefits. The very idea of banks profiteering from activities from whose consequences they had to be rescued and of whose impact the public is still suffering is despicable. Nevertheless, Wolf thinks the VR is not the best way to go.
2. *Workable?* Here, many doubts arise. Where do you draw the line (and police it) between legitimate bank activities and activities unrelated to serving their customers? Various technical considerations begin to blur the line. Further, how is bank size to be measured? Definition technicalities get more complicated.

3. *Relevant?* Wolf argues persuasively that vast affiliated parts of the financial system that have evolved from deposit-taking are vital, and indeed, represent well-coordinated component parts of the entire system. These have become so interconnected that the system operates as one integral whole. Then, there is "shadow" banking (institutions with promises to repay liabilities on demand), which is vulnerable to a "run" as well. The list extends to money-market funds, finance companies, structured investment houses, securities dealers, and so on. Surely, this chain of shadow institutions can't be ignored in any reform exercise. Ironically, during the crisis, banks' investments in hedge funds, private equity, and even proprietary trading were not, at the core, what went terribly wrong.

Mr. Gapper argues, "Volcker has the measure of the banks."[7] For the first time, he states: "A government is attacking the size and complexity of the over-mighty institutions." Impractical? No way. Hedge funds and private equity can be readily hived-off from banks with access to the Fed window and Federal Deposit Insurance Corporation (FDIC) insurance. Granted the definition of proprietary trading can be technically tricky. But, in reality, banks know what a proprietary desk is. Indeed, Volcker assured US Congress that "bankers know what proprietary trading is and is not. Don't let them tell you different. . . . I don't think it's so hard." He emphasized: "What I want to get out of the system is taxpayer support for speculative activity."[8]

Mr. Gapper didn't think much of Wolf's idea that the VR would not fit outside the United States where Europeans are not only wedded to the universal bank model but love big banks. Hence, there will be difficulties in international coordination of regulation. This is an overreaction. Gapper argues that the VR does not prevent the investment houses from—indeed, they are already taking—big risks. What is important is for the US system to be reformed and made stable. The VR would not curb innovation or stop hedge funds and private equity from making money. Curbs on very large financial institutions are compatible with—indeed, can stimulate—a thriving and stable financial system.

It is noteworthy that Volcker himself concedes that the proposals would not have prevented the debacles at AIG and Lehman at the heart of the 2008 crisis. But he stated emphatically that not adopting the proposals would surely "lead to another crisis in the future."[9]

Can Big Banks Really Walk Alone?

Both Wolf and Gapper agree that the VR is not perfect—its implementation needs sharpening. As I see it, serious bank reform is a global problem. Other central banks should offer ideas. It's worth trying to forge reform that is smart and practical. Lest we forget, contagion risk and counterparty failure globally have been the main hallmarks of the crisis. Human nature being what it is, I don't think we have seen the last of "gung-ho" traders and their quants who just want to drive profits. Right now, such activity is already back to up-profits in some big banks. Since we don't (and won't) really learn, the separation of commercial banking functions from such high-risk activities is what the VR is all about.

I gather that the Organisation for Economic Co-operation and Development (OECD), a developed nations group, has also been looking at options.[10] One concerns structuring systemically important financial institutions (SIFIs) under a variant of nonoperating holding companies on a global basis, as follows: (1) parent is nonoperational—only raises capital and invests transparently in legally separate SIFIs; (2) profits are flowed up through parent to shareholders; (3) parent is not allowed to shift capital among subsidiaries in crisis and can't request special dividends to do so. Such a structure allows for the separation of prudential risks and use of capital. In this way, regulators and investors can spot potential weaknesses. It creates a non-subsidizing environment for the riskier business; and (4) in the event of failure, the regulator shuts it down without affecting its commercial banking sister—obviating the need for even "living wills." This offers an innovative, transparent way to achieve globally what both Volcker and King wanted but without being extreme. Whatever the final outcome, a right balance needs to be struck between an appropriate size that's conducive to benefit from purposeful diversification and strong global competition to meet sustainable consumer demands at reasonable cost.

What, Then, Are We to Do?

In the end, realistically, I can't see how the VR or its variants, including what the OECD is working on, can really prevent another crisis, human nature being what it is. History is full of repeats where greed eventually overwhelms prudence and common sense. Nevertheless, it could make one less likely, less often (we have had one every three years), and less costly if it did occur. To this, I think Winston Churchill would have added: Such a measure would make finance less proud but the industry more content.

Singapore
February 10, 2010

Notes

1. First published on February 13, 2010.

2. Jean-Claude Trichet, interview with the *Wall Street Journal* in Frankfurt, Germany, on January 26, 2010.

3. Mervyn King, governor, Bank of England. At a hearing before a Parliamentary Treasury Committee, on January 26, 2010, in London, United Kingdom.

4. Joseph Stiglitz, "Too Big to Live," commentary, *The Edge*, Malaysia (December 14, 2009).

5. Secretaries John Snow, Paul O'Neill, Nicholas Brady, George Schultz, and W. Michael Blumenthal wrote in a letter published by the *Wall Street Journal* (February 22, 2010).

6. Martin Wolf, "Volcker's Axe Is Not Enough to Cut the Banks Down to Size," *Financial Times*, London (January 27, 2010).

7. John Gapper, "Volcker Has the Measure of the Banks," *Financial Times*, London (January 28, 2010).

8. Paul Volcker, in a statement to the US Senate Banking Committee on February 2, 2010, in Washington, DC.

9. Ibid.

10. Adrian Blundell-Wignall, "How to Break Up the Banks," op-ed, *Wall Street Journal* (November 24, 2009).

CHAPTER 81

"Too-Big-to-Fail" and the Volcker Rule Faces Fresh Challenges[1]

The public still asks: What's this Volcker Rule we hear so often these days? I wrote about it on February 13, 2010 (Chapter 80, "Whatever Volcker Wants, Volcker Gets?"), not long after it was first proposed. It took the US Congress close to four years to make it operational. Even so, it remains controversial. I sense there is widespread interest and concern about too-big-to-fail (TBTF). So, here goes. To reduce risks of bank failure, the intention is to prevent banks from gambling with deposits, including small deposits guaranteed by the US federal government, Federal Deposit Insurance Corporation (FDIC). The resulting Volcker Rule (named after its proponent, Paul Volcker, former chairman of the US Federal Reserve Bank—Fed) prohibits "proprietary trading," that is, making bets with the banks' money purely for the bank's own gain rather than to serve its clients. US President Barack Obama described it as a "simple and commonsense reform to strengthen the financial system."

On December 10, 2013, as authorized by the 2010 Dodd–Frank law overhauling the regulation of US financial institutions, five different regulatory agencies (viz. the Fed; the Office of the Controller of the Currency [OCC]; FDIC; the Securities and Exchange Commission [SEC]; and the Commodity Futures Trading Commission [CFTC]) approved the Volcker Rule (VR) to come into force on April 1, 2014. Ironically, during the long 1,419 days of "sausage making" between conception and birth, the VR evolved finally into something far larger and more complicated than originally envisaged (the final version is reported to have 963 pages, with 2,826 footnotes and 1,347 questions, reflecting a preamble addressing public comments that will help guide its implementation).

The immediate impact is not expected to be too significant, since much was already anticipated. Most big US banks have by now eliminated the most obvious forms of proprietary trading. Indeed, Wall Street welcomed the certainty that the VR is now settled (more or less) to be not as burdensome as originally anticipated. Its effectiveness will depend on the enforcement by banking and market regulators. Banking-focused regulators (the Fed, OCC, and FDIC) work to ensure and monitor the safety and soundness of banks and the financial system, while securities regulators (the SEC and CFTC) work to protect investors and the broader smooth functioning of financial markets. They all bring different perspectives to their supervisory roles. So, interagency coordination becomes critical to its effective implementation.

The Volcker Rule

Although the Dodd–Frank reform legislation was passed in 2010, nearly two-thirds of its many other regulations remain incomplete. So, the VR can be regarded as the barometer for the overall strength of the entire law. The main objective, as I see it, is to prohibit regulated large banks from using customers' money to trade for their own gain. It is based on Mr. Volcker's simple idea: Don't let government-insured banks gamble in the securities markets. Taxpayers shouldn't be forced in the end to stand behind Wall Street's trading desks. The VR needs to be strict enough to prevent banks from making risky bets with their depositors' money. They enjoy the upside on the risks taken, while others (depositors and taxpayers) share the downside. This is aimed at preventing future trading blowouts on Wall Street.

The prohibition draws a bright line, making it clear that banks' business is about lending, not speculating. At its core, the VR distinguishes between trading that banks are allowed to do—to serve their customers and offset their own risks and the prohibited trading done solely for their own profit, known in practice as proprietary trading (one of Wall Street's most lucrative and riskiest activities). In so doing, the VR hopes to prevent the buildup of risky positions that nearly sank Wall Street in 2008.

But drawing the line has proved contentious. In the end, the VR will allow banks to assume their traditional role as market makers: It allows buying and selling securities if they can show that these deals are made to meet "reasonable expected near-term demands of customers and counterparties." This concession helps to preserve vital market liquidity. However, it opens up a loophole for banks to mask their proprietary bets as market making; banks to do proprietary trading in bonds issued by governments (including Treasuries and municipals), as well as bonds issued by foreign governments (another concession); banks to place trades meant to offset the risks posed by positions they hold—that is, run-of-the-mill hedging that can also resemble proprietary trading. The VR would prefer banks to tie each hedge to the risks of specific positions that hedge has taken.

In practice, however, there are few perfect hedges. So, banks resort to "portfolio hedges," to protect against broad economic risks or unspecified risks (a Black Swan event). Such hedges are deemed risky proprietary trading (JPMorgan Chase's "London Whale" trade, which cost it more than US$6 billion in losses, is instructive).[2] The VR now requires banks to identify the risks and then conduct technical "correlation analysis" and "independent testing" to ensure such hedging will "demonstrably reduce the risks." It also requires banks to conduct "ongoing recalibration of the hedges" to ensure they are not prohibited proprietary trading; banks to require their chief executives to annually attest that they have "in place processes to establish, maintain, enforce, review, test and modify the compliance program" to show they are not engaged in proprietary trading; banks to require traders engaged in market making and hedging not to be paid based on the profits made; banks to own not more than 3 percent of hedge funds and private equity funds; banks to be granted extension of time until July 2015 to comply; and "community banks" with less than US$10 billion in assets to be exempted.

"Too Big to Fail"

The VR was not meant to deal single-handedly with the dangers posed by large banks. Recent reports indicate that the VR did come out stronger than Wall Street had expected. That's good. But is it strong enough to prevent "too big to fail" (TBTF)? Lest we forget: JPMorgan Chase (JPMC), the largest US bank, had US$2.4 trillion assets as at June 30, 2013, and debts of US$2.2 trillion: US$1.2 trillion in deposits and US$1 trillion in other debt. The six largest US banks together owe US$8.7 trillion (about the size of China's gross domestic product [GDP]). Only a fraction of this represents loans.

Risk taking is a vital part of free enterprise—it's necessary for innovation and growth. Healthy enterprises rarely carry debts more than 70 percent of their assets. Many do with much less. Banks, in contrast, have liabilities exceeding 90 percent of their assets. JPMC's debt represents 91 percent of its assets. European Basel III rules allow banks to borrow up to 97 percent of their assets; proposed US requirement for the largest bank holding companies is up to 95 percent. It seems to me that if banks' equity (i.e., own money) is only 5 percent, even a small loss of 2 to 3 percent of assets could lead to a bank run! If a number of the big banks are distressed at the same time, systemic failure will ensue.

Conventional wisdom states that banks' high levels of borrowing are acceptable because banks are good at managing risks and regulators know how to measure them. Both failed to manifest in the 2008 crisis. Yet, we ignore the lessons. Recent scandals point in the same direction: JPMC's latest US$2.6 billion Madoff fraud settlement, coming on the heels of a string of legal penalties totaling US$20 billion on the sale of troubled mortgage securities and the "London Whale" trading debacle; HSBC's US$1.9 billion money-laundering fine; some of the biggest banks' (including Barclays, UBS, and Deutsche) more than US$5.8 billion fine for manipulating LIBOR; inappropriate sales of credit-card protection insurance that resulted in a US$2 billion settlement by British banks—they all suggest that big banks are also "too big to manage, control, and regulate."

Implicit guarantees of government support encourage banks to overborrow, take risks, and become TBTF. VR can help to lessen bank risks, and Dodd–Frank is supposed to spell an end to bank bailouts. Don't count on it. Historically, finance's share of the US economy has been about 4 percent. Today, it's easily twice that—at its peak, it was 9 percent. Finance's role has become pivotal. In the end, banks need to rely much more on equity and much less on borrowing. I understand there is now a serious move to raise the leverage (capital to assets) ratio to at least 6 percent (3 percent now under Basel III). Tougher leverage will force the largest US banks to hold more capital.

The 8 largest US banks' ratio averaged 4.3 percent (against 3.86 percent among 16 largest overseas banks); together, they hold nearly US$15 trillion in assets (about 90 percent of US GDP), making the United States more vulnerable than ever to their miscalculations and mistakes. I share the view of Professor Anat Admati (Stanford University) and Martin Hellwig in *The Bankers' New Clothes: What's Wrong with Banking and What to Do about It*" and Professor David Skeel (Pennsylvania Law) in *The New Financial Deal: Understanding the Dodd-Frank Act and Its (Unintended) Consequences*" that raising equity requirements substantially (as proposed by the US Brown–Vitter Bill) is the single best step for making banking safer and healthier.[3]

Potential Loopholes and Challenges

The VR will usher in change on Wall Street. Indeed, the way Wall Street does business has since changed in both the make-up of its trading units and its personnel policies. In anticipation, the pure proprietary trading units have long gone. The remaining businesses centered on the profit engine, fixed income, currencies, and commodities (Ficc) have been restructured and retooled, given the restrictions imposed by the VR. High-performing traders have moved on. Professional managers have moved in. The way the business is managed has also changed. Businesses that remain are likely to see a reduction in the peaks and troughs in Ficc's profitability. They will become more predictable, though less profitable in good years but also less prone to blowing up, as they did in 2008.

The changing of the guard is already in motion. As William Silber, author of Mr. Volcker's biography, *Volcker: The Triumph of Persistence*, said to the *Wall Street Journal* in New York on December 16, 2013: "If a firm like Goldman Sachs, which is now a bank, can't speculate, then the pendulum will swing." Indeed, the pendulum has been in motion for a while. Further, the VR will help improve the compensation culture of Wall Street, long based on profit sharing with traders. It now prescribes how traders are paid—they can only receive a discretionary bonus. No more rewards from prohibited proprietary trading.

The VR draws a line between everyday banking and Wall Street wheeling-dealing. Critics say the VR doesn't go far enough. On its part, Wall Street is expected to scour for loopholes to challenge it in court; they regard the VR as too severe, constricting the flow of capital so badly needed to oil the economy. Supporters want the VR to prevent the buildup of the kinds of risky positions that nearly sank Wall Street in 2008 and led to the recent US$6.2 billion "London Whale" trading loss at JPMC, resulting from a sprawling speculative position under the guise of hedging that spun out of control. Also, critics worry whether the VR is strict enough to force banks to stockpile securities only for customers and not mask their proprietary bets as market making or hedging. This appears to be one of the most challenging rules to get done in a balanced way.

Regulators say they have worked in good faith along this path. In the end, Treasury Secretary Jacob Lew sums it up best: "Regulators should err on the side of doing a little more, and then correct it if you've gone too far."[4] Nevertheless, unpleasant surprises have since emerged: (1) the American Bankers Association has raised concern that the VR unintentionally bars small "community banks" from investing in trust-preferred collateralized debt obligations that currently form a large part of their capital;[5] and (2) the US Chamber of Commerce has urged a rethink on the VR to avoid "unintended consequences," including "impeding the ability and increasing the cost of nonfinancial businesses to raise capital and manage risk." It "places the American economy at a competitive disadvantage."[6]

What, Then, Are We to Do?

The starting point of the VR is a good one—with a guarantee on small deposits, it makes good sense not to allow banks to gamble with their deposits. The ultimate aim is to stop taxpayers from having to bail out feckless financiers once again. The VR is good, even though imperfect—a good start toward getting banks back to being banks. The VR has lots of potential gray areas that banks may be able to exploit. Nevertheless, many believe that inventories of stocks, bonds, and derivatives are likely to get leaner, reducing the probability of them becoming a significant source of bank losses. Indications are that Wall Street's inventories have since shrunk considerably. But the VR may not be tough enough over time to stop banks from adding on, once again, excessive amounts of risky assets under the guise of market making or hedging. The VR provides considerable leeway.

Risks remain. Five years after the Lehman Brothers bankruptcy, we are no safer. TBTF continues. The lessons of the crisis have slipped by. Outgoing Fed Chairman Ben Bernanke has acknowledged that the TBTF problem has not been solved. The VR will help limit risks, but until banks are pushed to rely much more on money from the owners and shareholders to finance their loans and investments, TBTF will continue to haunt us, VR or no VR. That's today's reality. We have to learn to live with it.

Kuala Lumpur
January 9, 2014

Notes

1. First published on January 11, 2014.
2. After JPMorgan Chase & Company's more than US$6 billion loss in 2012—nicknamed after the bank's huge (hence, whale) positions taken out of its London office, which highlighted the perils of speculative trading.
3. Anat Admati and Martin Hellwig, *The Bankers' New Clothes: What's Wrong with Banking and What to Do about It* (Princeton, NJ: Princeton University Press, 2013); David Skeel, *The New Financial Deal: Understanding the Dodd–Frank Act and Its (Unintended) Consequences* (Hoboken, NJ: John Wiley & Sons, 2011).
4. Jacob Lew, speaking at the *Wall Street Journal*'s CEO Council Meeting in Washington, DC, on November 19, 2013.
5. In a motion filed on December 24, 2013, in federal court in Washington, DC, seeking urgently to suspend one part of the Volcker Rule.
6. In a letter dated December 4, 2013, to the five regulatory agencies involved, together with the US Business Roundtable and three other business trade groups in Washington, DC.

CHAPTER 82

LIBOR Scandal Fuss[1]

Since the outbreak of the LIBOR scandal, public reaction has ranged from the very basic, What's this LIBOR?, to the more mundane, How does it affect me? Some friends have raised more critical questions: Barclays appear to have manipulated LIBOR to lower it: Isn't that good? The problem first arose in early 2008: Why isn't it resolved by now? To demystify this very everydayness at which banks fix this far-reaching key rate, this chapter will be devoted to going behind the scandal—starting from the very basics about the mechanics of fixing the rate, to what really happened (why Barclays paid the huge fines in settlement), to its impact and how to fix the problem.

What's LIBOR?

The London Interbank Offered Rate (LIBOR) was first conceived in the 1980s as a trusty yardstick to measure the cost (interest rate) of short-term funds, which highly rated banks borrow from one another. Each day at 11 a.m. in London, the setting process at the British Bankers' Association (BBA) gets moving, recording submissions by a select group of global banks' (including three large US banks) estimates of the perceived rates they would pay to borrow unsecured in "reasonable market size" for various currencies and for different maturities. LIBOR is then calculated using a "trimmed" average, excluding the highest and lowest 25 percent of the submissions. Within minutes, the benchmark rates flash onto thousands and thousands of traders' screens around the world, and ripple onto the prices of loans, derivatives contracts, and other financial instruments worth many, many times the global gross domestic product.

Indeed, it has been estimated that the LIBOR-based financial market is worth US$800 trillion, affecting the prices that you and I and corporations around the world pay for loans or receive for their savings. Anyone with a credit card, mortgage or car loan, or fixed deposit should care about their rate being manipulated by the banks that set them. In the end, it is used as a benchmark to determine payments on the global flow of financial instruments. Unfortunately, it turns out to have been flawed, bearing in mind LIBOR is not an interest rate controlled or even regulated directly by the central bank. It is an average set by BBA, a private trade body.

In practice, for working purposes, LIBOR rates are set essentially for 10 currencies and for 15 maturities. The most important of these relates to the 3-month US dollar (i.e., what a bank would pay to borrow US$ for three months from other banks). It is set by a panel of 18 banks with the top 4 and bottom 4 estimates being discarded. LIBOR is the simple average (arithmetic mean) of what is left. All submissions are disclosed, along with the day's LIBOR fix. Its European counterpart, Euro Interbank Offered Rate (EURIBOR), is similarly fixed in Brussels. However, EURIBOR banks are not asked (as in LIBOR) to provide estimates of what they think they could have to pay to borrow—merely estimates of what the borrowing rate between two "prime" banks should be. In practice, "prime" now refers to German banks. This simply means there is in the market a disconnect between the actual borrowing costs by banks across Europe and the benchmark. Today, EURIBOR is less than 1 percent, but Italian banks (say) have to pay 350–400 basis points above it. Around the world, there would similarly be TIBOR (Tokyo Inter-Bank Offered Rate); SIBOR and its related SOR (Swap-Offered Rate) in Singapore; KLIBOR in Kuala Lumpur; and so on.

What's Wrong with LIBOR?

Theoretically, if banks play by the rules, LIBOR will reflect what it's supposed to—a reliable yardstick to measure what it costs banks to borrow from one another. The flaw is that, in practice, the system can be rigged. First, it is based on estimates, not actual prices at which banks have lent to or borrowed from one another. They are not transactions based, an omission that widens the scope for manipulation. Second, the bank's estimate is supposed to be ring-fenced from other parts of the bank.

But unfortunately, walls have "holes"—often incentivized by vested interest in profit making by the interest-rate derivatives trading arm of the business. The total market in such derivatives has been estimated at about US$554 trillion in 2011. So, even small changes can imply big profits. Indeed, it has been reported that each basis point (0.01 percent) movement in LIBOR could reap a net profit of "a couple of US$ million." The lack of transparency in the LIBOR setting mechanism has tended to exacerbate this urge to cheat. Since the scandal, damning evidence has emerged from probes by regulators in the United Kingdom and United States, including whistleblowing by employees in a number of banks covering a past period of at least five years. More are likely to emerge from investigations in other nations, including Canada, Japan, European Union, and Switzerland. The probes cover some of the largest banks, including reportedly Citigroup, JPMorgan Chase, UBS, HSBC, and Deutsche Bank.

Why Barclays?

Based on what was since disclosed, the LIBOR scandal has set the stage for lawsuits and demands for more effective regulation the world over. It has led to renewed banker bashing and dented the reputation of the city of London. Barclays, a 300-year-old British bank, is in the spotlight simply because it is the first bank to cooperate fully with regulators. It's just the beginning—a matter of time before others will be put on the dock. The disclosures and evidence appear damaging. They reveal unacceptable behavior at Barclays.

Two sorts of motivation are discernible. First, there is manipulation of LIBOR to trap higher profits in trading. Its traders—very brazenly—pushed its own money-market dealers to manipulate their submissions for fixing LIBOR, including colluding with counterparties at other banks. Evidence points to cartel-like association with others to fiddle LIBOR, with the view to profiteering (or reduce losses) on their derivative exposures. The upshot is that the bank profited from this bad behavior. Even Bob Diamond, the outgoing Barclays chief executive officer, admitted that this doctoring of LIBOR in favor of the bank's trading positions was "reprehensible." Second, there is the rigging of LIBOR by submitting "lowered" rates at the onset of the credit crunch in 2007 when the authorities were perceived to be keen to bolster confidence in banks (to avoid bailouts) and keep credit flowing, while "higher" (but more realistic) rates submission would be regarded as a sign of its own financial weakness. It would appear in this context—as some have argued—that a "public good" of sorts was involved. In times of systemic banking crisis, regulators do have a clear motive for wanting a lower LIBOR. The rationale behind this approach was categorically invalidated by the Bank of England. Like it or not, Barclays has since been fined £290 million (US$450 million) by UK and US regulators for manipulating LIBOR (£60 million fine by the UK Financial Services Authority is the highest ever imposed, even after a 30 percent discount because it cooperated).

Efforts at Reform

Be that as it may, LIBOR is something of an anachronism, a throwback to a time long past when trust was more important than contract. Concern over LIBOR goes way back to early 2008, when reform of the way it is determined was first mooted. BBA's system is akin to an auction. After all, auctions are commonly used to find prices where none exist. It has many variants: from the "English" auction used to sell rare paintings to the online auction (as in e-Bay). In the end, every action aims to elicit committed price data from bidders.

As I see it, a more credible LIBOR fixing system would need four key changes:

1. LIBOR must use actual lending rates.
2. False bidding must be outlawed (penalized)—bidders need to be committed to their price.
3. Nonbanks must be encouraged also to join in the process to avoid collusion and cartelization.
4. An outside regulator must intrusively monitor the process to ensure tougher oversight.

However, there are many practical challenges to the realization of a new and improved LIBOR. Millions of contracts that are LIBOR-linked may have to be rewritten. This will be difficult and a herculean exercise in the face of lawsuits and ongoing investigations. Critical to well-intentioned reform is the will to change. But with lawsuits and prosecutions gathering pace, the BBA and banking fraternity have little choice but to rework LIBOR now.

As I understand it, because gathering real data can often pose real problems especially at times of financial stress, the most likely solution could be a hybrid. Here, banks would continue to submit estimated costs, but would be required to back them with as many actuals as feasible. To be transparent, they might need to be audited ex-post. Such blending could offer a practical way out.

Like it or not, the global banking industry possibly faces what *The Economist* has since dubbed its "tobacco moment," referring to litigation and settlement that cost the US tobacco industry more than US$200 billion in 1988. Sure, actions representing a wide range of plaintiffs have been launched. But, the legal machinery will grind slowly. Among the claimants are savers in bonds and other instruments linked to LIBOR (or its equivalent), especially those dealing directly with banks involved in setting the rate. The legal process will prove complicated, where proof of "harm" can get very involved. For the banks, they face asymmetric risk because they act most of the time as intermediaries—those who have "lost" will sue, but banks will be unable to claim from others who "gained." Much also depends on whether the regulators "press" them to pay compensation—or, in the event legal settlements get so large as to require new bailouts (for those too big to fail), to protect them. What a mess.

What, Then, Are We to Do?

Eighty years ago, banker J. P. Morgan Jr. was reported to have remarked in the midst of the Great Depression: "Since we have not more power of knowing the future than any other men, we have made many mistakes (who has not during the past five years?), but our mistakes have been errors of judgment and not of principle."[2] Indeed, bankers have since gone overboard and made some serious mistakes, from crimes against time-honored principles to downright fraud. Manipulating LIBOR is unacceptable. So much so bankers have since lost the public trust. It's about time to rebuild a robust but gentlemanly culture, based on the very best time-tested traditions of banking. They need to start right now.

Kuala Lumpur
August 23, 2012

LIBOR Scandal Revisited[3]

"The system is broken and needs a complete overhaul," declared Mr. Martin Wheatley, head of UK Financial Services Authority, as he delivered the 10-point plan to fix LIBOR.[4] His tough job is to restore confidence, since more than US$300 trillion of contracts and loans today, from US mortgages to Malaysian US$ bonds to Japanese interest-rate swaps, refer to LIBOR. As far as I can gather, the Wheatley Review proposals comprised:

- Oversight by a new panel (likely to be the Financial Conduct Authority, a new regulator to be created in 2013).
- "The British Bankers' Association . . . should take no further role in the administration and governance of LIBOR. . . . The new administrator should be appointed through a competitive tender process."
- LIBOR (meant to reflect rates at which banks borrow from one another) will be based on actual borrowing transactions.
- Banks contributing data used to calculate the rates will be subject to audit.
- LIBOR rates set daily will fall to 20 from 150. Infrequently traded rates will be phased out; infrequently used maturities will be ended.

- More banks will participate in submitting borrowing rates.
- A more transparent pricing mechanism is to be adopted to ensure rates are credible and robust.
- Authority is being sought to criminalize the manipulation of rates.
- Regulators will draw up a set of overarching principles to underpin construction and calculation of all sorts of financial yardsticks used to determine price of assets, performance of indices, and obligations due from different parties in financial contracts.
- Work will be undertaken by international organizations, benchmark sponsors, regulators, and others to ensure associated important benchmarks are appropriately robust and credible.

The British government and the Bank of England have since declared that the changes should proceed without delay.

Concern continues to be expressed that LIBOR may still be manipulated, since in a financial crisis, banks will be reluctant to risk lending to other institutions so that the process will still have to rely on some level of judgment when hard data are not available. On such occasions, there just isn't enough transaction data to calculate LIBOR. Furthermore, implementation problems will need to be resolved. Existing contracts based on LIBOR face many issues when the new system is switched on, including those involving the calculation and payment of interest, and asset values, which could result in out-of-pocket losses; legal suits can arise for "breaking" contracts; then, the consequences of unanticipated changes, and so on. Nothing is perfect. Let the changes begin, and soon.

Kuala Lumpur
October 4, 2012

Postscript: LIBOR Rigging Scandal: Action at Last[5]

It has dragged on for seven years. Much uncertainty remains. I first wrote about it in the first section of this chapter, "LIBOR Scandal Fuss," and subsequently with a follow-up section, "LIBOR Scandal Revisited." Readers are still interested; they now ask: What's going on, since the scandal affects borrowers and bondholders and eventually, taxpayers (a matter of moral hazard)? One reader was most blunt: Am I still being screwed?

As far as I can gather, at least 12 enforcement agencies in the United States, Canada, Europe, Japan, and Singapore are examining whether bankers and dealers/brokers colluded to rig LIBOR—the benchmark interest rate used for some US$350 trillion worth of financial products today—and other widely watched benchmark rates to boost profits for their in-house trading positions or for personal gain. Regulators have been scrutinizing whether certain banks submitted artificially low rates to mask their own mounting financial woes during difficult times in 2007–2008 and beyond. Very simply, LIBOR, EURIBOR, KLIBOR, TIBOR, SIBOR (the Singapore equivalent used to price debt ranging from term loans to mortgages), as the main rates are known, are supposed to reflect daily measures of how much banks are paying to borrow US dollar, euro, yen, and other major currencies from one another for preset lengths of time.

Rigging

For the past 28 years, the rate-setting process has offered an indication of the overall health of the financial system. The benchmarks also served as a point of reference for interest to be paid on many financial products, including bonds and mortgages. Because these rates are derived from banks' estimates and not actual transactions, banks have the incentive in times of stress to "lowball" their submissions (i.e., to deliberately use low rates to deceive the market) in order to appear healthier.

To date, three large international banks (Barclays, UBS, and Royal Bank of Scotland) have been fined in total over US$2.5 billion by US, UK, and Swiss regulators for LIBOR rigging. More than a dozen financial firms and individuals are still under scrutiny as part of the worldwide probe. It's widely reported that Dutch lender Rabobank, the United Kingdom's Lloyds Banking Group, and London-based interdealer broker ICAP Plc have also settled. It is now clear that LIBOR has been really "readily and pervasively rigged."[6]

EURIBOR

EURIBOR (pronounced "yur-eye-bore"), the euro interbank offer rate— LIBOR's lesser-known European cousin, is similarly subject to widespread efforts by banks to rig it. The European Banking Federation (EBF), comprising 31 national banking associations, created EURIBOR in 1999. By the early 2000s, it had become the basis for an estimated US$250 trillion of financial contracts. It is trying to avoid the fate of the British Bankers' Association (BBA), which run LIBOR in London. However, unlike LIBOR (based on estimated borrowing costs of 18 banks), EURIBOR is derived from more than 40 banks based on how much it costs a theoretical "prime bank" to borrow—hoping thereby to avoid any deliberate understatement of rates to conceal its financial problems.

But this didn't make EURIBOR tamper-proof—it didn't stop the likes of Barclays and UBS from manipulating it. Also, unlike the Bank of England, the European Central Bank relies on EURIBOR as a data point in setting eurozone's monetary policy. Governments, institutions, and individuals borrow based on EURIBOR. Europe's top banking and market regulators have since directed EBF to strengthen its governance and supervisory framework.

Spillover Impact

LIBOR rigging has since turned out to be the tip of the iceberg. The probe into dealings of assets from derivatives to foreign exchange showed that wherever opportunities arise, someone will always try to rig the benchmark rates. The Monetary Authority of Singapore (MAS) had sanctioned in mid-June 2013, 20 banks at which 133 traders tried to manipulate SIBOR, and ordered them to set aside as much as US$9.6 billion in total.[7] In addition, the United Kingdom's market regulator, the Financial Conduct Authority (FCA)—which oversees markets and prosecutes financial crimes in the United Kingdom—is reported to be looking into potential manipulation in the US$4.7 trillion a day foreign exchange market. This is by far the biggest in the financial system but also the least regulated because transactions occur outside exchanges.

Rigging in this market has the potential to affect the buying power of consumers, while manipulation of rate benchmarks can distort prices and raise the cost of homes, cars, or any products purchased with borrowed money. Furthermore, while benchmark indices in securities are little known to the public, their influence extends to trillions of dollars in securities and derivatives. I also understand that regulators are probing the ISDAfix, a measure used in the US$370 trillion interest rate swaps market, as well as how prices of some oil products are set.

The International Organisation of Securities Commissions (IOSCO)—a Madrid-based group that harmonizes global market rules, has since identified a set of benchmarks that could impair the global economy if they were found to be manipulated. Along with LIBOR, ISDAfix, and energy market prices, IOSCO has flagged measures used in the market for overnight lending and repurchases, equities, bonds, and alternative investments such as hedge funds. IOSCO is expected to propose guidelines to improve transparency and oversight for such benchmarks.

New LIBOR Administrator

After revelation of market rigging besmirched the reputation of London, the financial center, the United Kingdom's FCA assumed the responsibility to regulate LIBOR in April 2013 as part of the overhaul. The British Treasury has since announced on July 9, 2013, that New York Stock Exchange's Euronext would replace the BBA as the new administrator and supervisor of LIBOR.[8] "This change will play a vital role in restoring the international credibility of LIBOR," according to Baroness Sarah Hogg, chair of the independent Tendering Advisory Committee for LIBOR. Supervision will still be based in London.[9] This was one of the principal recommendations of the Wheatley Review, which was set up in June 2012 in the wake of the LIBOR probe. The New York–based Euronext already operates the London International Futures and Options Exchange (LIFFE), Europe's second largest derivative exchange, which offers derivatives based on LIBOR.

What, Then, Are We to Do?

LIBOR has come to stand for everything that is wrong with the banking system. Sir Mervyn King, former governor of the Bank of England, is reported to have quipped that LIBOR is "the rate at which banks do not lend to each other."[10] Indeed, benchmark rates (like LIBOR) that are not anchored in observable transactions entered into at arm's length between buyers and sellers, undermines market integrity and leaves the financial system with rates that are prone to misconduct. Since the 2007–2008 crisis, there has been so little interbank lending that the LIBOR numbers have often become imaginary—obscure rates like Singapore dollar for nine months are just simply made up, since typically there are no trades. Manipulation was easy. Reform is more difficult.

The UK Parliamentary Commission on Banking Standards recommended in June 2013 that: (1) manipulation of LIBOR and other financial benchmark rates be made a criminal offense; and (2) the regime be reinforced by a new "senior persons" arrangement that ascribes designated bank functions to a specific individual who would be held personally liable when things go wrong: "Top bankers dodged accountability for failings on their watch by claiming ignorance or hiding behind collective decision-making," which is unacceptable.[11] This stand is certainly tougher than what is now on offer in Wall Street or other financial centers.

Coming in close is Singapore, where MAS has now proposed criminalizing such offenses and forcing the "administrators and submitters of systematically important benchmark rates to become licensed," starting with SIBOR and SOR.[12] The intention is to "enhance the integrity of benchmarks set in Singapore." Granted, the idea of putting rogue bankers and brokers behind bars is politically most appealing. But actually putting them there remains a huge challenge in practice. Still, we need to do the right thing.

Kuala Lumpur
September 1, 2014

Notes

1. First published on August 25, 2012, as "The LIBOR Fuss."
2. "The LIBOR Affair—Banksters," *Economist* (July 7, 2012), p. 12.
3. First published on October 6, 2012, as "LIBOR Revisited."
4. Martin Wheatley, *The Wheatley Review of LIBOR: Final Report* (London: The Crown, September 28, 2012).
5. First published on September 13, 2014.
6. Gary Gensler, chairman, US Commodity Futures Trading Commission, at a conference in New York on February 27, 2013.
7. Monetary Authority of Singapore, in a statement on June 16, 2013, in Singapore censuring banks for manipulating Singapore's SIBOR, SOR, and other financial benchmarks.
8. UK Treasury, in an announcement in London on July 9, 2013.
9. Sarah Baroness Hogg, chair, Tendering Advisory Committee for LIBOR, and chair, Financial Reporting Council, United Kingdom, in an announcement in London on July 9, 2013.
10. Mervyn King, former governor, Bank of England. Quoted by James Mackintosh in the *Financial Times*'s "Short View" column on May 2, 2013.
11. UK Parliamentary Commission on Banking Standards, London, announcing its recommendations on June 19, 2013, in London of measures to curb manipulation of global financial market benchmarks.
12. Boon Ngiap Lee, assistant managing director at the Monetary Authority of Singapore, announcing new proposals on July 29, 2014, in Singapore to regulate financial benchmarks.

CHAPTER 83

Wall Street Stock Market Rigged: HFT "Cheetahs" Only Take 13,000ths of a Second to Turn a Profit[1]

Iam inundated with requests to help unravel the mysteries surrounding high-frequency trading (HFT). The Commodities Future Trading Commission (CFTC) calls its traders (HFTs) "cheetahs"—they are always first to the kill in the markets: "If markets are going to be efficient and effective and less volatile, we need to cage the cheetahs."[2] Most readers are not familiar with their dealings—who are they? How different are they in making deals? Is what they do legal? Do they play fair? and so on.

Recent interest in them was generated by Michael Lewis's new book, *Flash Boys—A Wall Street Revolt*, which I read recently while in Melbourne.[3] Lewis is doubtless a compelling storyteller. His new nonfiction thriller unfolds the complex, fascinating world of this largely invisible market icon. Indeed, he alleges that the enabling policies of Wall Street exchanges and regulators did little to discourage what HFTs do best. More bluntly, Lewis (of *Liar's Poker* and *The Big Short* fame) claimed on CBS's *60 Minutes* in early April that the United States' $22 trillion stock market is rigged by HFTs. It's not surprising that some Wall Street titans, including Charles Schwab (founder of the old, established discount brokerage house), agreed, describing the practice of HFT as "a cancer undermining confidence in the free enterprise system."[4]

To be fair, other high profiles on Wall Street also insist that few investors are actually hurt by the activities of HFTs; in fact, these "New Barbarians" do have redeeming features, including injecting competition, generating market liquidity, and lowering transaction costs.

As I see it, in a market-based competitive environment, any violation of the spirit of the rules undermines the larger game, regardless of how few investors are directly or indirectly hurt by HFTs. Imagine a similar defense by an Olympic gold medalist's illegal use of performance-enhancing drugs, which, after all, do not hurt a large number of other athletes. Bringing intensive competition does not automatically bring about ethical performance. As far as I am concerned, the absence of strong principles and sound enforcement often lead to criminal-like behavior and lame rationalization. It is a pity that financial markets sometimes reward malfeasance rather than merit. However, it's good to know that regulators have since showed renewed interest in them. Both US and New York State Attorney Generals and the Securities and Exchange Commission (SEC) have started to target their investigations at the relationship between stock exchanges and HFTs to determine whether it violates insider trading and market manipulation laws ("Insider Trading 2.0"), or brings about a level playing field.

The Vocabulary

Use of certain terms defines the manner current literature is written:

- **Algorithmic trading**—or automated trading; the use of electronic platforms to execute trading orders in a predetermined, robot-like manner, often without human intervention. HFT represents a special class of such trading.
- **High-frequency trading**—uses highly sophisticated technological tools (including drones) and computer algorithms to very rapidly trade securities. They exploit an arsenal of lightning-speed computing, using high-powered servers, ultrafast fiber-optic cables, and a vast trove of microwave transmission towers to reduce trade execution time to microseconds ahead of everyone else to capture tiny price changes. HFTs can close a deal in 13,000ths of a second—a blink of the eye! HFT takes different forms: (1) paying exchanges for faster access to data on order flows to give HFTs a head start; and (2) using algorithms to analyze unfilled orders to enable HFTs to trade stocks ahead to take advantage of pending price changes. Profits from HFT have been reported to be in the region of US$1.25 billion for 2014 as a whole, down 35 percent from 2013 and 74 percent lower than the peak of US$5 billion in 2009. HFT accounted for 51 percent of total stock trading on Wall Street in 2012, against 61 percent in 2011.
- **Flash crash**—a very rapid and deep fall in stock prices occurring within a very short time and recovering just as quickly. It last occurred on May 6, 2010, when a US$4.1 billion trade on Wall Street resulted in the Dow Jones Industrial Index falling over 1,000 points and then quickly bouncing back—all over in 15 minutes.
- **Front running**—closing a deal on own account, taking gains from unfair advantage of advance inside knowledge of pending orders

from clients and of access to an ultrafast network revealing specific trades other people are trying to make. Akin to insider trading, it's illegal except when HFTs do it.

■ **Dark pools**—private forums or exchanges for trading securities that are not open to the public; usually used for large off-market block trades, so that investors don't have to show their hand until the deal is done.

■ **Lit-pools**—unlike dark pools, here, bids and offers are transparent to all.

■ **Insider trading**—a misuse of confidential information for one's own benefit, which constitutes a breach of fiduciary duty. It's illegal.

■ **Layering or spoofing**—a form of market manipulation; orders are made for the appearance of activity to induce others to deal, only to be canceled later.

■ **Pinging the markets**—multiple orders are sent out to determine whether any will be filled, to gauge the share's direction; 90 percent are then canceled.

Wall Street Is Rigged

Mr. Lewis contends that certain firms have built technical advantage in terms of a few microseconds to trade ahead of others to reap unfair profits. Investors realize that whenever they order to buy or sell, the price just moves against them as though someone is one step ahead. That's HFTs at work—their edge emanates from two sources, exploiting: (1) time differences (investor wanting to deal signals the broker, who searches exchanges for the best price; but order arrives at different exchanges at separate times—HFTs steps in to arbitrage; they race ahead, buy the stock and sell it back for a bit more than the investor had hoped to pay—all in a matter of microseconds, millions of times a day to millions of investors); and (2) the usage of dark pools (HFTs are allowed access for a fee to the flow of orders in order to prey on investors).

So Mr. Lewis claims HFTs rig the stock market. Their algorithm-driven real-time trading works like the old Wall Street scam of front running, except it's entirely legal—an unintended consequence of well-intentioned SEC Regulation NMS 2005, which discontinued the long-standing practice of going for the "best execution" of a trade in favor of the "best price" for the client. Technological advances meant the best price in the exchanges is as determined digitally over milliseconds.

In 2005, 85 percent of US stock market trading was done on New York Stock Exchange, the rest on Nasdaq. By 2008, there were 13 different exchanges, mostly stacks of computer servers in Chicago and New Jersey. Critics say HFTs make markets less stable and more volatile because of their speed and high volume. Its technology architecture has brought about a flash crash and other market hiccups.

HFT, an Unfair Game

HFT's problem is that its business model doesn't fit comfortably into classical theories of securities fraud used to pursue misconduct. There are five types of abuses:

1. **Insider trading (ITG)**—HFT appears to fall outside the ban on ITG as currently defined because firms pay exchanges for access to order-flow information; no laws are violated since data is legitimately purchased.
2. **Front running**—Mr. Lewis likens HFT to "computerized scalping," allowing firms with the fanciest software and speediest machines to front-run (i.e., where a broker buys or sells before executing a client's order). Since HFTs trade on their own account, they have not traded ahead of their clients. It is paradoxical that exchanges profit from selling access to data, which are then used for trades akin to front-running, in the face of rules that clearly prohibit brokers from this practice.
3. **Layering or spoofing.**
4. **Pinging the market**—such market manipulation (MM) in layering and pinging is being cracked down. Proving MM, including wire-fraud statutes, means showing either an intent to artificially affect stock prices, or to defraud others: (1) HFTs seek out the best price to trade ahead of others, but not to drive the price up or down; and (2) proving intent to defraud requires depriving the victim of property; indeed, HFTs make split-second price decisions that have nothing to do with the shares' underlying value.
5. **Other scams**—SEC allows HFT firms to "colocate" their computers inside the exchanges to secure their speed advantage, and to buy data-feeds and have early peek at business news releases—data they can use to trade before others—all in the name of providing equal market opportunity.

Flash Boys concludes that HFTs are given unfair advantage to rig Wall Street. Ironically, the intent was to rig SEC rules to favor individual investors. IEX—an upstart alternative (HFT-proofed) exchange—now offers to "play fair" by staggering trade requests from other exchanges using "speed bumps" to level the playing field, thereby bypassing HFT electronic front running.

What, Then, Are We to Do?

HFTs appear to be off the hook in not violating current rules on permissible trading. Even so, it does not entitle them to use lightning speed to grab best prices. That's not right: The tactic smells to high heaven. Markets have simply become too complex, thereby creating advantages for the sophisticated like HFTs. Hence, the growing concern for regulatory distortions and conflicts of interest as regulators continued to flounder. To me, information is key. Regulations have to move toward more open and more transparent markets. When they do work, investors are better off. But we can't turn back the clock. HFT is here to stay. After all, we are all HFTs now.

The issue is how to resolve at least the perception of fairness in the markets without denying the benefits brought on by HFTs—improved liquidity through bringing in more buyers and sellers, narrower spreads between bids and ask prices, which in turn lower trading costs for all. In the end, regulators need to figure out a way to balance these benefits while combating the widespread view that markets are rigged. Markets need confidence to thrive. More needs to be done to calibrate the obligations and privileges of HFTs.

Fixing the market through leveling the playing field certainly helps, including creating more lit pools, making market data freely available on a timely basis to all; it's estimated there are 40 dark pools and 13 exchanges—either every market is allowed to discriminate or none should; and requiring brokers to protect the integrity of customers' orders. The goal is to ensure the benefit of speed does not overwhelm the benefits that come with transparency, liquidity, and stability. What's really needed is to simplify the operations of markets to restore confidence and instill fairness for all. European Union's soon-to-come curb on HFTs hopes to "strike a decent balance" so that HFT "doesn't cause instability and isn't a source of market abuse." We'll have to wait and see.

> Melbourne, Australia
> Kuala Lumpur
> April 17, 2014

Notes

1. First published on April 19, 2014.
2. Bart Chilton, commissioner of the Commodities Futures Trading Commission, in a speech entitled "Caging the Financial Cheetahs," to the American Soybean Association Legislative Forum in Washington, DC, on July 12, 2011.
3. Michael Lewis, *Flash Boys—A Wall Street Revolt* (New York: W.W. Norton, 2014).
4. Charles Schwab, as reported by Nancy Folbre, under "The Front-Runners of Wall Street," in the *New York Times* on April 7, 2014.

CHAPTER 84

Shadow Banking: The Global Bogeyman[1]

The lure of shadow banking is ever present. Governor Mark Carney, Bank of England, points to shadow banking in emerging markets as the greatest danger to the world economy.[2] That's serious. Indeed, I receive regular requests to unravel this phenomenon and why it creates such an all-round "con-attitude" every time the concept surfaces. Why did it evolve? How large and pervasive is it? Will it lead to instability and precipitate a systemic crisis? One thing is certain: Its operations are not necessarily shadowy; it's global, it's huge, it's fast-moving, it's popular, but it's poorly understood. It can be a powerful tool for good, but if badly managed, it can be explosive. Following are some definitions to clear the air.

■ **Shadow banking**—defined by the Financial Stability Board (FSB) (the United Kingdom's watchdog to preempt financial crises) as "lending by institutions other than banks."[3] In most countries, banks are the only authorized depository of savings with last-resort support by the central bank to stabilize the impact of their lending. In return, they are subject to lots of restrictive rules and regulations. But monies can and do bypass the banks from savers directly to investors. Viewed broadly, shadow banking includes any bank-like activity undertaken but not regulated, including via mobile payment systems by, for example, Vodafone or Alibaba's Alipay; technology-based bond-trading platforms; investment products sold by Chinese trusts and Black Rock. Academics' usage is narrower: forms of credit that closely track what regulated banks do, for example, direct lending, private equity, investment funds, and money and bond markets. But many bankers do regard any encroachment on their business as shadow banking.

- **Structured investment vehicle (SIV)**—a legal entity created by banks to sell loans repackaged as bonds. When loans go sour, banks are pulled down.
- **Money market funds**—attract spare short-term cash of firms and individuals because they give a high return and are deemed risk-free; once they realize these are not (because of poor liquidity management), they are prone to runs.
- **Chinese shadow banking**—encompasses a huge network of lending outside formal channels and beyond the reach of regulators, such as trusts, leasing, business-to-business lending, credit guarantee outfits, and money market funds, including online finance platforms, pawnshops, and microcredit. This vast volume of shadow banking activity was valued at US$4.4 trillion at end-2012 by the Chinese Academy of Social Sciences, or about one-half of China's gross domestic product (GDP). It accounted for one-third of new social lending in 2013. That's huge by any standard.
- **Peer-to-peer (P2P) lenders**—a series of websites that directly match savers with borrowers, usually via online auctions. Some platforms even slice, dice, and package the loans. This business is exploding globally. Value of loans chaperoned by, for example, the United Kingdom's Lenders Club and Prosper (the two biggest, with 98 percent market share) has doubled yearly since its launch in 2007; its total exceeds US$5 billion today. Their success is based mainly on marketing oomph.
- **Trust beneficiary rights products (TBRs)**—banks set up firms to buy loans from a trust; they then sell the income-flow rights from the loans to other banks, creating TBRs. This gives the illusion that the corporate loans are "safer," being lending between banks—they bypass regulatory requirements.
- **Entrusted loans**—involve cash-rich companies (mainly well-known state-owned enterprises—SOEs) lending to firms with poor credit standing using banks as intermediaries to get around regulations preventing such lending, exposing the banks to yet more risks. Such loans have become increasingly popular; they have risen sharply in the first quarter of 2014.

Market Niche

FSB has estimated that shadow banking accounts for about one-quarter of global finance. I think more. Shadow banks (SBs) proliferated because US and European banks came out of the recent financial crisis battered, bruised, and beset with heavy regulation, high capital requirements, and endless legal battles. They retrenched and became risk averse—cutting credit and downsizing operations. SBs moved in to fill the gap. Orthodox banks faced two real problems: (1) maturity mismatch (borrowing short and lending long); and (2) high leverage (building larger credit positions with minimum capital exposure). So they got into trouble and taxpayers had to bail them out because governments guaranteed deposits, and are just too frightened to let big banks fail lest they bring about systemic failure and deep recession. But growing economies need a consistent flow of credit. So, SBs move in. This should make on paper the financial system safer. Ironically, SBs are by definition unregulated. As such, once they really proliferate, they can be just as dangerous and then become unstable. So we are back to square one.

The real question: How to make SBs safe? No one knows for sure. But one thing is clear. Even Jamie Dimon (chief executive officer of JPMorgan Chase, the world's second largest bank by value) acknowledges that SBs have become a real competitor, which is a boon to consumers.[4] Like it or not, banks operate in a changing environment where the boundary lines are blurring and orthodox banks, with stricter rules and capital requirements, will have to compete for turf with non-banks, especially SBs. The outcome should be lower pricing and better services for their clients. To the extent that SBs can make the financial system safer, regulators should encourage the evolution of certain SBs to help widen access to social credit, for the benefit of both consumers and the economy as a whole. These desirable effects can be achieved by preventing the resurgence of the forms of SBs that brought about the last crisis. What's certain is that they should not be disguised as appendages of banks. Not ever again.

Trusts on the Run

At the recent Fudan University Shanghai Symposium, I drew attention that whether we like it or not, SBs are today a force to be reckoned with. Many of them are respectable, others less so because of their blatant attempts to sidestep the many rules about how much banks can lend to which companies and at what rates. Indeed, China's concern is centered on trusts. They offer savers, frustrated by the low caps placed on bank deposits, returns up to 10 percent. They on-lend at much, much higher rates to firms with poor access to banks because of their low credit standing or they are in frothy industries (property or steel or coal) that regulators have judged to be over-invested, so banks are "curbed" from lending. With the economy slackening, several trust products have since defaulted (e.g., China Credit Trust's "Credit Equals Gold No. 1 Trust Product" sold US$500 million through big banks), although most investors have got their money back, one way or another. I am told more than US$400 billion worth of trust products will mature this year. Regulators now worry that investors will lose faith in trusts, prompting a run that might, in turn, spark a crisis of confidence in the face of overall economic slowdown. Ironically, trusts are regulated by the same agency, China Banking Regulatory Commission, that supervises banks. So trusts are now subject to tightening oversight, forcing monies to flow to less closely watched but weaker SBs. Fear of a downward spiral in which pricking the property bubble or the collapse of commodity prices can lead to panic among SBs, pushing housing and commodity prices and overall growth down further. Something has to be done.

What, Then, Are We to Do?

The dilemma for China's regulators is that while the impact of maneuvers by SBs can spread to the real economy, many trust loans are secured with decent enough collateral, mainly property, so that losses should be manageable. The problem is timely access to liquidity. The real threat remains moving too forcefully by regulators to rein in shadow lending in the face of default, accidentally precipitating a run on SBs. The irony is that China can really benefit from the activities by certain forms of shadow banking, especially securitization. After all, China needs to develop deep capital markets, and here SBs can be managed to make finance safer. Unfortunately, shadow banking has already made quite a mess. Regulators have so far moved warily; in my view, allowing an occasional minor real default can do some good. Calibrating their activities is tricky. Realistically, there is no easy way out of this mess. Here, regulators need to be creative; more important, they have to be bold.

Shanghai, People's Republic of China
Kuala Lumpur
May 29, 2014

Notes

1. First published on May 31, 2014.
2. Mark Carney, Governor of the Bank of England, and Head of the Financial Stability Board, an international watchdog set up to guard against future financial crisis, responded, when asked in London recently to identify the greatest danger to the world economy. As reported in the *Economist* (May 10, 2014).
3. Ibid., p. 7.
4. As quoted in "Do it Right" of the *Economist* (May 10, 2014), p. 15, Special Report on "International Banking: Shadow and Substance."

Going Green

Going Green

CHAPTER 85

Blue Ocean That's Also Green[1]

For some time now, I have advocated that we need a sufficiently large second stimulus plan to meet two major policy objectives: Create (and retain) jobs for Malaysians by adding value (up the value chain) and launch a new initiative to restructure the economy (especially manufacturing) with a strong tinge of green. These are both short- and long-term goals. They overlap and are mutually reinforcing. Current circumstances call for it. We need to act now, because preparation takes time, and their multiplier effects are known to have a lag over time. But its announcement impact is immediate—and helps to build confidence that firm leadership is there for better prospects.

What does adding value mean in practice? The starting point is, of course, innovation. Empirical evidence has shown that, historically, innovation is needed to drive rapid, and, more importantly, sustainable growth. Simply put, innovation refers to new products or services, new business processes or systems, and organic changes that add value to whatever we do to create wealth and social welfare. We definitely need fresh thinking and approaches to add (i.e., create) value. That's what we should be doing.

In addition, if we can get to do all this and at the same time reduce waste and the carbon footprint, we can help protect the environment in a very sustainable way (go green). One practical way to go about doing this is to create blue oceans that are also green. W. Chan Kim and Renee Mauborgne pointed to a counterintuitive way forward in the *Harvard Business Review* by making competition irrelevant. They suggested, "In blue oceans, you invent and capture new demand, and you offer customers a leap in value while also streamlining your costs. Results? Handsome profits, speedy growth and brand equity that lasts for decades while rivals scramble to catch up."[2] In so doing, you should endeavor to go green at the same time.

Green Glove

Consider the humble single-use glove. On November 19, 2008, the 2008 European Medical Devices Green Excellence Product Innovation Award was presented to the world's first made-in-Malaysia reusable latex glove, which created a blue ocean of uncontested market space with a strong tinge of green. It introduced a unique system that will move glove supply from simple commodity-style purchasing to a full-service-based approach. According to the announcement by Frost and Sullivan (a global growth consulting company), this innovation will provide a consistently high-quality glove at lower overall cost, resulting in better quality control and reduced import burdens. At the same time, it addresses important issues of waste management and overuse of resources, especially in the healthcare arena.[3]

What lessons can we draw to help add value? Offering customers more value will, in the process, create a new business (and industry) through Schumpeter's innovative concept of creative destruction. Today, about 150 billion disposable gloves are used annually just once and then turned into more than a million tons of landfill (most are not biodegradable). Their sustainability is increasingly called into question with pressures from government, regulators, and green activists to reduce emissions and waste. The new reusable glove is expected to transform the conventional low-margin "box moving" glove supply into a high-value-added service business, delivered by local service providers with improved margins for all stakeholders in the supply chain and with built-in customer loyalty.

What makes this new product so unique in the value-added business? (1) It's *traceable* (using state-of-the-art information technology), providing vital data for statistical analyses and management use; (2) it's both *safe and clean* (100 percent pinhole tested, decontaminated, almost allergy free, and packed by size automatically—using newly patented scientific and engineering processes); (3) it's *patented* as reusable and flexible and of high quality (reconditioned at high speed for multiple use without sacrificing quality and integrity of the glove); (4) it's *green*, so it is also eligible for carbon credits (its cleaning uses novel innovative processes, slashes waste, and cuts energy use), while rejected gloves are shredded and sold for reuse in other forms (no more landfills); (5) it's *cost-effective*, providing significant savings for users; (6) its *logistics simplification and environmental consciousness* underlie the gloves' ability to translate conservationism into a successful business model; (7) its *cleaning processes* use a completely automated and information technology–managed glove-use reconditioning unit (GURU), including automatic packing; and (8) it's *virtually superbugs free* (helping hospitals better manage contamination and hospital-acquired infection from microbes and endotoxins).

Spreading Value Added

I know this list provides more than you really want to know about any glove. Nevertheless, the details are important since practically every element adds to its uniqueness. Each layer upon layer of added value helps to raise the efficiency of the production and supply chain in this new, uncontested market space. More important, the entrepreneur makes additional profits every time he adds value, while the user receives new benefits, and the regulator, enhanced comfort in greater safety and less carbon emissions and waste. The main intention is to show that the processes do add significant value that is sustainable. Sure, it is not rocket science.

The underlying structure of most of the Malaysian economy needs to be overhauled—value added is too low for far too long, especially in manufacturing. More important, we have come to use, and rely on, too much imported unskilled labor—generally, they add little to gross domestic product (GDP) but bring on high economic costs. Many industries are oversubsidized; most rely on the old-growth model of continuing capital injection with diminishing marginal returns; and few are blue oceans. Indeed, most compete in overcrowded red oceans with dim prospects for innovation and for breaking out to create a leap in value for themselves and the global marketplace. For example, value added in the electrical and electronic components industry—despite its very large size—is low.

Consider the value-added linkages in the manufacture of Notebook PCs. To take full advantage of the entire value chain, you will need to develop Notebook original design manufacturing capability, including base manufacturing capability in batteries, keyboards, memory, and wireless cards; motherboard and chassis integration capability, LCD modular assembly capability; design and testing capability; global procurement and e-supply chain capability; and research and development capability. The list is not exhaustive.

Malaysia is currently engaged in mainly the lower end of this supply chain. Similarly, in the construction industry, the adoption of industrialized building system (IBS), essentially prefabrication, will significantly raise value added and reduce, most certainly, the use of imported unskilled labor. Malaysian workers' income will be a clear beneficiary. It is encouraging that the government has now agreed to build 70 percent of all its projects through IBS.

What, Then, Are We to Do?

Look at all the other industries in this same light: from plantations to transportation to construction; and from forestry to agriculture to services. They all tell the same story—the predominance of low value added. The current economic slowdown provides the best opportunity to restructure and reform the system with two main objectives: (1) create jobs (including green-collar jobs) with high value added for Malaysians; and (2) incentivize the training and retraining of Malaysians for high-value-added jobs. In the final analysis, human resource management holds the key to higher and rising value added.

Where expertise is lacking—be it the creation of high-value-added businesses or in high-value-added training—the liberal import of expertise (brain gain) and technology should be actively promoted in practice. For this purpose, I had previously suggested the setting up of a sizable Restructuring Fund (RM10–15 billion) as part of a much larger second stimulus package, to help existing industries and businesses restructure, add value, and find their own blue oceans. This fund should actively promote the inclusion of all the green elements in a very sustainable manner. The common glove example shows a way of doing this—not the only way. It is meant to demonstrate what is possible, even with a very simple product. Malaysia Boleh!

Kuala Lumpur
January 14, 2009

Notes

1. First published on January 17, 2009.
2. W. Chan Kim and Renee Mauborgne, "Blue Ocean Strategy," *Harvard Business Review*, Cambridge, MA (October 2004).
3. Kavitha Ravikumar, program manager for Frost and Sullivan, London, in a statement in London on November 19, 2008.

CHAPTER 86

The Crimson Goes Green[1]

I am back at Harvard, marking my fortieth anniversary at the university (crimson, by the way, is its official color). I have since attended the summer meetings of the Graduate School Alumni Council (as its chairman emeritus), the Board of the Harvard Alumni Association (regional director for Asia), and the University's 358th Commencement—that is, graduation (representing Asia alumni on the podium). As I write from the Faculty Club, Harvard celebrated its many achievements and successes in the face of a year that has gone drastically bad for the United States. For Harvard, too; it now faces an extended period of austerity since it "lost" 30 percent of its endowment (still leaves about US$28 billion). Fortunately, its flow of contributions rose 40 percent in the first half of 2009, including a single benefactor for US$125 million. Despite this, the 373-year-old university remains committed to high-quality education. In the midst of frozen academic pay and deep cuts in expenses, new ways to support and afford scientific research are being initiated, and stipend for graduate students (its core) was modestly raised (a surprise) to ensure scholarship is sustained. A record 13 senior faculty joined the Obama administration. Harvard conferred 6,777 degrees, of which only 1,562 (23 percent) were first degrees (with only 4 percent awarded summa cum laude or first-class honors). The university remains highly competitive—only 6 percent of 29,000 applications for its college were accepted for 2009–2010.

For me, the week presented the best opportunity to network and rub shoulders with Nobel and Pulitzer laureates, textbook-name academics, Washington-based policy makers, and bigwig corporate alumni. Every alumnus who is somebody in high academia was here. As is traditional, the pomp of the Commencement procession was led by a fit 93-year-old alumnus (Class of 1939). Quite unlike the British, where it's the chancellor and his academic management team that leads. It was a resplendent scene, unfolding beneath white tents in the leafy courtyard of the red brick historical Yard and its adjacent lush greens. Through the wrought-iron gates behind the seated graduates, spectators could see boats cruise by on the nearby Charles River. Within the parameters, the historic chapel bell tower rises, and opposite stands the world-famous Widener Library, built in 1913.

There was the usual lineup of star-studded speeches filled with nostalgic touchstones, but this time with a rousing flourish of jazz. The highlight was those well-crafted words conferring honorary doctorates on 10 outstanding individuals, including the US Secretary of Energy Steven Chu, the world's greatest living mythologist, Wendy Doniger, the pioneer in AIDS research, Anthony Fauci, the most-cited engineer in history, Robert Langer, and my favorite, Wynton Marsalis—the world's great jazz trumpeter and composer. The speech that delighted me most was the Latin oration given after graduating the seniors—a 1642 tradition.

Chu, the 1992 Nobel Prize physicist, is a strong advocate of new alternative and renewal energy. He warned that if the world continued on a business-as-usual path, the resulting climate change will be so rapid that many species, including humans, will have a hard time adapting. Referring to the climate problem as the unintended consequence of success, he stated that "Energy is the fundamental reason for the prosperity we enjoy, and we will not surrender this prosperity. . . . Can we, as a world society, meet our responsibility to future generations?"[2] Chu concluded: "We will invent much-improved methods to harness the sun, the wind, nuclear power, and to capture and sequester the carbon dioxide emitted from our power plants. Advanced biofuels and the electrification of personal vehicles will make us less dependent on foreign oil."

Al Gore, another Nobel Laureate, was also in town to push global warming to his returning 1969 classmates.

As a member of its nomination committee, the Graduate School of Arts and Sciences (Harvard's largest graduate school) chose to honor four outstanding alumni with the coveted Centennial Medal: 2005 Nobel Laureate in economics, Thomas Schelling; 1993 Nobel Laureate in physics, Joseph Taylor; noted art historian, Svetlana Alpers (daughter of my mentor and teacher, Nobel prize economist Wassily Leontief); and 1969 Pulitzer Laureate David Davis, scholar on slavery and abolitionism.

As I reflect on a week of hectic talk shops, intense networking, and excessive eating, four themes strike me as typical of difficult times, against a backdrop at the epicenter where the rot began—the Wall Street–Washington Consensus, and to a lesser extent, its teaching and thinking powerhouses along the Northeastern corridor.

Universities Hit Hard

First, the impact of the global financial calamity on Harvard typifies what's happening to even the strongest of universities in the United States and Europe—unprecedented shrinkage of endowment funding, budget cuts, and new constraints on spending. Harvard's strategic response to protect essential investments meant sustaining financial aid, even growing vital initiatives in the life sciences, global health, energy, and environment.

Its commitment to do whatever it takes to sustain excellence and integrity in graduate education is impressive. Even in such hard times, Harvard remains resolved to ensure students continue to receive incomparable education, one that prepares them to make critical contributions to knowledge and to society. Above all, it injects a moral conscience into its mission as a university.

No Guarantee of a Job

Second, new graduates were reminded that a degree—even from Harvard—won't guarantee a job. Reflecting the times, fewer graduates were leaving with a job offer: less than 60 percent as against close to 70 percent in 2009. Like Harvard, they inhabit a new world of changing structures, assumptions, and values, as well as changed resources. This meant new opportunities to explore their passions and not just fall into what seemed comfortable or expected—like going for large paychecks on Wall Street. This time, only 25 percent sought careers in finance and consulting, compared with nearly 50 percent in previous years. Also, more were returning to graduate work on energy, healthcare, and environment.

Backed by Ethics

Third, there is an increasing awareness that their newly minted degree cannot be simply an economic driver. The past year had profoundly changed them, as if they had been given the mantle of the future, especially in shared values. Nowhere was this more evident than at the Business School. Second-year students (class of 2010) signed a pledge (the "MBA Oath," mirroring the medical Hippocratic Oath) affirming their commitment to transparency and accountability in business practices: "to act with utmost integrity and pursue their work in an ethical manner."[3] A grassroots designed-by-students-for-students initiative, most felt that if business leaders showed greater commitment to ethical behavior, the avarice that drove many business decisions in the past might be mitigated in the future. Most of all, corporates now need to exercise greater humility.

Consumers Eager for Good News

Fourth, by the end of commencement week (June 5), stocks on the Dow rose for the fifth time in six days. Analysts recommended buying bank stocks and higher oil prices boosted energy producers. They appeared to outweigh a slump in retailing following disappointing May sales as shoppers shunned full-price outlets. The lack of stimulus government flow-through cash continues to hurt consumer spending. Even though US consumer confidence index recorded a 69 in June (biggest rise since April 2003), the index was still way below 100 (first quarter of 1966). But, the number of Americans collecting unemployment benefits fell for the first time in nearly five months. Many, reflecting recession fatigue, chose to read this as a fresh signal that the worst of the labor market turndown has passed.

Separately, US productivity grew at a solid pace in the first quarter of 2009, despite a steep contraction in output (5.7 percent fall in gross domestic product [GDP] is lower than expected). The bright note appeared to be the frantic improvement in corporate profits, which rose 3.4 percent in the first quarter of 2009 (plummeted 16.5 percent in the fourth quarter of 2008).

Flat Is the New Up

I had occasion to meet many old friends and teachers and top corporates at the CEO alumni forum. Some see intermittent evidence the economy's slide is getting to be over. Last week's survey by the National Association of Business Economics pointed to the economy getting out of recession by year-end. "I don't think so," said Professor Martin Feldstein, one of my best teachers and president of the National Bureau of Economic Research.

Marty believes a sustained upturn is unlikely until 2010, at the earliest. Others felt even more despondent. In spite of some improvements, the recent "good news" still showed how far the US economy has slid since December 2007. The first half of 2009 was the weakest such period in 51 years. The US economy has not contracted for three consecutive quarters since the first quarter of 1975! Massive government stimulus and Fed support deserve credit for preventing the economy from sinking into a deflationary abyss. But avoiding disaster is not the same as enjoying recovery. Don't forget, the first quarter of 2009 also saw plunging exports and business investment, and collapse of spending in nonresidential construction, all of which was a drag on the economy.

What, Then, Are We to Do?

What's really missing is solid spending—a crucial element in any recovery. This remains of serious concern in the face of rising unemployment (9.4 percent, highest since February 1983). On the whole and at a time of graduation flurry, many have also taken on hope from scattered signs that the pace of downturn may be slowing or even becoming flat. That the impact of aggressive stimulus will surely lift the economy out of the worst slump sometime next year, hopefully earlier than later. As Nobel Laureate Schelling noted at the Commencement lunch: "While I am worried, I am hopeful Larry [colleague Lawrence Summers, President Barack Obama's number-one economic strategist] will solve the problem soon enough." Good luck!

Cambridge, Massachusetts
Kuala Lumpur
June 6, 2009

Notes

1. First published on June 13, 2009.
2. Steven Chu, US Secretary of Energy, addressing the June 2009 Harvard University Commencement in Cambridge, MA.
3. Rakesh Khurana and Nitin Nohria, "It's Time to Make Management a True Profession," *Harvard Business Review* (October 2008).

CHAPTER 87

The Road to Copenhagen[1]

Today, I write from the Kahala, Honolulu, along Waikiki Beach. Its lagoons house six Atlantic bottlenose dolphins within a secluded long stretch of clean, sandy beach and tropical gardens, amidst blue skies and lots of sunshine. With time on my hands, the setting gets me thinking about climate change. All eyes are now on Copenhagen, where the forthcoming UN Climate Change Conference will soon take place.

This presents a precious chance to save the planet from rising seas and advancing deserts. So much so it has created a wave of eye-catching demonstrations, such as the globally coordinated protest on October 24, calling for carbon concentration in the atmosphere to be kept at 350 parts per million. Inconveniently, there are already signs that sentiment in some high places in the United States could well be moving in the other direction.

The Dangers

Global warming gases have built up to record levels that match scientists' worst-case scenarios: Carbon dioxide concentrations, currently hovering at 385 parts per million, are on the way to above 390 next year. The past million years have never seen 390! If this goes on unchecked, concentrations will hit 450 in 30 years. This means global temperatures will rise 4.3° to 11.5°F by century's end, on top of the 1°F rise in the past century. This has dire consequences on world climate patterns, to the detriment of mankind. Such warming will cause more extreme weather events, spread drought and floods to new areas, kill off plant and animal species, and make seas rise from heat expansion and the melting of land ice.

Perspective to Copenhagen

For more than 100 years, the United States has been the world's biggest carbon emitter: producing 40 percent of the global total in 1990, for about 5 percent of the world's population. In 1900, Western Europe emitted 60 percent. The industrial nations thus carry a huge baggage for the carbon dioxide already in the atmosphere. Admittedly, this liability was recognized in the first global warming meeting in 1992: Nations had common but differentiated responsibilities. This line was reflected five years later in the Kyoto Protocol—where the rich nations agreed to do the cutting, while the developing economies were allowed to continue business as usual. The United States unfortunately failed to ratify the agreement (bowing, I think, to the "big carbon" oil lobby). Since then, global carbon dioxide emissions have grown by 25 percent.

In truth, "Kyoto" had no teeth. With the UN Intergovernmental Panel on Climate Change fourth report in 2007, the underlying science is now definitive. Still, deniers abound. Saving the environment will need unprecedented action, and lots of luck. As I see it, not even the most optimistic feel confident enough in meeting the goal of peaking greenhouse gas emissions by 2020, and then reducing them by 50 percent (1990 as baseline) by 2050.

- **Targets vs. commitments:** The Bali roadmap of end-2007 had agreed that (1) those responsible for the accumulated pollution (the developed nations) would face binding targets to reduce total emissions; while (2) developing economies made commitments (verifiable actions) to bring down their greenhouse gas emissions below a "business as usual" level.
- **What we can look forward to:** (1) a set of financial arrangements, including support of adaptation and mitigation for the poorest developing nations; (2) a political agreement on deforestation; and (3) practical language to effectively implement real technology (as a public good) transfer.
- **President Obama's dilemma:** (1) the US House of Representatives approved a yearly tightening cap on national carbon emissions to fall to 17 percent below 2005 levels by 2020, through operating a carbon-trading scheme (cap-and-trade); but (2) the US Senate had since proposed a tighter target of 20 percent. What is the president to do? To be sure, the rest of the world will not be forthcoming without a binding US target. The sooner this is made known, the better. US clarity is vital.

Threats of Denial and Despair

A major enemy of inaction has always been the deniers (especially President George W. Bush since 2001), no matter how compelling the scientific evidence. The Great Recession made the skeptics an even more powerful pressure point for inaction. The other threat encourages despair—you can't do everything, so why do anything? Besides, there are too many free riders who will duck out of commitments.

But I do sense that all is not lost. While most are irritated by the US stance, I think it's more about timing than substance. Of course, the Europeans have been much more positive—they are bound to show up US recalcitrance. They now talk of a 30 percent cut below the 1990 level, and up to 95 percent cut by 2050. For Japan, it's a 25 percent cut.

The Gridlock

Copenhagen offers an opportunity to fix the problem (of cutting emissions of heat-trapping gases driving climate change) that has derailed successful cooperation so far. In part, because of different interpretations about what is fair. The overall focus has been on carbon dioxide emissions, and on who should cut them, by how much, and when. The US focus has been (1) on total emissions; and (2) it regarded China and India as large co-offenders. Whereas the China and India focus is on the high US per-capita emissions (20 tons), as against five for China and two for India, making it unfair for them to be asked to cut emissions at all. Moreover, they are unhappy the United States even thinks of trade sanctions to induce such cuts.

The recent Barcelona climate talks pointed to other sore points of contention: (1) on finance: no positive reaction so far on the new climate fund, which requires developed nations to contribute 1 percent of GNP (US$400 billion annually); (2) on technology transfer: setting up of the Technology Action Fund to transfer climate-friendly technologies has not been well received; (3) on adaptation (that is, raising developing nations' capacity to cope with the effects of climate change—here again, no real progress); and (4) on shared vision and long-term goals; clear global goals by 2050, especially for developing countries, remain a serious big challenge.

A Copenhagen "Political Agreement"?

The November 2009 G-20 Summit in Pittsburgh had committed to take action: to tackle the threat of climate change and work toward an ambitious outcome in Copenhagen. This was reaffirmed at the Singapore APEC Summit in mid-November. President Obama stated that instead of a legally binding treaty, world leaders would aim instead for a "political agreement" on substantive issues. This would set out four main goals:

1. Targets for developed economies to make big cuts on emissions by 2020.
2. Commitments by developing nations to take measures at curbing future growth of their emissions.
3. Financing from rich to poor countries to help them effectively curb their emissions and cope with climate change.
4. Outline of governance structures to monitor and deliver them.

At Copenhagen, up to 192 negotiators are expected to sign such an agreement with no legal force, but that would be politically binding. A fully articulated treaty would be ready for signing possibly by June (in Bonn) or at the next climate change summit in Nov./Dec. 2010 in Cancun, Mexico.

"One Agreement, Two Steps"

APEC members, which account for two-thirds of global emissions, did reach consensus in mid-November 2009 on this "one agreement, two steps" approach as laid out by Danish Prime Minister Lars Rasmussen. This compromise makes practical sense in a difficult situation, where the United States is unable to be on time to commit to specific targets (with the US Senate unlikely to conclude its work before Copenhagen). The Europeans are understandably unhappy, since they have set out a reasonably good package for Copenhagen—promising tight restrictions on emissions. China and Brazil, as I understand it, have since signaled greater willingness to cut emissions relative to a "business as usual" baseline, with actions that are measurable, reportable, and verifiable. Even India now looks less of an outlier. Sure, there are real dangers to this approach. There are still too many obstacles to overcome. But, to leave Copenhagen without a global framework for tackling climate change would be morally indefensible. At Copenhagen, we need to feel that the long-term vision and short-term politics would be mutually reinforcing and actively supportive. Otherwise, we'll be in big trouble.

Climate Change in a Hungry World

Climate and food security are two sides of the same coin. Indeed, the UN Secretary General's recent warning that failure at Copenhagen will result in a further rise in hunger must be seriously heeded. Moreover, it is sobering to note that over the past 18 months, food insecurity had led to political instability in more than 30 countries. As the weather gets more extreme, today's food crisis is a wake-up call for tomorrow.

What, Then, Are We to Do?

The world has more than one billion who are undernourished, mostly in Africa and South Asia. The proportion of undernourished people in the developing world has risen to almost one in five—the level of 1990. Three other developments are strikingly noteworthy: (1) by 2050, the world needs to grow 70 percent more food; (2) water is fast becoming a scarce commodity; and (3) child malnutrition will rise 20 percent by 2050. The world cannot achieve food security if climate change is not effectively tackled. This reality matters. It's dispiriting. Surely, this must be of global concern. Yet, I am not hopeful. It's a real pity.

Honolulu, Hawaii
Kuala Lumpur
November 24, 2009

Note

1. First published on November 28, 2009.

CHAPTER 88

RIO+20: What a Huge Disappointment[1]

Rio+20 (UN Conference on Sustainable Development, Rio de Janeiro, June 13–22, 2012), billed as a once-in-a-generation chance to save the planet, was a huge disappointment—even an embarrassment, given that almost 200 countries were present, with many leaders, including from Brazil, France, Australia, and India, attending. A friend at Rio likened the meeting to a rally race of backseat drivers. Everyone is sitting in the backseat and no one is taking responsibility.

This meeting was named after the one held 20 years ago (the 1992 Rio Earth Summit), which launched a number of landmark agreements and treaties, including one to limit the extinction of species and acceptance of the human right to safe drinking water. There had been very little progress since then. According to the UN Environment Programme (UNEP) June 2012 Report: Only four of the world's 90 most important green goals and objectives have seen significant progress. There has been "little or no" improvement on goals to address 24 key problems, including decimated fish stocks, climate change, and deteriorating coral reefs. "Nature," the world's preeminent scientific publication, graded the implementation of three of its many vital treaties—climate change, biological diversity, and combating desertification—with a resounding F.[2]

Looking back, I must say the agreements that had emerged from Rio 1992 were thoughtful, far-sighted, public spirited, and focused on global priorities. Yet, they have not saved us because of poor political support and ineffective implementation all round. This time, Rio+20 produced final documents filled with weasel phases and untidy compromises. As I read them, buried among the caveats in the endless clever use of words and gobbledegook, the final approved document, "The Future We Want," is so diluted and tentative that it makes, I am afraid, the entire exercise quite meaningless.

Someone tweeted soon after agreement was reached: "Nobody in the room adopting the text was happy." That's how weak it was.

Expectations were simply set too high, despite a long string of clear indications on the endless difficulties encountered in reaching ambitious deals among such varied interests and such diverse groups of nations. And, the loud political "noise" from the evolving European debt crisis in particular distracted attention from the main focus on real issues. It will take more than the volumes of words crafted to restore public confidence in the Summit's outcome, or the lack of it. In the end, the world just got a bad deal at Rio+20.

What Happened at Rio+20?

Rio+20 was intended to reaffirm political commitments made 20 years ago and to initiate new action plans and strengthen the implementation framework to resolve the crises confronting the world's environment, which has deteriorated and become much more serious since. Sounds simple enough. But it was not to be. As documented in detail by columnist Martin Khor, negotiations were bogged down by new concepts (including the "green economy") and second thoughts even about reaffirming the original equity principles or in recommitting previously agreed arrangements on finance and technology transfer.[3] So, not only were there no major breakthroughs this time around, but even initiatives to bring on new ideas to strengthen institutional delivery capabilities and to introduce new goals and roadmaps were subject to unduly harsh scrutiny. Six key issues had needed renewal or serious consideration:

1. To reaffirm the underlying original Rio principles of equity, in particular the common but differentiated responsibilities (CBDR).
2. To provide adequate finance to developing economies to set them on to environmentally sound development paths.
3. To transfer technology on concessional and preferential terms to emerging and developing economies.
4. To identify and set sustainable development goals (SDGs) as key deliverables.
5. To introduce and adopt the concept of "green economy."
6. To strengthen the institutional framework for sustainable development (IFSD) to ensure more effective implementation.

The first three issues had already been resolved and accepted at Rio 1992, but needed to be renewed and reaffirmed, and made more relevant to meet present pressing needs. Even these encountered enormous problems.

"The Future We Want"

As I understand it, the United States and Europe gave early notice that all issues were on the table—nothing was to be taken for granted just because political commitments were made at Rio 1992. I well recall the issue of equity and CBDR was hotly contested in 1992. I was there. Although all nations must act to protect and preserve the environment, developed economies have to do the most and assume leadership in global environmental actions. This made sense then, and still does today. The United States in particular, however, had wanted emerging nations (except the poorest developing ones) to take on a similar burden as the advanced economies. In the end, the United States relented and the final document reflected global reaffirmation of the Rio 1992 principles.

Similarly, the second and third issues were once again seriously revisited. On finance, G-77 and China (representing developing countries) had insisted on renewal of the original commitments of new and additional financial resources, including meeting the aid target of 0.7 percent of gross domestic product (GDP). In addition, they also proposed that advanced nations (1) provide at least US$30 billion a year in 2013–2017 and US$100 billion annually from 2018 onward; and (2) establish a working sustainable development fund (SDF). Not surprisingly, all these were rejected by the North, who introduced new references to secure funding from "a variety of other sources and new partnerships." What was finally agreed was to restart discussions at the United Nations to review options for an appropriate financing strategy.

I was chairman of the UN Experts Working Group on Finance for 10 years. Even then, realistically, political support for funding was not as forthcoming. If anything, today's politics has hardened. Chances are slim the political will to act is there at all. Rich nations are already experiencing funding fatigue. On technology transfer, the North had insisted that their prior commitment to transfer technology should now be voluntary and on mutually agreed terms.

Finally, the United States agreed to "recall" the text used at Rio+10 in Johannesburg, stating technology transfer would be on favorable terms to developing countries. The United Nations was also requested to present a report on the technology facilitating mechanism for further debate at the General Assembly.

The concept of SDGs was of concern among Europeans, who had insisted that certain SDGs (energy, water, climate, oceans, and land) should be listed as priority goals. G-77 and China, while accepting SDGs as an operational tool, wanted SDGs to be represented in a more balanced way consistent with the three agreed key pillars—social, economic, and environmental.

In support, my friend, Professor Jeffrey Sachs (president, Earth Institute at Columbia University), advocated a worldwide call for action:

> *Around the world, the cry is rising to put sustainable development at the center of global action and thinking, especially to help young people solve the triple bottom-line challenges—economic well-being, environmental sustainability and social inclusion—that will define their era. Rio+20 can help them do it. Let's adopt a set of SDGs that will inspire a generation to act. The SDGs can open the eyes of today's youth to climate change, biodiversity loss and the disasters of desertification. We can still make good on the three Rio treaties, by putting people at the forefront of the effort.*[4]

Rio+20 agreed to set up a 30-member Working Group nominated by governments, to identify and list these SDGs in a balanced manner.

The Europeans had also pushed hard to endorse a UN green economy roadmap with clear environmental goals, targets, and timelines in the hope of changing the way economies are organized. G-77 and China were concerned that its acceptance would (1) be used to divert attention away from sustainable development as the key focus for policy design, (2) be misused as grounds to justify trade protection, (3) be used as an excuse for greater aid conditionality, and (4) lead to imposition of new green economy obligations. It was finally agreed that this concept would be used only as one of the tools for sustainable development and subject to, according to Martin Khor, safeguards along 16 principles to protect real environmental interests against abuse.[5]

On strengthening the IFSD, the final document agreed to (1) strengthen and upgrade UNEP, including universal membership on its governing council, and increased financing (but not as a UN specialized agency); and (2) set up a high-level political forum on sustainable development (to replace the Rio 1992 Commission on Sustainable Development) to provide political leadership, design the agenda, facilitate regular dialogue, consider new challenges, review progress in implementation, and improve coordination within the UN system.

Cost of Not "Greening"

The old conventional wisdom of "grow first, clean up later" approach to industrialization no longer works. Environmental concerns hardly played a role until the 1960s. Even so, the Kyoto climate change protocol exempted all developing nations from obligations to cut greenhouse gases. The cost of waiting for the cleanup has since risen. The Chinese Academy of Social Sciences estimated that annual damage to the Chinese economy was as much as 9 percent of GDP. On the average, World Bank studies pointed to the cost of environmental degradation as being 8 percent of 2012 GDP for the world. Bad sanitation and water pollution already cost India 6 percent of GDP. The impact gets more serious as nations grow richer.

Over the next 40 years, most of the rise in the world's population will be in developing nations. Two to three billion more will become middle class. That's two to three times as many as was achieved in the past 150 years. They all want higher living standards and improved material comforts. All these simply put greater stress on natural resources, water, land, and food. In short, the world will get more polluted. Avoiding such an outcome is a problem for today, not just tomorrow. Development needs to be green from the start. It's the new mantra for businesses and policy makers. Green growth plans are proliferating. The World Bank, in support, published *Inclusive Green Growth* by Marianne Fay (its principal author), which likened the work of today's environmentalists to antipoverty economists in the 1990s. China's recent smog-choked skies prompted new calls to cut greenhouse gas and approve a carbon tax by 2015. The real challenge is whether the circle of conflict between greening and growth can be squared. Green growth advocates regard the environment as a form of capital: It makes a measurable contribution to output and should be accounted for, invested in, exploited efficiently, and (ideally) made to work to create value. It's controversial—indeed, even regarded by some as greenwashing capitalism.

What, Then, Are We to Do?

Twenty years ago, Rio 1992 tried to address environmental degradation through a series of agreements, treaties, and international law. Unfortunately, these documents lived in the shadow of our daily politics and media. All we managed so far were widespread neglect, immense delay, political bickering, and disputes over legalities. We now have at least three failing grades to show for our efforts.

Rio+20 has come and gone. We are no better off. Indeed, we have failed to inject life into simple down-to-earth concepts to determine our own survival. "The Future We Want" misses much of what we really want. It fails to speak plainly about what we need in order to save ourselves and our children. All we want is to end extreme poverty; decarbonize the energy system; slow down population growth; promote sustainable food supplies; protect the oceans (and what's in them), forests, and dry lands; and redress inequalities of our time.

That's the future we truly want. The world is poised to act and Rio+20 was supposed to unleash a generation to action. This was not to be. But, there is still time, just barely. Waiting for the politicians to save us despite ourselves is to wait too long. We urgently need to heed Sachs's call for global action. President Barack Obama says it best: "Change will not come if we wait for some other person or some other time. We are the ones we've been waiting for. We are the change that we seek." So, for heaven's sake, let's get going.

Kuala Lumpur
February 6, 2013

Notes

1. First published on February 9, 2013.
2. Jeffrey Sachs, in an article calling on the world to act and to help unleash a generation of action: "A Rio Report Card," published in *The Edge Financial Daily*, Malaysia (June 18, 2012).
3. Martin Khor, "Key Issues Facing Rio+20," *The Star*, Malaysia (June 11, 2012).
4. Sachs. "A Rio Report Card."
5. Martin Khor, "Follow-up Is Key after Rio+20," *The Star*, Malaysia (June 25, 2012).

PART VIII

Social Issues of Concern

CHAPTER 89

9.6 Billion[1]

The world's population is likely to reach 9.6 billion by 2050 from about 7 billion today, an increase of 38 percent, mostly concentrated in poor nations. Today, up to 1 billion people are so undernourished they can't do modest manual work. Can the world be fed? That's the challenge. Food prices reflected the Malthusian vision of population rising too fast to feed itself. Rising consumption of grains is draining global stocks fast and pushing prices to levels that fueled riots four years ago, and widespread discontent more recently. In 2007 and 2008, food prices soared and led some 30 poor nations to deal with food-price-related riots, and Russia started to restrict exports. Again in the summer of 2010, world wheat and rice prices spiked. Riots resumed and Russia once again banned wheat exports. The oil price is at its highest since October 2010, just shy of US$127 per barrel in early April 2011. By end-2010, world food prices were already back at their July 2008 peak. Beginning in mid-2010, world grain prices exploded. Prices rose to an all-time high in February 2011.

High prices were among the triggers of street protests and even revolutions that recently swept North Africa where wheat dominates the region's diet. Egypt is the world's biggest importer of wheat. The United Arab Emirates import more than 50 percent of its wheat needs. Despite massive subsidies and price controls, high prices still filtered through to consumers, building a tinderbox for unrest and discontent. In Tunisia and Egypt, housewives are shown screaming on TV about high food prices. I believe this marks the end of cheap food.

Supply and Demand

The US role in keeping a global food shortage at bay hinges, in the short run, on the weather and harvests from US farms, the world's biggest agricultural exporter. Most expect world wheat supply to recover later this year as drought conditions ease in the Black Sea region, which should moderate prices. But, the long-term expectation is still for food prices to remain high. Climate change has set the stage for severe weather disruptions. Importers have limited places to shop: The United States controls 55 percent of world trade in corn, 44 percent in soybeans, and 28 percent in wheat. What lies ahead abounds in the US farm belt. February farm products price index (covering 48 commodities) was 24 percent higher than a year ago, but has since risen further. China gobbled up about one-quarter of the US soybeans crop. Due to rising oil prices and government mandates, 40 percent of its corn is brewed into ethanol, which US Senator Tom Coburn described as not a green fuel: "It consumes as much energy as is used to make it, as when it is burnt."[2]

By the time the fall 2011 harvest begins, the United States is left with enough corn to satisfy only 18 days of the nation's appetite—tightest position since the 1930s Dust Bowl era. This is despite farmers producing larger record crops of wheat, soybeans, and corn. Demand for corn is so strong that a 10 percent rise in harvest will lengthen reserves by only five days. If the long-overdue drought hits US Midwest's corn and wheat output, food prices will skyrocket again. The 1988 drought slashed US corn crop by as much as one-third. Major wheat producers (Canada, Australia, and Russia) saw output fall 5.5 percent last year. Food demand is confronted with strained supply. High prices or shortages could further destabilize poor countries, and trigger a global scramble for scarce foodstuffs. The bad experience of 2008 remains fresh.

In essence, growing global affluence underlies the squeeze. The Food and Agriculture Organisation of the United Nations (FAO) estimated wheat prices rose 60 percent so far this year; corn gained 92 percent and rice recorded new highs in Indonesia, Thailand, Vietnam, and Bangladesh. With modernization comes diet change—shift from eating grains directly to consuming them indirectly as meat and dairy products. From 2000 to 2030, per-capita meat consumption is estimated to rise 50 percent in China, 80 percent in India, and 22 percent in Brazil. This, in turn, will boost grain demand as feedstock. Research shows for cattle, it takes eight pounds of feed grains to gain one pound of beef; for chicken, it's between two and three pounds. This simply means demand for food will continue to outpace supply. In the last 7 of 10 years, world wheat consumption has outpaced output. Grain reserves have since grown very, very thin. I believe the era of crop surpluses is over.

What's Enough?

The Food supply needs to rise sharply by 2050 to feed a 9.6 billion population. FAO estimated in 1996 that the world can produce enough food to provide for everyone with 2,900 calories a day, well above the minimum required. The *Lancet* (British medical journal) indicated people need 90 grams of meat a day (they eat more than that now). Scientists believe the world can feed itself. Allowing food for biofuels and wastage along the way, farmers are already producing enough.

So what's the problem? In a 1981 essay, Harvard Nobel Laureate Amartya Sen concluded that the main reason for famines is not shortage of basic food but problems on wages, distribution, storage, even democracy.[3] This is still valid today. Part of the answer lies in prices. When output falls below demand for whatever reason, prices rise. That happened in 2007–2008 and it's happening today. Volatile prices are bad for producers (not knowing what and when to invest), who need high and stable prices to keep investing, and for consumers, especially the poor who risk not affording basic food.

Second, it's a daunting task to improve distribution (storage, logistics, refrigeration). Often, food is not available where it's needed most. In the end, it's the balance between production and consumption. By 2050, another 2.6 billion mouths need to be fed, equivalent to two extra Chinas. If you add the billion-odd people who are hungry today, we are talking of another three Chinas! Putting this in perspective: By 2050, world population will rise by 38 percent; that's much less than in the 40 years to 2010, when it rose over 80 percent. Consumption of wheat, corn, and rice historically tracks people growth but at a higher level. So demand will add at least another billion tons to the 2 billion produced in 2005–2007. That's much less than in the previous 40 years when cereals output rose by 250 percent.

These headline numbers do not reflect the real situation. Over time, population becomes more urban based, richer and able to afford pricier food, such as meat. So meat demand will rise strongly. In 2000, 56 percent of all the calories consumed in developing countries was provided by cereals, and 20 percent by meat, dairy, and fats. FAO estimates that by 2050, the ratio will be 46:29. To match the fast demand, meat production will need to double its current level. FAO estimates that total demand for food will rise 71 percent between 2006 and 2050, more than double the demand for cereals. That's still only half as much as the rise in food production between 1962 and 2006. On paper, producing enough food to feed the world in the next 40 years appears not to be more difficult than in the previous 40. Realistically, it won't be as easy simply because of yields, which have slowed down from 3 percent a year for staples in the 1960s to about 1 percent today. With advances in plant genetics, producers of staples can push up growth in yields to 1.5 percent per annum.

Waste

FAO estimates that in both rich and poor nations, 30 to 50 percent of all food produced is wasted—mostly gets rotten or thrown away uneaten. In poor countries, much food is wasted on or near the farm. Mice, locusts, and rats eat the crops in the field or in storage. Milk, vegetables, and fish spoil in transit. These are often regarded as losses. They can be easily reduced by one-half, equivalent to raising output by 15 to 25 percent. But it's more an investment matter: building enough storage and silos, better infrastructure, more refrigeration, and better logistics.

Rich countries waste as much food as the poor ones—up to one-half of production—but differently. Studies concluded that a quarter of food from shops ends up as rubbish or thrown out by restaurants. Top of the list are salads—about one-half is thrown away; a third of all bread; a quarter of fruits; a fifth of vegetables. If the global rich nations waste like the United States and United Kingdom, roughly 100 kilogram per person per year, that's equivalent to one-third of the world's entire supply of meat! If this waste could be halved and distributed to where it is needed, the problem of feeding the world would be much easier. But that won't happen. Spoilage reflects bad behavior and regulation. In the end it's a matter of prices. Food is cheap. Prices are unlikely to rise enough to change attitudes.

Can It Be Done?

Environmentalists believe it can't be done. Climate change, declining water tables, and eroding topsoils limit the possibilities. It's not just weather disruptions. With a real carbon price, farmers will commit fields in terms of carbon embodied in crops and soil. That, in turn, influences what they grow (perhaps, elephant grass instead of wheat). Competition for crops is already keen. Then, there is disease. The return of stem rust (taken as wiped out in the late twentieth century), if not dealt with properly, can prove disastrous for wheat, the most widely planted crop, providing one-fifth of world's calories.

Science offers the solution. Farmers and breeders need every tool, including genetically modified (GM), in the constant battle against disease, predation, and complacency. Then, there are structural problems involving market failure. Imbalances in supply and demand reflect the essence of agriculture. In 2010, global wheat harvest was the third largest of all time. Yet, supply shocks often happen, as in the summer of 2010, when harvest failure in Russia (just 8 percent of world wheat output) led to embargoes and panic buying. Markets are supposed to have acted to absorb it. But they failed. This led to such headlines as "Don't trust markets" and "Food security begins at home," which are counterproductive.

Self-sufficiency is grossly inefficient and shallow markets make prices more volatile. Climate change will worsen volatility. Existing proposals should be seriously considered: (1) the United States, Europe, and Japan should cut farm protection and release food for trading across borders; (2) World Trade Organization should provide some insurance against export bans; and (3) create a global system of food stocks as Keynes had proposed after World War II.

On the bright side, astonishing advances in biotechnology have since quintupled corn yields and quadrupled wheat yields. Use of "smart seeds" (making crops more resistant to weeds, bugs, and drought), improved fertilizers, better irrigation, and efficient farm practices have led to huge gains. By 2030, smart seeds are expected to double output of US corn and soybeans. These seeds are being increasingly used in Brazil, Russia, India, China, and South Africa (BRICS) as they emerge as significant food producers, while Europe declines. Eurozone's Consumer Agriculture Policy (protection costs €55 billion in 2009) and rejection of GM will soften yields further, and thus it is in danger of marginalizing itself. But the United States will remain the global leader.

What, Then, Are We to Do?

Given the strains and politics of food, efforts to feed the world can sharpen geopolitical conflicts and speed up shifts that are already happening. So there are enough reasons to worry about food supply: political uncertainty, volatile prices, continuing waste, and hunger amidst plenty. Success depends on nature and technology restoring a better balance between supply and demand. All said and done, I sense the emergence of a new agriculture revolution to better feed the world led by technology. Genomes of most major crops have been sequenced and benefits are being felt. BRICS and others like Indonesia and Vietnam have shown use of smart technologies and sensible policies can free more food for global trade—and with some luck, they can transform themselves into bread baskets instead of being basket cases. Indeed, the consequences of failure on human suffering and political conflict are fearsome.

Obiter Dictum

Readers wonder why I use a wheelchair. Reminds me of a leading journal's interview with Professor Paul Johnson (bestseller: *Modern Times*) who asked Winston Churchill in 1946: To what do you attribute your success in life? Churchill promptly answered: "Conservation of energy. Never stand up when you can sit down. And never sit down when you can lie down."[4] That's why.

Kuala Lumpur
April 21, 2011

Notes

1. First published on April 23, 2011.
2. Senator Tom Coburn has since proposed an amendment in April 2011 at the US Congress to scrap the subsidy on the production of ethanol from corn.
3. Amartya Sen, *Poverty and Famines: An Essay on Entitlement and Deprivation* (New York: Oxford University Press, 1981).
4. Brian M. Carney, "Why America Will Stay on Top," *Wall Street Journal*, London (March 7, 2011).

CHAPTER 90

The Seven-Billionth Baby Is Born[1]

It's not everyday we welcome the next billionth baby. According to the United Nations, the seven-billionth baby was "born" on October 31, 2011. The last time it happened was 12 years ago on October 12, 1999—Adnan, the six-billionth baby, born in war-torn Sarajevo. When it comes to counting population, the United Nations is regarded by most as setting the gold standard. But there is already controversy: US Census Bureau reckons the milestone will not be reached until March 12, 2012. However, the two dates are within 0.4 percent of each other. Even the United Nations concedes its estimate is subject to a 1 percent margin of error. It's not easy to get to 7 billion: According to the *National Geographic*, it will take more than 200 years to count to it out loud; or, if you took 7 billion steps, you would have walked around the globe 133 times.

How Did We Get Here?

It took the entire human race until 1804 to reach the first point at which the whole of one billion persons lived at the same time on Earth. The second billion was reached in 1927, 123 years later; and the third, another 32 years in 1959. The fourth billionth baby was born 15 years on in 1974, and the fifth, in Zagreb in 1987, 13 years later. The sixth billionth came in 12 years after that, and the seventh, after another 12 years. Since modern man appeared around 50,000 BC, an estimated 108 billion people lived on this Earth—implying about 6.5 percent of all humans ever born are alive today. The eighth billionth is not expected until 2025 (14 years from now—the first time the next billionth has taken longer to reach than the one before) and then the ninth not for another 18 years in 2043.

Rapid world population growth is a recent phenomenon. About 2,000 years ago, the population of the world was only 300 million. It took more than 1,600 years for it to double. It all began in the 1950s when rapid growth came about through reductions in mortality in the less-developed regions, resulting in an estimated population of 6.1 billion in 2000, nearly two and a half times that in 1950. However, with the decline in global fertility (by more than 50 percent in 50 years) but remaining high in the developing economies, global population growth has been declining since its peak average of 2.0 percent in 1965–1970. Still, the world today adds 80 million people a year; at this rate, it experiences the numerical equivalent of another United States in terms of population every four years.

The Demographics

For the first time this year, the United Nations is reported to have attempted to look as far ahead as 2100, using different assumptions about how fertility and mortality would behave over time. The average of these estimates suggests that (1) global population will exceed 10 billion by 2085; (2) by 2100, 22.3 percent of population will be aged 65 or more (7.6 percent in 2010); (3) the bulk of population growth is expected in the developing countries, with Africa's rising to 3.6 billion in 2100 (1 billion in 2010); and (4) the rich will only account for 13 percent of world population (32 percent in 2011).

Asia remains the most populous major area today. But Africa is gaining ground as its population more than tripled, passing 1 billion in 2001. In 2011, 60 percent of world population lived in Asia and 15 percent in Africa, whose population is growing at 2.3 percent per annum, double Asia's 1 percent. Population in the others (Americas, Europe, and Oceania) totaled 1.7 billion in 2011, projected to rise to nearly 2 billion in 2060, and then decline. Europe is expected to reach a high at 0.74 billion in 2025 and then fall. Asia's population, at 4.2 billion today, will peak around the middle of the century (to reach 5.2 billion in 2052) and start to slowly decline.

The underlying demographics include: (1) males account for 50.4 percent of total population; (2) 50.5 percent of people live in urban areas; (3) median age: 29; (4) 33 percent of them are Christian; (5) per-capita gross world income: US$10,290; (6) under 25s make up 43 percent of the total; (7) average life expectancy: 68 (48 in the 1950s); (8) 13 percent of the world is found in China; (9) infant mortality is 46 per thousand deaths (133 in the 1950s); and (10) fertility fell to 2.5 births (6.0 in 1950s), still above the replacement level of 2.1 children, one of them a girl. In East Asia, the fertility rate in 1950 was 6; today, it's 1.6—well below replacement level. The rate in Africa continues to be at more than five since 1950.

Demographic Imbalance

With 7 billion, humanity is on the verge of a huge milestone. In the last 50 years, humanity more than doubled—a rate without precedent. The UN Population Division anticipates 8 billion people by 2025, 9 billion by 2043, and 10 billion by 2083. Experts complain demographic imbalance has placed serious strains on towns and cities across the globe, as mostly middle-class blue-collar migrants move from the poorer rural areas to richer urban centers. Beijing, for example, already the world's 13th most populous city, doubled its population over the past 10 years, reflecting a worldwide trend, particularly in emerging nations.

Cities in Africa, Asia, and South America are bursting at the seams from migrants seeking better jobs or as farmers flee drought, food, and other environmental disasters. By 2009, 3.5 billion people already live in cities (only 730 million in 1950), and in four decades it will bulge to 6.3 billion according to the United Nations. This explosive growth stretches limited resources and infrastructure and places megacities on a collision course with a predicted increase in extreme flooding, storms, and rising sea levels from climate change. Today, Bangkok is a classic example. Worldwide, I am afraid the lack of national and international coordinated planning is exacerbating the problem.

Demographic Dividend

Although fertility rates (children a woman can expect to bear) have fallen from the 1960s peak, there is now a demographic "bulge," a boom of young people. The generation that matters is the one before fertility fall begins to bite, which in Europe and the United States was the Baby Boomers, who are now retiring. In the case of China and East Asia, it is the generation now reaching adulthood. That is, the generation with lots of children and fewer surviving grandparents. This is Europe in the 1950s and East Asia in the 1970s. And as this generation enters the labor force, the nation starts to benefit from the "demographic dividend." This happens when there are fewer kids (reflecting falling fertility), relatively few older people (reflecting higher mortality earlier), and lots of economically active adults, including women. That's Europe in 1945–1975 and East Asia in 1980–2010.

Today, people 24 years old and younger make up nearly half of world population (with 1.2 billion between 10 and 19). Their share in some major developing nations is already at its peak, according to the United Nations. Indeed, ratio of the young between 10 and 24 has begun to fall in many places, in the rich and also in middle-income nations. In Mexico, where fertility has fallen sharply, its population "pyramid" has been steadily shrinking at the bottom, with 14 years old and below accounting for 29.3 percent of the national count in 2010, from 38.6 percent in 1990. Its median age consequently rose from 19 to 26 over two decades. The "bulge" moves upward into middle age, reshaping the pyramid. For now, they are a fantastic resource. Yet this opportunity of a one-off "demographic dividend" is a fleeting moment that needs to be claimed quickly to raise productivity, where economic growth can jump by as much as a third.

Demographic Silver Lining

The coming revolution where the gilded generation turns silver is well underway in the rich nations. It exists in Japan and is arriving fast in Europe and the United States, and soon will reach East Asia. It will become global in the next 50 years. Part of China's rapid growth reflected its low dependency ratio: just 38. That is, the number of dependents, children and persons over 65, per 100 working adults. In 1950, for each person 65 and older, there were six kids under 15. By 2070, the elderly will outnumber them, and there will be only three people of working age (15–64) for every two persons under 15 or 65 and older. Pressure to extend the working age beyond 65 will grow more intense as a result of this anomaly.

Sharing Earth's Resources

With 7 billion and rising, resources are under more strain than ever before. Worries are on how to provide basic necessities in the next 50 years.

Water

Water usage is set to rise by 50 percent between 2007 and 2025 in the developing world and 18 percent in the developed, with much of the use centered in the poorest nations as more move to the cities. The problem: 97.5 percent of the world's water is salty, and of the 2.5 percent that's fresh, two-thirds of it is frozen. So, we are left with little fresh water to start with. Only 8 percent of the planet's fresh water goes to domestic use; 70 percent is used for irrigation and 22 percent in industry. Today, over a billion people lack access to clean drinking water, and over 2 billion live without adequate sanitation, leading to 5 million deaths, mostly children. Drought and insufficient rainfall make up the water risk, along with floods and contamination. The world will face a 40 percent water shortfall between demand and supply by 2030. No doubt, water will quickly become a limiting factor.

Food

Nutritious food is in short supply. The world produced 2.3 billion tonnes of cereal grains in 2009 to 2010, enough calories to sustain 9 to 11 billion people. But only 46 percent went to human consumption; domestic animals took up 34 percent of the crop, and industrial use, 19 percent (biofuels, starches, and plastics). Still the World Bank estimates nearly 1 billion people are hungry today, partly due to high food prices since 1995, lack of access to modern farming techniques, and waste (at production and consumption). Recent high food prices drove an additional 44 million into poverty. Another 1 billion experience food insecurity or chronic malnutrition.

I am convinced the world can feed itself (refer to Chapter 89, "9.6 Billion," for details). To feed 2 billion more, as predicted by 2050, food production will need to rise by 70 percent, according to the UN's Food and Agriculture Organisation. This is not as much as it sounds, since from 1970 to 2010, farm productivity rose far more—by over three and a half times. What's worrisome are signs that productivity may be leveling out. New farmland is limited; water shortages are chronic, and fertilizers overused. They suggest that the big problem has more to do with supply, not demand.

Climate Change

Climate change poses the biggest impediment to meeting the food target as rising temperatures and droughts dry out farmlands, which are then invaded by intense floods and storms. Humanity's ecological footprint is already large. This footprint measures how much land and water area a person requires to produce the resources he consumes and to absorb carbon dioxide emissions, using existing technology.

We already have an ecological "overshoot." It now takes the Earth one and a half years to regenerate what we use in one year. According to United Nations' *State of the World Population 2011* report: One-half of the global footprint in 2007 was attributable to 10 countries, with the United States taking up 21 percent of the earth's bio-capacity, and China, 24 percent. The newborn American would, over time, produce an eventual carbon footprint 7 times that of the extra child in China, 55 times the child in India, or 86 times the child in Nigeria. It's overconsumption, not population growth, that is the problem.

What, Then, Are We to Do?

Where is this taking us? The next 50 years will see huge shifts in the geo-political–economic balance of numbers: further falls in fertility, smaller but more numerous households, rising elderly and greater dependency, pressure on food and water, and growing megacities. But as of now, the International Labour Organisation[2] warns that two-thirds of the advanced and one-half of emerging nations are already experiencing a slowdown in job creation at a time when worldwide unemployment exceeds 200 million. "We have reached a moment of truth. We have a brief window of opportunity to avoid a major double-dip in employment."[3] Already, 81 million or 13 percent of 620 million economically active youth (15–24) globally are unemployed in 2009, mainly because of the financial crisis.

It will take at least another five years for employment in the advanced economies to return to pre-crisis levels. Even so, the world is likely to create only 50 percent of the 80 million jobs needed over the next two years. As I see it, the risk of greater social unrest is real, notably in Europe. Discontent is fueled by lack of jobs and perception that the burden of the crisis is not being fairly shared. Further, fiscal austerity is viewed as a threat to social protection and workers' rights.

Kuala Lumpur
November 4, 2011

Notes

1. First published on November 5, 2011.
2. International Labour Organization (ILO), Geneva. In an October 2011 report released on October 31, 2011, ahead of the November 2011 G-20 Summit in Cannes.
3. Raymond Torres, director of ILO's International Institute for Labour Studies, in a press statement on October 31, 2011, in Geneva.

CHAPTER 91

The Ominous Demographic Dilemma[1]

Demography matters. But it's not destiny as the French philosopher, Auguste Comte, would have us believe. Other things also matter. Certainly its impact endures longer and has wide-ranging effects. Nevertheless, even demographic trends do change. What's happening right now is extraordinary. The United Nations' "State of World Population 2011" pointed to ominous trends. The world's population reached 7 billion on October 31, 2011, of which only 1.2 billion (17 percent) live in the rich world; 5.8 billion (83 percent) are found in developing economies, including 851 million in the least developed. More than 4 billion (57 percent of the world) reside in Asia and the Pacific. What's remarkable today is that about 900 million people are over the age of 60 worldwide; by 2050, they will rise to 2.4 billion as population ages and lives longer, and birth rates slide further.

The twentieth century was marked by the greatest fall in death rates. Low birthrates look likely to be the defining demographic event of the twenty-first century. Total fertility rate (TFR) now averages below 2.1 in more than 70 nations (representing 50 percent of world population). This level of TFR measures number of births that the average woman would need to bear over her lifetime to prevent population from falling in the long run.

All European nations have low TFRs today, and so do many Asian economies, including Japan, China, South Korea, and Taiwan. Russia, Japan, and Italy now have the lowest TFRs—typically not more than one child during a woman's lifetime. Without strong immigration, their populations will fall. The United States, by contrast, still has a growing population because its TFR is at about the 2.1 replacement level and it continues to attract significant immigration.

Not long ago, many were concerned, and some still are, about the rapid rise in population. This poses an ominous policy dilemma—while the falling population brings with it the benefits of inverse correlation between fertility and income per capita, which should please neo-Malthusians (those who still believe population will rise faster than the means of sustenance, bringing with it war, famine, and epidemic), the current trend of low TFR and rising life expectancy will result in, eventually, falling economic growth and rising costs, including health and related spending on social safety nets, as the workers pool supporting retirees falls. Today, four workers support one retiree in the European Union; by 2060, the number of such workers will drop to just two.

Dispelling the Myths

- **Overpopulation is a problem.** Is 7 billion too many? No one knows for sure—not economists, not demographers. UN forecasts world population will reach 9.3 billion in 2050 and more than 10 billion by the end of this century. So? Population density can't be used as the yardstick: Monaco has more than 16,000 persons per square kilometer, whereas Bangladesh has only 1,000. Some scholars even tried to determine the "optimum population." Part of the problem lies in uncertainties forecasting the impact of future technologies on food production. Using resource scarcity isn't helpful, either. Real prices of corn, rice, and wheat fell during the twentieth century when world population exploded from 1.6 billion to more than 6 billion. Since prices are supposed to reflect scarcity, the world should be less "overpopulated" today than 100 years ago, right? Doesn't match common sense, does it?
- **High population growth keeps poor nations poor.** Experience of Asian tigers South Korea, and Taiwan doesn't bear this out. In 1960, they were poor with fast-growing populations. Over the next two decades, South Korea's population will rise 50 percent, and Taiwan's, 65 percent. Between 1960 and 1980, these nations boomed; income per capita rose an average 6.2 percent a year in South Korea, and 7 percent in Taiwan. That's not unique. Between 1900 and 2000, world population exploded but per-capita income grew faster by fivefold.
- **As population declines, so does growth.** Again, empirical evidence showed otherwise. Between 1940s and 1960s, Ireland's population collapsed, falling from 8.3 million to less than 3 million. Yet Ireland's per-capita income tripled. More recently, most of the former Soviet-bloc nations experienced depopulation since the end of the Cold War. Yet, today, economic growth has been rather robust in this region; for example, Bulgaria and Estonia suffered sharp population contractions of close to 20 percent—but their income per capita rose 50 percent and 60 percent, respectively.

- **Small is beautiful**. A contrarian view is that Japan should accept a smaller population and, hence, less competition for space and resources. "Support a smaller Japan with a higher quality of life" (Professor Akiko Matsutani). This challenge to the orthodoxy urging Japan to reexamine its social and political priorities could yet gain ground. The call to "populate or perish" remains compelling for most developed nations, including Japan.
- **China's one-child policy boosts growth**. This restrictive policy and China's adoption of Deng Xiaoping's pro-market reforms began in the late 1970s. Since then, China's per-capita income rose more than eightfold. Both outcomes are not necessarily linked. Before the one-child policy, China's TFR was 2.7; today, it's 1.6, or 40 percent lower. Between 1960s and 1970s, Chinese TFR fell from 5.9 to 2.9, a sharper 50 percent drop. Yet, China's per-capita income only rose modestly. Its falling trend in fertility reflected also the experience of many East and Southeast Asian societies. Myanmar also experienced very low fertility, but without state intervention. Nevertheless, reform is in the cards even though many exceptions are already being granted to minority groups—rural families whose first child is female, and couples who are both from one-child families.

Tale of Two "Bellies"

The demographic divide between nations ("bellies") with high and low population growth has enormous economic and political significance. Today, Europe is following the traditional normal demographic path: As it became richer after the 1950s, its TFR fell sharply to 1.4 today, below the replacement 2.1 rate. The United States followed a similar pattern until the 1980s. Then the TFR reversed its fall and even rose to about the replacement rate. With immigration, US population actually rose. The United Nations expects US population to rise from 315 million today to 350–400 million over the next 25 years, and to 400–550 million by 2050. Europe's population will likely peak at 740 million in 2025 and fall thereafter.

So what? With a fertility rate of 50 percent higher than Germany, Russia, or Japan, and well above China, South Korea, and Italy, and virtually higher than all of Eastern Europe, the United States is the outlier among its traditional competitors, all of whose populations are destined to eventually fall after 2035. Today, Russia's low TFR (1.3) suggests its population will drop 30 percent by 2050 to less than one-third of the US population. Equally serious is the emerging gap between the United States and East Asia.

By 2050, a third or more of East Asia's population will be over 65 years old (30 percent in China). A slowdown in population growth can offer short-term economic and environmental benefits, but will soon cut deep into the nation's savings and income. Between 2000 and 2050, the US work-force will grow 42 percent, while the same will decline 10 percent in China and 25 percent in Europe, and 44 percent in Japan. Unlike Europe and East Asia, the US imperative is not in meeting the needs of the aging but in promoting jobs and opportunities for its expanding workforce.

What the United States does with this "demographic dividend" derived from its new "sweet-spot" of a robust young workforce will depend on the entrepreneurial spirit of and innovative initiatives taken by the private sector—an issue that's worrisome even now as more than 15 million are already unemployed. But the eventual loss of human capital as Generation-Y ages means that this dividend has to be repaid. Similarly, Europe and East Asia's aging demography also needs to set their agenda—to find ways to ease pension and health burdens and grow productivity at the same time. Both regions need to bring new sparkiness into their midst through entrepreneurial vigor. They have to become more open to immigration.

Asia is home to more than 4 billion. Its population will peak at 5.2 billion in 2052 and then start a slow decline. It claims the world's two billionaires: China with 1.35 billion (and TFR of 1.6) in 2011, and India, 1.24 billion (and TFR, 2.5). China's population will stabilize in 2025 (its workforce had started to shrink for the first time in 2012), and India, in 2060. In 2028, India will overtake China (with 1.39 billion) as the world's most populous nation with 1.46 billion. China's population will stop growing by 2032 and then decline to 1.3 billion by 2050, while India will continue to grow to 1.7 billion by 2060 before it begins to fall.

Global population shrinkage is real: Russia's population will fall by 22 percent in the first half of the twenty-first century, Ukraine by a staggering 43 percent. This is creeping all over the rich world: Japan has started to shrink (from 127 million to 100 million by 2050); Germany and Italy will follow soon. By 2050, populations will be lower than today in 50 nations. Demographic decline is worrisome because it is perceived to be accompanied by economic decline. When population contracts, growth will slacken. Companies worry because domestic markets shrink. People worry about their economic welfare. Yet all these need not happen. Productivity growth will keep per-capita growth up through the smart use of technology and the free spirit of entrepreneurship. With political will, the new demographics can herald a golden age.

Aging Time Bomb

The world is graying, and Japan is graying at an unprecedented rate. Fifty years ago, only 5 percent of its population was over 65, well below the United States, United Kingdom, France, or Germany. Today, it's risen to 20 percent, the highest in the world, and is forecast to reach 30 percent by

2025. After World War II, it had a more defined population pyramid than the United States. Now, its demographic profile looks more like a Japanese lantern. Soon, it will turn into a narrow-based urn, with serious consequences. Soon enough, there will be fewer productive workers, and more and more dependent elders.

Also, the demographic shape of the workforce will eventually assume an inverted pyramid, with fewer young workers at the base where once there were many. The old consume more resources than the young, mostly in health-related resources. The Baby Boomers have now started to retire and become custodians of years of accumulated technical and managerial skills. They will be sorely missed by Mama-san at Ginza bars.

Japan, at least, had a chance to grow rich before it grew old. Most developing economies, including China, are growing old before they even get rich. Bear in mind that China's per-capita income is only US$6,000 in 2012, against US$50,000 in the United States, US$36,800 in Hong Kong, and US$22,600 in South Korea. China's low TFR means that by 2020, 20 percent of its population will be over 65 years old (14 percent in 2012); on current trends, it will reach 30 percent by mid-century. It is estimated that by 2038, there will be as many people over 65 as there are below age 20. Post-2038, older consumers will outnumber younger ones. Today, 1.4 percent of Chinese is over 80 years old; by 2050, 7.2 percent will be.

The implications on state finances are stark. The nation's social security system, which covers only a fraction of the population, already has debts far exceeding its ability to repay. It also needs reform to put social spending, especially on healthcare, on a more sustainable footing.

What, Then, Are We to Do?

Yes, demography does matter. The new demographic trends are worrisome. Birthrates are low for good reasons, particularly the high time cost involved in raising children (especially for career women) and the desire to invest more in each child than in another. Birthrates can be raised by incentives and generous subsidies, but they are found in cross-country studies to have only modest impact. I am of the view that once nations (like Japan and Russia) have TFRs far below the replacement level of 2.1, even the most generous financial support will not significantly raise TFR in the next few decades. The viable solution to an aging and falling population is to open the immigration gates.

US studies have shown that significant inflows of immigrants have proven to: (1) be active venture capitalists; (2) start ventures that create jobs and investment; (3) often act as critical catalysts in high-tech manufacturing and in information technology; and (4) also make up a large portion of new

graduates in engineering and computer science, who are crucial in supporting growth of the finance and IT sectors. Immigrants help expand the pool
of intellectual capital. Sure, immigration can create political, economic, and
social problems. That's why Japan and Russia face a worrisome demographic and economic future. It's not surprising that people ignore the Greek
philosopher Plato's keen insight: "We easily forgive a child who is afraid of
the dark; the real tragedy of life is when men are afraid of the light."

Kuala Lumpur
August 22, 2013

Note

1. First published on August 24, 2013.

CHAPTER 92

The Quality of Life[1]

This chapter represents a complete change of pace. I was in Singapore undergoing surgery on my spine—a procedure called Trans-foraminal Lumbar Interbody Fusion (TLIF). My doctors tell me because of wear and tear over the years, not to mention prolonged youthful excesses, my lower backbones have degenerated badly to cause severe spinal pain and discomfort. I do make light of this but it's a big deal—any orthopedic surgeon will tell you that addressing degenerative lumbar kypho-scoliosis affecting simultaneously four lumbar vertebrae involves a major operation that is not to be taken lightly. Simply put, the surgeon has to decompress—enlarge the vertebrae space to remove undue pressure on the nerves, repair, rebuild, and fuse with instrumentation in order to stabilize that part of the spine. In the final analysis, titanium nuts and bolts and plates are used to put my vertebrae together; and *voilà!* I now have a new lumbar spine. And, I feel great, mobile, but most important, increasingly pain free. I am even slightly taller! It involves seamless teamwork, intricate "carpentry," meticulous surgery, and sensitive dexterity in managing the patient to avoid, in the worst-case scenario, paralysis.

Soft Options

The injuries to both my cervical and lumbar joints date back to the 1970s as a student at Harvard. It was only in the past 20 years—got worse still in the last 10—that the pain and discomfort deteriorated. I decided very early on—like most 50-somethings—that no surgeon is to touch my spine. To "heal" myself, I learned "wu-qi" (older version of tai-qi) and qigong. I had great teachers. They helped to relieve pain—even some resistance to it—and build increasing ease of mobility. Off and on, I had to rely on the chiropractor, traction, and other sophisticated "heat" treatments to feel more comfortable. Indeed, I even managed to "cheat" pain through a coordinated program I had developed for myself using a loose combination of the famous Mckinsey (New Zealand) method, qigong moves, and adopting time-tested exercises based on the vast experience of many friends. They worked well enough to give "false hope" in association with painkillers. The mix of Western and Eastern methods helped.

I also started consulting with experts at the Cleveland Clinic and Harvard Medical School. You will be surprised how widespread "back pain" afflicts 50- to 60-somethings! When the pain got progressively worse, I tried "special" acupuncture techniques from Beijing and Nanjing, and lately, epidural—which worked very well for five to six weeks at a stretch. By July 2009, my bag of tricks had begun to run out of workable options. Pain became more intensive and more prolonged, often occurring at the most inconvenient of times, and ease of mobility became more difficult and more painful, with no end in sight. I was getting desperate—even attempted aggressive pain management. I realized soon enough I need to consider the hard options. Most friends—well intentioned, no doubt—still think I have not exhausted the soft-Eastern options. Western medicine decided long ago that surgery is the only answer.

Mind you, I have had a good run without invasive surgery of any kind. For the past four to five years, my work takes me up to five working months—off-and-on—in a year abroad—mostly Asia, also involves periodic trips to New York/Boston, Tokyo, and Australia. Most of the trips include flying (in-and-out of airports) frequently. In other words, lots of multiple moving around and rushing about. So much so I am convinced if you don't miss flights, you have spent too much time at airports. But with determination and a very positive mind, I managed to keep working—pain free most of the time, but at the expense of the future. By the way, I retired from Bank Negara Malaysia in mid-1994!

Risk Management

By early July 2009, I was placed between the unenviable rock and the hard place. For me as an economist, I now have on hand a classic case of risk management. Except that the critical elements involved are not quantifiable at all—on the one side, there is inconvenience, continuing pain, uncertainty, overdependence on others, immobility, and at worse, paralysis. On the other, a set of rebuilt lumbar vertebrae even though fused (and hence, offer limited flexibility), painless mobility, managed flexibility, a "can-only-get-better" mind-set, and taking charge once again. To be honest, you still have to deal with the difficult odds attendant upon what can go wrong in a major surgery, including paralysis, which can be frightening. Indeed, the risks go beyond the expertise of the key person—the surgeon. However, for me, I place greater risks at the work of the anesthetist—not always factually based, I admit. You hear horror stories of not waking up from the table or waking up as a vegetable. Just as important is your own medical condition; can your heart take it? Are your kidneys in a good enough condition? What is the quality of your blood, your bone structure? All your other illnesses in combination are also likely to weaken you at surgery. The list goes on. So you see, the risk matrix to be managed gets rather multidimensional and complicated to offer a clear-cut solution. What am I to do?

The Quality of Life

The solution lies in the big picture. I will be 70 very soon. Today, Malaysian males have a life expectancy of close to 72 (76.5 in the case of females). This is an average—as they say, you can drown in an average 4 feet of water! Based on hereditary lineage, I have a good chance of outliving the average female to reach 80—and with some luck and clean living, even to 85. So another 10 to 15 years on this earth is within reach. But what sort of quality of life would I have for the next 10 to 15 years if I continue as I am, even assuming my lumbar (and cervical) spine condition doesn't deteriorate? There are other questions. Turn the question around. What if I did what the surgeons consistently suggested and break free to enjoy a new regime of painless living with a newly reconstructed lumbar spine? Of course, the risks are high. To me, the choice was obvious. If I were to live another 10 to 15 years, I want and need a good quality of life—this can't be negotiable; it has to be the incentive for me to move forward. Put this way, I opted for surgery.

How to Go about It?

When buying property, the three simple rules of thumb to follow are "location, location, location." In the case of surgery, it's "reputation, reputation, reputation"—i.e., the reputation of the surgeon and his team. This helps you narrow down your options. The advice of your physician (who knows you best medically) and the spine and associated experts is critical from here on—the Key Performance Indicator is obvious: high success!

Not long ago, I chaired a Working Group for the Prime Minister's Economic Action Council on Medical Tourism. This gave me a good feel of what's available in India, Thailand, Singapore, Hong Kong, and, of course, Malaysia. I had planned to have the surgery in Kuala Lumpur for obvious reasons. It also helps when I have my brothers and sisters who are doctors, and they, in turn, know the reputation of leading surgeons, and so on. The identified hospital facilities in Kuala Lumpur are good; so is patient care (both pre- and postoperation) here. Kuala Lumpur also has good orthopedic surgeons, neurologists, anesthetists, endocrinologists, urologists, and nephrologists who can back up the principal surgeon—considering the operation is complex and can take up to 8 to 9 hours, even 10.

At the last minute, the operation was shifted to Singapore for four key reasons: They have a world-accredited spine center; a renowned spine surgeon; a fully operating team of experienced supporting specialists, technicians, and nurses who constantly work together as a team, capable of seamless work; and state-of-the-art ability and access to the latest tested techniques, instruments, and drugs. Together, they become more than "the sum of the parts"; indeed, as an effective team, they offer value added to raise the odds on success. It's that simple. Ironically, the lead surgeon and most of his team are Malaysians—indeed, very few Singaporeans.

Talent Management

With nothing better to do during recovery, I revisited the same issues, which I presented in my recommendations to promote medical tourism. All things being equal, we in Malaysia can be just as successful as our immediate neighbors in marshalling extensive value added from a dynamic medical tourism industry. But we need to want this passionately enough. The surgeon who led the surgical team is a Malaysian—most of his team members, not just the specialists but also the technicians, nurses, and so on, are non-Singaporeans. This should not be a surprise—the saying goes: Open your eyes, and you see a team of Malaysians helping you recover, even though you are in Singapore!

Singapore has placed itself where it wants to be today by (1) embracing the entire value chain—taking two bites off the same cherry: first, the value added by each specialist and then a second bite as a team; (2) practicing talent management—it consciously draws expertise from top surgeons to technicians to nurses from the world over; (3) nurturing development of a state-of-the-art presence, including providing facilities of excellence (e.g., spine center); and (4) providing 360-degree-service orientation. From the time you arrive at the hospital until you leave (in my case, straight to the airport), they have made it one seamless exercise. The convenience is awesome. Most important, Singapore understands the consumer (patient in this case) is king and gives him what he wants, all things being equal—that is, reputation, reputation, reputation. Reputation built tirelessly on world-class expertise, professional integrity and reliability, and building a successful track record. I asked my Kuala Lumpur surgeon how many cases like mine has he done so far: 50 to 60; my Singapore surgeon (who is younger) had already done close to 300! Sure, we can improve, but competition can only get keener; time and tide wait for no man.

What, Then, Are We to Do?

This is intended to pass on an experience—albeit one that is unique to me. My real medical condition is more complicated and, unlike many, I firmly believe a disciplined mind can help affect the well-being of the entire body. Mine had been one where short-term ends were allowed to overwhelm my long-term interests. This, however, is not unique to me. In the end, my decision to go for surgery at 70 is late—I wish I'd had the wisdom to give my long-term good much higher priority than I did. It's never easy. I know there are many out there having the same predicament as I had—many much younger. All I can say is this: Listen to your physician—he should be less biased than your surgeon, even though the surgeon knows more about what ails you than the physician. The ability to piece together the big picture is critical—not to miss the woods for the trees. Give your close friends and family a good run for their advice. Good luck.

Singapore
Kuala Lumpur
September 10, 2009

Note

1. First published on September 12, 2009.

CHAPTER 93

The Emerging Bourgeoisie[1]

For Karl Marx, "the bourgeoisie . . . has played a most revolutionary part" in history. He is right. In the past two decades, the new middle class (NMC) has surged forward, silently producing a revolution within emerging markets in wealth creation and in lifestyle. By and large, they are a product of growth.

Who Are They?

There is no best definition of the NMC; it all depends on what the objective is. US$2 a day is commonly accepted as the poverty line in developing nations; beyond this, people join the middle-class in the sense they have moved out of poverty. My old friend, Homi Kharas (formerly with the World Bank and now a senior fellow at the Brookings Institute, a US think tank), had promoted the definition of today's global NMC as households with disposable income (or daily expenditure) of US$10 to US$100 a day (RM30 to RM300) per person at 2005 purchasing power parity prices (i.e., their domestic buying power at 2005 prices).

Two recent reports tell their story: "Global Trends 2030," just published by the Paris-based European Union Institute for Security Studies (ISS), quoted in the *Financial Times*,[2] and "Perspectives on Global Development 2012—Social Cohesion in a Shifting World" by the Organisation for Economic Co-operation and Development (the rich world's think tank, also based in Paris).[3] According to them, the NMC is global and on current trends, its members will rise from 2 billion in 2013 (split about 50–50 between developed and emerging nations) to almost 5 billion in 2030 (of an estimated world population by then of above 8 billion); among them, 3½ to 4 billion are likely to live in emerging economies representing 65 to 80 percent of the global population. Viewed differently, for the first time in human history, more people will be part of the NMC than poor! No matter how one looks at this, the irrevocable redistribution of income and economic power is undeniable. China is the main driver of this change. The Asian Development Bank forecasts Chinese NMC will rise up to 80 percent of the population by 2030. India has similar potential, with as much as 300 million in the NMC today.

One-Third Rule

By definition, middle-class members are neither poor nor very rich—they are sort of in-between. Middle class, whether lower or upper, describes more than an income category—it reflects a set of attitudes, indeed, a new lifestyle. A key characteristic is that they possess a reasonable amount of discretionary (spend at will) income: As a rule of thumb, people turn middle class once they have about one-third of their income left for purposeful spending, after providing for basic food and shelter. This allows them not just to buy a house and durables (TV, car, fridge) and improve health and leisure, but also plan for the future. Usually, this means having some form of employment with a predictable income stream and benefits. That's the second characteristic.

In practice, the 2009 special report by *The Economist* identifies two types of middle class in emerging economies: (1) *global middle class,* who by any standard carry recognizable hallmarks of being middle class—they have confidently made it and are fast growing but account for only 10 to 15 percent of emerging world; and (2) *developing middle class* (loosely, also known as lower middle class) who have just made it and are more numerous; they are recognized as such but by evolving standards of the developing world and are not as rich as the global middle class; they have grown very fast and are now 60 percent of world population, against only 30 percent in 1990.[4] The NMC are not really a coherent, homogeneous group—they vary even from place to place, yet are recognizable by most standards as being middle class. This heterogeneity distinguishes them.

NMC Surges

For another, the NMC don't grow incrementally, unlike the process of economic growth. Empirical evidence from World Bank studies show that in 1980, there was hardly a middle class in the developing world (including China). With sustained economic growth, incomes rise and they move hurriedly toward the annual income threshold (US$3,500–4,000 per person), and before you know it, vast numbers cross into middle class. This shift in income distribution was most evident between 1990 and 2005 in China. Once past a certain stage, it surges. During this period, Chinese NMC share of population soared from 15 percent to 62 percent. This is only being reached in India at the end of the 2000s.

Kharas characterizes this mass crossover as the "sweet spot of growth"— when developing nations reap maximum benefit from utilizing cheap labor through expanding global demand and trade. But the process slackens as they price themselves out of world markets. It also marks the period of rapid urbanization when underemployed farmers abandon what Marx often refers to as the idiocy of rural life to work in manufacturing nearby urban areas. They soon become the NMC sitting somewhere between rich elite and rural poor. Their numbers are expected to double by 2030, with profound social consequences. Karl Marx wrote in *The Communist Manifesto*: "The bourgeoisie, by the rapid improvement of all instruments of production, by the immensely facilitated means of communications, draws all, even the most barbarian, nations into civilisation."[5]

New Habits

As income of the NMC rises, spending habits change. In a 2012 study, HSBC Global Research concluded: "Two things stand out, viz. impact of the 'threshold effect' and the massive rise in discretionary spending" as personal annual incomes rise from below US$1,000 to between the US$3,000 and US$5,000 threshold.[6] The "S-curve" effect quickly sets in, demand radically changes, and thereafter, beyond a certain income, behavior tends to moderate to become more incremental. China, India, Indonesia, and Russia all went through this process. The NMC acquire new (often bad) habits: Consequently, spending on (1) basic food falls from 40 percent of total income to 10 percent; (2) meat, fish, and dairy rises; (3) alcoholic drinks and tobacco also rises; (4) fuel to power a more comfortable living goes up; and (5) health, social protection, and financial services get higher priority (from 5 percent to 15 percent).

This significant shift triggers the development of a vast array of new services and service providers. Over time, as demonstrated in China, India, and Brazil, discretionary spending picks up markedly (as income rises further), especially on "cooked food" (restaurants), clothing, and footwear (shopping) as well as on travel, recreation, and personal care—all growing at high multiples. Consistent with massive transformation, emerging markets' NMC are expected to buy up to 55 percent of all audiovisual, photographic, and communication and computing equipment in 2050, from 24 percent today.

Social Cohesion

The current wave of protests and demonstrations (stretching from United Arab Emirates to Hong Kong and South Korea to Brazil) reflect just the beginning of this trend. For the NMC, fostering cohesive societies holds the key to achieving their dreams. Indeed, the rise of global NMC is already transforming the world's social, political, and economic landscape. Overall, NMC will demand more and better public services, a fairer division of growth's benefits, and more responsible political institutions. As I see it, what's happening today suggests that the wealthier and more educated they become, the NMC increasingly identify and bond with a broad set of universal values. This political awakening has begun to ferment. To stabilize this process, I think four key issues need to be addressed:

1. Institute more extensive social protection.
2. Create more and better jobs; these are desperately needed especially in states like Greece and Spain, where youth unemployment reached 57 percent.
3. Formulate a robust social contract calling for better delivery of public services and greater government accountability.
4. Provide more private "space" for citizens, especially the NMC, to exercise their voice, including a more extensive role for social media.

The NMC and Growth

The NMC make distinctive contributions to the growth process. First, NMC are committed to education. Human capital accumulation is vital to the growth process. This means more kids at school and university and more adult continuing education. Education remains high on the agenda of NMC values, more so than the poor or even the rich. Second, the NMC spend proportionately more on their children's education. Part of their extra spending goes to keep children longer at school, and increasingly, they do not take their children out of school to work. The same commitment is made in health and personal care, as the NMC desire healthier lives. Third, the NMC contribute to entrepreneurship. Indeed, new entrepreneurs readily emerge to create employment and contribute to productivity growth. They are more likely to invest in new businesses and more willing to learn new ways of doing things. As a class group, they are known to produce both a mass of hardworking businesspeople and some exceptional entrepreneurs. Above all, the NMC can act as a moderating influence on social conflicts that can help restart growth. By definition, a growing middle class can act to reduce income inequality because they can moderate the stark divide between rich elite and rural poor that is so often a source of conflict. Additionally, the NMC also tend to be inclusive, which is good for growth.

Scary New Rich

Unfortunately, rising incomes often do not yield shared values. *Newsweek* reportedly calls the emerging bourgeoisie "a patchwork of contradictions." Rather scary, I think, as they are known to behave differently: clamorous but seldom confrontational politically; supporting globalization yet highly nationalistic; proudly upward-mobile but fearful of falling back; fiercely individualistic yet still reliant on government patronage; often socially conservative and supportive of powers that be so long as they deliver the spoils of growth.

The 2009 Pew study was reported to show that the NMC are often prepared to give up their ideals for prosperity; indeed, most are politically risk-averse.[7] In Brazil and Russia, the NMC are more worried about "freedom from hunger than freedom of speech." In Malaysia, Turkey, and Indonesia, much of the NMC are devout Muslims who do choose to vote wearing Islamic headscarves. The NMC are often psychologically driven by an odd mix of individualism and insecurity. In China, India, and Russia, they became NMC the hard way. Nearly 30 percent of Brazil's NMC owes its livelihood to the "gray" market, where income is irregular and social safety nets nonexistent. For most, they are unsure how sustainable the new status is going to be.

What, Then, Are We to Do?

Transformative power is the hallmark of the NMC. Within the last 30 years a world that was predominately poor is now mostly middle class. Rising wealth is unlikely to replace cultural and national identities. It might even reinforce them. Not surprisingly, the transformation is set to be most pronounced in Asia. China already has more than 160 million NMC consumers, second only to the United States. But they represent less than 12 percent of the Chinese population. By 2030, the ISS projects this ratio to rise to 74 percent.[8] On the back of growing paychecks, China's retail sales rose 17 percent in 2011. Consumption is expected to make up 45 percent of gross domestic product by 2015 (up from 15 percent in early 1990s). By 2025, as much as one half of India could cross the threshold to become middle class.

This tide goes beyond Asia. ISS estimates more than two-thirds of Brazilians are likely to become middle class by 2030;[9] by then, Central and Latin America can have as many middle-class consumers as North America. The process will take more time to come to pass in Africa. Even there, the numbers will more than double by 2030. Sure, this new group of consumers will still total much less in disposable income than their North American and European counterparts. But the rich nations' share of global middle-class consumption is likely to fall, by more than one half from 64 percent to 30 percent by 2030. The Chinese already buy more cars than Americans did since 2009. The Arab Spring suggests that existing and authoritarian elites will come increasingly under strong pressure. Transformative change will come—the NMC demands it, amplified by widening access to education (especially for women) and by the impact of digital revolution. Internet users in China and India have already far exceeded those in the United States. Will growth be more stable and sustainable, or can the world become more peaceful? No one knows for sure how this will finally play out, or how the gap between NMC expectations (with its new "fire power") and lack of political will of states to act, can be bridged. Whatever the outcome, the increasingly more affluent NMC won't let go! Transformative power remains in their hands. Time will tell what the final outcome will be.

Kuala Lumpur
January 23, 2013

Notes

1. First published on January 26, 2013.
2. Philip Stephens, "The Great Middle-Class Power Grab," *Financial Times*, London (March 30, 2012).
3. Johannes Jutting, Head, poverty reduction at the Organisation for Economic Co-operation and Development (OECD) Centre, Paris; "The Middle-Class Goes Global," *The Edge Financial Daily*, Malaysia (February 27, 2012).
4. "Burgeoning Bourgeoisie," a special report on the new middle class in emerging markets, *The Economist*, London (February 14, 2009).
5. Ibid., p. 9.
6. Jutting.
7. "Burgeoning Bourgeoisie," p. 12.
8. Stephens.
9. Ibid.

CHAPTER 94

Rising Income Inequality and the Piketty Blockbuster[1]

It is undisputable that the richest 1 percent in advanced economies has captured a disproportionate share of overall income growth over the past three decades—so says the Organisation for Economic Co-operation and Development (OECD), the 34-rich-nations' club. The lowest wage earners have scarcely progressed, and some have even fallen behind in real terms over this period. This gap will widen without direct policy action. So much so that President Barack Obama identified income inequality as "the defining issue of our time" in his 2014 State of the Union speech. In the United States, real income of the top 1 percent rose 47 percent.

Looked at differently, 95 percent of gains of the recent recovery have flowed to the richest 1 percent of US households and in which social mobility has stagnated even as inequality has widened. Indeed, the top 1 percent is close to full recovery from the financial crisis, while the bottom 99 percent has yet to really recover.

In 1912, an Italian statistician, Corrado Gini, invented the Gini coefficient (GC)—used ever since as the universal measure of income concentration anywhere. On a scale from zero (representing perfect equality) to 100, where all income flows to a single person (perfect inequality), as a rule of thumb, at over 40 a society is regarded as increasingly unequal. The US index now "ranks with Jamaica and Argentina," so says President Obama. Latin America's GC is about 50, well above emerging Asia's 40, with Singapore at 47, China 51, Malaysia 46, Philippines 43, and India 40, according to the Asian Development Bank (ADB) 2012 Report.

Another measure looks at its functional distribution—that is, ratio of gross domestic product attributable to labor (wages and benefits) as against capital (profits, rent, interest). Labor's share in Asia's largest economies has steadily fallen over the years: China, from 60 percent to 48 percent; Malaysia, from 42 percent to 30 percent; even South Korea, from 48 percent to 43 percent despite its low GC.

Piketty, Kuznets, Marx

The notion of inequality is not new. Americans have, over the years, regarded the gap between haves and have-nots as a European obsession. But stung by a jobless recovery in the face of excesses on Wall Street, the rich, capitalism, and redistribution have become of foremost concern. Thomas Piketty's recent book, *Capital in the Twenty-First Century*, painstakingly analyzes the evolution of income and wealth over 300 years, particularly in the United States and Europe.[2] He argues that rising inequality is not merely a feature of history. It is the historical norm, concluding that growing wealth concentration is inherent in capitalism. He offers a simple, readily understandable explanation for rising inequality, viz. wealth generally grows faster than the economy. The French economist summarizes his contention simply as $r > g$ (rate of return on capital, r, exceeds rate of economic growth, g), resulting in wealth accumulating over time at far higher rates than wages, which just tracks growth plus productivity, if any.

Conventional wisdom holds that inequality will eventually stabilize and subside on its own. Piketty disagrees; he sees few economic forces strong enough to counteract this natural tendency for wealth to become increasingly more concentrated, as greater wealth brings greater opportunities to save and invest. So inequality persists and prevails. This cuts hard against the grain of economic orthodoxy shaped during the Cold War by my teacher and mentor at Harvard, Nobel Laureate Simon Kuznets, whose "Kuznets curve" on inequality had ruled since 1964—widening in the early phases of growth when transition from preindustrial to industrial civilization was most rapid; becoming stable for a while; and then narrowing at later stages. This boosted capitalism, suggesting the market economy can distribute its fruits equitably, without any need for state intervention.

Nevertheless, deep concern remains about distributive justice regarding income and wealth that inspired nineteenth-century thinkers like Ricardo and Marx at a time of enormous wealth and deep squalor, an era that gave us *Les Miserables* and *Oliver Twist*. Today, it is difficult to put aside their ideas when US real wages have been depressed for years while the richest 10 percent take an increasingly larger share of the economic pie since 1913. This has now become a global phenomenon. It appears the distribution of economic rewards in the twenty-first century is taking on significant nineteenth-century features.

Inequality versus Growth

Most economists would agree that some degree of inequality is good for growth, creating incentives for hard work, driving entrepreneurship, and fostering risk taking. For over 20 years, the gap between Asia's rich and poor has widened, including in China, India, and Indonesia, nations that powered the region's growth. For the entire Asia, its GC rose from 39 to 46. Had it remained stable, according to the ADB, another 240 million would not be poor. Widening inequality threatens Asia's growth sustainability—it can lead to instability, and certainly, poor political choices: often opting for populist subsidies on food and fuel.

Ironically, its main drivers of growth—technology, globalization, and market reforms—also worked to widen this rich and poor divide. Asia is changing. Since World War II, Asia has delivered unprecedented growth. Never before have so many people been lifted out of poverty and at such unprecedented speed. Yet income disparities have also worsened.

Other than questions of political and social tensions, this matters for growth: (1) it's a drag on productivity; and (2) it encourages inefficient populist policies that stunt growth. What's driving this is unclear. It may simply reflect the nature of the growth process, driven by manufacturing instead of services. Demographics—reflecting an aging population—could have depressed the rise in wages. Others include poor social-safety net programs.

What's clear, however, is that as income inequality rises, growth gets traded off. History shows that prolonged spells of rapid growth often come to an abrupt end when inequality rises significantly. International Monetary Fund researchers have added some clarity, concluding: "It is the duration of spells of growth that is most important for long-run economic performance; getting an economy growing is much easier than keeping the growth spell rolling. When growth falters, inequality is often the culprit."[3] Other studies reckon inequality is mildly bad for growth. If Latin America closes its inequality gap by 50 percent, its typical growth spurt might last twice as long.

What, Then, Are We to Do?

Piketty's conclusion on how policy should best respond to rising inequality has provided widespread disagreements, even disappointment. He prescribes a progressive global tax on wealth (a levy starting at 0.1 percent and hitting a maximum of up to 10 percent of the greatest fortunes), which is widely dismissed as politically unfeasible (which he concedes). He also proposes a punitive 80 percent tax on incomes above US$500,000. He glosses over the issue of whether such redistribution of wealth weakens growth and puts off entrepreneurs and risk taking, and punishes those with imagination and other positive traits that have so far brought great financial success. The politically feasible solution, however, centers on the standard recipe of "education for all," mandating the less wealthy to quickly acquire an ephemeral form of capital—knowledge—that can bring enormous returns. But this is no match, according to Piketty, for the powerful forces driving inherited wealth even higher. He says his fiscal solution provides a "less violent and more efficient response to the eternal problem of private capital and its return."[4] He adds: "The fiscal institutions to redistribute incomes in a balanced and equitable way have been badly damaged." He is right. He offers twentieth-century France as an example: "France was a democracy and yet the system did not respond to an incredible concentration of wealth and an incredible level of inequality. The elites just refused to see it . . . claiming that the free market was going to solve everything." It did not! For Asia, governments need to ensure the dividends of prosperity are more equitably shared at ground level. This requires three things: (1) tax systems aimed at a more active but effective redistribution of income; (2) quality education, and healthcare and housing that's affordable and accessible to all; and (3) inflation (which hurts the poor the most) must be tamed. This requires, on occasion, tough fiscal and monetary policies—the price to pay to ensure sustainability that makes a difference between a healthy, sustainable growth path and one that's decidedly subprime.

Kuala Lumpur
May 15, 2014

Notes

1. First published on May 17, 2014.
2. Thomas Piketty, *Capital in the Twenty-First Century* (Cambridge, MA: Harvard University Press, 2014).
3. "Up to a Point, Redistributing Income to Fight Inequality Can Lift Growth," *The Economist* (March 1, 2014), referring to a 2008 International Monetary Fund Report by Andrew Berg, Jonathan Ostry, and Jeromin Zettelmeyer, *What Makes Growth Sustained?*
4. Piketty.

CHAPTER 95

Has Undergraduate Education Lost Its Way?[1]

The excesses since 2000, especially the latest financial meltdown from Wall Street to the City of London, and from Paris and Frankfurt on to the other end of Asia, Tokyo, have broken the public trust. *Madoff-proof* is the new byword. Yet, those responsible are educated in some of the finest and smartest global universities. It just doesn't make sense. What went wrong? I know it's always difficult to generalize. So, let me pick the best—Harvard University (okay, I am biased). Also, I happen to know more about the goings-on at this university than any other. I have been associated with it through a number of formal Harvard appointments as an active alumnus since 1993, both at the University in Cambridge and in Asia. As I see it today, Harvard's challenges are not unique—they are as relevant to us in Malaysia as they are to the best British, French, German, and Japanese counterparts. In his insightful book, *Excellence without a Soul*, former Harvard College Dean Harry Lewis dwells critically on why today's universities have lost sight of their core mission.[2] That Harvard teaches students but doesn't make them wise.

Harvard College (its undergraduate wing) has an overarching role to educate students to be independent, knowledgeable, reflective, and creative thinkers with a sense of social responsibility. Toward this end, it should provide students with the knowledge, skills, and habits of mind to enable them to enjoy a lifetime of learning and to adapt to changing circumstances. It does all this through repeated reaffirmation of its commitment as America's oldest university (since 1636) to a liberal education in the arts and sciences. I have observed that Harvard strives to be the best in many things; it often succeeds.

Yet, over the years, according to Lewis, it has allowed its key mission to drift: (1) from education toward, increasingly, stakeholder satisfaction, (2) developing more and more as an international brand, and (3) assuming the role of an education market enterprise—that is, from harvard.edu to harvard.com, so to speak. Mind you, Harvard remains consistently the first-rate world-class research university. Developmentally, 17- to 23-year-old youngsters are ripe to become immersed in the life of the mind, and to draw energy and inspiration from their evolving independence, as they begin to shift the burden of responsibility from dependency on parents to caring for themselves and society. Yet, it would appear that universities seem oblivious to the opportunity to shape their lives.

Why This Drift?

According to Lewis, relentless competition among universities for research excellence has produced a university system optimized for research. Of course, this has brought untold prestige and prosperity through scholarly discoveries and scientific inventions. But, I think, at a price to the real quality of undergraduate education. For example, there are no key performance indicators for effectively imparting knowledge and inculcating committed habits of mind to make students wiser and more productive adults. Universities' teaching rarely consciously promotes responsible citizenship and an obligation to leave the world a better place. Professors are rewarded for academic excellence. But no credit is assigned to help students live meaningful lives, with a sense of their eventual place in society. Simply put, no one appears to be looking at the big picture. No one was monitoring for systemic failure—from the students' point of view. T. S. Eliot (Harvard class of 1909) wrote in *The Hollow Men*:

> Shape without form, shade without color.
> Paralyzed force, gesture without motion.[3]

Herein lies the entrepreneurial challenge to the rest of world: how to capture the creativity of top US research universities, like Harvard, without importing their aimlessness as well.

What Universities Forgot

It is not that the great universities have been complacent. Indeed, according to Lewis, over the years, deep and profound changes have taken place:

- **Curriculum**—now certainly richer, deeper, and broader, but without clearly identifiable ideals.

- **Grading**—now more disciplined, even though grade inflation still exists; but grades have become more credentials for employment and graduate schools, rather than instructional feedback from teacher to student.
- **Extracurricular activities**—broader and more diverse, with competition going beyond the required academic ideals; unfortunately, they are now greatly motivated by eventual materialistic incentives.

In the process, I agree with Lewis that great universities, including Harvard, have forgotten their basic job: to turn restless 18-somethings into stable 20-something adults—to help them grow up; learn who they are; search for a larger purpose in life; and leave university as better, more balanced human beings. The only trouble is that the more famous the university, the more intense is market competition for faculty, students, and research funds. Increasingly, at the university level, there is less serious talk of developing good character, of building personal strength, integrity, kindness, cooperation, and compassion. Indeed, so totally has the goal of scholarly excellence overwhelmed the university's education role that they forgot both aims need not be in conflict. It must be recognized that this is not a zero-sum game.

Curriculum Reform

The answer must lie mainly in curriculum reform. I am one of those who believe that education should be more than what we learn. Pedagogy in the world's best universities is often good, also, often not so good. Frankly, with age, we only remember the brilliant teacher but not what he actually taught. "Education is what is left after all that has been learnt is forgotten"[4] (James Conant, Harvard president, 1933–1953).

At Harvard, I learned that the undergraduate mission has remained largely intact: to transform teenagers, whose lives have been so strictly managed by their families and schools, into adults with enough education to take responsibility for their own lives and for civil society. The intent is to reflect this new curriculum onto their system in order to realize their potential—they won't be able to (and can't) get it anywhere else. Fortunately, for Harvard, its strength lies in having the best students, first-class faculty, and excellent research. Emphasizing strength of character and scholarly excellence, the new curriculum is intended to (1) help students understand the complexities of the human condition; (2) challenge them with issues that are disturbing in society; (3) come to grips with the basic questions of life; and (4) fit seamlessly into its multitalented, multiethnic, multicultural, and multinational student body. In the process, the idea is to turn dependent adolescents into wiser adults.[5]

Dignity, Honor, and Responsibility

In my view, restoration of the right balance between scholarly excellence and its education role requires developing in students a *philosophy of life* that brings dignity, honor, and responsibility to oneself. For Malaysia, this means helping them to believe in themselves as individuals, and not to see themselves first as members of any identity group. This simply entails creating community out of diversity. The building of self-understanding and confidence in one's own principles and judgment remains key to the type of educated person and leader we all want to emerge from our universities. Within this context, universities need to proceed to redesign curriculum that includes seven basic requirements:

1. More flexible purposeful-course requirements
2. Written and oral communication
3. Foreign language, including English
4. Quantitative skills
5. Basic science
6. Moral reasoning
7. Specialization

Hopefully, in being able to engage the increasingly complex world, new graduates should by then have the (1) ability to compose a literate and persuasive essay; (2) knowhow to interpret a famous humanistic text; (3) capacity to link history to the present; (4) understanding of foundation science and scientific methods to unravel mysteries of the real world; and (5) needed quantitative reasoning to sharpen analysis of problems.

In essence, it has to be recognized that tomorrow's world will not accept graduates not knowing the difference between a gene and a chromosome. Or, not familiar with select Nobel Prize–winning works in literature. The building of confidence involves a capability to speak cogently, including in English, persuade others, and reason on moral and ethical issues. They are also expected to know how to collaborate with others on divisive issues, and to engage each other in a civil manner.

Balance between the Sciences and Humanities

After World War II, the sciences and humanities became the foundation for curriculum thinking. The sciences were regarded as the transforming force, while the humanities were seen as both the conserving element and the secular instrument for moral uplift. In the United States at least, the power of the disciplines has since become overwhelming: They have become increasingly autonomous and self-justifying. There is little choice in this. Students will need to know how to use disciplines outside their academic context, indeed, to put a "human face" on whatever they learn. They must appreciate the global context and temporal depth of the human experience. And, they must develop and build capacity to analyze without being intimidated by the disciplines. Like it or not, science will grow in stature. As a practical matter, the basic understanding of science and technology is a crucial element of being an educated person.

At the same time, how can universities nurture and inspirit the humanities? Especially when humanists today feel increasingly marginalized. Critics retort that the humanities have lost their way by indulging in obscure postmodern theorizing about race, gender, and class. Such tensions are easily exacerbated by the growing emphasis on science. This leaves humanists feeling more and more neglected. This should not be.

What, Then, Are We to Do?

New advances in the sciences offer possibilities of prolonging human life, destroying human life, transforming human life artificially in ways that challenge the very meaning of what it is to be human. With such a prospect, traditional focus of the humanities on questions of value, of meaning, of ethics is now more important than ever before. Unfortunately, they do not lend themselves to testable theories or to empirically verified results. If we are to make sense of the thrusts life sciences place on us, we need a society in which scientific advances are made to serve humane purposes. Science will always need a human face.

Obiter Dictum

Any meaningful reform is complex and difficult. Former president Derek Bok of Harvard compared just such an exercise in his time to moving a cemetery. But I cannot see a higher priority than this awesome task at real undergraduate reform. President Barack Obama is reported to have said: "Change will not come if we wait for some other person or some other time. We are the ones we've been waiting for. We are the change that we seek."[6] Our world is shaped by leaders, good and bad—even the mediocre. They say we get the leaders we deserve. Yet, leaders develop their thinking, their ideas and beliefs, their biases, attitudes and capacities for change, including their advisors, at the universities. Let's give our future leaders a fair shake. We all deserve better.

Kuala Lumpur
July 9, 2009

Notes

1. First published on July 11, 2009.
2. Harry Lewis, dean, Harvard College, 1995–2003, *Excellence without a Soul* (New York: Public Affairs, 2006), p. 255.
3. Ibid., p. 1.
4. Ibid., p. xvi.
5. Ibid., p. 255.
6. President Barack Obama, "Our Time Has Come," speech in Chicago to supporters, February 6, 2008, transcript in "Obama on Super Tuesday: 'Our Time Has Come,'" *Washington Post* (February 6, 2008).

CHAPTER 96

The MBA: Is It Still Relevant?[1]

I was in Manila for the gathering of governors and trustees of the Asian Institute of Management (AIM). They comprise the cream of the Makati business community (including the Ayalas, Lopezs, Ocampos, del Rosarios, and of course, Cory Aquino until 2008), and a cross-section of entrepreneurs and scholars from India to Korea and Japan as well as from the United States, United Kingdom, and Australia. AIM was founded 42 years ago, supported by the Harvard Business School (HBS), which provided its first president. It's the oldest postwar business school (B-school) in Asia. This sets me thinking about the master of business administration (MBA) degree in the wake of the financial crisis.

You Are Angry, I'm Angry, Too!

A 30-something asked, Don't we ever learn?, referring to Generation Y's concern about negative perceptions about banks and bankers, following big bankruptcies in early 2000s, and now exacerbated by the financial crisis. We seem to be stuck in an evolving quagmire of intense rage against big business's bloated profits and outlandish bonuses. To be blunt, there is loss of confidence in financial institutions—investment banks, credit rating agencies, and regulators even, including B-schools. Surely, MBAs have lost a bit of luster.

I'm angry because many people at the heart of the crisis, from Christopher Cox (former US Securities and Exchange Commission chairman) and former Treasury Secretary Henry Paulson (ex–Goldman Sachs chief) to Paul O'Neal and John Thain (former Merrill Lynch chief executive officers), and Rick Wagoner (ex–General Motors), carry a Harvard MBA. They should have known better. To be fair, although some of the worst culprits had MBAs from other schools, lots of others involved didn't (Bernie Madoff, for one). It is easy to confuse correlation with causation. Also, I am angry because the teaching of ethics and values-based leadership was not taken seriously enough. Critics point to many MBAs being not well equipped to make good judgments, without enough good sense to take corporate social responsibility (CSR) to the next level. I am still angry because many MBAs have a dangerous overdose of quantitative models, with underexposure to management of system-wide risks. MBAs are good at analysis, not always at managing. Still, greedy appetites in a "corrupt" ecosystem can overpower even the best management education. For comfort, CEOs (with MBAs) of Canada's two largest banks did just fine. While Wall Street bankers had no qualms in gearing their borrowing at 34 to 1, Canadian institutions played it safe with 18 to 1. They are doing well, of course, while their US counterparts are on life support.

A Little Bit of History

MBA started life in the 1900s (HBS, 1908). The aim was to train professional managers to run large institutions (like US Standard Oil and General Motors) so that they wouldn't take undue advantage of markets and consumers. CSR was also strongly advocated. Giant enterprises need to be managed for the public good, not for short-term gains. After World War II, the Ford and Carnegie foundations supported serious reviews to modernize the MBA. It was a time of market liberalization. Milton Friedman (Nobel laureate 1976) and the Chicago School increasingly dominated business thinking. Their ideology glorifies markets as efficient, capable of regulating themselves, and all managers have to do is to maximize shareholders' value. Critics argue this very thinking got us into so much trouble today. This is the point made by HBS Professor Rakesh Khurana in his 2007 book on the history of MBAs, *From Higher Aims to Hired Hands*, which concluded B-schools have veered from their original purpose of "training managers to rule in the name of society."[2] This new preoccupation with quantitative methods and mathematical models, including the use of advanced analysis, unfortunately gave MBAs the illusion of being able to control financial risks. Moreover, their teaching was flawed by ignoring a good sense of ethics ("largely a waste of time," anyway) and imparting lots of moneymaking knowhow. I overheard at MIT-Sloan last summer: In physical science, three laws explain 99 percent of behavior; in finance, 99 laws can explain at best only 3 percent.

The Trouble with Rankings

As I see it, business-school rankings (BSRs) are part of the problem. Sure, market pressure from BSRs exerts the needed competition to improve curricula and teaching. But undue attention to drive up BSRs can have unintended consequences: (1) higher starting pay means admitting the more mature; (2) stress on higher-paying sectors skews the curriculum to favor Wall Street; (3) funds are misdirected to coach students to perform well at interviews to raise job offers; and (4) focus on professional education is undermined—instead, students ask: How can I make the most money? Ratings target short performance drivers, and needlessly bias B-schools' marketing efforts. Professor Joel M. Podolny (Apple University and formerly Harvard, Yale, and Stanford) was emphatic: "I do object to the manner in which rankings have legitimized most business schools' myopic focus on the short term."[3]

Management Education Adds Value

When asked, Is the MBA still relevant?, HBS professor Quinn Mills's response was quick and crisp: "Yes and more than ever."[4] According to Mills, business has become more important as financial crises challenge political stability and economic welfare. MBA training helps students better understand the ecosystem and master developments. The education has two elements: One is about business and economics; the other, management and leadership. The first looks outside the firm to its context (customers, suppliers, regulators, markets); the second looks inside the firm to its effectiveness, efficiency, planning, and implementation. Both are important to the success of individuals in a leadership position.

Mills is convinced problems in financial markets involve more the business element. Problems arise in what financial firms are doing to others and to each other, not in how efficiently they are managed. Many say it's all a leadership problem. If Wall Street firms were better led—less greedy and more responsible—these problems would not arise. Many major MBA programs emphasize technicalities of finance—training people to work in banks, not to lead them. It is in financial engineering that problems have arisen.

Unfortunately, nations have yet to reform financial regulation. Sad to say, B-schools have not sufficiently revised curricula to reflect lessons from the crisis—though in individual courses and cases, there is much that is now up to date. Financial engineering continues to be taught, but also updated to reflect disasters that have occurred (complicated securitization, credit default swaps, and complex derivatives) so similar errors might be avoided in the future. Also, ethics courses have been strengthened in response to dramatic cases of fraud (Madoff, Allen Stanford, etc.). Hopefully, students are better prepared to meet the world as it now is. Through it all, acceptances to MBA programs are significantly up in 2009. In the end, this simply means more business as usual.

Too Little Core Revamp

Nevertheless, there has been since a lot of soul searching, including at HBS. Professor Nabil El-Hage (HBS senior associate dean) has this update: We concluded teaching critical thinking skill is one area we must do better. Our students go on to be leaders; they need to know how to think and challenge the status quo in a clearly analytical fashion. He adds: The other, perhaps more mundane area, is risk management. This is difficult to teach. It is not exciting, it is not fun, and it is not so much about leadership. But if businesses focus strictly on the upside and lose sight of inherent risks, then crises are bound to recur. So, we are thinking long and hard about how to deal with this. In the final analysis, I believe real change will come through punishment by the one factor B-schools understand best: the market.

A Promise to Be Ethical

The original sin of B-schools is that there has been no real focus on business ethics and CSR. In the post-Madoff era, this has now become urgent. But quality teaching is a problem since these "were kind of shunted in" after early 2000s scandals, wrote Philip D. Broughton in his tell-all book about his years at HBS, *Ahead of the Curve*.[5] Khurana confirms ethics was brought in like "academic theatrics," and has been since "quietly abandoned or marginalized."[6] But students are not happy. Last summer, I attended Harvard's Commencement when new HBS graduates took the "MBA oath," saying essentially: Greed is not good. This is a voluntary student-led living pledge to "act with utmost integrity and in an ethical manner," and to guard against "behavior that advances my own narrow ambitions but harms the enterprise and society it serves."[7] This is not unlike that at Columbia: "I adhere to principles of truth, integrity and respect. I will not lie, cheat, steal or tolerate those who do."[8]

What's being done appears serious—mirroring the Hippocratic oath of doctors to "do no harm" or the US lawyers' pledge to "uphold law and Constitution." When I was there, 200 (graduating class of 800) had already signed up. This movement has been contagious. Diana Robertson, professor of business ethics at Wharton, doesn't think it will just fade: It's coming from students; we've not seen such a surge of activism since the 1960s.[9]

For Khurana, it is now timely to transform business management into a true profession. This will involve licensing and an oversight body to police members. But he is not optimistic this will happen. It's still very much work in progress. Quinn Mills doesn't see how business can really gain. The management/leadership element of MBA, he says, is too much an art for it to be professionalized.[10] The finance side is already governed by a quasi-professional standard—the fiduciary responsibility rule (a financial adviser is legally bound to put clients' interests above all). In practice, this rule is already not much honored by financial advisers, money managers, and courts. Mills sees little reason new professional rules will perform better. He has a point.

How Best to Regain Trust

We may not feel it as much in Asia. But even on Wall Street, there is resentment building on the way MBAs are educated. The world has changed. B-schools have yet to change with it. To reduce distrust, MBAs need to show they value what society values. As I see it, what is not taken seriously enough are the "soft" disciplines (leadership, values, and ethics) and greater attention to detail (big-picture education is not good enough). Leadership responsibilities need to be brought to the forefront—not just the rewards. There are no quick fixes. Podolny pointed to five possible ways:

1. **Foster greater complementarity**. Integrate the mix of disciplines, linking analytics to values.
2. **Appoint team teaching**. Ensure "hard" and "soft" disciplines are jointly taught, giving a holistic understanding of problems and solutions.
3. **Incentivize qualitative research**. Cultivate a more eclectic approach, encouraging faculty to better weave "soft" disciplines into the main fabric of education.
4. **Stop competing on rankings**. Regain professional focus and downplay money as the end-all of business.
5. **Withdraw the degree**. Oaths work when behavior is monitored and credentials withdrawn on violations.[11]

What, Then, Are We to Do?

I think these warrant serious consideration. They are difficult to accept and hard to implement. Once upon a time, kings engaged jesters to bring them down to earth. Maybe it's now timely for B-schools to do likewise, encouraging faculty and students to prick bubbles, expose management fads, and even rough-up "hero" managers. Yes, in a sense, to bite the hand that feeds them. Realistically, I am convinced such changes are unlikely since it requires B-schools to reinvent themselves. HBS Dean Light thinks:

"The crisis has not resulted in a systematic reinvention of curriculum, nor should it." After all, as in every crisis, enrollment is up. So what's your problem?

Manila, the Philippines
Kuala Lumpur
March 11, 2010

Notes

1. First published on March 13, 2010.
2. Rakesh Khurana, *From Higher Aims to Hired Hands* (Princeton, NJ: Princeton University Press, 2007). Also, with Nitin Nohria, "It's Time to Make Management a True Profession," in *Harvard Business Review* (October 2008).
3. Joel M. Podolny, "The Buck Stops (and Starts) at Business School," *Harvard Business Review* (June 2009), p. 65.
4. Quinn Mills, in a private note exchanging views on this subject on March 2, 2010.
5. Philip D. Broughton, in a widely cited piece in the *Sunday Times* of London in early 2009.
6. Khurana.
7. The 2009 HBS oath: I promise:
   - I will act with utmost integrity and pursue my work in an ethical manner.
   - I will safeguard the interests of my shareholders, co-workers, customers and the society in which we operate.
   - I will manage my enterprise in good faith, guarding against decisions and behavior that advance my own narrow ambitions but harm the enterprise and the societies it serves.
   - I will understand and uphold, both in letter and in spirit, the laws and contracts governing my own conduct and that of my enterprise.
   - I will take responsibility for my actions, and will represent the performance and risks of my enterprise accurately and honestly.
   - I will develop both myself and other managers under my supervision so that the profession continues to grow and contribute to the well-being of society.
   - I will strive to create sustainable economic, social and environmental prosperity worldwide.
   - I will be accountable to my peers and they will be accountable to me for living by this oath.

8. Leslie Wayne, "A Promise to Be Ethical in an Era of Immortality," *New York Times* (May 30, 2009).
9. Ibid.
10. Mills.
11. Podolny, pp. 66–67.

CHAPTER 97

375 Years and Still Number One[1]

The year 1636, the first liberal arts college was founded in the British American Colonies, known simply as the College at Cambridge. It was renamed Harvard College three years later after a young Puritan minister endowed it with one-half of his estate and all 400 of his books. The College was already 140 years old when the Colonies became the United States. It commenced 375 years ago with just a dozen young scholars.

Today, Harvard has been transformed into a world-class research-based university, with a full-time enrollment of close to 20,000, where more than 13,000 attend its 12 world-famous branded graduate schools. Harvard has a very large global presence—about 25 percent of its 320,000 alumni are overseas. I was just there, invited to participate at the close of a year of commemorating Harvard's 375th birthday.

It ended with commencement (or what the British call *convocation*) on May 24, when 7,500 were conferred degrees for academic excellence. I also attended the traditional summer meeting of the Graduate School of Arts and Sciences Alumni Council (a member since 1993 and its chairman, 2003–2005), at the end of which the 2012 Centennial Medals were presented to four distinguished alumni scholars—for contributions to society as they have emerged from one's graduate education at Harvard.

Rites of Passage

To celebrate commencement, Harvard reaches back through the centuries to recall some of its time-honored—and, quaintly curious—graduation rituals. According to *Harvard Magazine*, among them:

1. **Here comes the sheriff:** "Sheriff, pray give us order!" With this cry, the city of Cambridge's own sheriff—clad in top hat and morning coat—pounds his staff three times and declares, "This meeting will be in

order," to officially begin commencement. According to lore, the sheriffs were invited in the seventeenth century to control rowdy students and alumni who had overindulged in punch and ale.

2. **The happy committee:** Members of the committee for the Happy Observance of Commencement escort dignitaries, guests, alumni, and students at Commencement, assist in managing the alumni "spreads" (or lunches), and marshal the procession. They are (even today) recognized by their regalia: top hat and tails for men, all-black outfits adorned with crimson cockades for women, and batons for both.

3. **Three legs are better than four:** During graduation, the president of Harvard reposes in a three-legged richly carved chair, crafted from European ash and US oak from the eighteenth century. In 2011, a college graduate mused that its lack of a fourth leg signifies: "Our learning opportunities are not over."

4. **Badges of honor:** Graduation gowns are adorned with a feature unique to Harvard—embroidered "crow's feet" emblem. Graduands wear two, while honorary degree recipients get three. Different colors signify the graduands' faculty or school: purple for law, light blue for education, and so on.

5. **Bona fortuna:** Reflecting its classical roots, one graduand is chosen to deliver the Latin oration (only graduating seniors are provided with a translation). *Quandocumque officium vocat!* (Whenever duty calls, listen!).

6. **Bells:** At just past 11:30 a.m., the tintinnabulation of bells from nearby churches and institutions celebrate the end of commencement.[2]

Harvard through the Years

Great universities endure—none more so than Harvard. Indeed, Harvard is consistently ranked number one among world universities. Its alumni include 45 Nobel Laureates, some 50 Pulitzer Prize winners, and scores of other just as reputable prize winners in the sciences and the liberal arts. At its heart is Harvard College. Today, it has some 7,000 male and female students from all 50 US states and 6 continents—10 percent are international, 5 percent Asian. They represent a spectrum of socioeconomic, ethnic, and religious backgrounds that is unsurpassed by any other global institutions.

To become truly global, Harvard partnered with MIT to create EdX, an online learning platform that will allow students around the world to take virtual courses from the two institutions for free. The program has had 120,000 students enrolled since its debut in February 2012. It represented a "college education revolution," Thomas Friedman wrote in the *New York Times*. It will democratize education, technology, and teaching, supported by the influential Harvard and MIT brands.

Over the past 25 years, one to three Malaysians were admitted annually to the college. Unfortunately, there was none in 2011, and none again in 2012—worse, this year (2013), none of the Malaysian applications was deemed fit by Harvard to be even interviewed. This is sad, and reflects, I am afraid, the poor state of the Malaysian education system. Sure, admission at Harvard remains very competitive. In 2011, 35,000 applied but only 6.3 percent was admitted. All told, as of June 1, 2012, Singapore has 18 students studying at the college, Thailand 7, Vietnam 6, Malaysia 5, and Indonesia 2.

Make no mistake, studying in Harvard is expensive. But Harvard still offers the best deal there is anywhere—tuition finances only 25 percent of the cost of a Harvard education. It receives no government monetary support. The rest, the university subsidizes: 60 percent of its students are granted scholarships worth a total of US$172 million this year, which are blind need-based. But, Harvard is now accessible and affordable.[3] If the family income is less than US$60,000 a year, the student pays nothing. If it's less than US$180,000 a year, the student pays only up to 10 percent.

You can't get a better deal than that. Of course, students are also expected to contribute to the cost of their education through part-time and summer work. Harvard just looks for the best and the brightest there is to admit. That's how it remains the world's No. 1.

Too Selective?

For its graduating class of 2016, Harvard will admit 2,032 students this fall, or 5.9 percent of the applicant pool of 34,302, dipping below 6 percent for the first time. It expects an 81 percent yield (percentage of acceptance), the best turnout since 1971 and the highest among the Ivies.

Harvard remains heavily demanded—is it getting too exclusive? For sure, it casts its net wider and wider each year to attract ever-more qualified applicants. This year's pool is remarkable: (1) 3,800 were ranked first in their class; (2) 14,000 scored 700 or more on the SAT critical reading test, with 17,000 scoring 700 or above on the SAT math test; (3) extracurricular interests cited by students were outstanding (e.g., 41 percent with music and performing arts); (4) minority representation remains strong (21 percent Asian Americans, 10 percent African Americans, 10 percent foreign—but including US dual citizenship and permanent residents, 19 percent); and (5) 53 percent are men. With applicants getting perfect SAT scores far exceeding the number of places available, personal qualities and character remain central in the final decision to admit. In the end, those admitted reflect Harvard's commitment to diversity and excellence.

Divergent Global Presence

According to the Harvard *Crimson*: Two years ago, Yale University caused a stir by co-sponsoring a new campus in Singapore with National University of Singapore (Yale-NUS)—the first by an Ivy-league school overseas.[4] Harvard, however, remains committed to keeping its student body firmly rooted in Cambridge. Yale's decision is controversial even today. "We don't want to just focus on one area of the world and put a disproportionate part of our attention on one location in which we invest a huge amount of our effort. We would rather support activity much more broadly," said Harvard's President Drew Faust.[5] "If you take Harvard out of Cambridge, it's no longer Harvard," observed an education expert.

The Crimson had reported that Faust believes that Harvard's goals are best achieved by connecting the Harvard community with programs, collaborations, and partnerships abroad. She launched EdX (with MIT) to use technology to cross borders. At the same time, she is an advocate of tempered expansion overseas (e.g., setting up international offices to serve as a "home base" for students and faculty). Its venerable Renaissance research at Villa I Tatti (outside Florence) is complemented by the business school (HBS) centers in Hong Kong, Buenos Aires (with branches in Sao Paulo and Mexico City), Tokyo, Paris, and Mumbai. The vast Shanghai Centre is the first to have teaching facilities to conduct HBS executive education. Its other outposts—devoted to Hellenic studies, AIDS care, and training programs—are scattered from Greece to Botswana to Ho Chi Minh City. *The Crimson* had concluded that questions remain over the benefits of physical expansion abroad. Many at Harvard remain convinced that such a step would diminish the meaning of the brand "Harvard." Indeed, Harvard Yard is regarded as a global hub.

Constancy of Change

Harvard has constantly been changing over a generation of its now 375 years, and promises more change. Through five presidents, Harvard stressed interdisciplinary scholarship, championed diversity, and launched an imaginative international initiative. In the process, it used its vast resources to underlay investments in facilities, faculty growth, financial aid, and the sciences. With the severe financial downturn, it refocused attention on teaching and learning, and brought university governance into the twenty-first century, and set in motion an imaginative capital campaign to advance its academic agenda.

Throughout this period, the presence of international students probably quadrupled, to more than 4,100 of its total 19,200 in 2009. Foreign students' presence became far more common in the professional schools as the University population got more global. A foreign born is now the university's vice provost for international affairs, and three top schools have foreign-born deans (Public Health, Design, and Business). At these three schools, 32 percent of students come from abroad. Only the Graduate School of Arts and Sciences (36 percent) and the Kennedy School (42 percent) have a higher foreign presence. Even as the college opened itself to more foreign students and a more diverse slice of America, it has since become more selective. There is now almost gender parity at the undergraduate level.

This year's graduating class's job choices are also changing—as much a reflection of the changing economy as of their own changing priorities. The College's 2012 seniors survey estimated that 68 percent already have jobs (73 percent in 2007), still far better than at the height of the financial crisis. Just over 20 percent will head for consulting (12 percent) and finance (9 percent); in 2007, it was 47 percent—that is, in the two sectors synonymous with big-bucks Wall Street. Fewer will enter law or health and medicine. This reflects the enduring legacy of the recent financial crisis.

What, Then, Are We to Do?

Harvard has changed and flourished—it emerged as a research institution in the late nineteenth century; then transformed into a national university; and developed after World War II into an engine of innovation to power rapid economic growth and became a force for human development. During the past generation, it has evolved in the context of globalization and immense technological change to emerge as a champion of innovation in the sciences and biotechnology, and to renew itself to help students and faculty bring new ideas to life to raise a better world. It also began to reinvent itself, reform its curriculum to reflect the deepening of global inquiries, and modernize its governance to make it more outcome oriented, providing opportunities for more coherent strategic thinking about the future.

Its students have developed into global citizens, able to appreciate the international dimensions of whatever problem they seek to focus on in their lives. Harvard already has a large global footprint. It opens up lots of opportunities to its students and faculty to enable them to be challenged enough to bring new perspectives to their scientific enterprise.

It makes sense for Malaysia to be a part of this endeavor. "This world demands the qualities of youth: not a time of life but a state of mind, a temper of the will, a quality of imagination, a predominance of courage over timidity, of the appetite for adventure over the life of ease" (Robert Kennedy). Our youth must be back on Harvard's radar screen next year. For a start, the Harvard Club of Malaysia now helps to sponsor "Teach for Malaysia" to encourage young professionals to take time off to teach, and share in the passion for education excellence.

Cambridge, Massachusetts
Kuala Lumpur
May 31, 2012

Notes

1. First published on June 2, 2012.
2. *Harvard Magazine*, vol. 114, no. 6, July–August 2012.
3. Drew G. Faust, president, Harvard University, letter dated November 11, 2008, to alumni and friends on Harvard and the economy, Cambridge, MA.
4. Michael C. George and Alyza J. Sebenius, "Between Harvard and Yale, a World of Difference," *Harvard Crimson* (May 24, 2012).
5. Drew G. Faust, quoted in ibid.

CHAPTER 98

Onward the Harvard Connection [1]

"Fair Harvard": That's the university hymn I heard when I first set foot on the Yard from Harvard Square during the summer of 1969. Harvard inspires. It's also contagious. This is not surprising, since the university is consistently judged number one globally. QS Rankings and *London Times* Higher Education Survey place Harvard as the world's top university (mean rank position) over the past 10 years.[2] Mind you, personally, I attach little significance to such rankings—though it does please me as an alumnus to find Harvard right there on top. I know of many who regard this as "invidious, crude, and meaningless."

Still, looking at the top 10 or even 50, Harvard does lead the world in basic science research and is at the cutting edge of the social sciences. Indeed, students the world over seek to enter in large numbers. Since its founding in 1636, 140 years before the United States became a republic, Harvard has built a solid reputation of being among the best and finest there is. It has won 44 Nobel and 46 Pulitzer prizes. Much of its staying power can be traced to the unusual characteristic of US private university life of being competitive (against the English, European, or Asian "continental model"). In the United States, it is not unusual for institutions of similar stature to actively compete for faculty, research funds, students, and peer recognition, and much else. Stanford, Chicago, and Harvard, for example, aggressively compete for the best students. It is not unusual to hire professors away from another university (offering higher compensation and benefits) to enhance quality. Competition has prevented complacency and pushed the drive for excellence and change. This assures quality at the top—whereas "continental model" professors tend to be civil servants, subject to bureaucratic regulations, where "logrolling" is said to replace competition.

Tenured Professor

The appointment of professors with tenure, or permanent employment, is vexatious, even annoying to the point of being agitatingly controversial. But in the United States, the granting of tenure is taken most seriously.

Tenure is given after a long period of probation, and extensive inside and outside peer review. It involves a highly competitive selection process. At Harvard, Professor Henry Rosovsky was chairman of the Economics Department in the early 1970s when I was a doctoral student, and later dean of Harvard's largest school, the Graduate School of Arts and Sciences, for 11 years (responsible for 9,000 students, 6,000 employees, a budget today exceeding US$1.2 billion, and 1,500 teachers). Rosovsky said:

> At Harvard, we ask a traditional question: who is the most qualified person in the world to fill a particular vacancy, and then we try to convince that scholar to join our ranks. We may . . . not succeed in attracting our first or even second choice, but our goal is elevated. . . . The best faculty attracts the finest students, produces the highest-quality research, gains the most outside support.[3]

In practice, the process to appoint a tenured Harvard professor takes no less than two laborious years of international search, review, and selection.

I recall reading it in the *Economist*, which once described professors with tenure: as if they can think (or idle) in ill-paid peace, accountable to nobody. That's the general feeling. Professors have academic tenure—that is, "without limit of time"—and can only be removed for misconduct or neglect of duty, or a serious moral lapse. In essence, tenured professors enjoy independence and security. Indeed, tenure is defended, according to Professor Rosovsky, in four ways: (1) as the principal guarantor of academic freedom—to teach whatever one believes without fear of retribution; (2) as a source of internal discipline since the selection process is subject to extraordinarily rigorous standards; (3) as a practice contributing to institutional stability—preventing unfair personal advantage; and (4) as a social contract preserving the quality of professors who trade off lifelong security for lesser economic rewards. But there are serious minuses, too.[4]

Professorship Funds

A year ago, I wrote, at the close of Harvard's 375th anniversary, of how the university has changed and flourished since World War II into one identified as an engine of scientific discovery and economic growth, as well as a force for significantly broadening social opportunity.[5] Harvard already has the most reputable global footprint. Today, education is more vital than ever to the well-being of economies and societies.

President Drew Faust reflected recently:

Knowledge is the most important currency of the twenty-first century. And universities are the places that, more than any other, generate and disseminate that knowledge. . . . We need the knowledge and understanding that research generates. . . . We need the support and encouragement for the students (and faculty) who create our scientific future. We need the economic vitality—the jobs and companies—that these ideas and discoveries produce. We need the nation to resist imposing a self-inflicted wound on its intellectual and human capital. We need a nation that believes in and invests in its universities because we represent an investment in the ideas and the people that will build and be the future.[6]

That's exactly what Malaysia really needs to get out of "the middle-income trap." So, I congratulate the Jeffrey Cheah Foundation (JCF) for the US$6.2 million initiative to establish at Harvard two Jeffrey Cheah Professorships of Southeast Asia Studies, the Jeffrey Cheah Fellowship, and the Jeffrey Cheah Travel Grants. The agreements to effect the arrangements were finalized in July between Tan Sri Jeffrey Cheah (as chairman of JCF) and Professor Jorge Dominguez, Harvard's vice provost for international affairs (acting for president of Harvard). According to JCF:

[These funds are intended] to support the best and the brightest faculty and students from around the world (including Malaysia) as they advance teaching and research focused on Southeast Asia (SEA), including Malaysia. . . . These funds will work in tandem to advance academic discovery focused on SEA, further define (the pro-active role of Malaysia in advancing) the growing influence SEA has on our global community, and strengthen ties between Harvard, Malaysia and the region.[7]

The investment, administration, and distribution of each of the following funds shall be managed at the discretion of Harvard's president. The university will provide an annual report within 90 days after the end of each fiscal year.

Jeffrey Cheah Professorship (JCP)

Jeffrey Cheah Professorship (JCP) endows a US$4 million Harvard chair in SEA Studies in perpetuity (i.e., forever), to be awarded to an eminent scholar focused on advancing teaching and research on societies and cultures of SEA countries, among them Malaysia. The Jeffrey Cheah Professor may focus on any of the following themes: governance and public policy; political economy; economics and development particularly of the region; business and management; public health and healthcare; urbanization; innovation; education; and the study of SEA's peoples and cultures. The first appointment, to be made at the discretion of the president of Harvard, will be in economic development, and the professorship may reside in any school of the university. The professor's title may also reflect the incumbent's field of specialization (e.g., Jeffrey Cheah Professor of Southeast Asia Studies and Political Economy).

Jeffrey Cheah Visiting Professorship of SEA Studies

Jeffrey Cheah Visiting Professorship of SEA Studies involves an expendable gift of US$200,000 to enable Harvard to appoint soonest possible a visiting professor for a specified term while the recruitment for JCP proceeds. It will also support at least one early conference related to SEA studies to be coordinated in consultation with Sunway University (SUY), Malaysia. Excess monies can be used to support a second appointment, other conferences, and workshops.

Jeffrey Cheah Fellowship in SEA Studies

Jeffrey Cheah Fellowship in SEA Studies endows US$1 million in perpetuity to support a Harvard graduate student conducting research focused on SEA. The Jeffrey Cheah Fellow may be appointed from any School at Harvard. Excess income may be used to appoint another Fellow.

Jeffrey Cheah Travel Grants (JCTG)

In order to advance teaching and research focused on SEA by faculty and students of Harvard University—and to support engagement with Harvard by SEA-based scholars—JCF will underwrite a continuing series of grants to support research and education-related travel to and from Malaysia and SEA. Up to US$100,000 annually will be made available for the next 10 years to support this JCTG program. The grants will better enable members of the Harvard community to travel to SEA (with Malaysia as priority) for research or study, and for scholars and practitioners on SEA studies from institutions in SEA (especially the Sunway Education Group—SEG) to travel to Harvard to present lectures and conduct research utilizing the university's library and museum collections and its faculties' expertise. The grants will be administered in practice as collaboration between Harvard's Asia Center (HAC) and JCF. HAC will select the most competitive applicants for approval by JCF. HAC will also publicize the grant program to Harvard faculty and students, and will coordinate with JCF on publicizing the program under SEG. Harvard-based applicants will know that travel to Malaysia (solely or in addition to travel to any other SEA nation) is a prerequisite for receiving an award.

JCF hopes that Harvard faculty and students will utilize the facilities of the Sunway Group of Companies—including SEG—and will engage with the students, faculty, and administrative leaders of all Sunway institutions, notably through teaching, scholarly research collaborations, joint publications, and joint research grant applications. This offer of hospitality is intended to strengthen the connection and collaboration between Harvard University and all Sunway institutions, and to help extend the reach and impact of JCTG.

Benefits

Trustees of JCF are right that teaching and research on SEA studies are important and timely to fill the present vacuum left by the concentration of academic and other interests and pursuits in Northeast and South Asia. It should further define the growing influence that SEA has on the global community and strengthen the connection and collaboration between Harvard University and Malaysia, and SEA in general. It is essential that the gifts generate an active two-way flow of scholars between Harvard and SEG (which also administers SUY and Monash University Malaysia–MUM) to support research, conferences, and workshops related to SEA studies, as well as through other scholarly collaborations.

The partnership should encourage development of Malaysian academic talent to upgrade their studies and research at Harvard, and the injection of Harvard expertise to help develop and improve standards in teaching and research at SEG in SEA Studies. This collaboration should also benefit higher education generally, and help establish a new benchmark of excellence to improve, and become a world-class education and research Hub in this region. These gifts provide unique opportunities to link up with Harvard University and its highly coveted Harvard brand. It will surely raise Malaysia's standing in education globally.

Indeed, it brings to bear at home the much-coveted association with Harvard, which rarely lends its name to any such ventures outside the United States. It also helps to extend the reach and impact of Harvard to SEA, which will eventually benefit and enhance the academic standing of SEG. That's good.

What, Then, Are We to Do?

Tan Sri Jeffrey has always been passionate about education. He has since set aside all his education assets, valued in excess of RM720 million (in addition to SUY and MUM, SEG comprises Sunway College, Jeffrey Cheah School of Medicine and Health Sciences, and Sunway International School), into JCF to promote education and help the disadvantaged. To date, more than RM100 million have been given out in scholarships.

JCF is by far Malaysia's largest social enterprise. Jeffrey often likes to say: "I aspire to inspire before I expire." He is fascinated by Harvard's global success, so much so he aspires for his modest SEG to become, someday, the Harvard of the East, and he is prepared to invest to make this happen. So, I am delighted that SUY will soon establish the Jeffrey Cheah Institute of SEA Studies (JCI) to act as a catalyst in promoting SEG as an attractive hub for studies on SEA.

It's noteworthy that JCI is being set up with the help and advice of Harvard Emeritus Professor Dwight Perkins, who was at one time chairman of Harvard's reputable Economics Department, and for 16 years thereafter, as director of the renowned Harvard Institute of International Development and, before his recent retirement, as director of Harvard's prestigious Asia Centre.

The aim of JCI is to be a top-notch, independent research outfit, initially to bridge the gap in research and teaching in SEA studies, collaborating and cooperating with other world-class institutions (including Harvard) and leveraging on research efforts at similar institutions worldwide, reflective of the best traditions of world-class think tanks. Malaysia badly needs such an initiative, and Tan Sri Jeffrey's bold effort is timely.

The challenges facing us today are too consequential. The need for knowledge, imagination, and deep understanding of SEA is just too great, and the opportunity to improve the human condition is too precious for us to do anything less than rise to the occasion. Tan Sri Jeffrey has sown the seeds to instill in our scholars what it means to be world-class. The inventor Alexander Graham Bell reminded us: When one door closes, another opens. However, we often look so long and so regretfully upon the closed door that we do not see the one that has opened for us. Tan Sri Jeffrey, thanks for opening the new door. With inspiration and a helping hand from no less than Harvard, and—I hope—strong support of our national leaders, we will prevail. We must. Let's keep this door wide open.

Kuala Lumpur
July 25, 2013

Notes

1. First published on July 27, 2013, as "Fair Harvard! Here We Come."
2. QS World University Rankings 2012, and *London Times* Higher Education World University Rankings, 2012.

3. Henry Rosovsky, *The University—An Owner's Manual* (New York: W.W. Norton, 1990).
4. Ibid., pp. 179–186.
5. Reproduced as Chapter 97, "375 Years and Still Number One."
6. Drew G. Faust, president, Harvard University, speech delivered at Harvard's commencement on May 30, 2013, in Cambridge, MA, pp. 6 and 8.
7. Jeffrey Cheah Foundation, press statement, "Realising the Vision: The Harvard of the East," July 27, 2013.

CHAPTER 99

The Future of University Education: What It Takes to Be Educated[1]

The inaugural Conference on Southeast Asia held in conjunction with the official launch of the Jeffrey Cheah Institute on Southeast Asia (JCI) by the Deputy Prime Minister of Malaysia on March 18, 2014, had as its theme: Overcoming the Middle Income Trap and Keeping Balance Amid Global Turbulence. I presented a paper on "Human Capital Needs for the 21st Century: The Role of Higher Education." The president of Harvard University talks of knowledge being the most important currency of the twenty-first century.[2] Indeed, I do believe that knowledge, innovation, and creativity, which together reliably drive increases in productivity, holds the key to releasing nations from the middle-income trap.

Higher Education

It is well acknowledged the delivery of quality education is the principal "takeaway" on higher education. As I see it, it is quality education that enables youth to develop (1) the ability to think clearly and critically, (2) the ability to communicate, (3) a strong set of ethical principles, (4) a commitment to fulfill civic responsibilities, (5) the ability to adapt and respond to a globalized society, (6) a breadth of interests to better cope with life, and (7) dependable instincts to prepare for a lifelong career.

Tensions

Along the way, the evolution of education confronts a number of tensions (pulling in different and, often, opposite directions) reflecting:

1. Requirements versus flexibility
2. Research versus teaching as a priority
3. Concentration (specialization) versus being "too" concentrated (i.e., less discipline-based and more focused on applications and professions)
4. Sciences versus humanities and social sciences (also, the shift in content)
   - Sciences: the transforming force
   - Humanities: the conserving element and instrument for moral uplift
5. How best to humanize the sciences?
   - Connecting theory with practice
   - Cannot divide student lives into what they study versus what they do; students want to be treated as a whole
6. Class curriculum versus extracurricular athletic and public-spirited outside activities where they learn to take initiative, build teamwork, display discipline, and exercise leadership—these can't be classroom taught
   - Mentored in nonacademic skills to tackle cases in business and economics, or compose music and write poetry—they build character and instill confidence
   - National versus international experience

This simply means: fundamental curriculum and pedagogy reforms.

End Product

The outcome, in practice, requires the end product (graduates) to at least have the ability to compose a literate and persuasive essay; sufficient insight to interpret a famous humanistic text; a capacity to link history to the present; the know-how to understand foundation science and scientific methods to unravel the mysteries of science and technology as they affect the real world; and enough quantitative reasoning ability to sharpen analysis of everyday problems. As I see it, tomorrow's world will not accept graduates "not knowing the difference between a gene and a chromosome or not familiar with select classics or Nobel Prize–winning works in literature."

So, the first challenge has to deal ultimately with building self-confidence, the lack of which figures prominently in local graduates' poor performance at job interviews—indeed, to be able to go beyond the ability to simply read and write. This must involve a capability to speak decent English and to articulate cogently, to persuade others, and to be able to reason on moral and ethical issues. They are also expected to know how to collaborate with others on divisive issues, and to engage each other in a civil manner. The task ahead is daunting. We need to start now.

Second, students need to rigorously consider the level of mastery we ask of them and how flexibly we should allow them to acquire it, given the complexity of the world they have to deal with. Take science, for example. Traditionally, nonscientists of my generation could manage to understand enough about cutting-edge science 50 years ago, which is not remotely possible today, certainly about tomorrow's world. Yet, given the dynamics that science holds for progress in various domains, science and scientific thinking are fast coming to dominate an ever-widening range of human activity. Looked at differently, decisions on how to manage economic policy, or how to respond to a public health crisis, or how to handle a national disaster (e.g., recent Malaysia Airlines' "missing" flight or having its plane blasted from the sky), or market a new drug, or even to evaluate the national bid to host the next Olympics—all once based on hunch and art, are today conducted in increasingly rigorous and more analytical ways. The challenge here is that it is no longer adequate for students to have just some "exposure" to science and its methods. They will need reasonable working knowledge of, and some dexterity with, its means of measurement, analysis, and calibration. Science and technology are here to stay. Students have to be equipped to engage them.

Third, yet another challenge concerns the future of society in the face of the tremendous prospects for change arising from the impact of science and technology. *In a world* where the database will know every phone number that I have ever dialed; *in a world* where researchers have cooperated in a multinational project to successfully sequence and map the human genome and in understanding the impact of this work; and *in a world* where cloning is changing what it means to be human, we are going to increasingly need people who understand that science is just too important to be left to scientists. The challenge here is to address the need to educate students who can think through the social problems and political challenges posed by science, with not just a reasonably good scientific and technical understanding but also a grounding in the deepest human values. Education in the sciences, adapting our modes of research to an era of life science, thinking about the interactions between science and society vis-à-vis the future of mankind, if we are to meet the challenge, that is one of the ideas our universities have to appropriately order. There are more. This offers just a taste of what's involved.

To adequately prepare students, I cite Harvard's new curriculum (reviewed and since reformed over a period of 10 years), which has been designed to meet four goals that link up to life after graduation:

1. Prepare for civic engagement.
2. Understand the traditions of art, ideas, and values.
3. Respond to deep change.
4. Appreciate ethical dimensions.

So, today, Harvard graduates have to complete courses in (1) aesthetic and interpretive understanding, (2) culture and belief, (3) empirical and mathematical reasoning, (4) ethical reasoning, (5) science of the living system, (6) science of the physical universe, (7) societies of the world, and (8) the United States in the world.

What, Then, Are We to Do?

World Bank's recent 2013 Report was rather critical of Malaysia's education system—putting on paper what most of us already know.[3] The four major conclusions are:

1. Malaysia performs very well with respect to access to education.
2. The quality of education has not kept pace. Among East Asian countries that participated in the 2012 PISA, Malaysian students only outperform their Indonesian peers, and lag even lower-income countries (including by a wide margin, Vietnam).
3. Performance also appears to be declining. Although the latest PISA scores showed improvement in math, most other recent indicators point in the opposite direction. Evidence also suggests that English proficiency has deteriorated over time.
4. The key constraints to improving the quality of basic education thus relate not to the quantity of inputs but institutions: (a) highly restricted levels of autonomy, (b) low parental involvement and therefore accountability, and (c) shortcomings in teacher recruitment and performance management.

Teacher numbers are ample, but there are significant concerns about teacher quality. Malaysia's education system is among the most centralized in the world. The report concluded: "There is an urgent need to transform Malaysia's education system so that it produces the quality graduates required by a high-income economy."[4] For years, the government has been in denial. Now, we know for sure.

Five Questions

As I look forward, five key questions first posed by Derek Bok, former president of Harvard University continue to bug me, and they should bug universities enough to come up with the answers:[5]

1. **Who** are our students? **Whom** should we educate? Need for lifelong learning and executive education, and technology's ability to extend

access beyond the classroom to the world: how should universities respond?

2. **How** can we best teach them? Given advances in technology and cognitive psychology, and growing interconnection among disciplines (requiring a more university-wide, interdisciplinary approach to learning).

3. **How** can we effectively reach a more global interconnected world? Bowing to the inevitable, stand-alone instruction online start-ups, through massively open online courses (MOOCs), have gone ahead (e.g., Harvard-MIT's EdX now reaches millions worldwide free of charge; Harvard's own HarvardX and AlumniX also put its best forward and have proved to be popular).

4. **How** can we infuse science usefully into everyday life, so that scientific advances do not overwhelm us?

5. **How** can we humanize science? The role of humanities on key questions of *value,* of *meaning* of life, and of *ethics* assumes critical importance.

Kuala Lumpur
March 20, 2014

Notes

1. First published on March 22, 2014.
2. Drew G. Faust, president, Harvard University, 2013 commencement speech at Harvard, Cambridge, MA, May 30, 2013, pp. 6–8.
3. World Bank. *Malaysia Economic Monitor: High Performing Education* (Washington, DC: World Bank, December 2013).
4. Ibid., pp. 103–104.
5. Derek Bok, former president, Harvard University, 2007 commencement speech at Harvard, Cambridge, MA, June 7, 2007.

CHAPTER 100

Schumpeternomics: Gotta Keep on Learning[1]

I just returned from the summer meeting of the board of governors (on which I am a long-standing member) and the board of trustees of the Asian Institute of Management (AIM) in Makati, Manila. It celebrated its 45th Anniversary—first set up in 1968 with assistance from the Harvard Business School (HBS), which provided a tenured HBS professor as its inaugural president, and financial support from the Philippines' business elite, including the likes of the Ayalas, Lopezs, and Del Rosarios, under the leadership of the venerable Washington Z. Sycip. To mark the occasion, AIM held its second Asian Business Conference in July 2014 against the backdrop of an emerging ASEAN Economic Community (AEC) by 2015. It was well attended by a wide cross-section of Asian businesses, research institutes, and universities, under the banner: "2015 Approaching: Priming for ASEAN Integration." I spoke at the strategic session on banking and finance with particular focus on the need for Asia (and indeed, ASEAN) to keep on innovating to create a truly learning society, in order to maintain its competitive edge and remain relevant in an increasingly hostile and uncertain world. To survive, we just gotta keep on learning!

Technological Progress

I learned early as a Harvard graduate student in the 1970s, from no less than Nobel Laureate Robert Solow at MIT down the Charles River, that rising output and incomes can only come about in a sustained way from technological progress (TP), not from mere capital accumulation. Put simply, Solow repeatedly emphasized that TP comes from learning how to do things better; indeed, there's always a better way. As a practicing banker and economist at Bank Negara Malaysia (central bank) after my PhD studies, I quickly learned that much of the productivity increases we see come from small incremental changes—they all add up—rather than the lumpy gains arising from dramatic discoveries or from unpredictable phenomena. It all starts with nurturing our education system and the process of its development to ensure youths are properly educated, not just in terms of literary, quantitative, and scientific skills, but also with the right moral values and civic outlook. Broadly, along what Nobel Laureate Joseph Stiglitz has been advocating—it always makes good sense "to focus attention on how societies learn, and what can be done to promote learning, including learning how to learn."[2]

Innovation and Creative Destruction

The seeds of the critical role of innovation in economic growth were first planted about a century ago by Harvard's economist and political and social scientist, Joseph Schumpeter, a contemporary of John Maynard Keynes. His economics (hence, Schumpeternomics) is based on the ability and capability of the market economy to innovate on its own. I recall reading his 1939 book, *Business Cycles: A Theoretical, Historical and Statistical Analysis of the Capitalist Process*, where he wrote, "Without innovations, no entrepreneurs; without entrepreneurial achievement, no capitalist returns and no capitalist propulsion. The atmosphere of industrial revolutions—of "progress"—is the only one in which capitalism can survive."[3]

Schumpeter went about challenging conventional wisdom in three areas: (1) misplaced focus on competitive markets. He contended that what matters was "competition for the markets, not competition in the markets," as rightly pointed out by Stiglitz. It is competition for the markets that drives innovation. Sure, this can (and does) result in the rise of monopolies; still, this would lead to improved living standards over the long haul (e.g., Microsoft, Nokia—acquired in 2013 by Microsoft); (2) undue focus on short-run efficiency, which can be detrimental to innovation over the long term—classic example is helping "infant industries" learn. But governments should not be in the game of picking winners; the market can do this better (witness President Barack Obama's failed "clean energy" projects or Malaysia's wasteful car-maker, Proton). Sure, there are exceptions where government invests in research that has since led to development of the Internet and discovery of DNA with enormous social benefits; and (3) innovation leads to creative destruction—it can (and does) wipe out inefficient industries and jobs.

The Internet has turned businesses from newspapers to music to book retailing upside down. In their place, more efficient businesses have popped up. In his biography of Schumpeter—*Prophet of Innovation*—Thomas McCraw wrote:

Schumpeter's signature legacy is his insight that innovation in the form of creative destruction is the driving force not only of capitalism but of material progress in general. Almost all businesses, no matter how strong they seem to be at a given moment, ultimately fail—and almost always because they failed to innovate. Competitors are relentlessly striving to overtake the leader, no matter how big the lead. Responsible business people know that they ignore this lesson at their peril.[4]

In 1983, the 100th anniversary of the birth of Schumpeter and Keynes, Peter F. Drucker proclaimed in *Forbes* that it was Schumpeter, not Keynes, who provided the best guide to the rapid economic changes engulfing the world, according to McCraw.

Higher Education

The business of higher education has changed little since Plato and Aristotle taught at the Athenian Lyceum. With government patronage and support, close to 4 million Americans and 5 million Europeans will graduate this summer. Emerging nations' universities are expanding even faster. I was told in Shanghai last month that China has added 30 million university places in the past 20 years. Indeed, I do see a revolution coming for three main disruptive reasons: (1) rising costs—Baumol's disease has set in (i.e., soaring costs reflecting high labor intensity with stagnant productivity); for the past two decades, costs have risen 1.6 percentage points above inflation annually; (2) changing demand—a recent Oxford study contended that 47 percent of occupations are now at risk of being automated and as innovation wipes out jobs and drastically changes others, vast numbers will be needing continuing education; and (3) fast-moving TP will change the way education is packaged, taught, and delivered.

Massively open online courses (MOOCs) today offer university students a chance to learn from the world's best and get a degree for a fraction of today's cost. HBS will soon offer an online "pre-MBA" for US$1,500! The reinvention of universities will certainly benefit many more than it hurts. Elites like Harvard, MIT, and Stanford will gain from this creative destruction process, but others may suffer the fate of newspapers and traditional retailers. Education is now a global digital market.

What, Then, Are We to Do?

Corporate giants come and go in a competitive economy. Microsoft and Nokia used to rule the digital world. Now they don't. No monopoly is permanent, unless enforced by government, which, as everyone knows, hardly changes, even as the rest of the world passes it by. In the United States, it is reported that the Administration wants to prevent Apple's iTunes and App Store from abusing the network "lock-in" created by Apple's tech ecosystem. But US District Judge Denise Cote has since ruled, "I want Apple to have the flexibility to innovate."[5] That's something, isn't it? My old professor at Harvard, Nobel Laureate Kenneth Arrow, used to extol the importance of learning by doing. So, those who want to innovate, let them just do it—hopefully with no government intervention, even though there is a compelling "infant" argument for industrial protection, which can be a two-edged sword when it comes to learning and innovating. Most of the time, the infant fails to grow up. But reinventing the ancient institution of higher learning will not be easy.

EdX, a nonprofit MOOC founded (and funded) in May 2012 by Harvard and MIT, is now a consortium of 28 institutions worldwide. No one knows how big the online market will eventually be. It's more akin to online airline-booking services—expanding the market by improving the customer experience. Still, innovation at MOOC will definitely reduce the cost of higher education, grow market size but with widespread creative destruction collateral damage, and turn inefficient universities on their heads. MOOC estimates that university employment can fall by as much as 30 percent and as many as 700 to 800 institutions could shut down. The rest have to reinvent themselves to survive. Our learning society will change forever, whether we like it or not.

Manila
Kuala Lumpur
July 10, 2014

Notes

1. First published on July 12, 2014.
2. Joseph Stiglitz, "Creating a Learning Society," *The Edge*, Malaysia (June 16, 2014).
3. Joseph Schumpeter, *Business Cycles: A Theoretical, Historical, and Statistical Analysis of the Capitalist Process*, Vol. II (New York: McGraw Hill, 1939), p. 1033.
4. Thomas McCraw, *Prophet of Innovation: Joseph Schumpeter and Creative Destruction* (Cambridge, MA: Belknap/Harvard University Press, 2007).
5. Chad Bray, "Judge Plans to Narrow Scope of Proposed Oversight in Apple E-Books Case," *Wall Street Journal* (August 27, 2013).

Malaysian Transformation and Innovation

CHAPTER 101

Getting "Cangkul-Ready"[1]

Bear Stearns went belly-up in March 20, 2008, and by September, Merrill Lynch had collapsed (and was taken over), but Lehman Brothers was allowed to fail (eliminating three of the big five New York investment banks), while bankrupt Fannie Mae and Freddie Mac were nationalized. The crisis that exploded seemed like a fire troubling essentially Wall Street. But few realized that the US economy was already in recession ("a significant decline in economic activity" since December 2007, as determined by the US National Bureau of Economic Research).

It is remarkable that a 73-month economic expansion that started in November 2001 had ended in a whimper. Experts I am acquainted with now expect a long and deep downturn. Indeed, it could mark the first time US gross domestic product (GDP) will contract for four consecutive quarters since the third quarter of 2008. That puts the likely contraction at 18 months, the longest period of activity decline since the Great Depression. However, its intensity is harder to tell and compare at this time. Latest surveys don't expect the United States to recover before the fourth quarter of 2009. The US Chapman Report last week suggested that the pain is likely to persist until 2010. It would appear that the worst is yet to come.

Financial Impact

The financial impact of this meltdown has been disastrous. Panic seized markets. Stock exchange prices have plummeted and credit markets are today still frozen. Worse, the US financial system became dysfunctional, so much so that the government and the US Federal Reserve Bank (Fed) had to step in and use unconventional tools and extend emergency lending to prevent systemic failure. One estimate placed the US government and the Fed's pledged involvement to the "bail-out" at about US$7.5 trillion, more than 50 percent of US GDP. That's unprecedented. Yet, the story has not fully unfolded. The prospect of another package to rescue the US auto Big-3 and the unraveling of the

US$50 billion Madoff Ponzi scam this week (mid-December 2008) add to more worrying possibilities. It is not surprising that Franklin D. Roosevelt's famously calming words, We have nothing to fear but fear itself, don't seem too reassuring today. Stability will not come quickly. Things are still in a state of flux. Expect new market incidents, institutional failures, and policy mistakes ahead.

The pain of the Wall Street crisis has, with a lag, ratcheted up to Main Street USA. In addition to the sharp loss in wealth (and pension savings) following the deep malaise in stock prices—the broad S&P 500 index is down 48.8 percent this year (2008). But this recession has centered so far not as much on businesses (not yet) as on consumers who are being hit also by dwindling home prices and, more crucially, job losses. The jobs market looks ugly and will not be "pretty," either, by next year (2009). In past recessions, labor market contraction continued for months after the downturn's end. The unemployment rate could well peak at 8.5 percent (4.4 percent at its low in March 2007) this time at end-2008. The spiraling crisis has now begun to hit US businesses where it really hurts: exports—October 2008 exports fell for the first time in three months.

But in an interconnected world, this meltdown's transmission can deliver the shock anywhere and to anyone linked to it financially and commercially. Europe has since been equally devastated; its financial fires are just as fierce and still breaking out, and with recession, the economic impact on spending, wealth, and jobs has been just as severe. As in the United States, rescue and stimulus packages are widespread and, now, somewhat coordinated as best they could.

The blaze is still spreading. Asia, with lagged effects, has not been spared. Export-dependent nations like Japan, China, India, South Korea, and Taiwan (including Singapore and Hong Kong) bore the brunt of the first blow. As in the United States and Europe, a waterfall-like drop in global demand exerted widespread damage. Fortunately, their banking systems are strong and stable (the legacy of the Asian currency crisis 10 years earlier), and they have accumulated enough international reserves to cushion the adverse impact from the export markets. Nevertheless, the impact is real, especially on financial markets. Across Asia, stock exchanges are just as battered, especially China and India. One fallout of the meltdown was the withdrawal of foreign portfolios from many emerging markets, with impact beyond stocks and socks. Their currencies—especially Korean, Brazilian, and Mexican—depreciated significantly against the US$ in recent months.

Closer to Home

Malaysia entered the crisis in relatively good shape, thanks to high external reserves, limited leverage and low indebtedness, and entrenched counter-cyclical monetary and fiscal policies and risk-averse financial markets acting to insulate it from the meltdown, especially the fallout from fast-moving illiquid derivatives (especially collateralized debt obligations and the credit default swaps). Unlike the United States, there was no collapse in growth and consumption; no widespread defaults; and a government retaining core-policy creditability. Yet, I sense a calm before the storm; that sinking feeling is still very evident. Just look around. Most of Asia, the BRICs (Brazil, Russia, India, and China), and other ASEAN nations (Brunei, Indonesia, Malaysia, the Philippines, Singapore, Thailand, Vietnam, Cambodia, Laos, and Myanmar) are hit in varying degrees, some more than others. But the worst is yet to come because the lag effects have not yet played through. The outlook remains treacherous. For us, the worst will hit after Chinese New Year in early 2009. Two worrying possibilities emerge:

First, the epicenter of the crisis is still in Wall Street, anchored in the world's largest economy (albeit now weak), which also provides the only reserve currency. Despite the gargantuan bailout efforts, markets remain fragile, with many cracks largely papered over. We still need to "jaga well" (i.e., take good care) lest we fall victim to the vagaries of an unstable, uncertain, and fast-moving crisis. Cash is still king at a time very few are lending in the face of lots of liquidity. Equity markets may look good now, but bear in mind that foreign portfolio investors, facing large losses at home, have been known to scramble to repatriate funds at the same time with unwelcome side effects.

Second, public policy response needs strengthening—Malaysia's RM7 billion stabilization scheme is insufficient for the time being. Short-term stabilization must now give way to a much larger stimulus package with strong doses of ready-to-go public works that are "cangkul-ready" (i.e., can be readily implemented on the ground), and broad-based programs to restructure the economy (adding real value through technology and innovation). At this time, government cannot force consumers and businesses to spend. That leaves only the government to keep activity going. To have the desired impact, such a package has to be large (do more, rather than less)— in the order of RM30 to RM40 billion over 2 to 3 years—and be credible. The stimulus push should also take on a green tint. I don't think financing will be a problem. I am convinced there are enough savings (augmented by pump-priming resources) to aggressively drive growth through the expenditure multiplier (hence, employment but for Malaysians). At this time, the priority must be growth; the least of our worries is inflation (and indeed, some of it might even be good to stave off any deflationary forces). Some essential elements include the following:

1. Vast array of ready-to-go public works programs (e.g., resurface most roads in the major cities—they badly need to be done anyway; flood and pollution mitigation works; sewerage; maintenance for schools and

hospitals; "wire up" (broadband) the universities and schools; rebuild mass transit and upgrade city transportation; and the like).

2. Train Malaysians with value-added skills (don't cut jobs to save costs; cut costs to save jobs) through government grants and incentives, and support in a purposeful way.

3. Assist the middle class (the real consumers) by temporarily lowering their tax incidence (especially income tax).

4. Set up a RM20 billion restructuring fund to restructure and "green" manufacturing in particular (value add through greater use of technology—automation, innovation, and greening). Push for more "green-collar" jobs. In addition, train Malaysians for higher value-added jobs in the new services growth sectors through government grants to support their restructuring efforts. Essentially to build a more efficient economy.

What, Then, Are We to Do?

The timing is right for this. Costs are down. Projects are now cheaper. To succeed, more than ever, we will need strong leadership, less politicking, firm commitments to move, and to adopt a "do-it-now" work ethic. Ask our businesses and workforce—they are all "cangkul-ready"! Let's get to work.

Kuala Lumpur
December 18, 2008

Note

1. First published on December 20, 2008.

CHAPTER 102

Now the Real Pain Begins[1]

Since the collapse of Bear Stearns in March 2008 (now part of JPMorgan Chase) culminating in the meltdown and panic on Wall Street in September 2008, and the subsequent series of rescues by the US government and the US Federal Reserve Bank (Fed) on the subprime and related fallout (all told with a price tag of US$7.5 trillion by an estimate), the entire world has panicked. Needless to say, the storm clouds have spread, and Europe is just as hot in the collar. Not to be outdone, its responses have been swift and firm, and intervention definitive, including massive injections of liquidity, coordinated interest rate cuts, and partial nationalization of certain financial institutions. Although policy responses all round have been bold—even unprecedented—the situation is far from stable. The sands of change are still shifting. The global system—if there is still one—clearly lacks a reliable anchor. One fallout has been the serious erosion of trust between buyers and sellers in many markets, adding a new dimension of uncertainty between and among banks, and opening up unexpected exposures to new third-party risks. All this adds on uncertainties to the conduct and cost of doing business. Going forward, this crisis still has a capacity to surprise. The plight of the Big-3 US automakers (they have since been given a brief lifeline) and the recent unfolding of the purported US$50 billion Bernie Madoff fraud case are reminders.

Impact

The transmission of problems from Wall Street to Main Street has been swift. In the face of massive losses in personal wealth, the economies of the United States and Europe are already in recession. Unemployment is rising, housing foreclosures are spreading, business investment appears not as forthcoming, and consumer spending is weakening—and weakening fast. Manufacturing is cutting production, and inventories are rising. Capacity utilization is also sharply down. Exports and imports have since started to shrink. Clearly, despite

exceptionally low interest rates (and still falling) and oozes of bank liquidity—
few are lending. A global recession is in the offing. In Asia and the BRICs
(Brazil, Russia, India, and China), the mood remains somber. Whatever the
causes (and the list is long), the global prosperity of nations is being fundamentally threatened. The world will not be the same again. That is why most
nations in Asia and ASEAN (Brunei, Indonesia, Malaysia, Philippines, Thailand,
Singapore, Vietnam, Cambodia, Laos, and Myanmar) have acted swiftly, not just
to protect themselves, but becoming proactive in acting to stimulate.

The massive stimulus programs of China, India, and Japan are classic.
What's worrisome is Columbia's Professor Nouriel Roubini's recent observation that the risk of a hard landing in China is sharply rising. It is in this
context that China needs to spend, and spend big! Indeed, Asia has a vested
interest to ensure China (and others in Asia) forges ahead and helps pull
the East Asian locomotive forward. This crisis has led the world into unchartered waters. In this regard, the recent summit by China, Japan, and Korea
augurs well for Asia to forge a coordinated regional engine to counter any
spillover from the global turmoil.

Malaysia remains in relatively good economic health so far. But I sense
that the lagged effects are only beginning to take hold. Indications are that
the fourth quarter of 2008 gross domestic product (GDP) growth will still be
positive in the face of gathering growing weaknesses here and there. The main
surprise is that usually reliable expected orders in manufacturing, in particular,
have suddenly more or less disappeared. I hear of rather widespread, waterfall-like drops in demand. Chipmakers and the electronics industry are already
feeling the heat, not to mention the sharp fall in demand for palm oil and petroleum exports. Indeed, the dismal export performance in October is another
indicator. Capacity utilization is falling fast, especially in manufacturing of both
final and intermediate goods. Inventories (at higher earlier prices) are rising, but
their need for top-up financing is not as forthcoming. Further, trade financing
has tightened. Consumer demand is softening as well. Construction and property development are badly hit. Housing demand at the lower end is reported
lately to be down one-third; at midrange, down one-half; and at the high end,
lower by up to 70–80 percent. Demand for services has also softened and the
postponement of decisions on even firm orders is rather common.

Businesses are already reviewing plans on capital spending—many
working to postpone them until late 2009 or 2010; lots of right sizing of
built-up capacities is going on. Petronas's shutdown of many petrochemi-
cal plants reflects the state of play in many businesses. Capital spending is
clearly slackening. Indeed, approved foreign direct investments are being
reviewed by their principals as the global recession takes hold. Consumer
spending is struggling to stay positive in view of the coming holidays stretching until the Chinese New Year festivities in late January 2009. Producers
and retailers are offering aggressive promotions for a last "spurt" drive.

Impact of the world recession will come home to roost in the first quarter of 2009. Reports of hiring are muted; almost across the board, many businesses are barely hiring. Retrenchments are already ongoing—but quietly. It is good that unskilled labor is being repatriated (hopefully, never to be seen again). The worrisome aspect is the influx of new graduates in the first and second quarters of 2009 who will find problems in getting hired.

All said and done, I think the worst is yet to come. There are many risks still out there. Recession in the United States and Europe has yet to mature. The fallout on the frontliners like India, China, Japan, Taiwan, and Korea has not yet been played out. The situation as we move forward can be full of surprises—we see Avian flu resurfacing with the onset of winter; tourist arrivals affected by security and newly emerging concerns; the bloating of credit card receivables posing a potential threat as banks review overall credit and individual overdraft limits come year-end; the reshaping of trade flows given emerging supply chain and logistics complexities brought about by earlier high oil prices; and growing difficulties in trade financing casting a long shadow. The list goes on. The move from trouble to turmoil has left too many things still in a state of flux. Stability will not come easily. So, be prepared for the unexpected.

Need for Stimuli

In this fast-evolving crisis, government cannot force businesses to invest nor consumers to spend and banks to lend. What is unfolding is unprecedented. Frankly, no one knows what's going to happen, even early in the new 2009. Bold and steadfast government leadership is needed to restore sustained confidence and create new job opportunities from growth—indeed, this must take top priority as the main object of public policy. What's really needed is a credible and substantive (doing more rather than less) stimulus plan to restore and improve living standards—indeed, pushing to change the parameters of our present comfort zone. There is the urgent need to send a strong signal that there is political will and the ability to move ahead despite the turmoil. Government needs to light a bright candle instead of cursing the darkness. But there appear to be three main concerns.

Large Budget Deficits

First, the burden of large budget deficits: Paul Krugman (Nobel Laureate in economics 2008) is right: "Under current conditions there is no trade-off between what's good in the short run and what's good for the long run; strong fiscal expansion could actually enhance the economy's long-run prospects."[2] As I see it, the fiscal worriers are mistaken, for four important reasons:

1. Government borrowing will not crowd out private investment and drive up interest rates (indeed, fiscal austerity will push the already-low rates still lower).
2. Fiscal austerity at a time of a clear deficit in business and consumer spending can be deflationary (e.g., 1937 in the United States and 1996–1997 in Japan aptly illustrate this). Government has to take up the slack in expanding public investment (hence, enriching nations in the long run); otherwise the economy will slacken further and even possibly into negative territory.
3. Inflation (if any) is now the lesser evil.
4. Today provides the opportunity to build potential GDP (in the 1960s and 1970s, it was up 10 to 12 percent per annum but fell to about 6 percent after the 1998 currency crisis) to at least 9 to 10 percent per annum through demand-driven research and development (R&D) spending and human resource development (HRD), including attracting home-skilled Malaysians working abroad. This is a sure way to strengthen future productivity. The bottom line: Fiscal stimulus à la Keynes at this time will not burden future generations.

Size of the Stimulus

Second, how big a jolt will it take? At this time, size matters—more is needed as the economy weakens. Spending smart also matters. This is not rocket science. In uncertain times, doing more is better than less to ensure a robust expansion. Such a plan will require a mix of spending and tax breaks. The rule of thumb today is to have more spending (60 to 70 percent) than tax cuts (because the tendency is to save more instead of spending more). Every RM100 million spent in this way will generate about RM160 million more in economic activity (less in value-added terms). For example, resurfacing a road means hiring workers, who spend their salaries at supermarkets and for services, who in turn hire salesclerks, cooks, and so on, who then spend more, and so on. The multiplier effects are especially good when there is little import leakage. With a tax break, however, the multiplier is likely to be smaller if most of it is saved or much of it is used to settle debts. To be effective, stimulative spending must be large enough to build public confidence (i.e., in believing that its overall impact will make a difference).

Design of the Plan

Third, the plan must focus on job creation for Malaysians (not imported low-skilled workers), with a strong focus on the restructuring of manufacturing and services for higher value added, through practical innovation and the effective use of technology. Value added is far too low in Malaysia. Adding value to all that we do is the only way up to achieve higher living standards.

Today presents the best time to embark on this mission. Innovation and R&D spending when times are good tend to yield low successes because they insulate innovators from market realities, and the chances of them getting it right the first time out of the gate are very low. Professor Clayton Christensen (Harvard's innovation guru) teaches at Harvard Business School that in an environment where you have to push innovation out of the door quickly and resources are limited (like now), that's when people are actually a lot more open to new thinking and rethinking about the fundamental way of doing business, resulting in higher success.

Stimulative Package

An adequate stimulative package must have size and impact: RM30 billion to RM40 billion (even up to RM50 billion), implemented within two to three years (more upfront) with a "green" tint. The essential elements should include four features:

1. **Substantial "ready-to-go" job-creating works program.** This includes massive and pervasive resurfacing of city roads; repairing highways; and schools, hospitals, and universities; irrigation, flood and pollution mitigation works; rebuilding mass transit and city transportation; sewerage rehabilitation; river basin improvements, including sufficiently large infrastructure and information technology works to reconnect the nation (if needed, bring forward 10th Malaysia Plan projects). Since quick implementation is key, we should learn lessons from the Middle East in fast tracking the implementation of large infrastructure projects (including bridges and airports) through the use of reputable and experienced private project managers to assist government and to ensure value for money. Also, there is a need to move fast to take advantage of low materials costs and growing unutilized construction capacity. Domestic multiplier effects of such spending can be readily maximized.

2. **Large-scale training programs.** Train and retool the Malaysian labor force (old and new) across the board with value-added skills through the purposeful use of grants and soft loans, including tax incentives. Avoid the conventional wisdom of "cut jobs to cut costs"; instead, "cut costs to save jobs," mainly through intensive training in new skills to further add value, with government assistance and financial support.

3. **Strengthen the financial position of spending middle-class Malaysians.** Raise their purchasing power by lowering their tax incidence (especially income tax).

4. **Establish a RM20 billion to RM50 billion industry restructuring fund (IRF).** Promote the restructuring of low value-added production into higher value-added and "greener" plants and processes, including automation. Push for more "green-collar" jobs. Also, hire skilled Malaysians working abroad (where economic conditions have since sharply deteriorated) to push for more demand-oriented R&D spending at a time of low activity through smart use of government grants and soft loans, including tax incentives. This is a rare opportunity to assist industries to build skills (soft and hard) for longer-term benefit.

What, Then, Are We to Do?

In purely economic terms, a traditional infrastructure building and repair scheme could provide the biggest bang for the buck, capturing the imagination of the private sector with a quick shot of confidence. But government badly needs to move fast on the ground. Improving government's delivery system is a necessary and sufficient condition. At the same time, manufacturing, in particular, needs to be restructured to add more value for the benefit of Malaysians, not imported unskilled labor. Hence, IRF is critical. This exercise is urgent—indeed, rather Darwinian, really (yes, survival of the fittest).

Kuala Lumpur
December 22, 2008

Notes

1. First published in *The Edge* on December 29, 2008.
2. Paul Krugman, "Fiscal Expansion," *International Herald Tribune*, New York (December 2, 2008).

CHAPTER 103

Mahathir's Challenge[1]

The public has been asking with increasing frequency why the biggest banks in the world are in such a sorry state of affairs. Was it because of a black swan?, referring to Nassim Taleb's unlikely but not impossible catastrophe that no one ever seems to plan for, but that does not mean it does not exist.[2] Indeed, I have heard it quoted in a recent issue of *Time* that it is not just one black swan; it is a bunch of black swans that have hung out for a while and since created this gigantic problem.[3]

Twelve days ago, I had one of those rare opportunities to spend some quality time with Tun Mahathir at a private brainstorming session with select experts (including some from abroad), and on February 4, 2009, participated in his strategy session on the global financial crises. Tun's challenging query was simply this: Why did the US financial meltdown—not just its scale—happen so very swiftly (most were caught unaware), wreck so completely (US financial system in particular), and reduce so systemically (the efficacy of the global financial international mechanism)? How could subprime mortgages provoke such worldwide dislocation? These are legitimate but very difficult questions to answer.

I have since thought about it a lot, and shall now try to unravel, as best I can, the mystique of this upheaval (which the *Financial Times* called, with tongue-in-cheek, Asia's Revenge), in so far as I have managed to string the sometimes rather incoherent parts together.

The Big Picture

Professor Charles Kindleberger's classic book, *Manias, Panics, and Crashes: A History of Financial Crises*, suggests that in history, financial crashes shared one trait—excessive expansion of credit, which feeds on itself.[4] The current bubble is no different. The US Federal Reserve Bank (Fed) kept interest rates too low and for too long.

George W. Bush became president following the dot-com bust in 2000. His tax cuts plus Fed Chairman Alan Greenspan's push on the monetary accelerator (in rapidly cutting interest rates) helped spur housing and consumer spending. Even as the second tax cut became law in late May 2003 and with economic recovery beginning in earnest, the Fed funds rate was further cut to a mere 1 percent and kept there for a year. This stimulus worked well—indeed, too well. Professor John Taylor of Stanford called this a monetary mistake: By pushing so much excess credit into the economy, the Fed created a consumption and housing mania that Wall Street took full advantage of, with many banks abandoning normal risk standards.[5] Taylor demonstrated by comparing the actual Fed funds rate for this decade with what the rate would have been if the Fed stayed within the policy experience of the previous 20 years. This has now come to be known as the Taylor rule for determining how central bank rates should be adjusted. "This extra easy policy was responsible for accelerating the housing boom and thereby, ultimately leading to the housing bust," according to Taylor.[6] It was a party no one wanted to end, but it did nevertheless in 2008.

The System That Failed

The banking business is based on trust—some may even call dealing with a bank an act of faith. Over the past decade in particular, the system that has evolved was underpinned by four articles of trust:

1. **Trust in regulators** (central banks, securities and exchange commissions, and inspectorates), who apparently have done such a great job that it can be safely assumed the Western banking system is extraordinarily strong and much more advanced than a decade before. The track record of the crises management skills of central banks and financial authorities is so well regarded, even the authorities are convinced that any glitches (big and small) can be readily contained— indeed, the system always emerges stronger and more sustainable after a crisis.

2. **Belief in the viability of modern capital markets** (especially New York and London), which are always liquid and which have become so deep and dependable that banks and investors can readily trade with confidence in debt securities—so much so that this has encouraged banks to let down their guard to arrogantly assume that risks can always be passed on. Indeed, in times of abundant liquidity, most have overestimated the markets' ability (and expertise) to assume risk.

3. **Confidence in credit rating agencies** (assumed wrongly by investors to be strictly regulated) as a reliable compass to guide investors
   through the workings of the complex jungle of derivative products,
   which most don't understand.
4. **Trust in the intellectual capital and capital muscle of Wall Street,**
   based on the assumption that any "slicing and dicing" of debt into
   derivatives of all hues has made the financial system more resilient
   and more stable, supported by the banks' ability to churn out so much
   profits in the process. This assumption that pain emanating from any
   potential default would be spread over millions of investors, rather
   than concentrated in particular banks (since these are off-balance-
   sheet activities) is naïve, of course. The opacity of the derivative products left much to be desired. This shift from bank balance sheet to
   the off-balance-sheet realm of securitization and derivatization in Wall
   Street might not have been so bad if they actually worked to spread
   risk and encourage creative destruction, bringing the best minds to
   bear on resolving the underlying banking problems. Instead, they created a bubble, diverting capital to the least productive use, and, worst
   of all, fed the pangs of greed.

Derivatives

A word about derivatives: They are what they sound like; their worth is
derived from a stock or a bond or a mortgage or a collection of them. The
most common (and dangerous) is the credit default swap (or CDS)—a
sort of insurance policy. A third party assumes the risk of the debt (say,
mortgage) going into default; in exchange, the insurer receives payment (like a premium) from the issuer bank. Created by whiz kids from
MIT and Cambridge for JP Morgan in 1994, they have since ballooned
into a US$62 trillion market, before racheting down to US$55 trillion in
September 2008 after AIG defaulted on US$14 billion of CDSs (it held
US$440 billion). Warren Buffett called them financial weapons of mass
destruction. Since CDSs are privately negotiated between the parties,
they are not regulated.

There are others—for example, collateralized debt obligations (CDOs),
derivatives linked to corporate debt. These are essentially made for insurers,
banks, and others to invest in a diversified portfolio of enterprises without
actually buying into their stocks and bonds. This market could be as large
as US$6 trillion. The entire derivatives market (all forms) is very large. Lat-
est estimates point to US$668 trillion (gross), or about 15 times the size of
the world economy. Their underlying worth is about US$15 trillion, slightly
larger than the US gross domestic product.

Relevant Developments

The US banking system has evolved dramatically in the past 40 years. Consider six changes that have since worked to significantly undermine the system:

1. Forty years ago, 90 percent of all loans were backed by bank deposits; today it's 60 percent.
2. Regulators require lower capital on loans not backed by deposits. But the US Securities and Exchange Commission (SEC) removed in 2004 the leverage cap of 15 to 1 for investment banks (e.g., Bear Stearns, Lehman Brothers, Merrill Lynch, etc.), which allowed them to expand lending vigorously without raising capital.
3. By then, regulatory separation between investment and ordinary banks was long removed, encouraging the likes of Bank of America and Citibank to move more and more of their lending to their investment arms. Leverage took off—by end 2007, 30:1 was not uncommon. Lehman's leverage, when it collapsed, exceeded 40:1.
4. Stock buybacks, especially funded by borrowings (impact: upped leverage and lowered capital), boosted profits.
5. Adoption of sophisticated computer models with advanced risk management controls was intended to reduce capital requirement per loan.
6. Regulatory and accounting changes (including mark-to-market rules) resulted in banks' capital bases eroding much faster than expected.

All these meant that while US banks went on a lending spree so far this decade, their capital base had lagged behind, leaving the system vulnerable and in jeopardy of collapse (US$13.6 trillion in assets as against US$0.82 trillion in tangible equity, or less than 7 percent, as at September 2008).

Trust Undermined

To be fair, the Bank for International Settlements (the central banker's bank) did express concern over the extraordinary burst of innovation as bankers implemented novel ways to slice and dice their loans (including the now-controversial subprime mortgages), and then sell the resultant derivatives under the cover of prime names and high credit ratings to investors all over the world.

Despite many early warning signals (including by notables Professor Robert Shiller of Yale and Professor Nouriel Roubini of Columbia), the US Fed appears convinced that these "deals" have changed the system in a fundamentally beneficial way. No question that there was denial all round, even though the four articles of trust underpinning the system and supporting the credit boom had started to collapse since the summer of 2007.

For example, two hedge funds linked to Bear Stearns got into heavy losses related to US subprime mortgages. This led to a series of downgrades and raised doubts among investors. Soon, the European Central Bank injected substantial cash and the Fed embarked on emergency measures. By year-end, banks started writing losses and the United Kingdom had its first bank run in 140 years. In the new year (2008), there were more writedowns and downgrades, culminating in the nationalization of Northern Rock and the collapse of Bear Stearns; and then, the big ones fell—Lehman, Fannie and Freddie, and then Merrill Lynch. In the first half of 2008, the financial system suffered US$476 billion in credit losses and raised US$354 billion in new capital. This was only the beginning.

What, Then, Are We to Do?

Basic trust has since crumbled and shook faith in banking and finance. Western banks found themselves running out of capital in a way none of the regulators had imagined. The Fed initially estimated that subprime losses were unlikely to go beyond US$50 billion to US$100 billion—a fraction of the total capital of Western banks or assets held by global investment funds.

As it evolved, banks started hoarding cash and stopped lending to each other; bankers lost faith in their ability to assess the health of other institutions—sometimes, even their own! Then, a vicious deleveraging spiral got underway as banks scurried to improve their balance sheets—selling assets and cutting loans, especially to hedge funds. All these started with eight years of cheap and plentiful money (liquidity). Sure, easy money provided the fuel. But it soon became evident that the real problem in the banking system was not so much liquidity, but toxic assets and inadequate capital. Regulators lost credibility; the SEC's relaxation of the leverage capital cap proved to be a huge mistake.

It also became clear that the global capital markets (especially New York and London) were not what they seemed—they could not stay really liquid when required. Neither did the ratings generate the confidence required of them. These rating agencies started downgrading even supposedly ultra-safe debt—causing prices to crumble (e.g., in July 2008, Merrill Lynch sold a portfolio of complex derivatives at 22 percent of its face value, even though they were rated triple A). Investors lost faith in the ratings and stopped buying, thus created a funding crisis. Worse still, the notion that banks should be better protected because of risk dispersion also cracked. In the end, everything came back to haunt the banks with a vengeance.

Obiter Dictum

More than a year into the credit crisis, America's broken banks are an eyesore. Banks are still struggling to respond to investor demands for larger capital cushions and an effective way out to rid themselves of toxic assets. The system did crack, and banks remained fearful of their own solvency. Trust remains a rare commodity after eight years of easy money. This trust was broken when the underpinnings of twenty-first-century finance turned out to be dangerously flawed. In a crisis born of greed and undiscipline in the face of the myth of a rational marketplace (markets know best, remember?), pity is in short supply.

To answer Tun Mahathir: In an environment of easy money (Greenspan cut interest rates too far, too fast), banks, borrowers, and investors lost their cool and self-discipline; in an environment where free markets ran amok, trust in the banking system (and its collaborators) was shattered as regulators let their guard down, and bankers let the pursuit of profits undermine the integrity of the system that they were charged to protect. *Result:* The entire system failed in the face of denial, undiscipline, and greed.

Kuala Lumpur
February 13, 2009

Notes

1. First published on February 14, 2009, as "Mystique of the Global Crisis Unraveled."
2. Nassim Nicholas Taleb, *The Black Swan: The Impact of the Highly Improbable* (London: Penguin Books, 2008).
3. Stephen Gandel, "America's Broken Banks," *Time* (February 2, 2009).
4. Charles Kindleberger, *Manias, Panics, and Crashes: A History of Financial Crises* (New York: John Wiley & Sons, 1978).
5. John Taylor, "The Bush Economy," *Wall Street Journal* (January 20, 2009), p. 19.
6. Ibid.

CHAPTER 104

Stimulating Times[1]

On March 10, 2009, Prime Minister and Finance Minister Dato' Sri Mohd Najib bin Abdul Razak introduced the much-awaited Second Stimulus Package (2SP), worth RM60 billion, or about 9 percent of gross domestic product (GDP).[2] Its size surprised many, considering the first package (1SP) in November last year was only RM7 billion. And, size matters. This is as it should be. The risks of doing less are far higher than the risks of doing more.

The world has changed dramatically since Christmas 2008. The recession that started in the United States and followed soon after in the United Kingdom, eurozone, and Japan has become global; indeed, the recession that is being felt across the world is now globally driven. World trade is shrinking for the first time in 50 years. Recession in the developed world has grown deeper and wider in the first quarter of 2009. The International Monetary Fund (IMF) had in January 2009 forecast slow global growth in the course of the year. On March 8, it now expects world growth to be negative for 2009 for the first time since World War II.[3]

Continuing instability (coupled with massive deleveraging) in the financial world, combined with a growing lack of confidence among consumers and businesses is depressing domestic demand across the board. Everywhere, governments are stimulating: Eurozone governments have committed €1.2 trillion to protect financial systems and had since pledged a combined €200 billion to lift their economies out of a worsening slump. The US economic stimulus package (US$787 billion) to revive the economy was passed in mid-February 2009; this is in addition to an estimated US$8 trillion of funds made available to provide liquidity/save/guarantee/bail out/recapitalize in order to protect its "lifeblood" financial institutions from systemic failure. As it stands now, it would appear that despite these massive efforts, a near-term strong economic recovery (especially in the United States) appears unlikely.

There is no question that the macroeconomic situation in Malaysia has since sharply deteriorated. Things can, and will, get worse. The public likes signs of action even though they know—deep down—that there are no easy cures to what challenges the nation; there is no silver bullet. But the psychodynamics of the recession isn't difficult to understand. People need (and now demand) firm leadership—they want a leader on their side with a vision they can share, who gives them hope; a leader who is prepared to play out concrete strategic and tactical initiatives to make them feel better and confident about investing in the future. This is where I see Najib is coming from—instilling confidence in the face of an economic situation gone the wrong way and, in the process, managing expectations in a manner that consumers and businesses can begin to feel they have some mastery (however illusionary) over their future.

2SP

The 2SP comprises a balanced combination of fiscal spending and tax relief, as well as ready private access to credit and assistance to restructure private productive capacity. Although not explicit, I gather the split is about 50:50, so that the direct impact on the budget deficit is readily manageable. I see no real problems in its financing. I also agree that this can be done without any material crowding out of private initiatives' access to credit. The 2SP is not just a shot in the arm. That is not what is wanted. Fiscal spending and tax relief are good; they will help to create jobs, generate income, and hence, raise demand (with the attendant multiplier effects). This is what the good doctor (John Maynard Keynes) ordered. I particularly like the proactive ideas of: (1) ensuring businesses, especially small and medium industries, are kept active with the needed "lifeblood" of credit; (2) government assuming, at this time, the role of lender of first and last resort; (3) helping businesses and industry restructure and build lasting value-adding capacity, raising productivity along the way; (4) creating green-collar jobs; and (5) ensuring Malaysians are the true beneficiaries. All these will, in the end, strengthen the underlying fundamentals of the economy, and stand it in good stead when recovery emerges.

The 2SP, however, can't do much to spur economic activity in the first half of this year. We are already in mid-March and much of the spending, relief and lending takes time to plan, organize, and get off the ground. Hopefully, the head start provided by the 1SP is advanced enough and sufficiently robust today to fill this vacuum. But all is not lost. If needed, another window is still open. In private consumption spending, the dynamo has always been the middle class—they are usually overtaxed (especially indirect taxes) and often, not really appreciated. To ease their cash-flow problems (and encourage them to spend), two options are still available: (1) tax rebates of up to RM2,000 for each individual with chargeable income of up to RM200,000; or (2) equalize the individual's income tax rate with the corporate rate. With tax returns due at the end of April 2009, the benefits can be in their hands within six weeks—simple, fast, and easy to implement. However, there is a third "costless" option: Defer tax payments by six or nine months. This will definitely help their cash flow (and raise potential disposable income).

Impact

The 2SP is a necessary but not sufficient condition to push recovery. The inclusion of a bucket of measures to reduce the cost of doing business is a wise move. It will go some way toward ensuring a fast-acting stimulus plan. Like most plans, the real unknowns are many, including how soon a recovery can start and how fast it will take hold once it does. This lag time—unfortunately, experience points to a rather long one, depending on the passion of the implementers to act (or lack of it)—does hinge ultimately on policy makers facing up to three contentious but inexorable situations:

1. The macroeconomic impact of packages 1 and 2 on job creation over the next two to three years remains rather opaque: Up to 163,000 jobs/training positions were mentioned; in the end, up to 250,000–300,000 could be made available in both the public and private sectors. The impression is certainly given that most of the immediate job/training opportunities will be generated within the broad public sector (including government-linked companies). This is not good enough. The private sector needs to be actively engaged to play a strong partnership role. Over time, this number needs to be pinned down to properly assess their impact.

2. The very nature of the stimulus requires that Malaysians are the main beneficiaries of the job creation and training. Usage of the levy in a progressively prohibitive manner on imported unskilled labor can be a powerful tool to ensure this. It is unfortunate that foreign workers in the construction and plantation industries are to be exempted. At stake is the government's desire to raise the incomes and living standards of all Malaysians—that's what stimulating development is all about. That's why the new fund to help restructure our industries is timely and badly needed. No industry should be allowed to persist on the back of the continuing flow of cheap imported labor. This is unhealthy and unstable. The nation's future must lie in constantly adding value (and hence, higher incomes) through innovation, automation, technology, mechanization, and smart, soft managerial and IT skills. In this context, only the imports of talent and housemaids justify exemption from the levy. Plantations and construction industries, like all others,

must be constantly persuaded to raise productivity and compete efficiently through persistent outlays, not just in research and development (R&D) but also in innovative practices, processes, and systems, automation, the widespread use of machines and equipment and advanced process engineering, and the entire range of managerial and organizational skills using IT, computerized software, and other technological advances (and fully supported by fiscal incentives), to compete globally, including in services. If properly executed and passionately committed to by private enterprise (including going "green"), there will be no jobs Malaysians will not want to do, since these will be value-adding jobs that attract competitive wages, consistent with rising living standards. Granted, time is needed to help them restructure, and this time of recession provides the best opportunity to do so (with positive encouragement by government assistance). But the national mission is clear: In time, with limited exceptions, no more imported unskilled labor through a progressively more prohibitive levy is the way to go.

3. Confidence is best won when all the elements of the stimulus are quickly packaged and made ready to go. Prompt implementation is critical, with all intended beneficiaries (especially the poor and disadvantaged) clearly identified in the myriad programs to be put into place on the ground. It is also vital that the measures to help those affected by the sharp economic downturn are painstakingly designed and smoothly executed. It is encouraging to note that some of the measures are already ready for implementation (e.g., the two guarantee schemes worth a combined RM10 billion to assist private enterprise will accept applications on March 16). In the end, it is not enough that the impact of both 1SP and 2SP are effectively cleared to give a "bang" for your buck. They must also be closely monitored to ensure public policy objectives are met. Just as important, these outcomes will need to be made highly visible, transparent, and accountable to command continuing public confidence.

What, Then, Are We to Do?

At a time like this, the pressure to perform is immense. The public must realize that these are unusual times. Stimulus programs of any kind are difficult—more so in times of growing uncertainty and when expectations are sky-high. I am reminded of US President Franklin D. Roosevelt, whose New Deal from 1933 was based on his belief in "bold, persistent experimentation." It is the same legacy that Najib now inherits from Prime Minister Tun Abdul Razak's (his father) halcyon days of success in post-merdeka (independence) development. This approach simply means doing what will work on the ground. Programs need time and effort to be put into place and then to implement; parts will require reevaluation and, maybe, redesign— sometimes, even some experimentation. If things don't work out, it's back to the drawing board—and then proceed to work on something else that will work. That's in the nature of being bold. And, to be able to experiment is part of the game. In the end, given goodwill, it should all work out. Commitment (on the part of government) and patience (from the public) are required. At this time, both appear to be in short supply.

Kuala Lumpur
March 13, 2009

Notes

1. First published on March 14, 2009.
2. Mohd Najib Abdul Razak, prime minister and finance minister, Malaysia, in introducing The Supplementary Supply (2009) Bill, 2009, at the Dewan Rakyat, the lower house of the Parliament of Malaysia, Kuala Lumpur, on March 10, 2009.
3. International Monetary Fund's (IMF) Managing Director Dominique Strauss-Kahn: "IMF expects global growth to slow below zero this year, the worst performance in most of our lifetimes," announced at the African central bank governors and finance ministers in Dar-es-Salaam, Tanzania, on March 2, 2009.

CHAPTER 105

Price Fixing, Market Sharing, and Collusion Are Illegal[1]

Three words should take us out of the middle-income trap: *Be more competitive*. But that's going to be tough despite the economic transformation already in train, because price fixing, market rigging, and collusion are so commonplace. With the coming into effect of the Competition Act (since June 10, 2010, and enforced on January 1, 2012), anticompetitive practices are now illegal! The act[2] is intended to promote and safeguard "the process of competition, thereby protecting consumers." It states that because competition "encourages efficiency, innovation and entrepreneurship," it will reward consumers with: (1) competitive (lower) prices; (2) improved quality of products and services; and (3) wider choices. That's why the act serves "to prohibit anti-competitive conduct."

To oversee the effective implementation and enforcement of the act, the Malaysia Competition Commission (MyCC) was established. MyCC is charged with investigating any anticompetitive practices and is also empowered to impose strong financial penalties. The act applies to all commercial activities in Malaysia and abroad that affect competition in the Malaysian marketplace. However, decisions by MyCC may be appealed to the Competition Appeal Tribunal, on which I have been appointed as a member. In addition, MyCC also: (1) advises government and public regulatory authorities on all aspects of competition; (2) advises government on the impact of laws governing competition; (3) undertakes studies and market reviews; and (4) issues guidelines governing the conduct of competition.

Competition Act 2010 (Act 712)

Act 712 provides a framework for identifying and dealing with anticompetitive practices by all enterprises, ranging from multinationals to other large as well as medium- and small-scale enterprises. Activities in communications and multimedia and energy are exempted, as these are regulated by their respective governing laws. In essence, the act can be expected to promote competitive markets by leveling the playing field for all. Its focus is to safeguard the market against all anticompetitive and unfair practices (including cartel-like and restrictive initiatives).

In so doing, benefits will accrue to consumers through: (1) lower entry barriers into the marketplace; (2) encouraging competitive forces to drive enterprises to become more efficient; (3) promoting innovation and investment in research and development to create new products and processes; (4) enlarging domestic markets; and (5) promoting efficient allocation and utilization of scarce resources. Anticompetitive practices are centered on two main prohibitions.

Anticompetitive Agreements (ACAs)

Act 712 prohibits ACAs whether horizontal (i.e., among enterprises operating at the same level of the production or distribution chain) or vertical (i.e., among enterprises operating at different levels of the production or distribution chain), with the object or effect to significantly prevent, restrict, or distort competition in Malaysia. Agreements mean any arrangement or understanding among enterprises, including decisions by any association and concerted practices. Enterprises refer to any entity carrying on commercial activities to provide goods or services. Prohibitions include price fixing (agreements to fix, control, or maintain prices of goods and services), market allocation (enterprises agreeing to divide customer markets geographically or by customer-type or to sell only to allotted customers), bid-rigging (agreements on who should win a tender), and limiting production (enterprises maximizing profits by limiting or controlling supply).

Abuse of Dominant Position

Act 712 prohibits any abuse of dominant position by enterprises occupying a dominant position in the market (i.e., dominant in their ability to adjust prices or dictate trading terms without effective constraint from competing enterprises or consumers). They include price discrimination (practice of selling the same products to different customers at different prices simply by exercising market power), excessive pricing (enterprises using market power to dictate prices beyond the effective competitive level), and predatory pricing (enterprises exercising market power to drive down selling prices of their products or services with the aim of driving competitors off the market or creating barriers to entry of new competitors).

Exclusions and Relief

Act 712 provides for certain activities to be excluded from these prohibitions, including: (1) exercise of government authority; (2) agreements and conduct to comply with legal requirements; (3) collective bargaining activities and collective agreements; (4) purchase of goods and services not for economic activity; and (5) services of general economic interest. However, the Act allows for relief of this liability for engaging in listed prohibitions, provided all four reasons are met simultaneously: (1) there are direct significant identifiable technological, efficiency, or social benefits; (2) the benefits could not reasonably be provided without such restrictions; (3) detrimental effects of such anticompetitive agreements are proportionate to the benefits; and (4) such restrictive practices do not lead to the complete elimination of competition.

These, I dare say, are rather onerous conditions. But, it is worthwhile noting that in the European Union, an additional criterion must be met to qualify for exemption; that is, benefits resulting from any agreements must be passed on to the consumer. This seems fair. Nevertheless, each enterprise or block of agreements may apply for exemption. I am told MyCC has not granted any exemption so far.

Furthermore, to assist consumers to better understand the process of competition, MyCC is empowered to conduct market reviews to determine whether any feature or combination of features in the marketplace prevent, restrict, or distort competition. All reviews would be made public. In the end, the intention is to promote a more competitive and efficient marketplace to maximize consumer welfare, resulting in lower prices, more choices, better quality of goods and services, and a higher standard of consumer services.

Current Situation

Act 712 comes on the heels of similar laws put into place in Singapore, Indonesia, Thailand, Vietnam, and Hong Kong. It is still common practice in Malaysia for trade associations, guilds, and professional regulatory bodies to indulge in a wide range of anticompetition practices, including open price fixing, market sharing, supply limitations, bid-rigging, and scale-fees setting, as well as the sharing of price and supply of sensitive information.

These represent "hard-core" cartel offenses under the act. For a long time, the association of banks and insurance companies, for example, have fixed prices, as have product-based associations on the sale of cars, flowers, food and beverages, and steel, and so on, while professional guilds have set scale fees for their membership to comply. Also, producers and distributors have gathered to share commercially sensitive information. These must remain of grave concern to MyCC, who worry about open offenses breaching the act.

Entrenched in Malaysian business is a culture of collusion to fix things in the name of advancing the common good, including arrangements having the effect of preventing, restricting, and distorting competition. This has gone on for so long that it has become something like second nature in business discourse. Thus, change won't come easy. However, rigorous enforcement of competition laws can help bring about badly needed change.

Already, Malaysia Airlines Cargo was reported to have been penalized to pay A$6 million (plus legal costs) by the Australian Federal Court for price fixing as part of a cartel. As I understand it, other airlines including Singapore Airlines, Cathay Pacific, Air New Zealand, and Thai International are also being pursued for a similar offense. Cartel conduct is both a civil and criminal offense in Australia; it is particularly damaging because it usually inflates prices for consumers. MyCC needs to act boldly. It has to begin building a body of traditions of robust adherence to the law, enforcing it without fear or favor to protect the greater good of consumer interests; of absolute integrity and technical competence; of dependable expertise that readily accepts absolutely the dictates of the national interest.

The act has yet to be really tested. Like most global competition laws, the act contains presumptions and deeming provisions. In Malaysia, prohibitions can arise either because a restrictive agreement has the "object" or "effect" of preventing, restricting, or distorting competition, similar to competition legislation around the world. What's unclear at this time, according to Professor Richard Whish (King's College, London), is whether such prohibitions will be interpreted in the same way as in European Union and United Kingdom, such as where agreement restrictions "by object" are presumed per se to have anticompetitive effects without a need to go through the process to demonstrate such impact, thereby injecting legal certainty and conserving the use of resources at MyCC.

Clarity on other issues is also important, including the standard of proof required; use of effects analysis and how to prove effects; quality of empirical analysis and economic evidence; adoption of time-tested best practices; and jurisdiction over the impact of mergers and takeovers on competition, even though "the government is of the view that for the time being, the act should not regulate mergers and acquisitions."

Dawn Raids

Like its European counterparts, Act 712 provides MyCC with the authority to conduct surprise onsite inspections, commonly known as dawn raids. This serves as an important avenue for MyCC to gather (check on and coordinate) information particularly early on in a cartel investigation. Such a move includes wide-ranging powers, and combined with a court warrant, has proved invaluable to investigations especially in cases focused heavily on compiling deep documentary (including corporate records) evidence. The rigor of enforcement is often enhanced by suitably timed dawn raids. This has proved to be an indispensible tool for national competition authorities to investigate hard-core infringements of competition rules and their presumed negative market effects. In practice, based on European experience, any secret agreement or understanding among competing enterprises that seek to fix prices, limit output, or share markets, customers, and sources of supply (i.e., involving cartel behavior) will inevitably attract intense regulatory scrutiny sooner or later. Such hard-core price fixing must inevitably attract dawn raids.

What, Then, Are We to Do?

Competition remains at the heart of economic policy. The act relates to only behavioral prohibitions, not structural ones. Indeed, the act says little about the structure of markets and the structure of pricing or the profit margins derived. For example, it has been reported that the Honda Insight, which retails for less than US$20,000 in the United States, is priced much higher in Malaysia, at around RM100,000 (even without excise or import duty). So, we are still far from fair and competitive pricing. Besides, philosophy also matters. In markets where the invisible hand (forces) of supply and demand are allowed free play à la Adam Smith or Hayek tradition, competitive pricing inevitably reflects the maximization of profits, not necessarily the maximization of consumer benefits. But in a truly utilitarian regime or under egalitarian communism, the greatest good of the greatest number prevails in assessing real social benefits.

In the end, the outcome is to be reflected in lower prices, better products, and wider choices for consumers. The final test of competition must rest on consumer benefits, even though it can harm inefficient enterprises in the process—but that's creative destruction. Like the United Kingdom and Hong Kong, MyCC smartly adopted a phased-in approach to implement the act. Relevant implementing guidelines have already been issued, and more are expected. But it must avoid overregulation at all cost. Realistically, I don't see rigorous enforcement of the prohibitions in the Act in practice any time soon. This remains MyCC's major challenge. Ultimately, Malaysia badly needs to be more competitive to get out of the middle-income trap. The sooner, the better. No two ways about it.

Kuala Lumpur
May 30, 2013

Notes

1. First published on June 1, 2013.
2. Competition Act, 2010 (Act 712). Percetakan Nasional Malaysia Berhad, 2010.

CHAPTER 106

Najib's New Way Forward[1]

On Wednesday, August 12, 2009, Universiti Sains Malaysia (USM) celebrated its 40th convocation, capping what was by any measure an extraordinary year. Indeed, the class of 2009 was historic. From the time most of these students first entered the USM campus, their years there have been momentous beyond imagining. In the past year alone, theirs was one of great political fluidity—of dramatic changes in State administrations and the retirement of the once-most-popular prime minister; the year of new Prime Minister Najib Razak—not to mention the high expectations even here of the year of President Barack Obama; the year of financial failures and turmoil unseen since the Great Depression; the year of recession at home, something not seen since 1997; the year of imminent pandemic; the year the world became something very different from anything ever expected. Yet, it was also the year of triumph for USM when it was named by the government as the only Apex university in September 2008.

The Newly Minted Graduates

Unfortunately, this unexpected past has led to a more uncertain future—for everyone, and quite immediately for the newly minted graduates (NMGs). Last year, as I spoke to the class of 2008 as its pro-chancellor, I thought the timing of their graduation was not the most convenient. Not knowing, of course, that this time around, 2009 is turning out to be even more inconvenient. Jobs have not been easy to come by; and where available, they are keenly competed for. At this time last year, most graduates expressed uneasiness as they headed off to the job market—a market they found offering less of a choice than grab-what-you-can-get. Today, the job situation appears to have worsened. As someone who sat next to me on the plane from the Kuala Lumpur International Airport said: We only have a choice simply because the really real choices are just too risky. This year, the world at large and the world in Malaysia have changed drastically. We are in the midst of a major paradigm shift. Prime Minister Najib has called for no less than the adoption of a new economic model to ensure survival in the aftermath of the Great Recession—one that will be innovation driven in order that Malaysians can compete more efficiently, and in a more sustainable way, if we are ever to get out of the middle-income trap. For this purpose, innovation simply means fresh thinking that creates value in terms of more income or wealth or societal well-being.

The Way Forward

Najib's New Way forward extends an open invitation to the NMGs in particular to turn crisis into opportunity. They are now given the mantle of the future. And, challenged to boldly inhabit this new way to create and to innovate. For them, a new whole world has opened, offering new choices. If they are not motivated enough to get moving to create and innovate, it's partly the university's shortcoming—because that's what USM is expected to have prepared them for. Indeed, if this university did its job right, the NMGs should have received an education that cultivates habits of mind, an analytic spirit, a capacity to judge and at least, ask the right questions that will enable them to adapt to any new circumstance or take on any vocational direction. Looked at differently, I am reminded (no less by the president of Harvard) that the new circumstance presented an opportunity for the NMGs to be allowed to have their "midlife crisis in advance." Instead of waking up when you are 45 or 50, suddenly wondering what your life means, you get to try something adventurous and uncertain while you are young and resilient. I think, it would be "cool" to be able to now take on new risks to help fix aspects of climate change, to teach a new curriculum in English to a group of kids who have no clue what you are talking about, to be part of an effort to end malaria or AIDS, or to continue research to nurture new stem cells to save lives.

New Economic Model: Three Pillars

Embedded in the new economic model, as I see it, are three national areas of priority, namely: (1) education, (2) health and the life sciences, and (3) energy and environment—three areas that confront challenges any nation must address. By the same token, these are the same great issues any top-notch university and leading enterprise will need to contend with. Equally important is the state of the ecosystem framework within which the overarching policy of innovation has to evolve and develop. Indeed, it is vitally important to get this ecosystem right. On the one hand, are the tools—the sciences, engineering, ICT, the arts, humanities, and languages, and, of course, management and politics. But, it has always been too much politics that throws the system and investors off. On the other hand, there are the mind-sets to change, the creativity that must reckon with the values, cultures, and religions of the diverse communities, and the intense intolerance of corruption, injustice, discrimination, and crime. This coming together of the ecosystem and its innovation-based economy, strongly supported at the base by the three pillars of priorities, will have to blend and interact seamlessly, to generate over time a society that is not only efficient and competitive but also sustainable in tomorrow's ever-changing, volatile world.

Education

At the heart of innovation are education and the mind. Now more than ever, Malaysians have to jump the learning curve, after a few generations have lost their way. This requires a firm political commitment toward building excellence and integrity in primary, secondary, and tertiary education. Even in these hard times, Malaysians should not lose sight of ensuring that the young students receive an incomparable education—one that prepares them to make critical contributions to knowledge and to society. Generations past are depending on them to keep that flame of commitment alive. This commitment must also be about interdisciplinary opportunities—to give students the kind of depth but also the ability to think critically about other methods, strategies, and orientations to learning. In the end, what really matters are the ideas, the engagement with these ideas, and the development of these ideas. Lots more will need to be done. Malaysians badly need a pair of fresh eyes and strong constitutions.

Health, Energy, and Environment

Also, the emergence of pandemics, development of new drugs, vaccines, and devices to treat difficult diseases, the prospect for new life from stem cell research, and the impact of these and other discoveries on diverse populations are centrally important to where Malaysians are going. Similarly, the development of newer, cleaner, cheaper forms of energy and energy storage, the more efficient use of scarce energy, and the many challenges posed by climate change are extremely significant concerns for the young in particular.

As intellectual matters, what's so exciting is that they touch on everything from basic research and scholarship to challenging the important applications that engage all professions. These three key pillars cross the boundaries of the natural sciences, engineering, social sciences, and the humanities. It's not uncommon, for example, for biological discovery and technological development to be stymied, if these are not fused with a good understanding of political science, anthropology, and religion. Above all, the challenges posed by these three important areas connect us to the underlying problems of the real world. The new economic model recognizes the importance of such endeavors. I am afraid we have to rely on this new generation to engage them after graduation. At this time of great disruption, volatility, and uncertainty, it is not too much to ask that the NMGs be the architects of change, not its victims. It is vital that as they join the labor force, they will need to pause to remember what defines them—and how they have come through, hopefully, stronger and wiser, more resilient, more adaptable, and better prepared to lead fulfilling lives.

Confucius Says

Finally, I well recall the wisdom of the great Master Kŏng-zi (Confucius):

There are nine things of which a new graduate should be mindful: to see clearly as he uses his eyes; to hear distinctly when he uses his ears; to be gracious in expression; to be respectful in demeanor; to be sincere in speech; to be serious in the execution of his duties; to seek advice when in doubt; to consider the consequences when he is angry; and to think of what is right and just when he is faced with advantage or gain.

What, Then, Are We to Do?

To these, I should add a tenth: to be ethical and act with utmost integrity when dealing with the enterprise and society in which he or she serves. In my entire public life—as in private—I have insisted on these 10 things for myself. And now, as the NMGs and many others take up the challenges of Najib's New Way, I wish them for you.

Kuala Lumpur
August 21, 2009

Note

1. First published on August 22, 2009.

CHAPTER 107

We Still Don't Get It[1]

The Great Recession started in the United States in late 2007. It brought in its wake the biggest bubble since the Great Depression, 1929 to 1932. The past two years were difficult. I have been in the business of government and of private entrepreneurship for a total of almost 50 years—never saw anything quite like it. World recovery still has a soft belly. In the United States and eurozone, the rebound is uneven, even anemic. We are now in 2010. When I last checked, doubts still encircle the vigor and rhythm of this nascent global recovery. But one thing is certain, the world has changed. So much so that we don't know what's normal anymore. Indeed, it is now cool to talk about the "new normal"—views differ on what this really means. For us in Malaysia, much appears to have changed over the past 25 months—in partisan politics, investor behavior, business perception, economic outlook, even the art scene. Or, has it?

On the heels of the most harrowing period for exporters in particular, there was a convergence of resolve: never again! I well remember a senior multinational enterprise executive yelling his head off at the golf club on his unexpected new experience in late 2008—the "waterfall" drop in demand for what he produces and exports: Today it's here, tomorrow it's gone! For politicians, businessmen, and investors, the talk was for review, restructure, and reform in a fundamental way. Often enough, we hear senior government officials remark: We have been able to successfully identify, appreciate, debate, and think out of the box on the systemic issues; our job is to go back to basics, change and implement a new game plan. The Malaysian prime minister's new economic model (NEM) is seductive and to the point: He is pushing to change the parameters of the nation's comfort zone. That's leadership: to have the serenity to accept what cannot be changed, the courage to change what cannot be accepted, and the wisdom to distinguish one from the other (Reinhold Niebuhr, US author). For more details, refer to Chapter 106, "Najib's New Way Forward," and Chapter 115, "Export-Led Growth Model: Quo Vadis."

As I look back, it is striking how little politics and business have really changed. Indeed, even amid any so-called change, much more has stayed the same.

Talk, Not Change

How loud does the prime minister have to get? His vision of NEM was first mooted in early 2009. His overarching strategy: to build an innovation-based economy with the clear objective of creating a high-income society. Since then, much water has passed under the bridge. No doubt, reaction has been positive. This shift in direction is refreshing; the rakyat is thrilled with renewed expectations for a better life. Businesses and investors liked the idea and promised—together with the civil service—to assist in its design and delivery.

I understand the details of the NEM framework—to form the basis of the 10th Malaysia Plan, 2011–2015 (to be announced in June 20, 2010), which will be unveiled in February. But on the street and in corporate boardrooms, it's still very much business as usual. The momentum of change doesn't seem to catch on. The power elite appears consumed with its incessant, discordant fiddling over money politics, vested business interests, old-school petty squabbles over turf, and the "blame game" over the delivery of public services. In all of this, the hardworking middle class and the very poor got pathetically short shrift.

As I write, I wonder whether most politicians, civil servants, and businessmen fully grasp the depth of the crisis and fully understand what the NEM really means and can accomplish. Implicitly, some even question: If it ain't broke, why fix it? Trouble is, the system has cracked once too often. Underneath, there are just too many cracks. All that is needed is for something to happen, and bang, the entire system breaks down. We definitely have to fix it. No question.

What's at Stake?

I travel quite a bit these days. Fulfilling speaking engagements, engaging academic interests, networking Harvard alumni (as the university's regional director for Asia), and occasionally, fostering business ties and ventures. I feel the dynamism of Asia—refreshing, vibrant, and invigorating. It is an Asia that never fails to amaze.

Malaysia has had a good run for nearly two generations. Now, it is slipping, squeezed in the middle by China and India, and failing to find a firm footing among its more dynamic Southeast Asian neighbors. In the Asian market space, standing still is not an option. Simply keeping up is no better. Malaysia is a small nation. We need to run faster than most to preserve our place in the sun. Today, Northeast Asia and India are changing so fast; what a difference a year makes. Today, geography is history!

What's at stake is our ability to compete and grow in a sustainable way to raise living standards. Clearly, we need to realize the following:

1. Time is not on our side—we must be able to move at a pace that meets stressed (not soft) targets.
2. The world (especially Asia) moves on, whether we like it or not—it waits for no one.
3. The window of opportunity (to move up the value chain) is still open, but we are already late—if not taken, we'll be left behind.
4. For inward foreign direct investment from the United States, eurozone, and Japan, Malaysia is beginning to be off the radar screen—we have to work real hard to really get back in.
5. Our best bet is to aggressively build on our long-standing relationship within the region and with China and India; to really succeed we need to be small and medium enterprise (SME) focused and innovation based.
6. We must be seen to be real "hungry"—be prepared to compete and fight for our niche-space.
7. Only private initiative and enterprise can make us efficient and sufficiently competitive to bring out the "animal spirits" so critical for success in entrepreneurial endeavors.

NEM Is Pivotal

That's why NEM is so pivotal; it's the change that it brings to bear on our society. For NEM to work, the innovation-based economic engine functions best within an ecosystem that fosters its own incubation—an environment that: (1) promotes the rule of law and a clear sense of security; (2) builds unity in the face of diversity; (3) embraces family values and a sense of community; (4) practices transparent democratic politics; (5) inculcates a fair and open society; (6) fights corruption; and (7) prioritizes education. It grows, draws, and retains talent, especially in science and technology. Indeed, we need to work much harder at creating a more hospitable ecosystem.

But, this is just a necessary but not sufficient condition for NEM's success. The new 1Malaysia drive helps. We will need to do better in practice. Sure, it is an ongoing process. For without it, even the best of economic models will be suboptimal. But, it is important we get this right. The US experience has shown that given the right environment, innovation has driven more than one-half of its productivity growth over the past 50 years. As I see it, innovation simply means fresh approaches that create value and societal well-being. While easier said than done, innovative value-added has to permeate every facet of our economic life—from responsible politics to government policies and procedures, to business methods and organization, and to household practices and systems.

Finally, there is always the issue of focus—on new growth areas. These not only lend support to the innovative-based economy but, equally important, provide a new source of strength to capitalize on new opportunities to expand both the gross domestic product and gross national product. It must involve a sharper shift to expand the services sector, where the real stimuli are expected to emanate from vibrant entrepreneurial SMEs—the very essence of middle-class progression.

There are four major services pillars of support:

1. Health (wellness) and life sciences
2. Tourism
3. Education and human resource management
4. Renewal energy and the environment (green growth)

Education remains our first and last defense—the acquisition and management of knowledge capital remains key in building a pool of global-savvy talent and niche skills.

The Nasi-Lemak Principle

The centerpiece of the NEM is to drive innovation. This is particularly timely. History teaches that promotion of and spending on innovation must be sustained through tough times in order to better compete when the new cycle of growth emerges. I see this being done by private enterprise in Japan, China, India, South Korea, and Taiwan, where research and development spending remained aggressive despite recession. For more details on this, refer to Chapter 111, "Innovation: Catalyst for Recovery." To think about it, innovation is really rather simple, for the mark of true innovation is not the grand gesture but the simple things done well. I call this the "nasi-lemak" (a popular fragrant rice with fish or meat, commonly consumed by most Malaysians) principle. It has done well for the folksy "nasi-lemak." It will do well for NEM.

What, Then, Are We to Do?

There are no quick fixes. Building strong fundamentals helps. But they are not enough. Sure, we have lots of problems. So do others. What's important is to make continuing progress: The trick is to make sure today is better than yesterday, and tomorrow, better than today. The direction is vital. In no time, we can be on our way. Similarly, leadership is important. But it is not enough. Leaders have to make serious political commitments to build unity out of diversity, and to use a lot of political capital to bring about real change. It is important that change is made clearly transparent and highly visible. That change is seen in everything we do—applying the nasi-lemak principle in processes and procedures, systems and regulations, organizations and methods. This is the only effective way to deliver. And, we need to deliver with a great sense of purpose and passion!

Concommitedly, two traditions need to be immediately revived and actively inculcated:

1. A tradition of predictability in public policy, consistency in its application, and transparency on the ground. This builds credibility.
2. A tradition of integrity, strong work ethic, hard work, and always, value-added service. This strengthens credibility.

In the final analysis, NEM works only if the ecosystem—within its bosom the model is conceived and in turn reinforced—is soundly grounded in innovation and creativity and solidly anchored in private enterprise.

Kuala Lumpur
January 28, 2010

Note

1. First published on January 30, 2010.

CHAPTER 108

Creativity: The Key to NEM's Success[1]

The New Economic Model (NEM) was unfolded in March 2010 and the 10th Malaysia Plan (2011–2015) in June. These aim to transform Malaysian life and fortunes. At its heart is innovation. The prime minister takes every opportunity to drive this home—indeed, to succeed innovation must be pushed harder and harder until it becomes an integral part of the nation's culture. As a concept, innovation simply means the nurturing of talent for creativity. Here creativity can be likened to producing something original and useful. Viewed differently, to be creative means getting the classic creative challenge of divergent thinking (producing unique ideas) and convergent thinking (putting ideas together to improve life) to work in tandem. According to Professor E. Paul Torrance (who created the gold standard in creativity assessment), a creative person has an "unusual visual perspective," matched with an "ability to synthesize diverse elements into meaningful products."[2] That's what creative talent is all about—essentially getting the left and right brains to operate as one. A recent IBM chief executive officers' poll identified creativity as the number-one "leadership competency" of the future.[3] Unfortunately, we don't have such a culture.

Creativity: A Culture Thing

In practice, despite former Prime Minister Tun Dr. Mahathir Mohamad's Look East policy, Malaysia has yet to succeed in emulating Japan's innovation culture. Three main elements of this culture remain alien:

1. It has a mentor system of management.
2. Japanese accept starting at the bottom in order to understand a firm's workings at every level.

3. Japanese function in unison as a workforce and are bonded to the future of the firm.

Whatever we have since achieved is still very much work in progress. Singapore's former Prime Minister Lee Kuan Yew's assessment is right. Not unlike Singapore, we just don't have the culture. As a matter of public policy, we did try to create a Malaysian way to develop our own brand of creativity culture by: (1) making Malaysia an attractive place to live, with security, good infrastructure, and communications, within a unique and relaxed way of life that is multiracial, multireligious, and multicultural, where foreigners can easily adapt; and (2) trying to position the nation as an attractive base for foreign direct investments (FDI) to come, expand, and prosper, with the widespread use of English. These we tried to do—but with only limited success to make up for what is special to the Japanese. We just don't have the culture. Besides, we can't (and won't) change readily enough to quickly develop such a culture.

Education: The Issue of Our Time

Chapter 112, "On Productivity and Talent Management," says: Human capital lies at the core of innovation. Raising productivity requires a labor force of high caliber—committed, motivated, and skilled enough to drive transformational change based on excellence over the long-term. It's about trapping potentials through acquisition of new skill sets in designing new products and services, and devising new processes and systems to do things smarter and more efficiently. All these need ready access to a talent pool of critical skills and expertise. Frankly, we don't as yet have such a pool (certainly not enough of it). To create and nurture one, we need to go back to basics. This means transforming our education system into one that emphasizes meritocracy and lays the foundation for creative thinking and analysis from day one. For a start, teaching curriculum, pedagogy, and management of education have to be reformed. President Barack Obama is right: If we want success for our country, we can't accept failure in our schools.

Fortunately, as evident from a recent issue of *Newsweek* magazine, creativity can be taught.[4] It starts with recognizing the new view that creativity is part of the normal brain function. The trick is to get the classic divergent-convergent creativity challenge working as a matter of habit. First, we need to get rid of some baggage: Discard emphasis on IQ in favor of CQ (creativity quotient). It is already proven that Torrance's creativity index is a good predictor of kids' creative accomplishments as adults. According to Professor Jonathan Plucker of Indiana University, using Torrance's massive database, the correlation to lifetime creative accomplishment was more than three times stronger for childhood CQ than childhood IQ. However, unlike IQ scores (which rise 10 points every generation—known as the Flynn effect, because presumably, enriched environments produce smarter kids)—CQ scores in the United States and many rich nations have fallen of late. No doubt, this reflects more and more time kids now spend in front of TVs and playing video games, rather than engaging in creative activities. Also, there is a growing lack of creativity development in schools and at home. This has become so serious that the United Kingdom and the European Union are making creativity development in education a national priority—even in China, where "drill-and-kill" teaching is prevalent.

The same decline appears to be happening in Malaysia. Reform must adopt a problem-based learning approach, where education is revamped to emphasize ideas generation; where curricula is driven by real-world inquiry; and where pedagogy acquaints teachers with the neuroscience of creativity. Critics argue our kids already have too much to learn. This is a false trade-off. Creativity thrives on fact finding and deep research. High global curriculum standards can still be met—but they need to be taught differently. True, creativity is prized in Malaysia, but politically we don't seem to be committed to unlocking it.

Continuing Denial

We have not produced (and are unlikely to produce) the talent in sufficient numbers we need to take us to the next level in becoming a high-income nation. For sure, what got us to where we are today will not get us to where we want to go. To begin with, we have to broaden the human capital base. For this, we need to transform our education system to secure at least a quality supply flow in the next generation. Over the medium term, we will have to make do with a real commitment and practical flexibility to turn our 18-to-30-somethings, on the margin at least, into as productive a workforce, given past damage. And retain them. By necessity, this will be suboptimal. Better late than never. In the end, it's not just about sustaining economic growth. We are surrounded with matters of national and international importance crying for creative solutions—from striving for excellence to raising productivity to delivering quality healthcare. Such solutions emerge from an open marketplace of ideas. These can be sustained by a workforce constantly contributing original ideas and receptive to ideas of others. What is required is real leadership to effectively harness the vast energies engendered.

Prime Minister Najib Razak is right in highlighting government as a key component of the creative ecosystem, in what he calls: "bringing innovation into government and government into innovation. . . . This will enable them to formulate framework, regulations and policies that support and not hinder innovation."[5] A great policy move, but in reality, government at large has yet to buy in on this transformational change. If you ask around—as far as talent development and retention goes—much of government remains in denial. US President Ronald Reagan once said jokingly that the nine most feared words in the English language are: "I'm from the government and I'm here to help." This rings all too true!

Come on, Get Real

Studies by an old friend, Professor Rajah Rasiah, at the University of Malaya identified three underlying causes for Malaysia's poor showing in the 2009 FDI inflows in Unctad's 2010 World Investment Report: its narrow human capital base, absence of synergy between research and development (R&D) labs and industry, and inadequate technological absorption in the face of intensifying competition in Asia, especially for talent. Like it or not, the talent game is dynamic as it is intense.

It is not good enough to have a set of policy responses to attract and retain talent. Weaknesses have to be dissected and addressed, and practical solutions neatly designed for effective implementation in a well-coordinated fashion. Most policy pronouncements reflect incentives offered by government that it considers attractive. Nobody bothers to ask targeted talent what they want and what it takes to make them want to move home. The tendency is to assume that, given the right incentives, Malaysian talent overseas would move back and foreign talent is readily attracted to come to Malaysia. Hence, the dismal failure of its "brain-gain" program. The approach is all wrong. Get real!

The Talent War

Be that as it may, the bar on talent has since been raised. Fueling the war for talent, enterprises in Asia are providing higher salaries and perks (external inequity of compensation is a common cause to move). A sea change is taking place in the way businesses organize themselves, create wealth, and market their brands and wares worldwide. The rise of the web and tech-based professions in logistics, biotech, life sciences, and information technology put a premium on scientists, engineers, finance analysts, and computer geeks. In Asia, soft skills, which were previously sidelined (viz. adaptability, English and Chinese skills, ease to fit into other cultures, negotiation, and political savvy), are now in demand. It's no longer enough for talent to be conversant with Oracle and Java; talent needs to have global experience and an ability to lead multicultural teams, and in multitasking, diplomatic knowhow to move seamlessly across borders, even though these skills are in short supply. The globalized economy has changed everything. Indeed, businesses will ultimately have to rethink the way they recruit and steward talent. Today, China and India are fast becoming sources of innovation, and R&D is moving global. Already, these nations are benefiting from "brain-circulation," with capital and talent returning after value adding in skills and experience abroad. This is occurring without government incentives. National ecosystems are evolving nicely for them. It's happening simply because it makes good business sense. There is much Malaysia can learn from the new reality.

As wealth and power change hands, talent is no longer a buyer's market for the traditional rich. By 2015, the International Monetary Fund projected Asia-Pacific will make up 45 percent of global gross domestic product, as against 20 percent by the United States and 17 percent by eurozone. The talent drain can only get more intense. We now have a world where talent can be found anywhere. The problem is particularly acute in rising Asia and Latin America, where breakneck growth is pushing management to the limit. The talent crunch is real. Throwing money and incentives at talent won't necessarily solve the problem. We need to think long term and rethink old ways. To do that, corporations are already investing to raise supply—that is, to create the talent they lack—going so far as to found their own universities to shape raw recruits into corporate leaders.

What, Then, Are We to Do?

In the end, nations need to have a workable process to recognize talent, fast-track careers, and provide fresh opportunities—essentially, to understand what makes them (talented people, that is) tick. It needs high-potential programs to attract and retain key talent within an ecosystem, which provides for high living standards, where security and rule of law are taken for granted. But, risks remain in the global economy. Concerns of citizens must be addressed by developing and investing in them. The quality of tertiary and vocational education has to be raised as a matter of priority. Imported talent can only reinforce local talent; yes, bring in people who can contribute. Striking the right balance is vital.

Kuala Lumpur
August 12, 2010

Notes

1. First published on August 14, 2010.
2. Po Bronson and Ashley Merryman, "The Creativity Crisis," *Newsweek* (July 19, 2010), p. 25. Refers to the creativity tasks first designed and tested by Professor E. Paul Torrance in 1958.
3. Ibid.
4. Ibid., p. 27.
5. Mohd Najib Abdul Razak, Prime Minister of Malaysia, speech at the National Innovation Summit on July 21, 2010, in Kuala Lumpur.

CHAPTER 109

The Mystique of National Transformation[1]

I am often asked: What's this new economic model (NEM) all about; how is this related to the economic transformation program (ETP) and to the government transformation program (GTP); what has all this got to do with creating a high-income society; what is this middle-income trap we are caught in; and why the urgency for national transformation?

Since the idea of NEM was first mooted by Prime Minister Mohd Najib Abdul Razak in mid-2009, our vocabulary has been enriched (or debased) by a barrage of upbeat words (economic roadmap, transformational journey, squeezed-in-the-middle, social minefields, talent management, managed liberalization, catalyzing change, etc.), some of which boggles the mind. New acronyms include NEAC, GNI, NKEAs, NKRAs, SRIs, EPPs, BOs, 10MP, IEB, Pemandu and GOA, Greater KL/KV, and many more. This is more than most can remember—let alone know what they stand for and to understand the complex web of interrelationships among them. No wonder the public seems confused. Many businessmen, investors, civil servants, and even academics are not sure they understand enough to lend a deep insight into how the various parts fit together and how they relate to what they are doing.

It is tough to fully appreciate the whole scheme of things in order to be able to buy in. After all, the entire framework, strategies, and policies and the manner they are stitched together are rather complex. Going through the maze of close to 2,000 pages of interrelated technical reports and discourse, and understanding what they really mean in terms of practical implementation, can be rather onerous and tiresome. It can put many off. Unless stakeholders appreciate enough to buy into and take ownership of the array of programs, no amount of political will and leadership commitment can see them through in practice. That's the challenge, I guess.

Middle-Income Trap

It is a fact that middle-income economies (MIEs) have grown less rapidly than either most rich or poor countries, which accounts for the lack of convergence in the past 100 years. So, middle-income nations get squeezed in the middle, between low-wage poor nation competitors (who dominate in mature or old industries) and the rich country innovators (who dominate new activities based on technological change). Southeast Asian nations today face this challenge, especially Malaysia. Conventional economic theory postulates that MIEs face three transformations as they evolve: (1) diversification slackens and then, reverses as they get more sophisticated and specialized; (2) fixed investment assumes less importance as the process of innovation gathers steam; and (3) quality of education shifts to enable workers to absorb readily new skills and technologies to increasingly add value to the production process.[2] These are observable outcomes as MIEs successfully shift their growth strategies.

But in the absence of economies of scale, smaller East Asian MIEs will need to struggle uphill in their attempt to maintain previous high growth rates. Strategies based on continuing capital accumulation will deliver steadily worse results, simply because the law of diminishing returns soon sets in. Many nations in Latin America and the Middle East are examples of MIEs that have not been able to get out of this middle-income trap.

For East Asia, however, I see room for optimism. World Bank studies have shown that some MIEs in East Asia have successfully made this transition from middle income to rich under proper environments driven by private enterprise, and adopting correct policies. Studies show some MIEs (e.g., South Korea and Taiwan) had remained successful manufacturers even in rather mature industries. Also, China, Taiwan, South Korea, and India had shown that success in knowledge-based industries and services can be had. For these MIEs, the tactic has been to straddle both strategies. Clearly, exploiting economies of scale does offer a way out. World Bank experience shows that "the pattern of trade, the flow of ideas and innovations, the new financial architecture, and the performance of cities are all consistent with East Asian economies displaying a shift toward growth that is founded on economies of scale."[3] However, it comes at a price—distributional consequences in terms of rising inequalities, widespread corruption, persistent crime, and lack of social cohesion are symptomatic of this model. Be that as it may, transformational change is what is needed if we are to get out of the middle-income trap. There is no other way.

NEM,[4] ETP, and GTP

Hence, NEM for Malaysia. Designed to provide a "concerted, holistic roadmap" to raise income and living standards over the next 10 years, its goals are anchored on strategies outlined in ETP and GTP. It targets growth in gross national income of at least 6 percent a year. By 2020, income per capita is expected to reach US$15,000 (RM48,000), enough to become a developed nation. To achieve this, ETP identifies eight strategic reform initiatives (SRIs) to propel transformation and growth: (1) promoting a private-sector led economy; (2) creating a quality workforce; (3) instilling competition; (4) strengthening the public sector; (5) building knowledge-base infrastructure; (6) enhancing sources of growth; (7) ensuring growth sustainability through innovation; and (8) implementing transparent and market-friendly affirmative action. Strategically, this makes a lot of sense. But, it's a tall order by any standard.

On the ground, ETP roadmap identifies 12 national key economic areas (NKEAs) in its drive to maturity—these represent growth engines identified to bring about high incomes through constant value adding: (1) oil, gas, and energy; (2) financial services; (3) palm oil and rubber; (4) wholesale and retail trade; (5) tourism; (6) electrical and electronics; (7) business services; (8) education; (9) communications, content, and infrastructure; (10) health tourism; (11) agriculture; and (12) the Greater Kuala Lumpur/Klang Valley. ETP needs to be private-sector driven, with government shifting its role from financier to facilitator.

Implementation of ETP complements the transformational push of SRIs; the outcome is expected to be a more balanced and more sustainable economy. Bear in mind that SRIs are intended to deal with foundational economic issues underpinning transformation and growth. However, success of ETP rests on four key underlying thrusts. The first involves the creation of an innovative and creative culture. To thrive, this needs an ecosystem that inculcates private enterprise and risk-taking, which flourish best in a competitive and regulatory friendly environment. The second addresses the presence of a reliable flow of quality workforce incubating in a conducive workplace. The third deals with a revamped government able to transform its service delivery system. This requires a government "embedded" in support of private initiatives, but not "in bed" with investors. Only a quality civil service instilled with fiscal discipline can deliver this. The fourth tackles the issue of inclusiveness and the need to reduce disparity—often collateral damage from unfettered laissez-faire private participation, in the absence of checks and balances. This thrust is critical for social cohesion in the face of a strong push for growth. For without growth, there will not be enough to redistribute.

GTP in conjunction with ETP forms an integral part of NEM. GTP is intended as the implementation roadmap to improve performance of the government engine. Here, six national key result areas (NKRAs) have been identified as critical: (1) reducing crime; (2) fighting corruption; (3) transforming education; (4) reducing poverty; (5) improving rural infrastructure; and (6) providing modern urban public transportation. To me, as a matter of priority, early outcomes must be measured against the goal of zero tolerance of corruption and crime, and building a modern education system. To retain talent and to attract more, Malaysia needs to transform the fight against corruption and crime with a passion in order to create livable cities to act as "talent magnets" that are open, tolerant, safe, and liberal, with attractive lifestyles.

A Lesson from History

European renaissance started first in Italy in the fifteenth century. It rapidly spread to Western and Central Europe. Outcomes were centered on (1) absorption of knowledge (mathematics) from India and Arabia; (2) notion of good living; and (3) rapid transmission of ideas through advent of printing. But undesirable social conditions (poverty, strife, and corruption) deteriorated in the midst of a golden age of plenty. What's happening in East Asia mirrors the renaissance—swift absorption of knowledge from the United States and Europe, focus of living well now, and widespread dissemination of ideas emanating from ICT and the computer. The lesson is clear—transformation changes must be accompanied by greater social cohesion to avoid problems from the worsening of social maladies.

Important How the Public "Feels"

The Malaysian prime minister declared that success of the ambitious blueprint hinges on its effective implementation: Execution needs to be flawless.[5] As I see it, discernible progress in four areas of priority concern to the public and investors needs to come early enough to build confidence. They are corruption, crime, education, and private enterprise. It is not enough to show that during the first nine months of 2010, crime fell by 16 percent (but there are still 132,355 unresolved reported cases), and street crimes fell 38 percent (18,299 unresolved reported cases), or that 648 persons were arrested for corruption. The public and investors (with ears to the ground) have to "feel" any improvement. Raw and biased statistics can't tell the real story, and don't impress. At this time, it would appear the public and investors don't feel any material improvement in the crime and corruption situation. That matters. But they don't rush to judgment. What they want to feel is for today to be better than yesterday, and tomorrow to be better than today; and come tomorrow, their expectations are fulfilled.

Incidents from personal experience reinforces this. Damansara Heights (DH) is rated a top spot to work and live in greater Kuala Lumpur. I stay there and my office is in nearby busy Plaza Damansara. Last week, my car was parked three doors away from my office, and within 10 minutes (no joke), the car was gone—stolen (sophisticated antitheft gadgets didn't help). Although a police "pondok" (base) is quite nearby (about 200 yards away), I still had to go to report at a police station miles away (which has jurisdiction over where my office is situated) and it took altogether three hours just to get a police statement taken. Many more steps still have to be made before I can file an insurance claim. That's another story. Because my car was a popular brand, we were told that four such cars were stolen in the DH area in recent days. Not so long ago, my associated office in DH was broken into and computers were stolen. When friends and neighbors learned of my predicament, I had an earful of equally unfortunate incidents nearby, including muggings, holdups, and handbag snatching. The point is simple—crime remains a problem of serious concern, even in the most livable area in Kuala Lumpur. People and investors just don't feel safe, whatever the data (whether true or not) may show.

Human Capital and Innovation

Key to NEM's success is ready availability of quality human resources. At its foundation is the education system and how it can be made to deliver. So far, none of the SRIs, NKEAs, and NKRAs point to confidence that this will be done holistically and comprehensively any time soon. Time is of the essence. The competition for talent is getting more intense worldwide. Bear in mind that it takes at least a generation to finish one cycle of "production." On mathematic reading and science tests given to 15-year-olds in 65 countries in 2009, Shanghai teenagers topped all three worldwide. Near the top were: Singapore, Taipei, Finland, South Korea, and Japan. Malaysia was not on the radar screen. The United States was, once again, in the middle of the pack in science and reading, but below average in mathematics. The Organisation for Economic Co-operation and Development (who runs these tests) attributed Shanghai's success to being a "leader in reform," citing the city's near-universal education system, its competitiveness in admissions, high level of student engagement, modern assessment system, ambitious curriculum, and a program to assist weak schools. Until now, China has not even surfaced as a threat!

Human capital lies at the core of innovation and the taking of risks. Raising productivity requires a labor force of high caliber—committed, motivated, and skilled enough to drive transformational change based on excellence over the long term. Only private initiative can deliver this. Lest we forget, there is a big difference between incremental improvements and transformational change. French President Nicholas Sarkozy says it best: The invention of the light bulb did not come about from incremental improvements to the candle. Make no mistake, transformational changes necessarily involve the taking of risks. Tom Watson (the founder of IBM) once said: If you want to succeed, raise your error rate. As I see it, a government that takes no risk in promoting innovation is one that is likely to make the bigger error of not trying hard enough. Getting private initiative back as the engine of growth is hard but critical. Bold steps need to be taken. Incremental changes such as getting government-linked companies (GLCs) to gradually sell down equity won't get us there. Private investors need to accept the Schumpeterian "creative destruction"[6] impact of innovation and stand fired up enough to deal with it as the only route to sustained growth. In the end, what's really required is to squeeze out their entrepreneurial juices: "Without innovations, without entrepreneurial achievement, no capitalist returns and no capitalist propulsion. The atmosphere of industrial revolutions—of 'progress'—is the only one in which capitalism can survive."[7] To be serious, government needs to get out of the business of doing business. GLCs and other federal and state enterprises are a serious source of unfair competition. They only work to hold back the prompt reemergence of real private initiative.

What, Then, Are We to Do?

I should end with a quotation from my favorite poet, E. E. Cummings: "America makes prodigious mistakes, America has colossal faults, but one thing cannot be denied: America is always on the move. She may be going to hell, of course, but at least she isn't standing still." This is no time to stand still in undertaking bold transformation change. In the end, that's what statesmanship is all about.

Kuala Lumpur
December 13, 2010

Notes

1. First published on January 1, 2011.
2. Indermit Gill and Homi Kharas. *An East Asian Renaissance: Ideas for Economic Growth* (Washington, DC: World Bank, 2007), p. 4.

3. Ibid.
4. Mohd Najib Abdul Razak, Prime Minister of Malaysia. Launching the concluding part of the nation's New Economic Model (NEM) Report on December 3, 2010, in Putrajaya, Malaysia, "New Economic Model for Malaysia—Concluding Part," National Economic Advisory Council, Putrajaya, December 2, 2010.
5. Ibid., p. 8.
6. Thomas K. McCraw, *Prophet of Innovation: Joseph Schumpeter and Creative Destruction* (Cambridge, MA: Belknap/Harvard University Press, 2010). Schumpeter said: Creative destruction is the driving force of capitalism.
7. Joseph Schumpeter, *Business Cycles: A Theoretical, Historical and Statistical Analysis of the Capitalist Process*, vol. II (New York: McGraw Hill, 1939), p. 1033.

CHAPTER 110

Toward Quality Undergraduate Education[1]

The National Economic Advisory Council (NEAC) March 2010 Report stated: "Malaysia faces an exodus of talent. Not only is our education system failing to deliver the required talent, we have not been able to retain local talent of all races nor attract foreign ones due to poor prospects and a lack of high-skilled jobs."[2] This simply does not make sense. Human capital lies at the heart of any high-income economy. It is key to Malaysia's transformation agenda. Success in structural reform relies heavily on skill-intensive and innovation-led growth. Not surprisingly, human resource development features prominently in the new economic model. Simply put, this means it will need to develop, attract, and retain talent. Yet, the brain drain—that is, the cross-border migration of talent—runs counter to the compelling domestic need for a more skilled, more innovative, and more entrepreneurial labor force to be able to constantly add value.

Against this backdrop, the Malaysian experience is not unique. The World Bank estimated that in 2010, 215 million people live outside their country of birth, 80 percent from developing nations, with 43 percent living in high-income advanced economies.[3] Within Asia, the most pronounced brain drain is in Southeast Asia. Malaysia's brain drain is intensive, not because too many are leaving but because the skills base is narrow. This is compounded by the lack of compensating inflows. It is also concentrated in Singapore. A large part of Malaysia's problem reflected the poor quality of graduates from public universities. It progressively eats into the quality of its human capital stock. No Malaysian university was in the 2010 QS World University Rankings Top 200:[4] Among its top research universities, Universiti Malaya was ranked 207 (2009: 180); Universiti Kebangsaan was ranked 263 (291); Universiti Sains, 309 (314); Universiti Teknologi, 365 (320); and Universiti Putra, 319 (345). This poses a particular challenge.

673

Historical Perspective

For years, the classic Ivy League American college envisages learning based on foundational knowledge of key disciplines or fields ("core") and in-depth study of a key area of specialization ("concentration"). This approach has been variously described as an unstable compound arising from the marriage between the German research university and the English liberal arts college. Unlike the United States, however, the British Commonwealth public universities started following the British model. Today, these universities are, in practice, more akin to the already much deteriorated German experience, which for decades prided themselves on their egalitarianism in education. With the adoption of the 1963 Robbins Report, the United Kingdom and Commonwealth public university system has become geared to advance this holy grail. As a general rule, vigorous selective admissions of the 1950s and 1960s, with exceptions, have since gradually disappeared. A degree from one university is deemed to be worth about just as much as the other. Every university will be run more or less the same, turning most of the once-proud older universities into virtual extensions of government bureaucracy. Again with exceptions, professors and staff become public servants, earning more or less the same pay at almost every university, based not on merit and academic excellence.

And so, just this one idea, equality, which turns out to be a bad one, is attributed to its undoing. This idea promotes the anti-elitist belief in equality of access to university education and equality of standing of every university. The consequence is for the State to pay to see this idea through. Since the best receives the same funding as the worst, the result in the United Kingdom has been—according to Robert Stevens—"to homogenize English universities and dumb them down to a lower, mediocre mean."[5] It reflects a system designed to protect the weak instead of rewarding the best.

Understandably, this phenomenon has since led to a disentangling of intellectual privilege from social privilege. This new academic elite was led by Prime Minister Tony Blair based on the principle that some students are academically better and, thus, deserve greater resources directed to their development. Otherwise, England would be in danger of turning into an incubator for the likes of Yale and Harvard (according to Oxford Professor Alan Ryan). Unlike the British system, the United States maintained an elitist rewards system, designed to develop the best and the brightest. Here, competition is the name of the game. Top US universities stayed mainly independent of government funding. With independence comes the ability to compete for academic success with the best the world can offer. In practice, this means vigorous competition for funding, the best students, and the best staff.

Liberal Arts Education

A liberal arts education pursues a spirit of free inquiry undertaken without concern for finding a job.[6] It accomplishes two main objectives: (1) sharpens students' awareness of the world; and (2) provides them with the tools to engage the forces of change. The breadth of subjects they study and the skills and habit of mind they acquire are intended to shape their lives after graduation. This is best exemplified in the overarching role of the US Ivy League colleges to educate students to be independent, knowledgeable, reflective, and creative thinkers with a sense of social responsibility. Towards this end, they are made to think and act critically. Their sense of history and theory enlightens and empowers them to act with great self-confidence. Harvard educates—but does not make them wise.

What's Wrong?

Five things have gone wrong, as described in some detail in Chapter 95, using Harvard, consistently the best of the lot, as an example. It is in Harvard's DNA to always strive to be the best; and it often succeeds. Yet, I think it has since the 1960s, first of all, allowed its main mission to drift toward evolving education increasingly to promote stakeholder satisfaction: to developing its international brand, and to assuming the role of an education market-enterprise. Through it all, Harvard continues to remain consistently the top rated world-class research university.

Second, in meeting relentless competition for research excellence, it has brought about a university system primed for research. Of course, this brought untold prestige through scholarly discoveries and scientific inventions. But, I think, at the expense of underlying student quality. For example, performance outcomes for effectively imparting knowledge are left unmeasured; teaching doesn't consciously promote responsible citizenship; professors are rewarded for academic excellence but not for helping students find meaningful lives.

Third, deep and profound changes have taken place: (1) in curriculum—now richer, deeper, and broader, but without a clearly identifiable link between what is taught in class and what they do outside class; (2) in grading—now more disciplined, but grades have become more credentials for employment and graduate schools, rather than instructional feedback from teacher to student; and (3) in extracurricular activities—which have now become broader and more diverse with competition going beyond intellectual undergraduate ideals; they have since become more motivated by materialistic incentives.

Fourth, I think great universities have forgotten their basic job—to turn restless 18-somethings into stable, well-balanced 20-something-adults—to help them grow up. The greater the university, the more intense is market competition for faculty, students, and funds. Increasingly, there is less attention on: (1) developing good character; (2) building personal strength and integrity; (3) inculcating kindness, cooperation, and compassion, and (4) offering extracurricular experiences that link up to formal learning.

Fifth, the sciences and humanities have long been the foundation for curriculum thinking: the sciences being the transforming force while in the humanities the means for moral uplift. No question, science will grow in stature. How can universities nurture and inspirit the humanities? Humanists today already feel marginalized. This should not be. New advances in the sciences offer possibilities to prolong human life, destroy life, and artificially transform life in ways that challenge the very meaning of what it is to be human. As such, traditional focus of the humanities on questions of value, of meaning, of ethics, has assumed more importance. Somehow, there is this growing urge to ensure scientific advances are made to serve humane purposes.

Reform

I believe education should be more than just what we learn. At Harvard, as I know it, the undergraduate mission remains largely intact: to transform teenagers (whose lives have been so protected by their families and schools) into adults with the learning and education to take responsibility for their own lives. That's why it has taken Harvard the greater part of the 2000s to review its curriculum. In 2009, it replaced the existing 30-year-old core curriculum with a new Program in General Education (PGE).[7] Emphasizing strength of character and scholarly excellence, the new curriculum is focused to (1) help students understand complexities of the human condition; (2) come to grips with the underlying questions of life; and (3) learn how to fit seamlessly into its multitalented, multiethnic, multicultural, and multinational student life. To work, it has to gel with new commitments to pedagogical innovation and to activity-based initiatives linking extracurricular activities to classroom experience.

Make no mistake. The academic experience is its centerpiece, comprising: (1) the concentration (in-depth pursuit of a disciplinary interest); (2) the electives (broadening interest beyond the focus); and (3) the PGE (connects and helps appreciate the complexities of the world). In contrast to the previous core curriculum—which exposed students to a number of different "ways of knowing"—I am told the new PGE seeks to provide new opportunities to learn (and faculty to teach) in ways that cut across departmental and intrauniversity lines.[8] Its four main goals link up to life after college: (1) prepare for civic engagement; (2) understand the traditions of art, ideas, and values; (3) respond to deep change; and (4) understand ethical dimensions.

To pursue these goals, students are asked to complete courses in: (1) aesthetic and interpretive understanding, (2) culture and belief, (3) empirical and mathematical reasoning, (4) ethical reasoning, (5) science of living systems, (6) science of the physical universe, (7) societies of the world, and (8) United States in the world.

Dignity and Honor

As I see it, restoration of the right balance between scholarly excellence and its education role requires developing in students a philosophy of life that is intended to bring dignity, honor, and responsibility. Harvard has, in my view, set the new gold standard in undergraduate education. Its first graduates under the new curriculum will emerge in 2013. Malaysia, too, badly needs to reform its education system and policies. But it need not reinvent the wheel in order to jump-start its own undergraduate uplift. There are valuable lessons to be learned from the Harvard experience. For Malaysia, this means there is already a ready blueprint to help students: (1) to believe in themselves as skilled individuals; and (2) to place themselves first, above members of any identity group. This entails creating community out of diversity, based on confidence in tested owned principles. This remains key to raising the quality of an educated person and leader. This is something Malaysia wants to emerge from its universities.

Adding "Breadth" in Australia

It is noteworthy that since 2008, Melbourne University has adopted the US academic model, requiring all students to take "breadth" courses from outside their faculty and embark on more specialized training as professionals in medicine, law, and engineering at the postgraduate level. That is, three years for a broad-based bachelor's degree and thereafter two extra years for a master's to be a professional. Most of these pathways add an extra year, but they graduate with greater personal confidence plus higher satisfaction and higher quality. After all, what's another year in a student's lifetime? In Malaysia, life expectancy has been already lifted to 75 in 2010, rising past 73 in 2009. As former Harvard president Derek Bok said: If you think education is expensive, try ignorance. Worse is to be stuck in denial.

What, Then, Are We to Do?

In the end, we have now readily available a tested experience to engage the increasingly complex world. As I see it, the Harvard PGE should enable new graduates to have: (1) the ability to compose a literate and persuasive essay; (2) the insight to interpret a famous humanistic text; (3) the capacity to link history to the present; (4) the know-how to understand foundation science and scientific methods to unravel mysteries of the real world; and (5) enough quantitative reasoning to sharpen analysis of problems.[9] We have to believe that tomorrow's world will not accept graduates, according to former Harvard President Lawrence Summers, not knowing the difference between a gene and a chromosome; or, not familiar with select Nobel Prize-winning works in literature. This building of self-confidence must involve a capability to speak English well; and to articulate cogently, persuade others, and reason on moral and ethical issues. They are also expected to know how to collaborate with others on divisive issues, and to engage each other in a civil manner. The job ahead is daunting. We need to start now.

Kuala Lumpur
July 14, 2011

Notes

1. First published on July 16, 2011.
2. National Economic Advisory Council (NEAC), *New Economic Model for Malaysia*, Part I (Kuala Lumpur, March 2010), p. 105.
3. World Bank, *Malaysia Economic Monitor: Brain Drain* (Washington, DC: World Bank, April 2011), pp. 11–13.
4. QS World University Rankings, 2010.
5. Author of "University to Uni: the Politics of Higher Education in England since 1944."
6. Harry Lewis, *Excellence without a Soul* (New York: Public Affairs, 2007), pp. 253–255.
7. Harvard University. "Program in General Education," in *Handbook for Students, 2010–11*' (Cambridge, MA: Harvard University Press, July 7, 2011).
8. Harvard College, *Report of the Task Force on General Education*, Faculty of Arts and Sciences, Harvard University, Cambridge, MA, 2007.
9. Lewis.

CHAPTER 111

Innovation: Catalyst for Recovery[1]

History teaches that spending on innovation must be sustained through tough times in order to better compete when recovery resurfaces. Otherwise, companies will emerge from the recession with obsolete products or services—with nothing new in added value and no initiatives in modernization, automation, and intellectual property to compete for markets. General Electric (GE), for example, failed to keep up in the 2001–2003 recession, with rivals developing more efficient LED lighting technology now competing with incandescent bulbs. Investments sow the seeds of innovations, including software in new/improved systems, processes, and methods that enhance their competiveness globally. Innovative products like iPod (Apple) and RAZR cell phone (Motorola) were hatched during the downturn of the early 2000s. Despite plunging sales, GE spent billions following the end of the Cold War to develop new engines with blades lighter than titanium. This paid off handsomely in the 2000s, earning billions more from servicing these engines. Of particular interest is Corning's "rings of defense" strategy in the face of the current recession—innovation spending was placed in the innermost ring, making it the last to be cut.

Recession and Research and Development

With growing interdependence, the United States and eurozone face keen competition from China, India, Japan, and South Korea, which have continued to invest. According to the latest private US survey by consultant Booz & Co., research and development (R&D) spending in 2008 rose by 4 percent in North America, rose 2 percent in Japan, and fell 1 percent in the eurozone.[2] In India and China, it rose by 7 percent each. The US Battelle Memorial Institute (which tracks R&D outlays) estimates that such spending by government, companies, and universities will rise more than 3 percent in 2009, perhaps slowing down in 2010.[3] Indications are that Japanese, Chinese, Indian, and Korean R&D spending will remain aggressive despite recession. Sure, economic conditions are now bad and not getting better anytime soon. Still, many consider this to be the best time to innovate. That's what is needed to drive growth coming out of the downturn.

According to Professor Clayton M. Christensen, the Harvard Business School guru on innovation (his book, *The Innovator's Dilemma*, was a *New York Times* bestseller), hard times are good for innovation because (1) it forces innovators not to waste so much scarce resources on innovative endeavors (especially R&D); (2) in an environment where there is growing pressure to push innovation "out of the gate" fast and keep the cost of such activity down, the chances of success increases (Christensen argues that under normal circumstances, 93 percent of all innovation that ultimately becomes successful started off in the wrong direction); and (3) breakthrough innovations often come when pressure is greatest at a time when resources are limited.[4] That's when innovators and entrepreneurs become more realistic and more open to promptly rethink their business model to best translate new ideas into commercially viable ventures.

Of course, things won't happen overnight. It will take two to three years to notice the difference, perhaps, four to five years to see real successes. But the opportunity presents itself now to generate a new wave of innovation initiatives to spur business investment, job creation, productivity gains, wealth accumulation, and sustainable gross domestic product (GDP) growth. But important preconditions for success need to be met. Government needs to foster a more hospitable environment including: (1) good education fundamentals; (2) high levels of technological readiness and ICT savviness; (3) innovation and ICT diffusion capabilities; and (4) clear fiscal incentives for public–private partnership to deliver.

Jobs, Skills, and Talent

Above all, availability of human resources is critical: The nation will need a reliable and steady flow of good quality personnel from tertiary and vocational education facilities, and imported talent (when needed). Indeed, hard times offer the best opportunities to acquire, train, retrain, upgrade, and retain the broadest range of skills. This will need—at this time—broad-ranging and generous incentives to hold and acquire technically competent staff, and aggressively promote R&D and ICT innovation initiatives—especially in process engineering, systems design, and software computing and development. The main objective is to build capacity when others are retrenching and cutting spending.

The focus of public policy at this time of crises must be to create higher-paying value-added jobs for all Malaysians. This is vital, especially in occupations where Malaysians have preferred not to participate (unskilled labor-intensive jobs). We see this in land development, plantations, agriculture, construction, public works, and many services industries. This is understandable, especially in menial jobs. Nevertheless, that is why spending on innovation and R&D is so critical.

Unskilled occupations can be readily retrained and transformed to higher and higher paying jobs through systematic value adding. This can be done through the application of even simple technology, mechanization, and automation (from the simplest to the most complex); process engineering, and the adoption of new methods, systems, procedures, and processes (i.e., new and better ways of doing old tasks and doing new and better things to replace old ways), including turning services into software. The opportunities for these initiatives are wide ranging. Moreover, Moore's Law[5] and its flipside (i.e., today's sophisticated computing technology and software; instead of providing ever increasing performance and holding it at a particular price, they now provide a particular level of performance at an ever lower price) do offer a cost-effective way to do so.

In practice, this has resulted in a geometric rise in the processing power of desktops, laptops, and mobile phones without increases in price. If needed, talent should be imported to accelerate the process of change. Of course, all stakeholders need to be persuaded to "buy in," and implementation of the entire process will take time. More important, the political will to change and hold the course is vital. Change, in practice, may require a transitional period to bring this about. But it is vital that the objective of public policy is held steadfast and politicians are sufficiently convinced and committed to withstand outside pressures to keep the status quo.

Indeed, expect strong vested interests to put lots of pressure to bear to keep the comfortable old ways. A practical way out during transition is to tie companies to progressively wean themselves (within a committed time frame) from importing unskilled labor. It should be based on a definite plan to restructure and to adopt innovative ways to significantly add value to their processes (and employ more and more Malaysian labor). Besides, many of them already depend on subsidized gas and government incentives. For the nation to compete and grow, this is the only viable option left to raise incomes and lift living standards.

What, Then, Are We to Do?

The centerpiece to promote recovery and quality growth during hard times is to drive innovation. It is comforting to note that the first and second stimuli programs have embodied significant elements in spending on training, restructuring, and funding (at this time with government as the lender of first and last resort). Indeed, hard times are also the best time to revitalize, restructure, and rebuild. However, realistically, such stimulative spending (and lending) will only raise productivity over the medium and long run.

Above all, they have to be effectively implemented. It must be recognized that these are not intended to be government consumption (i.e., one-shot pump priming). Their attendant multipliers can be expected to raise private spending, create value-added jobs, and ultimately raise incomes. And, to the extent that imported unskilled labor is no longer needed, they also strengthen the nation's external payments position and even the federal budget (since their claims on more social services will be significantly reduced). The key element has to be the government's will to make these fundamentally vital changes—involving not just the commitment of substantial funding (which the nation can well afford), but also a stubborn resolve to change mind-sets in order to instill and build (and effectively put on the ground) a creative and innovative culture, and a national entrepreneurial spirit, especially among the young.

What's next? We see today a worldwide wave of new innovation that presents opportunities of a lifetime, like green technologies, nanotechnology, voice-over Internet protocol virtualization, cloud computing, wireless broadband mobility, software to value add in the services sector, and social networking. The financial and social benefits that can flow through will be wide ranging. If done well, they will propel Malaysia to become more competitive, especially when we are being "squeezed in the middle" (between India and China). We need to recognize that creating good-paying jobs is worth pursuing as an object of public policy. The only way is to restructure the economy.

This involves persistence and commitment by the civil service in particular, to stand steadfast behind the cause to give it their all to support the government of the day. Above all, it may involve new commitments of funding and incentives if what's already in the stimuli plans proves insufficient. It will be monies well spent (up to the civil service to see to this) since it raises the economy's capacity to produce more and more efficiently. This is doubly worthwhile if it also reflects an understanding of shared responsibility and opportunity with investors and entrepreneurs to meet this bold challenge together. What remains to be done now is to pick up from the national innovation roadmap and operationalize it for early implementation in all its facets. Start by integrating the key strategies into the two stimuli programs, including an "early bird" attraction to create green-collar jobs. After all, there is much to be said about a "blue ocean" strategy that's also green.

Kuala Lumpur
April 23, 2009

Notes

1. First published on April 25, 2009.
2. Referred to and reported on in Justin Scheck and Paul Glader, "R&D Spending Holds Steady in Slump," *Wall Street Journal* (April 6, 2009).
3. Ibid.
4. Clayton Christensen, *The Innovator's Dilemma* (Cambridge, MA: Harvard Business School Press, 1997).
5. Derived in 1965 by Gordon Moore (a cofounder of Intel, now the world's biggest maker of computer chips). In practice, it simply means that the cost of a given amount of computing power falls by roughly one-half every 18 months. Looked at differently, the amount of computing power available at a particular price doubles over the same 18-month period.

CHAPTER 112

On Productivity and Talent Management[1]

For 50 years, sustained growth in Malaysia was based on ever expanding use of manpower and accumulation of fixed capital assets. Basic economics tells us that this business model will eventually give way to the law of diminishing returns: when increasing injections of labor and capital lead to lower rates of additions to output with each passing year. The message: We can't be expected to grow efficiently by simply doing more of the same. To become an increasingly higher-income nation, we need to shift from the "old" resource-based economy to one that is innovation led. Empirical evidence suggests the old strategies have delivered steadily worse results.

On the other hand, innovation is known to have driven one-half of US productivity growth over 60 years. Notes the McKinsey Global Institute: Those innovations—in technology as well as products and business processes—boosted productivity. For us, only innovation can be relied upon to drive exponential growth. By innovation, I mean fresh thinking and approaches that add value to consistently create wealth and social welfare. In the end, innovation drives productivity, and productivity drives the flow of real income. History teaches that a burst of productivity growth can make the years ahead much more prosperous. With higher pay, workers can still save and yet have enough left over to spend more to raise living standards.

Productivity

However, economics is unsure about the predictability of innovation and productivity. Investors are notoriously fickle, and entrepreneurs' serendipity, usually random; then, there is the speed new products and services can be rolled out and brought to market. Research findings over the years confirm that productivity is never an accident. It is always the result of a commitment to excellence, intelligent planning, and focused efforts. Perhaps this can help make productivity growth somewhat more predictable. In the United States, studies by my econometrics professor at Harvard, Dale Jorgenson, pointed to technology advancing less fast than in the decade before the recent recession.[2]

Consequently, productivity can be expected to slacken to around 1.5 percent annually, yielding potential gross domestic product (GDP) growth for the United States as a whole of up to 2 to 2.5 percent a year over the next few years. Nothing spectacular, but much better than Japan during the recent lost decade. As of now, continuing high unemployment and rising US GDP growth in the fourth quarter of 2009 and the first quarter of 2010 have resulted in an abrupt 7 percent annual rate gain in productivity. This reflected in part a reluctance to hire given uncertainties. A similar knee-jerk reaction also happened in the 2001 recession. Rebound in electronics demand suggests perhaps the wave of technology advances that fueled productivity in years prior to 2008 may have some steam left.

Most now see Asia reviving nicely this year—the first quarter of 2010 results and forecasts for the year are rather robust, thanks to government stimuli. The Asian Development Bank (ADB) and World Bank now talk of 7.5 to 8.5 percent growth for the year (5.5 to 6 percent ex-China). But India and East Asia (China, South Korea, and Taiwan) display more impressive productivity growth. Within ASEAN (Brunei, Indonesia, Malaysia, Philippines, Thailand, Singapore, Vietnam, Cambodia, Laos, and Myanmar), the underlying productivity profile remains anemic, especially the more mature among them. For Malaysia, productivity growth averaged below 1 percent a year over the past 20 years. That's a setback.

Hence, resurgent talk of reform and rebalancing in search of new directions. The ADB suggests finding ways to "shift the drivers of growth." Singapore pushes a new focus to double workforce productivity growth from 1 percent now to 2 to 3 percent in the near future. That's easier said than done—even for Singapore. Thirst for new ways to competitively value add has to be quenched. Today, China and India are where the action is—they provide the learning laboratory for innovative practices and processes. It was management guru Peter Drucker who predicted China to have the next management revolution in innovation. As Professor Bill Fischer of IMD (Switzerland) puts it: Whereas Japan's management revolution was all about "lean," China is all about "speed"—faster to produce, faster to market, faster across markets, faster to expand. Today, China uses its competitive advantage and "Chineseness" to do things better, but not through conventional blockbuster innovation. In a still-emerging economy, being good enough (or acceptable enough) but less expensive reflects a determination to raise productivity. We see this success in Alibaba and Taobao (B2B and C2C market space), Dangdang (e-commerce, similar to Amazon), Chery (cars), and Diao (detergent). The bet is to be one up on someone else's established success to gain market share.

Government as an Enabler

There is no prescription for how a country can create a culture of innovation and competitiveness. According to Nobel Laureate Joseph Stiglitz in 2001: But government does have a role—in education, in encouraging the kind of creative and risk taking that the scientific entrepreneurship requires, in creating the institutions that facilitate ideas being brought into fruition, and a regulatory and tax environment that rewards this kind of activity. Ironically, US prowess in innovation owes much to government support. As Harvard Professor Josh Lerner tells it at his MBA class, early development of Silicon Valley emanated from Pentagon contracts, as did the Internet, which grew out of a Department of Defense project initiated in 1969.

Even today, US Department of Energy disburses US$40 billion in loans and grants to stimulate private development of green technologies. In Malaysia, development of new industries and restructuring of old ones (creative destruction) often requires a nudge from government in terms of subsidies, loans, infrastructure, and other support. In order to be successful, government needs to (1) create a conducive climate for public–private collaboration—as Harvard's Dani Rodrik puts it: requires a government "embedded" in the private sector, but not in bed with it; (2) incentivize innovations with "rental" rewards through a credible patent system; and (3) ensure "public goods" serving society are promoted in a transparent fashion.[3]

Venture Capital

From ASEAN to Northeast Asia and from India to Japan, the big risk to innovative ventures remains the lack of ready access to finance at reasonable cost. The onset of the Great Recession and damage done to the financial system have exacerbated this risk. Firms that depend on bank credit and private equity have been particularly vulnerable. A recent International Monetary Fund study of North American manufacturers estimated that a 100 basis points (1 percentage) rise in corporate bonds rate can lead to a 25 basis points (0.25 percent) fall in productivity.[4] This is a big deal. Worse hit is venture capital (VC). In the best of times, VC funds are already hard to come by. In recent years, reflecting big losses (by foundations and endowments) on hedge funds, private equity, stocks and shares, venture financing has become more risk averse. Holding back by university endowments is a great setback. Harvard's Josh Lerner estimated that although such VC funding accounts for a fraction of total research and development, the R&D such VC supports produces three to four times as many patents per US$ spent as regular corporate R&D.[5] The same story hits Asia since innovative ventures are forced abroad for financing, even in cash-rich Japan. Worse hit are angels, early start-ups, and intermediate-stage start-ups. In risk-averse Japan, odds really stack up against start-ups. In normal times, only 10 percent of VC in Japan goes to start-ups. In the United States, as much as 20 percent is invested in start-ups and another 15 to 20 percent in later-stage ventures. In Malaysia, the situation is worse. The bulk of VC monies come from government and private start-up funding is virtually nonexistent in practice. Not only are governing boards and top management of VC funds risk averse, their fear of loss on their watch scares them. Furthermore, the environment is set in a culture that does not take on risk readily. Thomas Watson, founder of IBM, is widely reported to have once said: If you want to succeed, raise your error rate. As I see it, a government that takes no risk in promoting innovative ventures is one that is likely to make the bigger error of not trying hard enough.

Ironically, all is not lost. Studies at Harvard Business School have shown that venture financing during and soon after recessions is more successful per dollar spent in practice, than during booms when money flows easily. Indeed, entrepreneurship is resilient to business cycles, partly because many turn to self-employment when laid off or offered a chance to take on risk. I am told 40 to 45 percent of corporates listed in Fortune 500 were born in recessions. As one who is actively involved with VCs, I find little comfort in this. I certainly won't bet on it.

Talent Management

Human capital lies at the core of innovation. Raising productivity requires a labor force of high caliber—committed, motivated, and skilled enough to drive transformational change based on excellence over the long term. It's about trapping potentials through acquisition of new skill sets in designing new products and services, and devising new processes and systems to do things smarter and more efficiently. That's what talent management is all about. In terms of outcomes, this simply means encouraging businesses to invest in R&D, design, automation, software, training, and the accumulation (also acquisition) of intellectual property. Concomitantly, Malaysia also needs to pursue initiatives on the flipside—promote angel investors and start-ups through an incentive regime that rewards risk taking. Angels nurture start-ups very early. Their involvement goes beyond funding. They provide handholding, mentoring, coaching, and access to business networks.

Indeed, this link turns innovative ideas into commercial propositions. All these need ready access to a talent pool of critical skills and expertise. They make the difference between success and failure; the difference between quality and quantity. In the end, they deliver products and services better, smarter, and faster. That's what productivity is all about.

Global Talent War

The Economist Intelligence Unit's August 2009 global survey on talent strategies identified critical constraints on talent in an enterprise's capacity to innovate—External: (1) intense global competition; (2) rapid turnover; and (3) rising cost. Internal: (1) lack of collaboration and resource sharing within an organization; and (2) business and talent strategy not aligned.[6] They reflect the war on talent out there.

In today's world (which isn't "flat," contrary to what Thomas Friedman says), I believe competitive enterprises can't afford to be insular. Indeed, they need to look outside for talent to survive. China and India are wooing their national talent from North America where they have been entrepreneurial drivers. Other parts of Asia are doing the same. Indications are host advanced nations are fighting back. They may not have to fight too hard. Between 1997 and 2002, I am told, close to two-thirds of foreigners who earned PhDs in science and engineering in the United States are still there. The *stay rates* are much higher among Chinese and Indians (80–90 percent).[7]

Talent scarcity is a global issue. It's not confined to developed nations where it's very serious. By 2050, for the first time, 60+-year-olds will exceed 15-year-olds or younger. Even population-rich nations like India and China lack skilled professionals. The high skills-gap reflects inadequate quality education and education mismatch—output can't meet domestic demand; also, highly skilled are not prepared for global companies. Malaysia is reported to have lost up to 400,000 people (mostly professionals) to emigration over the past two years. We are told 1 million to 2 million Malaysians work abroad (again, mainly professionals).

What, Then, Are We to Do?

In his book, *The Flight of the Creative Class*, Professor Richard Florida states that skilled immigrants gravitate to global "talent magnets" centered in major cities that are open, tolerant, and liberal with attractive lifestyles. As a "third-tier" global city, he argues that Kuala Lumpur cannot engage successfully in the war on talent. To evolve into a human creative hub, Kuala Lumpur's ecosystem and outlook on excellence need to be radically transformed to reflect the true spirit of Malaysia's New Economic Model. This will require strong leadership, steadfast political will, and lots of time. Until this commitment is translated on the ground, Malaysia's success in the talent war remains a serious challenge. Yet, without an adequate talent pool, innovative-led growth can only be suboptimal.

Kuala Lumpur
April 22, 2010

Notes

1. First published on April 24, 2010.
2. Quoted in "Trying Harder," a special report on the US economy in *The Economist* (April 3, 2010), p. 13.
3. Dani Rodrick, "The Case for Industrial Policy," *Straits Times*, Singapore (April 16, 2010), p. A18.
4. Trying Harder, p. 13.
5. Ibid.
6. As reported in *The Edge Financial Daily*, "Talent Management Essential in Driving Innovation," on November 3, 2009, Kuala Lumpur.
7. As reported in "Most Foreign PhDs Remain in US," *Wall Street Journal* (January 27, 2010).
8. Referred to and reported on in Nazrin Hassan, "Reversing the Outflow of Human Capital," *The Edge*, Malaysia (April 12, 2010).

CHAPTER 113

Finance for Innovative Ventures: Broken Dreams?[1]

The new economic model (NEM) characterizes Malaysia in 2020 as market-led, entrepreneurial, and innovative. A deliberate move toward a more competitive society, dedicated to value adding to achieve high-incomes. In Chapter 111, "Innovation: Catalyst for Recovery," I wrote: "The centerpiece to promote recovery and quality growth during hard times is to drive innovation." The key element here is government's will to make some fundamental changes, including "a stubborn resolve to change mind-sets in order to instill and build (and effectively put on the ground) a creative and innovative culture, and a national entrepreneurial spirit." A year later (April 2010), I wrote in Chapter 112, "On Productivity and Talent Management": "We can't be expected to grow efficiently by simply doing more of the same. To become an increasingly higher-income nation, we need to shift to an economy that is innovation-led." Innovation simply means fresh thinking and approaches that add value to consistently create wealth and social welfare. In the end, "innovation drives productivity, and productivity drives the flow of real income." I ended with a remark on venture capital: "From ASEAN to Northeast Asia and from India to Japan, the big risk to innovative ventures remains the lack of ready access to finance at reasonable cost." Policy makers have turned to creating tomorrow's jobs rather than saving yesterday's. The buzzwords in government are entrepreneurship, innovation, and venture capital.

Asian environment is set in a culture that does not take on risk easily. Thomas Watson (the founder of IBM), when asked about risk taking, is widely reported to have said: If you want to succeed, raise your error rate. I believe the Malaysian government has to become a bold enabler when it comes to nurturing the buildup of risk capital. I also believe any government that takes no risk in promoting innovative ventures is likely to make the bigger error of not trying hard enough. Accept the hard-headed Sun Tzu rule that making omelets will require breaking eggs.

Venture Capital versus Private Equity

Venture capital (VC) and private equity (PE) are not the same. VC provides development funding to early stage firms mainly in high-tech and biotech. By contrast, PE backs established enterprises using equity and debt. They can't be more different. VC helps fund innovation—to grow seed and start-ups into major breakthroughs that dazzle. PE thrives at the other end of the spectrum—offering equity and leveraged finance to spin deals. PE-backed enterprises are usually run by the same executives who ran them before PE moved in. Essentially, PE teams up with entrepreneurs to create value. However, VC managers bring professional advice and managerial and organizational support to the table, and help manage start-ups and "teenage" ventures.

PE executives make money from fees; capital gains are just a bonus. The standard "2 and 20" fee structure, whereby managers charge investors 2 percent on monies managed and 20 percent of profits earned, is lucrative. They also charge transaction fees, and fees for monitoring portfolios. In contrast, VC takes are more modest since their fund-size pales in comparison. VC ventures do fail, but occasionally they get a hit—returns of 10 to 50 times. In the end, VC is all about real big, big successes. PE is never easy. Indeed, funding and executing private investment is hard. Competition is fierce and much financial engineering has already been tried. Only operators who are talented—and lucky—can keep on producing high returns. Similarly, VC funding is difficult in terms of staying power. The easy-to-profit schemes of the 1990s created impatient investors.

But building new ventures take perseverance. Most 100 largest publicly traded US software companies took six years or more to generate enough revenue to reach IPO (initial public offering). Microsoft and Oracle both went public in 1986, but were founded in 1975 and 1977, respectively. VC fuses innovators and entrepreneurs with intelligent capital (and business knowhow) in a combination that's capable of spectacular successes, such as Apple, Google, Intel, and FedEx. This also needs enlightened government policies. That's how wealth creation actually takes place.

Be that as it may, the NEM needs a dynamic VC and PE industry to meet its goals. Innovation and finance go hand in hand. With economic recovery, VC and PE must get back to providing growth capital—from seed to start-ups and then on to expansion, refinancing, and buyouts in the drive to maturity. Indeed, recession has left them with lots of "dry powder" (uninvested committed capital) before they need to raise new money. Yet, many have fallen victims of a worldwide reshuffle. Survivors will have to get used to a diet of smaller deals and lower returns, at least until economies fully recover.

Venture Capital in Malaysia

In Malaysia, chronic risk aversion defines the financial landscape. So much so the VC industry remains grossly underdeveloped, unwilling to take on seed and early-stage big-bang bets. In the 1970s, Bank Negara Malaysia took deliberate small steps to set up venture capital funds. The first real move was Bank Industri's joint venture fund with San Francisco–based Walden International to finance nascent ICT ventures. The joint venture later set up two additional venture funds in the 1980s. Since then, government became more proactive and led the way to promote VC businesses, introducing a wide array of VC funds, soft loans, and tax incentives. But according to Professor Noriyuki Takahashi of Musashi University, Malaysia today ranks very, very low among 54 countries with way less than 0.5 percent of those aged 18 to 64 involved in start-up activities, compared with 10 percent in the United States, 6 percent in Britain, and 4 percent in Japan.[2] Structurally, the VC industry in Malaysia is very skewed and weak. Among 113 players, 104 were 100 percent locally owned, nine joint ventures, and one, 100 percent foreign owned. Together they manage RM5.36 billion of funds at end-2009 (less than 1 percent of gross national product [GNP]), of which only 48 percent (RM2.6 billion) is invested. In 2009, only RM597 million were invested; 80–85 percent of committed funding came from government and only 12.6 percent from banks, financial institutions, and individuals. Of the funds invested in 2009, only 24 percent went to seed (3 percent), start-ups (6 percent), and early stage (15 percent). The bulk was utilized to fund expansion (53 percent) and bridging (17 percent). Not only is VC funding highly reliant on government, but the ecosystem presents difficulties in private fundraising because of risk-averse institutional investors; restricted regulations on asset allocation; and VC firms lack a credible track record.

Although entrepreneurs recognize that there are improvements in start-ups, changes are in small increments and many barriers remain. The lack of "real" venture funding is a problem, and funds are highly risk averse. About 85 percent of venture capital funds are provided by government, whose providers are conservative. Since their mandate is to lend and/or invest, they just do so and quickly take them to IPO, rather than take on the risk to nurture them, as in the United States and Europe. In government, the culture is to avoid taking risk. Malaysia is not unique here. VC companies in Japan have long suffered from a dearth of "risk" capital with a conservative attitude.

According to Professor S. Kagani of Tokyo University, Japanese VC firms ironically do not take risk even though they offer risk capital.[3] Typically, they invest with other VCs, scatter their funds widely, and keep them small to minimize risk. Japan invested US$2 billion in 2008 (as against US$25 billion in the United States), of which only 10 percent was in start-ups (18 percent in the United States). In Malaysia, the ratio is 6 percent. Like Japan, Malaysian VC still has much "dry powder" in hand, totaling RM2.7 billion (or 52 percent of capital committed). Indeed, they still have money to spend.

Compelling Challenges

US President Ronald Reagan used to joke: The nine most terrifying words in the English language are: "I'm from the government and I'm here to help." To be fair, government has helped to ignite entrepreneurship—as well as providing vital innovation infrastructure, investing in education and directly driving entrepreneurship itself. It also helped to develop the VC industry— warts and all.

Indeed, most great entrepreneurial hubs, from Bangalore to Hangzhou, from Singapore to Seoul, bear the stamp of public intervention. In *Boulevard of Broken Dreams: Why Public Efforts to Boost Entrepreneurships and Venture Capital Have Failed—and What to Do About It*, Harvard Business School Professor Josh Lerner points to two foolish tendencies that politicians find hard to resist. First is the temptation to spread wealth to regions and interest groups.[4] France, for example, tried to transform Brittany (a backward region) into a hive of high-tech activity but failed miserably. Second is suspicion of foreign investors. In the 1990s, Japan lavished billions on start-up VCs but was reluctant to embrace foreign VCs or invest in non-Japanese VCs. Today, Japan has the rich world's weakest VC market. Sound familiar?

Start-Up Nation, by Dan Senor and Saul Singer, tells the story of how Israel plugged itself into the global VC market in 1992 with a US$100 million publicly funded VC.[5] It was designed to attract foreign VC and foreign expertise to do the job. This market-driven fund attracted foreign VC to participate. The nascent high-tech industry boomed, domestic VCs learned from this experience, and foreign expertise was passed on. Its VC industry flourished. In 2009, Israel attracted as much foreign VC as France and Germany combined, and had more companies listed on Nasdaq (New York exchange) than China and India combined.

New Approach to Venture Capital

The Malaysian VC community is too government-centric: Government provides funding and calls the tune on what to invest, whom to invest in, how to invest, and whom to manage. Funds are risk averse in practice, reflecting conflict between its developmental and commercial agenda. But, they are risk averse by necessity because VC lacks risk management skills; activities are largely insulated from global interconnectivity, with only a limited window abroad.

As a result, it has poor deal flows. Its overall performance has been dismal. The fundamental weakness lies in a lack of focus on seed and start-up enterprises; these account for 9 percent of total VC funding. Including early-stage, their combined share is about 24 percent. But there are only a handful of professionally managed, genuine early-stage VC funds—targeting prerevenue, unproven businesses. Organized angel investing, where affluent individuals invest in seed and early start-ups, is rare. Yet, early-stage funds play a critical role; they create jobs and new industries as well as generate high returns. More important, without continuing flows of early-stage funds, later-stage funds would be starved in subsequent years.

So why aren't there more early-stage funds? There are two main reasons. First, there is genuine lack of expertise. Second, most VC funds effectively force them to do deals of RM2 million or more to ensure a manageable number of investments. Indeed, a few smaller-ticket early-stage deals are done as an afterthought. While VC investing traditionally has been a "home-run" business, venture firms are backing far safer investments. What's needed are smaller funds of RM50 million and a fresh outlook from investors willing to take calculated risks on small but good opportunities and strong teams, and patience to wait for real value creation.

What, Then, Are We to Do?

To succeed, VC has to dramatically change direction. Creating a more dynamic environment must be high on the agenda. Here, taking risk and managing risk have to be seen in a more positive light in Malaysian business culture. To begin with, VC needs to be market driven. To survive, the business must be risk driven, people driven, and most of all, innovation driven. Government will be needed to act as an enabler—a funder with private investors and markets and a provider of incentives to deepen business commitment. VC focus must be on seed and start-ups. To better serve and service the business, VC's structure and organization (systems processes and skills) have to be revamped, within an ecosystem to be made much friendlier. Also, VC must be regionalized and globalized in scope. Finally, to complete the chain, PE must also be restructured but approached differently to complement VC growth in vital areas of refinancing, mergers and acquisitions, and buyouts.

All these simply mean a complete mind-set and culture change. In the end, VC and PE business must be seen to be talent and skill oriented, with the world as its marketplace. Transformation of the VC–PE landscape (restructured to up-skill with due emphasis on generating deal flows) becomes critical. Finally, VC–PE needs to find its niche business on the Islamic finance radar screen.

Kuala Lumpur

June 4, 2010

Notes

1. First published on June 5, 2010, as "Whither Finance for Innovations?"
2. Cited in "Risk-Averse Japan, Odds Stack Up against Start-ups," *The Edge Financial Daily*, Kuala Lumpur (April 20, 2010).
3. Ibid.
4. Cited in "Policymakers Are Turning Their Minds to the Tricky Subject of Promoting Entrepreneurship," *The Economist* (October 31, 2009).
5. Ibid.

CHAPTER 114

Venture Capital Initiatives to Boost Entrepreneurship[1]

I attended the 22nd meeting of the Asian Shadow Financial Regulatory Committee (ASFRC) held in Sapporo, Japan, last month (October 2013), hosted by the University of Tokyo. The group comprises university dons and bankers whose main mission is to take a considered analytical position on current policy issues of public concern, especially in the area of monetary economics. Its focus this time was on corporate venture capital (VC) initiatives in Japan, viewed as a key element of the Abenomics strategy to stimulate long-term economic growth. This is important because according to a recent survey of investment as a proportion of gross domestic product (GDP) by venture capital firms, Japan ranked 35th out of 37 countries surveyed, well below China (11th) and South Korea (14th) and behind many other Asian nations.

In a sense, poor VC initiatives in Japan have become an embarrassment besides being a drag on growth. Despite its high domestic savings, Japanese financial institutions traditionally avoid funding risky businesses—just simply being risk averse. Even its taxation regime is hostile toward the use of stock options (sweat equity) as an incentive. This lack of risk capital and a robust VC community in the face of a business environment that discourages the taking of risks has led to falling competitiveness and productivity so detrimental to sustainable income growth. Japan badly needs to aggressively develop VC markets, promote entrepreneurship, and build deep VC management skills through encouraging new start-ups and foster, over time, an appetite for risk taking. To create an environment conducive to promoting the buildup of broad-based VC capacity, fundamental economic reform is needed to transform inflexible labor markets (and relax employment protection laws), redesign existing policies to encourage immigration (which can help to inject much-needed entrepreneurship), and open up the economy by incentivizing and commercializing innovation; discarding restrictive protective professional practices (which crowd out new entrants); and freeing up agriculture and liberalizing participation in medical services.

The ASFRC made a number of suggestions. On the demand side: (1) stimulating growth of innovative new ideas by encouraging greater interaction between academicians and industry. For example, by allowing faculty members to serve on the boards of private companies (particularly start-ups), and inviting industry leaders to serve on the advisory boards of universities, schools, and think tanks; (2) opening up those areas in the economy that currently face restrictions and stop protecting ailing companies and allow for-profit incorporation in all sectors, especially the agricultural and medical sectors; (3) granting strong incentives to encourage eventual commercialization of research findings when reviewing applications for government funding; and (4) reviewing immigration laws to encourage skillful foreign workers to move to Japan and qualified foreign students to study and work in Japan for a minimum of two years as is common practice in other countries.[2] On the supply side: (1) government should invest in foreign and local VC funds operating and investing in Japan, including a willingness to take a lower return than its VC partners; (2) incentivize banks to provide more funding for start-ups through their investment bank arms with tax incentives; and (3) reform the labor market to allow more flexibility in the hiring and laying off of staff in new start-ups.

Private Equity

For me, a focus area of research and study is venture capital. I last wrote on it on June 5, 2010 (reproduced as Chapter 113, "Finance for Innovative Ventures: Broken Dreams?"). I have since been requested to elaborate on the various concepts and terms used to help better understand what's going on in this industry. I'll paint with a broad brush, drawn from the research of many eminent scholars, notably Professors Andrew Metrick and Ayako Yasuda.[3] Venture capital (literally "high-risk" capital) refers to financing of small ventures, which lack resources, but whose activities point to potentially high future profits. It plays a vital role in the development of technologically advanced industries as well as the growth of entrepreneurship, much of these through the formation and activities of new ventures or "start-ups," and at its later "mezzanine" stage (when they begin to generate some revenue, but not enough to be profitable as yet). Both require entrepreneurs and investors to assume great risk. Related to them are buyouts (BOs), where ventures need ownership change or to be rescued. It is convenient to group the VC and BO segments as subsets of the broader private equity (PE) industry as against public equity (stock and shares) markets. Key characteristics that bind PE, VC, and BOs together are (1) the illiquid nature of their capital; and (2) the information asymmetry between insiders (entrepreneurs) and outsiders (investors) of the firms as well as VC's full access to information compared with others, including the banks. Then there is venture debt (VD), which complements high-growth VC firms by helping them preserve their ownership (and value) of the firms.

Like PE, both VC and BO as well as VD investors are financial intermediaries that raise funds from institutional and other investors and invest in private illiquid ventures. They are all activist investors and aim to maximize returns for their investors. It is worth noting that worldwide, PE funds have as much as US$3 trillion under management. While BOs account for one-half to two-thirds of PE investment by value, VC represents the most investments by number of deals. The industry experienced extraordinary growth in the last 15 years, starting with only US$100 billion in 1994. The industry's impact on innovation, competition, and employment has been far reaching; it has also rapidly globalized, with China receiving the highest investment flow after the United States and United Kingdom, followed by France and India.

PE (with some exceptions) has four main characteristics:

1. It's a financial intermediary (mobilizes investors' capital and invests the funds directly).
2. PE invests only in private companies (i.e., not traded on public exchanges).
3. It actively monitors and assists in managing investee companies.
4. Its primary goal is to maximize financial returns through sale or exiting via IPO (initial public offering).

PE is different from angel investors (sponsors of early start-ups) and private investment firms, which use their own capital. Within PE, there are four main subclasses, of which VC (and mezzanine) and BOs are by far the largest and most important. The last segment covers distressed investing, which is really a specialized adjunct of BOs. It is common practice among PE funds not to mark-to-market, and fund returns are not finalized until the end of its lifetime. Finally, PE funds are different from hedge funds (HFs) and mutual funds (MFs) in five ways:

1. PE funds have a finite life, usually 10 years (both HFs and MFs are open ended).
2. PE investors are committed to illiquidity until the end of the fund's life (unlike HFs and MFs, both of which allow redemptions on demand).
3. PE investments do not allow reinvestment (HFs and MFs have options to reinvest dividends, etc.).
4. PE fees are often highest first and decline in later years (HFs and MFs fees are a flat ratio of assets under management).

5. Profits are earned only when realized—that is, only after sale or exit (while HFs' carried-interest or profit participation is a fixed percentage, usually 20 percent, of market value in excess of cost).

In summary, VCs are specialists with superior preinvestment screening capability, a distinct ability to handle risky start-up and later-stage mezzanine activities in high-tech sectors, and expertise in governance during the holding period, making them a cut above other bankers. In contrast, BO specialists are engaged primarily in private-to-private transactions and usually require great restructuring sophistication and skills. These are high-risk operations. Both VC and BO backing assume a critical role in monitoring and advising investees' companies, including provision of independent and hands-on boards to bring on higher-quality earnings.

Crowdfunding

Crowdfunding or the collaborative effort to raise funds online has been going on for some time. Latest data by Massolution indicated that the overall crowdfunding industry raised US$2.7 billion in 2012, across more than one million individual campaigns globally. In 2013, the industry was projected to raise US$5.1 billion. New developments include investment crowdfunding (becoming a shareholder), localization (focused on specific cities and neighborhoods), mobile solutions, and group-based approaches. But the bulk of funds raised involves donations where the "crowd" of investors funds projects, including charities and causes like liberalizing Egypt.

Funders donate via a collaborative goal-based process in return for products, perks, or rewards. Sites include Kickstarter, which has since mobilized US$830 million in 50,000 projects from some 5 million donors. However, the new approach centers on investment crowdfunding, where businesses seeking capital sell ownership stakes over the Internet in the form of equity or debt. There is Somolend (lending to small businesses), AngelList (a tech start-up), and Crowdfunds (offering a blend of donation-based and investment crowdfunding). Here, investors become shareholders, with a potential for return.

On September 23, 2013, the US JOBS Act (Jumpstart Our Business Start-ups Act) came into force to encourage the growth of a new source of business funding. It is intended to help small businesses raise significant capital without too much hassle (including open advertising for private placements via social media). Prior to this, funds have to be raised privately until the business is ready to enter the public domain. However, there are safeguards to limit risk and prevent abuse: (1) there is a US$1 million limit, which each entrepreneur can raise annually; (2) they can take money only from accredited investors, including people with personal net worth exceeding US$1 million or those whose annual income is above US$200,000; and (3) if a company raises more than US$500,000, it will have to produce audited accounts.

Crowdfunding helps to grow a market for impact investing in social enterprises, managing the worlds of entrepreneurship and philanthropy and helping a broader base of investors to back enterprises for both purpose and profits. It has become popular in promoting angel investing and creating a new market. No one knows how this facility would develop. Already, there are measures to lower the bar further to widen the net of investors. We will have to wait and see.

What, Then, Are We to Do?

Empirical studies confirm that institutional frameworks do matter in the sustainable development of VC markets. Key "institutions" include the legal environment, financial market development, taxation, labor market regulations, and research and development spending. Among them, taxes, the legal environment, and financial deepening correlate best with robust VC activities across nations. Increased financial liberalization and progressive government policies can help VC markets take off.

In Japan, entrepreneurs—unlike those in United States—are usually unwilling to cede formal corporate control to make VC really work. While differences in cultural values and norms play their part, other complementary reasons also matter, including different market situations, different social norms, and different legal systems. Also, unfriendly tax laws against the use of sweat equity as incentive do impose an undue risk burden on Japanese entrepreneurs. They all limit the efficacy of VC activities. Be that as it may, in his book, *Boulevard of Broken Dreams: Why Public Efforts to Boost Entrepreneurship and Venture Capital Have Failed*, Harvard Professor Josh Lerner advocated that governments can only play a limited role in spurring innovation and entrepreneurship.[4] I can't agree more. Indeed, numerous empirical studies have concluded that government initiatives are usually characterized by poor design and a lack of understanding of VC processes and systems.

Professor Lerner's conclusions make good sense: Governments would be better placed to limit their role as catalysts by: (1) ensuring an environment that is conducive to entrepreneurial development; and (2) providing direct investments through an independent VC fund (as in Germany and Japan). This way, they hold out better prospects for creating a dynamic and sustainable network of start-up ventures and corporations, including parallel investments in VCs operated by third parties.

Strong international VC presence can bring numerous benefits to VC market development, including injection of human capital and foreign expertise, building the network for creating new capabilities and initiatives, and acting as role model and mentor for locals. Above all, it is vital that governments understand the importance of hands-off independence, and how VC investing really works. My experience has been that government is neither ever ready nor suitable as a direct participant in VC industry management. Japanese VC history has proved it to be too conservative, and its development efforts too restrictive.

In essence, government lacks the entrepreneurial tradition and culture of Silicon Valley. Its role should be confined to facilitating rather than controlling. Equally important is its pivotal role in building trust in VC. Trust is key to its ability to attract risk capital and remain competitive; success of alliances and collaborations among private corporations, VC specialists, and traditional investors depend on it. Performance risk is high in this industry, which relies on active competition.

In the last 10 years, London has surely become the most mature among European tech hubs. It's attracting the new generation of start-ups, centering in the neighborhood of Shoreditch in East London. Start-ups have to be always competitive—that's how they survive.

Sapporo, Japan
Kuala Lumpur
October 28, 2013

Notes

1. First published on November 2, 2013.
2. 22nd Asian Shadow Financial Regulatory Committee Statement, Sapporo, Japan, September 6, 2013.
3. Andrew Metrick and Ayako Yasuda, "Venture Capital and Other Private Equity: A Survey," *European Financial Management* 17 (4) (2011), pp. 1–36.
4. Josh Lerner, *Boulevard of Broken Dreams: Why Public Efforts to Boost Entrepreneurship and Venture Capital Have Failed—and What to Do About It* (Princeton, NJ: Princeton University Press, 2009).

PART X

Emerging East Asia, ASEAN, and BRICS

CHAPTER 115

Export-Led Growth Model: Quo Vadis?[1]

I leave very soon for Harvard in Cambridge (H1N1 flu notwithstanding) for my biannual Graduate School of Arts and Sciences Alumni Council meeting at the University, and to join the 358th commencement exercises (marking my 40th year since joining the university). Also, I have accepted the invitation to attend the Yale CEO Leadership Summit at the Stock Exchange in New York City. My hope is to gain a fresh perspective from the epicenter of our current problems.

Asia

For now, I want to discuss what it takes for Asia to change the parameters of each nation's comfort zone—away from the export-led model that has brought such great prosperity to the world; and yet in recent times, so much misery. Indeed, the current state of play in the global economy bears testimony that this model has broken down. After all, what can you expect: Emerging countries in Asia are twice as dependent on exports as the rest of the world; and, as much as up to two-thirds of their gross exports eventually lands in the United States, eurozone, and Japan. The International Monetary Fund's (IMF) regional forecast earlier this April expects even relatively resilient countries like South Korea, Taiwan, Singapore, Malaysia, and Thailand to be in recession this year.[2] Some are in a similar dire situation as Singapore, which recorded its 12th consecutive monthly export decline—falling as much as 19 percent by April 2009.

Even sophisticated exporters like Germany and Japan are not spared: German exports were down 23 percent in February 2009, and for Japan by an unprecedented 26 percent in the first quarter of 2009. Particularly badly hit is China; exports fell off the cliff by 26 percent in February 2009, after a 29 percent decline in January 2009. In the case of India, exports in March 2009 fell by 33 percent (against –22 percent in February). For Asia as a whole, the Asian Development Bank now forecasts a 10.5 percent fall in exports in 2009 (as against +15 percent in 2008).[3] World trade in volume terms will contract for the first time since World War II by as much as 9 to 10 percent, according to the World Trade Organization.

The world remains a risky place. How the global recession will play out depends critically on when the epicenter (United States and eurozone) stabilizes in respect of its financial system, housing situation, unemployment, and confidence by consumers and businessmen in the leadership to do what it takes to bring this about. Any of the risks—financial strains becoming more severe, premature withdrawal of support in macroeconomic policies, continuing deep corporate losses, global deleveraging turning out as more destabilizing—can tilt the outlook on the downside. Prolonged global recession is not good for Asia, even though the risk of deflation (e.g., Japan in the late 1990s) is low at this time. For export-led Asian economies, there is the additional real risk of a continuing structural decline in demand from the industrial West, and, of course, the presence of protectionism. Asia has learned through bitter experience that it cannot rely on foreign capital inflows (especially portfolio) after the 1990s currency crisis. This time around, the collapse of the international trade and payments system in the face of global recession makes Asia wonder if it can still rely on continuing export demand from the West.

Export-Led Growth

One thing is clear: Export-led Asian nations need to become more self-reliant—each as a country in Asia and as a member of the Asian community. This has been the direction to which they have been moving since the Asian currency crisis. Most have emerged leaner but stronger, with more stable economic credentials, including a firmly based financial system, large accumulated reserves, stable public finances, and high savings. Many have credible stimulus programs to bridge the gap in consumption and investment spending. In particular, the largest among them (Japan, China, and India) have been at the forefront in pump priming to make up for the slowdown in private spending in the face of weak income growth, depleted wealth, tightening credit, and high household debt. Also, cooperation in the region has been stepped up, with significant moves toward freer, better focused, and more purposeful intraregional trade and investment. To provide ready access to adequate international liquidity, the swap-arrangements were expanded to US$120 billion (part of the Chiang Mai Initiative) for mutual help in times of need. This impetus to the pooling of risks reflected a common concern about greater independence of action in an environment of continuing uncertainty.

At the heart is the growing urgency in Asia to find a new growth model. One that places greater emphasis on the evolution of a dynamic intra-Asian market, capable of absorbing more and more Asian goods and services. The prospect that Asian growth is still largely dependent on how quickly the United States and eurozone recover is rather scary. After all, given the many risks, even the more optimistic scenario still envisages expansion in the West to be rather sluggish and bumpy as it recovers in 2010. The real concern is that global recovery might be too slow for Asia to get the type of boost it needs, given the region's huge (and growing) excess capacity. This leaves Asian countries with little choice but to work together and quickly scale up domestic spending through more purposeful fiscal stimulus (if needed), and more forceful (and innovative) measures (including monetary) to lift the region out at a much faster pace.

Imports Aren't So Bad

Theoretically, export cannot be an end in itself. We need foreign exchange to pay for imports, which are needed to raise living standards. That's the gain from international trade we learn in basic economics. In reality, however, there is a strong bias in favor of exports, and imports are generally frowned upon. A soon-to-be-published study[4] by four American economists showed how such prejudice in India has no basis in fact. In the IMF's 1991 US$25 billion rescue package for India, a condition precedent imposed sharp tariff cuts across the board, which India implemented: from an average of 90 percent cut in import tariffs in 1991 to 30 percent in 1997. India protested that the resultant flood of imports would destroy Indian manufacturing. Not true. As expected, imports doubled in value over the period. But manufacturing output rose 50 percent. More important, cheaper and greater access to imports gave a huge boost to domestic industrial growth in the 1990s. It gave India ready access to a wide range of less-expensive intermediate and capital goods. Intermediate imports rose 227 percent, while consumption imports increased 90 percent over 13 years to 2000. This transformed Indian manufacturing by increasing access, lowering cost, opening new ways to produce existing goods, and promoting new goods to be made more efficiently and competitively. Indeed, the benefits extended beyond manufacturing into other activities (including raising the quality of Indian movies), especially services. Between 1991 and 1997, this liberalization was responsible for 25 percent of India's manufacturing output through more competitive pricing, higher quality of goods, and increased efficiency in production methods and systems.

There is an important lesson here. The broad multiplier effects (both in substitution and on income) of imports liberalization (both quantitatively and in lower tariffs) offer a worthwhile way to rapidly expand domestic demand through raising productivity and promoting creativity in transforming the way goods and services are produced. But first, we need to get rid of this prejudice against imports. And, creative destruction can be beautiful.

The Paradox of Thrift

As to be expected, sluggish consumption in the United States, eurozone, and Japan is holding back early return of stabilization and recovery in the global economy. Although there may be some indications, of late, of a return of some life in consumer spending, I think there is every chance it will remain depressed for a much longer while. This is so because of (1) weak real income growth, (2) vastly depleted wealth, (3) tightening credit conditions, and (4) ongoing widespread deleveraging.

For example, the negative wealth effect will depress consumption in the United States by about 2 percent this year. On top of this, continuing uncertainty and rising unemployment have made consumers more cautious about the future, prompting many to save more. Clearly, households are beginning to rebuild their balance sheets. Spending less and saving more are good for the individual, but disastrous for the economy since they create what Keynes is often reported to have called a vicious spiral of increasing unemployment. Hence, the paradox of thrift. Personal savings in the United States was below zero in mid-2008; it rose to 3.9 percent in December 2008 and to 5 percent in January 2009 (5.6 percent being the 30-year average high). Keynes recognized this in a BBC radio talk in 1931, when he denounced this urge to save more in recession as utterly harmful and misguided. This led him to conclude that government spending is the only viable way to resolve the paradox of thrift.

What, Then, Are We to Do?

In the end, Asia will need to be more innovative and creative. Perhaps, use even bolder and more forceful fiscal measures than the anticipated policy responses. This approach is called for in order to emerge faster and firmer from the recession, at a time when economic and social costs are potentially low given the absence of inflationary pressures. Ultimately, a new growth model will need to emerge to lift the region out of this stubborn recession.

New York, NY
Cambridge, MA
Kuala Lumpur
May 23, 2009

Notes

1. First published on May 30, 2009.
2. International Monetary Fund (IMF), *World Economic Outlook* (Washington, DC: IMF, April 2009).
3. Asian Development Bank (ADB), *Key Indicators for Asia and the Pacific* (Manila, Philippines: ADB, 2009).
4. Penny Goldberg, Amit Khandelwal, Nina Pavcnik, and Petia Topalova, "Multi-Product Firms and Product Turnover in the Developing World: Evidence from India," *Review of Economics and Statistics* (April 2009).

CHAPTER 116

"Go East, Young Man"[1]

I spent the year-end holidays with my entire family, plus two new grandkids in tow, on a nostalgic "balik kampong" trip to Ipoh (my hometown), the state capital of Perak, Malaysia. Our target was the Banjaran, a new resort and spa perched at the foot of limestone hills and caves in Tambun (world famous for its pomelos) outside Ipoh. It's a world-class hot-springs retreat with only 25 villas (each with its own hot-spring Jacuzzi and swimming pool). It's an eco-friendly resort with lots of green (even a spice garden) and picture-perfect surroundings. It comes with a fantastic wine cellar set inside natural high-ceiling limestone caves, complete with Malaysian-style Bali-Thai-type spa that provides complete relaxation. It also has a pool of garra rufa fishes that love to chew up dead and excess hard cells your feet may spare. This venture is the brainchild of Tan Sri Jeffrey Cheah (of Sunway Group), who must be congratulated for creating a visionary retreat, using to the maximum all that nature has endowed around the scenic caves. It's a treat.

Ipoh

Ipoh was built on the riches of tin mining. With tin now a distant memory, Ipoh is at the heart of a thriving industry of small and medium-size businesses besides nearby palm oil plantations, thriving E&E foundries and chip makers, and small farms growing groundnuts (world-famous Menglembu), pomelos, star fruits, and seedless guava. Ipoh has always been famous for its food, especially hawker food, offering the best there is in Asia—from fresh large-headed Tualang udang gala (prawns) to its thick and juicy bean sprouts, from delicious baby-bottom-soft sa-hor-fun (flat rice noodles) to its amazing chicken-feet preparations; from the smoothest ice-kacang (shaved ice, red beans) there is to its best spread of traditional hawker food imaginable. It is not uncommon to eat five times a day here (we did six!).

What impressed me is the vibrant spirit of private enterprise of which Ipoh has come to be now famous—innovation in biscuit making, coffee and charcoal toast, ornamental fish, delicate tow-fu-fa (soft bean curd dessert), unusually large tropical fruits, and ready-to-serve food, including exotic seafood. For me, a must is dry curry-mee and sui-kau (Chinese dumplings) for breakfast and sa-hor-fun soup plus beef tendon balls for lunch, dunked down with lots of Ipoh white coffee. The last time I was here, most shops were small, dirty, and crowded (but with long queues).

At my favorite place in old town, the owner has since embraced technology—new and bigger premises, now clean and spacious, computerized ordering from a long wish list, and spreadsheet billing and accounting. Business is thriving. There is also Ipoh's famous biscuits, like the delicious curry-puff-shaped pastry with steamed coconut–egg jam filling—sells like hot cakes: most buying 5 to 10 boxes of 10 each; only Singaporeans buy them by the 100s (for them, these are cheap and so good). No doubt, private entrepreneurship is thriving—no government assistance (want government to remain hands-off and just improve service delivery). It's not just local business—they export and attract tourists. Unfortunately, the town remains rundown with little renewal. What a pity. But its new suburbs are modern. Looking forward to 2011, they are an optimistic bunch. It's this optimism about what they do in Ipoh that impresses me. They are transforming. Better government facilitation in terms of ready availability of finance, quick access to land for expansion, and improved infrastructure and logistics are what is needed to solidify this transformation. In Ipoh, the beginning of transformation is on the move. This is as it should be throughout Malaysia. There is hope yet.

Shift in Optimism

Hope and *change*—overused words since the Great Recession. For the past 400 years, the West monopolized optimism. Their intellectual discourse on enlightenment eventually led to harnessing of technology and modern management to impose their will on the world. US founders offered not just life and liberty but also the pursuit of happiness. Optimism is now shifting—you want to prosper, go East; that's where the action is. Growing pessimism in the United States is overwhelming politics, as shown in the midterms. Winning Republicans are hardly optimistic—reflecting, I think, rather more anger and resentment. Europe is no better, with mass demonstrations from Athens to Dublin, London to Paris, Rome to Madrid.

I sense there is pessimism even at the eurozone core. The best seller in Germany is reported to be Thilo Sarrazin's *Germany Does Away with Itself.* [2] The French have Jean-Pierre Chevenement's *Is France Finished*, and *French Melancholy* by Eric Zemmour.[3] In contrast, modern art in China is colorful and bright, portraying rising materialism, growing prosperity, and emerging open lifestyle. Painting is aggressive and innovative, always ready to experiment. The contrasting attitudes have become more marked since the recession, which shook the very foundations of the system the West built, and has now lost confidence in.

The growing growth gap is stark. China and India will each grow by close to 10 percent in 2011 (like in the previous two years). With recovery, the United States is expected to close the year with growth of 3 percent, and eurozone, 2 percent. Unemployment is, however, worse: near 10 percent in the United States, where more than 1 million may have given up looking for work. Europe again is even worse—unemployment is very high among youth in Germany; 41 percent of Spanish youth are unemployed. The malaise goes deeper. Growing numbers of US parents worry that their children's living standards may be worse than theirs. After all, median workers' real income has remained more or less the same since mid-1970s. They worry that failing schools and lack of suitable jobs will handicap them in pursuit of the American dream.

European dreams are different—they remain cozy in their European Union cocoon with generous welfare security. But high debt and rising social discontent in the context of an aging population are not making it easy to continue carrying the burden of unaffordable entitlements. Nevertheless, I know the French elite will continue to leave Paris on Thursday for a long weekend in the countryside—come hell or high water.

Emerging Asia is in constant motion—building infrastructure and logistic hubs, and institutes of higher learning. China's university population has quadrupled in the past 20 years. UNESCO estimated that 38 percent of world scientific researchers is based in emerging nations in 2007 (30 percent in 2002). Chinese and Indian world-class enterprises now compete aggressively with their western counterparts. In technology, these firms are redefining the boundaries of the possible. My teacher at Harvard, Professor Dale Jorgenson, sees Asian emerging markets as the "most dynamic . . . eclipsing others such as Brazil and Russia; . . . the size of the Chinese economy (will be) on par with the United States by early 2020."[4] This may be difficult for many Americans to swallow. He warns the United States should brace for social unrest amid blame over who lost US global economic primacy.

US Growth Prospects

The US "new normal" remains: sluggish growth, stubbornly high unemployment, and weak inflation—the same as last year. The growth forecasts have since shifted higher for 2011 to 3 to 3.5 percent. This is driven by extraordinary policy measures, including a second quantitative easing by the Fed pumping US$600 billion into the economy by buying government bonds

(QE2) and the second stimulus package (US$800 billion through extension of the Bush-era tax cuts and a temporary reduction in payroll tax). However, my mentor at Harvard, Professor Martin Feldstein, believes the outlook is less sanguine. Indeed, the impact of fiscal expansion will be modest at best.[5]

The dire situation of state and local governments is likely to be a drag on growth. Growth was boosted in 2010 by a fall in household savings. But households now worry about uncertain future, return to paring back debt and stocking more away—purely precautionary saving. Professor S. Johnson of MIT puts it more bluntly: Damage from the crisis and its aftermath have dealt US prominence a permanent blow—"The age of American predominance is over."[6]

I believe the new normal will stay for some time, mainly because the US and European governments are unwilling to grasp the nettle on exit strategies. The policy dilemmas before the major governments are clear:

- In the United States, there is no political will to restructure—I see continuing resistance to the new reality of sluggish growth.
- In Europe, governments were forced to intervene with their balance sheets, which implications are now being played out.
- In China, management of continuing rapid growth has to deal now with rising pressures on inflation and the yuan. This has led Mr. Mohamed El-Erian of PIMCO (the largest global bond investor) to conclude: "You see the muddling through approach continuing. Everybody might now want to kick-the-can-down-the-road. The problem is that the longer you muddle through, the more you create problems. I see the new normal as being stable for a while yet."[7]

Impact of Rising Debt

More serious is contagion of the European debt crisis, which started with bailout of Greece and then Ireland. Will this reach Portugal and Spain? The problem is likely to widen: (1) how far reaching this will impact other parts of Europe; and (2) it's just a matter of time before this concern assumes macro-proportions covering the entire national debt, including private sector. Soon, the worry will shift to banks and companies as they will now find it harder to borrow.

The risk is that if Spain is not protected, bigger nations will be next in line. Unlike Japan and Italy (where private sectors are net savers), Spain remains vulnerable even though its government debt is relatively lower, but it carries enormous company and household debt. The debt to gross national product ratios of government and banks combined in the United States, United Kingdom, core eurozone, and peripheral Europe are all at 150 to 200 percent. That's higher than at any time in the past century.

How big is this problem? Harvard's Professor Kenneth Rogoff and University of Maryland's Carmen Reinhart's research suggests a country's growth potential slows significantly once the debt/gross domestic product ratio exceeds 90 percent—a level the United States is at today.[8] I agree with Rogoff and Reinhart at this time that the crisis will not affect the United States and the majors—they still have cards to play. Psychology, too, plays a big part, since the United States is grounded more in growth than inflation, and Europe, being dead set against inflation, will trade off growth. Between the United States and Europe, my bet is on Europe to be the first to raise interest rates. So, more pain for Europe.

Looking forward, some nations are unlikely to handle their debt overhang without restructuring, à la Argentina 2002. This is a messy process, with other high-debt nations swept into the contagion. In a globalized world, how big the problem becomes depends on confidence. So we do have a fragile situation not only in Europe but the United States as well. This situation is serious: In the event creditors and debtors worldwide erupt into a full-scale war, debt-financed growth will become history. Creditors do get tired of kicking-the-can-down-the-road and debtors can get adjustment/austerity fatigue. Such an impasse can only be resolved in the long run through a transfer of wealth from creditors to debtors. I think the fear of default will eventually get creditors to blink first.

Fault Lines Haven't Gone Away

While it is clear the world economy has now recovered, it is also clear the crisis is far from over. This is because the deep fault lines uncovered during the crisis are still within the Western economies and global economic structure. According to Chicago's Professor Raghuram Rajan, they present two risks: (1) structural export dependency, particularly in Japan, Germany, and China; and (2) unresolved clash of financial systems, making it difficult to forge integration.[9] They will threaten global stability in two ways: (1) premature tightening of monetary and fiscal policies poses the danger of tipping the world back to recession; and (2) failure to secure a medium-term structural shift to fiscal austerity, so vital for sustainable global recovery. So, the world remains a dangerous place, but nothing moves in straight lines.

One thing is certain: The West is not the power it used to be; its consumers cannot be relied on as they used to be; and its financial standing is not as good as it used to be. Structural reform is needed to avoid another global crisis ahead. At the heart of it all is the United States—it may have missed the chance to rein in its largest financial institutions, many of which remain too big to fail and are getting bigger. In the long run, the United States must face reality—inevitably, it will be overtaken by China as the world's largest economy; and the center of economic power will gravitate to Asia. But America as the biggest mover will be in place for a long time.

What, Then, Are We to Do?

As 2010 ends, Asia moves on aggressively. Manufacturing in South Korea and Taiwan accelerated in December, even as expansion in China and India slowed, with the United States and Europe supporting the region's exports. Overall, the world had a good fourth quarter of 2010 as the US economy also continued to grow, although the underlying fundamentals remain weak. But the world wakens to new challenges. The Internet now provides ready access to information for all, which previously was reserved for just a few. Medical advances are making strides in overcoming diseases and extending the life span for the benefit of all. History reminds us that for so long only the privileged few can look forward to a better life. Today, the masses in Asia can. Prudent growth and benevolent management will make this possible. Surely, that's good enough reason to be optimistic.

Ipoh
Singapore
Kuala Lumpur
January 13, 2011

Notes

1. First published on January 15, 2011.
2. Cited in *Time*'s leader: "The Redistribution of Hope" in its December 18, 2010, issue, London.
3. Ibid.
4. Leading economists speaking at an annual convention in Denver, as reported by *Reuters* and published in Singapore's *Business Times* on January 11, 2011, p. 16.
5. Ibid.
6. Ibid.
7. "Champions of 'New Normal' Are Sticking to Their Guns," *Financial Times*, London (December 22, 2010).
8. "Debt: On Their Heads Be It," *Financial Times*, London (January 6, 2011).
9. Martin Wolf, "The Fault Lines that Underlie the Crisis Have Not Gone Away," *Financial Times*, London (July 15, 2010).

CHAPTER 117

Asia Feels the Heat[1]

The eurozone crisis has been hitting Asia. It has since escalated sharply. Asian economies are hit hard in multiple ways, including slackening external demand, sluggish trade, weakening financial and supply chain linkages, volatile markets, and deteriorating risk appetite. Developments in Greece and talk of a Spain bailout have been negative. Concerns over the future of the euro and the rising possibility of Grexit (Greece exit from the euro) deepened on new evidence of policy inertia and a fresh spate of dire economic news that points to whatever remaining support for business activity in the eurozone splintering away. The strong headwinds from Europe coupled with fresh signs of a slowdown in the United States, China, and India have since effectively erased whatever gains global stock markets had gathered since end-2011. The huge market declines have raised anxiety for investors, who are now girding for a worldwide slowdown. It is naïve to expect Grexit to resolve Europe's problems. As a result, Asia's emerging markets are under rising pressure to stimulate their economies just as investors, banks, and enterprises are moving in the opposite direction, scaling back on lending and investing on new projects, fearing a turn for the worse in Europe. There are worries that excessive stimulus will be counterproductive in the face of serious fiscal and political constraints.

Downswing in Sync

Latest reports are disturbing, indicating a new threat is emerging: Activity appears to be slowing in sync around the world. Europe, struggling with the rising risk of a Greek default and broader growth problems, is now the epicenter of global concern. But reports of slowdown are turning up in the United States, the BRICS (Brazil, Russia, India, China, and South Africa), and elsewhere.

As in a boom, global contraction can become interconnected and self-reinforcing, and likely to spread deep and wide. Eurozone's downturn deepened with business activity falling at its steepest rate in nearly three years. The purchasing managers index (PMI) fell to 46.0 in May 2012 (less than 50 indicates a month-on-month contraction in both manufacturing and services), against 46.7 in April, the fourth consecutive decline and lowest reading since June 2009 when the eurozone was last in recession. This is consistent with expectations of a fall of at least 0.5 percent in gross domestic product (GDP) in the second quarter of 2012—official data showed the economy had flattened in the first quarter of 2012, after falling by 0.3 percent in the fourth quarter of 2011. Signs of weakness in business activity are also reflected in the same index for Germany (49.6) and France (44.7). The Ifo Institute's confidence index for Germany fell to 106.9 in May (109.9 in April), indicating it is no longer growing fast enough to keep the wider eurozone out of trouble. Industrial production fell 2.2 percent in April (+2.2 percent in March) and construction output lost 6 percent (+26 percent in March), raising the risk of recession, with uncertainty weighing on sentiment. The outlook doesn't look good. Order books fell for the 10th straight month, hit by heightened political uncertainty.

The European Union is in a state of flux, apart from indicating that its priority remains in keeping Greece in the currency bloc. But there is a lack of strategic positioning to prevent the crisis from spiraling downward in the absence of a clear mandate to issue euro-bonds, or for the European Central Bank (ECB) to be the lender of last resort. Also, there are no signs ECB will do more to support growth and restore overall health to the fragile state of banking. The yield on two-year German bonds is close to dipping below zero (now trading at below 0.1 percent but on the plus side). This unique occurrence simply means investors are prepared to take a capital loss as trade-off for safety and liquidity. The euro sank to $1.2455 against US$ on June 6, 2012, its lowest level since July 6, 2010; it also lost ground against sterling and yen.

Indications are that in the event of Grexit, its new currency is likely to immediately depreciate 60 percent against the euro, unleashing massive contagion. Citigroup now puts the probability of Grexit, by the start of next year, at 50–75 percent (from 50 percent previously).

US Growth Corrects

The US economy has been expanding at an average 2.4 percent annual rate since the recovery in mid-2009. The weakest recovery on record continues to lose steam in the first quarter of 2012, now estimated at just 1.9 percent (2.2 percent previously), down from 3 percent at end-2011. A string of soft US data and lack of Fed resolve kindled renewed investors' focus on broader global concerns. Risk appetite of investors had turned more negative.

Over 60 years, the United States recorded 11 recessions and 11 recoveries; this recovery ranks near the bottom. Job growth was just 1.9 percent after 34 months into recovery, below the average of 6.5 percent. Cumulative gross domestic product (GDP) growth was 6.8 percent after 11 quarters into recovery, less than half the average (15.2 percent), the worst of all 11 quarters. Recent growth deceleration reflected sharp cutbacks in public spending and weaker business investment (–2.1 percent). However, consumer spending accelerated (+2.9 percent) in the first quarter of 2012 while the moribund housing showed positive signs. More damaging was the third slower jobs report in a row, raising the jobless rate to 8.2 percent (from 8.1 percent), marking three years of unemployment at or above 8 percent. It is clear that consumers can't keep on spending if investments are not forthcoming to raise productivity. Current unemployment also reflected the entry of 642,000 into the labor force, so its participation rate rose to 63.8 percent—still 2 percentage points (3 million fewer workers) below the norm.

Of particular concern is the report by the nonpartisan Congressional Budget Office (CBO) that the economy will likely fall into recession in the first half of 2013 if the large tax increases and scheduled budget spending cuts (popularly known as the fiscal cliff) are allowed to come into effect in January 2013. This has the desired effect of sharply reducing the fiscal deficit but would hold back economic recovery. The CBO projected that GDP would contract by 1.3 percent annual rate in the first half of 2013 (i.e., fall into mild recession), and then stabilize in the second half of 2013. Unemployment would rise to 9.3 percent at end-2013.

If none of these happened, the economy could expand 4.4 percent in 2013, adding another 2 million jobs. Early action including Fed support is needed to avoid the fiscal cliff. To complicate matters, the government will hit its US$16.394 trillion borrowing limit later on this election year; the ceiling must be raised to avoid default. Gridlock poses a real recession risk.

Asia Buckles Under

The impact of the global slowdown, especially the effects of Europe's woes, is felt all across Asia, including its most important industries ranging from finance and services to trade and shipping to technology to mining. As a result, the International Monetary Fund (IMF) now sees the global economy moving more slowly than 2011's 3.9 percent, reflecting new weaknesses and significant downside risks in the first half of 2012.[2] Emerging and developing economies, as of now, will expand 5 to 5.5 percent in 2012 (down from 6.2 percent in 2011), with significant slackening in China, India, Russia, Brazil, and in Southeast Asia. What matters is that the weakening, in turn, means investors are taking it on the chin—where it hurts most—that is, in equities. The MSCI World Index for stocks, which tracks global markets, is down more than 10 percent since mid-March. In Asia, the trade cycle is hitting home: Globally, new export orders have since started to contract. The flight to safety is boosting the allure of Asian sovereign bonds. The yield on 10-year Japanese bonds fell to a low of 0.79 percent, the lowest since 2003. Investors are abandoning equities with recent sell-offs. Leading the decline early last week was Taiwan's Taiex (−3 percent); Shanghai Composite (−2.7 percent); Japan's Topix (−1.9 percent); and Malaysia's KLCI (−1.2 percent). The Japanese Nikkei is down 19 percent from March's peak, and the Hang Seng, 16 percent below the February 2012 high. From year-to-date highs, South Korea's Kospi was down 11 percent, and Australia, down 15 percent. Despite a recent solid bounce-back, weak exports, growing uncertainty, and lower risk tolerance are expected to further slow down Asian expansion.

China Out of Steam

The Chinese economy is losing steam in the second quarter of 2012 based on a slew of disappointing indicators. China's official PMI fell to 50.4 in May (from 53.3 in April), close to 50, which separates growth from contraction. Its first-quarter 2012 GDP rose 8.1 percent, its slowest pace since the spring of 2009. Based on current data, growth in the second quarter of 2012 will dip below 8 percent, down from 8.4 percent before the April data release; for 2012 as a whole, expect GDP to rise 8.2 percent, and in 2013, 8.6 percent, Growth in industrial production fell to 9.3 percent, (from 11.9 percent in March), the lowest level since May 2009, reflecting broad-based weakness across two main drivers of growth: investment and consumption. Investment rose 18.7 percent in January–April 2012, down from 23.5 percent in the first quarter of 2012 while exports rebounded to 15.3 percent in May, against 4.9 percent in April.

China's prime minister has since directed for "more priority to maintaining growth." It is now likely Beijing will front-load spending after easing monetary policy on May 7, running a budget deficit of 1.5 percent of GDP for 2012. It has scope to ratchet up spending or cut taxes to support growth. China's debt-to-GDP ratio was 25 percent in 2011; adding on local government debt, it's 47 percent. Expect more spending on social welfare, and quickening of construction of social housing and infrastructure ahead.

Japan Growing Again

A nascent recovery is at last on the way. Japan is headed for a moderate recovery as rebuilding from the March 2011 earthquake and tsunami gets into full swing and government subsidies for low-emission vehicles support demand for cars. Latest data point to a 4.1 percent GDP growth in the first quarter of 2012; private consumption (70 percent of GDP) rose 1.1 percent while exports were 2.9 percent higher. Public investment jumped 5.4 percent on mainly reconstruction work. Corporate capital spending, however, fell 3.9 percent, reflecting the shift of production offshore in the face of the strong yen. Bank of Japan's Tankan survey showed business sentiment had remained at a pessimistic –4 in March, against December (calculated by subtracting the percentage of companies saying business conditions are bad from those saying they are good). Businesses are still concerned with power shortages and the strong yen amid a highly uncertain outlook for exports to the eurozone. Overall, GDP would grow 2 percent in the current year.

India's Self-Inflicted Slowdown

GDP rose 5.3 percent in the first quarter of 2012, the slowest in nine years, from 9.2 percent in the first quarter of 2011. Inflation is at 7 percent and the rupee is Asia's worst performing (depreciated 25 percent against US$ since the third quarter of 2011). India's predicament is largely of its own making: (1) kept interest rates high for two years to keep a lid on inflation (with little impact since prices were driven by supply constraints in food and energy, not demand); (2) did little to encourage foreign investment; (3) suffered political paralysis; (4) subjected to widespread corruption; (5) lacked business confidence; and (6) stalled reforms. For the year, GDP is expected by the IMF to grow up to 7 percent, but it's likely to fall far short.

ASEAN Pushes Forward

ASEAN-5 (Indonesia, Malaysia, the Philippines, Thailand, and Vietnam) is particularly vulnerable to European uncertainty, but strong domestic demand helped to cushion the impact of falling external demand, especially Indonesia. Growth in the first quarter of 2012 averaged about 6 percent, with a strong Thai recovery as it rebounded from the flooding devastation last year. Consumption remained the dynamic stabilizing force. Growth for 2012 should be robust enough to average 5.5 to 6 percent, with GDP expanding 6 percent plus in Indonesia and 5.6 percent in Thailand while Vietnam struggles to grow. Indonesia is best insulated against external shocks because of its large domestic market, extensive natural resources, and limited reliance on European and US demand.

What, Then, Are We to Do?

Emerging Asia needs to brace itself to manage risks posed by global uncertainty to safeguard regional growth that, despite recent gains, still remains home to most of the world's poor. For the second time in four years, Asia is hit with an external demand shock emanating from recession in Europe, which could turn ugly and become something far worse, triggered by contagion arising from a possible Grexit. Their impact cannot be taken for granted—or even lightly. The best defense remains supporting and expanding internal demand—just as economic rebalancing is the only sensible way out for China, this must be so for its partners in the Asian supply chain. Few realize private consumption fell to a record low 45 percent of developing Asia's GDP in 2012. This won't do. Asia's intraregional exports—trade flows within the region—have expanded sharply in recent years: from 36 percent of total exports in 1998 to 44 percent in 2012. This trade needs to be actively promoted to bring about an increasingly more autonomous Asia, especially in final goods and services, not just intermediate inputs. Therein lies the challenge, and China definitely holds the key.

Kuala Lumpur
June 11, 2012

Notes

1. First published on June 16, 2012.
2. International Monetary Fund (IMF), *World Economic Outlook: Growth Resuming, Dangers Remain* (Washington, DC: IMF, April 2012).

CHAPTER 118

QE3 Exit and Asia's Trilemma[1]

W e are on the threshold of possibly another crisis in 2013. An impression is already being created in Chapter 41, "An Inconvenient Truth: QE Withdrawal Syndrome," that financial and currency markets in emerging nations (ENs) have started to feel the full force of US Fed's moment of reckoning (initial phase of quantitative easing [QE] tapering). Indeed, these markets have begun to react to expectations of reduced money creation (at best "lite tapering") and eventual significant interest rate increases. No decoupling has taken place—if anything, there is now talk of recoupling.

Since May 2013, emerging markets (EMs) from India to Turkey to Brazil have been the focus of sell-downs, triggered by events half a world away. In recent weeks, kept buoyant by (and now reliant on) foreign capital inflows (following the massive injection of QE3 monies), EMs have exhibited more violent price amplifications to adjustments in US macroeconomic policies than the US itself. True, US Treasury yields have spiked and Wall Street has been wobbly, but it's nothing like what's happening in EMs following capital flows out of Asia in particular.

Policy Trilemma

As global investors adjusted to a world eventually without ultra-cheap money, currencies and shares tumbled. EMs' shift to become involuntary capital donors has left policymakers with what some analysts call a *trilemma:* three unpalatable policy choices: (1) higher interest rates, which run the risk of choking-off investment and hence the push for growth; (2) faster growth with the attendant risk of generating higher inflation; and (3) imposing capital controls to stem outflows with the concomitant risk of scaring off investors and cooling business confidence. Any of the three options is likely to be "equity market negative." Be that as it may, the outlook for equity markets in ENs, especially those with current balance of payments (BoP) deficits, is kept hostage to future prospects for US bond yields.

The higher the yield (an inevitable consequence of QE exit or tapering), the lower would be equity prices. What's ironic is that when the Fed started QE monetary expansion in 2010, ENs from China to Brazil cried foul, accusing the United States of waging "currency wars" by pushing the US dollar down (i.e., depreciating) with zero interest rates. Now, the same nations are again hit hard by a reversal to meet "what they had wished for"; yet they cry foul again, prompting the Mexican central bank governor to recently call for implementation of "a more predictable exit . . . and to coordinate as much as possible in order to make it easier for emerging markets" to adjust.[2] Be careful of what you wish for!

Impact on Asia

The influence of Asia, as the world's growth engine, has since waned as the major ENs across the region weaken and investors pull out billions from financial markets as anticipation of the scaling back (tapering) of US QE draws attention to the region's slackening growth and rising debt. They sent Indonesian equity tumbling and pushed the Indian rupee down to new record lows. The impact is worldwide: Brazil's real fell 20 percent since 2009; the Turkish lira, 10 percent since its February peak. The most dramatic activity was centered on Southeast Asia's ENs when Indonesian stocks fell 9 percent on August 19 and 20, 2013, declining 20 percent from May, wiping out all its gains in 2013 so far. Thailand's stocks fell 6 percent to its weakest level this year, while Malaysia's stock market fell as the ringgit hit a three-year low. Malaysia posted its second straight quarter of sub-5 percent growth. Shares in Japan, Hong Kong, and China fell as well.

China is reported to have sold US$6.7 billion in foreign currency in June to stabilize the yuan, against net purchases of more than US$10 billion in May. Nevertheless, the yuan has risen close to 2 percent so far this year. Signs are growing that Asia's economy is losing its shine. Thailand has entered recession while Indonesian economic activity weakened amid worsening trade imbalance and as the second quarter of 2013 gross domestic product (GDP) sputters along at its lowest pace (5.8 percent) in three years. Overall, Indonesian rupiah is trading at its lowest level since 2009. Indian rupee has since lost about 20 percent in the past three months. But pressures on these economies are unlikely to abate anytime soon.

This time, however, the rout is selective. Sure, the eye of the storm has moved firmly above ENs for now, as liquidity tightening and China's slowdown (curbing demand for basic commodities and goods) are fueling a sell-off of EMs' stocks. This resulted in a reverse flow of money (estimated to date at US$7.6 billion so far) backward, favoring nascent recoveries in the United States and Europe. No question, the period ahead is proving tougher and more difficult for Asia. Even so, the impact has been uneven. Mexico and South Korea, which were at the locus of past EM meltdowns, have been relatively unscathed this time around. Investors have chosen to punish nations with large BoP imbalances and heavy foreign borrowing (viz. India, Indonesia, Brazil, Turkey, and Malaysia). The situation worsened, with worries of possible US military strikes against Syria. Nevertheless, economies that used the era of easy global money to reform underlying structural problems are reaping benefits. That's why South Korea and Mexico have emerged stronger. Fundamentals are key—they can't overstate the importance of sound economic management, strong fiscal positions, credible pro-active monetary policy, and vigorous financial sector oversight. Many of the struggling nations' currencies were down 15–20 percent over the past year. However, the South Korean won and Mexican peso remain in positive territory. During the good times, they had a window to undertake pro-growth reforms and they did. In Asia, the economy of South Korea had gotten stronger. While Mexico's growth is still sputtering, it is expected to pick up speed on the back of a US recovery that's trying to strengthen. Mexico has little exposure to China. Overall, EMs in Asia are still extremely fragile and can easily get buffeted by negative developments and headlines. Monies had flowed out of EMs in recent months. Selling of equities by foreign investors totaled US$3.1 billion in August. What's being witnessed is a reaction from expectations being unrealistically positive a year ago to now becoming more realistic and more down to earth. Asia still has much potential, but market pressure is unlikely to abate any time soon.

Dicey Dominoes

Recent market volatility has done little to ease uncertainty about whether it will blow into a bigger crisis. Indeed, investors are resigned to witness more volatility from now on. Since the global financial crisis began in 2007, the notion that a "risk-on, risk-off" cycle in which asset prices all move together in response to global shocks (like the Fed scare we just had) is back. This means asset prices will reflect investors' risk appetite. So, as soon as the Fed's tapering comes on, it will hit all asset classes with its impact dependent on its speed of implementation—the more decisive and faster it acts, the more disruptive it can be and hence the greater the damage from prompt adjustment. It's uncertain. Here, I was intrigued by the reaction of longtime bearish global strategist at Société Générale, Albert Edwards, who has since warned that market volatility will not be confined to EMs: "I see this as the beginning of a process where the most wobbly domino falls and topples the whole, precarious, rotten, risk-loving edifice that our policymakers have built."[3] This is scary in the face of a world that has since witnessed the biggest capital outflows from the United States since QE began. It is estimated that investment portfolio inflows into EMs (excluding China) had exceeded US$78 billion since 2009. But, I do believe a large bulk of the "tapering" is already priced in—markets just need to see it start, for sure. Besides, Japan's aggressive and massive QE expansion, which will continue to drive global liquidity flows, is likely to make up for what the Fed does take out. My hunch is that a domino run is unlikely to start anytime soon. In similar vein, I share Nobel Laureate Paul Krugman's view that there will be no repeat of the Asian 1997–1998 financial crisis.[4] The parallel is tempting. The poorly performing currencies are today floating (fixed during Asian crisis); their nation's current BoP deficits and high debts are but only one part of the story; and they have ample foreign exchange reserves and access to more "standby" liquidity for backup; many still have credible lines of defense. As for the recipient developed world, the influx of new capital is likely to find its way into higher yielding opportunities (including junks and bonds) and possibly equity. As I see it, this could prove temporary, since some I know are already being tempted back into EMs by their bargain prices and potential for future capital gains.

BIITS and CRASH

Recent e-mails brought to my attention the "acronym anxiety" of John Authers of the *Financial Times*.[5] First, there were "PIIGS" (Portugal, Ireland, Italy, Greece, and Spain) that can't fly. Now, there is the Fragile Five BIITS— that is, Brazil, India, Indonesia, Turkey, and South Africa, representing the gang of five that was humbled in the recent currency and stock market rout following the shift of focus and the pullout of riskier assets in EMs, sending their currency rates and stock and bond prices spiraling downward. Conditions have since stabilized, but it's an uneasy calm. Markets are still confused.

Second, there is CRASH—that is, Conflict, Rates, Asia, Speculation, and Housing, which originated from Bank of America Merrill Lynch (BoA). This brings me to the August 22 annual retreat of central bankers and academics in the mountains of Grand Teton National Park at Jackson Hole, Wyoming, to brainstorm latest thinking on matters of growing concern surrounding the EM turbulence and on how best to avoid risky future accidents and shocks. August is a month when investors "sell and go away." Historically, September and October are prone to market shocks and accidents.

CRASH is a commonsense approach by BoA's Michael Hartnett to assess the risk of an accident.[6] Conflict scares markets and inflicts severe economic damage. Rate spikes are equally damaging, especially for the Fragile Five saddled with serious BoP financing gaps. Another sharp uptick in rates could prove disastrous. Asia matters. Its recent turmoil, however, indicated that its impact is differentiated. MSCI Emerging Markets indices were already down 13 percent for the year; for Latin America, they were down 20.2 percent in May, suffering more than Asia (11 percent). However, South Korea, with strong exports, was unscathed, whereas India (–25.8 percent), Indonesia (–30.7 percent), and Turkey (–35.8 percent) suffered sharp falls. Speculation magnifies the risk. Margin debt (money borrowed to fund short-term speculation) on the New York Stock Exchange hit a record in April, while indications of leverage have also spiked. Even though BIITS account for only 7 percent of global GDP, it can readily trigger a generalized crisis. After all, Thailand (a mere 0.5 percent share of global economy in 1997) did trigger a global crisis, following widespread contagion. Housing has been a clear plus for US recovery, which, in turn, affects ENs' well-being. Unmistakably, higher interest rates add fresh uncertainty for housing. In all, the analysis points to a world that's still a rather dangerous and risky place. Nevertheless, world stocks are up 5 percent for the year. I see no immediate possibility of a real crash. Certainly, no impending crisis—not yet. But the warning signals are on red.

What, Then, Are We to Do?

Indications are that momentum is appearing to shift away to the developed world from ENs that had since led global growth. For once, since mid-2007, the United States, Europe, and Japan together are expected to contribute relatively more speed to growth of the US$74 trillion global economy than ENs, including BRICS (Brazil, Russia, India, China, and South Africa) as well as Mexico. World conditions have slackened to a much greater degree than expected. This turnaround is bound to change the dynamics of world capital flows. The forces driving this shift include: (1) resurgent Japan, with a new confidence to beat deflation and to reform the economy for sustainable growth (second quarter of 2013 GDP up 2.6 percent); (2) a slowly recovering United States (GDP up 2.5 percent in the second quarter of 2013) that is gaining traction even though unemployment (at 7.4 percent) remains stubbornly high; (3) euro economy is struggling to grow (GDP up 1.1 percent in the second quarter of 2013) after contracting for six quarters previously, and hoping to recover with better momentum; and (4) a new China where economic slowdown appears to have stabilized and is heading for a soft landing (GDP at 6–7 percent in 2013), with a newfound confidence that growth can pick up. The other EN big guns (Brazil, Russia, India, and South Africa) are still ailing or ratcheting back slowly.

While there is optimism, there are good reasons for caution: Recovery in Japan and Europe remains tentative; and new China cannot be expected to spur global growth. So any broad rebound globally that depends on the

United States has to be fragile and undependable. Global conditions have slowed down too much to take things for granted. The recent EM rout is still simmering. Frankly, ENs still lack sufficient lines of defense to prevent potentially huge capital outflows from causing domino-like systemic failures. The looming Fed "tapering" is worrisome. Amplifications, feedback loops, and sensitivity to risk perceptions can complicate the process of exit. That's why International Monetary Fund's commitment to "stand ready to provide financial support if needed" makes a lot of sense at this time. The fund's standby arrangements and flexible credit lines are intended to be set up in advance of a crisis to prevent a crisis. This support may be needed sooner than we think.

Kuala Lumpur
September 5, 2013

Notes

1. First published on September 7, 2013, as "QE3 Exit & Asia's Policy Trilemma."
2. Agustin Carstens, governor, Bank of Mexico, speaking at the Jackson Hole (Wyoming) Symposium organized by the Reserve Bank of Kansas City on August 23, 2013.
3. Ralph Akins, "Fed Taper Is Dicey Dominoes Game," *Financial Times* (August 31, 2013).
4. Paul Krugman, "The Unsaved World," *International Herald Tribune* (August 31, 2013).
5. John Authers, "Piigs in Biits as Markets Suffer Acronym Anxiety," *Financial Times* (August 31, 2013).
6. Ibid.

CHAPTER 119

Focus of Concern:
Emerging Asia at Risk[1]

For much of the past five years, emerging Asia (EA) has been host to cheap money inflows. This came about as a result of quantitative easing (QE) measures by the US Federal Reserve Bank (Fed), augmented by the European Central Bank's (ECB) own QE actions, and lately, sustained through Japan's unique QE program following "Abenomic" thrusts to undeflate its 20-year period of deep sleep. Most of these monies reflected deliberate moves by global institutional investors, leery of low yields in Western markets, as they poured cheap borrowed funds into the region.

While the going was good, EA was in the midst of shifting to a more precarious phase of evolution as its pace of growth slackens, certainly in China and India, not unlike their non-Asian BRICS partners (Brazil, Russia, and South Africa). China could still hit its official target 7.5 percent growth in 2013 (7.7 percent in the first quarter of 2013 and 7.5 percent in the second quarter of 2013). Growth in India has slipped to 4.4 percent in the second quarter of 2013 (against below 5 percent for fiscal year ended March 2013 and at one-half its annual rate between 2005 and 2008). Russia and Brazil (each at 2 to 3 percent) are barely expanding against what they did in boom times, while South Africa has surely slipped away—less than 3 percent in 2013. Collectively, BRICS will still grow 4 to 4.5 percent in 2013, while ASEAN-5 (Indonesia, Malaysia, Philippines, Thailand, and Vietnam) will also decelerate to 5.6 percent in 2013 (6.1 percent in 2012).

EA is now expected to grow at about the same pace (6.9 percent) as it did in 2012 (against 8 percent in 2011, when it helped pull the global economy forward in the face of financial crisis). To be fair, that still sounds fast compared with what's going on in the rich West; but it is nevertheless the slowest rate of expansion in a decade. The focus of concern is whether it's a temporary loss of form or EA has permanently lost its mojo.

Take a Deep Breath

As I see it, the year marks the beginning of EA's second phase of transformation when emerging markets as a group already accounts for just over half of world gross domestic product (GDP) (in terms of purchasing power parity—PPP—that is, as reflected in real local purchasing power), against less than one-third in 1990. As I see it, this represents one of the greatest economic transformations in modern history. In the first phase, industrialization and globalization changed the world. Resource-rich nations (including Australia) flourished as they satisfied the growing appetite of the likes of China, which flooded the world with low-priced manufactures, hollowing out job markets worldwide. In the process, they helped to hold down inflation by making readily available a wide range of consumer goods at affordable, stable prices around the world.

Benefiting from the knock-on effects, 6 of the world's 10 fastest-growing economies are now found in South Africa. The upshot: Incomes rose significantly all round. Ten years ago, China's per-capita income (in PPP terms) was only 8 percent of the United States'; today, it's 18 percent and rising. Catching up will go on but the pace will decelerate, because (1) its workforce is falling; (2) its population is aging; (3) its currency is up and stabilized; (4) wages are rising; and (5) its total debt (as a ratio of GDP) is also rising.

The current second phase is more transformative, involving hard structural reforms. For China, this means rebasing the growth model to one that's more balanced and inclusive—pushing consumption on to assume the front-row seat ahead of investment and exports (which together propelled the economy for the past 40 years), and developing the services sector while industry shrinks.

Indeed, resource-based mass production processes dependent on cheap labor will give way to greener, cleaner, and technology-savvy ways to produce goods and services. Value added is expected to come through a better-educated, more productive, but increasingly smaller workforce, harnessing new and innovative IT methods that will be hopefully homegrown. That's the plan, anyway—away from the old-style borrow-and-build policies, emblematic of China's penchant for overbuilding. But these overhauls will be tough. Resistance is already building. As long as money is cheap and plentiful, vested interests will push to slow down the reform process—so the need for restructuring change becomes less pressing.

This is happening because EA on the whole is now better positioned than they were at the time of the last crisis in 1997–1998. China today has fiscal strength both to absorb losses from undue "knocks" and to stimulate, if needed. With the rich economies still feeble, chances are low that global monetary conditions will suddenly tighten. Even if they did, EA now has better defenses based on flexible exchange rates, larger stashes of forex reserves, and relatively less debt in foreign currencies; their banking system is also stronger and relatively more stable after having been restructured at the last crisis. But it's clear the back-breaking speed of development is over.

EA has come a long way—with still a long way to go. It's being realized that room for catch-up is now less—but it'll go on, only at a slower clip; only its quality gets better. For EA and BRICS, slowdown has become a reality. This simply means EA can no longer make up for any weakness in the rich West. Without stronger recovery in the United States, Europe, and Japan (whose outlook as a whole, in my view, still remains dire), the global economy is unlikely to grow any faster than today's lackluster pace in the region of 3 percent. So, things will remain and even feel sluggish.

"Fragile Five"

Chapter 118, "QE3 Exit and Asia's Trilemma," talks of the trauma for EA of the impending Fed's QE3 tapering. Of course, it didn't happen as was widely anticipated. But the damage is done. Interest rates have risen (already up 100 basis points and rising). Bond yields have risen faster. Indeed, analysts and markets have, since June 2013, highlighted concern over the stability and volatility of particular markets. So much so that Morgan Stanley (a major Wall Street investment bank) has since identified Brazil, India, Indonesia, Turkey, and South Africa (two in Asia and three among BRICS) as the "Fragile Five." They share one thing in common: All experienced excessive short-term capital inflows (StCI) in the face of growing current balance of payments (BOP) deficits for too long. Such easy financing has made governments tolerant of high growth rates, even as their exchange rates appreciated, making them less competitive.

With the recent reversal of fortune, their growth rates and exchange rates tumbled. EA as a whole is in trouble because (1) credit and commodity booms, which led to high growth rates, are not sustainable; (2) StCI has become too large and their reversal too unpredictable, with negative effects on stability; and (3) surge in inflation becomes inevitable. Some even tried to defend falling exchange rates, but at a high cost on reserves.

Like it or not, governments have to reform to deal with the impending end to StCI sooner than they think. Further, the world has to cope with two approaching down cycles, the 15- to 20-year credit cycle and the even longer commodity cycle. EA benefited from both that have now peaked. Its long decline has started. Most vulnerable are economies with persistent BOP deficits, high foreign debt, and stubborn budget deficits, which are the first to suffer. Similarly with large commodity exporters. That's why Russia, Brazil, South Africa, and Indonesia are particularly vulnerable. Many who ignored the needed structural change during boom times are likely to now experience low growth for prolonged periods.

In the circumstances, those who allowed state and crony capitalism to thrive in the process have locked themselves in the middle-income trap. Those that paused and committed to reforms (e.g., South Korea, Chile, and Mexico) are likely to do better. The next round of reform will be hard and difficult. There's no other way out. It has to be done.

Coping with Cheap Money's End

Traveling around Asia, I gathered few realize the full implications (not to talk of even being aware) of the strengthening US$ against EA's currencies. Indeed, few Asian companies even bother about it, let alone hedge against it. The combination of China's slackening growth in the face of transforming its investment-heavy strategy, and the prospect of imminent Fed "tapering," is taking its toll on EA. India and Indonesia have been the hardest hit. The rupee is down 20 percent since May, and the rupiah, 13 percent. As the Great Unwind (so called by Morgan Stanley) proceeds, it brings in its wake higher capital costs.

But the Chinese RMB (yuan) is holding stable, despite pressure from a dramatically weaker yen (down 30 percent from its high). Hedge funds managers tell me how profitable it was for them this year just borrowing yen and investing in RMB short-bonds and certificates of deposit (CDs), picking up gains from RMB appreciation and from attractive interest differentials. But, it's possible RMB can weaken to put pressure on regional competitors. More volatility is likely. Uncertainty still looms.

EA also faces sobering and tightening alternative funding options as deposit growth slackens and bank lending tightens. With outflows from emerging market equity and bond funds rising further (more than US$60 billion in the past three months), EA is bound to face more market volatility and increasingly more expensive capital costs. Swings in global bond markets this year have been violent: Until May, bond yields hit record lows; from May to September, the sell-off pushed yields to two-year highs. With the Fed not yet ready to "taper," yields have since moved lower. Eventually, they will head higher again. The risks and math get more daunting. It is said that the biases and rigidities of capital markets pose once again the paradox of thrift. As capital withdraws from emerging markets, some EA nations will be forced to adopt austerity measures and run BOP surpluses. But who will then be able—and willing—to run deficits? It's either China (RMB wants to be a reserve currency) or eurozone (its euro is already a reserve currency). Unfortunately, they both also want to continue to run surpluses. Since it's a zero-sum game, this simply means the United States must resume its role as the consumer of last resort—that is, run deficits. So we are back to square one, with imbalances threatening the system's stability once again.

Rising Cost of Capital

Not surprisingly Asian Development Bank (ADB) recently expressed concern that money will be harder and more expensive to tap.[2] It's a pity, since this is happening at a time when EA investment needs are huge and when European banks have significantly withdrawn from lending to the region. Indeed, ADB estimated EA needs to invest some US$8 trillion in transport, communication, and energy infrastructure by 2020. This is critical for the region as its poor state of infrastructure hampers future productivity growth prospects and poverty eradication efforts. "A slower growth outlook for the region has also contributed to capital flowing out with the withdrawal of funds, leading to rising bond yields and depreciating currencies. The turmoil in global financial markets has made it harder and more expensive for companies to issue foreign currency bonds; it has also made it harder and more expensive for EA companies—particularly lower-rated firms—to borrow in key foreign currencies such as US$, euros and yen."[3] In the first five months of 2013, US$81 billion were issued, but in June and July, only US$7.5 billion were raised.

ADB is right to be worried about EA's rising interest rates (already by Indonesia in mid-September) in an effort to stem capital outflows (and fight inflation as India just did recently), resulting from feared monetary "tapering" by the US Fed; bond yields will also rise, causing the value of bond portfolios of banks and businesses to fall. These constrain the growth of bond markets, which, at the same time, cause the cost of capital to rise. To soften the blow, I agree with ADB that EA clearly needs to (1) develop more stable sources of funding, including foreign direct investment; and (2) widen the range of bond investors, including pension funds.

What, Then, Are We to Do?

It is easy to conclude that EA now has hit a wall, undermined by China's slackening growth; end of the commodities super cycle; and as the clock winds down on a possible US government shut-down and the potential debt default by October 17, so that short-term outlook for interest rates (while trending upward) is decidedly murky. Despite the recent continuing sell-off in markets across Asia and Latin America, it will be unfortunate to write off EA. In my view, EA is now better placed to resume its vital role in global growth over the long term. While growth is bound to be more measured, ongoing efforts at reform (especially in China) to shift to a more consumer-driven economy and toward deeper and market-oriented financial markets provide a more reliable base from which to meet challenges ahead. What's making the difference is its rising middle class.

Indeed, it will include people who had managed to get out of poverty taking better care of their health, enjoying a better living standard, and seeking better education and social amenities for their young. EA has come a long way and is now better prepared. There has been a sea change from the past. Observed Nobel Laureate Paul Krugman: "The good news in Asia now is that the levels of external debt are much lower than the 1997 levels and Asian countries are not as financially vulnerable, adding that in comparison, eurozone nations today mirror the forex debt levels last seen during the Asian currency crisis."[4] Still, many worry about China. True enough, China is now experiencing a tough transition in serious reforms, including allowing banks to set interest rates to reflect market forces and allowing free flow of investment into and out of China. I regard this more as a sign of maturity than of weakness. Indeed, more pressure being placed on getting on with structural overhauls would lead to a higher likelihood of tough social reforms happening.

So far, signs are that economic slowdown has stabilized. People should not unduly overreact to China's changing condition. All's well that ends well.

Kuala Lumpur
October 2, 2013

Notes

1. First published on October 5, 2013.
2. Asian Development Bank (ADB), "Part I—Special Chapter: Asia's Economic Transformation: Where To, How and How Fast?" *The Key Indicators for Asia and the Pacific 2013* (Manila: ADB, August 2013).
3. Dr. Iwan Azis, head of Asian Development Bank's Office of Regional Economic Integration, press statement, *Asia Bond Monitor—September 2013* (Manila: ADB, September 26, 2013).
4. Paul Krugman, keynote address at the Julius Baer Next Generation Summit in Bali, September 9, 2013.

CHAPTER 120

ASEAN Stimulus[1]

Over the past two weeks, I have had the opportunity to make brief study trips to the other main countries in ASEAN (Singapore, Indonesia, Philippines, Thailand, and Vietnam), and more recently, ASEAN+3 (Japan, China, and South Korea) to update (and learn first hand) the impact of the ongoing global financial crisis and the attendant global recession.

I also participated in the Asian Economic Forum in Jakarta (March 22–24, 2009) organized by the Indonesian Ministry of Trade; Universiti Indonesia and Centre for Strategic and International Studies (CSIS) Indonesia; Columbia University; Keio University; Korea Institute of International Economic Policy; and University of California, Davis. The broad range of contributors came mainly from the principal ASEAN+3 nations, comprising academics, economists, and practitioners, including the Ministers of Finance and Trade, Indonesia. The theme was "The World in Crisis: National Strategies in an Interdependent World," with a one-day session on East Asia's response to the global economic crisis.

In addition, while visiting these countries, I also tapped on the Harvard alumni Asia-network comprising academics, professionals, entrepreneurs, and graduate students, who are well informed, well connected, but a rather random group. They provided me with a valuable second opinion, embracing an all-round cross-sectional "feel" of the current state of the political economy in ASEAN+3, which I so very badly needed.

My position as regional director for Asia, Harvard Alumni Association at Harvard University accorded me with the unique privilege to do this very pleasant task of making an assessment of what's going on, which I now intend to share. This chapter will concentrate on the principal countries of ASEAN as a group (Indonesia, Malaysia, Philippines, Singapore, Thailand, and Vietnam, known as ASEAN-6). In Chapter 121, I will share my impressions of ASEAN+3 (Japan, China, and South Korea).

The views expressed are independent after considering many viewpoints and hearing a very wide perspective of opinions. In many respects,

I benefited from the findings of scholarly empirical manuscripts and authoritative statements of persons who are really in the know, as well as insights of education-based nongovernmental organizations and respected academics, all of whom naturally have their biases. They all share a common characteristic: distrust of official data, which they dismiss in most cases as unusually optimistic, and officials who are often in denial. I was particularly pleased that an old professor of mine at Harvard, Barry Bosworth (who now researches at and writes from Brookings), provided an authoritative discourse on "Financial Crisis American Style." All errors are mine.

The Perspective

First, the broad brush. For many countries in ASEAN, the effects of the now-global recession were felt on the ground with a rather long time lag for structural/seasonal reasons:

1. East Asia, in varying degrees, was devastated by the Asian financial crisis in 1997–1998. Stock markets fell like a waterfall; banks and financial institutions were highly stressed and distressed; exchange rates were significantly devalued as international reserves declined; fiscal deficits mounted and external debts for many became difficult to service. As expected, growth decelerated and many nations even experienced brief periods of negative growth. But unlike now, world demand for East Asia's exports did not collapse at that time since the crisis was essentially "Asian born." Painful stabilization and recovery efforts took a heavy toll; indeed, the financial systems had to be fundamentally restructured, toxic assets disposed, and its institutions recapitalized and, in some cases, merged. To their credit, all of them took the bitter pill, and their banks and capital markets had since emerged leaner but stronger—so much so that when the US financial crisis struck in 2008, it had little impact on the integrity of ASEAN's financial system and infrastructure. The irony is that in 1997–1998, flight to quality meant deposits and prime borrowers moved to the foreign banks. This time around, deposits and prime borrowers switched to the domestic banks for cover! Nevertheless, ASEAN paid a high price for its financial resilience today. For example, Malaysia (a relatively well structured and stable nation, even then) took 8 to 9 years to regain its 1996 annual per-capita income of US$4,500. Today, it stands at US$7,700.
2. Advanced economies, which account for about two-thirds of global gross domestic product (GDP), was in recession for most of 2008. The impact of this sharp contraction in demand (and getting worse) was

transmitted (in an increasing globalized world) to ASEAN with varying degrees of rapidity and severity depending on each nation's openness to, and composition of, trade. For Singapore (total trade being 350 percent of GDP), its growth rate flattened in the third quarter of 2008, and then on to recession. In the case of Indonesia (less than 50 percent), the impact on growth was milder and less pervasive; it still recorded a growth rate of 6 percent in 2008. Malaysia (160 percent), Vietnam (140 percent), and Thailand (120 percent) felt it by the fourth quarter of 2008; so did the Philippines (75 percent). Nevertheless, all four countries registered decent growth rates of 3 to 5 percent for 2008 as a whole.

3. With the exception of Singapore, the widespread impact did not really hit home until after the first two months of 2009, mainly because of continuing consumer spending (albeit at an increasingly decreasing rate) during the Christmas, New Year, and related Chinese festivities. But the situation since then had deteriorated rapidly—most now begin to "feel" the recession, and consumers and businesses are becoming more cautious in their spending. Throughout ASEAN, growth had slackened in the first quarter of 2009 simply because the same period a year ago was rather buoyant.

Second, exports have become the principal casualty of the sharp drop in global demand. For the quarter ended February 2009, ASEAN exports fell by significant double digits, with the rate of decline in succeeding months steeper than in the previous month. By February 2009, ASEAN exports as a whole had fallen 30 to 40 percent, compared with the same period the year before. The collapse of global demand calls into question the sustainable viability of the export-led growth model that had helped to jump-start the transformation of East Asia into the often-regarded "model" collection of dynamic economies they are today.

Third, the currency crisis of 1997–1998 had since made most businesses and consumers (especially their bankers) quite risk averse. For the banks in particular, the bad experience with toxic assets (high nonperforming loans [NPLs]) and the hard scramble for fresh capital left an indelible mark on their psyche. This also explains why the banks have managed to remain well capitalized with low NPLs—at least so far. Except for Singapore, the world of collateralized debt obligations and credit default swaps hardly entered their books. Similarly, for most investors, even though the financial systems in ASEAN had liberalized enough for them to have ready access to foreign exchange accounts and to invest abroad. By chance, this has insulated most of ASEAN from the recent excesses and toxic influence of Wall Street.

Fourth, they often say "once bitten, twice shy." For ASEAN, the need to accumulate international reserves was (and still remains) a major driving force for recovery and revitalization in order not to be painted into a corner once again with insufficient "working capital" cushion to cover black swans, unscheduled unforeseens, and bloated debt servicing. With the onset of global recession, all the main ASEAN nations saw to it that they are well stocked with reserve funds to help support (when needed) jittery markets and unstable and unwelcome situations. Today (end-March 2009), the 12 central banks in the region hold close to US$4.5 trillion in international reserves, of which China (PRC) has about US$2 trillion, and Japan, US$1 trillion. Each nation has managed to maintain a comfortable reserves position to meet contingencies on a rainy day.

Global Recession Persists

Unfortunately, it looks like the global recession is still gathering momentum. Latest data on employment in the United States and eurozone and Japan have not been encouraging. Neither are the latest data on the US housing market (with declining prices picking up speed, showing that contraction is still deep). The International Monetary Fund (IMF) forecast last week that the eurozone will shrink 3.5 percent this year (and about 3 percent in United States), after contracting by an unprecedented 5.8 percent in the fourth quarter of 2008.[2] Japan's Tankan survey showed sentiment among big manufacturers had worsened; it hit the worst-ever low in the first quarter of 2009.

Despite US Federal Reserve System (Fed) Chairman Ben Bernanke's recent reference to "green shoots" of hope, I am convinced this recession will be prolonged. The IMF's September 2008 study (of 17 developed nations over three decades) had concluded that recessions preceded by financial crises are always deeper and longer; recessions tend to be worse if the crisis is in banking; and recessions linked to banking crises last two times longer, and the cumulative GDP loss, four times more.

The lesson to be learned points to a severe and long recession this time. World trade will slump 9 percent this year, according to the World Trade Organization (WTO). G-20 now targets return to growth by end-2010. There is tremendous downside risk in the global outlook. So, it makes sense to plan ahead based on the worst-case scenario. As I see it, the prudent approach is to prepare for more difficult times ahead. Global GDP is set to shrink 2 percent in 2009 (World Bank) and modest recovery in 2010 is uncertain. I can't see the United States, eurozone, and Japanese recessions stabilizing until toward year-end 2009, at the earliest. The road to recovery is still a ways off. The situation in ASEAN appears somewhat better. As a group, growth at an anemic 2 to 3 percent is possible, bearing in mind Singapore, Malaysia, and Thailand could post negative rates. None of the even modest recovery can be taken for granted. The outlook for 2010 continues to be surrounded by extreme uncertainty globally.

Stimulus

Like the industrial nations, the ASEAN+3 have individually embarked on a stimulus program (à la Keynes) to revitalize their lagging economies, especially their battered export industries. Massive numbers of jobs have been lost or are at risk. Each national program has been designed to suit its particular purposes, especially in providing the needed social safety nets and creating jobs. International demand has collapsed. In ASEAN, because their economies are dynamically export oriented, domestic consumption (though expanding) has not been as dependable a countervailing force in stressful and unusual circumstances. This is so simply because incomes are low and savings high (a cultural thing?). The stimulative packages put in place reflect this reality.

Among the ASEAN-6, Singapore and Malaysia have been the most aggressive in their "policy-induced recovery" programs (pump prime to the equivalent of 8 percent of GDP in Singapore and 9.5 percent in Malaysia). Singapore is into this for obvious reasons since it is the worst affected (contraction could possibly even be at –8 to –10 percent in 2009). Malaysia used the slowdown to also push for value-added investment to restructure and revitalize its low productivity labor-intensive industries. Manufacturing in both nations is the worst affected. Singapore was confident enough to finance 25 percent of its stimulation package by drawing down on its vast international reserves. Malaysia, just as confidently, relied on its vast domestic savings to do the job.

As I see it, since both countries have large unutilized capacity and low inflation, the dangers emanating from deficit finance are remote. In the end, it is vital to ensure that government borrowing and lending do not crowd out private initiative. As regards Indonesia and Thailand, I am convinced that their relatively modest stimulus push would soon be significantly enhanced, given the rapidly deteriorating economic situation, especially in Indonesia. Like Malaysia and Singapore, their manufacturing activities are also the worst affected. In addition, Thailand's fragile political malaise weighs heavily on the success in pushing through a badly needed second stimulus as most nonpoliticians (a powerful force) are worried that the monies so created will be politically diverted or misdirected. The Philippines, with just 30 percent of its economy driven by exports, relies more on remittances from millions working overseas in industries (healthcare and education) less vulnerable to recession. Its current stimulus program at 4 percent of GDP appears adequate and intact. In Vietnam, the situation is rather different, having just emerged from coping with overheating and high inflation. Monetary and fiscal adjustments are being worked through to one of relative easing. Most (including the World Bank) expect 5 percent growth in 2009 (6.5 percent in 2008).

Overall, the ASEAN-6 appear set to ride the recession storm, marshaling resources (human and financial) to create jobs, strengthen social safety nets, aggressively promote training and retraining to build future capacity, and foster lasting confidence among consumers and businesses to spend again.

What, Then, Are We to Do?

Recent experience tells me that to succeed, any stimulus package in Asia has to be more than just a "shot in the arm." Keynes's way envisages the integration of two key approaches: (1) pump priming—significant fiscal spending in the face of growing impotent monetary policy; and (2) reinvigorating "animal spirits" (AnS).

- AnS relates to building consumer and business confidence, but much more.
- It refers also to a sense of fair play; to a sense of trust (this is critical); and to a sense against bad faith and corruption.
- When AnS is at the ebb (like now), consumers withhold spending, and businesses don't invest and don't hire.
- For Keynes, AnS drives the business cycle. Swings in trust/confidence are not always logical. In good times, people are trusting and this emotional state (and associated feelings) contribute to building an ecosystem of confidence. They can make decisions spontaneously; they follow their instincts to gain success, even suspend suspicions. As this state spreads and people believe in the system, they can even become rash and impulsive. Recent display of trust in the mortgage/housing system in the United States drove real-estate prices to unattainable heights—the most dramatic case of unbridled AnS that has ever been seen. The case of Thailand is also a classic example. So is the Bernie Madoff scam case.

In the end, active stimulation to revive AnS must involve firm leadership; targeted policies; bold action; and visible implementation. There is nothing like seeing action on the ground.

Kuching, Sarawak
Kuala Lumpur
April 3, 2009

Notes

1. First published on April 4, 2009.
2. International Monetary Fund (IMF), *World Economic Outlook: Crisis and Recovery* (Washington, DC: IMF, April 2009).

CHAPTER 121

ASEAN+3 Stimuli[1]

Chapter 120 dealt with the outlook for ASEAN (centered on ASEAN-6, i.e., Indonesia, Malaysia, Philippines, Singapore, Thailand, and Vietnam). And, the country efforts to stimulate (à la Keynesian style) in the face of a menacing recession that has become globally driven. Successive monthly releases point to a worsening situation. Last week, the World Bank talks of more pain as widespread unemployment hits home.[2] Growth in 2009 for East Asia is now revised downward to 5.3 percent (from 6.7 percent in December 2008). Excluding China, the region as a whole will hardly grow within a global perspective that will see an overall contraction of close to 2 percent (first-ever decline since World War II (WWII). Transmission, at an astonishing speed, of the effects of the recession in the United States and Europe is spreading uncertainty and destroying business and consumer confidence.

East Asia

ASEAN+3 (i.e., plus China, Japan, and South Korea)—often loosely called East Asia—is determined to do better. At the recent Asian Economic Forum held in Jakarta, I left with the impression that there is sufficient political will in the region to help themselves; that firm leadership has since emerged to prevent a fait accompli; and that the way to go is to stay the pressure to stimulate, to reinvigorate the animal spirits, and to do "more rather than less" in order to reverse this psychology of worrying more about dangers than rewards, and to unshackle our entrepreneurs as fear overcomes greed. This is not easy, given the gloom and the many constraints that surround the region. If anything, what's happening today clearly debunks decoupling as a myth. Consider global consumer spending. In 2007, US private spending was about US$10 trillion, and eurozone, nearly US$9 trillion. In Japan, the world's second largest economy, private consumption was just about US$2 trillion, and China was struggling to reach one trillion. Consumers in Japan and China combined spend less than one-sixth of what their counterparts do in the United States and Europe. So, no matter how rapidly Chinese consumers raise their spending, they can't offset more than just a small fraction of the "loss" in the Western world.

Look at it another way. Over the past 30 years, Asia has so perfected its export machine that by 2007, exports reached close to 50 percent of gross domestic product (GDP), compared with only 17 percent in 1980. This business model has been so successful in bringing prosperity and rapidly rising incomes in Asia that private consumption as a percentage of GDP fell from 65 percent in 1980 to just above 45 percent in 2007. Much of this has to do with the US consumption binge. Since WWII, US consumers had significantly improved their living standards; private spending averaged 67 percent share of GDP during 1975–2000, having risen steadily from 61 percent in 1960.

Because of easy money, they consumed 72 percent of their gross earnings by 2007! With the onset of recession at the end of 2007 and its aftermath, US consumption has begun to collapse under the weight of sharp falls in income and wealth. With capital loss alone estimated at US$11 trillion in 2007, a permanent consumption fall of 3 percentage points of GDP can be expected in the United States. This will surely lengthen the recession in the United States. The US consumer at risk today has become a source of concern to underlying recovery in Asia.

Japan

In the ASEAN+3 region, China and Korea are among the most aggressive "stimulators." Ironically, it is Japan that really needs this, as the economy is in a bad way—logging its worst performance in 35 years in the fourth quarter of 2008, contracting at an annualized rate of 12 percent. For 2009, the World Bank expects GDP in Japan to contract by as much as 5.5 percent, regarded as not "off the mark" by the government (Organisation for Economic Co-operation and Development says, by –6.5 percent). After being in a "deep-sleep" for about 10 years following the collapse of stock market and real estate prices in early 1990s, Japan is experiencing "stimulation fatigue."

With public debt at 180 percent of GDP, Japan finds itself increasingly constrained from issuing more government debt to finance further fiscal stimulus measures. Being painted into a corner, it now has little choice (with the lost decade still a sore point) but to inject fresh stimulus. The expectation is for a new package equivalent to about 3 percent of GDP, doubling in aggregate the total stimulative spending to about 5 percent of GDP, in the face of a deepening recession that is worse than in the United States and eurozone. Indeed, this will be Japan's worst since WWII. It should be noted that after its lethargy of 1991–2002, Japan had only managed to grow at an annual average rate of 2 percent until 2007.

As far as stimulus goes, Japan is a veteran. Even prior to its problems of the 1990s, public works spending was twice as large in Japan as a share of GDP (6 percent) than in the United States. This was raised in the mid-1990s to a high of 8 percent, with Japan finding less and less worthwhile projects to spend on (bridges to nowhere actually originated here!). Hence, the deep Japanese distrust of fiscal spending and the ensuing rising public debt. For the new stimulus, I will not be surprised if most spending on infrastructure will be financed by the issue of revenue bonds, utilizing private-sector funding. This has broad-base support among academicians. Typically, the government bears a portion of the construction costs with the remainder financed by private initiative through issue of revenue bonds. Interest and principal will be repaid from revenue generated by the project, especially suited for infrastructure, very much like Malaysia's private finance initiative (PFI), which is sometimes used for public projects.

China

In East Asia, China is doubtless in the best position to withstand the impact of global recession. It has been (and will continue to be) painful; unemployment is a big worry with its attendant social ills. China's social infrastructure is not sufficiently mature to absorb the shocks. Just as the world outside is facing increasingly difficult times, business and consumer sentiment in China had continued to plunge, eating steadily into public confidence in the leadership's ability to withstand the surrounding onslaught. The World Bank[3] last week forecasts China will expand 6.5 percent this year (down from 7.5 percent earlier in the face of 9 percent growth in 2008); it is expected to bottom out in the second half of 2009. As the vast stimulative package kicks in, China is expected to recover somewhat to grow about 7.5 percent in 2010.

There are significant downside risks here; the outlook still weighs heavily on the success of the United States, Europe, and Japan stimuli. China scholars and observers I met recently in Jakarta, Shanghai, and Beijing are generally rather optimistic about the outlook because: (1) the fourth quarter of 2008 contraction of 6.8 percent reflected sharp inventory destocking, following the collapse of global commodity markets and exports; (2) the vast stimulus package (12 percent of GDP), not counting additional stimulative spending by local government (estimated to have the potential to double that of the central stimulus), should be able to generate visible multipliers especially in late 2009 and certainly 2010; (3) its fiscal position is strong; and (4) the banking sector is relatively sound and healthy.

In short, China's determined stimulus has the capability to boost domestic demand, offset some of the impact of the "waterfall"-like falls in exports, create new jobs, and over the next 18 months generate a sustainable recovery of 7.5 to 8 percent by end-2010. Continuing growth will enable the government to strengthen its social safety net and broaden access to healthcare and education.

But there are many risks and just as many areas of concern. First, some critics have called the stimulus "legless" in that it contains great potential, but its epic scale and scope make it difficult to effectively implement at the grassroots. That is, job creation will be found wanting and the risks of crowding out private initiative (especially small and medium enterprises) are high. Second, continuing reliance on the investment-driven growth model would further favor industrial expansion to the detriment of the less-buoyant services sector, which badly needs priority support and attention. Third, the needed structural adjustment away from excessive reliance on exports—underlying cause of the downturn—is likely to be delayed. Fourth, the virtual size of the stimulus makes it difficult in the short run to generate the needed stream of worthwhile projects flowing at a sufficiently high rate without lowering the efficiency of investment. Subprime projects will raise the risk of nonperformance. Finally, the stimulus risks worsen the steady buildup of excess capacity, especially in manufacturing.

Already, China's investment share of GDP had risen to 43 percent. At their peak, Japan's and South Korea's industrial investment averaged less than 40 percent. China has been investing more since the early 2000s as a share of the economy than Japan and South Korea did even at the height of their industrialization. With the export crash, significant excess capacity has now emerged in China, so much so that by the year 2010 (even without the stimulus), the output gap will have reached 4 percent of GDP. The vast stimulus will significantly widen this gap, which raises serious problems of waste, oversupply, and low returns. As I see it, China's drive to recovery is still on "first gear." Success will center on its ability to significantly expand the services sector and get the Chinese to consume more and more to improve living standards. But, there are already indications that China is instead saving more. This dilemma cannot be easily resolved.

Above all, China needs to robustly expand and build a large domestic market. Its future stability depends on it. Already, the drastic shrinkage of export markets abroad has exerted enormous pressure on the government to redirect priority and incentives to strengthen domestic demand. Policy makers recognize that deficiencies here have hindered job creation and the rise in living standards. Friends in Shanghai and Beijing tell me that entrepreneurs focusing on meeting and building demand in the expanding domestic market are flourishing. A good number who are recently established now expects this year to be (in their own words) "their best ever!" And, I believe them.

South Korea

Very much like China, the impact of the global recession on South Korea has been severe: Exports now account for more than two-thirds of its near US$1 trillion GDP, up from one-third at its last recession in 1998. Major markets are the United States, eurozone (with a combined share of 25 percent), and China (22 percent). The core problem today is lack of aggregate demand. The Korean economy had already been slowing down since 2006. By the fourth quarter of 2008, growth fell 4.5 percent (quarter-on-quarter), the worst since the Asian currency crisis. Both private consumption and investment recorded negative growth, with a current payments deficit driven mainly by falling exports. Nevertheless, for 2008 as a whole, there was still growth of 2 to 2.5 percent.

Prospects for 2009 are rather poor—recent consensus points to a 4 to 4.5 percent contraction. Both consumer and investment sentiment remain weak—and exports look bleak as long as the United States, eurozone, China, and Japan struggle to cope with global recession. The first quarter of 2009 export shipments have not been encouraging. Rising unemployment is weighing the nation down, and help from its weakened currency will be limited. South Korea still has much capacity to further stimulate (existing package is about 2.5 percent of GDP), and serious steps have been taken to keep credit flowing and to ensure its banking system is adequately pro-growth. Success of East Asia's fiscal stimuli as well as US leadership in aggressively pushing growth and job creation are crucial to South Korea's recovery efforts. Unfortunately, its export-driven growth model is too entrenched to be readily restructured. The endgame in South Korea will surely become more painful—more jobs will be lost and social unrest can only delay the steady turnaround in consumer and investment sentiment.

What, Then, Are We to Do?

Last week, the World Bank forecasts more pain for East Asia. That's nothing new. No doubt, East Asia is a continent adrift. My worries go beyond Asia, indeed to the world, which has so far lagged behind expectations in terms of progress and performance. From my vantage point in Asia, the eurozone seems to be still somewhat in denial. I mean, its reluctance to respond firmly and decisively to the financial meltdown (in the face of adverse recessionary forces just as severe as in the United States) is quite astonishing. In my view, Europe's fiscal and monetary response has fallen short of what is needed (with a response time longer than necessary). It is important for Asia to have growing confidence that both the United States and Europe do act boldly and in sync, and to stimulate in good measure to effectively combat a deepening recession that has become global.

Be that as it may, ASEAN+3 is on the move. China's leadership is boldly stimulating growth to recovery. Since the G-20 meeting last week, Japan now appears ready to lead a new aggressive stimulus plan to lift the gloom that has engulfed its entire economy. Certainly, ASEAN is reaching out to better coordinate regional initiatives, with a common purpose to expand intraregional and domestic demand. There is need for further stimulus, especially in Indonesia and Thailand. Even South Korea. There are signs that beggar-thy-neighbor policies can only hurt. It's a zero-sum game. Quietly, ASEAN+3 works. It has reached a crucial turning point and the region needs to do more at this time. The global meltdown requires it to fundamentally change the way each nation approaches and cultivates development. The export-drive model has outlived its usefulness. Ironically, the United States wants to be net export driven as well. East Asia badly needs a vibrant domestic engine, with increasing reliance on expanding a dynamic domestic market and reducing excessive dependence on export markets so very vulnerable to disruptions.

ASEAN+3 have proven to have the capacity and resources (human and financial) to do this. It is in their collective self-interest to get this done with some haste. Most individual nations within the region are already setting this in motion, committing firm leadership behind the move to change. Plans of action will need to be more focused and be better coordinated for greater cooperation in the region. This can only help. Indeed, the risks of doing less are far higher than the risks of doing more. East Asia badly needs a big push to help themselves. The time is now.

Kuala Lumpur
April 9, 2009

Notes

1. First published on April 11, 2009. It was edited down because of space constraints. This is the full and unedited version.
2. World Bank, *East Asia Pacific Economic Update* (Washington, DC: World Bank, April 2009).
3. Ibid.

CHAPTER 122

AEC Is on the Way, but It's No Big Deal[1]

Many ask: What's this ASEAN Economic Community (AEC) all about? If it's that important, why do we know so little about it? Can you help explain? Here goes: ASEAN (Association of Southeast Asian Nations) kicked off as a political entity some 46 years ago.[2] It has since evolved over time, standing today on three pillars: (1) political-security, (2) economic, and (3) sociocultural. Experience from the 1997–1998 financial crisis highlighted the necessity for closer economic collaboration to protect mutual national interests. This is reinforced by the recent rise of China and India, strengthening ASEAN's determination to create a stronger and more cohesive community.

The 1997 ASEAN Summit in Kuala Lumpur brought this into sharper focus with the ASEAN 2020 Vision Declaration to transform the region into a stable, integrated, and competitive region. By 2003, the Bali Summit committed the group to accelerate the establishment of the AEC from 2020 to 2015. Since then, the 2007 AEC Blueprint sets out clear timelines for ASEAN members to strive toward becoming an integrated economic community by 2015 with: (1) a single market and production base; (2) a highly competitive economic region; (3) increasingly more equitable and inclusive economic development; and (4) a region fully integrated into the global economy.

The endgame will finally revolve around (1) a core ASEAN center; (2) an inclusive ASEAN; (3) an efficient and transparent operational framework; (4) harmonized rules and regulations; and (5) a strong linkage to the global supply and value chains. These characteristics are interrelated and mutually reinforcing. At the heart of AEC is the overarching objective to promote the free flow of goods, services, investment, and skilled labor; the free flow of capital; and the free and open integration of clearly identified priority sectors, as well as in food, agriculture, and forestry. To help deepen ASEAN market integration are clear commitments to formulate milestones under the Roadmap to Monetary and Financial Integration, as well as the operationalization of the US$485 million ASEAN Infrastructure Fund Limited to facilitate sustained economic growth and address poverty alleviation in the region.

ASEAN

ASEAN's uniqueness needs to be highlighted; it has:

- A combined gross domestic product (GDP) of US$2.2 trillion, with a capacity to grow at 5 to 6 percent a year.
- A population exceeding 600 million, with relatively young demographics and a per-capita income averaging about US$3,800.
- A young workforce (aged 15–64), exceeding 310 million in the face of a contracting working population in China; this labor force totals 115 million in Indonesia, 50 million in Vietnam, 40 million each in Philippines and Thailand, 27 million in Myanmar, and 12 million in Malaysia—most now hit the demographic "sweet spot."
- A vast difference in their stages of development and levels of income:

Rich	Rich in resources, attracting continuing inflows of foreign direct investment (FDI) (US$110 billion in 2012).	Brunei, Singapore
Middle-Income	An external trade totaling US$2.5 trillion in 2012; but trade among themselves (intra-ASEAN trade) remains small—at only 26 percent of the total, against 75 to 80 percent in the 28-nation European Union (EU) and 55 percent under the North America Free Trade Area (NAFTA).	Indonesia, Malaysia, Philippines, Thailand
Poor	Relatively open borders among themselves, allowing vast numbers of young workers to move within ASEAN seeking higher wages and better employment opportunities, helping to level the playing field across the region. But domestic political pressures reflecting growing nationalism and social infrastructure constraints are working against fuller and faster integration any time soon, limiting progress to only baby steps.	Cambodia, Laos, Myanmar, Vietnam

AEC Scorecard

According to Datuk Dr. Rebecca Fatima Sta. Maria, secretary-general of Malaysia's Ministry of International Trade and Industry, nearly 80 percent of the targeted measures have already been implemented (Malaysia: 88 percent).[3] Details include the following:

1. **On elimination of import duties:** It's 88 percent completed; what's left involves making the flow of trade seamless through smart trade facilitation and faster Customs' integration.
2. **On liberalization of services:** The ninth package will be finalized in 2013 and tenth package is on track for 2015; equity ownership of 70–100 percent is now allowed for most sectors.
3. **On investment flows:** ASEAN Comprehensive Investment Agreement (ACIA) is already effective in 2012; it provides investment protection and transparency in investment regimes.
4. **On labor mobility:** Agreement on the movement of natural persons was signed in 2012. The report card looks good—but only on paper; it merely records meeting compliance metrics and does not reflect actual outcomes, which really matter.

At best, they simply reflect work-in-progress as ASEAN continues to engage, consult, and interact. Much more needs to be done at the ground level. As the measures begin to take hold (and slowly, to bite), adverse effects will emerge—most serious being the effects of Schumpeter's "creative destruction," with inefficient businesses checking out as they fail to effectively compete, victims of innovation by their competitors. And with it, the wreckage it leaves behind—unemployment, bankruptcies, and fortunes lost, together with their dire social consequences.

Global Trade

World trade is expected to grow in 2013—for a second time in a row—at about the same pace as in 2012 (2 to 2.5 percent), that is, below this year's rate of global output growth (estimated at 2.9 percent, compared with 3.1 percent in 2012). This is unusual—indeed an anomaly. Historically, going back to the late nineteenth century, global trade had expanded at about twice the rate of world GDP growth. It remains uncertain if this phenomenon will happen a third time this year. Forecasts by the World Trade Organization (WTO) and International Monetary Fund (IMF) suggest the numbers are close. Since the Industrial Revolution, the only time world trade lagged behind global growth was in 1913–1950—a period between two world wars, which saw the disastrous impact of the Great Depression. Some even dubbed this the "era of de-globalization." The *Financial Times* recently asked if the world is merely "experiencing a blip or a more fundamental structural twist in global commerce."[4]

It's just too early to tell—no one knows for sure. Quipped economics Nobel Laureate Paul Krugman: "Ever-growing trade relative to GDP isn't a natural law, it's just something that happened to result from the policies and technologies of the past few generations."[5] It's quite clear that the world has changed. I sense the low-lying fruits of global trade expansion have been plucked. The WTO's recent World Trade Report[6] concluded that many of the big factors that had driven trade growth over the past three decades had been exploited, like an exhausted mineral resource. It would appear even globalization has lost much of its steam. Nations, including the United States and Europe, have begun to turn inward. Who is to champion globalization? There is also the issue of whether real reform in China—now the world's biggest trading nation—will really take place; on it rests the question of whether China's market will remain open to the outside world, since any setback in reform would slow down the process of globalization, and with it world trade.

Beyond ASEAN

At the same time, when AEC is being actively pursued, resources are distracted and redirected at negotiations on three other large trade arrangements:

1. The Trans-Pacific Partnership (TPP) negotiations involving 12 countries (including the United States and Malaysia) to form a vast free-trade market for 800 million people in the Pacific Rim, with a combined GDP of US$27 trillion, or about one-third of world GDP. This partnership has been called a twenty-first-century free-trade pact, providing a blueprint for global economic engagement by facilitating foreign investment with transparency, and environmental and intellectual property safeguards beyond traditional free trade.
2. The Regional Comprehensive Economic Partnership (RCEP) or ASEAN+6 (i.e., plus China, India, Japan, South Korea, Australia, and New Zealand). It envisages broadening and deepening ASEAN's AEC with its large Asian trading partners to create a free-trade zone that would cover over one-half of the world's population. If both RCEP and TPP were to come together, they would be similar in economic size to the European Union. They will begin to form the building blocks over the long run to meet the goal of the 21-member Asia Pacific Economic Cooperation (APEC) group to deepen trade liberalization, bringing the

United States and China together into a single Asia-Pacific free-trade region, succeeding in putting together more than a mere "spaghetti bowl" deal, which 10 years of talks at the WTO have since failed to do.

3. The old story of the long-stalled 2001 Doha Development Round, now trying to sign a last-ditch "slimmed-down" deal to clear red tape at world borders, focused on "trade facilitation." Indications are that talks have again stalled.

All three arrangements have set the year-end as the deadline. It's a challenge, particularly for the United States, which needs "fast track" Trade Promotion Authority (to prevent the US Congress from amending prospective trade deals) to assure trade partners that any agreements will not be reopened. Under such a mechanism, the US Congress could only vote "yes" or "no" on the deal. In addition, the United States is also trying to conclude a historic US–EU deal to forge by late 2014 the world's largest free-trade accord—covering some 40 percent of global GDP and 50 percent of world trade. EU estimates that such a deal would generate annual benefits of US$200 billion to 500 million Europeans, and slightly less for the United States. The deal would also cover services, investment, energy, and raw materials; but its key aim is to harmonize regulatory regimes to further reduce barriers to trade.

I sense much of the lethargy in growth of world trade can be traced to the impact of recent US financial crisis and the prolonged recession in Europe (especially collapse of imports), as well as effects of business slowdown of multinational companies dependent on global supply chains. As growth regains normalcy in the face of heightened activity in regional trade integration, global trade can be expected to regain its former dynamism over time. Granted, globalization has retreated and there has been a steady increase in "stealth" protectionist measures (including nontariff barriers) since 2008. Granted also, world trade has since veered into unchartered waters. Be that as it may, the quickening pace of regional trade will expand market access, draw in investment and capital, and help build capacity and expand global supply chains.

What, Then, Are We to Do?

What's missing so far is that the world has avoided the surge in protectionism that marked the Great Depression during the interwar years. But worries of competitive devaluation have assumed a different form—a consequence of a series of quantitative easing (QE) measures by the US Federal Reserve System (Fed) in recent years, followed by the adoption of a similar policy stance by the European Central Bank (ECB), and this year, by the Bank of Japan (BoJ), leading to the debasement of currencies. Global currency wars are heating up again as central banks embark on a new round of QE to combat slowdown in growth. The ECB cut interest rates in early November in a move interpreted by many as intended (in part at least) to curb the euro after it soared to its highest level since 2011. The ECB had been talking down the euro for some time. On the same day, Czech policy makers intervened for the first time in 11 years to weaken the koruna. Both New Zealand and Australia publicly noted that their dollar was "uncomfortably high." With the IMF downgrading global growth, countries are revisiting policies to boost competitiveness through weakening currencies.

In Asia, emerging currencies skidded and shares tumbled following mixed signals from the Fed raising fresh concerns about imminent "tapering" (rollback) of its asset-buying stimulus, and from the recent QE measures of ECB and BoJ. The Indonesian rupiah hit its weakest in four and a half years, while the Indian rupee sagged to a two-month low. Most other Asian currencies (including the ringgit) weakened across the board, except for the Chinese yuan (or RMB), which held steady. Both the rupiah and rupee had remained weak throughout the entire month. In recent days, the Philippines peso and Thai baht have weakened further. While the coming on of AEC is welcome and contributes to the easing of global trading conditions, the rising risk of competitive devaluation is much more serious. Bear in mind intra-AEC trade remains relatively small.

What's of real concern and is becoming increasingly more worrisome are: (1) the persistent withdrawal of capital (on the rising risk of Fed tapering), which in turn, places at risk future FDI flows and the availability and cost of funding especially of up to US$1 trillion of Asian major infrastructure projects; (2) continuing QE flows of cheap money—raising risks on the prospect of "currency wars," and rising protectionism (especially "stealth" protectionist barriers); and (3) growing political pressures emanating from nationalist vested interests to water down regional integration and liberalization efforts, especially on the free flow of skilled labor. Viewed in this perspective, AEC is really no big deal!

Kuala Lumpur
November 28, 2013

Notes

1. First published on November 30, 2013.
2. ASEAN was founded in 1967 by Malaysia, Indonesia, the Philippines, Singapore, and Thailand. Its membership has since expanded to include Brunei (in 1984), Vietnam (1995), Laos (1997), Myanmar (1997), and Cambodia (1999).

3. Rebecca Fatima Sta. Maria, "ASEAN Economic Community 2015: Will We Get There?" paper delivered at the MICPA-Bursa Malaysia Business Forum 2013, Kuala Lumpur, November 19, 2013.
4. "Trade: Into Uncharted Waters," *Financial Times* (October 25, 2013), p. 7.
5. Ibid.
6. Ibid.

CHAPTER 123

South Korea Emerges More Competitive[1]

L eft booming Shanghai on Sunday for South Korea (Asia's fourth-largest economy) to attend a gathering of social scientists in the future city of Incheon and its adjacent port. This ancient city is South Korea's first Free Economic Zone (1,000 km^2), designated in 2003. It is already fast becoming an intelligent high-tech city with state-of-the-art infrastructure and facilities to house world-class businesses, schools, universities, hospitals, meetings, incentives, conferences, exhibitions (MICE), and cultural complexes. This sets Incheon as the next northeast Asian hub for global logistics and center for investment.

What I saw was most absorptive—a far cry, I thought, from Malaysia's Port Klang Free Zone that failed to be. You can't but be impressed with the South Koreans' determination to do what it takes to seriously compete with its two towering neighbors—China and Japan, and, somewhat further, India. It's the beginning of spring in Incheon, but it snowed! First time in 40 years, I am told. A rare treat. This meeting of a mix of some smartest analysts in economic affairs and public policy from the United States, Europe, and ASEAN+3 provided the needed warmth to fascinate each other on the prospective state of goings-on in the world, especially Asia. The collaborative research of young South Koreans was an eye opener. I intend to share some of their analytics and findings in the hope that we can learn from their lessons and policy action experience.

South Korea before Global Crisis

South Korea was hard hit in the 1997–1998 financial crisis. But it rebounded with V-shaped recovery in 1999. Since then, economic fundamentals had consolidated and strengthened to grow at over 4 percent a year in the 2000s. Reforms were undertaken to restrategize underlying macroeconomic structures and the financing framework of banks and enterprises. The objective was simple: Transform the economy and inject sufficient resilience to withstand the next crisis. The focus was to allow private enterprise and initiative to take the lead, with increasing reliance on the market for price discovery and to sharpen competitiveness. Indeed, South Korea has since relied on market power to drive adjustment to basic macroeconomic soundness but with varying success. It significantly liberalized the financial market. Restrictions against foreign investment were lifted; the exchange rate was allowed to float; foreign capital was encouraged to move in (foreign investment was soon 40 percent of total listed shares); and banks were pushed to restructure, recapitalize, and improve basic soundness.

South Korea's corporations and industry responded by strengthening governance and balance sheets, reducing debts, and restructuring and reinvesting to raise productivity. With newfound confidence, South Korea raised its share in some global markets as weaker competitors exited (e.g., in semiconductors and LCDs). South Korea autos penetrated deeper into the US, European, and Asian markets. Indeed, South Korea had the audacity during the crisis not just to reform, restructure, and rebuild, but also to invest in new private productive capacity for sustained future growth. Their rising competitiveness was reflected in strong export growth for 10 years since 1997. By end-2007, South Korea's foreign exchange reserves rose to US$262 billion, as against only US$20 billion in 1997.

Shocks from the Global Crisis

Not unlike its neighbors, the 2007–2008 global turmoil hit South Korea hard, even though it had restructured its economy and built some resilience. Impact of the severe shocks was visible in the virtual collapse in export demand and the tightening financial markets and liquidity crunch. Effects were as sudden as they were severe. This "double whammy" from both export loss and large capital outflows drastically weakened its external payments position. In 2008, South Korea recorded its first current as well as capital account deficits since 1997–1998 crisis. Collapse of global demand reduced exports by 12 percent in the fourth quarter of 2008, despite the sharp depreciation in the South Korean won in 2008. However, imports also declined, reflecting weakened manufacturing output, which fell by 12 percent. Poor business sentiment led to a 16 percent fall in private investment. Private consumption declined by 5 percent. As a result, gross domestic product (GDP) recorded a negative 5.6 percent in the fourth quarter of 2008.

The devastating impact was centered on financial markets, with capital flows dripping in red. In 2008, foreign exchange outflows totaled US$55 billion, comprising both foreign direct investments (FDI) and portfolio outlays.

Sharp deleveraging prompted domestic businesses to borrow massively short-term; by end-2008, short-term foreign debt rose to the equivalent of 97 percent of national reserves. This mismatch of long foreign assets and short liabilities remains until today a source of concern. These simply meant tightening domestic financial conditions, considering that in 2008: The stock index (KOSP1) fell 41 percent, loan–deposit ratio rose to 135 percent, and bank profits declined by 47 percent. The severe credit crunch reflected the 50 percent depreciation of the South Korean Won from early 2008 to the fourth quarter of 2009. Overall, South Korea's balance of payments looked awful: current deficit of US$6 billion, and on capital account, US$51 billion. As a result, South Korea's national foreign reserves fell by US$57 billion to just over US$200 billion at end-2008. That's a far cry from a position of persistent surpluses since 1998 (reserves at end-1997 being only one-tenth of 2008).

Policy Response

Like its Asian neighbors, South Korea had learned well from prior experience in successfully handling crises. More important, it had previously credibly reformed and restructured the economy. It was better placed than most in terms of technological infrastructure to effectively deal with what came along. The policy mix adopted this time comprised four rather traditional thrusts:

1. Expansive monetary policy to ease liquidity crunch, including very low interest rates and accommodative quantitative measures (including purchase of long-dated assets).
2. Aggressive expansionary fiscal policy to raise domestic demand directly, with tax reductions and front-loading large spending.
3. Ready access to substantial official financing, and guarantees to relieve pressure on the exchange rate and other asset prices, especially in stabilizing forex markets (using new swap arrangements with the United States, Japan, and China).
4. Strengthening restructure and reform mechanisms to reduce inefficiencies in debt workouts, bank recapitalization, and small and medium enterprises (SME) credit support.

These measures are still ongoing. Since the crisis, this mix of policies has worked reasonably well, with intended objectives being increasingly met. The banking system appears to have stabilized, with most indicators looking sound enough. Improvements are visible in bank asset quality, and

SME support looks solid, with low nonperforming loans ratios. True, the forex market continues to be of concern, but measures to address uncertainties are working sufficiently. Others like direct forex liquidity provision (US$55 billion), government guarantees to banks (US$100 billion), currency swap lines with three majors (US$90 billion, with usage already repaid), and the Chiang Mai Initiative (reserve pool of US$120 billion) have proved adequate to help calm markets. Short-term foreign debt has slowly declined (now below US$150 billion), as has the foreign debt ratio (39 percent of GDP). On the fiscal side, economic stimulus spending since 2008 reached 5 percent of GDP by end-2009, with the three-year total for 2008–2010 at 7 percent. This was made possible because of its solid fiscal position until 2008—with a public debt of 36 percent of GDP (lowest in the Organisation for Economic Co-operation and Development, average being 72.5 percent).

South Korea Post-Crisis, 2009–2010

It now appears South Korea's policy responses have had most of its desired effects. Financial markets are certainly more stable. However, forex markets are still not yet calm enough, with continuing currency maturity mismatches, which need time to unravel. Nevertheless, the overall situation remains vulnerable. South Korea still does not have a completely convertible currency, even though its exchange rate is market determined. Its recent experience showed off vast volatility in the won, which impact cuts both ways.

Certainly, the sharp depreciation since mid-2008 helped boost exports in 2009. But the speculative massive capital movements inflicted high costs on the nation's finances. Overall, the economy is in recovery—a V-shaped one at that. GDP expanded 6 percent in the fourth quarter of 2009 (–5.6 percent in the fourth quarter of 2008). Latest forecasts point to a 4.5 to 5.5 percent growth this year. Between February 2009 and January 2010, the KOSPI was up 51 percent, the won appreciated by 24 percent against the US$, consumer prices were down 25 percent, Bank for International Settlements (BIS) capital ratio of banks, up 15 percent, and currency reserves, up 36 percent to US$273 billion, even higher than previous peak at end-2007.

Exports are doing particularly well, up 19 percent in 2009. It's significant that South Korea's export markets have become more diversified (China now accounts for 24 percent of total trade; ASEAN, 19 percent); so have the products-mix (semiconductors, 8 percent of total; autos and parts, 11 percent; flat TV panels, 5 percent; and ship building, 10 percent). South Korea's share of global LCD market is now 50 percent, and autos, close on 15 percent.

South Koreans have done rather well for themselves.

Nothing Is Overoptimistic

As you get familiar with South Koreans—academics, policymakers, businessmen and consumers—you know they know they have come a long way. Indeed, they have successfully evolved from passive followers to becoming active agenda setters. This role befits a country on the move: from destruction in the 1950–1953 Korean War to being one of Asia's richest nations. With per-capita income now above US$20,000 a year (China, US$3,300, and Asia, US$4,000), it's within earshot of its former colonial master. But it has a much healthier economy than Japan, and is growing much faster to be merely catching up.

For South Koreans, "nothing is overoptimistic," notes an observer. Global brands acknowledge how quickly South Korean names have risen. They are already well known for innovativeness and efficiency in electronics, cars, LCD display panels, and ships. And, are rising rapidly in building high-speed railways and atomic power plants. But new successes will not come easily. Its economic model needs to be regularly updated to boost productivity and develop a more competitive service industry to move rapidly up the value chain. Otherwise, they will be squeezed by low-cost producers from China, India, and other Asia, and out-innovated by the likes of the United States, Japan, and Germany. Under pressure on costs, South Korea knows it has to move into more advanced areas, like clean energy technology, including wind tunnels and hybrid electric cars. They are making strides in low-carbon industries (already commands one-fifth of global lithium battery production). Its well-developed technological infrastructure is a plus. After all, South Korea is the world's most wired nation—95 percent of homes have broadband (60 percent in Japan, 58 percent in Germany) with the highest connection speed (14.6 Mbps).

What, Then, Are We to Do?

Overseas, South Korea's top brands are making new breakthroughs. Samsung (the largest of Korea's 60 biggest business groups) already outsells Hewlett-Packard in electronics. According to a recent report, Samsung is on track to make more profits in 2010 than the top 15 Japanese electronics firms combined. Similarly, South Korean autos already have 8 percent of the US market. Given Toyota's predicament, Hyundai cars may well make further significant strides. Still, South Korea has a way to go. It has not yet arrived. But the South Korean spirit is no longer just one of catch-up. Its enterprises have demonstrated with increasing frequency a determination to compete almost anywhere and with almost anyone. They deserve the credit of always trying harder. They most certainly set a great example for the rest of Asia to follow.

Incheon, Seoul, South Korea
Kuala Lumpur
March 25, 2010

Note

1. First published on March 27, 2010, as "A More Competitive Korea Emerges."

CHAPTER 124

The Philippines: Its Turn Is Next[1]

I spent last weekend in Manila. I attended the 45th anniversary festivities of the Genting Group, including the opening of Resorts World Manila and the senior managers meeting of Genting Malaysia. The celebration culminated with a performance by Philippines' finest, world-renowned artist Lea Salonga. The presence of the president of the Philippines was not conspicuous, while his senior ministers passionately promoted their case at Invest Philippines. I was pleasantly surprised at the effective manner in which this forum was managed by senior officials, as well as international bankers who truly believed that the time has come for the Philippines to be noticed as a global investment destination. I should share with you the impressive case put together on: why invest in the Philippines. No doubt, there are valuable lessons to take on board.

New Broom, New Strategies

The Aquino administration's social contract with the Filipinos involves inclusive growth strategies to actively promote an enabling environment for private investment and entrepreneurship; equal access to development opportunities; and effective and responsive social safety nets leading toward high and sustained growth of real gross domestic product (GDP) of 7 to 8 percent in 2010 and 9 to 10 percent in 2011–2016. To make this happen, President Benigno "Noynoy" Aquino pledged to repair and make good what had troubled investors during previous administrations: (1) enforcing the rule of law for a peaceful and orderly society; (2) instituting effective anti-corruption measures; (3) promoting a stable macroeconomic environment; (4) implementing sound and consistent public policies; (5) providing adequate investment infrastructure; and (6) putting into place efficient investment programming processes.

These are bold promises. After all, the Philippines was ranked not so long ago in the World Economic Forum's bottom quartiles for organized crime, cronyism, and bureaucracy. Landing in Manila, the still-unfinished international airport is visible, mired in disputes for the past eight years. Continuing budget deficits mean the government is in no position to increase investment on its own, even with sovereign bond yields at record lows. Corruption and widespread bureaucracy discourage overseas investors, who have simply shied away. Of late, foreign direct investment has begun to improve; still, it's on course to reach only 0.3 percent of GDP, much below the average for the past 40 years. Realistically, this is what the new president has to reckon with since he took office in June, as he "plots to turn the ship around."

As Mr. Aquino begins his charm offensive, there is good news. GDP growth in the first nine months of 2010, at 7.5 percent, was the highest "honeymoon growth" in 20 years. The economy had contracted by 0.7 percent in the first three months of the Ramos administration; it grew by 1.3 percent during Estrada's debut, and by 5.6 percent when it was Gloria Arroyo's turn. Growth in the third quarter of 2010 was 6.5 percent, compared with 7.9 percent in the second quarter of 2010 and 6.7 percent in the first quarter of 2010. That's something when growth was 3.7 percent for 2008 and only 1.1 percent in 2009.

Inflation has been kept low. It recorded a 10-month low of 2.8 percent in October, and indications are that it will be below 2.9 percent in November 2010. The average for the first 11 months will be around 3.8 percent. For the full year, it's likely to settle at the lower end of the Central Bank's cap of between 3.5 percent and 5.5 percent. The appreciation of the peso helped. It certainly made imports cheaper. In early November, the peso hit 42-to-a-dollar territory—the strongest in two years, on the back of a surge in inflows of foreign portfolio investment. A benign inflation environment is expected over the next two years. With interest rates kept low, investors have turned bullish. The stock market soared to all-time highs—reached 4,397 on November 4, 2010 (last historical high was on October 8, 2007, at 3,873). That's up 44 percent since the beginning of the year, with three-quarters of the gain happening since June 30.

Why Has Growth Stalled?

Since Cory Aquino's "yellow" revolution in the mid-1980s, the Philippines has been marred by political uncertainty with generally unpopular presidents, especially in the 2000s. Politics has since become a structural constraint, joining other equally serious constraints to stall growth, including deteriorating budgetary positions with high debt-to-GDP ratios (exceeding 100 percent in the early 2000s; between 70 and 80 percent since then); debt servicing (interest payments) as a ratio of the budget exceeding 35 percent (now about 28 percent); dysfunctional government; and lack of funds to do anything significant. Growth was essentially consumption driven, rising 3.5 to 5 percent a year in the 2000s. Glaringly absent was demand from government spending and from private investment. In the 2000s, government output and private investment rose at a cumulative average growth rate of less than 1 percent a year—thus denying the economy of any stimulus from two otherwise strong pillars of any vibrant economy. In addition, bank lending was anemic; total bank lending accounted for only 38 percent of GDP in 2009, against ratios of between 100 and 120 percent in China and Malaysia. That is a lot of pent-up demand waiting to be satisfied.

Growth Framework

President Aquino is bent on turning the tables and unleashing this pent-up demand. He intends to push the macro-drivers really hard—ensuring political stability, improving fiscal affairs, pushing bank lending, getting the government to begin to pump prime, and incentivizing private investment and entrepreneurship. He has a reasonable chance of success, as the economy is in a sweet spot, characterized by strong stable growth, low inflation, a still undervalued peso, an increasingly diversified export base, and a rather robust outlook on its basic balance of payments position, reflecting possibilities of a further rising peso.

Unlike its peers, the Philippines enjoys two sweet spots, which underlie its stability. First, less external exposure. For Malaysia and Singapore, net exports account for about 15 percent of GDP; China, India, and Taiwan, 5 to 6 percent; Thailand and Korea, 3 percent. For the Philippines, its net exports are a negative 3 percent, not unlike India (–6 percent). Second, its benign inflation trajectory places it at an advantage of not being compelled to tighten monetary conditions anytime soon (as South Korea, India, Thailand, and Indonesia had to). Adding stability are another two reliable sources of growth, which are stable and recession proof, viz., remittances, which should bring in close to US$20 billion in 2010, and its US$9 billion business process outsourcing (BPO) industry, second only to India. Consequently, its external reserves strengthened to an all-time high of US$57 billion at the end of October 2010, close to 10 times its imports and 5 times its short-term foreign debt. That's a far cry from what it used to be.

A key element of its growth strategy is to promote investments. The focus is on (1) creating a better business environment; and (2) promoting key priority industries. The centerpiece is to improve infrastructure through public–private partnerships. Also included are new efforts at cutting red tape and reducing corruption. Priority industries being actively promoted include BPO/call centers, electronics, and tourism. A decade ago, the BPO/call center services barely existed. By 2011, total revenues could reach

US$12 billion (US$9.4 billion in 2010) employing 750,000 full-time personnel (560,000 in 2010). Big names include IBM, Accenture, and Convergys.

Electronics is also relatively new. Today, the Philippines is home to some of the world's top electronics firms, including top chip makers and four of the world's largest HDD companies (Hitachi, Toshiba, Fujitsu, and NEC). Their exports accounted for 58 percent of total exports in 2009. I well recall the Philippines was one of Asia's top tourist destinations in the 1960s and 1970s. They were so successful then that the Asian Development Bank (ADB) decided to site its headquarters in Manila. Today, Thailand attracts 1.4 million to 1.5 million tourists a month, Indonesia, 600,000. Monthly tourist arrivals in the Philippines totaled less than 300,000. Asia is expected to represent 32 percent of global travel spending by 2020, up from 21 percent at present. The Philippines plans to reposition itself to capture a significant part of this business.

Thinking out of the Box

For President Aquino, public–private partnerships (PPPs) hold great promise of lifting his country from the yoke of poverty. He realized that the government simply does not have the resources to build or to upgrade infrastructures like highways, airports, and power plants so essential to propel the economy. So, he invited private investors to provide the funding and expertise. This pro-investor stance is vital because of the delays in the negotiation and execution (and payment) of high-value contracts—or worse, investors spending loads of money on research, going through the bureaucratic maze of consultations and submissions, participating in long-winded bidding, and, after winning the contract, being unable to proceed due to some legal challenge. These have hounded most big-ticket projects undertaken by past administrations.

To resolve this, the president took the bold step to assure participants of PPPs that the government will give their money back if the regulators, Congress, or the courts stop their projects due to questions regarding their contracts or, worse, ordered them canceled by judicial fiat. To resolve this and get PPPs moving, he now promises reasonable returns and protection from "regulatory risks." Mr. Aquino explains: "If private investors are impeded from collecting contractually agreed fees—by the regulators, courts or legislators—then our government will use our resources to insure that they are kept whole."[2] He added that investors "cannot deal with a government where the right hand is offering a handshake and the left hand is trying to pick (their) pocket." This bold approach reflects, I think, the president's committed resolve to move forward, even if it meant being harrumphed as "heretical" in protecting investors from duplicities. It's an eye opener.

What, Then, Are We to Do?

The president's first test comes as he lures US$17 billion worth of PPPs to upgrade infrastructure and build new ones. His new assurances to investors have to work. He badly needs to rebuild credibility in fiscal affairs. In spite of persistent fiscal deficits, the Philippines remains a reputable borrower. It helps that Standard and Poor's gave it its first upgrade in 13 years this November, with a stable outlook. This simply means the rating will stay unchanged for at least a year. It's positive that spreads on Philippines debt paper have since fallen to 261 basis points, below the global average of 337 basis points. I am told that external debt markets are already treating Philippines a notch or two higher in ratings. Of course, Mr. Aquino still faces many risks, not least a possible prolonged global recession and political vested interests determined to thwart his many bold initiatives. In the end, the proof of the pudding is in the eating. As Lex (*Financial Times*) noted recently: "Even so, the challenge for "Noynoy" is daunting," at best.[3]

Manila, the Philippines
Kuala Lumpur
December 2, 2010

Notes

1. First published on December 4, 2010.
2. Artemio V. Panganiban, "Protection from Regulatory Risks," *Philippine Daily Inquirer* (November 28, 2010).
3. The Lex column, "The Philippines," *Financial Times* (November 25, 2010).

CHAPTER 125

Indonesia Losing Its Footing?[1]

Since Susilo Bambang Yudhoyono (SBY) came to power, I have been a fan. Mind you, Indonesia remains today a nation full of problems: political, economic, and social. His reputation was built on sustaining a predictable regulatory environment. Despite its problems, Fitch rerated Indonesia in December 2011 with an investment-grade credit after 14 years in junk status, followed by a similar move in January 2012 from Moody's Investors Service. Indonesia—like many in Asia—expects sluggish global demand to slow its rapid growth, to 6.43 percent in the first quarter of 2012—after posting gross domestic product (GDP) growth of 6.5 percent in 2011, the quickest pace since the 1997–1998 currency crisis. During my last visit in March 2012, I gathered investors are still flocking to Indonesia simply because there is a deep affiliation that "tomorrow will be better than today"; and today is pretty good—so far. Indonesia must realize that a good reputation is fragile. It is built over years, but can be destroyed overnight.

Resource Nationalism

Not long after Suharto's 1998 fall from power, Indonesia was transformed from a tightly controlled autocracy to become one of the world's most vibrant democracies. With the run-up to the 1999 elections, the military has since stayed on the sidelines. Sweeping political and fiscal decentralization devolved real power and resources to the nation's hundreds of districts and municipalities. The government created new, independent political institutions to provide for checks and balances, including a constitutional court, a judicial commission, and a corruption eradication commission. Constitutional reform formalized a presidential system under a direct one-man-one-vote regime, making Indonesia among the most democratic. The nation's economic turnaround has been no less dramatic.

Despite all the progress, there are decidedly many discordant notes. As US scholar Karen Brooks rightly pointed out: Indonesia's ports are

767

overstretched, its electrical grid is inadequate, and its road system is one of the least developed in the region.[2] These conditions make the Indonesian economy inefficient and will stifle its future growth. The president's new master plan (2011–2014), which emphasizes infrastructure development, is deemed inadequate. The government's dysfunctional regulatory framework and weak enforcement have discouraged private sector participation. Besides, the inability to acquire land and endemic corruption have held back development. Indeed, corruption now runs deep at all levels of government since the devolution. The SBY administration's promotion of Indonesia as an open, investor friendly economy has slipped—indeed, the gap between pronouncements and reality is rather wide. In fact, the backslide has reversed some of its international commitments.

The government's most recent Investment Negative List, which lays down limitations on foreign investment, is the most restrictive so far. The late-2010 rule requires foreign companies that open new mines to sell stakes to Indonesian participants starting with 20 percent by the 5th year. In late 2011, this would be progressively raised to 51 percent by the 10th.

It all started in 2009 when a new mining law changed the system based on contracts to one regulated by licenses. This gives bureaucrats more discretionary power. The latest proposal imposes a coal and base metals export tax of 25 percent this year, rising to 50 percent in 2013. As I understand it, this is ahead of a ban to be imposed on some unprocessed metals due in 2014. Its aim is to force the "beneficiation of minerals" in order to raise the value of exports as well as domestic employment. This policy is directed at extracting more from its resource base, particularly thermal coal (it being the world's largest exporter), diverting it largely to domestic use. These various moves have "upset" foreign direct investment (FDI). From their vantage point, these are reflective of: (1) evolving domestic political maneuvers; (2) government making policy on the run (ahead of presidential elections in 2014); and (3) growing resource nationalism. Given the government's frequent backflips (e.g., recent scaling back of gasoline subsidies), investors are expecting likely policy flip-flops. Indeed, indications are that some of the more extreme regulations are unlikely to be implemented. Jakarta had previously proposed minority ownership caps in banking, but has since apparently reversed its stance. Nevertheless, investors have reason to be nervous when regulators are known to be working with politically well-connected businessmen.

Economic Poster Child

During the Asian currency crisis (1997–1998), Indonesia looked like a state on the brink of collapse. The chaos left this nation, the fourth largest in the world—covering a sprawling archipelago of more than 17,000 islands,

240 million people, and the world's largest Muslim population—without hope. Today, Indonesia is hailed as the darling of the international financial community. In 1988, its economy contracted by more than 13 percent. Since then, it has expanded more than 5 percent a year, including 4.5 percent in 2009, when GDP in most of the rest of the world shrank. Last year, its economy expanded the fastest in 15 years, spurred by strong consumer spending and rapidly rising private investment outlays. Aggregate domestic consumption, which accounted for close-on two-thirds of GDP, rose by 4.7 percent in 2011, while private fixed capital formation expanded by 8.8 percent. FDIs ploughed in US$20 billion in 2011, up from US$17 billion in 2010. Singapore, Japan, and the United States were among the top investors, centered mainly in mining and telecommunications, as well as in much-needed infrastructure works.

Exports, too, had done well: They posted a 29 percent surge in 2011, exceeding the government's US$200 billion target. The current balance of payments continued to show a modest surplus. Its international reserves remain sizable, reaching close to US$120 billion at the end of 2011, its highest ever, covering 2.3 times its short-term external debt. The basic domestic forward-looking indicators have continued to look strong: Inflation fell to 4.1 percent in 2011 (6.3 percent in 2010) and held steady in the first quarter of 2012 (4 percent) although inflationary expectations are likely to stay elevated on uncertainty over the government's fuel-subsidy policy. The budget deficit had remained restrained (2 percent of GDP in 2011) and expected to fall to 1.5 percent in 2012. Reflecting the steady inflows of FDIs and strong exports, the exchange rate of the rupiah strengthened by about 3 percent in 2011. The industry sector has continued to expand—up 5.2 percent in 2011 (4.7 percent in 2010), with strong performance from the non–oil and gas manufacturing moving up by 7 percent for the first time since 2005.

Demographic Dividend

Sustaining growth in manufacturing has helped Indonesia create more jobs, especially higher value-added jobs to raise living standards and provide productive employment for the growing 2 million new entrants into the labor force annually. Indonesia already faces significant underemployment and poverty. In 2011, unemployment was 6.6 percent, while 12.5 percent still live below the poverty line, against unemployment of 9 percent and poverty off over 16 percent in 2004. But an estimated 65 percent of Indonesians are employed informally, mainly in agriculture. However, graduate unemployment has since dropped to 8 percent in 2011, from 11.9 percent in 2010. In recent years, the elasticity of employment growth to GDP has been around 0.5. That is, every 1 percentage point of GDP growth brings about a 0.5 percentage point rise in employment (i.e., creating about 500,000–600,000 jobs). But Indonesia has a young population, with a significant portion of its population still under the age of 30. This simply means that the proportion that is of working age will rise significantly over the next decade.

Economists like to link this with the prospect of a "demographic dividend," providing a comparative advantage over aging societies such as Japan and China. The younger generation will consume more, and contribute to a more productive labor pool. To reap this benefit, Indonesia will need to create more and more higher-quality and better-paying jobs to transform this into a real dividend. Herein lies the challenge. Nontraditional sectors such as finance, real estate, and manufacturing (including oil and gas) have increased their contribution to employment growth over the past three years. Potentially, they can provide important sources of higher productivity and higher wage jobs. For the government, realizing growth with quality job creation will require improvements in skills, education, and training, and a supportive regulatory environment. That is why attracting more and more FDIs must remain key to Indonesia's success in meeting this challenge. It is estimated that the nation requires more than US$400 billion up to 2025 to build the needed infrastructure and manufacturing base to create the jobs required.

The Outlook

Indonesia's growth has been remarkably stable and robust in recent years. GDP in the fourth quarter of 2011 expanded 6.5 percent, driven by strong household spending and private investment. Indications are that lower global demand for its exports had slowed its rapid pace in the first quarter of 2012. However, the outlook for 2012 remains clouded by uncertainties in a Europe already experiencing recession. Industrial production in the eurozone (accounting for 20 percent of its GDP) slumped in February 2012 by the steepest decline since end-2009. In the United States, growth remains tentative, while the rise in China's GDP would slacken to 8.25 percent this year (9.2 percent in 2011 and 10.4 percent in 2010). Its GDP rose 8.1 percent in the first quarter of 2012, the slowest in 11 quarters. According to the Asian Development Bank, emerging Asia's growth will "cool somewhat" to 6.9 percent in 2012, down from 7.2 percent in 2011, before edging higher again to 7.3 percent in 2013.[3] The region is shifting to a "more sustainable long-run growth path," based on strong domestic demand instead of exports, which have been hit by wobbly Western demand. For Indonesia, the median forecast of 11 leading economists was 6.48 percent in 2012, against a recently downgraded World Bank forecast of 6 percent.[4]

In recent years, Indonesia has benefited from political stability under SBY's administration, conservative fiscal management, and deep reserves of natural resources. Its debt-to-GDP ratio had fallen from a high of 100.3 percent in 2000 to only 26 percent today, which compares favorably with its Southeast Asian neighbors. Inflation was at a high of 77 percent in 1998; it now hovers at just about 4 percent in 2011. The rupiah, which lost over four-fifths of its value in 1998, is at its strongest since 2004—and up 31 percent since 2008. The recent upgrades by Moody's and Fitch are a testament to Indonesia's economic fundamentals, making demand for its bonds more attractive as yields are trending lower.

What, Then, Are We to Do?

Looking forward, domestic capacity constraints and the recently "turned adverse" business climate remain key development challenges, which can pull down Indonesia's growth outlook and diminish its ability to create quality jobs. Furthermore, budget execution difficulties carry the risk of poor disbursements and ineffective spending. According to my old friend, Dr. Arifin Siregar, a highly respected former Bank Indonesia governor: "It is now up to Indonesia to transform foreign businessmen's increasing interest in investing in our country into reality. We have to improve the efficiency and effectiveness of our bureaucracy. . . . Essential infrastructure facilities should be improved significantly to create a sound and competitive environment."[5]

Yet, as one market analyst recently observed: The only thing . . . certain about Indonesia's policies on resources is that there is no certainty whatsoever. On this, Jakarta appears to have dug itself into a hole. Indonesia used to be an easier option for many FDIs, but this may no longer be the case. As Siregar had concluded: "We should be prepared for the worst and at the same time to seize likely opportunities."[6] Indonesia deserves credit for what it has done. Some gains are now under threat. Continued success requires a new wave of reform. But if the risk and cost of investing continue to rise and be cloaked in legal uncertainty, Indonesia would be hurting only itself. Time has come for change and reform. Indonesia deserves firm and steadfast leadership.

Kuala Lumpur
April 19, 2012

Notes

1. First published on April 21, 2012.
2. Karen Brooks, "Is Indonesia Bound for the BRICS?" *Business Times,* Singapore (November 11, 2011).

3. Asian Development Bank (ADB), *Asian Development Outlook, Supplement* (Manila: ADB, December 2011).
4. World Bank, *Indonesia Economic Quarterly—Enhancing Preparedness, Ensuring Resilience* (Washington, DC: World Bank, December 2011), pp. 4–5.
5. Arifin M. Siregar, "The Challenge of Serious and Complex International Financial Developments: Indonesia's Position," *Economics and Finance in Indonesia*, vol. 59 (2011).
6. Ibid.

CHAPTER 126

Indonesia and India: Under New Management[1]

For historical reasons, no one seriously considers India and Indonesia as neighbors, although at their nearest points, these two nations are barely 100 miles apart across the Straits of Malacca. But the two economies have taken steps forward since Indian Prime Minister Narasimha Rao's 1991 policy of "Look East." Today, both are under new management. In India, Prime Minister Narendra Modi took charge soon after the landslide victory on May 17, 2014. In Indonesia, President-elect Joko "Jokowi" Widodo will assume office on October 20, 2014. Both leaders have promised to turn their slackening and staggering economies around, with high expectations that advancing growth will be given top priority in the early days of their administrations. Last week's Asian Development Bank updates trimmed its forecasts for Southeast Asia while keeping its July forecast for India, in the face of a slower world economy (the International Monetary Fund now forecasts growth at 3.4 percent, down from 3.7 percent in July), with extended stagnation in Europe as its main stumbling block.[2] With poor global demand, the export-led strategies of India and Indonesia will become more difficult to implement successfully.

India

Modi's stock is high; he exudes optimism—helping to spread the much-needed confidence India so badly needs. Yet his first budget mostly underwhelmed and failed to offer big reforms. "The Indian public is not ready for broader reforms," warns his finance minister.[3] Much of Modi's success rests on his platform of reform and growth. I am afraid if his administration doesn't set clear but attainable policy goals, his vast political capital can ebb away. Labor reform is worth fighting for because it is key to the success of his new economic model to create export manufacturing industries. After all, he needs to create 10 million new jobs a year. That means overhaul of labor laws and market regulations reform to incentivize business to expand and hire more to reap that "political dividend." I understand Modi has articulated a clear enough vision for the first time since Nehru. But he needs to rid old legacies that still linger—differences with its neighbors (Pakistan and China)—and ditch protectionism to promote India as a truly global trading nation. He has yet to face up to lowering fuel and fertilizer subsidies and tackling high food inflation—which means scrapping rules that persist in making agriculture unproductive and to support free trade. He has to shake up the noncompetitive, dreary retail trade in the broader context in letting in foreign expertise and capital. There is still no tax reform.

India today is remarkably similar to China in 2001. China's growth spurt was planted in 1978; India, in 1991. India's per-capita output in 2013 (adjusted for inflation) is about China's in 2000. But China, even in 2001, was much more manufacturing-export oriented than India is today, which is fueled by services (software and outsourcing). So, India arrives late at a party that is already very crowded mainly with Southeast Asia nations and Bangladesh. Still, India's advantage rests with its young. In 2000, the median Chinese was aged 30; the same Indian today is 27. Much to catch up.

The Reserve Bank of India (RBI) reported that economic recovery is uneven.[4] Gross domestic product (GDP) rose 5.7 percent in the second quarter of 2014 (against 4.6 percent in the first quarter of 2014), the quickest pace in two years. The road ahead remains bumpy. Although strong exports and better auto sales suggest recovery is on the way, fixed investment spending was disappointing. Investment needs to pick up. Modi has to follow through on his pledge to address structural bottlenecks that constrain industrial development, and more needs to be done to fix infrastructural regulations and implementation. I don't see how India can catch up without everything coming nicely together. Business and consumer confidence has since improved. Consumer prices are too high at 7.8 percent in August (8 percent in July). RBI's target is to stabilize retail inflation at 8 percent by January 2015 and 6 percent a year later to build enough confidence before it loosens policy to push private investment.[5] It's tough going.

India has been struggling with slowing growth and rising inflation for more than two years. The economy grew 4.7 percent in year-ended March 2014—first time in 25 years GDP expanded below 5 percent two years in a row. Optimists say even the mere anticipation of change will lift the economy. Mr. Modi has already opened up railways to foreign investment; allowed more foreign ownership in defense; and got rid of the Planning Commission. But many also gripe that the razzmatazz glitters more than the real substance. Sure, inflation has softened, but things can just as easily reverse—lower than normal rains can boost food prices or oil and gas prices can climb on new Middle East turmoil. Inflation remains of deep concern—as it should. Another spoiler could come as US or European monetary policies could reignite uncertainties to destabilize the rupee. But inflation flare-ups aside, India badly needs real reform change—the sooner the better.

Indonesia

Investors can't wait until Jokowi assumes office. The anticipation is catching. Already, he is reported to be busy placating allies and building a government as transformational as his candidacy. Still, he has to deal with his rival's majority control of the national legislature. Nevertheless, the government and parliament have since agreed to withdraw the cap on foreign ownership of plantations at no more than 30 percent, from up to a maximum 95 percent at present.[6] Scrapping the cap will improve the business climate. But Jokowi will need to take difficult early decisions. Foremost is how to trim the nation's disastrous fuel subsidies, which threatens to undercut its own programs. The fuel subsidy costs US$31 billion in 2014, 18 percent of the budget. At about US$2 a gallon, it carries a 50 percent subsidy. Eliminating it will trigger inflation and raises the price of anything shipped by road, rail, sea, and air. The impact can be far reaching. Much of the subsidy is, however, enjoyed by the growing middle class. Subsidizing fuel has also created a lucrative opportunity for smugglers.

Jokowi takes over a nation whose finances are dire—its external current payments (balance of payments, or BOP) deficit more than doubled in the second quarter of 2014, reflecting not just slowing growth but also rapidly rising fuel subsidies. Bank Indonesia had estimated that the BOP deficit of US$9.1 billion in 2014 represents 4.3 percent of GDP (2.06 percent in the first quarter of 2014)—its worst ever. GDP growth in the second quarter of 2014 slackened to 5.12 percent (5.22 percent in the first quarter of 2014, and 5.7 percent in the fourth quarter of 2013), the weakest in five years.[7] The widening payments gap exerts pressure on the rupiah, even though inflation has slowed significantly (realistically estimated to be 6 percent for 2014 as a whole). Headline inflation was reported to be 4.53 percent in September. Bank Indonesia seeks to keep inflation within 3.5 to 5.5 percent in 2014. The World Bank reckons the 2014 fiscal deficit will be 2.8 percent of GDP, close to the legal limit of 3 percent, but still vulnerable to rising oil prices and a depreciating rupiah.[8] Subsidies already account for about 3 percent of GDP.

Jokowi inherits a budget that leaves him little room to maneuver. Yet, he had pledged to raise GDP growth to 7 percent within two years by attracting foreign investment, especially in manufacturing and cutting red tape; to boost infrastructure investment (fix dilapidated ports, roads, and utilities); and to expand access to education and healthcare that is ultimately causing the severe shortage of skills and lack of productivity gains. As a result, the budget will be even more squeezed. As a trade-off, fuel subsidies are best eliminated to provide fiscal space to accommodate and support structural policy changes.

Trade-offs does mean hard choices. He already has his hands full trying to meet three critical challenges: Reverse the twin external and budget deficits, contain inflation, and bolster the rupiah in the face of four vital imperatives: (1) holding monetary policy tight; (2) maintaining protectionism to retain more resources for domestic use; (3) cutting fuel subsidies; and (4) boosting investment especially in infrastructure. Given these obvious short-run constraints, Jokowi will have to trade off for lower growth in order to get the economy back on an even keel, after weaning Indonesians off their dependence on resources. Nevertheless, I am sure he'll still do his darnedest to push investment in infrastructure and cut red tape in order to truly deliver. Realistically, I expect growth to moderate to between 5 percent and 5.5 percent, with inflation holding at 5 to 6 percent over the next year. Getting the economy to grow at 7 percent by 2017 remains a serious challenge.

What, Then, Are We to Do?

Both India and Indonesia are at the crossroads, trying to reduce their twin external and budget deficits, bolster their currencies, and battle to contain inflation, while holding on to stabilize growth in the region of 5.5 to 6 percent, which they both badly need to create enough jobs. The key rests on strong political will to curb (even scrap) fuel subsidies, which they cannot afford. If they succeed, inflation will soar and, with it, possible political unrest. If they waiver, the budget deficit will worsen and their currencies will weaken. The policy dilemma is difficult, but both leaders have sufficient political capital to take the high road and do the right thing to conserve badly needed resources to promote investment and growth. For both leaders, building infrastructure provides both a business opportunity and an enabler for long-term development. Surely, India and Indonesia deserve better.

Kuala Lumpur
October 1, 2014

Notes

1. First published on October 4, 2014.
2. Asian Development Bank updates to the 2014 outlook were released in Singapore on September 26, 2014, as reported in *The Edge Financial Daily* on September 27, quoting Reuters; Christine Lagarde, managing

director, International Monetary Fund, at a news conference in Cairns (Australia) during the G-20 meeting on September 21, 2014.

3. Arun Jaitley, minister of finance, India, presenting his 2015 budget to the Indian parliament on July 10, 2014, New Delhi.

4. Raghuram Rajan, governor, Reserve Bank of India, at a banking conference in Mumbai on September 15, 2014, quoting the latest data released by India's Ministry of Statistics on August 29, 2014.

5. Reserve Bank of India, in a statement issued after the bank's regular policy meeting in Mumbai on September 30, 2014.

6. Reported on September 15, 2014, by Indonesia's news agency Kontan and published in *The Edge Financial Daily* (September 18, 2014).

7. Bank Indonesia, as reported by Reuters and published in the *Jakarta Post* (August 14, 2014).

8. Karen Brooks, "A Daunting Agenda for Jokowi," *Asian Wall Street Journal* (August 26, 2014), p. 11, quoting the World Bank.

CHAPTER 127

Vietnam Wakes Up:
Ding Dong Dung[1]

I was back in Hanoi in early October 2012 after a long absence. Change is all over, reflecting the impact of breakneck growth. It so happens my revisit coincided with the Vietnam Communist Party's (VCP) 175-member Central Committee (CC) meeting, preoccupied with two main issues: the political future of its prime minister (PM), Nguyen Tan Dung, and what to do with recent financial scandals amid slackening of its once-red-hot economy in the face of a depreciating dong (its currency).

Word around Hanoi was that Mr. Dung, generally regarded as a pro-West liberal, was under immense pressure to convince his CC colleagues that he deserves a second chance to put the nation back on a firm footing and get the economy onto high gear once again. Mr. Dung is a survivor. A former governor of the State Bank (Vietnam's central bank), Mr. Dung is a street-smart politician, having fought with Vietcong guerrillas against the United States, and who once served as the nation's public security chief. He was first appointed PM in 2006 and charged with continuing economic reforms that pushed the war-torn backwater nation into a promising emerging economy. In 2007, he steered the nation into the World Trade Organization (WTO), which triggered a new wave of foreign direct investment (FDI) inflows. Unfortunately, the nation was caught in an inflationary spiral (reaching a high of 23 percent in August 2011), driving the government to tighten policies, slow down growth, and force a series of devaluations of the dong. Mr. Dung stood for reelection to the CC and Political Bureau (PB), the nation's top policymaking body, and was reappointed PM for a second term in May 2011. He survived it all despite the damaging VCP Political Report and Socio-Economic Report—containing "criticism and self-criticism, as part of the party's rectification campaign" against poor economic management—both of which were nevertheless approved at the 11th Party National Congress in January 2011.

The Politics

Vietnam politics is unique. I sense from talking to friends in Hanoi at the time of its CC meeting that top leaders from the PM to the VCP president to its party chief all acknowledge the government's shortcomings in managing the economy in recent years. Specifically, they all talk openly of the slowest pace of economic growth in 13 years, amid signs of unease over high levels of bad debts in banks and the widening wealth gap. As a result of poor supervision, some of the largest and most influential state-owned enterprises (SOEs) racked up multibillion losses (e.g., Vinashin, a vast government-owned shipbuilding group, which almost sank in 2010 after straying far from its core business). Growing corruption has led to loss of confidence following a recent series of arrests (and some convictions) of financial executives for wrongdoing, including a prominent tycoon at Asia Commercial Bank close to Mr. Dung. All of these have exposed a series of long-simmering political tensions within the highest echelons of the ruling VCP.

All these serve to underscore why top officials are getting increasingly concerned and sensitive to how they are being perceived by investors and an economically anxious public, especially its growing middle class. Indeed, signs are everywhere: (1) new rules on "no more lavish weddings"—to the extent of limiting the number of guests allowed to be present and avoiding hosting banquets in luxury hotels; (2) new laws (for the first time) empowering the National Assembly to force incompetent leaders to step down or face a vote of no confidence; (3) recent convictions against bloggers (and songwriters) for online "anti-government propaganda"; and (4) crackdown on new popular Internet sites in recent months (Vietnam has 34 percent Internet penetration) such as "Quan Lam Bao" (or Officials Doing Journalism)—its anonymous contributors purportedly provide inside "goings-on" information at the highest echelons of power. All of these point to the lack of transparency and accountability in public governance.

I am told the PM managed to survive because:

- He has enough "support votes" at CC.
- There is no credible successor in sight.
- His ouster would destabilize the party, so best not to allow "enemy forces to exploit the regime's current problems."
- The government team bears collective responsibility for poor management.
- It is best to retain the PM to correct mistakes and move forward.

I am also told "repeated forgiveness" is a commonly accepted way to settle complex problems—as Vietnamese as a bowl of pho. Forgiveness heals and prevents the party from splitting. The show must go on. But for how long, where corruption poses a major threat to the legitimacy of one-party politics?

The Economy

Vietnam was Asia's new poster child for development. With the war a distant memory, progress achieved since 1986 when it first embarked on the new path of Doi Moi (reform) has been nothing but spectacular. It has well surpassed the milestone per-capita income of US$1,000. Vietnamese now enjoy their newfound wealth. Until lately, Vietnam was among the least impacted by the second round global crisis, with private consumption and diversified exports driving domestic activity. Retail experience in Hanoi and Ho Chi Minh City includes shopping in malls, like Malaysia's Parkson, for Gucci, Louis Vuitton, Chanel, and so forth, and relaxing with refreshments at Starbucks or Circle K, and dinner at Hard Rock Café. The lifestyle is fast changing. But all has not been rosy—this hyperactivity came with a cost: high inflation and a growing trade deficit. But Vietnamese learn swiftly from past mistakes and they now appear to be addressing growing pains with the needed commitment, slowly but surely. Four compelling forces help drive the current revival:

1. **Political stability**—it's ahead of the BRICS (Brazil, Russia, India, China, and South Africa) according to the World Bank.
2. **Attractive demography**—with a population close to 95 million: low labor cost, high literacy (93 percent), and 65 percent within the working age.
3. **Domestic-demand-driven economy**—its large, young population riding on rapid early stage industrialization, realizing its newfound wealth, with a deep thirst for housing and consumption.
4. **Resource rich with a large agricultural base**—exports account for up to 70 percent of gross domestic product (GDP) (having risen two-and-a-half times in 2004–2008). It's the world's largest rice and coffee exporter, a net exporter of crude oil and gas, and exports a wide range of minerals, including bauxite, coal, nickel, iron-ore, gold, and tungsten.

No wonder it's labeled the "next China," or sometimes, "China plus One" (it's like China but is one-up with cheaper labor) to attract multinationals to spread their bets. But it badly needs more physical infrastructure (power, water, highways, ports); diversified social infrastructure (education, hospitals, housing, welfare safety net); sound financial infrastructure (money and capital markets); and a strong commitment to realistic macroeconomic planning.

Struggling Again

Today, Vietnam's economy remains weak and needs additional stimulus and "easier" policies to get back on track. The first quarter of 2012 growth at only 4 percent was the weakest in three years, slowing from 6.1 percent in the fourth quarter of 2011 and an average annual rate of 7.7 percent from 2003 to 2008. Latest indicators point to GDP growth in the first half of 2012 of 4.4 percent (4.7 percent in the second quarter of 2012), well below the government's 6 percent full year's target. FDI was down nearly 30 percent in the first half of 2012 and toxic "nonperforming loans" in the fragile banking system is at 8.82 percent as at end-September 2012 (up from 6 percent at end 2011). Independent analysts place the ratio at as high as 15 percent in the face of 8 to 10 percent suggested by the State Bank in August. For the year as a whole, GDP growth is now expected at 5.2 percent (against 5.9 percent in 2011).

No doubt, the economy is much weaker, but the International Monetary Fund anticipated it to rise to 5.9 percent in 2013. Following a series of determined monetary policy moves to contain inflation, consumer prices rose 7 percent in October 2012, against 6.5 percent in September having dropped to a three-year low of 5.04 percent in August (well off its 23 percent peak a year earlier).

With growth slackening, the government appears determined to keep inflation below 8 percent for the whole of 2012. "We have learned our lesson," declared the PM. In October, Fitch Ratings maintained its rating for Vietnam's major banks at "B" (junk status) with a stable outlook—among the lowest in Asia. The ranking "reflects difficult domestic operating conditions and other structural issues typically found in low-income emerging markets," Fitch said. Moody's Investors downgraded the nation's rating in late September 2012, citing moral hazard risks requiring the government to pump in substantial bank capital. Standard and Poor's talks of the need for fewer but stronger banks with credible risk management and a need for greater foreign participation to facilitate transfer of best practices and processes to strengthen domestic banks.

Moving Forward

To reset its growth path moving forward, Vietnam needs a second Doi Moi—moving away from reliance on cheap labor and capital and big government, toward serious reforms focusing on banks, SOEs, and public spending. The challenges will be absorbing—inflation has surged above 20 percent twice in the past three years, while foreign exchange reserves have slumped and the "ding-dong" dong has lost more than 20 percent against US$. Its external debt is more than 40 percent of GDP, and bank credit to GDP, 125 percent. Excessive investment in inefficient SOEs has misdirected capital, straying wildly into noncore activities such as property and stocks, both of which have badly faltered. Many of their problems can be traced to the mismanagement of SOEs: 10 largest SOEs ran up debts of US$50 billion, or about 50 percent of GDP in 2010. It is obvious they need more robust and rigorous supervision. Getting the party and politics out of the management and SOEs is the answer. It's about time to experience Schumpeterian "creative destruction."

The path back requires the restoration of the people's faith. Vietnam's 1 percent interest rate cut in June 2012 for the fourth time this year reflects the government's determination to revive the economy. This meant refinancing rate falls to 11 percent, discount rate to 9 percent, and overnight rate for interbank electronic payments to 12 percent—still high by international standards, but leaves much room for further cuts. Slackening growth will make the fight to contain inflation easier. With determined efforts, inflation will slow down over time. But the economy needs basic reform in major policy areas like healthcare and education, jobs creation, industrial policy, privatization (they call it "equitization"), social safety net, housing, and anti-corruption efforts through "smaller but smarter" government. In conversations with friends in Hanoi, I sense investors and the public have become more impatient as the government is too slow in delivering. Hence, their economic advancement since has been slow and hesitant. Yet, there is not a cohesive and united group of leaders to bring about the change that everyone talks about so passionately—this desire to restart serious reforms.

What, Then, Are We to Do?

I first visited both Hanoi and Ho Chi Minh City in the early 1980s. One thing hasn't changed over 30 years: Then, I heard of the Vietnamese dream for a strong, authoritarian, benevolent, and fair leader who can deliver to the nation its past glory. Today, they are still dreaming the same dream. Nothing has changed except the capital cities are buzzing with energy, swarmed by tourists and plagued with convoluted traffic jams—signs of growing vitality. But it masks symptoms of a nation with deep-rooted woes, desperately in need of firm and honest leadership. The young now find it harder to get jobs; small- and medium-sized businesses have a tough time coping; and public projects are often delayed or canceled. It's curious: When I was there, the best the CC, PB, and the party could do was to adopt a new motto for planning future weddings: "playful—healthy—thrifty." What a shame they are still dancing around the peripheral. The time for reform is now.

Hanoi
Kuala Lumpur
November 30, 2012

Note

1. First published on December 1, 2012, as "Ding Dong Dung, Wake Up Vietnam."

CHAPTER 128

Thailand on the Rebound[1]

The Thai economic rebound is beating expectations. February 2013 estimates by the National Economic and Social Development Board (NESDB)
point to robust private spending in both consumption and investment, which
pushed the fourth quarter of 2012 gross domestic product (GDP) growth to
close on 19 percent, exceeding 3.1 percent in the third quarter of 2012 and the
15.4 percent median by Dow Jones survey of economists.[2] Economic activity
was earlier brought down sharply by natural disasters of unprecedented proportions (first, the impact of Japanese earthquake and tsunami in the second
quarter of 2011 via supply chain disruptions, and later, massive flooding in the
fourth quarter of 2011, the worst in nearly 70 years) from a +7.8 percent clip
in 2010 to hardly any growth in 2011 as a whole (fourth quarter of 2011 contracted –9 percent). Total losses were estimated at 3 to 4 percent of GDP. The
Thai economy has since recovered nicely, although it is still affected by slackening global economic growth and trade. Nevertheless, positive signs abound.

V-Shaped Recovery

Against this backdrop amid heightened widespread fragility about the global outlook, NESDB now expects the Thai economy to expand at 6.4 percent
for 2012 as a whole (0.1 percent in 2011 and 7.8 percent in 2010), much
higher than 5.5 percent estimated by the International Monetary Fund (IMF)
in April 2012; 4.7 percent by the World Bank in December 2012; and a median 5.4 percent expected by private economists.

Growth was supported by an upsurge in household consumption and
much higher investment outlays by both government (reflecting mainly
massive disaster rehabilitation and the impact of consumption stimulation
measures) and private fixed capital spending as inflows of foreign direct
investment (FDI) capital resume. Inflation remained low and stabilized at
about 3 percent (+3.4 percent in January 2013), which is expected to persist. Core inflation has averaged at below 2 percent, well within Bank of

Thailand's target. Net exports were hit by production disruptions in the first half of 2012 and by a sharp slackening of demand in the second half of 2012 from the United States and Europe, as well as China, India, and Southeast Asia. Thai export growth is highly correlated with the rise in world trade, which rose only 3.7 percent in 2012 (6 percent in 2011). Export growth fell to 3.6 percent, and is expected to recover only moderately (+5.5 percent) in the course of 2013. The current external payments balance in 2012 will be just about flat. Cheap capital is flooding into Asia, including Thailand. The baht has since gained about 2.5 percent this year against US$. It remains one of Asia's strongest currencies and is helping to hold down inflation to complement the government's price control and subsidies' efforts, which as a whole cost the budget 3.5 percent of GDP. However, the budget deficit remains low (2.7 percent of GDP in 2012) and should stabilize in 2013 so that total public debt, including off-budget debt of government entities, would reach less than 50 percent of GDP in 2013, which is not considered excessive. Moreover, more than 90 percent of this debt comprised domestic long-term debt. The financial system remains stable.

The economy in 2013 is expected to continue to expand as manufacturing production fully recovers from floods and natural disasters, and as the global economy, especially China, tracks a modest comeback. Exports will grow somewhat faster, as will domestic demand, particularly investment outlays, sustaining the momentum as FDIs continue to rise. NESDB expects GDP to grow at 4.5 to 5.5 percent in 2013, with inflation stabilizing at 2.5 percent, and core inflation, no more than 2 percent. Domestic demand, especially private outlays on fixed investment, will pick up, complemented by strong public spending with implementation of massive water management projects initiated in 2012. In the near term, I concur with the IMF that Thailand needs to focus on the "challenge of rebuilding the economy in the near term, and restoring confidence while maintaining macroeconomic and fiscal stability and promoting inclusive growth."[3] Its near-term prospect is promising. January 2013 trade data support this outlook. Nevertheless, risks significantly tilted to the downside still remain and stem from both the volatile global economy and challenging domestic conditions.

The Risks

The Thai economy remains vulnerable to weak growth among its major trading partners, especially China and Southeast Asia. Domestically, political tensions and capacity constraints in public spending on reconstruction, including adverse climate change, could work against its growth outlook. Government's priority in making growth more inclusive is the right way to go. But higher wages will need to be accompanied by productivity gains to raise competitiveness.

Global Growth

Combined GDP of Organisation of Economic Co-operation and Development (OECD) (comprising 34 developed nations) is now shrinking (–0.6 percent) for the first time in the fourth quarter of 2012, after 13 consecutive quarters of growth. It's a sign of how fragile the global economy is, just when it appeared the recovery was gathering strength. It is unusual for downturns to be so widespread. Growth was negative in the United States, eurozone, the United Kingdom, and Japan. For 40 years, there have been only 13 such quarterly downturns: three in 1974–1975 following the first oil crisis; four in 1980s during the double-dip US recession; one in 2001; and four in 2008–2009 during the Great Recession, and now in the fourth quarter of 2012. Recent weakness is unusual in that there has been no countercyclical support from government in the face of a weak economy. Historically, it is most unusual for government spending to fall when economies weaken. In the United States, there was no single quarter in the first decade of this century when public consumption actually fell. But, that's now changing. It's the new normal in the United States and the eurozone because of fiscal austerity.

The World Bank forecasts almost flat OECD growth in 2013 (1.2 percent in 2012 and 1.5 percent in 2011), with eurozone growing marginally (if at all) against a contraction of 0.3 percent in 2012.[4] I now expect US growth to be closer to 0 to 1 percent than 2 percent (2.1 percent in 2012), and Japan, 1 to 1.2 percent (0.9 percent in 2012). As a result, global GDP will inch up 1.5 to 2.6 percent this year, against 2.3 percent in 2012; its June 2012 forecast had expected 2013 growth to reach 3 percent. The recovery (if any) is late in coming, expected now only in the third quarter of 2013. I agree with the World Bank that a drawn-out political battle in United States over raising the debt ceiling and sequestration (automatic budget spending cuts that became effective March 1) could hit growth, raise unemployment, spark a loss of confidence in US$, and unnerve financial markets.

The European Commission's latest downbeat forecast adds new gloom as Europe struggles with dual burdens of half-heartedly trying to stimulate growth while cutting public spending to pare deficits and debt. The credibility of its growth forecasts of 1.8 percent for the European Union (EU) in 2014 (1.4 percent in eurozone) is undermined by the fourth quarter of 2012 negative growth rates just reported for Germany, France, United Kingdom, and Italy in addition to Spain, Greece, and Portugal. Europe's insistence on austerity is creating a self-perpetuating cycle: Demand is diminished and growth falters; the negative impact on tax revenues will further exert strains on its fiscal finances.

The World Bank also cut its forecasts for developing economies as a whole to 5.6 percent in 2013 (from 6 percent in its June forecast) against 5.2 percent in 2012, its slowest pace in a decade.[5] Growth is likely to gradually pick up, reaching 5.75 to 6 percent over 2014–2015. Before the crisis, developing nations expanded at 7.5 percent. The World Bank projected Chinese growth to reach 8.4 percent in 2013, then slowing down to 7.9 percent by 2015 (against 7.8 percent in 2012 and 10.4 percent in 2010). The economy can grow briskly this year considering many infrastructure projects were fast-tracked by government in the second half of 2012 (new highways, ports, railways, sewage networks) and the built-in momentum of economic reforms. The World Bank did note, however, that many developing nations were already operating at near full capacity and additional measures to boost GDP risk rekindling inflation. I should add the growing "bitter" China–Japan territorial dispute can have long-lasting consequences on growth on both sides, with serious spillover effects across the region.

It is clear recovery remains fragile and volatile, clouding the outlook for an early return to robust growth. But bear in mind the volume of trade among developing nations has exceeded that of rich nations for the first time in 2011. Also, developing economies have since built up self-generating supporting activities on their own, creating a newfound engine. Still, many risks remain—a eurozone implosion could lead to another bout of devastating contagion; clumsy fumbling by the United States over the budget and debt stalemate could have unintended depressive side effects; substantial fall in investments in China could turn off private demand; oil and food prices could rise sharply to pull back consumption; and political tensions between China and Japan could spill into bouts of wasteful military adventures. These risks will not be easy to manage.

Minimum Wage

Rising wages represent a tough challenge for risk management amid sustained rapid growth. There is a global phenomenon, reflecting years of widening income gaps between rich and poor, and rising labor discontent. It's happening in China, Indonesia, and Malaysia. In 2012, Indonesian workers secured minimum wage increases above 20 percent. In Peninsular Malaysia, a minimum wage of RM900 (or US$300) a month will come into effect this January for the first time. Even in China, the prime minister just flagged plans to boost minimum wages this year following significant pay increases at many of the largest manufacturers in the past two years. In Thailand, minimum wages were raised 40 percent in April 2012, and this minimum increases to US$10 a day nationwide beginning this year, up 22.4 percent from the 2012 benchmark, a level that's competitive with Malaysia.

Currently, about 5.4 million workers (14 percent of labor force), mostly women and those with low levels of education and skills, earn below this minimum wage. In the past decade, minimum wages rose only 2.5 percent annually on the average, well below the rate of inflation. So this latest move represents a big deal for labor as well as business. To be sustainable over the longer run, however, labor productivity needs to rise in tandem to raise competitiveness. This simply means promoting more capital investments to boost productivity, more public spending on vocational education and training, and more incentives for wider workers' skill development. Empirical evidence across Asia points to a strong correlation between workplace skills and innovation, productivity, and growth.

Subsidies

Subsidies present yet another big risk. They now cost the Thai government the equivalent of 3.4 percent of GDP, comprising the cut in corporate income tax to assist business to better cope with the minimum wage hike; lower fuel excise tax to lift the poor; tax refund for first-time home buyers and car buyers; and rice price guarantee scheme to support farm incomes. This burden reflects the cost to government of alleviating income inequality, including discrepancies in regional income, which are large and growing; promoting more inclusive growth, tapping underdeveloped regions; and raising wages to help bridge income gaps. Over time, these supportive policies need to gradually unwind to allow sufficient time for the private sector to adapt and avoid inflationary pressures that would otherwise require tighter monetary policies.

Aging Demography

Thai population is aging—its old-age dependency ratio of 12 in 2010 (percentage of population exceeding 60 years old) is only second to Singapore within Southeast Asia. By 2050, the ratio would jump to about one-third! Already, public health spending will rise from 2.8 percent of GDP in 2010 to 3.9 percent in 2030. Though not alarming by international standards, growing pressure to improve the coverage and quality of social protection will rise as income rises. The challenge is to so manage this risk that healthcare and social welfare programs are sufficiently resilient to meet the evolving demographic changes.

What, Then, Are We to Do?

We often hear: The economy and markets now face more uncertainty, not less. So much so "uncertainty" has become the watchword for politicians and chief executive officers as an explanation (perhaps, even an excuse) for slow growth, rising market volatility, lack of commitment to hire, and so on.

Of late, uncertainty about sustainability of central bank largesse (the Fed— US Federal Reserve—printing cheap money) in the face of a fragile global economy left investors climbing up the "wall of worry." It even brought on, in late February 2013, the worst two-day fall in US S&P 500 stock index since November 2012, fearing the Fed will slow down or stop quantitative easing (QE3) through more bond purchases) from stimulating the United States and the world. None of this is new. It just goes to show that many still harbor the belief that Asia's success merely reflects continuing demand from the rich West. Like it or not, this risk is real and Asia learns to live with it. Be that as it may, at this time, it makes more sense for Asia, whether Thailand, Malaysia, or Indonesia, to focus its policies on time-tested underlying drivers of prosperity, instead of relying on stimulative quick fixes. They should look to themselves and implement previously successful productivity-enhancing policies in structural reforms, education and training, and the competitive use of resources.

Kuala Lumpur
March 6, 2013

Notes

1. First published on March 9, 2013.
2. As reported in "Thai Economy Beats Expectations," *Asian Wall Street Journal*, Bangkok (February 19, 2013).
3. International Monetary Fund (IMF), "Thailand—2012 Article IV Consultation," *IMF Country Report* No. 124 (Washington, DC: IMF, June 2012), p. 4.
4. World Bank, *Thailand Economic Monitor, December 2012* (Washington, DC: World Bank, December 2012), pp. 3–7.
5. Ibid., pp. 8–9.

CHAPTER 129

Myanmar: Not the Burma
I Used to Know[1]

A century ago, Rangoon (now Yangon) was one of Asia's great trading centers and home to a diverse ethnic mix. Its nineteenth-century population of 100,000 has since swelled to about 6 million in greater Yangon, which now suffers from cracking infrastructure, electricity brownouts, traffic congestion, and growing pollution. I first visited the city in the mid-1960s as a young central banker (and have been back often up until the 1990s), working alongside prominent bankers and economists at the then–Union Bank of Burma (the central bank). Its colorful history is reflected in the city's heart, where ancient Buddhist pagodas sit next to churches and cathedrals, Sunni and Shia mosques, Hindu and Parsee temples, and a Jewish synagogue. I well recall at its very center stands the magnificent Shwedagon Pagoda sitting serenely in gold glittering amid the city skyline. Then, Yangon was the home to hundreds of Victorian and Edwardian-era buildings, including the edifices of Lloyds and HSBC bank, and the all-teak Pegu Club where Rudyard Kipling stayed.

I am told many have since been demolished to make way for development. What a pity. But even then, I was glad the Victorian-era Strand Hotel (that once welcomed George Orwell) has been transformed from a run-down budget hotel into an elegant five-star. Before the makeover, I recall being seated at lunch in the sparsely furnished hotel café and being told that its original eight-page menu (dating back to pre–World War II) now carried only plain sandwiches—all else were just not available. Even so, the Yangon of today is nothing like the quaint 1960s Rangoon I used to know.

No More Burma

With the combined size of France and Britain, resource-rich Myanmar sits strategically between India and China and alongside Southeast Asia, with ports on the Indian Ocean and the Andaman Sea. As such, it is coveted by China's western provinces as a strategic energy-security asset. Bordering five nations (including Bangladesh, Thailand, and Laos) with Malaysia to the south, Myanmar offers multiple avenues for Asian engagement as the United States shifts its focus to the growth axis within the Asia-Pacific region. Yet poverty is jarringly endemic, especially outside Yangon. While the European Union has started to unwind sanctions, punitive US measures continue to cut deep into the domestic economy. Bear in mind that Myanmar was among Asia's most prosperous before the 1962 military coup ushered in the disastrous "Burmese Way to Socialism" that brought sweeping nationalization and rapid global isolation.

After 50 years of often-brutal military rule, Myanmar is today one of the world's poorest. One-third of its 60 million people live on less than US$1 a day! The International Monetary Fund (IMF) estimated its gross domestic product (GDP) to be just over US$50 billion.[2] Its neighbor, Thailand, with 67 million, has a GDP (US$350 billion) that is seven times larger. Similarly, Malaysia's GDP (US$285 billion) is nearly six times its size but has about one-half its population. Years of mismanagement by a corrupt and inept military regime have left Myanmar without a functioning economy. I am told a trip to the countryside can feel like a ride in a time machine back to preindustrial society—oxen drive ploughs where houses are thatched and use bamboo extensively. Most areas are devoid of sewage, paved roads, or cell phone reception. Residents power light bulbs with car batteries, even though there are few cars in sight.

Myanmar is poised at an important juncture in its often-tragic history. Reform, to paraphrase Victor Hugo, is an idea whose time has come. In the 12 months since he became president, U Thien Sein has led his nation down a radical path away from dictatorship to elections, vowing to "root out the evil legacies deeply entrenched in our society." By all accounts, the bookish 66-year-old leader is no radical reformer—I have heard visiting generals refer to him as the Gorbachev of Myanmar—prematurely, I think. An adviser to the former president described him as: "Not ambitious; not decisive; not charismatic; but very sincere." Despite the nascent signs of change, Aung San Suu Kyi sums up the outlook best early this year to a group of visiting Malaysians: "I don't think it's past the point where you can say it's irreversible. But we are going to have to make it irreversible. . . . I think, the (investors) should wait a little."

IMF Optimistic

The IMF's economic report in January 2012 concluded:

> *The new government is facing a historic opportunity to jump-start the development process and lift living standards. Myanmar has a high growth potential, and could become the next economic frontier in Asia, if it can turn its rich natural resources, young labor force and proximity to some of the most dynamic economies in the world into its advantage.*"[3]

Its recent efforts are in the right direction, starting with establishing macroeconomic stability, mainly at improving monetary and fiscal management. It has started the process with working plans to unify the exchange rate and to gradually lift exchange restrictions on current international payments and transfers. Modernizing the economy will also involve removing impediments to growth: from enhancing the business and investment climate, to modernizing the financial system, to liberalizing trade and foreign direct investment (FDI). However, foreign banks are unlikely to be let in before 2015. There is still much to change. Given decades of neglect, "You name it, we need to reform it," remarked a senior government adviser. Fortunately, they are open to outside help with the reform process, unusual for a regime that used to regard global institutions with great suspicion.

The IMF estimates GDP growth in Myanmar will rise by 5.5 percent in FY2011–2012 and then by 6 percent in FY2012–2013, stimulated by buoyant commodity exports and fixed investment reflecting improved business confidence. Inflation is expected at 4.2 percent currently with the recent fall in food prices, but anticipated to rise to 5.8 percent in FY2012–2013 as oil prices rise. The "market" exchange rate had appreciated by about one-third (to 830 in January 2011) since the end of FY2009–2010, following large foreign capital inflows.

International reserves rose to US$5.3 billion at end-FY2010, sufficient to finance seven months of imports. On the fiscal front, further improvements can be expected. Exchange rate unification should improve revenues, although the losses of state economic enterprises (SEEs) will become more apparent and transparent. The fiscal deficit had averaged 5 to 5.5 percent of GDP in the past two years, but should improve mainly due to new gas exports as they come on stream.

It is expected that additional revenues will go toward building human capital, healthcare, and infrastructure. Tax reform would emphasize direct taxation over indirect taxes to protect the poor. The FY2012–2013 budget has targeted a lower deficit of 4.6 percent of GDP. Privatization of SEEs would booster private-sector-led growth. Recent steps to improve competition in key sectors can be expected to reduce informal market activity and reduce prices.

New Exchange Regime

Reforming the highly complex exchange rate system is top priority, and rightly so. It will remove a constraint on growth. Indeed, its success will help establish a monetary policy framework for price stability. But the Central Bank of Myanmar (CBM) needs to be empowered with operational autonomy and policy independence to meet its mission, including bringing about market-determined interest rates to help build efficient financial intermediation, including a stock exchange. Myanmar is one of only 17 nations with dual exchange rates (i.e., different exchange rates for different purposes). Officially, US$1 = 6.4 kyats (pegged to the IMF's Special Drawing Rights since 1977). Unofficially (in the streets' "black market"), it had far exceeded 1,000 (in 2009) and now hovers around 800 kyats. The official rate is used for government revenue and for imports by some SEEs. As a result, state revenue is grossly underestimated. From April 1, 2012, the kyat was allowed to float against the US$, managed using an auction system. The CBM will conduct sealed bids for a given amount of US$, from 14 authorized domestic bank dealers. In practice, market forces will be allowed to determine the kyat's value, within a trading band of 0.8 percent on either side of the reference rate set daily by the CBM (at 818 on April 2). This move also calls for enhanced regulation and supervision of banks. From continuing trials over the next 12 months, interbank currency and money markets are expected to emerge. According to the IMF: "Certain exchange restrictions can be removed immediately, for example, by allowing the use of all foreign currency bank account balances for imports, easing import licensing requirements and access to the newly established foreign exchange retail counters."[4]

Currency reform is a delicate process and can have far-reaching impact on ordinary folks. People still remember 1987 when the cancellation of certain banknotes by the late dictator Ne Win wiped out people's entire savings, and led to pro-democracy uprising the following year, which the military crushed and killed thousands. Poor implementation could easily destabilize the economy. The business community remains nervous with the latest move: (1) the new rate could become unstable given the narrow market, or worse; (2) strengthen further to the detriment of exports; or (3) prove difficult to maintain stable due to speculative influences. To be successful, the value of the kyat has to be seen as determined by the orderly interplay of market supply and demand.

New Investment Laws

The new investment laws, while likely to significantly improve Myanmar's business climate, won't solve its massive infrastructure deficit, or answer concerns over its unpredictable legal system, its dysfunctional banking system (automated teller machines and credit cards are not widely used), and its opaque policy-making process. Still, the new laws are keenly awaited. Foreign investors will be (1) granted a 5-year tax holiday; (2) free from needing a local partner to start businesses; (3) free to form joint ventures (with at least 35 percent foreign capital); (4) allowed to lease land for up to 30 years, to be extended twice, 15 years each time; (5) required, after 5 years, to employ at least 25 percent skilled local labor; (6) exempted to export; (7) guaranteed against nationalization; (8) free to repatriate 100 percent of profits; and (9) allowed to import skilled labor.

A new telecommunications law is also expected to create four new phone licenses, open to foreigners to bid. Myanmar has only 2 to 3 million (some estimate much less) mobile phone users today. The number of Internet users is even smaller—estimated at 110,000. The government's target is 50 percent wireless penetration by 2015.

What, Then, Are We to Do?

The push is on for a really "open door" society. Developments are still evolving. All-round support is needed to accelerate and secure political and economic reforms. They have come a long way from where they were a year ago. Today presents a real opportunity for permanent change. We hear from Aung San Suu Kyi that the president is "sincerely motivated." He has since moved firmly on both political and economic fronts.

The challenge is for the West to recalibrate its response to reciprocate the bold reform initiatives. It would appear there is a new mind-set in Myanmar. The country has been secluded for so long that this time around, people with their newfound freedom may, understandably, have set their expectations too high to be realistic.

Implementation can easily fall short. They have lost everything over the past 50 years. They have nothing more to lose. They want—and deserve—more in terms of really improving the plight of their impoverished people. They expect much better healthcare and education. Quick reforms in land and agriculture are also badly needed. All this will require serious political effort by the West commensurate with that made by Myanmar. They urgently want to achieve enough progress to make the process irreversible. For them, there can be no turning back. "People have high hopes (and) . . . like to see progress on the streets." I wish them well.

Kuala Lumpur
April 6, 2012

Notes

1. First published on April 7, 2012.
2. International Monetary Fund, "Statement at the Conclusion of the 2011 Article IV Mission to Myanmar," Washington, DC, January 25, 2012.
3. Ibid., p. 1.
4. Ibid.

CHAPTER 130

Myanmar Spring: "Look, Listen, Learn, and Leave"[1]

These are early days still in Myanmar, the "final frontier." In the 30 months since the new regime assumed power, Myanmar has undergone a remarkable transformation. Rich in oil and gas, and minerals, investors are equally interested in what Myanmar does not have, which is pretty well everything else. So far, change has come largely to the center—the capital, Yangon. Around the periphery, home to numerous ethnic groups that make up two-fifths of the population, little has changed. Chapter 129, "Myanmar: Not the Burma I Used to Know," was written in April 2012. I revisited Yangon a month ago (January 2014). What really surprised me was the enormous traffic—full of jams, too many cars, and just not enough roads and bridges. Considering cars are not cheap, it's quite unbelievable. Except for the magnificent Shwedagon Pagoda, lovingly regilded for the benefit of visiting pilgrims and tourists, most of the city seems to have remained untouched for decades (reminds me of downtown Kuala Lumpur in the 1950s)—other than demolitions at strategic locations to make way for new shopping malls, offices, and high-rise residences, as well as hotels.

But my yearning was for a bowl of arguably Myanmar's national dish, Mohinga (*mont-hin-gar*)—a luxuriously rich and creamy fish-based broth with thin rice noodles (vermicelli), usually served steaming hot from massive cauldrons along the roadside (that's where I had my first taste of it in the 1960s). I found it again at Inya Lake Hotel's champagne buffet lunch—just as I had remembered, as best described by Nobel Laureate Aung San Suu Kyi in her 1995 *Letters from Burma*: "A steaming bowl of mohinga adorned with vegetable fritters, slices of fish cake and hard-boiled eggs and enhanced with the flavour of chopped coriander leaves, morsels of crispy fried garlic, fish sauce, a squeeze of lime and chillies is a wonderful way of stoking up for the day ahead."[2] That made my day.

I had wanted to taste it once more after spending the next day at Naypyidaw (the gaudy new capital built by the generals) as I checked in at the grand lady of Yangon, the Strand—originally built in 1901 by John Darwood and then acquired by the legendary Sarkies Brothers (of Singapore Raffles fame) as one of Southeast Asia's grand colonial hotels. From the beginning, the Strand was regarded as "the finest hostelry east of Suez" by Murray's *Handbook for Travellers in India, Burma and Ceylon* (1911 edition)—which I sighted at the hotel—patronized by "royalty, nobility, and distinguished personages." But made really famous by the likes of George Orwell, Somerset Maugham, Rudyard Kipling, and Sir Peter Ustinov. The hotel has been mostly restored to its elegant old self, but it was a great disappointment to find that mohinga was not on its dining menu! The new manager, Philippe, has since e-mailed that it's now back in where it should be.

Reality Check

There has been remarkable change. For years since the 1950s, Burma was a blank space. The generals ran it to the ground under the quasi-Marxist, "Burmese Way to Socialism," since 1962. Now it's finding its own space at a nexus between two giants (China and India, with a total population of 2.6 billion) and Southeast Asia (with some 600 million people). Its neighbors are its largest investors (Singapore, Vietnam, China, and Malaysia), putting in a lot of foreign direct investment (FDI) cash to work, while generals joked that Japan joined "NATO" instead: No Action, Talk Only!

I don't blame the Japanese for being prudent. My sense is that the leadership is sincere in their desire to tackle poverty, modernize the economy, and advance the democratic process. But much time is diverted to managing expectations—much of which is not realistic, bearing in mind that Myanmar hasn't had a proper business system for 60 years. Signs of ossification are everywhere, from on-off access to electricity to physical infrastructure shortcomings to the lack of skilled labor. After all, less than 30 percent of the population (mostly in cities) is connected to the grid, while Internet and mobile phone access is only about 10 percent. Telenor, the Norwegian service provider granted a license to set up the new mobile network, can't get it launched before the third quarter of 2014. The nation's once-excellent education system was all but destroyed. This left the Burmese with poor language and quantitative skills.

There is also too much reliance on cash for most settlements. Automated teller machines are rare, and banks' branch network is sparse. In an economy dominated by well-connected "cronies" with close ties to the still-dominant armed forces, it is not difficult to understand why motorcycles are banned in Yangon for security reasons. Nevertheless, we see that economic reforms are beginning to pay off. "The genie is out of the bottle." The World Bank's January 2014 global updates place Myanmar's growth at 6.8 percent in 2013 (6.5 percent in 2012 and 5 to 5.6 percent in 2010–2011).[3] Basic reforms will take time to filter through and distortions, unbundled. U Myint, the president's most senior adviser, told me: "It has not been the lack of resources but rather misconceived ideas and flawed policies that have been our undoing." But the basic shifts are taking place—military's share of the national budget is down to 12 to 15 percent (against more than 22 percent in 2010); while education and health budgets have nearly trebled from below 3 percent each. The third wave of reforms will focus on prudential financial regulation and land rights. It is more difficult to gauge the building of a nation that can celebrate religious and ethnic diversity and put an end to decades of conflict. The difficult part is to build trust between different religious and ethnic communities. This requires courage, creativity, and transparency, which don't readily lend to measurement. Above all, it calls for statesmanship.

No Turning Back

Most of the reform emanates from the nondescript "Ministry of the President's Office" in Naypyidaw, 320 km north of Yangon. This is the "super-ministers" headquarters led by two former military officers known to outsiders as the reformers: U Soe Thane, who oversees the economic ministries and the powerful Myanmar Investment Commission; and Aung Min, who leads peace negotiations with the ethnic groups. Together with two other ministers—Tin Naing Thein (coordinates reform strategy) and Hla Tun (budget reform and decentralization)—these four form the president's inner circle. I met them all. U Soe Thane, a former commander of the navy, is urbane and dynamic and a no-nonsense doer:

> *We have been planning for two years; we have changed many things. But this is our year of implementation, particularly for economic reform. Things are moving fast . . . you cannot tell us to stop or slow down now. . . . The Lady is the democracy icon, the president is the reform icon. . . . we must deliver for them, especially in critical things like infrastructure and electricity.*

I sense that there is this transformation also taking place among some generals—from uniformed junta members to civilian reformers, comfortable in suits or flowing longyi sarongs. Their open mind-set now reflects a keener appreciation of public expectations and needs, in the face of a combative parliament resistant to change, and of ever-growing demands by investors and businessmen. While not losing sight of the fight against entrenched corruption at the same time.

What Is Done and What Is There Still to Do?

Dr. Aung Tun Thet, an economic adviser to the president, believes the economy is heading in the right direction and will keep the momentum. GDP per capita, at about US$900, is 6 percent above the estimates provided for 2012 and 2011 for a population of 64 million (of which 46 million are of working age). As at end of the first half of 2013, FDI totaled more than US$42 billion, mainly in power, oil and gas, mining, and manufacturing. At the rate things are moving, Dr. Aung believes that the economy will have its best year yet in 2014–2015. This simply means ordinary people will begin to see real improvements in their daily lives. This is needed to develop an inclusive political culture, based on the rule of law and respect for human rights. Six critical reforms have since taken place:

1. Accession to the New York Convention on the Recognition and enforcement of Foreign Arbitral Awards 1958 on July 15, 2013, to protect foreign investors' interests in the resolution of disputes.
2. Passage of the new Central Bank of Myanmar law, 2013, to enable the Bank to become autonomous of the Ministry of Finance, and to open the door for the entry of foreign banks to spur competition.
3. Enactment of the Securities Exchange Law, 2013, to provide the needed framework to establish the stock exchange under the Securities and Exchange Commission, which will supervise and regulate the securities market.
4. Passed the land-use bill in 2012 to improve the rights for farmers, who comprise three-quarters of the population.
5. Enactment of the Foreign Investment Law, 2012, to establish the Myanmar Investment Commission to regulate and approve all foreign investments, giving foreign investors most of what they had wanted. Approved projects can apply for tax incentives, including five-year tax holiday.
6. Unification of multiple exchange rates and scrapping the 35-year-old fixed exchange rate on April 1, 2012, by implementing a market-based exchange system of managed floating for the kyat, Myanmar's currency. Work is in progress to free up capital flows and establish a monetary policy framework. Gross official reserves rose above US$10

billion in 2012–2013, up from US$3.1 billion in 2007–2008, according to the International Monetary Fund.

Together, these measures form the frontline of bold reforms taken. The European Union and Australia have since lifted their sanctions, and the United States has eased theirs. Despite these, the World Bank's 2014 "Doing Business" index ranked Myanmar poorly—among the very worst in the world to do business.[4] Starting a business involves 11 different procedures, takes 72 days, and costs nearly US$1,500, in addition to a US$58,000 deposit to get the final go-ahead. Long and costly approval procedures hamper much-needed construction work to rebuild dilapidated infrastructure.

Myanmar's electricity is the priciest in the region. A long road lies ahead. Although many reforms were taken, implementing them effectively remains a problem, given the chronic shortage of trained staff and professionals. There are also too many laws, including outdated ones still in the books (e.g., the 1914 Companies Law and, even older, the 1872 Evidence Act). It will take time to sort things out, says Dr. Aung: "Investors need to be patient." Myanmar also faces a general election in 2015: The transition period gets shorter with so much more to do. Be that as it may, reform efforts will need to continue. The greatest challenges include a still-evolving banking system, a developing network of infrastructures, and a weak education system.

Vietnamese Lessons

The rush into Myanmar to fill a business vacuum carries many risks. This is reminiscent of the Vietnamese experience a generation ago. I recall the 1986 opening of Vietnam when it rolled out "doi-moi"—its renovation program. Hanoi reduced trade barriers, showered FDI with attractive incentives, and adopted many reforms, including elimination of subsidies and allowing the private sector to compete along state-owned enterprises. It proved an early success: From 2005 to 2010, Vietnam was a hit with FDIs. Yet, Vietnam floundered and squandered early advantages as a result of lost reform momentum. The Vietnam case study showed (1) high failure rates, as early investors' tastes turned sour (as high as 90 percent); (2) too much FDI chasing too few good partners; and (3) too much optimism on potential consumption growth.

So Myanmar needs to heed the lessons: (1) sustain economic reforms; (2) aggressively pursue transparent and competitive privatization, and do so without undue delays; and (3) tear down bureaucracy and corruption. Ultimately, investors like strong rule of law and a vibrant private sector to drive sustainable growth.

What, Then, Are We to Do?

Myanmar reminded me very much of China during my second visit in 1979 (my first was in 1974 during the Cultural Revolution)—then, I recall, Deng Xiaoping was reported to have said: "We have to do something new." And China did. Myanmar, too, is doing something new. After all, it has a good size population, massive natural resources, agriculture, even rare metals—it has everything, including natural beauty and a wealth of Buddhist monuments and pagodas (notably, in Bagan, considered by many as equal to Cambodia's Angkor Wat). IMF saw "high growth potential."

It starts from a low base—its GDP is one-seventh Thailand's size, and Vietnam's is three times larger. Malaysia, which has one-half its population, is six times bigger. Experts at global consultants McKinsey estimated that Myanmar can quadruple its GDP to US$200 billion by 2030 if it presses on with reforms and embraces technology (lucky to have started reforms during the digital era). In the process, it can add 10 million jobs and lift 18 million (28 percent) of its population out of poverty. This plan calls for investment of US$650 billion, 50 percent in infrastructure alone—well and good on paper. Sure, there is a new sense of optimism amid an air of high expectations. But it's tinged with caution. Hopes have been dashed before. Everything remains in a state of flux. A lasting political solution still seems a long way off.

As I see it, everything hinges on four factors to get the job done: (1) progress toward democratization; (2) success at resolving ethnic conflicts; (3) sustaining political and economic reform efforts; and (4) marshaling enough skills and professionals when everything is in short supply. Beneath the thin veneer of expertise at the very top, I am told, is an ex-militia-based bureaucracy that is provided with sinecures—they make up the "green ceiling," which simply means that getting anything done takes a long time. Add to this, corruption. Everyone wants a piece of Myanmar—Western and Japanese businesses are keen to access its rich resources. Asians are definitely positioning for much greater access. But the path toward change depends critically on ethnic diversity—it has to end decades of conflict. The nation is split into 135 ethnic groups, many speaking different languages and practicing different religions. The army has engaged in border wars with the Rakhine, Kachin, Shan, and Karen. There has been no political settlement. Key to real change, however, rests on the behavior of the Army. Uncertainty and tension cause fear, often misplaced, even exaggerated, and sometimes unfounded. Building trust thus becomes critical. These are difficult issues.

To really transform, Myanmar has to bring about key political changes; the presumption of impunity has to end; and violence and hatred, cease. Until then, the gap between expectation and reality will persist. It must be bridged. All I can say now is that, perhaps, "the beginning of the beginning has begun." Until then, investors will continue to flock to Myanmar and follow the popular four *L*s: look, listen, learn, and leave. Will Burma ever begin to really bloom?

Kuala Lumpur
February 20, 2014

Notes

1. First published on March 1, 2014. It was edited because of space constraints. The version here represents the original, as first drafted before editing.
2. Aung San Suu Kyi, "Letters from Burma," 1995, cited in Robert Carmack and Morrison Polkinghorne, *The Burma Cookbook: Recipes from the Land of a Million Pagodas* (Bangkok: River Books, 2014), p. 204.
3. World Bank, *Global Economic Prospects: Coping with Policy Normalization in High-Income Countries* (Washington, DC: World Bank, January 2014).
4. World Bank, *Doing Business 2014: Understanding Regulations for Small and Medium-Size Enterprises* (Washington, DC: World Bank, October 29, 2013).

CHAPTER 131

The BRICS Are Coming . . .[1]

The term *BRIC* (Brazil, Russia, India, and China) was first used in 2001 by economist Jim O'Neill (Goldman Sachs) to call attention to four rapidly rising large emerging economies considered able to play a significant role in global affairs, championing the interests of developing nations. Very much like what G-7 does for the developed world. For years since, it was treated by investors and journalists as a shorthand for the big emerging markets. Adding South Africa to the group widens its focus to include more from outside fast-growing China and India.

The BRICs held its first summit in 2009 in Russia, discussing issues on international monetary reform, including possibilities of a new dominant reserve regime to replace the US-dollar-based system. In 2011, China played host and invited South Africa to join, formally naming the group *BRICS*. Together, they exceeded three billion people, nearly 45 percent of the world, and about 25 percent of the world's 2011 gross domestic product (GDP) based on purchasing power parity. China's total output is bigger than the other four put together. The economic clout of the BRICS is now growing as the developed world struggles to expand and pare debt. Indeed, they are starting to operate as a common bloc in the G-20, providing a counterpoint to the United States and Europe.

Building BRICS

But the group is vastly different. India, Brazil, and South Africa are vibrant democracies, in contrast to the more authoritarian Russia and China. BRICS needs to balance the interests of its members: three large commodity exporters and two huge commodity importers. For sure, they have to get used to obeying rules they played little part in shaping. China's economy, the world's second largest, is nearly 3 times the size of Brazil, close to 4 times that each of Russia and India, and 16 times that of South Africa. They also differ on exchange rate policies. Brazil is vocal against China's tight management of the yuan's value, keeping its exports relatively cheap. China is becoming prominent in BRICS' trade—already it is Brazil's and South Africa's largest source of imports.

Be that as it may, the group shares strong macroeconomic fundamentals going into 2012. China and India will grow 8.5 to 9 percent in 2011; Russia and Brazil, 4 to 4.5 percent; and South Africa, 3.5 percent. Their structural budget deficits are well contained, with low debt/GDP ratios, highest being in India (68 percent) and South Africa (65 percent). China continues to have a current balance of payments surplus (5.7 percent of GDP) while all others' deficits are each less than 5 percent. But they share a common problem—inflation: 6.5 percent in China, 9 percent in India, 9 percent in Russia, 7 percent in Brazil, and 6 percent in South Africa. Containing inflation remains a top priority of public policy. Still, they continue to struggle to deal with this threat.

BRICS Summit

The second BRICS Summit held in April 2011 reaffirmed the group's determination to transit from global Pax Americana to a new order in the "development of humanity." The BRICS' emphasis on cooperation in their call for reform of the US$-dominated international monetary system and for tighter supervision of commodity derivatives and markets and capital flows shows the group is seeking to refrain from too much assertiveness. Still the desire to shake off the old hegemony is there; it calls for a larger role in international fora. It condemns "the inadequacies and deficiencies" of global finance and the "excessive volatility in commodity prices." The Sanya (China) declaration underscored their concerns about underlying factors that fuel inflation and currency volatility in many emerging economies, as well as their strong desire to shift away from reliance on the US dollar. "We call for more attention to the risks of massive cross border capital flows now faced by the emerging economies. . . . Excessive volatility in commodity prices, particularly for food and energy."[2]

The BRICS took a new step toward cementing their global influence by: (1) calling for a broad-based reserve currency system "providing stability and certainty"—one that is more reliable and stable;[3] (2) welcoming discussion about the global role of Special Drawing Rights (SDRs), the International Monetary Fund's in-house accounting unit but a global reserve asset, and on the SDR's basket of currencies (now comprising US$, €, ¥, and £); (3) establishing mutual credit lines denominated in their home currencies among the state development banks of the group. To start the ball rolling, China Development Bank will issue loans worth 10 billion denominated in yuan this year to other BRICS nations, mostly to fund oil and gas projects;

and (4) forging a common emerging market negotiating stance on issues from climate change to world trade, and to act as a credible counterweight to the West in settings like the G-20.

BRICS and Asia

The Asian Development Bank (ADB) expects Asia to grow 7.5 percent this year (against 9.2 percent in 2010) and 7 percent in 2012; "if anything distinguished the region from the rest of the world, it is its strong macro fundamentals."[4] However, a dark cloud on the horizon is the slowdown in exports to its traditional markets in the United States, Europe, and Japan. Against this is the region's potential for rapid expansion in intraregional trade, amidst signs of rising domestic demand in Asia. True, manufacturing and services-related activity stalled across much of the world in August 2011, raising fears of another global downturn. True also, factory and services output throughout Asia, including China and India, slackened in August, pointing to growing evidence that weaker demand in the United States and Europe is weighing on Asia's export-driven economies.

Moreover, investor confidence dropped to the lowest in two years in September 2011 in the eurozone and the United States, and consumer confidence, already fragile, weakened further. Unfortunately, US anemic growth and Europe's worsening debt crisis have prompted governments to deepen budget cuts, undermining consumer demand and clouding growth prospects with uncertainty. Barring a full-blown double-dip in the United States and Europe, Asia will still suffer significant bruising from deepened dashed expectations, with most of the pain centered in highly exposed nations, in particular, Taiwan and South Korea. No doubt, BRICS economies are bound to face clear challenges in responding to the angst over weakened global conditions.

Missing BRICS

O'Neill has since suggested his original four BRICS be expanded to include Turkey, Indonesia, Mexico, and South Korea, to form the new "growth markets." A fresh look is taken to measure exposure to equity markets beyond market capitalization (GDP, corporate revenue growth, and volatility of asset returns); any emerging market accounting for 1 percent or more of world GDP should be taken seriously. Mexico and South Korea each represented 1.6 percent of world GDP, Turkey 1.2 percent, and Indonesia 1.1 percent. Among them, I particularly favor Indonesia. Like Brazil, Indonesia's success is based on the commodities boom: gas and coal to China and India, and palm oil to the world. Investments are flowing in.

With a population of 237 million (the world's largest Muslim nation), Indonesia is in the midst of a consumer boom. Indeed, it has the potential to become one of the world's biggest economies. But it has to get its act together. It will grow 6.2 percent this year (6.1 percent 2010) and hopefully 6.5 percent in 2012. Southeast Asia's largest and fastest growing economy is firing on all cylinders. It is today rated a notch below investment grade and should be upgraded soon. It will become a credible sixth member of BRIICs.

What impresses is Indonesia's growing middle class. The World Bank puts private consumer spending at close to one-half of GDP. The middle class (disposable household income exceeding US$3,000 a year) numbered 1.6 million in 2004; by 2011, Nomura (Japanese investment bank) estimated it to be about 50 million, more than in India and larger than in any of its nine other Southeast Asian neighbors. By 2014–2015, Nomura thinks it could reach 150 million. The nation is growing so fast, especially in the urban areas, that inflation is a major political issue at 7.2 percent for 2011. But it's stable, bearing in mind the rupiah appreciated 5 percent this year. Affluent middle-class Indonesians are spending, mainly on motorcycles (8 million sold in 2010, dwarfing sales in the rest of Southeast Asia), cars (750,000 in 2010), and smartphones. Indonesia is reputed to be the world's number two in Facebook members and world's number three in Twitter users. But Indonesia, to be frank, remains a difficult place to do business because of poor infrastructure (adding to production and distribution costs), and corruption ("nontransparent random regulations"). There are signs that things are changing for the better. It is still attractive to foreign investors: Nowadays, "if you are not here, you have to have a good reason." Most new consumer desirables are still imported.

A Wall of BRICS

As a group, the BRICS are growing fast. China has surpassed Japan as the world's second largest economy. India and Brazil are following fast behind. Catching up is always much easier, because the leader has already set the path and the pace. At some point, reliance on emerging nations as engines of growth begins to disappoint, as it becomes harder to sustain the pace. Growth will slow down (as did Europe, the Asian tigers, and Japan before them), or may even falter (as did Latin America in the 1990s). There is a lesson from history. A recent study by three scholars, Barry Eichengreen (University of California, Berkeley), Donghyun Park (ADB), and Kwanho Shin (Korea University)—EPS study—attempted to draw potential warning signs by examining economies since 1957 whose GDP per capita (on a purchasing power parity [PPP] basis) rose more than 3.5 percent a year for seven years, and then suffered a sharp slowdown when growth dipped two percentage points or more.[5] The focus was on economies enjoying sustained catch-up growth.

The common sense behind PPP is that the same amount of money should purchase the same product in any two countries (hence, the term *purchasing power parity*). That is, the purchasing power of money, expressed in one currency, should change pari-passu in different countries. If US$5 buys a cup of Starbucks coffee in New York and the actual cost of the same Starbucks coffee in Kuala Lumpur is RM12, then the exchange rate should be US$1 = RM2.40 according to PPP. But the actual exchange rate is close to RM3.00, or 20 percent cheaper. The use of PPP serves to neutralize any currency distortions.

What emerged was as follows: (1) growth slowdowns occurred when GDP per capita reached about US$16,740 per capita; and (2) the average growth rate then falls from 5.6 percent per annum to 2.3 percent.

In the 1970s, growth rates in Western Europe and Japan cooled off at about the US$16,740 threshold; as did Singapore in early 1980s and South Korea and Taiwan in the late 1990s. Thereafter, growth often continues and may even accelerate. Japan's boom lost momentum in early 1970s, then accelerated until it blew up in the 1990s. But, no one-size-fits-all—depends on circumstances. When the United States passed its threshold, it kept on growing rapidly consistent with its innovative prowess. Other risk factors matter, including openness to trade; lifting of consumption to beyond 60 percent of GDP; low and stable inflation; and high ratio of workers to dependents. On the other hand, an undervalued exchange rate raises the risks of a slowdown.

What, Then, Are We to Do?

The EPS study does draw interesting parallels. China is destined to reach the US$16,740 GDP per-capita threshold by 2015, well ahead of India and Brazil. Will it then slacken? The risk factors for China include: aging population, low consumption, and an undervalued currency. On these alone, the study suggests high odds (over 70 percent) of a definite slowdown by then! But China is unique. These risks can be managed by shifting development inland, leaving the maturing urban centers room to innovate. China is already in the process of reforming to become a more consumption-based economy, while its currency is being managed to reflect more and more market considerations. Prompt structural reforms help cushion the effects of any slowdown. Even so, a three-percentage-point drop in growth to 6 to 7 percent does not sound so scary. For China, it should not really be such a big deal. After all, that's still nearly four times the rate at which the United States is growing and up to six times that in the eurozone.[6]

Kuala Lumpur
September 8, 2011

Notes

1. First published on September 10, 2011.
2. The Sanya declaration issued at the end of the BRICS Summit on April 14, 2011, in Sanya, China.
3. Ibid.
4. Asian Development Bank (ADB), *Asia Capital Markets Monitor* (Manila: ADB, August 2011).
5. Barry Eichengreen, Donghyun Park, and Kwanho Shin, "When Fast-Growing Economies Slow Down: International Evidence and Implications for China," National Bureau of Economic Research working paper no. 16919, Cambridge, MA, March 2011.
6. International Monetary Fund (IMF), *World Economic Outlook* (Washington, DC: IMF, April 2011).

CHAPTER 132

BRICS Can't Run as a Herd[1]

BRICS—Brazil, Russia, India, China, and South Africa—held its fifth Durban Summit on March 27, 2013, under the overarching theme: BRICS and Africa: Partnership for Development, Integration, and Industrialization. They envisaged an inclusive approach of shared solidarity and cooperation, committed to "exploring new models and approaches towards more equitable development and inclusive global growth by emphasizing complementarities."[2] Back in 2001 during the dot-com bust, Goldman Sachs's Jim O'Neill created the acronym *BRIC* (without South Africa), proclaiming these emerging nations would drive markets in the next decade. He was right. In 2002, BRIC accounted for only 3 percent of World Federation of Exchanges market value. By 2011, it was one-fifth.

Historically, BRIC economic cycle moved in tandem with the advanced world. The gap in growth remained stable at 8.6 percentage points in BRIC's favor during precrisis 2007–2008. After that, the gap started to narrow, falling to 3.5 percentage points in 2012 in the face of slackening world growth. That's still significant. BRIC held its first summit four years ago and invited South Africa (smallest among them) to join the pack in 2011; and so, it became BRICS—accounting for 43 percent of world population and 27 percent of world gross domestic product (GDP) in 2012, with combined foreign reserves of US$4.4 trillion.

Trade among them surged past US$300 billion last year from only US$30 billion in 2002; it's expected to expand to US$500 billion by 2015. So BRICS does offer promise of clout. Indeed, BRICS's GDP could collectively become bigger than the United States by 2018 (about 80 percent, so far). BRICS could even surpass G-7's (the United States, Britain, Germany, France, Italy, Canada, and Japan) combined GDP by 2050. Russian President Vladimir Putin likened BRICS to Africa's "Big Five," the must-see trophy beasts of tourist lore—lion, elephant, buffalo, leopard, and rhinoceros. They certainly present a formidable potential counterweight to the advanced West. But, individually, they are very different and so very competitive that they are unlikely, in my view, to run like a herd; certainly they won't hunt as a pack!

eThekwini Action Plan

BRICS declared its commitment to forge a stronger partnership by adopting the Summit eThekwini Action Plan where it agreed to (1) establish the New Development Bank, with "initial substantial and sufficient contributions" for it to be effective in financing infrastructure (precise funding and location yet to be agreed); (2) form a financial safety net by creating a Contingent Reserve Arrangement (CRA) with an initial size of US$100 billion (details not yet available); and (3) work with both the "Multilateral Agreement on Co-operation and Co-financing on Sustainable Development" and the "Multilateral Agreement on Infrastructure Co-financing for Africa."[3]

It's still work in progress. Further, BRICS called to reform the Bretton Woods twins (the International Monetary Fund [IMF] and World Bank) to make them reflect the growing weight of BRICS; for international monetary reform with a broad-based currency system providing greater stability and certainty; to enhance the role of Special Drawing Rights (the IMF's reserve asset), including its currency basket composition; and to upgrade the IMF's surveillance framework to make it more even-handed. No doubt, as the United States gets more preoccupied with internal politics and with the European Union (EU) being mired in a debilitating growth and debt crisis, a vacuum is increasingly being felt in the global economic and trading system. This presented BRICS with an opportunity to emerge as a major global player. Unfortunately, overall momentum for BRICS is flagging. Growth in BRICS has since steadily slackened. At the heart lies structural disparities among them.

China's Dominance

There is no denying China's dominance. Indeed, China has grown so fast that others find difficulty in catching up. The Chinese economy is not only the world's second largest but also larger than other BRICS combined. The others are conscious of this. So they hedge their bets with alternative groups like IBSA (among democracies of India, Brazil, and South Africa). Still, China's dominance in BRICS trade is so overwhelming that others have difficulty getting a fair share. They openly complain about China's undervalued renminbi. Sure, economic ties between Brazil and China have prospered. But there are often frictions. Brazilians are losing market share even in Latin America—just can't compete with Chinese imports. It's also true that Russia and China often gang up against Western policies (e.g., Iran and Syria). But deep down, Russia worries about China's strong toehold in Asia's security landscape. Likewise, Sino-India ties remain strained—from land borders to maritime disputes. Although bilateral trade has risen sharply, India still worries about China's surplus. South Africa's growing trade imbalance with

China has long been a source of discontent. Indeed, China's stranglehold on the African continent has led to growing calls for a more equitable relationship. While it remains fascinated with multipolarity, it will be difficult for BRICS to transform itself into a truly unified global power force. It's a humongous task.

Remaining Resilient

The IMF estimated the big-4 BRIC's GDP rose 4.5 percent in 2012 against 1 percent for high-income nations.[4] Between 2000 and 2008, their growth averaged 8 percent, 6 percentage points above rich G-7 economies. This year, BRIC's growth is expected at 5.5 percent in the face of no growth in EU and less than 1 percent in G-7. That's not so bad for BRIC. Until 2008, emerging economies enjoyed average export growth of 20 to 30 percent a year. Then, the United States and Europe had consumption binges, soaking up imports that, in turn, fueled investment in emerging markets. Today, eurozone is in recession. The United States faces a stubborn jobless recovery, while still wrangling over deficits and debt. Demand in the West has virtually softened. Emerging markets exports will slacken, and so will investment in the face of much unutilized productive capacity. All this will hit the BRICS, with Brazil, Russia, and South Africa most exposed, being big-commodity exporters. Whereas Russia, Brazil, South Africa, and India have since suffered from low investments and high inflation, China relies excessively on investments to boost growth.

Russia

Russia presents a conundrum. Its corruption and demographic decline (shrinking working-age population) are well known. But at 6 times forward earnings, Russian stocks appear "a steal," against 15 to 18 times for other BRICS and 14 times for S&P 500.

Nevertheless, its two key influences—oil price and eurozone market demand—present huge risks this year. Already the economy has slackened for five consecutive quarters. In April 2013, central bank benchmark refinancing rate was left unchanged at 8.25 percent for a seventh month, in the face of an economy at near full capacity with unemployment (5.3 percent) at its lowest ever. Growth is expected to slacken to 2.4 percent (3.4 percent in 2012 and 4.3 percent in 2011) reflecting slowdown in industrial production and consumer demand, but with inflation maintained at 2012 level (6.5 percent). Capital flight remains of concern. Russia's most striking imbalance remains excessive reliance on oil (accounting for half of revenues and 60 percent of exports).

Brazil

Brazil's prospects are better than Russia. But 2012 was a bad year: Growth was only 1 percent, lower than 4.8 percent precrisis and 7.5 percent in 2010 and 2.7 percent in 2011. At 19 percent, Brazil's investment share of GDP is the lowest among BRICS. With its economy at near full capacity, inflation remains high at 6 percent (6.6 percent in 2011), which forces the central bank to keep rates high. But with corporate tax at 34 percent—highest among BRICS—it acts to dampen investment. Stocks are down 6 percent, also worst among BRICS. Brazil badly needs to recharge its internal engines to push investment's share of GDP to 20 to 25 percent, without fueling inflation.

South Africa

South Africa is the largest and most sophisticated in Africa. But recent mine killings and spreading labor unrest have tainted its reputation. Unless its natural resources (world's largest producer of gold and platinum) are better managed, South Africa risks growing negative investor sentiment. Growth slackened to 2.5 percent in 2012 with inflation at 5.5 percent, against 3 percent and 6 percent respectively in 2011.

GDP will expand by 3 to 3.5 percent in 2013 with inflation stabilizing at 5.5 percent. But South Africa needs to urgently address three ongoing problems: poverty (one-third of the population survives on US$2 a day); inequality (poorest 20 percent of population has just 2.7 percent of national income); and unemployment (25 percent; including those not actively seeking work, 35 percent). Moody's has since lowered its credit rating. It now faces the huge task of pushing for more inclusive growth.

India

India in many ways reflects the imbalances of Russia, Brazil, and South Africa. All four need to rebalance and push investment. Their central banks struggle to combat inflation, despite continuing high rates. Although India's investment is relatively higher, growth in private investment has sharply slackened reflecting lack of reforms, supply-side bottlenecks, and high borrowing rates. Like the other three BRICS, government spends far too much on welfare (on the 3 Fs: food, fuel, and fertilizers).

Inflation remains worryingly high (11 percent in February 2013), even though GDP growth is expected at 6 percent against just 4.9 percent in 2012, far below average 8 percent before the crisis. High fiscal deficits (5 to 6 percent of GDP since 2009) crowd out investment. Public spending has too meager investment content capable of boosting productivity and curbing inflation to provide more headroom to loosen policy to spur private capital outlays. Unfortunately, its biggest pains are self-inflicted (see Chapter 142, "India: The Outlook Dims"). Political logjam has thwarted Indian reforms, stalled meaningful decision making, and exacerbated the stubborn inflation.

China

China doesn't have a legacy of low investment. Far from it. Between 2003 and 2007, investment represented 42 percent of GDP—that's higher than Japan for the decade to 1974 and South Korea over 10 years until 1999 at the height of their industrial transformation. After the crisis, China unleashed a stimulus program that pushed the ratio to 48 percent with devastating impact on environment and inflation. Another side effect reflected growing trade friction, not only with the United States and Europe, but also with Asia and other BRICS due to overcapacity in manufacturing at home, as well as rising wages and growing nonperforming loans.

Fitch lowered China's yuan-denominated debt rating one notch to A+ with a stable outlook. Its new leaders have since taken these to heart. The new five-year plan calls for more effective rebalancing efforts in turning this huge domestic ship around (investment and net exports represent 51 percent of GDP) through pushing consumption spending (represents only over one-third of GDP). This is formidable, given that China's fixed investment in 2011 was as big as the GDP of Spain and Italy combined. Moreover, this turnaround runs the risk of slowing down overall growth and fanning the headwinds of social unrest.

Also, the transition would hit sectors tied to building and construction. China's new President Xi Jinping publicly declared before business leaders at the 2013 Boao Forum on April 8, 2013: "I don't think we will be able to sustain an ultra-high speed of economic growth and it is not what we want, either," citing the need to balance growth with sustainability and a clean environment. Asian Development Bank (ADB) expects China to expand by 8.2 percent this year (7.8 percent in 2012 and 9.3 percent in 2011), reflecting continuing strong manufacturing and services growth in the first quarter of 2013.[5]

What, Then, Are We to Do?

Dismal turn in data points to another disappointing year for the global economy, with growth in world trade slackening to only 3.3 percent this year (4.5 percent in 2012). The only European nation showing some resilience is Germany. Even that's borderline now. Impact of Japan's radical US$1.4 trillion monetary stimulus remains uncertain. Still, it's worrisome that continuing strong cheap capital flows will feed asset bubbles. Political discord emanating from US fiscal impasse, European austerity fatigue, and Asian border disputes are bound to jeopardize global sustainability.

They suggest that emerging Asia will have to do more to shift toward domestic demand and rely more on intraregional trade to help themselves. ADB's April 2013 forecasts rest on the uptick in China's continuing growth, and robust expansion in the Association of Southeast Asian Nations (ASEAN) to lead global growth. So, growth in emerging Asia is set to rise by 6.6 percent this year (6.1 percent in 2012), edging up 6.7 to 7 percent in 2014. ASEAN nations are also expected to shine based on robust private spending and strong intraregional trade, raising GDP growth to 5.5 percent this year (4.7 percent in 2011) and 5.7 to 6 percent in 2014.

Overall, world demand still needs to be nourished. Each BRICS must now reform in its own special way. Increasingly, political differences among them will become obvious. And, like the Beatles (which they outlasted), BRICS have to each go solo and rely on markets to set their fate. While Brazil, Russia, India, and South Africa will each have to rebalance in favor of investment, China's challenge is just the opposite. Each BRICS has to regain and sustain its own growth path before they can be expected to work together effectively as a group, to maintain global prominence again.

Fudan University, Shanghai
Kuala Lumpur
April 18, 2013

Notes

1. First published on April 20, 2013.
2. BRICS, *Fifth BRICS Summit Declaration*, Durban, South Africa, March 27, 2013.
3. Ibid.
4. International Monetary Fund (IMF), *World Economic Outlook: Hopes, Realities, Risks* (Washington, DC: IMF, April 2013).
5. Asian Development Bank (ADB), *Asian Development Outlook* (Manila: ADB, April 2013).

CHAPTER 133

Acronym Anxiety: BRICS Are Stumbling[1]

On April 20, 2013, I finished writing Chapter 132, "BRICS Can't Run as a Herd," concluding that "Each BRICS (Brazil, Russia, India, China, and South Africa) must now reform in its own special way. . . . Each BRICS has to regain and sustain its own growth path before they can be expected to work together effectively as a group, to maintain global prominence again."

What a difference a year makes. The International Monetary Fund's (IMF) October 2012 Outlook forecasted BRICS gross domestic product (GDP) for 2013 to rise by 5.0 percent (4.1 percent in 2012) against 1.5 percent by the advanced economies (AEs) (1.3 percent in 2012), yielding a gap of 3.5 percentage points.[2] Between 2000 and 2008, their growth averaged 8 percent, six percentage points above AEs. However, in January 2014, The IMF revised BRICS growth down to 3.5 percent for 2013, compared with 1.3 percent for AEs, with the gap narrowing to just over 2 percentage points, reflecting weakening BRICS economic expansion. Indeed, BRICS (ex-China) GDP expanded by only 2 percent in 2013 (same as in the United States); for 2014, it will expand within the same ballpark (2.2 to 2.5 percent) as AEs according to the IMF and the World Bank. Bear in mind that, collectively, BRICS GDP is close to 90 percent of the United States; they account for 43 percent of world population but much less than 30 percent of global GDP, with combined forex reserves at a whopping US$4.5 trillion. The economies of the United States, Europe, and Japan have gained some momentum lately. This has given rise to some optimism that both developed and developing nations will finally be strengthening together as they did before the crisis. Now, hopes of this happening have been dashed. Reasons behind the BRICS slowdown are myriad—from bank lending pullback in China to crumbling infrastructure, and rampant corruption in India and South Africa, to inflation and capital flight in Russia and Brazil. But they all share a common element: Cost of living is rising fast, sapping spending power, including the "go-get" spirit of even those who fared well since the crisis. It would appear at this time that BRICS can only help support the global economy, not drive it. Without China (whose GDP exceeded US$9 trillion in 2013, larger than all the other BRICS combined), they are quite a miserable lot today.

BRICS, MINT, and CIVETS

BRICS was set in motion by Goldman Sachs's Jim O'Neill in 2001, as a dynamic subset of fast-growing emerging economies but as an economic concept. It soon gathered enough interest to become an investment market, attracting monies into BRICS markets (which really have little in common beyond a broad market concept), as the group enjoyed turbocharged growth. In 2002, BRIC (without South Africa) accounted for only 3 percent of World Federation of Exchanges market value. By 2011, it was one-fifth. South Africa (the smallest among them) joined the pack in 2011.

But investment gains are not guaranteed, and underperforming local stock markets have since led some fund managers to flee in the face of Fed (US Federal Reserve Bank System) Chairman Ben Bernanke's May 22, 2013, talk about "tapering" quantitative easing (TQE). Since then, TQE has started with Fed's bond purchases being reduced to US$65 billion a month (from US$85 billion), beginning this February 2014. Assets under management in BRICS funds fell to US$12.2 billion (from US$28.4 billion at end-2010). It was reported that Goldman Sachs's own BRICS fund had lost 20 percent in value over the past three years. Undaunted, O'Neill now pushes a new acronym—MINT, for Mexico, Indonesia, Nigeria, and Turkey. Like BRICS, it's an economic concept, bearing in mind that the appeal of acronym investment is fast fading—giving way to what some call "acronym anxiety."

Unfortunately, O'Neill's timing appears off: Turkey is marred by corruption investigations and is in the midst of serious street protests since last summer. Nigeria is similarly in turmoil before vital elections next year. Indonesia, along with Turkey, is experiencing high inflation, capital flight, and a falling currency. Indonesia, along with many emerging nations, is also running large overseas payments deficits. Mexico, somewhat more stable, had a bad 2013, following a slump in manufacturing, construction, mining, and exports. Above all, all four MINT nations are not much connected. It would have made much better sense if the grouping involved markets where companies offered high-dividend yields. Investors in BRICS found out the hard way that rapid economic growth doesn't necessarily convert to stock market gains or a strong commitment to good corporate governance practices. BRICS markets are increasingly being ignored because they underperformed the broader MSCI index of emerging stocks (in dollar terms) over the past three years.

Another casualty is Hongkong Bank's (HSBC) CIVETS fund—covering another group of six emerging markets: Colombia, Indonesia, Vietnam, Egypt, Turkey, and South Africa—which the bank closed last year. Both CIVETS and MINT focus on demographics. These groups are expected to grow rapidly by the middle of this century because of their young population. In essence, most are at an earlier stage of development, sometimes referred to as "frontier" markets—smaller markets with more difficult trading conditions. They often take longer to pay off. Indeed, they remain long-term investment opportunities, but in the short run can be rather risky (like Egypt and Colombia); however, they do offer potential for robust future growth. Turkey has since moved to this category. As with Turkey, investors are wary of political risks in any exposure in Nigeria, Egypt, and South Africa, especially before the next elections and amid uncertainty over the future stability of political leadership. What's worrisome about both these groups is that their economic performance is not necessarily dictated by local developments, but very much so by the global economic outlook. In particular, these nations don't have an independent monetary cycle—so they do have to struggle in the short run, which raises undue risk.

BIITS

In the past year, Wall Street has stopped referring to BRICS as a catalyst for dynamic emerging markets. This has become so following eruption of protests from Brazil to Turkey in early summer of 2013, capital flight from BRICS thereafter, and most of all, broad slowdown across BRICS economies. Since then, and made popular by Morgan Stanley, the Street has started to refer to *BIITS* instead, or the "Fragile Five," viz. Brazil, India, Indonesia, Turkey, and South Africa, to raise concerns regarding the vulnerability of even the more dynamic emerging markets. I think it makes sense to exclude China and Russia, the two largest BRICS. The new five (three of them are commodity-based) share some common elements: All are soaked in too much short-term global capital, leading to excessive overseas payments deficits for far too long. Their consequent high-growth rates have made their governments complacent, even as they strengthen their currencies, making them less competitive.

Now their growth rates are slackening and their currencies, depreciating. Their currencies suffered dramatic declines last year (2013) and enjoyed some respite last September. But in the last week of January 2014, investors have once again found reasons to sell. The catalyst (but not the actual cause) of the current market remains the prospect of a rise in US interest rates that began with Fed's May 2013 reference to tapering. Since then, US 10-year Treasuries have surged by more than 1 percentage point and threaten to continue to rise as the Fed has begun to reduce the pace of its bond purchases. Bond yields of weaker emerging markets have risen even faster. This is so because the credit and commodity booms brought with it unsustainable high growth rates.

The common feature that did them in is their high overseas payment deficit, reflecting vulnerability to foreign creditors (i.e., capital outflows). By fall 2013, this deficit has begun to shrink in Indonesia and India, but remains high in the other three, dangerously so in South Africa and Turkey. This year, the five are likely to part ways as national elections are likely to play out with different and diverse implications. I think Brazil at best can hope to muddle through; India will continue to waffle in the face of slowing growth with high inflation, with an uncertain outcome; Indonesia remains on the lookout for a doer-leader who stands firmly behind reforms; Turkey's political and economic turmoil leave the future unpredictable; and South Africa's prospects for reform remain weak as its leaders continue to kick the can down the road. Author Ruchir Sharma's (of *Breakout Nations: In Pursuit of the Next Economic Miracles* fame) recent assessment best captures its essence: "So the prospects for post-election reform look best in Indonesia, worst in South Africa, muddled in Turkey and Brazil, unpredictable in India. . . . The Fragile Five are not equally fragile."[3]

Convergence Myth

World growth averaged 3.4 percent a year in 1980s and 3.2 percent in 1990s; in the first decades of this new century, it was 3.7 percent (despite recession in the latter years), reflecting in large part the dynamism of BRICS, following the impact of vast flows of cheap money and surging commodity prices, and consequently, market volatility and inflation. This led to excesses (clear sign of the world living beyond its means) with the crash of 2008–2009 as the inevitable cost they all had to bear. Be that as it may, the United Nations' (UN) goal of halving global poverty by 2015 was attained five years early. That's fantastic. This apparent higher growth trend has led to suggestions that the world is converging (i.e., incomes of poor nations will rapidly catch up and converge with those in the rich AEs).

After all, emerging and developing economies (EDEs) had expanded at three times faster than the United States, the world's largest economy. EDEs growth peaked at 8.7 percent in 2007 (US GDP up 2 percent) and tumbled to 4.7 percent in 2013 (1.9 percent in the United States). As indicated earlier, BRICS GDP (ex-China) is today growing at about the same pace as the United States, with GDP in MINT and BIITS rising in the region of 3.5 to 4.5 percent. This trend is unlikely to change significantly. Since 2011, the US share of global GDP has stabilized at 23 percent while EDEs' (ex-China) share has averaged at around 19 percent.

Historically, empirical evidence doesn't support convergence. Indeed, convergence is essentially a myth. Much of EDEs rapid growth reflected high investments (especially in China), which helped for a while, but which are not sustainable. Similar trends were evident at the beginning of Latin America's lost decade in early 1980s. As then, the world is now approaching a downward turn of two long cycles—the 15- to 20-year-long financial cycle (leading to credit booms) and the even longer commodity cycle (bringing benefits of booming prices) that have since peaked and begun a long-term decline of a decade or so. But commodity-driven economies like Russia, South Africa, and Brazil tend to stop catching up as soon as commodity prices spiral downward. According to World Bank, of the 101 middle-income nations in 1960, only 13 had become (and still remained) high income by 2008.

Among them, only one is commodity based. Unlike Latin America in 1980s, today's major EDEs have low inflation, limited budget deficits, mostly floating exchange rates, and large forex reserves to help cushion any downward adjustment and volatility. Global trends don't change often, but when they do, they do so abruptly and sharply. The high levels of EDEs growth since 2000 were artificial, driven by high commodity prices and Greenspan's global credit boom, and then, huge credit transfer from AEs. Last decade's mass convergence can't be repeated. I think the preboom period, 1980–2000, may be more representative of what's normal. This simply implies more economic divergence. For EDEs that ignored the needed structural reforms during boom years, the next round of reform will be harder—but change is the only way forward. Catching up is hard to do—and harder even to sustain.

What, Then, Are We to Do?

Looking ahead, I see the fickleness of capital markets posing once again the paradox of thrift. As capital withdraws from emerging markets, these nations will be forced to adjust and rebalance to try to achieve overseas payments surpluses. So we are back to look for nations willing (and able) to run deficits. Only two of the world's three biggest economies can do so—China and eurozone. But both are committed (and able) to generate surpluses! This leaves the United States to resume its old role as consumer of last resort—but that's how the world got into trouble in the first place. Its back to square one—stuck again with global imbalances. As a result, it is not surprising to see market turmoil acting up two weeks ago. Japanese stocks are down 13 percent since January 1, 2014. Other Asian stocks and currencies have tumbled. Global stock benchmarks have fallen in recent weeks. AEs markets are not spared. US stocks are coming off a banner year, looking fairly pricy even after a rough January. The Dow Jones has since fallen 5.3 percent from its end-2013 record. Indeed, recent events in Argentina and Turkey (and to a lesser extent, South Africa, India, and Russia) sent eerie echoes reminiscent of the early stages of the 1997–1998 Asian financial crisis.

Frankly, I doubt it will happen again. Today, emerging markets are far less vulnerable—given flexible exchange rates, higher forex reserves (a whopping US$7.7 trillion), smaller external imbalances, and lower debts denominated mostly in domestic currencies. Make no mistake. The days of easy money will soon be gone (slower than many would like) and diverse defense mechanisms are in place. The wild card is panic in the face of perceptions of crises, which do have a tendency of becoming self-fulfilling. So far, the pressure is on a few countries with glaring basic weaknesses— Argentina (high inflation and youth restlessness) and Turkey (high inflation and political upheaval).

Most central banks are taking precautionary steps and will likely do more. But they are not wholly in control, since capital flows are exogenous in origin, despite the Fed's policy of holding its policy rate near zero, and China's slackening growth is unlikely to bring on a slump. JPMorgan Chase had estimated that a 1 percent fall in China's GDP growth can lead to a 0.82 percentage point fall in South American growth, against 0.51 in Asia and 0.21 in AEs.[4] Then there's the politics—the political standoff in Thailand; anti-government protests in Ukraine; corruption probe in Turkey; and labor unrest in South Africa—which are most unsettling for businessmen. That's why investors are nervous—monies will flow out, currency rates will be volatile, and even gradual tightening will make businesses uneasy. Like it or not, most EDEs will need to change and rebalance to adapt to the fact that we are in for higher interest rates. It's just a matter of time.

Kuala Lumpur
February 6, 2014

Notes

1. First published on February 8, 2014.
2. International Monetary Fund (IMF), *World Economic Outlook: Coping with High Debt and Sluggish Growth* (Washington, DC: IMF, October 2012).
3. Ruchir Sharma, *Breakout Nations: In Pursuit of the Next Economic Miracles* (New York: W.W. Norton, 2012); Ruchir Sharma, "BIITS and Ballots," *Time* (January 1, 2014), p. 23.
4. Cited in "Plethora of Worries Drives Market Turmoil," *Wall Street Journal* (February 5, 2014), p. 5.

CHAPTER 134

China: Realities about Its BOP Surpluses[1]

Recently, I was in Shanghai to attend a research symposium led by Harvard's President Drew Faust. Participants included the university's best and brightest China-hands as well as luminaries from among China's elite academia. Deliberations took on "The Chinese Century?" "China: Dynamic, Important, and Different," "The Moral Limits of Markets," "Managing Crises in China," and much more. I came away wiser. Indeed, there is so much happening in China to experience, understand, and learn. Visiting Shanghai and Beijing, you cannot but feel China is under siege for running external payments surpluses.

A consequence—argued by politicians and others in the United States and Europe—of China's rigid exchange rate regime. The debate is as fierce as it is emotional. Of late, China is strongly criticized for artificially depressing (even manipulating) the value of its currency, renminbi (RMB), or yuan, to the detriment of its trading partners. Indeed, Nobel Laureate Paul Krugman even contended that China had since taken millions of jobs globally, especially from the United States.[2] To really understand requires going back to fundamentals. What caused China's recent balance of payments (BOP) surpluses?

Causes of Imbalance

For China, BOP surpluses are a relatively recent phenomenon. It used to have persistent deficits in the second half of 1980s. Surpluses only came in the early 1990s and rose sharply since 2004 (3.5 percent of gross domestic product [GDP]) to reach a high in 2007 (10.8 percent). The surplus has now moderated, but only modestly. Whereas serious US current deficits had started years earlier. The literature on China's surpluses is long. I came across a perceptive study by two young Beita (Peking University) econo-mists at its China Centre for Economic Research, Yiping Huang and Kunyu Tao, who attributed the main cause to asymmetric market liberalization.[3] Over the past 30 years, reform was much too focused on product markets (today, 95 percent of products are determined by free markets). But markets in factors of production, labor, capital, land, energy, and the environment remain highly distorted, driven by the government's growth-centered policy strategy to push exports. These cost distortions are equivalent to production and investment subsidies.

Both Chinese and foreigners invest massively because of China's cheap labor, cheap capital, cheap land, and cheap energy:

- **Labor:** China's abundant and cheap labor is key to its continuing suc-cess in manufacturing exports. But labor costs are distorted because (1) the separation of rural and urban labor leads to labor immobility and low pay for rural migrants; and (2) an out-of-date social welfare system (including health and pensions) means payrolls should be 35 to 40 percent more.
- **Capital:** The financial system remains repressed, with regulated interest rates and state control of credit allocation; external capital controls are restrictive on outflows. Moreover, the currency is kept undervalued.
- **Land:** State owns land in cities, and collectives, outside. No market mechanism exists to price land for industrial use; often, prices are set low to promote investment and growth.
- **Energy:** Key energy prices are state determined and usually subsidized.
- **Environment:** Enforcement is random since growth is given priority. Cost of pollution is not priced in.

All of these mean lower production costs and producer subsidies. They artificially inflate profits, raise investment returns, and improve compe-tiveness. Huang and Tao estimated that these subsidies are worth a hefty 7 percent of GDP. Capital market distortions are the most troublesome, con-tributing 40 percent of total; with labor subsidies, 25 percent. The upshot: These are structural imbalances. Factor distortions are deep. Any credible policy at rebalancing must tackle the root cause—that is, distorted incen-tives for investors, producers, and exporters. The undervalued RMB is but one element in the entire jigsaw.

The savings–investment gap is by definition the flip side of BOP sur-pluses. Attempts to explain the imbalance in terms of savings and invest-ment behavior will not be useful. Suffice to recognize the common belief that Chinese households save (HHS) too much is incorrect. For 15 years, HHS rate has been stable at about 30 percent; nothing unusual in Asia. Its stability suggests HHS is probably not a key cause of growing BOP surpluses in recent years. Because corporate savings are rising, households' income share is on the decline.

The Exchange Rate Option

Exchange rate reform in China is sensitive. For the United States and Europe, the yuan scapegoat is a political football, with attendant risks of a trade war. Among economists, there are vast differences in what needs to be done. The common prescription is to let the RMB rise by a certain margin (enough to eliminate the undervaluation), but no one knows precisely what this is. Views vary widely.

In April 2010, Goldman Sachs pointed out: At the moment, rather oddly, the bank's model suggests that the RMB is very close to the price that it should be. This has not always been the case. The model used to suggest the currency was undervalued by about 20 percent but it has moved by that degree over the past five years. However, the 2009 research of Morris Goldstein and Nicholas Lardy[4] at the US Peterson Institute pointed to a 12 to 16 percent undervaluation. Even if such an adjustment were taken, the West would still prefer it to be larger. Nor will the Chinese do so in one go, given the likely sharp negative impact on China's desire for exchange stability. But the weight of recent history looms large. Between mid-2005 and end-2008, the RMB exchange rate appreciated by 19 percent, after strengthening by 30 percent over 10½ years since January 1994. Yet China's BOP surplus surged during these periods. Despite the revaluation, US–China imports rose 39 percent during 2005–2008.

Japanese economic stagnation following US pressure in 1985 didn't boost confidence—US$1 fell from ¥240 to ¥160 over two years, and then to ¥80 by 1995. Consequently, growth slowed abruptly, forcing more government spending and low interest rates. The real estate bubble and a yearlong slump followed. The 1990s became a decade of lost growth. To this day, the intended aim to fix Japan's BOP surplus remains just that—an empty aim! Two lessons have emerged for China: Large forex adjustments cause long-term damage to the economy; and, it won't necessarily help eliminate BOP surpluses.

An often-suggested alternative is for China to adopt greater exchange rate flexibility. This looks reasonable enough, but will it resolve China's BOP imbalances? Empirical studies have shown there is no systematic or reliable relationship between its BOP position and exchange rate flexibility. Consider this, also. Even if a significant RMB revaluation could wipe off China's BOP surpluses, it still won't reduce US BOP deficits. After all, RMB features at only 15 percent of the Fed's exchange rate basket for the US$. This simply means a 20 percent RMB appreciation translates to only a 3 percent appreciation against US$. Furthermore, the market vacuum left by China would most likely be filled by exports from other low-income nations like India, South Africa, Indonesia, and Vietnam, or by even high-tech competitive South Korea and Taiwan. So be careful what you ask for.

And then, there is the crawling peg or gradual appreciation option. But this creates expectations that can lead to speculation and hot money inflows. China should have learned from RMB's rise in 2007 and 2008. A way out of this dilemma should be familiar—opt for the compromise it took in July 2005, when China moved off the peg to the US$ with a material revaluation, which eventually turned out to have little impact on its BOP surplus.

China's Neighbors Less Concerned

Unlike the United States and Europe, ASEAN (Brunei, Indonesia, Malaysia, the Philippines, Thailand, Singapore, Vietnam, Cambodia, Laos, and Myanmar), plus 4 (India, Japan, South Korea, and Taiwan), have remained "cool" on this issue because:

1. China's continuing growth provides a robust source of demand for the region.
2. Most neighbors have different export profiles from China; indeed, most of their trade complements rather well.
3. Japan, South Korea, and Taiwan have built large manufacturing capacities in China, thus sharing in China's dynamic exports.
4. Asia likes ready access to cheaper manufacturing equipment they badly need, which in turn keeps China's export machine running.

In the final analysis, many in Asia are likely to mirror any revaluation of RMB. This is already happening to the stronger Asian currencies as the US$ weakens.

United States Unlikely to Benefit

Students of economics know better. In the past two years, the United States had trade deficits with over 90 nations. Yet, the United States is pushing for a bilateral solution ("forcing" China to revalue or tax Chinese exports) to essentially a multilateral problem. Both China and the United States have large imbalances with the rest of the world. Any credible solution must lie in a multilateral approach. After all, China–US trade accounted for only 12 percent of Chinese total trade.

Nevertheless, empirical evidence suggests that a more expensive RMB is unlikely to reduce US bilateral deficit. Sharp appreciation of RMB between June 2005 and June 2008 in fact widened the US deficit: Contrary to textbook economics, US imports from China rose by 39 percent, offsetting increases in Chinese–US imports, which (even without revaluation) had been increasing since 2002. Moreover, higher import prices would mean a fall in the purchasing power of US income. But a stronger RMB raises the purchasing power of Chinese producers who rely on imported raw materials. Because imports are now cheaper, Chinese exporters can reduce export prices to maintain market share.

Realistically, it is not surprising that the relationship between exchange rate and BOP balance is, at best, weak. Weaker still is the relationship between BOP deficit and US job loss. Here again, empirical evidence is telling. An old friend, Professor Lawrence Lau of Stanford, pointed out in his 2006 research (and collaborated with others in 2008) that Chinese value added accounted for only one-third to half of US imports from China. This reflects the importance of efforts by workers and capital from other nations, including the United States. It has been reported the iPod costs US$150 to produce, of which only US$4 is Chinese value added. Most of the components are made in the United States and other countries. It is put together in China and exported to the United States for the full US$150 as imports from China, adding to the US deficit and exaggerating the US job loss! In reality, imported iPods support myriad US jobs up the value chain. Surely, prohibitive tariffs on iPod imports can't really hurt China. Why cut off your nose to spite your face?

What, Then, Are We to Do?

It does appear that slamming China as a "currency manipulator" does not help the US cause. It will probably backfire. Even assuming RMB is undervalued, exclusive focus on China's exchange rate policy is, I think, counterproductive. It will unlikely resolve the United States' persistent external imbalance. However, as I see it, there is growing awareness in Beijing that greater exchange-rate flexibility and a gradual RMB appreciation must be elements of any credible package of policy measures for China to seriously liberalize factor markets and remove cost distortions. This could well transit over time to a full market economy. Any exchange rate adjustment has to be viewed in this context.

Nevertheless, these are necessary but not sufficient. China has to embark also on other reforms, including redesigning macroeconomic policies that don't overemphasize growth, privatizing state-owned enterprises and liberalizing financial development, striking a better balance in income distribution from corporate to households, and aggressively promoting services sector development, especially small and medium-sized enterprises. Such a comprehensive rebalancing exercise can be made to work, but will necessarily take time. For now, it's steady as she goes.

Shanghai, China
Kuala Lumpur
April 9, 2010

Notes

1. First published on April 10, 2010, as "Realities about China's BOP Surpluses."
2. Paul Krugman, "Chinese New Year," *New York Times* (January 1, 2010).
3. Yiping Huang and Kunyu Tao, "Causes and Remedies of China's External Balances," draft paper dated February 20, 2010, presented at the Asian Economic Panel meeting in Seoul, South Korea, on March 22–23, 2010.
4. Morris Goldstein and Nicholas R. Lardy, *The Future of China's Exchange Rate Policy* (Washington, DC: Peterson Institute for International Economics, 2009).

CHAPTER 135

China: RMB Flexibility Not Enough[1]

Chapter 134, "China: Realities about Its BOP Surpluses," concluded with: "Exclusive focus on China's exchange rate policy is, I think, counterproductive. It will unlikely resolve the United States' persistent external imbalance. However, as I see it, there is growing awareness in Beijing that greater exchange rate flexibility and a gradual renminbi (RMB) appreciation has to be an element of any credible package of policy measures for China to seriously liberalize factor markets and remove cost distortions. This could well transit over time to a full market economy. Any exchange rate adjustment has to be viewed in this context."

Sure enough, the People's Bank of China (PBoC) announced on June 19, 2010, that it would allow greater flexibility for the RMB or yuan. Thereby, reverting to the flexibility it enjoyed before the RMB was effectively repegged at around 6.83 per US$ in mid-2008 to provide stability during the global crisis. In the three years following an initial 2.1 percent revaluation of the RMB on July 21, 2005, the currency gained a further 19 percent. But in those first remaining months of 2005, the appreciation was only 8.6 percent.

Credibility Requires Serious Action

China's decision to allow flexibility back into the value of the RMB was greeted with "grudging optimism." Few think, and rightly so, that the move will have a dramatic impact on rebalancing the global economy—partly because of its limited size. The RMB offshore forward market on the first trading day predicted an appreciation of just 2.3 percent by year-end, and 3 percent in 12 months. Based on an undervalued RMB estimated at between 25 and 40 percent, this will take more than a decade to eliminate—partly because most regard any RMB adjustment as a helpful but not critical part of shifting consumer demand from the United States to Asia. Previous experience in 2005–2008 was accompanied by a soaring Chinese current surplus instead. This was also the Japanese experience after the 1985 Plaza Accord, when Japan agreed to a major yen appreciation. Stanford Professor Ronald McKinnon found little long-term change in Japan's trade surplus with the United States as a result. The lesson China has taken on board is that rapid swings in the exchange rate can only be damaging.

The PBoC has yet to release details of the new regime. But it has hinted: (1) its focus is to guide the RMB against a basket of currencies, in order to foster a genuine two-way movement between RMB and US$; (2) the "basis did not exist for a large-scale appreciation" (i.e., big exchange rate fluctuations "are not in China's interest"), and any movement in RMB will be gradual; (3) flexibility to be in both directions—that is, instill interplay of two-way risks; and (4) make more use of existing trading-band from the RMB's central parity rate. In practice, the regime closely resembles a managed crawl. It is akin to the policy that let the RMB appreciate by some 21 percent against the US$ until the financial panic hit in 2008. Be that as it may, the expectation of a stronger RMB can only attract inflows of "hot money" betting on further RMB appreciation. That is why the PBoC had insisted that "it is not appropriate, given China's diversification of trade and investment, that the yuan is fixed solely to one currency, as it won't accurately reflect the real value of the yuan."[2]

Trading under the New Regime

To forestall undue expectations, the PBoC's weekend statement made clear that a big, onetime revaluation was not in the cards.[3] Indeed, the band under which the RMB trades daily will not be widened beyond 0.5 percent. In the short run, it's wait-and-see how far and how fast the PBoC will allow the currency to appreciate. On its first day of trading, the RMB rose to a new high against the US$, closing at RMB6.7976, up 0.42 percent from Friday's (June 18, 2010) close of 6.8262. It was the RMB's strongest level since the currency was regularly traded. The previous high was in July 2008, just before it was pegged to the US$ at around 6.84 and kept there for the next two years to help stabilize its economy amid global recession.

To be sure, the RMB had since appreciated 3.8 percent so far this year on a trade-weighted basis, thanks to a shrinking euro. On its second day of trading, the RMB weakened, reflecting the PBoC's message that the new regime doesn't guarantee a one-way bet on its currency. It ended at 6.8136, down about 0.23 percent from Monday's close. Indeed, the markets got the message: Two days of trading reinforced the PBoC's goals to allow market trading to drive the exchange rate, and to move it up and down, mainly to deter speculation. At this early stage, the PBoC is concerned—and rightly so—the perception of RMB appreciation as a sure thing will trigger massive capital inflows (hot money) to the detriment of Beijing's ability to maintain stability.

The PBoC's most effective means of control has been setting daily the rate for the RMB (i.e., central parity rate or CPR) to start off trading. Given that the RMB can only move 0.5 percent ± CPR, overall RMB movement is not set by intraday trades but by how the CPR moves from one day to the next. This way, the PBoC seldom needs to intervene directly in the market. On the second day of trading, the CPR was set at 6.7980 (almost where it closed on Monday)—that is, 0.42 percent stronger than Friday's close. This fueled expectation that the PBoC won't try to reverse Monday's gains. But early into trading, the RMB reversed and abruptly weakened, with heavy US$ buying by banks at around 6.8000. After a week of trading, the RMB closed stronger at 6.7922, up 0.5 percent from its close a week earlier. By Wednesday, June 30, it closed up 0.65 percent at 6.7817. To be fair, when the PBoC said there would be no dramatic movements, it wasn't kidding. But expectations are high. President Barack Obama anticipated the RMB would increase significantly. This expectation is being tempered by the International Monetary Fund (IMF): It will take time for the RMB to reach its normal market volume. Next developments will depend on the patience of the United States if the evolving RMB revaluation proves all too gradual.

"Hot Money"

The new regime has boosted Asian currency values. The South Korean won, Australia dollar, Thai baht, and Malaysian ringgit felt the biggest impact. Traders centered on these currencies they regard as proxies for China's growth and its appetite for imports with a stronger RMB. That, in turn, makes central banks in Thailand, Malaysia, Indonesia, and South Korea feel more comfortable about letting their currencies strengthen. It helps fight inflation because imported goods get cheaper, and reduces the need to raise interest rates. All over Asia, there is now greater tolerance for currency appreciation. While attracting foreign capital is usually good, short-term inflows can cause bubbles in stocks and property. And, when they pull out on the first hint of trouble, panic usually takes over.

South Korea and Indonesia imposed new measures recently aimed at moderating their impact. China's history of sharp and disruptive capital inflows during 2005–2008 offers an object lesson. The RMB's gradual strengthening (up 21 percent against US$ from 2005 to 2008) coincided with huge gains in Asian stocks (Hang Seng China Enterprises Index traded in Hong Kong rose 319 percent). Hence, China's concern over speculative risks complicating efforts to control money supply. To deal with this, the PBoC promotes the idea that the RMB–US$ exchange rate is unpredictable and can swing in both directions. Its management of the RMB in its first 10 days demonstrated this. This should help mitigate hot money inflows.

Non-Deliverable Forwards

China's State Administration of Foreign Exchange (SAFE), which manages its US$2.5 trillion in foreign reserves, is concerned that hot money investors are exploiting pricing differentials between domestic forward markets and offshore non-deliverable forwards (NDFs) market. But unlike South Korea, which recently imposed restrictions to reduce won volatility, SAFE opted to continue to monitor instead. NDFs are derivative contracts traded among foreign investors that pay out based on expectations on the value of the RMB against US$ in the future. Following the flexibility, 12-month NDFs moved sharply on Monday to a 3 percent rise of the RMB in the next year (compared with 1.8 percent on the prior Friday); 6-month forwards are up 1.3 percent.

Economists offer four reasons in believing hot money flows will be limited: (1) a 3 percent appreciation is too slim to attract investors unable to attract leverage; (2) fears the Chinese economy may "cool" and the bubble property market is about to burst; (3) expectations on asset prices have since "cooled down"—Shanghai stock market is already down 30 percent this year and housing sales are dropping sharply; and (4) a possible global double-dip recession.

Internationalization of the RMB

Concomitantly, the PBoC separately confirmed plans to expand its trial program to settle trade deals in RMB. It's part of a broader effort to modernize and internationalize its currency. First started in July 2009, it encouraged companies in Shanghai and Guangzhou province to use the RMB instead when trading with Hong Kong, Macau, and some foreign countries. After a slow start, Tuesday's announcement expanded the program to 20 of China's 31 provinces, and now, all foreign countries can participate. To date, the value of such RMB-based deals totaled only US$6.5 billion, or less than 1 percent of China's total foreign trade. The obstacle has been reluctance of many companies to hold RMB because of its limited use outside China. This has to do with China's reluctance to make the RMB fully convertible, a policy Beijing intends to hang onto. Increased RMB flexibility can make it more attractive to hold, provided it leads to appreciation. This program offers Chinese exporters a way out of worries on currency risks since their costs are mainly in RMB. The euro's recent volatility heightened this concern. Europe is China's biggest trading partner.

Despite the calmness of RMB trading under the new regime, the currency dispute in China has not gone away. But so far, reactions have been positive. At home, opposition to even a 3.5 percent appreciation of the RMB remains strong, especially within China's export lobby. The warning shot has come subtly: Water doesn't boil if it is heated at 99°C. But it will boil if it is heated by one more degree. Internationally, it's just more wait-and-see. Expect the initial euphoria to dissipate quickly as politics and reality set in. I am now reminded of former Chinese Prime Minister Zhou Enlai's response when asked, 175 years after the fact, what he made of the French Revolution. He thought for a moment and then answered (it was reported): "It is too soon to tell."

What, Then, Are We to Do?

I end as I began. The RMB revaluation is not China's most critical problem today. China has to embark also on other reforms, including redesigning macroeconomic policies that don't overemphasize growth, privatizing state-owned enterprises, and liberalizing financial development, striking a better balance in income distribution, and aggressively promoting services sector development. Such a comprehensive rebalancing exercise can be made to work, but will necessarily take time. For now, it's steady as she goes. We'll just have to wait and see.

Kuala Lumpur
July 1, 2010

Notes

1. First published on July 3, 2010.
2. In a statement issued in Beijing on June 20, 2010, the PBoC said that because the United States is but one of China's many trading partners, China should reassess how it valued the yuan.
3. Ibid.

CHAPTER 136

China: Much Ado about Nothing[1]

Headline: "Rising China Tops Japan as World's No. 2." Looks like a big deal. Officially, the news came out of Tokyo two weeks ago on February 14, 2011, when the Japanese government reported its economy shrank at a 1.1 percent annual rate in the fourth quarter of 2010, a period when China's gross domestic product (GDP) surged 9.8 percent from a year earlier. With those figures, Japan's full-year GDP amounted to US$5.47 trillion, about 7 percent smaller than the US$5.88 trillion China reported in January. Japan's real GDP for the full year (2010) expanded by 3.9 percent (–6.3 percent in 2009); for China, it's expected at 10.3 percent for 2010 as a whole, up from 9.2 percent in 2009. Thus, China became the world's second-largest economy in 2010, ending Japan's 42-year reign in that position. As I see it, it is something that is bound to happen, considering China's ballooning GDP and much, much larger population—just a matter of arithmetic and time. While China's economy has several times in the past surpassed Japan's based on quarterly data, February 14's reading marks the first time China has done so on a full-year basis, the standard used for global rankings. Indeed, China's recent success overshadows the fact that Japan's economy expanded for all of 2010. Growth in the first nine months meant that even with the poor showing in the fourth quarter of 2010, Japan's real GDP for the entire 2010 expanded at 3.9 percent.

Japan, China, and the United States

Still, Japan leads the pack among G-7 nations' growth, surpassing Germany (3.6 percent), the United States (2.9 percent), and the United Kingdom (1.4 percent). Lest it's forgotten, Japan remains dependent on exports. GDP growth could well fall off again if global trade tanks. That happened during the recent global crisis, when Japan's economy shrank 6.3 percent in 2009, the worst contraction among G-7 countries that year. Hobbled by continuing weak domestic demand, Japan's economic output is still about 5 percent smaller in nominal terms than it was in 2008, despite the rebound in 2010. In contrast, the US economy is today 2 percent larger than it was in 2008. But both Japan and China together remains considerably smaller than the US economy—still worth 23 percent less (at US$11.35 trillion) than the US 2010 GDP of US$14.66 trillion. Surely, the news marks the end of an era. For two generations since overtaking West Germany in 1967, Japan stood solidly as the world's number-two economy. Even now, Japan ranks way ahead of Germany (fourth), France (fifth), and the United Kingdom (sixth). The new rankings merely symbolize China's rise and Japan's decline as global growth engines. For the United States, as I see it, while Japan was in a way an economic rival, it has also been a geopolitical and military ally. China, however, poses as a challenger on all fronts.

China Continues Growing

But China remains, in many ways, poor, whereas Japan is an extremely wealthy nation. In terms of GDP per capita, Japan is number 1 in Asia and number 18 globally, between Canada and Germany, according to the World Bank. Japan's success after World War II—the economic "miracle" under-pinned by annual growth rates averaging 10 percent in 1960s and 5 percent in 1970s—is still looked up to by much of the world. China still lags behind Japan in many respects in the face of a reality that their growing interde-pendence makes them partners as well as rivals. By comparison, China's income per capita (at US$4,400) is only one-tenth of Japan's. The World Bank estimates that more than 100 million people in China—nearly Japan's entire population—live on less than US$2 a day.

Size, of course, matters. If you look at China's development, its standard of living is much like Thailand, even Indonesia. But if you look at China's mere size, besides being now the world's number-two economy, it's also its largest exporter (counting eurozone members separately); second largest importer; largest surplus nation (with current surplus peaking at 11 percent of GDP); and largest holder of the world's stock of foreign currency reserves (equivalent to 50 percent of its GDP). China's economy probably will sur-pass the US economy in outright size within 20 years. But, quite obviously, the GDP landmark can't reflect the true condition of Chinese society, which a friend of mine at Beita (Peking University) described as "rich country, poor people."

Still, China's continuing rapid growth points out the stark contrast with the United States and eurozone economies, which are still struggling to maintain growth and revive employment. US share of global output (20 percent), trade (11 percent), and even financial assets (30 percent) is shrinking, as emerg-ing nations continue to flourish. China's strong performance is in some ways good for the global economy. It reflects rising demand for Chinese goods in the United States and elsewhere. China's exports rose 31 percent in 2010, but its imports rose even faster at 38 percent. As China overtakes Japan, it also boosts its growth: Japanese exports to China hit a record ¥13 trillion in 2010.

Indeed, the rapidly growing Chinese market for a wide range of products (from cars and SUVs to high-tech electronics to Chinese tourists) is galvanizing corporate Japan and the rest of Asia. China surpassed the United States as Japan's largest trading partner in 2009. Masayoshi Son (CEO, Softbank) expects China's GDP to double Japan's in eight years. As of now, many in Japan and Asia view China's growing economic clout as benefiting all of Asia. Indeed, continued growth in China, as well as some pickup in the United States, is expected to help Japan bounce back in the first half of 2011.

Redefining Challenges

China's official rise to become Asia's top economy takes the spotlight off Tokyo. While some Japanese elite now look back to the era of Japan bashing with nostalgia, others found a new opportunity to help redefine Japan's image as number three. I well recall a recent *Asian Wall Street Journal* write-up on the book, *Do We Have to Be No. 1?* by Renho (a ruling-party politician), who suggested that Japanese should take comfort in the notion that Japan need not be a leader in everything (or anything) to be deemed successful.[2] Her notion of Japan is as a center of creativity and innovation (e.g., hybrid cars, and 3D video games), in contrast to its image 30 years ago as a copycat, which later outperformed the originals with excellent design, manufacturing, and craftsmanship. That label is now passed on to China. It's a matter of quality over quantity: "Japan is still a wealthy nation in many senses of the word."

China continues to grapple with challenges in achieving rapid, widely shared, and sustainable growth. Meanwhile, the rest of the world must learn to adjust to China's growing impact. In the aftermath of the global crisis, however, it is a rising China that feels time is on its side. Something rather Chinese considering its some 6,000 years of history. Like it or not, the United States' and China's economies are indeed deeply enmeshed—not at all a zero-sum game. To many Chinese (most are cool pragmatists), the United States will retain unchallengeable global power for the next generation, at least—given US capacity to adjust, innovate, and restore its dominance. In the meantime, Chinese attitudes have also changed in a world as it sees it today. There are already indications that the young are growing impatient and are increasingly ignoring the advice of Deng Xiaoping (architect of modern China) to "hide our capacities; bide our time . . . never claim leadership." China still has much to do just to keep pace with the people's aspirations for higher incomes and higher living standards.

GDP: Not Necessarily Happiness

I first met Professor Simon Kuznets at Harvard in the summer of 1969 (who won the Nobel Prize in economics two years later). A small but impressive man with piercing eyes, he educated me with his rare insights into development economics. It also taught me there is more to life than money. He once told me: The welfare of a nation can scarcely be inferred from a measure of national income. He should know—he invented national accounts and built them for the United States. So he knew their limits. Forty years on, where Kuznets led, others have followed, including US President Barack Obama, French President Nicolas Sarkozy, and UK Prime Minister David Cameron. Prime Minister Cameron sums it up best: We need to look for alternative measures that would show national progress not just by how our economy is growing, but by how our lives are improving, not just by our standard of living, but by our quality of life. I once read that in the 1960s, Robert Kennedy criticized GDP as measuring everything (including pollution, cigarette advertising, napalm, and nuclear warheads) except that which makes life worthwhile (the arts, wit, wisdom, and compassion).

Similar concerns underpinned the 2008 Commission on the measurement of economic performance and social progress set up by Sarkozy and led by Nobel Laureates Joseph Stiglitz and Amartya Sen.[3] It concluded that the level of GDP per capita was far from the best measure of material living standards. They emphasized greater usage of net national income (i.e., after adjusting for depreciation of capital, including infrastructure); stress more on the household instead of economy-wide measures; showcasing distribution of income and consumption; and evaluating nonmarket activities, including leisure. The second stage is to combine new measures of well-being (health, education, governance, environmental sustainability, and subjective measures of quality of life) into a single summary measure. The challenge remains how to summarize overall well-being using a simple set of indicators that most can understand and use.

Pursuit of Happiness

The trouble is, people do quite poorly at predicting what makes them happy. They focus too much on initial responses and overlook how fleeting moments of pleasure are, leaving them no happier than before. Granted, many studies have shown that wealthier nations tend to be happier than poorer ones; and rich people appear more satisfied than the less affluent. Yet, other studies on the United States and South Korea suggest that people are no happier than they were 50 years ago despite sharp rises in income per capita. Since happiness is what people finally want and wealth is only a means toward this end, Professor Derek Bok (former Harvard president) made it known that "the primacy now accorded to economic growth would appear to be a mistake."[4] A recent Canadian study concluded that the happiest people reside in the poorest provinces (Nova Scotia), while those in the richest (British Columbia) were among the least happy.[5]

What, Then, Are We to Do?

Based on latest research findings, two conclusions have emerged: (1) things that bring enduring satisfaction for individuals are also good for most others (e.g., helping others, and close relationships); and (2) experiences that bring lasting happiness do not feature as priority in government (e.g., medical afflictions, such as chronic pain, depression, and sleep disorders, give way to vast relief as sufferers are treated, but such people are often underserved in hospitals).

But is happiness research really reliable enough as inputs for public policy? For sure, people who claim to be happy tend to live longer, are less prone to commit suicide, don't abuse drugs, get promoted more often, and enjoy good friends. Their assessment of their own well-being lines up rather well with the views of friends and family. Researchers found that answers to questions about their well-being seem to correspond fairly well to more objective evidence. Be that as it may, it's still premature to initiate new bold policies on happiness based on research alone. Nevertheless, they can be useful in assigning priorities or identifying new possibilities for public intervention. At the very least, like the United Kingdom and France, governments should collect and publish regular data on trends in the well-being of citizens. Perhaps, public officials may even use these research insights as a basis for informed decisions. Surely, you can't go wrong with prioritizing happiness.

Kuala Lumpur
February 24, 2011

Notes

1. First published on February 26, 2011, as "Much Ado About Nothing."
2. "Rising China Tops Japan as World's No. 2," *Wall Street Journal* (February 15, 2011), p. 13.
3. Joseph Stiglitz (chair), Amartya Sen (chair adviser), and Jean-Paul Fitoussi (coordinator), *Report by the Commission on the Measurement of Economic Performance and Social Progress,* Paris, September 2009.
4. Derek Bok, "The Official Pursuit of Happiness," *Straits Times*, Singapore (January 6, 2011).
5. Ibid.

CHAPTER 137

The "China Dream"[1]

President Xi Jinping, general-secretary of the ruling Communist Party as well as chairman of the Military Commission, talked of the "China Dream" to unite an increasingly diverse nation of 1.35 billion people. What's Xi's vision, which incidentally sounds somewhat like the American dream?; it even evokes Martin Luther King's "I Have a Dream," reflecting some US-style aspiration. Since the revolution, China's goals have centered on unity, strength, and wealth. Mao Zedong tried to attain them through Marxism and failed: The Cultural Revolution ended with his death in 1976. Deng Xiaoping's catchphrase was more practical: "reform and opening-up." Then, Jiang Zemin pushed the more arcane "Three Represents" to embody the changed society, including allowing private businessmen to join the party. Lately, Hu Jintao championed the "scientific-development" outlook, which was about being greener and dealt with disharmony created by the divisive wealth gap. His Prime Minister Wen Jiabao dwelt repeatedly with the need to rid the economy of the four *uns*: "unstable, unbalanced, uncoordinated, and ultimately unsustainable growth."

Now, Xi talks of his dream of "the great revival of the Chinese nation," of a "strong army dream," and of our mission "to meet the people's desire for a happy life." He also alludes to ordinary citizens wanting "to own a home, send a child to university, and just have fun." The Chinese dream, he said, "is an ideal. Communists should have a higher ideal, and that is Communism." Frankly, even though short on detail, Xi's dream is different from his two predecessors' stodgy ideologies. I see practical politics at work here. With growth slowing, Xi's new vision appears to emphasize nationalism going beyond middle-class material comfort. Of course, there is the usual tough talk on the rule of law and on corruption ("fighting tigers and flies at the same time"); also on meeting the public's wish for "better education and more stable jobs." His dream seems designed to inspire rather than inform. In the end, "The China Dream is the people's dream," so he says.

Promises and Pledges

China's US$8.3 trillion economy went through its worst slowdown in 13 years in 2012 when weak exports and increases in interest rates dragged annual growth to 7.8 percent, the grimmest since 1999. The economy faces more headwinds as it struggles with surplus production capacity and underlying risks in the financial system. So it's not surprising that the new administration has called for sweeping reforms and lessening state control. Areas requiring pressing change include: freeing interest rates, promoting private investment, encouraging consumption and "greener" growth, and enforcing the rule of law. It has even declared: "Fair competition is our common goal," vowing to end subsidizing state-owned enterprises (SOEs) and leveling the playing field for private enterprise. The new leadership has since pledged to (1) slash bureaucracy; (2) commit to market-oriented reforms; (3) boost social spending and services; and (4) fight pollution. China is expected to rely on migration to the cities to boost domestic consumption and remake the economy to be less dependent on massive outlays on fixed investment at home and exports abroad. Such "rebalancing" needs to give markets room to operate competitively. In finance, market forces will be given freer play in setting interest and exchange rates, to ensure savers get a better deal and businesses have ready access to funding through more effective capital markets.

The Xi administration now puts China's fast-growing consumer class at center stage. Perhaps the most far-reaching change thus far is the urbanization policy being pursued. This involves reforming the rigid urban *hukou* household registration system by giving residency permits to some 220 million migrants to the cities, and allowing farmers to sell land at market prices to protect their land rights and boost incomes. Empowering a whole new class of consumers underpins the national drive to reorganize the entire economy from government to banks to SOEs. Such radical overhaul is needed to seriously expand domestic demand. China's plan includes adding nine million new jobs in urban areas to keep unemployment at or below 4.6 percent to ensure that real per-capita income for both urban and rural residents continues to increase. Its inflation target this year remains at 3.5 percent, lower than 4 percent in 2012. China's actual inflation last year came in well below that at 2.6 percent. But these achievements came at the cost of widening inequality and environmental degradation. China's Gini coefficient, a measure of income differences, was 0.474 in 2012, higher than the 0.4 level, which signals a potential for social unrest. A ratio closer to 0 indicates near full equality; 1 represents perfect inequality.

Transformation

China's gross domestic product (GDP) rose 7.7 percent in the first quarter of 2013 (down from 7.9 percent in the fourth quarter of 2012), slower than the median analysts' forecast of 8 percent. Given continuing weak US conditions and a eurozone locked in recession, disappointing Chinese data cast a long shadow over the global outlook. Frankly, I am not as worried, provided it reflects the transformation that's said to be already in train. Elements of this reform include: (1) shift from investment-export led growth to a new structure, providing widespread support for domestic private consumption; (2) this rebalancing will involve new initiatives emanating from services-led consumption; and (3) which in turn relies on more labor-intensive services—requiring 35 percent more jobs per unit of GDP compared with manufacturing and construction (thus ensuring rising employment and poverty reduction), with a much smaller resource and carbon footprint.

As I understand it, this services-led pro-consumption reform remains a core initiative in the current twelfth five-year plan. The agenda needs complementary support from implementing an enlarged and better-designed social safety net; reform of SOEs; and ending financial depression of households by raising the artificially low interest rates on saving. But there are strong headwinds coming from several directions: deteriorating credit quality affecting the integrity of bank balance sheets; weakening export competitiveness reflecting continuing rising wages; pollution, corruption, and inequality; and political economy missteps, including escalating disputes with Japan and others. China has come through two major crises in the past four years. Its economy remains robust and resilient, but it still needs to modernize. Make no mistake, the risks are real. Only purposeful transformation can provide China with the needed strength and resolve to pull through future crises. Reality check: As the economy matures, its pace of growth will surely slacken.

Urbanization

Urbanization (movement of rural population into cities and towns) has become a focus of China's reform plans. Its urban population reached 690 million in 2011, against 170 million in 1978. The percentage of urban population rose to more than 51 percent in 2011 (17.9 percent in 1978) and will touch 60 percent by 2020. Consequently, rural population fell from 82.1 percent in 1978 to 48.7 percent in 2011. This movement highlights the strategy to rebalance the economy: (1) it drives market demand; per-capita consumption ratio of urban residents to rural is about 3.3:1; (2) it pushes investment in infrastructure and social housing, which in turn creates employment and new incomes, which further raises consumption. A 1 to 1.5 percentage point rise in urbanization adds 15 to 20 million people to the city; (3) it promotes industrial restructuring and upgrading thereby raising the quality and productivity of employment; and (4) it also increases jobs in the service industry.

According to the World Bank, emigrants send home US$45 billion a year, with some sending as much as 80 percent of their income to support their families.[2] This leads to rising rural spending on better homes, education, consumer durables, and higher-grade groceries. Contrary to common belief, migrants actually maintain their rural shopper habits as they work and sleep in urban environments. The entire process will help to restructure the economy. It is projected that 400 million people will become urban over the next decade. Under the twelfth five-year plan (ending 2015), 36 million social housing units will have to be built in addition to the 7.2 million units built in 2012. To meet the growing demand for urban jobs, China created 10.24 million new jobs in the first nine months of 2012 (exceeding the 9 million target set for the entire year).

But urbanization comes at a cost. It is accompanied by chronic environmental degradation and worsening pollution, posing a serious threat to human health and social stability. Urban migration is drastically changing patterns of consumption and behavior: City residents use three times more electricity than rural dwellers; consume 10 times as much sugar; and require vastly more infrastructure and utilities to service their daily lives. Despite efforts to make cities greener, progress is slow because local officials are rewarded for high investment and fast growth, rather than for sustainability. Hence, repeated calls for urbanization to be "balanced with ecological security."

Additionally, there is fear that the surge of migration would turn cities into Latin-American-style slums. But urban reformers are pushing for "bigger-is-better"—the idea that cities gain by having people more tightly packed: forcing greater use of public transportation (hence, raising its effectiveness); forcing old-line high-polluting industries to relocate (thus raising productivity and freeing valuable social space); forcing new energies into a city; and thus, helping to create new businesses and investment.

Surprisingly, many of China's biggest cities are much less densely populated than Singapore, Seoul, Manhattan, and downtown Tokyo, all of which have made strong, successful transitions to the consumer-led service-industry model China wants. Beijing (20 million) has a density of less than 5,000 per square kilometers, and Shanghai (18 million), less than 6,000 against 11,000 in Singapore, 18,500 in New York, and 10,400 in Seoul. Rightly so, the Chinese leadership is worried about building super-size urban centers because they do create slums, worsen pollution, or spur pockets of political dissent.

What, Then, Are We to Do?

National unity requires China to be one big bed. But its people can, and do, have different dreams—indeed, as many as 1.35 billion. The challenge is to get them all to dream the same dream. President Xi hopes this would be his

"China Dream." China's rise in national strength is well known. It's already the world's second largest economy and the world's largest exporter. Over the past decade, the economy rose 9.3 percent on average, raising per-capita income to exceed US$6,000 in 2012.

Historians remind us that in 1820, China's GDP was one-third of the world. Then humiliation of the century brought it down to a low—so that by the 1960s, China's share fell to just 4 percent. Now, it has recovered to about one-sixth in purchasing-power parity terms. Xi's dream needs to reassure the new middle class that China can remain "rich and strong" in the hope of reigniting "the great revival of the Chinese nation."

From the "people first" approach to the "scientific outlook" on development, and then to campaigning for a "harmonious society" and "inclusive growth," the Hu-Wen administration shifted the single-minded pursuit of GDP growth toward more emphasis on balance, reorienting its strategies toward a stronger focus on social security (by 2012, 480 million were on pension and 1.3 billion covered by medical insurance); education (reforms at decentralization and addressing the need for innovation and entrepreneurship); urban–rural divide (reform of subsidies and taxes, and free and compulsory education in rural areas); and social housing (leading to massive building). Despite much progress, these areas remain of deep enough concern to require bold and innovative action by China's new fifth-generation leadership.

As I see it, gradualism (instead of cold turkey) is still the tone of future reforms. I see this manifested by the new emphasis on introducing pilot programs first to test their workability on the ground when carrying out major reforms. As part of reform, it does appear now there won't be any large-scale stimulus to boost growth as the government pares the state's role and relies more on workings of the market mechanism and the initiative of private enterprise. Many analysts have since begun to lower China's 2013 growth to 7.6 percent for the year as a whole, as the road ahead gets bumpy. It's unlikely to grow at 8.2 percent in 2014 (International Monetary Fund forecast.)[3] For the Xi administration, speed isn't everything. Better balance holds the key to unlocking China's dream.

Kuala Lumpur
May 17, 2013

Notes

1. First published on May 18, 2013.
2. World Bank, *Global Economic Prospects January 2013: East Asia and the Pacific* (Washington, DC: World Bank, January 2013), pp. 45–51.
3. International Monetary Fund (IMF), *World Economic Outlook: Hope, Realities, Risk* (Washington, DC: IMF, April 2013).

CHAPTER 138

China: Economic Slowdown: A Cause for Concern?[1]

Review just about any recent economic-social indicator coming out of China. They point to a clear slowing down of activity, reflecting poor exports and sluggish business performance, and increasing signs that credit-driven growth has run its course. China and ASEAN-5 (Indonesia, Malaysia, Thailand, Philippines, and Vietnam) have been providing the much-needed lift to the slackening global economy as US recovery stays stuck in the mud, with eurozone still mired in recession. I sense China's growth in the second quarter of 2013 to be around 7.5 percent, its slowest pace since the third quarter of 2012, as weak demand dented manufacturing output in the face of much excess capacity and weak margins, and slowing investment outlays.

The continuing weak global outlook (growth has since been further cut by the International Monetary Fund) is making life hard not just in China but also for ASEAN-5 exporters and manufacturers. In addition, recent turmoil in China's interbank market added acute stress, prompting central bank intervention to restore order and stability. The unprecedented money market crunch, which saw short-term interest rates spike to record highs, will eventually feed into the real economy through higher interest rates. This will further dampen growth, since higher borrowing costs will eventually shed jobs and lift unemployment, which is an important consideration in making policy. But the new leadership has flagged its commitment to shift gears toward a more sustainable growth path moving forward, emphasizing quality growth not reliant on extravagant investment funded by low-cost debt. It is supported, rather, by rising consumption based on improved wages driven by productivity gains. This stress on continuing reforms is good for medium-term growth.

China Worries

True, recent soft economic data reduced hopes for more stimulus, and concerns about interest rate liberalization, as well as the rapidly rising credit and debt, have added to China's worries. But there are positives:

- Focus on quality growth in the region of 7 to 7.5 percent is consistent with rather solid real growth—still the envy of most.
- The pair of purchasing managers indices (PMIs) for manufacturing and services remain in expansion territory, though weakening.
- Trade-weighted renminbi (RMB) appreciated by only 2 percent so far this year. Monetary policy remains somewhat tight, leaving room for some easing when needed.
- Soaring bank credit (i.e., total social financing including bonds and nonbank lending) has now expanded cumulatively to exceed 185 percent of gross domestic product (GDP) (against 125 percent in 2008), violating the so-called "5:30 rule," whereby nations whose stock of credit rises by above 30 percent of GDP within five years are prone to crisis. But no crisis has since ensued, reflecting the banking system's stability and robustness, with its accompanying high domestic savings rate. Fitch, the rating agency, had estimated this ratio to be 200 percent. Despite the double-digit credit growth, real GDP has slackened and will further slow down. It reflects China's commitment that future growth will be driven by reform, starting with market-based interest rates.
- Annual productivity has risen by 4.7 percent, but wages are growing faster. During 2008–2012, minimum wage levels across the nation rose 12.6 percent annually. To survive, manufacturers and service industries moved up the value chain and adopted management soft skills to keep pace. Migrant workers' wages rose 11.8 percent in 2012 (21.2 percent in 2011), while other wages gained 12 percent (17.1 percent in 2011), reflecting the policy to improve people's livelihoods.
- Price inflation (up 2.7 percent in June) remains below the official 3.5 percent target, also below the one-year deposit rate of 3 percent.

However, producer prices have been negative since March 2012. Indeed, prices of goods as they leave the factory gate fell 2.7 percent in June (the 16th month in a row they fell) amid lackluster demand and excess capacity as the economy cools.

Shadow Banking

China's four-year lending splurge saw its stock of credit expand 142 percent between 2008 and 2012. Much of this reflected the rise of its opaque "shadow banking system" (SBS), where activities have expanded so rapidly it accounted for nearly 15 percent of GDP in 2012 (with US$1.25 trillion in assets outstanding). Together with conventional banking, off-balance-sheet banking assets, comprising loans to property, local government, small and medium-sized enterprises (SMEs), individuals, and bridging loans, it was estimated to have totaled US$2.8 trillion, or one-third of GDP.

Shadow banking in China involves lightly regulated financial products that allow savers to earn more than bank deposits, which, in turn, channel funding for "subprime" borrowers. Essentially, they are loosely regulated (even unregulated) and don't comply with strict standards of conventional banking. The SBS consists of a mélange of trust companies, pawnbrokers, leasing companies, and a host of other unofficial lenders. Shadow banks first started to emerge in China in 1980s, and they reflect the closest thing China has to the culture of Wall Street. They assume risks traditional banks won't: "We do what banks don't do." That's what is commonly heard. Indeed, they mirrored the bad habits of US institutions during the subprime housing crisis, taking on assets in the capital market, including money market funds, asset-backed securities, and leveraged derivatives, funded mainly by investment banks, insurance companies, hedge funds, and large institutional investors. Their activities in the United States exceed those of conventional banking. Shadow banking is a worldwide phenomenon. The United Kingdom's Financial Stability Board had estimated total global shadow banking assets to exceed US$67 trillion in 2011, with the United States accounting for about one-third; eurozone, 30 percent; and China, 3.5 percent.

Chinese banks have been using cheap official funds to finance the vast shadow banking market, and the People's Bank of China (PBoC)—China's central bank—is concerned that its activities are crowding out legitimate access to bank credit by industry, business, and SMEs, and creating potential asset-price bubbles. They highlight the conundrum in managing a financial system that has racked up debts far too readily, yet remains in need of more liberalization. Indeed, savers are frustrated with deposit rates kept artificially low by fiat, thereby creating a demand for alternatives that shadow banks stand ever ready to provide. At the same time, mandated growth targets push local officials to seek out options to fund construction and other projects to expand economic activity and create jobs (providing opportunities for graft).

Shadow funds flow readily into local government projects that Beijing views as wasteful. But they benefit localities by pushing up land prices. The concern goes beyond managing liquidity risks, serious as these are in terms of product maturity mismatches. Many of the projects funded eventually turn sour. These remain an ongoing dilemma. Liberalizing interest rates on savings will weaken demand for shadow alternatives. But they squeeze profit margins, raise bad debt provisions, and affect bank profitability and viability in the end. I regard the latest credit crunch as a useful stress test. It did show up the deepening distress in China's financial system caused by shadow banking. High money-market rates simply reflect imbalances.

The benchmark seven-day repurchase rate touched a "nosebleed" 25 percent, showing up overextended positions, which forced banks found short to urgently bridge the gap. In past liquidity squeezes, PBoC would cut bank reserves and release funds into the system without much fuss—and rates would then naturally fall. This time, PBoC wanted banks to learn to better manage liquidity following reckless credit creation—a message in market discipline. Interest rates are now back to 3.4 to 3.6 percent. A lesson learned, I hope.

Reforms

China's reform refocuses, following President Xi's declaration that officials "shouldn't be judged solely on GDP figures . . . should instead place more importance on achievements in improving people's livelihood, social development and environmental quality."[2] This simply means slowing down credit expansion and growth, and shifting focus on structural reforms to the economy where wealth and income gaps have been widening and rapid industrial growth and infrastructure expansion have come at the expense of wasteful overcapacity and widespread pollution. It trades off short-term pain for more sustainable development over the longer-term.

The impact on supply and demand of the proposed structural reforms can be summarized as follows. Contractionary: (1) tax on natural resources, (2) higher utility prices, (3) liberalize exchange rate, (4) introduce market-determined interest rate, and (5) liberalize capital flows. Expansionary: (1) reform the "hukou" system, (2) emphasize social spending, (3) strengthen land rights, (4) reform value-added tax (VAT), (5) cut red tape, and (6) promote private investment.

They are intended to: help sustain growth of real productive capacity; improve efficiency in the allocation of capital and labor; rebalance supply and boost demand; get a grip on public finances by strengthening the funding capacity of local governments through issuing their own bonds; and rebalance growth favoring consumption and services. Above all, it signals that China will rely more and more on market discovery to sustain economic growth. A key component is the gradual adoption of market-oriented interest rates and ridding the system of the current low-interest-rate regime.

This has immense implications for the more than 100,000 state-owned enterprises (SOEs), whose return on assets has been reported to have fallen significantly since 2008 and where low-cost loans to support them have risen substantially. Interest rate liberalization will force SOEs to reform by stealth, mainly through privatization, or even closing down loss-making ones. Interest rate reform will also boost the flow of credit to those more creditworthy private enterprises where it has been reported that the return on assets employed is as much as three times that of SOEs. Since vested interest is strong and pervasive, reforms are being resisted. We'll have to wait and see.

Urbanization

China plans to unleash much purchasing power through urbanization—a process in which rural populations move into cities and towns. Of a population of 1.35 billion in 2011, 690 million, or 51 percent, is estimated to be urban; but only about one-half of them can claim urban residency status, due to an archaic national registration or "hukou" system that ties all citizens and public benefits to their hometowns. So, unregistered migrant workers have no access to education, basic health, housing, unemployment insurance, and other public services and benefits where they work. The system dates back to 1958, when the Communist Party wanted to regulate migration to ensure enough remain behind to till the fields. However, "hukou" has since evolved to become a major nightmare, and a source of growing inequality. It also forces migrants to save excessively to cover uncertainties, instead of spending to boost activity and employment.

Reform of "hukou" and land rights is now high priority. The plan is to make 60 percent of its population urban by 2020. Over the next 10 years, 400 million will move to the cities and towns. It's a gigantic task: US$6 trillion are earmarked for spending on infrastructure and social housing. To fund the plan, local governments would issue long-term bonds to ensure adequate funding for infrastructure and social safety nets; cheap and crowded neighborhoods are being cleared across China as part of the "stepped-up" urbanization program. In an ironic twist, the clearance of "villages within cities" removes the stock of cheap housing for the very poor without providing sufficient replacement units. This dilemma of a "net loss" poses hard choices for migrants living on the slimmest of margins (with many living in converted containers), but with no prospect of an affordable housing niche. Aggressive urbanization presents a powerful engine: pushes up investment; drives market demand; generates consumption; promotes industrial restructuring and upgrading; and creates more jobs in services.

What, Then, Are We to Do?

The global outlook has turned for the worse. New risks have emerged, including lengthening of the period of slowdown in emerging nations (as China, India, Russia, and Brazil face lower growth, slowing credit, tighter financial conditions, and rising interest rates); prolonged woes as recession deepens in Europe; growth-stunting spending cuts in the United States; and worsening tensions in the Middle East. Against this backdrop, reform in China appears to be slowly biting. As a result, financial conditions are tightening and growth is slackening as authorities seek to rebalance the interplay among forces of supply and demand, with increasing focus on using the market mechanism to improve economic efficiency and bringing about a more effective allocation of capital and labor. China will end up with higher-quality growth. The risk for policy makers is that financial stress and slowing growth are mutually reinforcing. Efforts to rein in China's shadow banking are taking hold as vested interests dig in. Planned reform will eventually filter in by stealth. No doubt, the current economic slowdown is a consequence of the push to reform. This stress on sustainable quality growth is good. It's short-term pain. Growth in the region of 7 to 7.5 percent is still to be envied. Deng Xiaoping once said at an earlier watershed moment: The only real choice is reform. But the main obstacle will remain politics. As I see it, the new round of bold, market-oriented reform is needed to meet the ambitions of the urban middle class. By all means, be concerned about the ongoing slowdown. But stay cool. Challenges abound.

Kuala Lumpur
July 11, 2013

Notes

1. First published on July 13, 2013, as "China Slowdown: A Cause for Concern?"
2. Jinping Xi, China's president, Xinhua News Agency, reported on June 29, 2013, in Beijing citing President Xi at a meeting on the work of personnel resources on the eve of the 92nd anniversary of the Chinese Communist Party's founding.

CHAPTER 139

China: The Third Plenum Reforms Are Well Received, but the New Deal Flashes Danger Signals[1]

On November 15, 2013, soon after the third Plenum of the Communist Party of China's Central Committee had completed deliberation on its massive document, "Resolution Concerning Some Major Issues in Comprehensively Deepening Reforms" (the Resolution), it published in Beijing an impressive 22,000-word blueprint of decisions for social and economic change over the next decade, unpromisingly titled "Decision on Major Issues Concerning Comprehensively Deepening Reforms" (the Decision): Its mission is to return the state to the golden era of wealth and power (fuqiang). Indeed, it attempts to resolve an ongoing contradiction—advance both power of the state and freedom of the individual.

Hints of this direction in reform were already made known in the "383 plan" of China's official think tank (Development Research Centre of the State Council, i.e., China's Cabinet). The symbol "383" reflects the plan's contents: interaction among the nation's three economic drivers—government, market, and business; the eight major areas of reform—competition, governance, finance, fiscal, urban–rural divide, state-owned enterprises (SOEs), liberalization, and innovation; and finally, the interplay of three interrelated objectives—inclusiveness, domestic–external balance, and eradication of inequality and corruption. True to its billing, the decision pledged wide-ranging reforms.

Now for the Action

I see at least four major breakthroughs. First, clarity on the relationship between the government and the market: to allow the market, in shaping the economy, to play a "decisive" role in allocating resources (as against just a "basic" role, when it first adopted the socialist market economy in 1993) while letting the government play its part better. And so, the market will determine prices of key resources such as water, oil, natural gas, electricity, and transport. In any event, government "should not make any improper intervention." Indeed, the role of government is to be confined to maintaining economic stability, providing public services, guaranteeing fair competition, ensuring well-functioning markets, and stepping in when there is market failure.

Second, the decision elevates the private sector's role in full recognition that both public and private sectors are important components of the socialist market economy. It is expected that business will be given bigger market access, and state monopolies will be held well in check.

Third, the urban–rural divide needs rebalancing, with a unified trading market for land to give farmers more proprietary rights to realize equal exchange of factors of production, achieve fair allocation of public resources, and promote healthy urbanization.

Fourth, accelerate the pace of opening up, both internally and externally, through widening investment access, relaxing investment barriers (including a "negative list" to attract foreign players), accelerating the building of more free-trade zones, and rapidly expanding the opening up of inland and border regions to the outside world. A major motive for SOEs to invest abroad, ironically, is to strengthen competitiveness at home. Competition from abroad will only increase in the domestic market if conditions improve for private investment, allowing SOEs to acquire strategic assets and opening up new industries to foreign investment.

Leadership Charts the Path

To unlock the middle-income trap with its potentially explosive social and political consequences, the Plenum called for comprehensive deepening of reforms but reflecting socialism with Chinese characteristics:

- Granting farmers their overdue property rights on collective land, making way for modern agriculture. They can now sell or mortgage village land.
- Accelerating moves to let the market determine interest rates and exchange rate of the renminbi (RMB or yuan), which will eventually lead to its full convertibility. Justifiable fears of destabilizing capital outflows will slow down the process. Banks are already allowed to determine lending rates. Soon, deposit rates will be similarly liberalized to benefit savers, who will be protected by deposit insurance. With the relaxation of interest rates, financial institutions (particularly state-owned large

banks) will be moved to compete for deposits and lend on the basis of risk-adjusted returns. This should drive credit toward the most productive enterprises and, over time, reduce the government's (and the party's) control over big business.

- Introducing more competition into financial services, especially at state-owned banks; this will ensure small and medium enterprises can have ready access to credit at a competitive price (and reduce shadow banking).

- Reaffirming the dominant role of about 100,000 SOEs, which contribute 26 percent of national industrial output, 80 percent of the value of Chinese-listed companies, and have near monopoly in energy, transportation, electricity, banking, and other sectors considered critical to economic stability. Reform of SOEs is contentious, with reformers pushing for (1) some of their assets to be passed on to the national social security fund; and (2) private investors to be given greater opportunity to engage in business dominated by them, including banking. All they got was for (1) SOEs to hand over, by 2020, 30 percent of their profits (US$400 billion today) as dividends to government (from up to 15 percent now); and (2) private sector to be allowed to invest up to 15 percent in SOEs. But the pledge to "incessantly strengthen" SOEs' vitality remains. New efforts at boosting competition should make SOEs more efficient, hopefully.

- Allowing mutually beneficial urban–rural integration whereby industry will promote agriculture development, and cities promote development in the countryside. This way, farmers have equal chance to share in the fruits of modernity and improve their livelihood. In 2012, 52.6 percent of China is urban; but only 27 percent of its population has *hukou* (or household registration) to fully enjoy public services available to urban residents. *Hukou* ties employment, healthcare, education, and welfare to the place where one is born. It deprives some 300 million migrant workers of social benefits. It is now being abandoned in small towns and cities; *hukou* restrictions will be gradually relaxed toward the large cities. This practice of experimenting—to "cross the river by feeling the stones"—is not uncommon in China.

- Setting up a sustainable social welfare system. China's national health insurance plan boasts nearly universal coverage but benefits are negligible, with wide disparities among regions and professions, and the scheme is underfunded. Its retirement scheme is equally inadequate, considering some 500 million (35 percent of population) will be aged 60+ by 2050.

- Revamping the fiscal and taxation system to optimize resource allocation in the face of the many reform measures being implemented, including a new tax base for local government (which can no longer rely on land transfers for revenue and need new property and resource taxes). Furthermore, there is overreliance on borrowing, especially by local government—often, overborrowing to invest in projects with very low returns. Financing of most infrastructures will need to be privatized and market funded.

- Building an "ecological civilization" involving a system of land development, which conserves resources, reduces emissions, and protects the environment through the extensive use of incentives rather than taxes and fees.

Early Concessions

Deng Xiaoping is reported to have said in 1992 that without further reform, China would reach a "dead-end." Holistically, reforms need social and political change to reflect government's sensitivity to dissent, and to demand for checks and balances. As China grows more complex and as more wealth is generated, the growth of civil society has not just become more obvious but begins to act as a bridge linking today's reforms to the politics of accountability tomorrow. The plenary Resolution noted: "Dare to grow through even tough bones, dare to ford dangerous rapids, break through the fetters of ideological concepts with even greater resolution." Hence, the decision to allow the emergence of "social organizations" (or nongovernmental organizations) but under the watchful eye of "government management," and to float the concept of "judicial jurisdiction systems that are suitably separated from administrative areas." Judicial reform will make officials more accountable. But the decision did allow two concessions on human rights: (1) to abolish "laojiao," the "reeducation through labor" camps; and (2) to relax the one-child policy by allowing couples to have two kids as long as one of the parents is an only child. The impact is not expected to be significant because of the high cost of housing, healthcare, and education.

Power to Implement

It's now all about execution. President Xi's credibility, his leadership's legitimacy, and China's future are all on the line. To ensure effective implementation, the Plenum established two high-level groups. The Central Reform Leading Group was charged to plan and carry out reform on modernizing China's "governance system" and "governance capability," with the view of designing and coordinating China's "great revolution" of reform and opening up. However, it threatens to marginalize the long-dominant technocrats of the National Development and Reform Commission, successor of the old

State Planning Commission. It is likely to be positioned at the same level as the Central Finance and Economy Leading Group. The second group is the State Security Committee to coordinate foreign and defense policy, as well as "improve the national security system and national security strategy to maintain and protect national security." It is intended to have the power to coordinate government organs at the highest level in order to respond to any major emergency and incidents that pose a serious threat to national security, such as border conflicts and major terrorist attacks, including social conflict due to the widening wealth gap and corruption. It seems likely that President Xi will head both groups.

What, Then, Are We to Do?

Overall, the reform package is robust and substantive. It's the most ambitious attempt at reform in two decades. Despite the stunning progress since Deng Xiaoping's historic opening up to the outside world in 1978, China still has a ways to go. So it's not surprising that in 2007, the then-Premier Wen Jiabao labeled China's economy with the four *un*s: unstable, unbalanced, uncoordinated, and unsustainable. Such a China is not good for Asia or for ASEAN (Brunei, Indonesia, Malaysia, the Philippines, Singapore, Thailand, Vietnam, Cambodia, Laos, and Myanmar). The five-year plan for 2006–2010 made little progress in rebalancing the economy as encapsulated in the much-reported "birdcage economy" (coined by Deng's ally, Chen Yun) where the free-market bird is given limited room to flutter within the confines of a centrally planned environment. The bird outgrew the cage soon enough as market forces began to surround and overwhelm Chinese life—not quite fully enough, though. This time the Plenum got it right—the market allocates resources far more efficiently than government can. Better still, China needs open, competitive, and well-functioning markets to perform. It is reassuring that China has embraced such far-reaching structural reforms. These are not perfect but seem workable. As now positioned, President Xi stands confident enough to deliver serious changes to a sclerotic system.

President Xi can expect stiff resistance. There is evidence that growing wealth has emboldened dissent, rather than stifled it. Beijing will set the overall policy direction, but it is the central and provincial government agencies who are charged with putting the plans into effect. Not unlike most bureaucrats, Chinese ministries are rife with conflicting interests and jealousies, wedded to traditional ways of doing things, and frequently beholden to vested interest that benefits from the status quo, which today also carries environmental problems, dangerous debt levels, and potential housing bubbles.

Implementation of strategic reforms is a hard slog; indeed, it's hard to push them past interest groups. There is already disappointment on the apparent lack of determination to reduce the dominance that SOEs hold and control over many areas of the Chinese economy. SOE reform appears timid, reflecting the old thinking that state ownership should remain as the mainstream. This is not sustainable. Without forcing SOEs out to really compete, private enterprise will remain disadvantaged in an unlevel playing field. Also, faster reform of the "hukou" system that denies rural migrants access to urban welfare will meet resistance, especially from local government (unless they get greater financial support for schools, hospitals, and other services) and middle-class urbanites who resent having to share resources with outsiders. SOEs, recalcitrant bureaucrats, and party ideologues will all resist market reforms that appear to threaten their interest.

To be fair, some reforms in the financial sector are already moving ahead; but many other changes are on a slower track, especially those encountering strong vested interests or that are involved in designing criteria to meet new environmental protection and healthcare standards, and technical innovation. Indeed, it is far from clear that they are able to come up with meaningful ways to quantify the new criteria or, worse, that officials will even take them seriously. The risks are high. History tells us that the last Chinese dynasty (Qing) fell after it reached the height of its power in the final years of the eighteenth century, after delivering living standards similar in some places to those in Britain. It was the familiar rot in terms of corruption, population pressure, internal dissent, and environmental exhaustion that undermined the Qing Dynasty. But China's success at reform is good for Asia and ASEAN. President Xi can take comfort from the French historian Alexis de Tocqueville, who wrote in *The Old Regime and the Revolution* that the French Revolution came about not from a popular clamor for change, but by the regime's own efforts at reform.

Kuala Lumpur
December 12, 2013

Note

1. First published on December 14, 2013, as "China's Third Plenum Reforms Are Well Received, but the New Deal Flashes Danger Signals."

CHAPTER 140

China: Multiple Policy Dilemmas[1]

Last November 2013, China endorsed a long list of bold reforms at its much-awaited "Third Plenum." I commented on them in Chapter 139, "China: The Third Plenum Reforms Are Well Received, but the New Deal Flashes Danger Signals." Reform is exactly what China needs to do to overcome the "middle-income trap"—failing to make the jump from an early stage of growth based on cheap labor and brute accumulation of capital, to the more sophisticated stage on the back of a well-educated workforce, innovation, and improvements in productivity. But no economy—not even one as determined to succeed as China, can move in lockstep from one growth model to another. Implementation is often a process of gradual diffusion—not abrupt transition. Besides, the policy environment and ecosystem have to be right.

Often, dilemmas (i.e., the risk of incoherence) arise as multiple policies are put into place; so trade-offs become inevitable: between long-term strategic focus and short-term tactical aims; between sustainable growth objectives and quantitative growth targets; between the role of market forces in determining the allocation of resources and the role of state-owned enterprises (SOEs); and so on. China's traditional emphasis on long-term strategic imperatives must continue to enable it to navigate these dilemmas (road bumps).

Outlook Still Dismal

The International Monetary Fund (IMF), World Bank, and Paris-based Organisation for Economic Co-operation and Development (OECD), comprising 34 rich nations, recently released updated forecasts for 2014—all see global growth firming, with the IMF expecting overall growth to rise to 3.7 percent this year from 3 percent in 2013—reaching its highest level since March 2011, and rising to 3.9 percent in 2015.[2] The World Bank and OECD are similarly optimistic. But the IMF cautioned that the world is "not yet out of the woods," given threats of deflation in the rich nations and of volatility in capital flows as they impact emerging nations. As expected, growth will be uneven, with the United States leading the pack (up 2.8 percent against 1.9 percent in 2013) and Japan jolted out of its long slump (1.7 percent; 1.7 percent in 2013); but with growth in the 17-nation eurozone remaining anemic, rising 1 percent against a contraction of 0.4 percent in 2013.

Developing economies will grow moderately at 5.1 percent in 2014 (4.7 percent in 2013), benefiting from a growing United States, a bottomed-out Europe, and a revitalized Japan. Growth in ASEAN-5 (Indonesia, Malaysia, Philippines, Thailand, and Vietnam) will stabilize at around 5 percent. For the first time in five years, the World Bank sees two engines (the United States and China) leading the train of global growth. Amid this new-year cheer, almost every year since the financial crisis, upbeat expectations have had to be eventually downgraded. The danger has to be undue optimism; downside risks remain a concern.

In this regard, it is sobering to note recent commentaries by Nobel Laureate Joseph Stiglitz and Columbia's Professor Nouriel Roubini on why there is cause for "muted optimism."[3] Their seven observations provide a valuable backdrop for a more balanced perspective, before we start to feel too upbeat:

1. While global economy will pick up modestly and tail risks (low-probability, high-impact shocks) will be far more subdued, growth in most advanced economies (except the United States) will remain anemic, and emerging market fragility can become a drag on global growth in subsequent years.
2. Inflation-adjusted real income per capita in France, Greece, Italy, Spain, United Kingdom, and the United States is lower today than before the Great Recession hit (2007); Europe will hardly grow in 2014 and with leaders wedded to austerity, its prospects remain fragile and bleak. I don't see how eurozone can enjoy real prosperity until its overhang of private debt is significantly reduced and its youth are brought back to the working labor force.
3. US median income (those in the middle) continues to decline; for most Americans, there is no recovery when 95 percent of the gains from growth goes to the top 1 percent.
4. The United States has a new problem in long-term unemployment, which affects 40 percent of those without jobs—as 2014 begins, about 1.3 million Americans who have since exhausted their unemployment benefits will be without a social safety net.
5. On both sides of the Atlantic, market economies are failing to deliver for most citizens.

6. Prospects for some emerging markets (India, Indonesia, Brazil, Turkey, South Africa, Hungary, Ukraine, Argentina, and Venezuela) will remain fragile in 2014, because of large external and fiscal deficits, slowing growth, higher than target inflation, and election-related and political tensions.

7. China's growth will hold firm and stable in 2014, given that the fourth quarter of 2013 gross domestic product (GDP) has moderated to 7.7 percent from 7.8 percent in the third quarter of 2013. Contribution to growth from tertiary industries (especially services) exceeded secondary ones (mainly manufacturing) for the first time in 2013. But the shift to a private consumption–based model, I am afraid, will occur too slowly—blocked by many vested interests, including local governments and SOEs (who are resisting change), as rising private and public debt run the risk of going sour, and hardline politics hold back the pace of reforms. So, although the latest data point to a softening of the economy (avoiding a hard landing), China's medium-term prospects remain worrisome.

GDP Worship

It is now clear that the focus of policy makers is being shifted from maintaining stability to deep-rooted reforms and a serious crackdown on corruption. In this context, confidence and transparency are important. As I see it, much of China's problems reflect its obsession with targeting GDP growth, what the official Xinhua news agency dubs "GDP worship," which has led to a ballooning of local government debt to US$3 trillion by end-2013 (US$1.7 trillion in 2011), or about one-third of GDP. Short-term targeting of GDP growth presents a dilemma for public policy, posing a trade-off between quantitative growth and quality growth; between the need to rebalance the growth process toward increasing emphasis on consumption and services, and away from building capacity in infrastructure, manufacturing, and construction; and between additional benefits from less-intensive resource demand, more subdued rise in energy use, and greater progress in addressing environmental pollution and income inequality. This simply means a trade-off for slower growth, which for China is not such a bad thing at this time. China is the only major world economy that sets specific growth targets—a relic of old Stalinist planned-economy tradition. It has become an anachronism that is not sustainable. Indeed, this go-for-growth mentality has had bad side effects in environmental devastation that has become a public health crisis and a serious political challenge for the government.

To be fair, the target is politically important in that it reflects its priority to grow the economy fast enough to provide full employment—part of the social compact of Chinese-style governance. But I sense that there is little "incentive" to change what is regarded more as a "bottom-line" aim rather than a serious goal to stretch forward. My guess is that the present presents the best chance to "jettison this socialist holdover."

There are political risks, of course, but it's an issue that needs to be addressed if China is to get a grip of the out-of-control local government debt. There are good reasons: (1) dropping the GDP target would serve as a clarion call that the nation now gives priority to a new growth model that is balanced and sustainable—no more growth at any cost; (2) signaling to all that the government is comfortable with slower growth; (3) timing is good as global economy is picking up; (4) setting a target distorts the efficient allocation of resources; and (5) with a falling workforce, China can still achieve its employment goals with slower growth. Yes, setting the strategic focus on sustainable long-term growth has to be the way to go.

Sustainable GDP

Another dilemma for Chinese policy makers is that in allowing market forces to play a "decisive role" in allocating resources within a competitive environment, they can get in the way of meeting the objectives of quality and sustainable growth. Indeed, the new sustainable growth model requires a stronger role for government. Air and water pollution can be addressed only by more government intervention at both central and local levels. Already, all provinces and municipalities are required to cut air pollutants by as much as one quarter. The dilemma posed is that meeting the demand for more effective pollution control and for more physical infrastructural makes it more difficult to rebalance and shift the growth regime from one based on investment and exports to one based on consumption.

More consumption today (auto sales were up 13 percent in 2013) aggravates the pollution problem in China and leads to rising demand for more infrastructure. This vicious cycle requires smart rebalancing, including urgent emphasis on more environmental investment. Other areas like network and utility industries in China (telecommunications, gas, electricity, and water) will require greater government oversight as well. If left to pure market interplay, these industries tend to become monopolistic or oligopolistic as the European experience shows. In the end, only effective regulation will prevent the emergence of cartels and anti-competitive practices, thus protecting consumers. Simply pushing "more market" is not always good. Stronger regulatory framework ensures markets maximize efficiency and social welfare.

Growth versus Debt

Officially, China's local government debt was estimated at US$3 trillion at end-2013, about one-third of GDP, whereas the Chinese Academy of Social Sciences now places total public and private debt at 218 percent of GDP, an alarmingly high figure—up 87 percent since the 2008 financial crisis. Total social financing (the broadest measure of credit), however, contracted 10.7 percent in the second half of 2013; still, the stock of outstanding financing rose 19 percent in 2013 (up more significantly in 2012), double nominal GDP growth, which means the ratio of debt to GDP continues to rise. But lending by shadow banking institutions (comprising banks' off-balance-sheet lending arms, trust companies, leasing firms, insurance companies, pawnbrokers, and other informal lenders) rose 43 percent in 2013—mostly to borrowers that traditional banks deem too risky (mainly local government, real estate developers, and corporations in industries facing overcapacity).

It is worth noting that since the global financial crisis, China's debt has been rising at a pace similar to the United States, South Korea, eurozone, and other economies, whose lending ballooned and then burst, leading to deep recessions. Between 2010 and 2012—a period when banks scaled back lending, Chinese shadow credit doubled to US$6 trillion, or nearly 70 percent of GDP in 2012. What's worrisome is that financial risks continue to rise as structural overhauls get delayed and debts get rolled over—creating "zombies," causing GDP to weaken and financial health to deteriorate. The rise of nonbank institutions over the past five years has changed the complexion of Chinese banking and finance, with banks now providing just over one-half of all new funding in the economy (more than 90 percent historically). The size of the shadow-banking sector now accounts for 40 percent of GDP. These banks are thinly regulated. If government cracks down too hard, too quickly, it can cause a panic. If it does not move forcefully enough to curb their "poor" lending practices, bad debts will proliferate and cause financial instability involving moral hazard. That presents a dilemma for policy makers.

There is a broader policy issue. When more and more lending coincides with slackening growth in today's China, it usually heralds the end of boom years and presents People's Bank of China (PBoC), the central bank, with a macroeconomic policy dilemma—how to rebalance, keeping growth on track while avoiding a debt-induced financial crisis as deleveraging begins. At this time, it makes sense to maintain slightly tight monetary policy in 2014, with a keen eye on its impact on the real economy.

Politically, policy has to keep the economy humming to enable the leadership to consolidate its power base as they work to forge ahead with sweeping economic and social reforms. No doubt, PBoC's efforts to restrain credit growth will create periodic liquidity squeezes in the interbank lending market, as it already did three times last year. Off-and-on cash crunches as banks scramble for fresh funds highlight the policy dilemma PBoC faces in 2014 as it pushes for financial reforms (including strengthening regulation of shadow banking) and rebalances the economy. Spikes in interest rates only signal PBoC's determination to reduce the alarming rise in debt but without braking too hard on legitimate credit demands. I note that PBoC has since sought to improve its communication with the market, including announcing in advance its short-term liquidity operations (SLO), through which it injects funds to relieve seasonal pressures by temporarily swapping securities for cash, in addition to offering short-term funds to small- and medium-sized financial institutions via the standing lending facility (SLF), a tool it launched last year.

It will not be easy for PBoC to meet its pledge to "maintain appropriate liquidity and achieve reasonable growth in credit and social financing, while improving credit structures." The reality is simply: If you control the price of credit, you cannot control the volume, and vice-versa.

Banking Reform

Market-driven interest rates can help wean the economy off its reliance on rising fixed investment. But there are structural constraints and potential risks. Controls in lending rates in China were removed last July. Freeing up long-depressed deposit rates (currently pegged at 110 percent of the benchmark) will push up borrowing rates, which can hurt manufacturers (many of whom are already operating on thin margins) in the context of an appreciating yuan (Chinese renminbi) and rising wages (expected to go up by a further 10 percent in 2014). No doubt, higher deposit rates will benefit savers and, ultimately, consumption. It will also discourage investment in speculative real estate or dubious wealth investment products that promise high yields.

Funds so mobilized are invested in shadow banking institutions and then on-lent to private businesses and local governments, which cannot get conventional bank loans because banks give preference to SOEs. Then, there are the constraints from debt workouts that will come with deleveraging as the economy slows down. Further, in a system with many—often implicit—government guarantees, it is not always the most efficient enterprises that are able to pay more to borrow. Liberalizing lending rates will enable those with guarantees to outbid smaller but efficient firms, resulting in more misallocation of capital. Until SOEs are barred (as in Europe) from receiving "unfair advantages," the market mechanism will not work.

What, Then, Are We to Do?

Beijing's reform drive will ultimately rest on turning words into deeds. Calls to accelerate financial and social reforms grew louder after the alarming rise and buildup of local government indebtedness were made public. To put it into perspective, many shadow banking loans go to local government-backed property and infrastructure projects, often of dubious merit. In short, this is a high-risk market where both its opacity and its rapid growth only magnify the probability of a nasty end, along the lines of the crisis that hit the US financial system in 2008. The reason behind all this is simple: Authorities created enormous demand from savers for high yields, and from borrowers for more credit. So, supply simply expanded to meet demand. Efforts to tighten regulations on shadow banking won't change that.

China badly needs to rebalance growth to create a sustainable, consumption-based society—the trade-off being slower growth, since deep-rooted reforms are necessary. Its biggest challenge is to adjust to a slower overall growth pace. Rebalancing must remain China's key strategic focus if it is to avoid messy policy dilemmas. In his highly acclaimed book, *Breakout Nations: In Pursuit of the Next Economic Miracles*, Ruchir Sharma postulates that growing annually at even 5 to 6 percent over the next 15 years, China's per-capita income will more than double to US$20,000 from US$7,000 today.[4]

A maturing China now creates up to 1.7 million new jobs for every 1 percentage point of growth (up from 1.2 million 10 years ago). So China will generate enough new jobs, bearing in mind the population is aging and fewer youth are joining the workforce. Whatever happens, it has to be accepted that the Chinese economic slowdown will end up becoming more painful, simply because of the failure to undertake reforms during the good years of the mid-2000s! It's better now than never.

Kuala Lumpur
January 24, 2014

Notes

1. First published on January 25, 2014.
2. International Monetary Fund (IMF), *World Economic Outlook—Transitions and Tensions* (Washington, DC: IMF, October 2013); IMF, *World Economic Outlook Update—Is the Tide Rising?* (Washington, DC: IMF, January 2014); World Bank, *Global Economic Prospects* (Washington, DC: World Bank, January 2014); Organisation for Economic Co-operation and Development (OECD), *Economic Outlook No. 94*, Paris: OECD, November 2013.

3. Joseph Stiglitz, "Advanced Malaise," *The Edge*, Malaysia (January 13, 2014); Nouriel Roubini, "Slow Growth and Short Tails," *The Edge*, Malaysia (January 6, 2014).

4. Ruchir Sharma, *Breakout Nations: In Pursuit of the Next Economic Miracles* (New York: W.W. Norton, 2012).

CHAPTER 141

China: Rebalancing Growth with Reform and Moving Up to the Next Level[1]

What's happening in China has a direct consequence on Southeast Asia, and Malaysia, in particular. Of late, China's growth has slackened—surprisingly subdued by normal standards. Its growth in fixed investment, housing, retail sales, and factory output has hit multiyear lows in the first quarter of 2014. This has rattled global investors, worried that this will soon become a drag on activity worldwide. Already, Asia's growth risks being dampened by China's slowdown. It so happens this sets the stage for China's recent annual sessions of the National People's Congress (NPC) in early March 2014. Even as the Chinese Prime Minister emphasized the urgent task of deep reform before the top legislature, as reflected in his Government Work Report (GWR) outlining the roadmap for China's economic and social reforms for 2014, he declared the growth target for this year to be "about" 7.5 percent (unchanged from the goal set for 2013 when the economy actually rose by 7.7 percent).[2] What's new is the addition of the word "about" alongside the target, compared with previous NPC sessions. It is supposed to signal some tolerance below 7.5 percent if it's tilted toward quality (i.e., so long as growth slides toward domestic consumption and so long as the fight against pollution continues. After all, "7.3 percent or 7.2 percent would count."

Growth and Reform

China's approach to reform is both cautious and gradual. It's intended to be this way. The GWR emphasized that "growth remains the key to solving all the country's problems; must keep economic development as the central task and maintain a proper growth rate." Employment is the government's

867

most important target—needing to create 10 million new urban jobs in 2014, keeping registered urban unemployment at no more than 4.6 percent. It also has the goal of keeping the rise in consumer prices to a maximum of 3.5 percent to protect the people's purchasing power. But there's no way China can get a free lunch. Reform consensus at NPC must be acted on. So, implementation will slow things down. The time has come to change its development mode so that a fall in gross domestic product (GDP) growth becomes unavoidable to improve the quality and efficiency of development.

Already, analysts have trimmed forecasts: 7 percent in the first quarter of 2014 as against 7.7 percent in the fourth quarter of 2013. For the full year, 7.2 percent appears to be the consensus given reform remains top priority. This seems to be Beijing's bottom line to keep employment from faltering. If the pace of growth does not pick up, backing for deep economic reforms will wane. On April 2, 2014, the government moved to arrest the slowdown—from lining up new infrastructure spending (on railways and low-cost housing) to tax relief for small businesses and, hopefully, to easing access to credit. For its trading partners, China's continuing growth is important. JPMorgan Chase estimated that a 1 percentage point fall in its GDP implies a 0.35 percentage point fall in world GDP. China remains an important destination for commodities from Asia and Latin America and for capital goods and electronics from the United States, Europe, and Japan.

Pragmatism at Work

On March 5, 2014, NPC confirmed that the central leadership will start implementing the comprehensive reforms this year. First, with the growth target for 2014 already set at "about 7.5 percent," fiscal policy will remain "proactive" and monetary policy "prudent." This simply means: (1) keeping official fiscal deficit unchanged at 2.1 percent of GDP; but the total fiscal deficit (including borrowings by local governments from banks and the shadow banking system) is likely to be significantly higher than in recent past; and (2) maintaining money supply growth target at 13 percent and "fostering a stable monetary and financial environment, and strengthening macro-prudential management to encourage an appropriate increase in monetary credit." Second, although the twelfth five-year plan (2011–2015) calls for rebalancing away from investment and industry in favor of consumption and services, the government's approach prefers raising domestic demand and boosting consumption, while wanting to "fully leverage . . . the key role of investment, regarding it as the key to maintaining stable economic growth." Put simply, consumption will become the main engine of growth, while investment will be used as the leverage to stabilize growth. It's like having the cake and eating it, too.

Third, being pragmatic on how fast to push reform. Although government is committed to "breaking vested interests," the GWR now calls for "a focus on areas where the public's call for reform is strongest and links on which there is extensive public consensus." This simply means that reform areas will be pushed where there is broad agreement and no strong resistance from vested interests. This is particularly so with the direction of financial and monetary reform—toward deposit insurance, liberalization of interest rates, broadening renminbi (RMB) trading band, and greater RMB convertibility. On the other hand, in the more difficult reform areas like fiscal and rural land reform and state-owned enterprises (SOEs), the approach will be more gradual and cautious.

Fourth, on the complicated area of improving the quality of urbanization and *hukou* (house registration) reform, the government is committed to "progressively grant urban residency to migrant workers and their families . . . and steadily extend basic public services to fully cover the permanent population of cities and towns so that the rural people who live in them can contribute to the development of modern urban life and enjoy it together with the urban people."[3] In simple terms, government has set for itself three tasks involving 100 million people: (1) granting urban residency to migrants; (2) rebuilding rundown urban areas; and (3) guiding further urbanization in the central and western regions.

Fifth, private investment (including mixed-ownership platforms) will be allowed for some projects in state-dominated areas such as banking, oil and gas, electricity, railways, telecommunications, resource development, and public utilities. In addition, the country will be opening up more service sectors to foreign capital, encouraging imports and leveling the playing field for Chinese and foreign companies to compete on fair terms, and ensuring China remains a top choice for foreign investment. China's inland and border areas will open wider to the outside world and turn these broad areas into hot spots for opening up.

Sixth, reform measures are also planned for areas including agriculture, urbanization, healthcare, education, and environmental protection. Above all, China has launched a resolute and deeper anticorruption campaign to root out both high-ranking "tigers" and low-level "flies." Its anticorruption mechanism will also help the market play a more decisive role in economic activity, maintain the order of competitive forces, and more effectively curb social unfairness. All these will lead to deeper reform and structural adjustment, and in the final analysis, enhance market competition.

What, Then, Are We to Do?

In the year of the Horse, reform will be China's main feature, even though it might not be all smooth sailing ahead. The reforms were all set out last November 2013 (refer to Chapter 139, "China: The Third Plenum Reforms

Are Well Received, but the New Deal Flashes Danger Signals," for details). Watch out for five things: (1) growth target remains unchanged at 7.5 percent, same as in 2012 and 2013. It shows that the central authorities will not allow radical reforms to hurt growth in a significant way. Such balancing is delicate. Let's watch; (2) China's surveyed unemployment rate (which better reflects the job market) is 5 percent (against registered rate of 4 percent); this rate is used internally for policy making. Let's watch if government has the confidence to regularly release this more accurate rate; (3) the Shanghai Free Trade Zone (SFTZ) is the test bed for deepening reforms—this pilot scheme needs more time to deliver. It is worth watching how this works out; (4) bilateral investment negotiations with the United States and European Union are well advanced. New trade talk with the United States is also possible. China uses these investment and trade deals as leverage to propel reforms at home. Let's watch what happens; and (5) Internet finance will inject competition and help break state monopolies. In the real world, innovation in Internet finance holds great promise for the benefit of consumers. We need to watch and see.

I recently came across James Fallows's book, *China Airborne* (nothing to do with aerospace), which I consider to provide a good inside account of modern China—that fundamental reform in China is on the way to change China fundamentally.[4] He cites the impact of deregulation, SFTZ, more competition in telecoms (11 licenses to new cellular telephone service providers), and Internet banking (new licenses to start private banks), which will bring about far-reaching radical changes that will spread because the multiplier (second and third round effects) can be expected to bring on long-lasting effects that will spur further economic growth.

For China, I believe the new vigor from deep market-based reforms now being played out will quickly spread. They will reinforce further reforms, creating a virtuous cycle of more changes to come. The reform now started, I am convinced, will show that China's possibilities are far greater than what outsiders can ever imagine. China will adapt to the wisdom of India's Gandhi: There is no way to reform. Reform is the only way.

Kuala Lumpur
April 3, 2014

Notes

1. First published on April 5, 2014, as "Moving Up to the Next Level: China—Rebalancing Growth with Reform."

2. Released on March 5, 2014, and tabled by Premier Li Keqiang before the opening of the annual sessions of the National People's Congress in Beijing.
3. Ibid.
4. Giles Chance, "China Moving Up to the Next Level," *China Daily*, Beijing (March 3, 2014).

CHAPTER 142

India: The Outlook Dims[1]

It's a pity India is slipping—it has lost much of its magic. I see two Indias over the past 40 years. The first is the economy of old, which brought forth slothful growth in the face of a suffocating bureaucracy and politics as usual. The statist model seen in the 1970s dragged along an economy stuck with the sluggish 4 percent "Hindu rate" of growth. The second evolved gradually after the 1990s liberalization, and surged with a burst of optimism by the mid-2000s—portraying a democracy that was vibrant, open, and fired by entrepreneurship that overcame a slowly retreating public sector, but undeterred to grow fast, supported by favorable demography, enthusiastic firms willing to save and invest, and prospect of a vast consumption-driven new middle class. The economy has since expanded at turbo-charged pace, culminating in 9 percent plus growth rate in 2007 and 2008. Growth averaged 8.5 percent over 2004–2008. Reserves reached a high of US$292 billion. What's worrisome now is that the India of old is making a reappearance—much like the Bollywood villain who tries to cheat death, clouding prospects with desperate and dangerous fragmenting politics.

"Rickshaw" Pace

India's growth trajectory has been impressive since the mid-1990s. Today, its projected economic growth (at "rickshaw" pace) is the weakest in a decade. Latest official data place growth at 5 percent in the current fiscal year ending March 2013 (against 6.2 percent in 2011–2012), down from 5.5 to 6 percent forecast in June 2012 and 6 percent predicted by the Ministry of Finance just last month. Growth slackened amid allegations by private businesses that government was suffering from policy paralysis. Inflation remained a problem at 10.79 percent in January 2013, although core inflation had eased to 4.1 percent. Both the rupee and Bombay stock index are also weaker. The outlook appears tentative: "You can't tell for sure," according to Dr. Raghuram Rajan, the Finance Ministry's new chief economic adviser.

The government is working to avert a ratings downgrade by Standard and Poor's and Fitch Ratings, which had since lowered their outlooks on India. The nascent recovery in 2013 and its growth prospects will depend on government's ability to reestablish confidence, promote investment, and continue liberalizing the highly regulated economy in the face of stiff political opposition.

The poll of 28 economists indicated India's gross domestic product (GDP) will rise 6.4 percent in 2013–2014, down from 6.6 to 7 percent polled in October 2012. Wilting demand is a major cause. There is no doubt India has the potential to grow: "Growth is a low-hanging fruit. But to actually pluck it and eat it, we have to accept a few home truths," according to Rajan. Let's face it. As Kaushik Basu (the World Bank's chief economist) recalled in his recent lecture, "India's Dilemma": India and South Korea had the same per-capita income in 1950.[2] Today, South Korea's per-capita income is 22 times India's.

What Ails India?

India's GDP is about US$2 trillion, the world's tenth biggest. It is young and restless (median age is barely 25; Japan's is 45), big (by mid-2020, its people will exceed China's 1.35 billion), and fast growing (even in tough times like now, it still grows at least 5 percent annually). Income per capita is rising; rural poverty is down; people are more materialistic, paved roads are getting more widespread; and so on. Sure, the economy is now going through a rough patch. Growth has slackened considerably. Prices are still too high for the Reserve Bank of India to significantly cut interest rates. Indeed, inflation risk limits room for monetary easing to bolster growth. Industrial output is declining, weighed down by weak demand, and the trade deficit, rising. Unemployment (9.8 percent) is still too high for comfort. So are the fiscal deficit and public debt (as percent of GDP in 2012); both ratios are the highest among BRICS (Brazil, Russia, India, China, and South Africa).

External problems also hurt, including weak global demand and high oil prices (India imports 80 percent of its oil, then subsidizes consumers big via the three *F*s: food, fuel, and fertilizers). But the biggest pains are self-inflicted: It badly needs foreign capital to fund the growing external payments deficit (at 4.5 to 5 percent of GDP); but the slowdown is equally visible in the corporate sector, which is increasingly being pushed to invest abroad. Political logjam has thwarted reforms, stalled decision making, and exacerbated a stubborn inflation. It's a result of bad politics and corruption. Fortunately, consumption accounts for 68 percent of the economy, insulating it from the worst of the global slowdown.

Netas and Babus

Core problem, as I see it? Governance: The very system governing reforms and investment decisions has broken down. The intricate processes involve the *netas*—politicians (who pass no significant legislation and are mired in sleaze)—and *babus*—bureaucrats working in an ossified system (who prefer to work by the rule book).[3] Like politicians, babus are worried about being fingered for or tainted by corruption and scandals, and consider it safest to do nothing. And so, the economy is stuck in all shades of politics—locked in over "graft and drift" in a system Rajan dubbed the *Resource Raj*—that is, a cozy alliance of well-connected entrepreneurs and public officials who, between them, acting in concert with politicians, carve up competitive "reform" measures of permissions and licenses that in the past helped to underpin and even push India's growth (with corruption being accompanied by investments). It enriched invested interests. Now, this process is collapsing. Hence, the present dysfunction in New Delhi.

As a result, widespread public anger with the corrupt and super-rich has risen, casting doubts over the future of market reforms—so much so that India appears to have lost much of its appetite for more reform. Indeed, in desperation, administrative improvisation is being resorted to as a substitute for genuine reforms to open up the economy. No doubt public outcry over corruption has changed the way Indian politics is conducted today. But like it or not, sustainable growth still requires a slew of big, second-round real reforms, including land acquisition and social housing, labor laws, and taxes.

Quality of Growth

India has become increasingly well connected. The latest census showed 63 percent of India's 247 million households have a phone (usually a mobile).[4] According to Ericsson, three-quarters of Indians have access to a mobile. The same census showed that two-thirds of Indians have electricity and nearly one-half have TVs. A similar number have bicycles but only 5 percent own a car. PricewaterhouseCoopers reported that in 2010, 470 million Indians had annual incomes of US\$1,000 to US\$4,000; this will rise to 570 million within a decade, creating a captive consumption market worth US\$1 trillion, at least.[5] Sustained growth could create a big mid-income economy.

In a perfect world, this could be true. But India is a grotesquely unequal world where millions of children struggle to get enough food or a decent education. Recent years brought high inflation, especially food prices. Roads, ports, and railways are already overwhelmed. Brownouts are common, and labor is getting as expensive as in China, even though the average Chinese is three times richer. Yet, the real benefits of growth are concentrated in a handful of states (especially in the South) and among a tight circle of businesses and the elite.

Harvard's Nobel laureate Professor Amartya Sen warned of how "stupid" it was for the Indian government to aspire to double-digit growth without addressing chronic undernourishment of millions of Indians.[6] Despite rising growth, the average caloric intake among India's poorest has been stagnant for the past decade. Eleven out of 19 states have more than 80 percent anemia and more than one-half of India's children under five suffer stunting and poor brain development from inadequate nutrition. The country is home to one-half of the world's severely malnourished children. Only 25 percent of Indians have a secondary education, which is more than twice as many have in China. Rather than driving growth higher, Sen proposed much higher spending on health and education and to take notice of how China has fed its people better. The quality of growth matters. To get there, the pie has to grow and, with it, reforms that don't come easy.

Indian Politics

My friend and renowned policy planner, Dr. M. Ahluwalia, is fond of telling me: In Indian politics, there is a strong consensus for weak reforms. That's why India never enjoyed the kind of benefits or "externalities" (like higher efficiency and productivity leading to even higher growth) that big-bang reforms can deliver. I am reminded of a report that likened India's political machine to being fitted with wheels of a bullock cart and brakes of a Rolls Royce. No matter how much change is introduced, the rest of the machine can't be made to work like a Rolls. But, India badly needs to reform. Already, the World Bank and Asian Development Bank (ADB) have separately warned India about the dangers of "halting modernization and liberalization of India's state-dominated banking system," and further, of the need to "strengthen its economic reforms, particularly deregulation in the service sector, including finance, and improve its infrastructure to promote manufacturing and unleash its economic potential." Because of the lack of real progress here, "delay in implementing the necessary reforms has hampered India's competitiveness." This delay also reflects the "unholy alliance" of some businessmen and politicians who block the changes it so badly needs. So, reforms now proceed only little by little. Even so, three recent episodes point to clumsy muddling at the top. Decisions to open the retail trade to foreign investment and the ban on cotton exports were reversed within days. The government's move to alter the tax code to tax foreign takeovers, retrospectively, raises worries about the rule of law, one of India's signal strengths. That's a real shame. Small wonder business is in a sulk.

What, Then, Are We to Do?

India has prospered despite government. To continue to do so, it has to build infrastructure, promote competition, protect property, and offer justice. In 2009, ADB published a report: "India 2039: An Affluent Society in One Generation" (2009). To get there, the report says India needs to radically upgrade the quality of government and focus on transforming seven intergenerational issues: (1) tackle disparities especially among social groupings, group-based entitlements, and group-based politics; (2) improve the environment; (3) eliminate infrastructure bottlenecks; (4) deliver quality public services; (5) renew education, technology, and innovation; (6) revolutionize energy production and usage; and (7) become a responsible global power.[7] There's nothing new that has not been said on the massive tasks ahead. For India, these remain difficult tasks. To these, I would add an eighth: Deregulate banking. Among the world's top 50 banks, none is Indian (China has 6). Indian banks have no scale because (1) three-quarters of them are government-owned; (2) they provide little long-term finance; (3) half of India's population have no banking access, and small and medium enterprises are ill-served; and (4) they have weak balance sheets and are saddled with serious problem loans. Public sector banks need to merge to create more dynamic and more efficient large banks. This would surely raise India's competitiveness. Frankly, government just needs to stop getting in the way. India needs government to deliver efficient and effective services. To do so, it needs competent technocrats and honest politicians, period. No more, no less.

The future belongs to the middle class. Chapter 93 discusses passionately about the emerging middle class and its transformative power. India today has a middle class of an estimated 300 million. But 900 million cell phones are in use. This means that there is also just as large a group of "virtual" middle class who, though still very poor, have access to a global voice to being treated as citizens with basic rights to electricity, clean water, public services, and generally, good governance normally associated with being middle class. This massive diffusion of cheap computing power via cell phones has significantly lowered the cost of connectivity and education, thereby empowering even the very poor with ready access to the kind of learning and a voice previously associated with being middle class. This newfound virtual middle class has begun to change the dynamics of pressure, pushing politicians to get their governance act together. I see this as a wake-up call to all politicians: Rise and recognize that a new generation has come of age. You don't need to have a middle-class income to be middle class any more, in order to have a voice and be treated as citizens with rights to fair play and decent governance.

Kuala Lumpur
February 19, 2013

Notes

1. First published on February 23, 2013, as "India Outlook Dims."
2. "Business Eyes Brightening Prospects for Indian Economy," *Financial Times* (January 11, 2013).
3. "Special Report on India—Aim Higher," *The Economist* (September 29, 2012).
4. Ibid.
5. Ibid.
6. "High Growth Fails to Feed India's Hungry," *Financial Times* (December 24, 2010).
7. Martin Wolf, "How India Must Change if It Is to Be an Advanced Economy," *Financial Times* (July 8, 2009).

CHAPTER 143

"A Passage to India": The Outlook Remains Dire[1]

E. M. Forster's book relates to "colonial India" of old, a romantic time of slothful growth, mind-bending bureaucracy, and suffocating red tape—a constant reminder of India before independence in 1947 in contrast with life after liberalization in the 1990s. The new India that had emerged by 2000 was robust and bursting in optimism. Of late, the magic appears to have slipped. After Chinese New Year 2013, I wrote Chapter 142, "India: The Outlook Dims," concluding, in effect, that India's sluggish "Hindu rate" of growth is self-inflicted in the face of an unmanageable bureaucracy and politics at its worst. Events have since moved swiftly. An update is due, as India's once-booming economy slides into a deep sleep. India's default risk is rising the most among emerging markets as it bucks a regional trend of budget tightening and reform, raising the prospect of a junk debt rating as the rupee (its currency) plunges to new lows.

Not on One Engine

India's gross domestic product (GDP) rose 4.4 percent in the second quarter of 2013 (against less than 5 percent for fiscal year-ended March 2013 and about one-half the annual rate between 2005 and 2008). The quality of growth is bad as well. The main source of growth came from government spending (up 10.5 percent), with household consumption trickling down to expand by only 1.6 percent while investments and exports shrank 1 percent each. It can't fly on just one engine, an unreliable one at that. The government expects the economy to grow at 4.5 to 5 percent for the year to March 2014. Paradoxically, the slowdown was the result of substantial fiscal and monetary stimulus that was injected into the economy in the aftermath of the 2008 financial crisis. The growth spurt led to rising inflation, so monetary policy has since remained tight, with high interest rates bringing about slowing investment and weakening consumption. What's of concern is that continuing government spending had not helped raise India's productivity nor raised its competitiveness. Over the past fiscal year, government spent three times as much on subsidies and salaries as on building roads and other badly needed infrastructure. India needed and deserved a better engine to help develop the economy—that means more private investment.

The economy now stands in disarray, with the prospect of worse to come. Economic decline has laid bare chronic problems, as the *International Herald Tribune* would have us believe: "An antiquated infrastructure, a sclerotic job market, exorbitant real estate costs, and bloated state-owned enterprises never allowed manufacturing, especially manufacturing for export, to grow strong."[2] I have said this repeatedly: Most of India's problems, including its high wholesale prices (hitting a six-month high at 6.1 percent in August), have domestic causes. During boom times in mid-2000s, capital moved in indiscriminately, overlooking India's many shortcomings. The recent turn of events in the United States, in particular, redirected investors' attention to fundamental problems plaguing most emerging markets.

It is a fact India has become less and less hospitable in recent years as more corruption scandals surfaced, more large infrastructure projects were mismanaged, more tolerance of the ballooning budget deficit was accepted (including wasteful subsidies), and more politics worked to sideline reforms in labor and education. Sadly, government leadership has become increasingly ineffective. Without reforms, economic performance will fall far short of its potential.

Rupee Shake-Up

The rupee has depreciated by 19 percent against the US dollar since May 1, 2013, hitting record lows in recent weeks. India's trade deficit, a key driver of its large external payments bill or current balance of payments (BOP) deficit, has become the sore point underlying the sell-off of Indian stocks and other rupee assets. Investors have become increasingly worried about India's ability to bridge this gap in the face of the US Federal Reserve Bank System's (Fed) impending scale back (tapering) of its easy-money program. Unfortunately, India has become too dependent on foreign capital inflows to finance this deficit. As a result, the rupee (together with the Indonesian rupiah, which slumped to its lowest level in four years) has become the focal point of the sell-down. Indian stocks have fallen by as much as 12 percent from this year's high before bottoming out lately. But both currency and stocks remain at risk. The rupee has suffered more than most others, partly because of loosening interest rates.

To stem the tide, the Reserve Bank of India (RBI) has since moved to tighten rupee liquidity (by limiting overnight borrowing), curtail trading in currency derivatives, and impose stricter import restrictions and some harsh capital controls. These measures include limiting foreign investment outflows (to 100 percent of an enterprise's net worth) and tightening restrictions on money outflows (especially to buy property). The situation has since improved somewhat, as reflected in lower swap rates—one-year borrowing cost retreated 110 basis points from a five-year high of 10.26 percent on August 20 to 9.16 percent.

For the longer term, though, India has no choice but to move in earnest to reduce currency volatility and stabilize the rupee, including attracting more foreign direct investment (FDI). From April 2009 to March 2013, FDI into India is reported to have shrunk significantly. FDIs are worried because of the host of major problems they face, including obstacles in securing mining rights, poor access to gas as input for production, cumbersome red tape, and problematic land acquisition rules. Only determined reform can resolve them.

Raghuram Rajan, the new RBI governor, recently listed three goals to help improve the situation:

1. Attract home US$ held abroad by nonresident Indians (NRI).
2. Double US$ borrowing capacity of Indian banks.
3. Widen the scope for exporters and importers to commit forward forex contracts.

"The bottom line is to increase the inflow of US$." These need to be viewed in the light of RBI's new commitment to a more open and competitive banking sector. But the rupee will benefit only if these measures are accompanied by visible signs of reform. Indeed, among the measures, the move to draw in NRI US$ deposits can have important short-term effects because the new RBI cover of 3.5 percent is about 50 percent of market rate. It could raise an estimated US$5 billion to US$10 billion, provided the environment is conducive enough. The irony is that such US$ inflows, if successful, represent taking on more debt!

Pressing Dilemma

As things stand now, foreign investors are cautious, even gloomy. The new RBI governor faces a pressing policy dilemma: If he raises interest rates to stabilize the rupee and stem inflation (as Indonesia and Brazil did), he could cripple industry, worsen the fiscal deficit, and raise banks' nonperforming loans. The sliding currency pushes up inflation. Indeed, it's estimated that every 10 percent fall in the rupee adds 80 basis points to inflation. Higher rates would stabilize the rupee and attract FDI. It could curb consumer price inflation as it approaches 10 percent, even before the impact of rising import prices takes hold. But higher rates could also work to choke off investment and growth. Already, India and Indonesia have the highest policy rates in Asia, at 7.25 percent. India's broad business community fiercely opposes further increases in interest rates—indeed, they are for lowering rates further! But the reality is that inflation is brewing hot steam—food and fuel prices are bound to rise as the impact of rupee depreciation sets in. Food inflation has accelerated to a three-year high of 18.18 percent in August 2013. Late planting and disruptions in the supply of vegetables and onions have fueled food prices. The policy options before RBI carry big risks that could antagonize large sectors of the public.

So far, RBI has merely tinkered. However, the new RBI governor's priority is clear—maintain monetary stability: Ultimately, this means low and stable expectations of inflation, whether that inflation stems from domestic sources or from changes in the value of the currency, from supply constraints or demand pressures. Unlike the situation in the United States and Europe, it's not going to be solely his call. RBI is required by law to consult closely and, finally, take direction from the central government where growth is still of top concern. But unless the rupee stabilizes, growth won't come. In the end, is there a case for stronger growth, given the many constraints faced by India at this time?

Currency Defense

India faces dual risks: a persistent BOP deficit (now at 5.1 percent of GDP and rising) plus a stubborn budget deficit (7 percent of GDP, one of the highest in Asia), and "suspected" opportunistic speculation that's causing the volatile market to overreact (à la Asian currency crisis). It's not unique to the rupee—it's happening in other parts of Asia and Latin America. How can emerging markets fight back?

India's idea is to mount a joint defense through regional coordinated intervention (CIV). No doubt, it is theoretically elegant, but in my experience, it's not workable in practice. The premise is simple enough: Emerging Asia has US$4.3 trillion in reserves; add another US$500 billion in reserves of Brazil, South Africa, and Turkey. By teaming up to sell US$ in a coordinated way, the region hopes to ease any targeted downward pressure on their currencies. The rationale is clear—their currencies are being depressed partly by rising US interest rates as a result of anticipated US Fed tapering, the timing of which is well beyond their control. This accords new opportunities for profit by speculators.

But the firepower is not evenly distributed. India has US$280 billion in reserves, of which US$70 billion are needed to bridge BOP gap and another US$170 billion to service maturing debts this year, whereas China has US$3.5 trillion in reserves but has no real cause to participate, since its own currency has remained relatively stable. For the others, their reserves are precious. Recent experiences in currency interventions have yielded mixed results. India's plan is to have regional CIV in offshore forward markets, which is currently punishing the rupee and rupiah. There is little cause for Malaysia, Philippines, South Korea, and Taiwan to take part, bearing in mind the high cost of failure. Indeed, they have better use for their reserves. In my experience, regional CIV can work when it's targeted and acted upon swiftly, and for a brief period. It requires expertise. But there are just too many risks in uncertainty out there to make it really work. The best way to deal with speculators is to stay cool, and undertake real reforms to improve the BOP and strengthen fiscal finances.

The Elephant and the Dragon

China's rise is given and accepted; the dragon in it is always fired up. But India remains very much the clumsy elephant—big, with soft power in abundance, it has a huge and talented diaspora, yet acts below its vast potential, simply because it can't quite put its act together. According to Harvard's Nobel Laureate Amartya Sen, what's worrisome is not whether India can overtake China in economic growth (which it clearly can't), but the wide gap between China and India in the provision of essential public services—a failure to bridge this gap would act as a drag on growth and depress living standards in India. Of course, income inequality exists in both nations.

For Sen, what matters is that China has done far more than India to "raise life expectancy, expand general education and secure healthcare for its people."[3] While China devotes close to 3 percent of GDP in public spending on healthcare, India allots only 1.2 percent. The same is true for education. Sen concludes: "For India to match China in the range of manufacturing capacity, it needs a better-educated and healthier labor force at all levels of society."[4] Here's a great lesson to learn. In addition, India must commit to reforms (Chapter 142 provides details), including service-sector deregulation and improvement in infrastructure to promote manufacturing, to unleash its economic potential. Delay will hamper India's competitiveness.

What, Then, Are We to Do?

As India's economy slackens, its poor suffer most. The threat of higher inflation erodes their meagre income as food prices rise. Fresh thinking is needed to protect their welfare, including providing welfare payments directly to poor families instead of through subsidized food grains, fuel, and other commodities, which feeds corruption. Direct transfers to the poor in Mexico and Brazil have proven to reduce poverty and cut down corruption and waste. As I see it, the situation is dire. The nation is in need of fresh and far-reaching solutions. Further, the droopy rupee also needs to be addressed.

The reality is that India is now a dual economy: Rural India and the "informal" economy are booming—beneficiary of expansionary high fiscal deficits between 2008 and 2011, which pumped huge subsidies into the rural areas. Food prices have risen more than 10 percent. However, the urban and industrial economy is in a slump, with manufacturing prices rising just 3 percent. This "split personality" presents a real challenge for nondiscriminatory public policy: to somehow gradually recalibrate policies to regain business confidence and stabilize the rupee, calm inflationary pressure and expectations, and at the same time set off a revival on growth through fresh new investment. It's a tall order at a time of increasing uncertainty. India is at a knife's edge.

Kuala Lumpur
September 19, 2013

Notes

1. First published on September 21, 2013.
2. "As Economy Slips in India, Root Causes Are Laid Bare," *International Herald Tribune* (September 6, 2013).
3. Amartya Sen, "Why India Trails China," *International Herald Tribune* (June 21, 2013).
4. Ibid.

Corporate Governance
and Management

CHAPTER 144

On Corporate Governance and Doing It Right[1]

Of late, the issue of governance has been in the limelight. I just returned from the Asian Shadow Financial Regulation Committee (ASFRC) annual meeting, held in conjunction with the Asian Financial Management Conference in Singapore. Corporate governance (CG) was the sole preoccupation of the 10 ASFRC members present. In order to better cope with the unique characteristics of corporate Asia, its communiqué emphasized real improvements in governance, which have since become ever more urgent and critical.[2] Furthermore, new recognition that financial institutions should "assist in protecting taxpayers . . . creates new challenges" for their boards of directors. This realization can result in a "potential dilemma" that requires a new mind-set to resolve.

The Big Picture

The recent financial crisis, triggered by bankruptcy of Lehman Brothers, raised serious issues on governance of the systemically important financial institutions (SIFIs) and how they are regulated and supervised. The massive injection of public monies in the United States and Europe—estimated by the European Commission at up to 25 percent of gross domestic product (GDP)—raised a huge outcry among taxpayers about moral hazard and the diminished responsibility of private stakeholders. Indeed, the European Commission's Larosière report highlighted three crucial gaps: (1) boards of directors (BoDs) and supervisory and regulatory authorities (SRAs) failed to understand the nature and scale of risks taken; (2) shareholders failed to effectively perform their role; and (3) lack of effective control mechanisms led to excessive risk-taking.[3] What's most worrisome is that CG determines and regulates business life. Which raises the question: Is existing CG deficient, or at best, badly implemented? Traditionally, CG is relied on (1) to chart the relationship among senior management, BoDs, shareholders, and other stakeholders (e.g., employees, society at large, and creditors); and (2) to determine the organization and means used to meet goals and monitor their implementation. But interdependence and connectivity among fast-growing SIFIs can lead to systemic risks. In the recent crisis, this led governments to shore up bad large banks with public funds. Consequently, taxpayers have since become reluctant stakeholders—adding a new dimension of CG.

At the heart of it all, as I see it, is greed, mostly at the expense of the innocent, perpetuated within organizations supposedly well run by professionals with business acumen. In reality, key management were found to be lying, living it up, and cheating, or just being downright suckered by liars and cheats around them. Those charged to notice didn't do so, or failed to raise their hands.

To reform, an effective CG system (based on smart control mechanisms with checks and balances) must make the main stakeholders (BoDs, owners, and senior management) assume greater responsibility with transparency. Bear in mind rule-based supervision focused on internal control, risk management, audit, and compliance structures could not prevent excessive risk taking by SIFIs. As I see it, to restore confidence, a number of critical issues have to be addressed.

Conflict of Interest

The model of shareholder-owner who looks to long-term business viability has since been severely shaken. The emergence of new shareholders with little long-term interest have amplified risk-taking for short-term gains (and contributed to excessive remuneration). This is reminiscent of the old Jack Welch adage that a firm's sole aim is to maximize shareholders' return, which dominated US business for the past 25 years. With the crisis, even "Neutron Jack" had since retracted: "[Maximizing] shareholders' value is the dumbest idea," he said last year, talking to the Business School class at Harvard. Traditionalists in the United States and United Kingdom showed disdain for stakeholder capitalism practiced in Europe, where interests of employees, creditors, and society at large are taken seriously. Such conflict came to the fore in the recent BP US oil spill—many BP shareholders were eyeing hefty dividends and didn't pay enough attention to environmental risks.

Given systemic risk and the high volume, diversity, and complexities of SIFIs' business, conflicts of interest can arise in a variety of situations, ranging from exercising incompatible roles and activities to clash on performance measurement between management and shareholders/investors.

The current travails of Goldman Sachs epitomize the conflict. When it went public in 1999, Goldman embraced the axiom of maximizing shareholders' value. As wooing sustainable customers became increasingly important, concentration on maximization over the short-term put at risk building stable relationships that rely on long-term success.

Or, when US senators questioned Goldman Sachs's executives on their fiduciary duty to clients when selling them sophisticated products, it admitted caveat emptor (Latin for "let the buyer beware") is the only rule. To improve CG, perhaps long-term shareholders (LTShs) should be given more clout. In the United States, shares traded on the New York Stock Exchange changed hands every three years on the average in the 1980s. Today, the average tenure is less than a year (10 months). Last year, a task force comprising seasoned investors (Warren Buffett, Peter Peterson, Felix Rohatyn, et al.) advocated in a report, "Overcoming Short-Termism," measures to encourage LTShs, including withholding voting rights for new shareholders for a year. The Netherlands is considering loyalty bonuses for LTShs. Roger Carr (Cadbury's ex-chairman) suggested that investors who bought shares in a takeover bid should not be allowed to vote on the offer. Would this work? As I see it, the real issue is not so much the length of time investors hold onto shares, but how to encourage them to take their duties as owners more seriously.

One Hat Is Enough?

The United States is unusual in lavishing power on chief executive officers (CEOs), who often also act as chairmen of boards of directors. Splitting the job is commonplace in the United Kingdom, Canada, Australia, and much of Europe and Asia. In Britain, 95 percent of FTSE 350 companies have outside chairmen; in contrast, 53 percent of S&P's 1,500 top companies combine the two jobs.[4]

Activists in the United States have since been up in arms against these "imperial bosses." In April 2009, they forced Ken Lewis to surrender his second hat (chairman) at Bank of America. The case for two different persons lies in the basic principle of separation of powers. How can the board monitor the boss when he sits at the head of the table? It conjures images of CEOs writing their own performance reviews and determining their own salaries. One of the notable steps taken by troubled US banks (Citigroup, Washington Mutual, Wells Fargo) when the crisis hit was to separate the two jobs.

No doubt, the arguments are compelling, but empirical evidence is not conclusive. Enron and WorldCom both split the jobs, as did Royal Bank of Scotland and Northern Rock. Separation has its problems: It is harder for CEOs to take quick decisions; ego-driven CEOs and chairmen do squabble over who's in charge; shortage of talent makes separation suboptimal. Be that as it may, BoDs have since become more independent; 90 percent of US S&P 500 companies now have a "lead" or "presiding" director to act as counterweight.[5] Indeed, recent changes make the old-style strongman an anachronism. However, I see no one-size-fits-all solution; the best way has to be evolutionary: Split, or explain why not ("comply, or explain").

Independent Directors

Independent nonexecutive directors (or Indies) are at the apex of CG. Widely criticized during the crisis, Indies failed to foresee troubles ahead or push management to find solutions. They are usually well connected and often sit on several boards as companies seek their experience and connections. SRAs now want them to be more diverse. Traditionally, when appointing new Indies, existing BoDs are inclined to look in the mirror—appoint in their image rather than look through the window and recognize diversity. This "old school tie" approach is just too cozy.

Also, BoDs need to be more transparent in recruitment. In the United Kingdom, the Financial Reporting Council code now requires firms to explain if Indies are not put up for reelection. More controversial is the annual election of chairman and other board members in an attempt to promote the best long-term performance in an intensively competitive environment. However, says its critics, this promotes a focus on short-term results, makes boards less stable, and discourages robust challenges in boardrooms.

Good CG relies on Indies to set smart checks and balances and fix the boundaries of organizational behavior. They hold the key to maintain confidence in the company's integrity. To do their job well, Indies need to be independent from management, business relationships, and substantial shareholders. In practice, they ensure that (1) internal and external rules of conduct are applied; (2) risks taken are commercially sound and consistent with the board's risk appetite; and (3) future success of the business is reasonably assured.

This is an onerous task. To succeed, its best practices code needs to operate under well-defined core values to which the board and management are committed. The case of Arthur Andersen is classic—no rules were broken with respect to Enron. But it failed by colluding with management, bankers, and lawyers in seeking ways to comply with the form but not the substance of accepted accounting standards. A true Indie knows how much work he can take on and still be effective. He needs no code on age, maximum appointments, terms served, or time spent to bind him. Integrity demands he will not accept a role he can't fulfill, unlike many who comply on paper. Companies and stakeholders cannot be readily protected from the vagaries of human frailty. Like it or not, their behavior reflects the ethics and mores of society. What is really needed is to rediscover moral values. SRAs just can't regulate for ethics and common sense.

Asia on the Go

Asian economies encounter two rather unique limitations in CG. First, cultural differences and being more "tradition-bound" place less emphasis on formal contacts but face greater subservience to authority and age. Second, Asia has a limited pool of qualified and experienced Indies, since CG is a relatively new phenomenon, gaining acceptance after the 1997–1998 Asian financial crisis. While it is desirable for Asia to recognize and learn from new codes of conduct being proposed in the United States and Europe, these need to be adapted and modified to fit local culture and experiences.

What, Then, Are We to Do?

In Asia, while CG sets the tone, it is imperative that Indies take individual responsibility to do the right thing not only by the firm they serve but also as individuals when it comes to ethical behavior. After all, Asia has 5,000 years of history, diversity, culture, and tradition. An evolutionary approach toward excellence in CG is what's really needed. Best practices work best in an ecosystem of "comply, or explain," augmented critically by purposeful continuing education to develop and improve skills and expertise. In the process, organizations build a culture of strict compliance, of rigorous risk assessment, and of commonsense ethical behavior. To succeed, CG and ethics must go hand in hand. No two ways about it.

Singapore
Kuala Lumpur
July 29, 2010

Notes

1. First published on July 31, 2010.
2. The Asian Shadow Financial Regulatory Committee's (ASFRC) Communiqué issued at the end of its Singapore meeting on July 14, 2010, at the Singapore Management University in Singapore.

3. Cited in the European Commission's June 2010 Green Paper: "Corporate Governance in Financial Institutions and Remuneration Policies," COM (2010) 284 final, Brussels, p. 2. The report cited is the "Report of the High-Level Group on Financial Supervision in the EU," published February 25, 2009. Mr. Jacque de Larosiere was chairman of the group.

4. Joseph Schumpeter (column), "Someone to Watch Over Them," *The Economist* (October 17, 2007), p. 70.

5. Ibid.

CHAPTER 145

The CG Blueprint 2011: "Let a Hundred Flowers Bloom"[1]

The maturity of the capital market is reflected in the quality of its corporate governance (CG). Most observers say CG in Malaysia has much to improve.

On the surface, we appear to have complied (with the myriad regulations to provide for good CG) and have a good record on paper in meeting international benchmark "good practices." But in substance, we don't do so well. Indeed, there leaves much to be desired. Still, we are told often enough, we need more rules to remain relevant.

So it's not surprising that we now have another Corporate Governance Blueprint 2011—a "major review and recalibration of controls is necessary," says the Securities Commission Malaysia (SC). This blueprint contains 35 new recommendations "to move from the normative tendency, which regards corporate governance as a matter of compliance with rules, to one that more fittingly captures the essence of good governance."[2] The chairman of SC further emphasized that the blueprint "**outlines strategic initiatives aimed at strengthening self and market discipline**" (highlighting is mine); yet its recommendation introduces more rules in the name of intending "to reinforce self and market disciplinary mechanisms."[3]

It's quite clear that what we need is time to build our own corporate culture. It's also strange that SC doesn't practice what it preaches—away from normative rules to greater reliance on self-regulation. The essence of good CG involves a state of mind. Human behavior is unpredictable. We just can't legislate good morals.

Since then, the SC issued on November 15, 2011, a public consultation paper seeking comments on two issues: (1) whether the chairman of a public listed company should be independent; and (2) whether poll voting should be extended for all resolutions requiring shareholders' approval.[4]

Both the blueprint and the recent paper raise important issues of wide public interest and concern. They deserve careful study and a frank public response in the hopes that SC will take them seriously enough to promote the best interest of companies and stakeholders. In this context, Chapter 144, "On Corporate Governance and Doing It Right," remains relevant. Frankly, we don't need more rules. Just more time to build our own corporate culture.

Independent Directors

The SC is right in saying independence is "inherently situational and is, more than anything, a state of mind."[5] It's in short supply. In this regard, the existing seven criteria for independent directors (Indies) under the Bursa Malaysia Listing Requirements still makes sense: "needs to be independent of management and free from any business and other relationship which could interfere with the exercise of independent judgment or the ability to act in the best interests of the company."

Ultimately, the qualitative evaluation, on a case-by-case basis, is made by the collective board. The Listing Requirements advise that "boards have to give effect to the spirit, intention and purpose of the independence definition." In the end, judgment rules the day, as it should.

The blueprint states from its survey that in 2009, 37.3 percent of companies had Indies whose tenure on the board exceeded nine years and concluded: "Long stretches of service may prejudice a director's ability to act independently and in the best interest of the company." This is only an impression, not backed by empirical evidence.

The finding is not alarming. It cuts both ways. It then refers to other jurisdictions' tenure limits (nine years on average). "Given the potential adverse effects of tenure on independence," SC recommends that a limit of up to nine years be imposed. This is, at best, a flimsy basis. It reflects "groupthink"—this safety in numbers is quite inconsistent with good culture.

Indeed groupthink is dangerous. It fails to consider our short historical CG evolution, imperatives of our Asian culture, our close-knit corporate community, the company's business cycle, supply and demand of experienced director expertise, increasing turnover of top management staff, inherent practical problems arising from frequent "sneaking in" of any other business (AOB) items at meetings, and important decisions via circular resolutions.

In the end, it's arbitrary and mechanical (okay at eight years, but gone the next). It's just a line in the sand (not even a straight line). Agreed, everyone has a limit. But it should not be set arbitrarily—it could lead to "musical chairs."

This is a contentious area, since it involves the individual's mind-set. Setting a quantitative limit on an issue that is largely subjective should be avoided. Ultimately, let the collective board decide on how to balance the company's needs with the individual's capacity to add value, but ensure transparency.

Multiple Directorships

As in the case of Indies, the Blueprint's rationale on limiting directorships held in listed companies to five is rushed. Bursa Malaysia data show persons holding more than five directorships are "extremely small" and concluded the issue is therefore "not about multiplicity of directorships held, but of capacity and commitment by directors." The logic gets simplistic from here on: "Taking both these points into account, we believe" the maximum directorships held in listed companies should be five.

Agreed, directorships represent significant time commitment. But it must be recognized that an individual's capacity for work varies, depending on the individual and his mental capacity to multitask; whether he is a full-time director; his work-and-leisure balance; within his work schedule, time committed to being an Indie; the company's circumstance, its business, size and state of finances; tasks entrusted to him; and amount of time he needs to spend to add value to the company.

All these point to his own assessment of the degree of care and diligence required of him, against the skills and experience he brings to the table, recognizing the practical reality of collective effort in making, and the responsibility for, board decisions.

In essence, it is only fair that this be left to the individual to decide, rather than being determined remotely by the SC. Real Indies will not accept a role they can't fulfill. Others merrily do so on paper but care little about their role. It is widely practiced in audit firms, for example, that the number an audit partner signs off varies, depending on the complexity of the companies and the individual capacity of the partner. In the final analysis, it should be based on the capacity of the individual to perform.

The existing system of ultimately letting the collective board (through its nominating committee) make the qualitative judgment and make the final call continues to make sense. SC should not dictate what should indeed be left to the individual—he knows best about his legal and fiduciary responsibilities.

Current data show this is not a problem. If it ain't broke, why fix it? Putting a limit on multiple directorships deprives companies of scarce board talent.

Separating Chairman and Chief Executive Officer

The SC makes a compelling case for separation and independence. Data presented show the underlying problem. Although 72.5 percent of listed companies on Bursa Malaysia in 2009 have separate chairman and chief executive officer (CEO), in substance, 15 percent of them do not practice it, reflecting the impact of strong family ties.

This is not surprising. After all, the practice of separation is not universal: in the United Kingdom, 95 percent of companies in the FTSE 350 have an outside chairman, but in the United States, 53 percent of Standard and Poor's top 1,500 companies combine the two jobs.[6] The case for separation is based on the simple principle of balance of powers.

Empirically, there is no solid evidence that splitting the job does any good. The past 20 years of research ended with inconclusive results. Enron and WorldCom both split the jobs; so did Royal Bank of Scotland and Northern Rock.

Splitting the job also brought undesirable consequences: CEOs find it harder to make quick decisions; ego-driven chairman and CEO squabble over who is really in charge; and the shortage of first-class CEO talent may mean bosses are often second-guessed by a chairman who has less knowledge of the business. The US solution: 90 percent of S&P 500 companies now have "lead" or "presiding" directors to act as counterweight to the executive chairman.[7]

In the end, there is just no one-size-fits-all solution.

After all, separating the jobs is only one aspect of CG. As I see it, the best solution is evolutionary, given our short CG history. In 1992, Sir Adrian Cadbury (Cadbury Report) introduced the "comply or explain" solution: If you can't comply (i.e., split), explain why. Seems like a sensible solution.

We should avoid groupthink just because the United Kingdom, South Africa, Australia, and Thailand have split. Singapore's compromise also sounds workable: Where the jobs are combined, ensure the majority of the board members are Indies. In the event a split is needed in the best interest of the company, an independent chairman makes more sense.

Mandatory Poll Voting

In this digital age, it makes sense for voting to go electronic. Poll voting accurately underlies the principle of one-share-one-vote. Because of the large number of diverse shareholders, poll voting can get cumbersome and time consuming, just as voting by show of hands is antiquated and inaccurate.

The technology is here to implement poll voting; it's just a matter of cost. Mandatory poll voting should be implemented once a credible electronic voting platform that is cost effective is found. This should not be an issue of concern.

Women Directors

Board diversity is good, including gender representation to harness diverse insights and perspectives. But the notion of "the goal is for women's participation on boards to reach 30 percent by 2016 and the progress toward this goal will be monitored and assessed in 2013" is discriminatory and bad policy. It's the wrong way to promote the role of women. Granted, women account for one-half of the population, but only 15 percent of board members at US big firms are women and 10 percent in Europe.

Empirical evidence shows mixed boards make better decisions. But quotas are a blunt tool and insult women with caliber. But I do understand why they are used: (1) men dominate boards and are incorrigible sexists; (2) talented executives are mentored by men, preferring males for fear of being misunderstood; and (3) globalization demands mobility, which disrupts families.

A recent study showed quotas place inexperienced women on boards, seriously damaging the firm's performance. Here again, there can be no shortcuts. Companies need to start by helping more women (1) gain the right experience up the ladder and (2) balance their family lives with the demands of the workplace. This is a slower process but is likely to be more meaningful, and it upholds the dignity of women.

Continuing Education

The growing complexities of modern business make it difficult for most directors to catch up. Professional directors need to be intellectually honest and robust; they need more than a fleeting acquaintance with new management techniques, including skills in risk management, strategic and business methods, and human psychology.

It's good that continuing education programs will be made mandatory—but in order not to encourage and entrench vested interests, the SC and Bursa Malaysia should not be involved in providing them. Let the private sector compete for the business operating under strict SC guidance stressing quality, competence, and international exposure.

It is important to get the best and brightest on board (here and from abroad) to teach. Otherwise, forget it. Directors are smart and intellectually curious—there is a need to get for them the best there is to make it worth their while.

What, Then, Are We to Do?

SC should practice what it preaches. Stop imposing more and more rules. The corporate community needs breathing space and time to build its own culture. President Ronald Reagan was fond of saying: "The nine most terrifying words in the English language are: I'm from the government and I'm here to help." So beware.

Hong Kong
Kuala Lumpur
November 30, 2011

Notes

1. First published on December 3, 2011.
2. Securities Commission Malaysia (SC), *The Corporate Governance Blueprint 2011: Towards Excellence in Corporate Governance* (Kuala Lumpur: SC, July 2011), p. vii.
3. Ibid.
4. Securities Commission Malaysia, Public Consultation Paper, "Independent Chairman and Voting by Polls," no. 1, November 15, 2011.
5. Securities Commission Malaysia, *The Corporate Governance Blueprint 2011*, p. 28.
6. Joseph Schumpeter (column), "Someone to Watch Over Them," *The Economist*, October 17, 2009, p. 70.
7. Ibid.

CHAPTER 146

Creative Destruction:
"Kodak Moment" No More[1]

En route to Harvard for the second time in mid-1976, I well recall the family's visit to Disneyland. At strategic places, the catchphrase for a precious "Kodak Moment" is identified for photo-shoots promising an unforgettable moment captured in time. The delight in posing against Cinderella's castle is one such "Kodak Moment." My grandchildren will not experience this. Eastman Kodak Co. (Kodak) filed for Chapter 11 bankruptcy protection in New York on January 19, 2012. Under US law, this provision allows for an orderly process of restructuring under bankruptcy, while being kept afloat in business to protect the company from being ripped apart by creditors. The struggling icon ran short of cash needed to fund a long-sputtering turnaround.

The 131-year-old enterprise had struggled for decades to cope with heightened competition, disruptive technology, and crippling legacy cost obligations. As one commentator observed, Kodak ceded the photography market to competitors such as Nikon, Sony, and Canon. It hung onto its identity, film, and watched it fade away before its eyes. Kodak still hopes to continue in business with the aim of emerging in 2013 after using the bankruptcy court to restructure and sell off some of its treasure trove of patents. Basically, it intends to bolster liquidity, monetize nonstrategic intellectual property, and resolve unsustainable pension and health costs to enable the enterprise to focus on its most valuable business lines. Can it succeed? To answer this, we need to get to where it has been and understand why it failed in the first place. Kodak's experience carries valuable lessons.

Kodak

Once ranked among America's corporate titans, Kodak launched its first "Eastman" camera in 1888 with the slogan: You press the button—we do the rest. Eastman Kodak was founded in 1881 by George Eastman, who developed a method for dry-plate photography from kitchen experiments in his mother's Rochester home. In 1900, it introduced the Brownie camera, selling it for US$1. Since then, Kodak has offered many firsts: first film designed for making motion pictures with sound (1929); Kodachrome film (1935); first commercially successful amateur color film; first instamatic camera (1963); first digital camera (1975); and first to record sales exceeding US$10 billion (1981). It launched a website to upload and share photos (1997); stopped selling reloadable film-based cameras (2004), and ended production of Kodachrome (2009) after a 74-year run. It invented the handheld camera and helped bring to the world the first pictures from the moon in 1969.

Kodak once dominated the industry, and its film was even the subject of a popular Paul Simon song, but it failed to quickly embrace modern technology. In 1976, Kodak accounted for 90 percent of film and 85 percent of camera sales in the United States, according to a 2005 Harvard Business School case study. Until the 1990s, it was regularly rated as one of the world's top five most valuable brands. Kodak's revenues peaked at US$16 billion in 1996, with profits of US$2.5 billion in 1999. Analysts' consensus forecast was for revenues of US$6.2 billion in 2011; it reported the third quarter of 2011 loss of US$222 million, the ninth quarterly loss, and headed for its sixth annual loss in the past seven years. Since 2008, Kodak's accumulated losses exceeded US$1.76 billion. In 1988, Kodak employed more than 145,000 worldwide; it now has barely one-tenth as many and is falling further fast. Moody's downgraded Kodak to a very low junk Caa3. Its share price has since fallen more than 90 percent to a low of less than US40 cents (it was a component of the Dow Jones Industrial Average from 1930 to 2004).

What Went Wrong?

Kodak's latest move represents the final reversal of fortune for a company that once had almost complete domination of its industry. Its troubles date back to the 1980s, when the enterprise struggled with competitors that hijacked its market share. It later had to cope with the rapid rise of digital photography and smartphones that double as cameras. Ironically, Kodak invented the digital camera (as early as 1975) but never managed to capitalize on the new technology, adopting a bad strategy of not cannibalizing itself (to be successful, digital photography will take market share from its own film business). It's perceived as though the "company is stuck in time." It allowed others to come in and eat its lunch.

Then, there were the restructurings, one after another, that found Kodak selling unrelated products and finally pitching head on into the highly competitive printer business. It got savaged. By the time Kodak realized this, it was five years too late to accelerate its shift back to the digital age, said

Antonio Perez, its chief executive officer in August 2011. The company's problems came to a head in 2011, when its strategy of using patent lawsuits and milking its family silver (patents for licensing deals) to raise cash ran dry. Hoping to plug the hole, Kodak put 1,100 digital patents up for sale in August 2011. By early 2012, the sale hit snags and faltered. When a company starts hacking off an arm here and a leg there, the end can't be far away.

Kodak versus Fujifilm

It is now clear that whereas Kodak suffered, its longtime rival Fujifilm did rather well. Both had a lot in common: (1) both enjoyed near monopolies at home; (2) both witnessed their common traditional business being made obsolete—while Kodak failed to adapt, Fujifilm transformed itself (its market capitalization in 2011 was US$12.6 billion against Kodak's US$220 million); (3) both saw different parts of the film market turn digital, yet Fujifilm adapted faster with new strategies involving a painful change of mind-sets, including bagging the 1984 Olympics, while Kodak dithered in complacency; and (4) both diversified—Kodak toyed with chemicals, cleaners, medical-test devices, and went big on drugs, which fizzled out (and were sold in the 1990s).

Fujifilm was more successful in cosmetics (its Astalift line is sold in Asia, and now, Europe), and in making optical films for LCD flat-panel screens, which paid off—in one that expanded the viewing angle, it enjoys 100 percent market share. Kodak was more nimble and creative with digital cameras, adopting Gillette's "razor-blade" business model (sold cameras cheap but made money from films). Kodak's success lasted only a few years before camera phones scuppered it. Furthermore, Kodak misread emerging markets, including the Chinese leap-frogging from no camera straight to digital.

At Fujifilm, technological change sparked an internal power struggle. By 2000, the leadership with a vision going forward won and adopted a new business model to propel Fujifilm to high profitability. "Surprisingly, Kodak acted like a stereotypical change-resistant Japanese firm, while Fujifilm acted like a flexible American one," observed a Harvard case study. Today, Fujifilm is up, and Kodak, down. Even so, one thing is clear. Without doubt, Nikon, Sony, and Canon are still far better placed to fight the digital battle, given their superior intellectual property and massive research and development spending.

Creative Destruction

It is said that Western capitalism quite often invents the technology that destroys its own business. Kodak's bankruptcy provides the perfect example. After all, it did build the first digital camera. That technology, followed by the onslaught of smartphones, battered Kodak's old film and camera-making business nearly to its death. Today, we see yet another tale of how easily a corporate icon can be felled by a single disruptive technology. Caught in a classic dilemma, Kodak stayed complacent and made bad business decisions, including its abortive move into pharmaceuticals. Its story remains that nothing lasts forever. In a free market, Schumpeter's creative destruction (the process where new technologies destroy the company but create in its place more vibrant new enterprises) benefits consumers, who no longer need to lug around clumsy digital cameras now that smartphones take (and store) such clear photos. Indeed, the destruction of companies and jobs also means the emergence of more competitive companies, offering higher-value-added jobs and better products and services at much lower prices.

Dominant market positions can prove fleeting in the era of Moore's law (every 18 months, the prices of products using sophisticated computing technology fall by one-half while digital capacity doubles). We see this throughout the twentieth century. It gets fiercer in the twenty-first century. Digital Equipment, the iconic dominant American computer maker, failed to spot the rise of personal computers—its managers were caught sleeping. Predominant firms in other industries have been killed by smaller shocks. Of the 316 department-store chains of a few decades ago, only Dayton Hudson adapted well and started an entirely new modern business to survive: Target.

That's what creative destruction does to businesses that change only gradually, if at all. Kodak's complacency follows a long list: Polaroid in 2008, Blockbuster in 2010, Nortel Networks (which also fell behind the technology curve) in 2010, and Borders (the largest bricks-and-mortar bookseller) in 2011. Unlike Kodak, Barnes and Noble is now seriously restructuring to separate its costly Nook electronic-book business in the highly competitive digital reading. The last numbers don't look good. Indeed, it's still unclear if it has a future. Neither is Kodak's eventual survival clear. Creditors will have to decide whether its consumer and commercial inkjet printing are worth supporting in a highly competitive and saturated marketplace, where it is still a bit player (2.6 percent market share), dominated by giants like Hewlett-Packard; or whether the bulk of its value really rests in its patents. We just have to wait and see.

What, Then, Are We to Do?

After 131 years, Kodak—along with many great companies before it— appears simply to have run its course. Many have died. Perhaps the challenges posed by new technologies are too overwhelming. Harvard's Clayton Christensen (of *The Innovator's Dilemma* fame) concluded that with the emergence of such a fundamentally different technology, there was no way to effectively use the old technology to meet the challenge. Kodak blinked against the headlights. Many saw change coming and got out ahead of it, often changing significantly. IBM bolted personal computers, and Milliken, much of its traditional textile production. In the process of creative destruction, IBM and Milliken lived the creative part; Kodak met with destruction.

There is also the legacy issue—pensions and health benefits have become too costly to sustain. In this, Kodak is emblematic of the postwar era: Kodak and the likes of General Motors bought labor by generous benefits, thinking revenues will always grow. Similarly with Greece and Spain. They proved crippling in uncertain times. Today, companies riding high on the technological wave need to heed Kodak's lesson: They aren't immune to business blunders or the impact of better or revolutionary technologies. Kodak had a good run for its money! Competition is brutal. Today, it's the iPhone or Android or Samsung. Can Microsoft, Google, AOL, or Facebook stay the course in the rest of the twenty-first century? Schumpeter observed: "Like the actual engines that loom so large in creative destruction—steam, electric, diesel, gasoline, jet—the capitalist engine can slow down, sputter, overheat, explode, or die."[2]

Kuala Lumpur
February 10, 2012

Notes

1. First published on February 11, 2012.
2. Thomas K. McCraw, *Prophet of Innovation: Joseph Schumpeter and Creative Destruction* (Cambridge, MA: Belknap/Harvard University Press, 2007).

CHAPTER 147

The F&N Saga[1]

I feel nostalgic this week. On July 18, 2012, the OCBC Group in Singapore sold to Thai Beverage Limited (ThaiBev) its significant interest in the F&N group of companies, Fraser & Neave Limited (listed on the Singapore Exchange Securities Trading Limited, SGX-ST). For the first time since 1883, management and control of F&N will no longer be vested in Singaporeans working closely with the Lee family group of companies (LFG). I have been associated with the LFG for the past 16 years, having served since 1996 on the board of directors of F&N Holdings (FNH) in Malaysia, its publicly listed company on Bursa Malaysia (the stock exchange in Kuala Lumpur), as well as at various times on the boards of some LFG in Singapore and Malaysia.

The Deal and the Man

ThaiBev (listed on SGX-ST) has since entered into sales and purchase agreements with OCBC Ltd., Great Eastern Holdings Ltd., and Lee Rubber Company (Pte) Ltd. to acquire 22 percent of the issued share capital of F&N for S$2.78 billion (at S$8.88 per share). F&N has three core businesses—food and beverages; properties; and publishing and printing. F&N's soft drinks and dairies business is generated through FNH with operations and investments in Malaysia, Singapore, China, and Vietnam while its beer business is conducted via Asia Pacific Breweries Ltd. (APB), listed on SGX-ST, operating 31 breweries in 15 countries in Asia Pacific. F&N's properties business is based on two SGX-ST listed real estate investment trusts, while its publishing and printing business is conducted through Times Publishing.

Concurrently, all three vendors sold their APB shares, or 8.6 percent of the issued capital of APB, for about S$1 billion (at S$45 per share) to Kindest Place Groups Ltd. This company is owned by Chotiphat Bijananda, son-in-law of Charoen Sirivadhanabhakdi, controlling shareholder of ThaiBev. Both companies are deemed legally independent of each other.

Mr. Charoen is a self-made billionaire (rated by Forbes as the second wealthiest man in Thailand, with a net worth of US$5.5 billion), who made his fortune in beer and whiskey and properties. He is known famously in Thailand for introducing, producing, and distributing the competitively priced "Chang" beer in a joint venture with Carlsberg, to rival market leader "Singha" beer. Though low profile, he is aggressive in expanding his business in the region, including the nonalcoholic segment. He has property investments in Thailand, New York, Singapore, and Australia. Mr. Charoen is known to have an interest in the English Premier League soccer club Everton, whose jersey advertises Chang beer. His acquisition of a significant stake in F&N represents a serious foray to expand his footprint deeper into East and Southeast Asia.

F&N: First 100 Years

F&N's 2011 annual report stated: "A household name to many, F&N has established itself as a leader in the Food and Beverages arena in Singapore and Malaysia since the 1930s. Beyond soft drinks, it has successfully ventured into brewing beer in 1931 and dairies in 1959. Today, the Group owns a portfolio of reputable brands, including F&N, 100-Plus and Seasons for Soft Drinks; F&N, Magnolia, Nutrisoy, Fruit Tree Fresh Juice and NutriTea for Dairies; and Tiger, Anchor, Baron's and ABC for Beer."

F&N (the popular abbreviation) has a long history going back to 1883, when John Fraser and David Neave formed "The Singapore and Straits Aerated Water Company" to produce aerated waters. As it flourished, a new public company, Fraser & Neave Ltd., was formed in 1898. The company set up its first branches in Kuala Lumpur and Penang in 1905. It weathered difficulties of World War I in rebuilding its productive capacity.

The interwar years represented two decades of significant diversification for F&N. Major milestones: diversification into brewing beer in 1931, and in 1936, F&N brought in the Coca-Cola franchise for Singapore and Malaysia. It was a difficult year—the world was in the throes of an impending double-dip recession. These two unrelated events helped transform F&N into a major company in the region. A joint venture with Dutch brewery, Heineken NV, gave rise to "Malayan Breweries" in 1931, producing Tiger beer.

At the outbreak of World War II, a rival German brewery (Archipelago Brewing Company) was set up in Singapore to produce Anchor beer. This was acquired by F&N after the war, and the two beers have been produced in their separate breweries ever since. After liberalization in 1945, the company survived unsettled conditions and rehabilitated, demonstrating its fortitude and resilience. Lion Ltd. was formed in 1948 to manage Coca-Cola. New productive capacities were built and exports revived. Both arms of the company's business expanded rapidly. Strategic acquisitions in the 1950s by Malayan Breweries expanded its business to span the South Pacific and New Zealand. In 1959, F&N secured another prestigious first—the 7-Up franchise.

The company enjoyed another decade of strong growth and diversification in the 1960s. In 1961, it set up a joint-venture factory with Beatrice Foods of Chicago, producing sweetened condensed milk (SCM). Later in 1966, Carnation International of Los Angeles joined the enterprise and the operation was enlarged and renamed Premier Milk (M). It integrated production combining SCM, evaporated milk, and the manufacture of its own cans in 1968. Although Malaysia and Singapore separated in September 1965, F&N forged ahead in expanding its businesses and investments in both Singapore and Malaysia seamlessly. By the end of the decade, F&N brought in new bottling capacities and investments to strengthen distribution networks and warehouses as well as in advances in technology.

The 1970s and the early 1980s continued to see phenomenal growth, including new franchises (Fanta, Sunkist orange, Schweppes); investment in high-speed manufacturing processes; entry into glass containers; launch of Meadow Gold ice cream; committing equity in Metal Box (S) Ltd.; and becoming the sole brewer in Papua New Guinea. In June 1983, F&N's 100-year book, *1883–1983: The Great Years,* stated: "A century ago, two enterprising printers sought to put more fizz into their business by diversifying into soft drinks . . . the project which they pioneered became a multi-million dollar organization that has since sold more than 12 billion bottles of soft drinks which, laid end-to-end, would encircle the globe 75 times. . . . But F&N is more than soft drinks today. It has established a spectrum of interests in the beverage, packaging and related industries, making it well diversified both in product and territory."[2]

The Last 30 Years

Since its centennial in 1983, F&N added two new pillars to its main core business of food and beverages—properties in 1990 and publishing and printing in 2000—reflecting the impact of its ever-growing legacy of enterprise. The history of its next 20 years, "F&N, Beyond the First Centennial," has been documented.[3] The company had since expanded and restructured in a robust and innovative manner. F&N's long history presents, in my view, a good case study of how a singular seed of an idea, nurtured with passion and perseverance with good follow-through, and some good luck to boot, can grow unfettered into a giant of an enterprise. F&N's performance over 10 years since 2001 is exemplary, as elaborated in its 2011 Annual Report for the financial year 2011:

- Revenue of S$6.27 billion, up 157 percent over 10 years.
- Profit (before interest and tax) of S$1.16 billion, up 185 percent: 32 percent came from beer business; 13 percent from non-beer business;

49 percent from property business (of which 35 percent was from property development).

- Attributable profit of S$621 million, up 209 percent.
- Earnings per share of S$0.44, up 227 percent.
- Market capitalization of S$8.75 billion, up 299 percent.
- Share price of S$6.20 as at November 16, 2011, against S$1.44 on September 30, 2001.
- Over these 10 years, revenue rose cumulatively at 10 percent a year.

Takeover Blues

Since the ThaiBev purchase, Heineken NV (F&N's joint-venture [JV] partner at APB) launched a swift defense of its interests, offering to purchase F&N's entire stakes at APB for S$5.1 billion, or S$50 a share (against a closing price of S$42, and 45 percent higher than its weighted monthly average). If successful, Heineken would follow up with a mandatory general offer at the same price for all APB shares it does not already own, for another S$2.4 billion. The market noted this to be a pricy offer, valuing APB at about 17.5 times 2012 earnings (before interest, tax, depreciation and amortization). The medium multiple for major brewery takeovers in the past five years was 13 times. Acquisition cost would total S$7.5 billion. But APB is a high-growth firm with significant strategic importance to Heineken.

At stake is the fast-growing Asian beer market (Tiger has 35 percent of Singapore's market, and Bintang, 42 percent of Indonesia), supported by young consumers with rising incomes, and holding rare brewing licenses in Islamic nations. Heineken is APB's largest shareholder (42 percent deemed interest), and F&N, its second largest at 40 percent. Their JV contains change of control, operations, and other terms designed to protect both parties. This makes it not easy in practice for APB to be sold to a third party. It's understandable why Heineken talks of a "consensual deal" with F&N, but "will review all options available to protect its commercial interests . . . to look ahead to the next chapter of its Asian business."[4]

OCBC's sale is understandable, in line with its strategy of divesting its noncore assets and reinvesting in its core financial business. It's a clean deal, bringing in S$3.216 billion of cash into the group, with a post-tax gain of S$1.153 billion. For ThaiBev, its purchase now gets complicated since it stands to lose its initial exposure to APB through F&N. ThaiBev is seen in the market as Heineken's key regional rival. But Kindest Place Groups could reap a handsome profit.

It would appear Japan's Kirin, F&N's second-largest shareholder at 14.96 percent, would likely lose its exposure to APB as well in the event F&N sold out. It is constrained in firepower to challenge Heineken, considering its net debt to equity is already at 102 percent in the fourth quarter of 2011, even though it has cash worth US$1.07 billion. So far, Kirin has stood at the sidelines. Surely, it can't just do nothing. It has hired Deutsche Bank for advice. At worse, Kirin and ThaiBev could act together (holding 37 percent of F&N) to try and block the Heineken deal.

What's F&N to Do?

F&N has a dilemma. Its beer and nonbeer beverage businesses account for 59 percent of total revenue in the financial year 2011. APB contributed one-third of total profits. Losing it would put a huge dent on its earnings, something it can ill afford after losing the Coca-Cola franchise last year. If the deal goes through, it brings in S$5.1 billion in new cash. But how can it best use this cash to rebuild? F&N's food and beverages will be left with just its Malaysian operations, where it has a 56.4 percent direct stake. For the financial year 2011, they contributed only S$150 million or 13 percent of group overall profits. If F&N stands firm on the status quo, Heineken could force a hostile bid for APB. This can get ugly and messy. Even if F&N sold APB, the possibility of F&N breaking up could be on the table. F&N Holdings, with its many soft drinks and dairies, household names, and a strong regional distribution network, offers an attractive base for Kirin and ThaiBev.

For some time, Coca-Cola is known to have interest in buying the firm, especially its brands and effective distribution network. It should not surprise if Pepsi-Cola also weighed in. After all, 100-Plus and Seasons are attractive, dynamic brands—bear in mind 100-Plus surpassed Coca-Cola in volume sales in recent years. The sum of the parts at F&N appears to be worth more than the whole of the company. In the end, F&N must decide what it wants to be. It has since engaged Goldman Sachs for advice. These are personal thoughts. I have no inside information. So the fun begins.

Kuala Lumpur
July 27, 2012

Postscript: The Outcome

A recap of the takeover battle between two billionaire families in Thailand and Indonesia: Charoen Sirivadhanabhakdi, which controls the TCC Assets Group and its Singapore-listed ThaiBev brewing and soft drinks business, launched an audacious S$8.9 billion bid to control Singapore's F&N in September 2012. But the Riady family of Indonesia, owner of the Lippo Group, launched a counteroffer in November through Oversees Union Enterprise (OUE), its property arm in Singapore. So the stage was set for a showdown. The sequence of events in 2012–2013:

Jul. 18, 2012	OCBC Bank and Great Eastern Life and associates agree to sell their combined 22% stake in F&N to ThaiBev for S$2.78 billion or S$8.88 per share. They also agreed to sell their 8.6% stake in brewer APB (Asia Pacific Breweries) to Heineken's Kindest Place for S$999 million, or S$45 per share.
Jul. 20	Heineken offers to buy F&N's interests in APB for S$5.1 billion or S$50 a share (F&N directly holds 7.26% in APB & 50% in Asia Pacific Investment Pte Ltd. (APIPL), a joint venture with Heineken that controls 64.8% of APB). Heineken also offers S$163 million for non-APB assets held by APIPL.
Jul. 24–25	ThaiBev acquires more F&N shares through married deals to raise its stake to 24.1%.
Aug. 3	F&N board accepts Heineken's S$50 per share offer.
Aug. 7	Kindest Place offers to buy F&N's direct 7.26% stake in APB for S$1 billion or S$55 per share. ThaiBev raised its F&N stake to 26.2% through the open market.
Aug. 17	Heineken raises its offer for F&N's interest in APB to a final price of S$53 per share or S$5.4 billion, valuing APB at S$13.7 billion altogether. F&N board agreed.
Sept. 13	Charoen's TCC Assets acquires 19.5 million F&N shares, raising the Thai bloc's F&N stake to 30.36%, triggering a general offer at S$8.88 per F&N share it does not own.
Sept. 28	F&N shareholders approve sale of APB with Thai support, in exchange for Heineken's promise not to take part in rival bids for F&N. Thais block F&N's capital reduction plan.
Oct. 10	OUE offers to buy F&N's hospitality and serviced apartment business for S$1.4 billion but F&N board does not respond because of the ongoing general offer. F&N independent adviser (JP Morgan) concluded that the Thai offer was "not compelling, but fair."
Nov. 15	OUE and fund managers (Farallon Capital Management and Noonday Global Management) announce plans to offer S$9.08 per F&N share, subject to gaining management control. Kirin (14.8% shareholder of F&N) agrees to sell its stake to the consortium, and to buy F&N's food and beverage business for S$2.7 billion if this consortium succeeds.
Dec. 6	OUE consortium sets January 3, 2013, as offer deadline.
Dec. 11	Thais extend the offer deadline to January 2 but keep their bid unchanged.

Jan. 18, 2013	TCC Assets raises its offer to S$9.55 per F&N share, valuing F&N at S$13.8 billion (deemed as "fair"—within the S$8.58 to S$11.56 range of values the independent adviser had ascribed for the share).
Jan. 21	Expected deadline for both parties to make final offers. Singapore's Securities Industry Council (SIC) triggered the "auction," since neither bidder declared a final offer by the deadline set. The SIC had stepped in after the Thais had extended their offer deadline seven times, and the OUE Group, twice—testing the patience of investors and the authorities. OUE finally decided not to raise its S$9.08 per share offer, thereby allowing the offer to lapse on January 21, 2013. As a consequence, Kirin's offer also lapsed. F&N board accepted TCC Assets' revised offer, setting the closing date on February 4, 2013. The Thais owned 46.4% of F&N as at January 25. Kirin finally accepted the offer as well for S$2 billion.

The Thais win.

So, Thai tycoon Charoen emerged as the winner of the F&N takeover tussle. His group controlled 90.3 percent of F&N as of end-March 2013. F&N shares resumed trading on the Singapore Exchange, SGX, on April 15 after a two-month trading coma. It has been granted an additional three months (until July 19, 2013) to restore the stock's public float to above 10 percent.

All's well that ends well. A new chapter begins for the 130-year-old F&N. This saga illustrates a new trend in which some of the region's largest and most powerful groups—backed by their billionaire families—are keen to expand beyond their home turfs to cash in on Southeast Asia's booming economies. Since the 2008 financial crisis, mergers and acquisition deals estimated at more than US$105 billion were either completed or pending completion in 2012, up more than 50 percent over 2011. The outlook for 2013 is good.

Kuala Lumpur
April 30, 2013

Notes

1. First published on July 28, 2012.
2. Published in 1983 by Fraser & Neave Ltd. in commemoration of 100 years of business in Singapore, p. 3.
3. Unpublished. The final draft remains in the company's files.
4. Emily Yap, "Heineken Bids S$7.5 Billion to Gulp Down APB," *Business Times* (July 21–22, 2012), p. 4.

CHAPTER 148

On Global Gaming, Aussie\$, the SGX–ASX Merger[1]

Just returned as a keynote speaker at the 2010 World Lottery Association (WLA) Convention in Brisbane, Australia. It's a grand affair, attracting 800 participants from around the world, most of whom are involved in managing the lottery business worldwide. It also coincided with the Melbourne Cup. Enjoying this special event by having a small bet, experiencing the party atmosphere, and watching the big race has become part of Australian folklore. Mark Twain is often reported to have said of the Melbourne Cup in 1895: "Nowhere in the world have I encountered a festival of people that has such a magnificent appeal to the whole nation. The Cup astonished me!" An estimated 120,000 people did watch "the horserace that stops the nation" at the Melbourne track this November 2 sunny afternoon.

Global Gaming

In 2010, the global gaming market attracted revenues of between US\$350 and US\$400 billion, with casinos, lotteries, and gaming machines accounting for close to 85 percent share. The online component is beginning to edge up to 10 percent within the next few years. Here, the push is led by the Organisation for Economic Co-operation and Development (OECD) group, representing three-quarters of this business. The worldwide lottery business alone is worth about US\$200 to US\$240 billion, growing lately at below 5 percent a year.

Growth is, however, uneven—20 percent in Latin America and South Africa; 10 percent in Asia (23 percent in China, where revenues in the first eight months of 2010 amounted to US\$16 billion); flat in Europe and the United States. In addition, global casino and other regulated gaming had revenues in the region of US\$150 billion in 2010, with 45 percent in the United States, 30 percent in Asia Pacific, and 20 percent in Europe, Middle East, and Africa (EMEA). But growth is fastest in Asia Pacific, up an estimated 20 percent per annum in 2008–2012, while US growth is expected at 4 percent, and EMEA, 5 percent. Casino gaming accounted for 90 percent.

In Asia Pacific, business in China (Macau) is growing the fastest, rising by 59 percent in 10 months of 2010 from a year earlier, with revenues passing US$21 billion for the entire year, while ASEAN-6 (Indonesia, Malaysia, Philippines, Singapore, Thailand, and Vietnam) expanded just as fast, with revenues of US$7 billion. Australia and South Korea have revenues of US$2 billion to US$3 billion each—growing much slower annually.

Conventional wisdom has it that the gaming industry is recession proof. This is a myth. During the recent Great Recession, the Bank of America Merrill Lynch (BAML) High Yield Gaming Index declined 56 percent from the beginning of 2008 to its trough in March 2009. However, since then, the index rose 136 percent until today. The ride has been anything but smooth.

Despite growing risks, Asia will lead economic growth this year and in 2011. Just today, the World Bank upgraded China's 2010 gross domestic product (GDP) growth to 10 percent.[2] At the same time, the OECD cut growth for its 33 members to 2 to 2.5 percent in 2011, downgrading the United States to 1.75 to 2.25 percent.[3] So growth in Asian disposable income will continue to expand; indeed, so will growth in Asian household consumption of goods and services. Since the beginning of this decade, Asia's gaming revenues have been the fastest growing—especially in Macau and Singapore.

The region possesses the richest potential for gaining profit. Latest record never ceases to amaze. I well remember back in 2007, most analysts figured the Macau market would be worth US$13 billion in 2010. Today, based on the third quarter of 2010 results so far, it's worth US$21 billion. I am told that in the United States, every available table and slot machine serves 250 people. In Southeast Asia and India, the number is as many as 45,000 to 50,000. So, Asian gamers are underserved.

It is estimated that Asians spend almost twice as much on gaming as Americans do. Singapore has gone from zero to near US$5 billion just this year alone. By 2012, Morgan Stanley estimated Singapore could generate revenues of US$7 billion to US$10 billion. Macau took about the same time to hit US$6 billion. Undoubtedly, Asia provides the best prospects in gaming and betting. It will utilize advances in technology to enhance its innovative and creative potential to lead in contemporary interactive gaming entertainment, in a socially responsible way. For this vibrant, exciting, and colorful industry, a bright future lies ahead.

The Aussie Dollar

As if the big race wasn't enough distraction, the Aussie dollar (A$) hits a 28-year high on the back of an unexpected interest rate hike on Melbourne Cup day. The A$ has been hovering just below parity with US$ for some time. Of course, the growing strength of the A$ benefited from the US Federal Reserve Bank System's (Fed) continuing efforts to drive US interest rates down (it's already near zero).

But its core strength is centered on a China-driven mining boom that has boosted its exports of iron ore, coal, and other minerals. Australia's terms of trade—its export prices relative to its import prices, have doubled in the past decade to record highs. So much so that its persistent current account deficit was all but eliminated last quarter. Above all, inflation is held well in check. The Reserve Bank of Australia had kept the benchmark interest rate unchanged since May and economists had predicted that the rate would stand pat again—indeed, swap traders betted there to be only a 23 percent chance of a rate increase, against a 60 percent chance before the third quarter of 2010 inflation rate turned weaker, thereby giving policymakers breathing space.

Historically, the Reserve Bank did raise interest rates on Melbourne Cup day four times in the past decade. True to form, in a surprise move, it raised interest rates by 25 basis points to 4.75 percent on November 2, 2010, in the face of expectations the US Fed will add massively once more to global money supply (on November 3 it unveiled plans to purchase US$600 billion of US government debt over the next eight months). The A$ promptly reached past parity against the US$, recording a high of US$1.0025.

Since deregulation in 1983, the A$ has never been higher. Many see the A$ as a proxy for Asia, and its worries about inflation reflect Asian central banks' concern as well. Regional currency also rallied—the Indian rupee (which also raised rates in a separate move), Thai baht, and Malaysian ringgit all gained against the US$. The euro traded above US$1.40, up 1.1 percent.

The rate hike shifted the Reserve Bank's focus to fight inflation with a preemptive strike, even though the rise in consumer prices in the third quarter of 2010 was well within its comfort zone. But like it or not, inflation is an obvious outcome of Australia's strong economic growth. In Asia, growing domestic demand and rising food and commodity prices can be expected to push inflation higher. Most forecasts place Asia's inflation in 2011 at 4 to 5 percent, up from 3.3 percent previously. India's case is more urgent—where inflation is running at above 10 percent and is too obvious to ignore. Tuesday's rate increase is India's sixth in just over seven months. It looks like its tightening cycle is not yet over.

SGX–ASX Merger

During the week I was in Australia, not a day passed without news about the controversial SGX–ASX merger (of the two national stock exchanges). For most Australians, this issue is divisive. Everyone has an opinion. It's understandable, as it touches lots of raw nerves. The central question remains: Is it in Australia's national interest to proceed with the merger? Actually, it's a takeover by the Singapore Exchange Ltd (SGX), which will pay A$8.4 billion (US$8.3 billion) to the Australian Stock Exchange operator (ASX Ltd) for it. According to the chief executive officer (CEO) of ASX: The combined exchange will be both more regionally relevant and globally relevant than the sum of its parts. So, "we can't see how this is contrary to the national interest."

The takeover requires the approval of both governments and regulators. For the deal to go through, Parliament needs to lift the ASX's 15 percent single shareholder cap, following a screening process by Australia's Foreign Investment Review Board. The deal is expected to cut costs and better place the merged exchange to fight growing competition. The takeover creates a US$1.9 trillion market to become the world's fifth-largest exchange, rivaling Japan and Hong Kong.

Politicians on both sides have voiced concern over the takeover. The leader of the Green Party (a member of the sitting Gillard government) is a vocal critic. Temasek, a 23.45 percent shareholder of SGX, has since stated publicly that this Singapore-controlled sovereign wealth fund is not involved in the governance, operations, or investment decisions of SGX. Frankly, Australians don't believe it in practice.

A Historical Perspective Is Helpful

Australia used to have a stock exchange in every state. In 1987, these markets were consolidated into the Australian Stock Exchange in Sydney—only after the Victoria government made what many still consider a "crucial" error in closing the Melbourne Stock Exchange. According to Professor Sam Wylie of the Melbourne Business School, the experience of Australian stock markets is best understood as a global process involving three discrete steps: (1) consolidation; (2) demutualization; and (3) mergers across national boundaries.

Australia has taken the first two steps, and the United States, all three, where trading is now concentrated in New York City in the New York Stock Exchange (NYSE) and Nasdaq. Inevitably, ASX will merge with a global exchange—if not SGX, then some other exchange. It would appear the global process of consolidation is unstoppable. Whichever group the ASX joins, it has to be run commercially, regulated to meet Australian standards, and free from government influence in its effective management.

It seems to me the main objections are centered on five points: (1) it's not in the national interest since it encourages shifting the processing, technology, analytical capacity, fund management, and investment bankers to Singapore, and more importantly, passing management of ASX to the Singapore government in the final analysis; (2) it forsakes Australia's ambitions to become an Asian financial hub; (3) Australia does not allow major banks to be controlled from offshore, so why tolerate this for its stock exchange?; (4) ASX is efficient, ahead in Asia in derivatives and in innovative products (initiated the Real Estate Investment Trusts market in Asia Pacific); and (5) benefits (technology sharing, colisting of stocks, and access to new pools of capital) can be enjoyed without change in ownership.

Supporters of the deal cut at the very heart of Australian capitalism: (1) it's an arm's-length business deal, and so long as both stock exchange boards deem it in their companies' best interest and vital domestic interests are protected, why not?; (2) then, it becomes a matter of a price—a 40 percent premium above market price of ASX is fair enough; (3) national interests are ultimately protected by the Corporations Act of Australia; (4) "The attractiveness of a combined pool of listings and a combined pool of liquidity would make this combination unique," according to ASX's CEO; and (5) for ASX, merger is inevitable—SGX is a good enough suitor.[4]

What, Then, Are We to Do?

In the end, it's the Australian government and regulators who have the final say. This simply means politics as usual, involving interaction of vested interests and self-interest. The real issue behind the fuss—as I see it—is slippage in the separation of business from politics. The final outcome? Discarding all the "noise"—anger and resentment and, no doubt, assurances to protect the national interest—the key issue focuses on national identity and how closely attached Australians are to its liberal free market system, which politicians so proudly and often identify with the national good. Only Australians can tell.

Brisbane, Australia
Kuala Lumpur
November 4, 2010

Postscript

On April 8, 2011, the SGX and ASX simultaneously announced the termination of the proposed Merger Implementation Agreement of October 25, 2010, following its rejection by Australia's Federal Treasurer, Wayne Swan.

Among Swan's list of reasons were concerns about relinquishing control of the nation's clearing and settlement systems, and Australian capital and jobs moving offshore.[5] Said Mr. Swan: "Becoming a junior partner to a smaller regional exchange through this deal would risk us losing many of our financial sector jobs. . . . So let's be clear. This is not a merger, it's a takeover that would see Australia's financial sector become a subsidiary to a competitor in Asia."

Nevertheless, in its announcement, the ASX Board "reiterates its ongoing belief in the need for ASX participation in regional and global exchange consolidation. ASX will continue to evaluate strategic growth opportunities, including further dialogue with SGX on other forms of combination and co-operation. . . . ASX also continues to strengthen its preparedness to operate within the proposed domestic competitive environment, which will include the offering of new products and services to its customers and new market operators."[6]

Notes

1. First published on November 6, 2010.
2. World Bank, *Global Economic Prospects* (Washington, DC: World Bank, November 2010).
3. Organisation for Economic Co-operation and Development (OECD), *Economic Outlook* (Paris: OECD, November 2010).
4. Robert Elstone, chief executive officer, ASX, in a statement on November 2, 2010, in Sydney, Australia.
5. Reported in the *Sydney Morning Herald*, April 21, 2011.
6. ASX announcement of April 8, 2011, in Sydney, Australia.

Epilogue

Epilogue

CHAPTER 149

In Search of Growth[1]

It's already six years since the Great Recession. Yet the world economy remains stuck in the doldrums—set on a course that is uncertain and unsustainable. World demand is still weak, as reflected in falling oil and other basic commodity prices as the once-dynamic emerging markets' slowdown fuels concern for the global outlook. Where spending had picked up, it is often the result of a dangerous new buildup of public and household debt.

Much of the financial reforms are still works in process—they have thus far only preserved the essence of an inherently fragile and unstable system. Too-big-to-fail remains a problem. Megabanks still don't have adequate equity capital.[2] The global system remains dysfunctional. The euro-crisis was simply papered over, with an array of underlying problems remaining unresolved. Many have since resurfaced. Japan may also be on the edge of a downturn. Emerging nations—resilient soon after 2008—now face slower growth and unsettling debt problems of their own. The economies of Russia and Brazil are stagnant at best. Even China is vulnerable. Much of the global mess is of policy makers' own making: in particular, the premature rush to fiscal austerity and the "kick-the-can-down-the-road" attitude in handling the series of euro crises. The pathway for this lopsided global economy to sustainable growth remains unclear.

October 2014 Assessment

Forecast updates were set for late September/early October 2014. On September 26, Asian Development Bank released its Update for 2014 and the 2015 Outlook for Asia.[3] It trimmed down its 2014–2015 growth forecast for Southeast Asia; however, its forecasts remained unchanged for India and China. Also, World Bank's Update released on October 6 similarly cut its forecasts for East Asia, citing risks to the outlook to include weaker global growth and slower growth in China and Indonesia.[4]

The International Monetary Fund's (IMF) release, *World Economic Outlook—Legacies, Clouds, Uncertainties,* on October 7 is by far the most comprehensive.[5] It talks about the need to address legacies from the past crises in the face of a cloudy future, as the interplay among them had resulted in the downgrading of forecasts. Yet, growing uncertainties bring on new risks, including risks associated with the search for higher yields, geopolitical risks, and risks that global demand could further weaken as eurozone growth stalls. The upshot: "Only a modest pick-up is forecast for 2015 as the outlook for potential growth has been pared down," according to IMF Managing Director Christine Lagarde.[6] She added that the global economy could get stuck in a much lower growth gear for years, warning the recovery is "brittle, uneven and beset by risks." Her somber outlook seems more realistic for once. After all, the IMF report did admit that it had to make "several downward revisions to the forecast during the past three years."[7]

Like most other international institutions, IMF does not have a good track record in forecasting, as reflected in what is now termed: "serial disappointments" in growth. My own feeling is that even the downgraded forecasts for 2014–2015 are optimistic. I won't be surprised if they will be further marked down come April 2015. Harvard's Professor Lawrence Summers's lament that the rich world now faces secular stagnation is worth thinking about.

The IMF expects the global economy to expand by 3.8 percent in 2015, better than 2014's estimated pace of 3.3 percent (it had expected 3.6 percent in April 2014), citing persistent weakness in the eurozone and a broad slowdown in several major emerging economies. Prospects for the eurozone's three largest economies, Germany, France, and Italy, remain poor. The eurozone is headed for its third consecutive year of recession, and the IMF now warns that the odds of it reentering a recession in the next six months have risen—doubled to 38 percent since its April 2014 outlook. It also sees disappointing prospects for Japan and lower growth outcomes in some big emerging economies, including Brazil and Russia.

In contrast, the outlook for growth in the United States—fresh from recent strong job reports in early October—was revised up to 2.2 percent (from 1.7 percent in July). For 2015, US growth will rise by 3.1 percent—outpacing all major "rich" nations and a number of emerging markets as well (which are supposed to grow at a more rapid clip). The United States is also expected to lead in corporate profitability and global competitiveness.

Hence, the chase for US$, betting it is now its turn to strengthen. Against seven of the world's most heavily traded currencies, US$ was up 6 percent since July 1, 2014; it recently hit a six-year high against yen (up 5 percent) and a two-year high against euro (up 6.4 percent), and against wobbly currencies like Russia's ruble (+19.7 percent), Brazil's real (+11.7 percent), and Turkey's lira (+6.8 percent). Ringgit weakened 2.3 percent. On most metrics, US$ has rallied faster than expected.

China's economic growth is forecast to slow down to around 6.5 percent by 2016 because of domestic rebalancing and reform, from 7.4 percent in 2014 and 7.1 percent expected in 2015, after averaging 10.5 percent before the crisis. However, growth in Brazil is expected to slacken to only 1.4 percent in 2015 (from practically no growth this year), reflecting poor policies. In the nine years before the crisis, it had expanded on average at 3.7 percent a year.

Ailing Europe

Growth in the eurozone, plagued by persistent banking problems and the prospect of deflation, will slacken to 0.8 percent in 2014 (still optimistic, I think) from 1.1 percent forecast in July 2014. For 2015, growth will rise by 1.3 percent (again, optimistic). Europe's "extended stagnation" remains a major stumbling block. The real problem lies in Europe still not coming to terms with the legacies from the financial crisis, continuing to be saddled with high government and household debts, poor banks' balance sheets, and persistently high unemployment. Italy has been in recession for two years and France's economy has been at a standstill for months. With Germany also in trouble, the chance of a Japanese-style deflationary spiral rises each week.

In addition, divergent monetary policies between the United States and Europe perpetuate the growth gap on both sides of the Atlantic. Furthermore, Europe can't cut (stick with austerity) and grow. Germany is being pigheaded in insisting that growth and fiscal discipline can go together, and that the key to economic revival rests solely on private initiative to create jobs. So far, this approach has not worked. As a result, Europe is simply left behind. Germany's now-slowing economy is no longer in a position to pull the eurozone out of the mud. The IMF downgraded Germany's growth to 1.4 percent (from 1.9 percent earlier), staying in the region of 1.5 percent in 2015. Germany needs to do more to stoke growth by stepping up spending on infrastructure to create jobs and stimulate private demand. I agree with the IMF that infrastructure investment, even if debt financed, can be economically justified. "Eurozone countries should be ready to do more." But, this has not gone on well with Germany.

Already, there is a rift between Germany, France, and Italy on how to revive growth—amid a warning that Europe risks a "lost decade" of low growth and low inflation but with high debt and high unemployment. It is clear the eurozone continues to suffer from lack of demand on top of its many supply problems in regulation, taxation, banking, and labor. It's also clear that monetary policy can't do the heavy lifting alone.

What is now needed is a coordinated push involving aggressive US-style quantitative easing (QE) actions by the European Central Bank (ECB), higher investment spending by Germany and European Union institutions (especially the European Investment Bank), and firm commitments to bolder reform measures in France and Italy.

Stock Sell-Off

For nearly two years, there has been a disconnect between what's happening in the markets and progress in the real economy. Spurred by expansive QE measures, financial and commodity markets (particularly in stocks and shares) have enjoyed their moment of magic, especially in 2013: US S&P 500 index on Wall Street rose by 30 percent, and Japan's Nikkei, 57 percent, buoyed by the vast pool of generous stimulus liquidity and growing optimism of revival of global growth.

By February 2014, some of the shine had worn off when some US$3 trillion was wiped off global shares in early 2014. After all, S&P 500 finished 2013 at a multiple of 25 times 10-year earnings (historical average being 16 times). Even so, by mid-August, S&P 500 was still trading at 15 to 16 times earnings, against an average of 14 times.

The Chicago Board of Options Exchange Volatility Index (or VIX, Wall Street's fear index), which is based on options prices on S&P 500, had been unusually low (<20) for a long period, reflecting a market that had experienced few hiccups over the past two years. But by mid-October, rampant market fear appeared to overwhelm all previous greed. There was a flight to safety from equities to haven bonds. Yields on 10-year US Treasury bonds slumped below 1.9 percent, and similar-maturity yen bonds, to as low as 0.47 percent.

The slide in the Dow Jones Industrial index and S&P 500 had erased all of this year's gains. Volatility was back: VIX>30. Similarly, European stocks tumbled. Relative calm returned on October 17. Still, the markets "lost" for the week. Nevertheless, the domestic US economy has been steadily improving. The negative vibes that had since emerged reflected markets catching up with the data, much of which investors don't even want to hear:

- Softening of growth in big countries like Germany, France, Japan, Italy, and China
- Tumbling oil and commodity prices, reflecting continuing weak demand
- Low inflation and prospects of it falling lower still
- Possibility of Europe going once more into recession
- Frenzy over the spread of the Ebola virus, and other geopolitical risks
- Prospect of higher interest rates
- Greece needing a liquidity injection once again, after being bailed out two years ago

The fear that any of them could provoke another market convulsion is real. The underlying problems haven't gone away. So after a week of turmoil and then some calm, uncertainty is back.

What, Then, Are We to Do?

The bleak outlook for the global economy is reviving divisions among governments on the limited policy options they have at their disposal: (1) greater flexibility in managing fiscal budgets in the short run, including spending in infrastructure to boost demand and create jobs; (2) immediately implement reforms, including opening up economies and labor markets; (3) ECB to adopt US/UK/Japan-style QE by buying government bonds directly (bound to be resisted by inflation-averse Germany); and (4) IMF mantra "to pursue bold and ambitious measures to revive growth, cut debt levels, and ensure stability in financial markets."

For six years, policy makers have tried but failed to make significant progress on all of them. Indeed, they have fewer tools at their disposal today than they did in prior bouts of stress. Early fiscal stimuli have led to rising debt loads, which the public now finds hard to swallow and for politicians to absorb, given years of slow growth and slow job creation. Even ECB's Mario Draghi couldn't make good on his vow to do "whatever it takes" to preserve the euro.

All these have been the consequence of underestimating the deep, underlying weakening that has taken place. In the end, Europe needs a compromise package deal: some fiscal stimulus, some reforms, some QEs, and some infrastructure spending. Chairman Tharman Shanmugaratnam of IMF's International Monetary and Finance Committee sums it up best: "To solve today's growth problems we have to lift potential growth . . . if we don't address tomorrow's growth problems today, we will be left with today's problems tomorrow."[8]

The world badly needs a consensus to act in unison to effectively grow— much rests on the shoulders of Europe, in particular, Germany. There's a lot that can still go wrong. So, get on with it. Voters are angered by years of austerity and declines in inflation-adjusted wages. Already, politicians find it harder and harder to ward off future calls for greater protectionism—the last thing the world needs now.

Obiter Dictum

I worry that central banks continue to deliberately push down to zero the cost of capital—that's price control, not monetary policy management. The consequences: They push up stock prices as well as bond and property prices. So many people are richer today because of officially sponsored "bull" markets.

Former Fed Chairman Ben Bernanke candidly called QE an exercise in "learning by doing." Investors benefit from zero percent funding big time; but savers suffer (for too long, I think), unfortunately in silence. Lest we forget, interest rate is a price. It functions as traffic lights for the market economy; it calibrates risk and reward. Analysts use it to establish investment benchmarks to guide decision making, and to discount projected future cash flows to determine the viability of projects.

When the rate is suppressed to zero (Keynes's "liquidity trap" sets in—rate can't be lowered further to induce higher investments), stock prices get inflated and investors cheer. But it acts to misdirect investments and screws up the market as being the efficient allocator of resources. So, price signals in the marketplace get badly misaligned.[9] Students are taught that true prices are discovered in the marketplace—not administered. That's why price control of any kind is a no-no.

The market price discovery mechanism is sacrosanct. When LIBOR was manipulated, the world was rightly outraged. Profligate banks and broking houses were (again rightly) fined billions. The system was reformed to prevent future repeats. Yet, why are central banks not censured for manipulating money market interest rates and bond rates? Just because they are well intended? Surely, being legal does not make their actions less subversive. Where do you draw the line between normal monetary policy and price (interest rate) manipulation—or, for that matter, currency (US$) manipulation, as the United States has been accused by China, Brazil, and many others. Well, it's the system, stupid!—which is, unfortunately, asymmetrical and dysfunctional. But, it's the only one we have. I know, it sucks! Now you know, too, why the world is so screwed up today!

Istanbul
Kuala Lumpur
October 18, 2014

Notes

1. First published as an abridged version: "In Search for Growth," on November 1, 2014.
2. Simon Johnson, "Two Views on Finance," *The Edge's Financial Daily,* Kuala Lumpur (October 10, 2014).
3. Update for Asia released in a statement in Singapore on September 26, 2014, and reported by Reuters and published in *The Edge's Financial Daily* (September 27, 2014).
4. Update for East Asia and Pacific released in Singapore on October 6, 2014, reflected in an article by Masayuki Kitano of Reuters and published in the *International New York Times* (October 7, 2014).

5. International Monetary Fund (IMF), *World Economic Outlook—Legacies, Clouds, Uncertainties* (Washington, DC: IMF, October 7, 2014).

6. Christine Lagarde, in prepared remarks for an event at the Georgetown University School of Foreign Service on October 3, 2014.

7. Ibid., p. xiii.

8. Tharman Shanmugaratnam, stated at the conclusion of the IMF's October 2014 meeting of the governing body of finance ministers and central bank governors on October 12, 2014, in Washington, DC, as reported in the *Financial Times*, October 13, 2014.

9. James Grant, "Low Rates Are Jamming the Economy's Vital Signals," *Financial Times*, October 13, 2014.

Postscript: On to 2015

CHAPTER 150

The Goat Straggles into 2015 amid Rising Risks[1]

2015 is the year of the lunar wood goat—renowned for moderation. In mid-November 2014, the world's most powerful economies pledged in Brisbane: "to lift G-20's GDP by at least an additional 2 percent by 2018. . . . If fully implemented, . . . this will add more than US$2 trillion to the global economy and create millions of jobs."[2] Brave words indeed after acknowledging: "The global recovery is slow, uneven and not delivering the jobs needed. . . . Risks persist, including in financial markets and from geopolitical tensions." G-20 emphasized that the extra 2 percent would be met only if Europe starts pumping billions into the stalling eurozone, given that Germany and France had just only narrowly avoided recession amid slowdown in most emerging economies, including China. It is clear the global economy is in for a rough ride. After all, the International Monetary Fund (IMF) had just trimmed world growth in 2014 to 3.3 percent.

Oil's Slide

For once, the betting is for plummeting oil prices to give an overall boost to the global economy by delivering a windfall to consumers and manufacturers, especially in countries with high-energy tabs. It is as though the world was given a significant tax cut. While part of the benefit will go to governments because of the way oil is being taxed (particularly in Europe) or used to subsidize (such as Malaysia and Indonesia), the overall global impact will be to boost consumption spending and lower production costs in countries that have been struggling to overcome prolonged malaise in growth and jobs. There will also be positive distributional effects within these economies, especially for lower income families, helping to offset certain forces that have since worsened inequalities in income, wealth, and

opportunities. There are risks as well: bound to be cuts in energy companies' investment budgets; could even accentuate deflation that is threatening Europe, although it is possible the favorable income effects can help
to counter this threat. The plunge in oil prices is proving disruptive for
financial markets. Worse—roiled by sanctions, a collapsing ruble, and large
capital flights—Russia now faces the impact of a sharp fall in oil revenues,
which strengthens the forces of recession, inflation, and financial instability.
What is really worrisome is this: In a complex global economy with many
moving parts, when markets experience a near 40 percent fall over a six-
month period for such an economically dominant commodity like oil, there
can be unforeseen spillover effects, often with unpredictable consequences.
Indeed, there are early warnings of a "harbinger of doom" as Europe flirts
with deflation—and even recession—as Japan tries hard to recover from its
own slump, and as China's already slackening growth risks morphing into
a steeper pullback in the face of slowing economic activities in many other
emerging nations, including Brazil and India. Still, the IMF's latest assessment is that on a net-net basis, the global economy should come out on the
plus side. Already, the IMF raised US growth in 2015 to 3.5 percent.

Wounded Bear Heads for #63

The story goes around in early December that Russia is headed toward #63:
President Vladimir Putin is 63 years old; the benchmark US oil price has already
touched US$63 a barrel; and the ruble has fallen past 63 percent relative to
US$ over the past year. Seriously, Russia is struggling. The economy did surge
on rising energy prices. Now that the oil price has tumbled from an average
of about US$110 a barrel in the first half of 2014 to well below the US$90 level
Russia needed to avoid a recession and keep its budget in balance, Russia is
doubtless, hurting. Then there are the coming debt repayments—firms owe
over US$500 billion in external debts, with some US$130 billion due before
end-2015. It is tough with biting sanctions in place. The ruble had performed
badly, despite being allowed to float because the market is simply not convinced the Russian Central Bank (CBR) is doing enough—using "a peashooter"
in its "reluctant" piecemeal interventions. It needs to significantly raise interest
rates or just let the ruble further weaken. All these spell trouble for Russia. It is
already in recession; gross domestic product (GDP) will shrink 1 to 2 percent
in 2015. In 2007, when the oil price was US$72 a barrel, GDP rose 8.5 percent.
In 2012, the price of oil averaged US$111—but brought on growth of just 3
to 4 percent. Between 2010 and 2013, with high oil prices, the net outflow of
capital was US$232 billion, 20 times it what was in 2004–2008. Empirically, falls
in the ruble closely track the oil price so that, in ruble terms, the monies that oil
brings in stay roughly the same. But its purchasing power is much less.

Europe, Japan Flagging; China Slowing

What a difference half a year makes. The IMF's April 2014 forecasts talk of "Global activity has broadly strengthened and is expected to improve further in 2014–2015."[3] Growth was expected to be strongest in the United States, positive in eurozone, growing in Japan, and in the emerging market, growth was projected to pick up—with, of course, significant downside risks. By the October 2014 update, forecasts had to be downgraded: "World growth is mediocre and a bit worse than forecast; . . . facing a cloudy future . . . the global economy has become more differentiated."[4] By December, economic prospects have been flagging across Europe, Japan, and the big emerging markets (including China, India, and Brazil)—a turn that presents fresh challenges to the robust US economy just as the world needed a dependable growth engine. Indeed, reports now point to slackening economic vitality across the globe. In Europe, consumer prices in December rose at its slowest annual pace in five years, deepening fears of tipping into deflation. Prospects are for inflation to hit zero in early 2015. In Japan, the core consumer price index in November rose at its lowest pace this year. Inflation is moving further away from Bank of Japan's 2 percent target. In both regions, the energy price fall has clouded a concerted push by central banks to boost inflation and stoke consumption and business confidence. The picture in emerging markets is not much better. Economic growth in China and India decelerated in the third quarter of 2014. Brazil managed to edge out of recession helped by government spending. But I sense that stagnation there is deep. China now faces a deflation risk as inflation in November grew at its slowest pace in five years; producer prices were down 2.7 percent from a year earlier. It is also striving to contain an explosion of debt—notably, risky borrowings by local governments as it rebalances the economy without crashing it. But the commitment to reform remains firm. Still, in different ways, China and Europe pose significant risks to the global well-being.

US economic growth at 3.9 percent in the third quarter of 2014 has so far been stronger than initially thought (+4.6 percent in the second quarter of 2014). The economy has now experienced the two strongest back-to-back growth quarters since 2003. Indeed, it was the fourth out of the past five quarters that the economy has expanded above a 3.5 percent pace. The United States remains a bright spot in an increasingly global gloomy economy, with Japan back in recession and growth in the eurozone and China slowing significantly. Overall, the US economy is better insulated from the global downturn because, among the world's major economies, it is less reliant on overseas export demand. Exports account for only 14 percent of US GDP, the lowest for any developed nation and well below the 51 percent for Germany and 26 percent for China. Furthermore, latest data confirmed a grim outlook for much of the eurozone's US$13.3 trillion economy, the world's second largest after the United States. Unemployment across the eurozone rose to 11.5 percent. Consumption spending fell in Germany, France, and Spain; retail sales also fell in Italy, where the jobless rate was 13.2 percent, the highest since 1977. The benefits for Europe of cheaper oil are being diluted by the euro's recent weakness against the dollar, which simply meant Europeans have to pay somewhat more for dollar-denominated imports.

Why the Differentiation?

Divergent policy measures have made a big difference: As a result (1) unemployment, which peaked at 10 percent in the United States, is down to 5.8 percent today.[5] Eurozone unemployment climbed to a high of 12 percent (11.5 percent today) and Japan is now back to recession; and (2) the United States aggressively adopted easy-money very early on (QE or quantitative easing). But Europe stuck steadfast to austerity and addressed bank weaknesses, softly; Japan chose to raise consumption tax to restrain deficits. So, easy monetary policy brought US short rates to near zero in late 2008 as QE (massive purchases of long-bonds) took aim to lower long-rates to spur activity. Japan only followed the United States in April 2013; Europe has yet to use QE. With the return of sustained growth, US interest rates will resume normalcy soon. The "feared" ill effects of inflation and bubbles did not materialize—even after six years! The second lesson learned comes from fiscal policy—adjust during good times in order to make "room available to maneuver" when times turn bad. Japan ran up public debt to 1.35 times GDP (0.8 time in the United States), leaving little room to adjust when adjust it must. In contrast, US fiscal policy was more flexible—it ran deficits over the short run and gradually adjusted after the crisis. Europe demonstrated that it can't cut (austerity) and grow. The third lesson concerns the recapitalization of failing banks. US banks raised substantial capital (US$203 billion) in 2009–2012, against only US$108 billion by European banks, which relied more on cutting risk assets (by US$1.5 trillion against US$154 billion for US banks). Both did raise their capital/risk assets ratios, but the United States ended much better capitalized. These lessons provide policy makers with valuable indicative best practices to navigate under difficult environments.

What, Then, Are We to Do?

I used to be asked, often, why the US$ is so weak. In 1971, soon after the US$ was delinked from gold, former US Treasury Secretary John Connally told a group of Europeans fretting over falling US$ value: "The dollar may be our currency, but it is your problem." This time around, the rising US$ is still America's currency, but it is now everybody's problem! That is because the strong US$ serves to crimp global liquidity, making financing more expensive and harder to get, markets more volatile, and emerging economies (especially those commodity-based), more risky. Today, big swings are back at the US$5 trillion-a-day currency market as traders grapple with sharply diverging central bank policies, a slackening China, stagnating growth across much of the world, tumbling commodity prices, and fear of deflation.

Of late, the rallying US$ pushed the yen to its weakest level in seven years; the euro slipped to a two-year low; the A$ fell to a four-year nadir; and the ringgit hit its lowest level in about five years. The Indonesian rupiah slumped to its lowest since 2008. The slide is far from over. Today, the market has become more sensitive to political unrest and changes in economic indicators because central banks are moving in opposite directions. Prospects of slowing growth are quickly reflected in currencies like the euro, yen, and those linked to commodity prices. They are set to face strong headwinds in 2015. We have not seen the last of the US$ strength. One thing is clear—so long as it remains the dominant currency and the US economy continues to perform, the US$ will stay strong (indeed, even stronger) to really become everyone's problem.

Kuala Lumpur
December 15, 2014

Notes

1. First published on December 27, 2014.
2. G-20 Leaders' Communiqué add accent Brisbane Summit, November 15–16, 2014, paras 1 and 3.
3. International Monetary Fund, *World Economic Outlook* (April 2014), p. xv.
4. International Monetary Fund, *World Economic Outlook* (October 2014), p. xiii.
5. Jon Hilsenrath, "What the Big Economies Got Right or Wrong," *Wall Street Journal* (November 25, 2014).

CHAPTER 151

2015: A Dismal World Where Oil and Currencies Are Causing Havoc[1]

Flashback 15 years to the time when the United States was in the midst of a disruptive digital revolution. By 1999, the United States was having the time of its life—gross domestic product (GDP) was up 4 percent (double the rate of advanced nations) and unemployment was down to 4 percent (a 30-year low). Foreign capital flowed in and US dollar and S&P 500 stock index were up: US stock prices reached 30 times earnings, and tech stocks went wild.

1990s All Over Again?

Sound familiar? Not unlike recent years, Japan slipped into deflation in 1997; Germany was then the "sick man" of Europe (now it's the entire euro-zone). Emerging nations were in crisis, culminating in the currency crisis of 1997–1998 when many currencies (especially from Asia—from Thai baht to Korean won to the ringgit) crashed as foreign capital withdrew and servicing US$ debt became unsustainable. The parallels with today are not dissimilar. In the 1990s, Harvard's Lawrence Summers warned that the world economy was flying on one engine. Today, Columbia's "Dr. Doom," Nouriel Roubini, echoes the same sentiment, stating only the Anglosphere (United States and United Kingdom) engine is functioning.[2] Eventually, the United States got sucked in: The tech-bubble burst in early 2000; business investment shrank and share prices fell and consumers cut back. By early 2001, the United States and the rich world had slipped into recession—albeit a mild one. This time, China is different in the two periods: It was a bit-player in 1999; now it's the world's second largest economy and the world's largest exporter.

Four trends were at work to destabilize the world economy—about the same as now. First, the growth gap between the United States and other advanced nations is stark, and is narrowing between the United States and big emerging economies, reflecting lack of demand in the face of a strong US dollar. Second, the outlook for the eurozone (reflecting the disastrous impact of austerity) and Japan (repeating the errors of 1997) is dismal. Third, while Asian nations are now better equipped (floating exchange rate, lower debt, and healthy reserves cushion), trouble is nevertheless brewing—Russia is a disaster; cheaper oil, low commodity prices, and variable currencies are hitting big emerging nations hard. Investors have become a nervous lot, as the US dollar gathers strength. Fourth, the messy geopolitical scene has gotten worse in the face of rising inequality, reflecting income redistribution to those with a high propensity to save (the rich and corporations), and exacerbated by capital-intensive, labor-saving technological innovation. Rising risks of upheaval are plaguing the planet. The Middle East is on fire, the Russia–Ukraine conflict is disruptive, Islamic terrorism is on the rise, together with geo-economic threats from the likes of Ebola and global climate change. All work to cause "secular stagnation" that is making structural reforms politically difficult. One thing is sure—they weaken global growth.

Oil Slide Resumes

The price of oil has slumped almost 60 percent since early 2014, as the Organization of Petroleum Exporting Countries (OPEC) resisted cutting output amid the US shale boom, exacerbating the glut by an estimated 1.8 million barrels a day. Having fallen from above US$100 a barrel to US$50 (and below), the price is still trying to find its place. Most analysts see US$50 as the floor, expecting a rebound to US$60–80 in the course of the year. History tells an analytical story of two distinct pricing regimes: (1) 1974–1985, and then, 2005–2014, during which the "monopolistic" US$ benchmark price fluctuated between US$50 and US$120; and (2) 1986–2004, with the "competitive" price settling at US$20 to US$50. The oil market is marked by a struggle between monopoly and competition. In this struggle, competitive pricing—recently led by low-cost Saudi Arabia and OPEC, and Russia—can go as low as US$20 (breakeven marginal cost of "old" oil), outflanking shale-oil producers (mostly costing US$50 to produce), who are now cornered into taking on the role as swing "commodity" producers. So, realistically, a much lower trading range could stretch all the way down to US$20. Oil on New York's Mercantile Exchange dropped to US$46.7 on January 20. I guess it can fall to US$38 to US$40 by the end of the first quarter of 2015 amid the continuing "war" for market share. Rising supply, slowing refinery demand, geopolitical shocks, and rising US$—these remain the factors driving prices.

Currency War?

It passed without much notice. On January 14, the euro slipped to US$1.17, the rate when it was first introduced on January 1, 1999. It then weakened rapidly. By early 2000, the euro hit parity with the dollar, plunging to US$0.83 by October 2000. Fearing competitive devaluation and worried about inflation, the big central banks coordinated to stem the euro's fall. Today, the euro's slide has been more orderly but definitely persistent. Deflation has set in in the eurozone (consumer prices fell 0.2 percent in 2014), and with Germany's economy wobbling and others in Europe either stumbling or stagnating, the region's prospects look ever so feeble.[3] Indeed, they're dead in the water. Parity with the US dollar is in the cards again. I am afraid both politics and oil are undermining the currency.

Immediate threat comes from this weekend's Greek elections. The possibility of Grexit (Greece exit from the euro)—though lesser than in 2012 and deemed by most to be unlikely—casts a wary shadow over the euro's value, with no political leadership to kick-start the single market. Policy makers are running out of options. Instead, all eyes are on the European Central Bank (ECB) and its willingness to engage in some form of quantitative easing (QE), even "a QE-lite" version, to create enough money to buy sovereign bonds (now deemed legal). This is really a copout. Europe definitely needs to reform and have a balanced recovery based on more investment and spending at home.

Meanwhile in Asia, the Japanese yen—as a result of Bank of Japan's unprecedented massive and aggressive QE—is considered undervalued against most currencies of emerging nations, including the Chinese yuan. It's now at US$1 = ¥117.5 compared with ¥80 in mid-2012. Japan's October 2014 move was perceived as unfriendly, beggar-thy-neighbor, provoking neighbors to react. China has since allowed the yuan to moderately weaken (down 3 percent in 2014). Beijing is in a bind as it seeks to grow its slackening economy in the face of ongoing structural reforms. It needs to deflate its previous wild lending boom and overheated housing sector, which rules out aggressive monetary easing. Fiscal policy runs up against the need to slow down capital spending and rein in local government excesses. For China, with growth slackening to 7.4 percent in 2014 (lowest since 1990), devaluation remains one clear policy option.

Most other emerging nations feel vulnerable, especially commodity-based economies like Indonesia, Brazil, Malaysia, South Africa, and Nigeria. Even Russia. Already, all of them have accordingly devalued. Malaysia, for example, has seen its ringgit fall close to 14 percent against the US dollar since last August. The real problem is that if everyone devalues, no one wins (a zero-sum-game). In the event this becomes aggressive and disorderly, it can create systemic risks worldwide, with disastrous consequences. US$ borrowers would struggle to find adequate funding. US firms would be furious to see their exports "evaporate." And emerging markets would be forced to raise interest rates to prevent their currencies from collapsing. Short of global monetary reform (unthinkable even today), nothing can be done to stop competitive devaluations once they begin.

Still, currency markets remain in turmoil. The recent abrupt move by Switzerland to remove the cap on its franc peg to the euro sent global markets reeling. This prompted the *Wall Street Journal* headline:[4] "Murder in Zurich." The Swiss franc has since revalued 20 percent against the euro. Pressure is now on the Danish krone peg. It signals an end to stable money and a setback for growth. It blew a hole in Japan's QE strategy by undermining the credibility of central banks. So, the Swiss National Bank had to move or get run over. Currency market tumult harms. How will China respond to the challenge posed by a much weaker euro, yen, and won? If Beijing caves in and adopts the already-in-vogue beggar-thy-neighbor stance, ripples can become tidal waves. As I see it, the world has little choice but to go for a globally managed suboptimal exchange regime.

What, Then, Are We to Do?

The political scene and economic dynamics have since changed——not in a good way. At the end of the 1990s, many in the advanced economies and in some of the big, emerging economies had enjoyed the fruits of the boom. Median US wages rose by 7.7 percent in real terms in 1995–2000. Since 2007, by contrast, they have been flat in the United States and fallen in the United Kingdom and much of the eurozone. There is much discontent, even anger, as a result. On top of this, the global geopolitical dynamics have also changed, the most serious being that we are now at war against unpredictable terrorism and radical Islamism.

The year 2015 may look much like the late 1990s, but the politics and economics have probably turned for the worse. String together indicators like weak gold prices, falling oil prices, and weak commodity prices, low gilt-edged bond yields, strong US dollar, and downward revisions to growth forecasts, and they point to deflation. The key question is: How to avoid deflation and promote growth in 2015? Given the failure of ultra-low interest rates to stimulate investment and growth, and recognizing that the United States is the only place where real demand is, policy makers in Europe and Asia are trying their darnedest to make exports cheaper to help their economies grow.

Although competitive devaluation is a zero-sum game, monetary easing is not purely zero-sum. Easy money can boost demand by lifting asset prices (equities and housing), reduce borrowing costs, and limit risks from inflationary expectations. The cause of currency turmoil is clear: As public and private sectors deleverage from their high debts, monetary policy (and QE) becomes the only game in town to boost demand and, hence, growth. All this only leads to further strengthen the US dollar, as growth in the United States expands and as the Fed prepares to raise interest rates sometime in 2015. But if global demand and growth remain weak, and the US dollar too strong, the Fed may defer (with growing "patience") raising rates to moderate US$ appreciation. The world is still flying on one engine. To navigate the menacing storm clouds, the pilot needs to be nimble (less fiscal austerity), bold (more public spending on infrastructure), but disciplined (less reliance on QE). But that's not what the world is doing. Small wonder global growth keeps on disappointing. Are we all Japanese now?

Obiter Dictum

Looking ahead, silent demographic shifts are taking place to redefine the future. Already in 2000, Germany and Italy had more people aged 60 and above than those below 20. In 2010, Japan joined them, as did many nations across Europe, including Switzerland and Spain. By 2025, 46 countries will have more old people than young. China and Russia will join by 2030, Indonesia by 2050, and India by 2070. That's not so far off. By 2050, old people worldwide will triple to 1.5 billion, 16 percent of the world's total. Much of this will take place in East Asia (China, South Korea, and Japan), where 1 billion old people will live. This means more wealth will be concentrated on the elderly, especially elderly women, and because of them, consumer behavior, product preferences, and social demands will change drastically. Societies now have the new task to prepare and deal effectively with the empowerment of this new class of consumers. Tomorrow, all eyes will be focused on the elderly.

Kuala Lumpur
January 22, 2015

Notes

1. First published on January 24, 2015.
2. Nouriel Roubini, "Single-Engine Global Economy," reproduced in *The Edge*, Malaysia (November 10, 2014).
3. International Monetary Fund (IMF), *World Economic Outlook Update* (Washington DC: IMF January 19, 2015).
4. "Murder in Zurich," *Wall Street Journal* (January 19, 2015), p. 11.
5. Juan Pedro Moreno and Albert Shen, "Aging Societies Redefine Banking," *China Daily* (January 2–8, 2015), p. 20.

About the Author

T an Sri Dato' Professor Dr. Lin See-Yan holds the following academic degrees and distinctions:

PSM, DPMP, DSAP, JMN, JSM, AMN, MM, BA, BA(Hons), MPA(Finance),
AM(Bus. Econs), PhD(Econs), C.Stat, C.Sci., Hon.PhD(Economics),
Hon.Dr.Economics, FRSS, FIBM, FMII(Hon), FMIM, FMEA
Eisenhower Fellow and Distinguished Fellow, ISIS, Malaysia
Professor of Economics (Adj), Universiti Utara Malaysia
Pro-Chancellor and Research Professor, Sunway University, Malaysia

A former banker, Professor Lin is a Harvard-educated economist and a British chartered scientist. He holds three graduate degrees from Harvard University, including a PhD in economics. Professor Lin is Malaysia's first UK chartered statistician. He continues to serve the public interest, including as a member of the Prime Minister's Economic Council Working Group, a member of the Competition Appeal Tribunal, and a member of some senior Ministry of Education Committees. He is the economic adviser to the Associated Chinese Chambers of Commerce and Industry of Malaysia.

In addition, Professor Lin sits on the boards of many publicly listed and private enterprises in Malaysia, Singapore, and Indonesia that are engaged in mining, oil and gas, plantations, manufacturing, real estate and housing, hospitality and entertainment, ICT, and power generation industries, as well as of universities and foundations. He served as pro-chancellor of Universiti Sains Malaysia (2000–2010). Professor Lin is Chairman Emeritus, Harvard Graduate School Alumni Association Council at Harvard University and is president of Harvard Club of Malaysia. He was the Harvard Alumni Association's regional director for Asia at Harvard University between 2000 and 2010.

Professor Lin has extensive experience in banking and finance. He was chairman and chief executive officer of a publicly listed diversified banking and insurance group (1994–1997). Prior to that, he was a central banker for 34 years, serving as the deputy governor (1980–1994). He was a founder and director of Malaysia's sovereign wealth fund, Khazanah Nasional (1994–2000), and chairman of its executive committee (1999–2000).

Professor Lin is also well recognized internationally, having served as chairman, Experts Group on Finance for Sustainable Development, United Nations (UN) Commission on Sustainable Development (UNCSD), New York (1994–2004); member, World Bank group of five international experts on Financial Reform in China (PRC) (1993–1994); chairman, Ad Hoc Inter-sessional Government Working Group of Experts on Finance, UN Commission on Sustainable Development, New York (1994–1999); chairman, G-15 (Commonwealth) Experts Group on Financial Mechanisms for Trade (1990–1991); chairman, International Experts Group on Financial Issues, UNCSD Agenda 21: Kuala Lumpur (1994), New York (1995), Manila (1996), Santiago (1997), Nairobi (1999), Prague (2000); member, UN Regional Roundtable of Eminent Persons (2002 Johannesburg World Summit) (2001–2002); member, International Monetary Fund (IMF) Working Party of Experts on World Payments Imbalances, Washington, DC (1985–1987); member, IMF Committee of Expert Balance of Payments Compilers, Washington, DC (1987); and member, Commonwealth Group of Experts on the Debt Crisis, London (1984).

He speaks, teaches, writes, and consults on strategic and financial issues, including contributing the column "What Are We to Do" at the widely circulated *The Star* in Malaysia.

Index

945